Changing the Immigration Policy of the United States

"What changes should be made in United States immigration policy?"

The Complete Resource Handbook

Changing the Immigration Policy of the United States

"What changes should be made in United States immigration policy?"

Lynn Goodnight
Terry Check
James Hunter

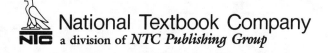

National Textbook Company
a division of NTC *Publishing Group*

Published by National Textbook Company, a division of NTC Publishing Group.
©1994 by NTC Publishing Group, 4255 West Touhy Avenue,
Lincolnwood (Chicago), Illinois 60646-1975 U.S.A.
Manufactured in the United States of America.

4 5 6 7 8 9 0 VP 9 8 7 6 5 4 3 2 1

CONTENTS

THE AUTHORS

LYNN GOODNIGHT is the Administrative Director of Northwestern University's National High School Institute and a freelance communications consultant. Ms. Goodnight is author of *Getting Started in Debate* and co-author of *Strategic Debate* and *Basic Debate*. While working on her master's, she was an Assistant Debate Coach at the University of Kansas. Ms. Goodnight was Director of Debate at Niles North High School from 1977 to 1980. She has lectured at high school debate workshops including the University of Kansas, University of North Carolina, University of Houston, Baylor University, Northwestern University, and the National Federation of State High School Associations Summer Workshop. She has been a member of the NTC writing staff for eighteen years.

TERRY "JER" CHECK is Assistant Debate Coach at the University of Pittsburgh. Mr. Check debated for Northwestern University and qualified for the National Debate Tournament in 1989. He also participated in the Northwestern Oxford Debates sponsored by the Annenberg School of Communication Policy Studies of Washington, D.C. He has lectured at the Baylor University Debate Workshop and the National High School Institute at Northwestern. This is Mr. Check's third year on the NTC writing staff.

JAMES HUNTER is Director of Debate at Oak Park-River Forest High School of Illinois. Mr. Hunter is also the Associate Director of the Debate Divisions of the National High School Institute at Northwestern University. Mr. Hunter qualified a team for the elimination rounds at the 1993 NFL National Speech Tournament. In 1990 he coached the Tournament of Champions winners. Mr. Hunter has worked at debate workshops across the country, including the Georgetown Debate Institute and the Wake Forest Debate Workshop.

Integrally involved in the preparation of this volume were Northwestern students and debaters. Tim Lakin, Carolyn Martin, Lisa Horstmann, Sheryl Wasserman, Jennifer Rapp, and Tony Yee have all made substantial contributions to the completion of this handbook. A special thanks goes to Betty Martin and Barbara Pollard at the National High School Institute for assistance during this project.

PREFACE

Once again we are about to embark on another debate season and another topic. For many it will be a new experience. For others it will be an opportunity to synthesize information gathered over the last few years. This handbook has been designed to help both the beginning and experienced debater as he or she begins to explore the ins and outs of programs and policies which affect immigration. **Changing the Immigration Policy of the United States** offers analysis and evidence on such areas as race relations, environmental impact, education, border patrol, health screening, refugees smuggling, visa, asylum, illegal immigraton, human rights, labor market, housing, etc.

This handbook has been written to serve as a resource tool. The debater should remember that **no** handbook can serve as a substitute for the continuous thorough research necessary for successful debate. We have discussed issues on their own merit. Rather than trying to graft them onto one or another of the propositions, we have presented a sampling of ideas and evidence. Since many of the issues and arguments are interchangeable on this year's topics, the outline and evidence for each chapter ma apply to any one of the three topics. We have outlined issues and questions that we feel will play a role in shaping this topic. It is our hope that the issues and questions we have raised will inspire debaters in their development of affirmative cases and negative approaches.

In addition to the handbook, **Changing the Immigration Policy of the United States**, debaters will want to consult **United States Policy on Immigration**, a basic overview of the topic, and **Immigration: New Directions for the Future**, a collection of critical essays, both published by National Textbook Company for the current debate year.

It has been a pleasure working with this staff of able authors and research assistants. The coordination and editorial assistance which I have provided will hopefully enhance the structural and stylistic unit of the individually prepared materials in this book. Terry Check prepared Chapter 3. Jim Hunter and Eric Truett prepared Chapters 2 and 4. Lynn Goodnight prepared Chapter 1. Ms. Goodnight also edited and organized the text upon completion.

L.G.

CHAPTER I

DETERMINING THE UNITED STATES POLICY TOWARDS IMMIGRATION

Problem Area: What changes should be made in United States immigration policy?

1. Resolved: That the United States government should substantially decrease immigration to the United States.
2. Resolved: That the United States government should substantially strengthen regulation of immigration to the United States.
3. Resolved: That the United States government should substantially increase protection of human rights in its refugee admission policy.

National Wording Committee Topic Summary

"Although the United States has been known historically as the world's melting pot, the American perception of immigration has changed. Debate today centers around three basic tenets of immigration policy: setting levels and goals in immigration, controlling illegal immigration, and dealing with the world's growing refugee crisis. Immigration is an area shrouded in myth and misunderstanding, which poses a timely and educational area of debate with abundant information available to support both sides of the issue. Affirmative cases could include policies concerning educational and professional qualifications of immigrants, limits on various categories of immigrants, visa modifications, screening of immigrants, deportation proceedings, or refugee policy. Negatives might make arguments regarding the positive role of immigration from an economic or ethnic viewpoint. Disadvantages might stem from the role immigrants play in many industries vital to U.S. economy, or effects of ethnicity on American culture. Overall, literature is widely available to support many divergent points of view on the issue."

The area of immigration policy is one of the most exciting debate topics offered in recent years. Human populations in the post-Cold War era are clearly in a time of circulation and flow not seen since the vast waves of immigration at the peak of the industrial revolution in the early 20th century. What are the best social, economic, political, and international policies to be adopted? These are not easy questions to answer. The United States has always been considered the "melting pot" of nationalities, and as a beacon of freedom she has welcomed all comers. The very social fabric of the United States is built on the myth of democratic co-operation. Yet, immigration has as often meant social problems and dilemmas as freedom for those who sought a newer world, and immigration policy has been troubled especially when brought into conflict with the costs of social welfare and the problems of class division within the United States.

This chapter examines the framing of questions for debating immigration. In it, we present some considerations over definitions of key terms for argument and some possibilities for dividing ground between affirmative and negative sides of the debate. The debater should note that issues pertaining to each of the topics clearly overlap, while the scope of issues and the division of grounds differ by virtue of the specific wording of the resolutions. We provide definitions of key terms and some tactical suggestions for debate.

Common Definitional Terms

THE UNITED STATES GOVERNMENT AS AGENT OF CHANGE

All three topics call for "the United States government" to act as a change agent for the action anticipated by the resolution. We offer the following definitions for consideration:

United States. "This term has several meanings. It may be merely the name of a sovereign occupying the position analogous to that of other sovereigns in family of nations, it may designate territory over which sovereignty of United States extends, or it may be collective name of the states which are united by and under the Constitution. Hooven & Allison Co. v Evatt, U.S. Ohio. 324 U.S. 652, 65 S.Ct. 870, 880, 89 L.Ed. 1252. (p. 1533)

Government. "From the Latin, gubernaculum. Signifies the instrument, the helm, whereby the ship to which the state was compared, was guided on its course by the 'gubernator' or helmsman, and in that view, the government is but an agency of the state, distinguished as it must be in accurate thought from its scheme and machinery of government.

In the United States, government consists of the executive, legislative, and judicial branches in addition to administrative agencies. In a broader sense, includes the federal government and all its agencies and bureaus, state and county governments, and city and township governments.

The system of polity in a state; that form of fundamental rules and principles by which a nation or state is governed, or by which individual members of a body politic are to regulate their social actions. A constitution, either written or unwritten, by which the rights and duties of citizens and public officers are prescribed and defined, as a monarchical government, a republican government, etc. The sovereign or supreme power in a state or nation. The machinery by which the sovereign power in a state expresses its will and exercises its functions; or the framework of political institutions, departments, and offices, by means of which the executive, judicial, legislative and administrative business of the state is carried on." (p. 695)

As the agent of change, "the United States government" would most clearly be those institutions of the federal government acting in concert. Such institutions include the legislative, executive, and judicial branches of government. Since the topic does not specify that the *entire* United States government act so as to effect policy, it might be assumed safely that the affirmative plan may direct legislative, executive or judicial changes in United States policy, or some combination thereof.

Note that there are differences in terms of the division of affirmative and negative ground among the topics in terms of what the agent of change can or cannot do as a result of the topic. In the topic that requires decreasing immigration to the United States, an affirmative might argue that such a policy can be accomplished in one of two ways: either the United States could pass further bans, prohibitions or restrictions or, alternatively, the United States could reduce the incentive for immigration by expanding economic aid to those countries whose populations are in flight. The first decrease is a direct consequence of the plan, the second is an indirect consequence of a plan. In some areas such topicality by effect is not seen as a valid argument, in other areas, so long as the main effect of a plan is to implement the resolution, such effects criteria are granted validity.

In the topic that requires the United States government to "substantially strengthen regulation of immigration to the United States," the question of effects topicality is not as clear. In the most straightforward interpretation, the quality of "regulation" is strengthened if mechanisms are put into place which affirm the objectives of the status quo. So, for example, if more resources were granted to the border patrol, or more money given to apprehension of illegal immigrants residing in the United States, or a more streamlined and fairer court process established, then regulation would be directly strengthened. However, it might be possible for an affirmative to argue that the only way to strengthen regulation is by dealing with causes of a problem—the purported flood of economic and political refugees from developing nations. The plan, then, might alter military, political or economic policies so as to reduce the incentives to immigrate to the United States. Incidentally, such plans often have the added benefits of reducing international instability, economic maldistribution of resources and the like—adding significantly to the affirmative side of the ledger. The problem with such cases is that they seem to veer from a direct discussion of immigration policy per se and verge on a discussion of improving international relations with foreign country X. On the other hand, the affirmative may have a point: that in order to "substantially" strengthen regulation one may have to deal with symptoms rather than causes. Clearly, the scope of action, whether directly or indirectly undertaken by the plan, will be a point of contention in this year's upcoming debates.

The question arises: What agents of change can the negative rely upon as residing outside of the topic? Thankfully, the term "United States government" is less ambiguous than the term "federal government." The former term clearly is distinguishable as a collective agency superior to individual state actions, while the latter is more ambiguous and may refer to a collectivity of state actions. Thus, the negative may be able to argue as a counterplan the "state government of California" should adopt policy X, if the affirmative area is only limited, say, to a single specific state. Yet, since the United States government sets immigration policy it may be difficult to rely on state action alone. This is especially the case since the federal government strongly influences welfare, medical care, the provision of educational resources and other standards of social welfare made available at the state level.

It is more likely that the negative may rely on international counterplans to offset immigration problems. If the root causes of immigration problems are disparities in the well-being among different national populations, then the solution to such issues may reside in transnational, even global, efforts directed at increasing human rights, economic growth, regional stability and so on. Rather than focusing on decreasing or regulation immigration to the United States, a negative might wish to examine the implications of more global activity. Whether such actions are "competitive" in the sense that the United States would have to be a presumed actor in any such scheme, is open to debate.

OBLIGATING TERMS OF RESOLUTION ACTION: "Should substantially"

An obligation term in a resolution is one that poses a particular standard or criteria by which the duties of the affirmative team are specified. Across all three resolutions for debate this year, the topic committee has required the affirmative to show that a change agent should do something substantial. Pause to consider the implications of these requirements. We offer the following definitions:

> **Should** 1. used in auxiliary function to express condition. 2. used in auxiliary function to express obligation, propriety, or expediency. 3. used in auxiliary function to express futurity from a point of view in the past. 4. used in auxiliary function to express what is probable or expected. 5. used in auxiliary function to express a request in a polite manner or to soften direct statement. (*Webster's Ninth New Collegiate Dictionary*, p. 1090)

Substantially. "Essentially; without material qualification; in the main; in substance; materially; in a substantial manner. About, actually, competently, and essentially. Gilmore v. Red Top Cab Co. of Washington 171 Wash. 346, 17 p. 2d 886, 887." (pp. 1428-1429)
Synonyms: important, notable, meaningful, and significant
Antonyms: trivial, unimportant, insignificant, incidental

The term should, in debate parlance, mean "ought to but not necessarily will" engage in resolutional action. The affirmative, therefore, has a duty to show that the plan has every prospect of being desirable and/or that the resolution is justified by due consideration of the affirmative arguments mandating change. The affirmative therefore is obligated to show that the plan should be enacted not that it will.

Each of the topics sets up a direction for what should happen in the case and plan advocating change. Topic #1 requires the affirmative to show cause to "substantially decrease" immigration; topic #2 requires the affirmative to justify the need or desirability to "substantially strengthen regulation" of immigration; and topic #3 asks the affirmative to "substantially increase protection" of refugees. What does this term "substantially" mean? If it is important enough to appear in all three topics, then it must be crucial indeed.

Unfortunately, there is no clear cut definition of what substantial means. Court decisions vary on the percentage of activity that is required to comprise a "substantial" portion of action, and court decisions that are not pertinent to the are of immigration may not be relevant for deciding what constitutes a substantial increase, decrease, or strengthening. For example, an additional million dollars in your allowance would be a "substantial increase" for you, but for the federal government that spends trillions, it is a relatively minor sum. Substantiality is a term that is in the eye of the beholder.

For the affirmative, their plan is by definition "substantial" insofar as its benefits are not trivial, insignificant, or unworthy of discussion. This point of view collapses the term substantial into the prima facie requirement of making a complete case for change. Note, though, this makes the affirmative potential vulnerable to a plan meet need or solvency argument as a topicality argument. If the affirmative defines a "substantial change" by virtue of the effects of its plans, then when the negative lessens the consequence of the plan by even a slight degree, the standard of "substantiality" is o longer met, or at least such a standard requires a shift of ground from the initial position. Under such circumstances, solvency arguments become more than incremental reductions of significance. They may be voting topicality issues.

While this kind of definition is confusing, other attempts to define substantial may be made by showing relative significance of the policy vis-à-vis the number of people, past and present, included by the plan. A plan that would reduce immigration 50% would be substantial, especially if many cases on the topic seemed not to reduce immigration at all. A plan that might not reduce immigration, but would effect a majority of immigrants—such as holding citizenship ceremonies—would be a substantial change from the point of view of sheer numbers covered by the plan. but would such a procedural change be a significant strengthening of regulation. Again, such an issue resides in the eye of the beholder.

The negative might argue that "substantial" is an inherently comparative term, and that the only way to differentiate reasonably the "substantial" from the "insubstantial" or the "significant" from the "trivial" is by comparative standards. One way of comparing issues is to read affirmative evidence on the nature and scope of immigration as a policy (a dangerous tactic) but one that might highlight minor procedural changes. Another way of establishing the argument is by referencing other cases run on the topic that are more common and more "substantial" comparatively to a minor procedural adjustment. In any case, a key term in the resolution is relatively difficult to define and will be highly contested.

ACTION REQUIRED BY THE RESOLUTIONS

All three topics under this year's problem area have common issues, centering upon the desirability of increasing or decreasing the total number of foreigners coming to the United States. However, depending upon which resolution you will be debating, the kinds of actions and the division of affirmative and negative ground varies a good deal. We have offered some basic definitions and will discuss each in context to give you an idea of the different kinds of actions anticipated by the resolutions.

Decrease."[T]o grow progressively less as in size, amount, number, or intensity." As a transitive verb "to cause to decrease." (*Webster's 9th New Collegiate Dictionary*, p. 331)
Synonyms: lessen, diminish, reduce, abate, dwindle, cut.
Antonyms: expand, augment, increase.

Strengthen. "[T]o make stronger." (*Webster's 9th New Collegiate Dictionary*, p. 1166)
Synonyms: enhance, improve, renew.
Antonyms: weaken, diminish, erode.

Regulation. The act of regulating; a rule or order prescribed for management of government; a regulating principle; a precept. Rule of order prescribed by superior or competent authority relating to action of those under its control. Regulation is rule or order having force of law issued by executive authority of government (e.g., by federal administrative agency). State ex. rel. Villines v. Freeman, Okl., 370 P.2d 207, 209. (p. 1286)

Regulate. To fix, establish, or control; to adjust by rule, method, or established mode; to direct by rule or restriction; to subject to governing principles or laws. The power of Congress to regulate commerce is the power to enact all appropriate legislation for its protection or advancement; to adopt measures to promote its growth and insure its safety; to foster, protect, control, and restrain. Virginian Ry. Co. v. System Federation No. 40, Labor, C.C.A.Va., 84 F.2d 641, 650. It is also power to prescribe rule by which commerce is to be governed, and embraces prohibitory regulations. United States v. Darby, 312 U.S. 100, 657, 61 S.Ct. 451, 456, 85 L.Ed 609. Regulate means to govern or direct according to rule or to bring under control of constituted authority, to limit and prohibit, to arrange in proper order, and to control that which already exists. Farmington River Co. v. Town Plan and Zoning Commission of Town of Farmington, 25 Conn.Sup. 126, 197 A.2d 653, 660.

Immigration. "The coming into a country of foreigners for purpose of permanent residence. The correlative term 'emigration' denotes the act of such persons in leaving their former country." (p. 750)

Increase. Enlargement, growth, development, increment, addition, accession, extension, production, profit, interest, issue. (p. 767)

Human Rights. "[T]he idea that each person is born with the moral claim on some political freedom which ought not to be denied by any government." (p. 341)

First of all note, that the directed action of the topics is quite distinct. Topics #1 and #3 are well-crafted and specifically delineate a fairly narrow and manageable affirmative ground, clearly distinguished from negative ground. Topic #1 asks that immigration be decreased. The affirmative must show that a decrease is desirable, and that its plan can accomplish this end without offsetting disadvantages. The negative can argue that either immigration should not be decreased or that it should in fact be increased. The only ambiguity in this kind of topic is whether or not a "net effect" standard can be used by a plan that mixes and matches some of its planks, by achieving retention of certain kinds of immigrants, say political refugees, while achieving an overall net reduction. This strategy is usually desired by the affirmative because it helps avoid plan disadvantages when proposals are constructed as blunt policy instruments. On the other hand, a negative may argue that any kind of standing pat or even increasing specific categories resides outside the rubric of resolutional action and must be stricken from the plan. Nevertheless the grounds dividing affirmative and negative are relatively clear.

Topic # 3 is clear, too. It calls for an "increase" of protection of human rights. Presumably, the standards for encouraging and granting asylum to political refugees would be increased overall. Affirmatives might pick out specific countries like Haiti to liberalize policy which overall increases protection of rights. Moreover, by narrowing the topic to "admission policy" the focus of the topic is directed away from the broader economic and cultural issues of immigration and toward the political sphere in particular. The negative has the ground of arguing that human rights policy is not a valid criteria for immigration or that such is not deserving in the particular case. This might be somewhat difficult because "increase protection of human rights" seems to be a somewhat loaded term. Nevertheless, the direction and action intended by the resolution are clear.

Topic #2, which will be debated by the widest number of schools, is by far the most ambiguous and complex. Note that it subsumes the first two topics, since numerical decreases and human rights issues are both sub-issues of an overall policy of "regulation." The topic tells us that the affirmative must present a case defending "strengthen[ing] regulation" of immigration to the United States. What does this mean? The resolution tells us noting about the direction intended by the topic. Since to regulate means something like to address with uniform standards or continue policy over time, the affirmative is free to argue for cases that encourage or discourage immigration, or better, cases that encourage and discourage immigration by virtue of special plan construction. All that is required is to keep like cases alike.

For an example, an affirmative could strengthen regulation by: (1) discouraging highly skilled professionals from entering the United States; (2) encouraging more human rights cases to come into the country; and (3) increasing enforcement against illegal immigration. What would be the net effect? Well, there might be marginally more or fewer people in the United States as a result of the plan. The thrust of the plan would be to "strengthen" regulation in the first case by having a more moral policy, that is, one that does not engage in draining talent from developing countries. In the second instance, regulation is strengthen from a political standpoint by liberalizing standards for political refugees. In the third case, regulation is strengthen by increasing the amount of resources that can be dedicated to the task of enforcement. Since "strengthen regulation" has no particular context, the affirmative is free to supply the specific context: economic, legal, political, moral, social "strengthen[ing]" of policy areas. The key term of the resolution is so ambiguous as to leave little negative ground.

As a test for available negative ground, consider the opposite of the resolution. "[T]he United States government should substantially **weaken** regulation of immigrants to the United States." What might this mean? Well, the negative could argue that in opposition to a regulatory approach, the United States should pursue an "open border" policy, letting everyone in or keeping everyone out. One could "abolish" immigration altogether by making citizenship an outmoded standard, as by a world government, or by making the United States isolationist. While quite radical, such counterplans are clearly competitive with a regulatory, incrementalist approach. Note that the topic specifically requires that the affirmative "strengthen regulation." It does not say: adopt radically new standards, abolish regulation, or anything like this.

Thus, the ambiguous "bi-directional" action term of this resolution leaves the negative with one of two choices: either it can research out every case that represents itself as "strengthening" regulation by increasing or decreasing legal or illegal, specialized or general, political, economic, social, or intellectual refugees or it can adopt a more visionary, global approach to the international exchange of populations as constructive grounds. A more narrow, well-crafted topic would be easier to debate insofar as it would encourage a direct exchange of issues by dividing opposing directions for change. This particular topic, however, offers an exciting opportunity to argue a range of issues.

THE UNITED STATES AS OBJECT OF CHANGE

Note finally, that not only is the United States government an agent of change in all the topics, that it is also the object of change in each topic. Topic #1 specifies that action must be taken so as to "decrease immigration to the United States." Topic #2 requires that "regulation of immigration to the United States" be strengthened. Topic #3 asks that the United States government should enhance "its [own] refugee admission policy." In all three cases, the topic committee is clearly focusing debate on internal domestic policy—what takes place in the United States. The question that is asked is whether more or fewer, the same kind or different, along one criteria of access or another, people are let into the United States as permanent residents. This is the issue that must be addressed.

CHAPTER II

PLACING A PRIORITY ON HUMAN RIGHTS

Resolved: That the United States government should substantially increase protection of human rights in its refugee admission policy.

Michael Cavosie in the *Indiana Law Journal* states the framers concern about U.S. refugee policies when he writes "The United States is a nation of immigrants, yet it has historically and paradoxically viewed newcomers distrustfully and sought to limit their numbers. This bipolarity has become more distinct as immigration and refugee levels have risen and is perhaps most acute in the area of United States refugee and asylum policy." (67, 411-412). This article will address the issues associated with defining the refugee population, the historical development of U.S. refugee policies, and the human right implications of the U.S. refugee policies.

United States refugee law is modeled after and governed by the 1951 United Nations Convention Relating to the Status of Refugees and the 1967 Protocol Relating to the Status of Refugees. The 1951 Convention, established after World War II in response to the large numbers of displaced persons in Europe, created an ideologically neutral and comprehensive means for contracting parties to protect refugees. According to Article 1(A)2 of the 1951 convention, the term refugee applies to any person who:

> As a result of events occurring before 1 January 1951 and owing to well founded fear of being persecuted for reasons of race, religion, nationality, membership of a particular social group or political opinion, is outside the country of his nationality and is unable or, owing to such fear, is unwilling to avail himself of the protection of that country (Rogers, 1116).

Although the 1951 Convention gave contracting states the option of limiting the application of the Convention to events in Europe, it defined refugee globally, without reference to specific nationalities and was designed to extend protection to as many refugees as possible. The language of the 1951 Convention establishes the minimum requirements for determining refugee status, and suggests that a demonstrated "well-founded fear" of persecution based on reasonable grounds is sufficient to establish refugee status. With this broad definition, the drafters of the 1951 Convention intended to grant protection to the international concept of human rights.

The 1967 Protocol adopted the 1951 Convention definition of refugee, but eliminated the temporal and geographic restrictions contained in the 1951 Conven-

tion, and extended the applicability of asylum to victims of all inhumane governments. United States asylum policy was brought into compliance with the 1967 Protocol through the Refugee Act of 1980, which amended the Immigration and Naturalization Act of 1952 and created a statutory basis for asylum. The Refugee Act of 1980 defines "refugee" as:

> Any person who is outside any country of such person's nationality…and who is unable or unwilling to return to, and is unable or unwilling to avail himself or herself of the protection of, that country because of persecution or a well-founded fear of persecution on account of race, religion, nationality, membership in a particular social group, or political opinion…(Cavosie, 426).

Adoption of the Protocol definition of refugee in the Refugee Act of 1980 broadened the class of people eligible for asylum under the Act by adding the categories of nationality and social group to the previous refugee definition. This broad definition of refugee satisfies the United States humanitarian concerns as well as international obligations to provide refuge to persecuted peoples.

Congressional regulations, defining the proof an alien must provide in order to demonstrate refugee status, further suggest that Congress intended to provide a flexible system for granting of refuge in the United States and to recognize that the persecution of groups can take many forms. The regulations require that an applicant establish that the individual suffered past persecution or has a well founded fear of future persecution. The well-founded fear standard is subjective as well as objective, and focuses on the perception of the applicant. The Board of Immigration Appeals and the courts have applied a reasonable person standard to define the objective evidence needed to render the subjective fear well founded. Thus an applicant establishes a well founded fear if the individual shows that a reasonable person in their circumstances would fear persecution if returned to their native country. The decision to grant or deny refuge status is based on the applicant's testimony and objective sources documenting the conditions in the country of origin.

The 1980 Refugee Act provides statutory protections for persons fleeing from persecution. The applicants applying under the 1980 Act are outside the numerical limitations that are established by consultation between the Executive Branch and the Legislative Branch. The consultation process is used as a means by which to evaluate the status of immigration "ebbs and flows", while allowing for communication between the two branches on potential new refugee producing conflicts and to communicate the views of the people on the status and responsibilities of accepting more immigrants. Most refugees would fall into one of four categories for the purpose of processing their claims. Refugees are those individuals that apply for protection while outside the United States at selected locations and must be "of special humanitarian concern to the United States" (Benoit, 1439). Withholding of Deportation is status for aliens that are within or at the borders of the United States at the time of application. Asylum status has the same determination process as Withholding status, but the applications must meet different standards of persecution. In asylum proceedings, one faces a subjective standard that evaluates the applicant's well-founded fears of persecution. In the proceedings for Withholding of Deportation, not only must the applicant prove that one's life or freedom would be threatened, one must meet an objective standard and show that it is more than likely than not that one will be persecuted if forced to return to their country of origin. The Supreme Court has interrupted that standard of proof in an Asylum claim to be an easier standard to meet than the standard for Withholding of Deportation (Mullane, 87). Furthermore, once attained, asylum and refugee status confer more benefits than Withholding of Deportation. An asylee or refugee will be paroled into the United States and may apply to adjust one's status to that of permanent resident. But Withholding of Deportation is country specific; thus, the Attorney General need only withhold deportation to the country in which the alien's life or freedom is threatened, and the alien may still be deported to any other country that will accept them (Benoit, 1441).

The federal agencies that oversee the process are coordinated under the auspices of the Attorney General. Immigration Judges conduct deportation hearings and make the initial determination on all matters raised at the hearing, including asylum and withholding of deportation requests. Appeals of the decisions of Immigration Judges are made to the Board of Immigration Appeals and are reviewable by the circuit courts.

One last immigrant category is known as Temporary Protected Status and is a collective status that is only granted to individuals. The Immigration and Naturalization Act authorizes the Attorney General to grant Temporary Protected Status to nationals of a country that meets one of the criteria that indicate that the country of origin suffers from extraordinary political or social unrest or disorder which prevents the aliens' safe return. Temporary Protected Status may be granted from six to eighteen months and is renewable.

The protection of human rights is the foundation on which United States refugee programs were created. Generally, U.S. policies were created to protect aliens whose rights are violated in their native lands on the basis of their race, religion, nationality, membership in a particular social group, or political opinion. During the Cold War, U.S. refugee policy was biased in favor of those who were fleeing oppressive regimes that were Communist and often ignored the applications from countries where the United States supported the leaders because of their anti-communist views, despite their repressive nature. With the end of the Cold War, former Communist states still produced the most significant numbers of refugees admitted to the United States, however for different reasons. The Lautenberg Amendment authorized guidelines for the adjudication of refugee status based on "the historically persecuted nature" of some social or religious groups. With the rise of xenophobic leaders within some former Communist states, this Amendment allowed for increased numbers of refugees to be admitted to the United States based on a lower evidentiary standard. The groups specifically recognized within the Amendment are Soviet Jews, Evangelical Christians, religiously active Ukrainian Catholics and certain categories of Vietnamese, Laotians and Cambodians (Feinstein, S467). The extension of this Amendment will be considered during the Fall term of the 1994 Congress.

Another area of expanding interest in protecting human rights applies to specific social groups. With the codification of the 1980 Refugee Act social groups were extended refugee status. New interpretations of the term "social group" has expanded consideration to groups like gays and lesbians. The implications of their inclusion into refugee status is highly controversial and thus is natural ground for the affirmative. Women who are persecuted because of their sex or because of archaic social or cultural norms also has been the focus of controversy in the development of United States refugee policies. This controversy hinges on the definition of persecution and the basis of the applicants "clear probability" of being persecuted.

U.S. policies in Haiti also have implications on the human rights role of U.S. refugee policies. The current U.S. policy of returning all Haitians who flee the island to Haiti to apply for refugee status violates the principle of nonrefoulement as articulated in the United Nations Declaration of Territorial Asylum and the 1967 Protocol. Despite being bound by the principle of nonrefoulement ("refouler" means to return), the Clinton Administration has not implemented a solution that meets the needs of thousands of fleeing Haitians, while upholding the principles of international law.

CHAPTER II

OUTLINE

I. GENERAL INFORMATION ABOUT U.S. REFUGEE POLICY

  A. Definitions
    1. Refugee (1-2)
    2. Immigrant vs. asylee (3)
    3. Refugee vs. Migrant (4)
    4. Asylee vs. Refugee (5)

  B. ASYLUM PROCESS (6-9)

  C. NUMBERS OF IMMIGRANTS, REFUGEES, AND ASYLEES (10-12)

  D. SOURCE OF REFUGEES (13)

  E. STATISTICS NOT RELIABLE (14-15)

II. STATUS AND SUBSTANCE OF U.S. IMMIGRATION POLICY

  A. GENERAL POLICY
    1. Favors open immigration (16)
    2. Hardline against immigration (16)
    3. Immigration policy racist and nativist (18-19)
    4. Refugee admissions restrictive (20)

  B. CLINTON'S REFUGEE ACTIONS
    1. On the spot hearings (21)
    2. Clinton cracking down (22)
    3. U.S. redirecting ships (23)
    4. Eliminating procedural processes (24)

  C. ASYLUM SEEKERS
    1. Standards for receiving asylum (25-26)
    2. Many fall through cracks (27-28)
    3. Well-founded fear too subjective (29)
    4. Work authorization too slow (30)
    5. UN war refugee definition too narrow (31-32)
    6. Torture victims deserve special protection (33)
    7. Refugee law not allow exclusion based on income (34)

  D. STATUS QUO DOES NOT PROTECT RIGHTS
    1. Backlash reducing procedural safeguards (35)
    2. INS does not protect due process rights (36)
    3. SQ denies rights to returnees (37)
    4. BIA ineffective in rights protection (30-39)

  E. BIAS IN ASYLUM PROCEDURE
    1. Admissions bias
      a. Cold war logic dominates refugee policy (40-41)
      b. Dominated by foreign policy concerns (42)
      c. Policy politicized (43)
      d. Immigration policy still biased (44)
      e. Victories of non-hostile country aliens rare (45)
    2. Appeals Bias
      a. Bias towards hostile state refugees (46)
      b. Process determined by politics (47-49)
      c. Special interest groups influence decisions (50)

  F. DUE PROCESS RIGHTS
    1. Aliens deserve due process (51)
    2. Not entitled to due process protection (52)

  G. SQ PROTECTS ALIENS' RIGHTS
    1. INS has humanitarian policy (53)
    2. Decisions not influenced by politics (54)
    3. Courts protect immigrant rights (55)
    4. Special interest groups protect aliens (56-57)
    5. Movements arise to challenge rights violations (58)

  H. MISC. ARGUMENTS
    1. Broad asylum standard not supported (59)
    2. Asylum does not solve human rights violations (60)
    3. Legislation fails (61)
    4. Decreasing discretion protects aliens (62)
    5. Activism response (63)

III. ISSUES IN INS ADMINISTRATION

  A. Structural problems with INS
    1. General problems (64-65)
    2. Overloaded with burdens (66-67)
    3. Tension between control and humanitarian goals (68-69)
    4. Information problems (70-72)
    5. Budgetary problems (73-75)
    6. Administration problems (76-77)
    7. Border patrol problems (78-79)
    8. Structural changes needed (80-83)
    9. Centralization efforts fail (84-86)

  B. NO PROBLEMS WITH THE INS
    1. Legislation not needed (87)
    2. Minor reforms solve (88-90)

C. DETENTION CAN'T BE AN EFFECTIVE
POLICY
   1. INS can't detain all aliens (91)
   2. Detention won't solve immigration
      problems (92-94)
   3. Smuggling plan does not solve (95)

D. DETENTION AND SCREENING
EFFECTIVE
   1. APSO expansion good (96)
   2. Screening solves refugee backlog (97-99)
   3. Must deter alien arrival to solve (100)

E. VWPP PROGRAM EFFECTIVE (101-105)

F. SYSTEM ABUSE
   1. System currently overloaded (106-112)
   2. Backlog increases immigration (113-116)
   3. Reforms solve backlog (117-121)
   4. Reforms can't solve, have negative
      consequences (122-127)

IV. INTERNATIONAL REFUGEE ISSUES

A. FORCES DRIVING INTERNATIONAL
MIGRATION
   1. Refugees increasing (128)
   2. Multiple trends ensure future increase
      (129-132)
   3. Economic growth key to resolving
      refugee crisis (133-134)
   4. Population growth creates refugees (135-
      136)
   5. Refugee problem is an LDC crisis (137)

B. INTERNATIONAL APPROACH NOT
WORKING
   1. International backlash to refugees exists
      (138-141)
   2. No international refugee protection (142-
      143)
   3. International procedures ignore aliens'
      rights (144-1450
   4. UN cannot solve (146)

C. NEED FOR COORDINATED DEFINITION
AND POLICY
   1. Opportunity exists for global policy
      (147-151)
   2. Current approach not cohesive enough to
      solve (152-156)
   3. Uniform definition solves (157-160)
   4. International cooperation only way to
      solve (161-165)
   5. U.S. leadership necessary to solve (166-
      167)

D. STATUS QUO ACTING TO SOLVE
   1. SQ solving in general (168)
   2. UN solving (169-171)

3. Humanitarian intervention will solve
   (172-173)
4. Non-governmental organizations solving
   (174)
5. No South-East Asian refugee crisis (175)

E. MULTIPLE BARRIERS EXIST TO
POLICY SUCCESS
   1. Need multiple actions to solve (176-177)
   2. Can't solve due to multiple causes (178)

F. ISSUES IN REFOULEMENT,
RESETTLEMENT AND REPATRIATION
   1. Legal obligations of states
      a. Asylum not mandatory under
         international law (179-180)
      b. Moving to a third country does not
         violate international law (181)
      c. Non-refoulement key to refugee
         protection (182)
   2. Barriers to Repatriation
      a. General difficulties in repatriation
         (183-185)
      b. Must evaluate change in host
         country situation (186)
   3. Resettlement difficulties
      a. Resettlement costly (187)
      b. Trade-off link-SQ protects against
         torture and women at risk (188)
   4. Miscellaneous issues
      a. Repatriation increasing in status quo
         (189)
      b. Repatriation can solve international
         crises (190)
      c. Should expand asylum options (191)

V. HUMAN RIGHTS VIOLATIONS

A. ASYLUM AND HUMAN RIGHTS
   1. Detention violates rights (19)
   2. Government obligated to help asylees
      (193-194)
   3. U.S. Policy violates human rights (195)
   4. Denial of access violates rights (196)
   5. Repatriation is a human right (197)

B. POSITIVE NEGATIVE RIGHTS
   1. Positive and negative rights distinct
      (198)
   2. Distinction arbitrary (199)
   3. Distinction does not apply to human
      rights (200)
   4. Positive rights key to dignity (201)
   5. Positive rights key to negative rights
      (202)

C. RAWLS
   1. U.S. immigration policy violates
      Rawlsian justice (203-205)

2. Rawls supports open borders (206)
3. Justice most important value (207)

D. U.S. HUMAN RIGHTS POLICY
1. U.S. does not support human rights (208-209)
2. Human rights policy cold-war based (210)
3. U.S. policy stops international human rights policies (211-212)

E. INTERNATIONAL ENFORCEMENT
1. No enforcement in SQ (213-217)
2. Aid solves (218-219)
3. Enforcement barriers don't justify ignoring human rights (220)

F. BENEFITS OF HUMAN RIGHTS
1. Human rights universal (221)
2. Moral imperative (222-223)
3. Human rights key to peace (224-226)
4. Human rights change social structures (227)
5. Cultural imperialism does not dejustify human rights focus (228)

G. NEGATIVE ARGUMENTS AGAINST RIGHTS
1. Natural and positive law trade off (229)
2. Basing human rights on necessity fails (230)
3. Lack of human rights theory dooms all moral theories (231)
4. Human rights violations have no significance (232)

H. ALTERNATE CAUSALITIES TO RIGHTS VIOLATIONS
1. Multiple threats to human rights (233)
2. Reducing SQ violations does not solve (234)
3. Nationalism kills human rights (235)

VI. FEMALE REFUGEES FLEEING GENDER VIOLENCE

A. SQ does not recognize women refugees (236-238)
B. Female refugees increasing (239-241)
C. Violence is persecution (2420244)
D. Violence against women is an attack on women as a class (245-247)
E. Social group category broad (248-249)
F. Genital mutilation harms (250-251)
G. Expanding social group definition solves (252-254)
H. Recognizing female refugees decreases rights violations (255-257)
I. Answers to expansion opens floodgates (258-259)

J. SQ acting to protect women's rights (260-262)
K. Many barriers to asylum—negative solvency take-outs (263-265)

VII. GAY AND LESBIAN REFUGEES

A. Gays not viewed as social group (266)
B. Moral turpitude used to exclude gays (267-268)
C. 1990 Act does not prevent deportation (269-271)
D. Gays want asylum (272)
E. Persecution of gays increasing (273-276)
F. Gays are a social group (277-278)
G. Sexual orientation immutable (279-280)
H. No support for behavioral view (281)
I. Answer to recognition opens the floodgates (282)
J. Sodomy laws not only basis for repression (283-285)
K. No barriers (286-287)
L. SQ protects gays internationally (288-290)

VIII. HAITI

A. What the SQ policy is—allows deportation (291-293)
B. Courts allowing repatriation (294-295)
C. SQ policy ignores human rights abuses (296-297)
D. ICP fails (298-300)
E. Detention camps bad (301-302)
F. Supreme Court Haitian decision sends signal of repression (303-305)
G. Excluding AIDS infected Haitians sends bad signal (306)
H. International Law Violations
   1. U.S. violates non-refoulement policy (137)
   2. U.S. policy violates 1951 screening agreement (308)
   3. Need even-handed policy to uphold international law (309)
I. Repatriation prevents human rights focus (310)
J. Root Causes
   1. Increasing refugees helps solve root causes (311)
   2. Interdiction prevents solving root causes (312-314)
K. HIV alien exclusion increases AIDS discrimination (315-318)
L. Solvency evidence on screening (319-320)
M. Inter-branch conflict (321)
N. Haitian policy decreases U.S. credibility (322)

CHAPTER II

EVIDENCE

1. Hugh G. Mullane. "Political Asylum: Determining Standards of Review." GEORGETOWN IMMIGRATION LAW JOURNAL, Vol. 6: 1993, p. 87. The term "refugee" means (A) any person who is outside any country of such person's nationality or, in the case of a person having no nationality, is outside any country in which such person last habitually resided, and who is unable or unwilling to return to, and is unable or unwilling to avail himself or herself of the protection of that country because of persecution or a well-founded fear of persecution on account of race, religion, nationality, membership in a particular social group, or political opinion.

2. Ellen Vagelos. "The Social Group That Dare Not Speak Its Name: Should Homosexuals Constitute a Particular Social Group for Purposes of Obtaining Refugee Status? Comment on RE: INSUDI." FORDHAM INTERNATIONAL LAW JOURNAL, Vol. 17: 1993, p. 234. To qualify as a refugee pursuant to the 1951 Convention and the Protocol, aliens must demonstrate three things. First, they must seek relief from outside their country of origin. Second, aliens seeking asylum in the United States must either be persecuted or have a well-founded fear of persecution in their country of origin. Aliens seeking asylum in Canada must have a well-rounded fear of persecution. Third, they must be persecuted or fear persecution on account of their race, religion, nationality, membership in a particular social group, or political opinion. Individuals qualify for asylum in the United States or Canada if they satisfy this definition of "refugee."

3. Rosemarie Rogers. "The Future of Refugee Flows and Policies." INTERNATIONAL MIGRATION REVIEW, Vol. 26, no. 4: Winter 1992, pp. 1127-1128. As was noted earlier, until the 1980s the classical immigration countries (which also have been the major countries of refugee resettlement) did not view themselves as countries of first asylum. Western Europe's relatively small number of asylum seekers came from Eastern Europe and the Soviet Union and were not expected to return to their home countries; if they were not resettled, the durable solution in their case was local integration. However, today Western Europe not only must respond to a growing number of individual asylum seekers from the east and the south, but Europe and the United States also are confronted with mass flows of people escaping persecution or violent upheavals in their home countries, as in the case of Bosnia and Haiti. In these situations, the individual status determinations based on the 1951 Convention and the

grant of asylum with the understanding that it means permanence no longer serve.

4. Michel Moussalli. "Prospects for Refugee Protection in the 1990's." IN DEFENSE OF THE ALIEN, Vol. 15: 1993, p. 127. Refugee issues are increasingly discussed in connection with migration issues. This is a welcome development in that it recognizes the complex causes of many contemporary population movements. However, we must always bear in mind the cardinal difference which separates refugees from migrants and gives refugees a special standing in international law. Unlike migrants, refugees are fleeing human rights violations, war and other armed conflict, serious internal disturbances or intolerable internal repression. The refugees' government cannot or will not protect them and indeed is often the agent of their persecution.

5. Barbara Yarnold. REFUGEES WITHOUT REFUGE: FORMATION AND FAILED IMPLEMENTATION OF U.S. POLITICAL ASYLUM POLICY IN THE 1980'S, University Press: Lanham, Maryland,1990, p. 11. While many immigrants come to the U.S. for employment and family reunification, refugees and asylees are those who flee their countries of origin since they fear or will likely experience persecution if returned. The only difference between the two is that refugees file their applications when they are outside the U.S., while asylees (both those who seek asylum and those who seek withholding of deportation) file their applications after they have arrived in the U.S. Since both refugees and asylees must convince relevant decisionmakers that they are in need of refuge, one expects that many of the same factors which influence U.S. refugee policy will impact its asylum policy.

6. Senator Lautenberg. CONGRESSIONAL RECORD, February 1, 1994. It is important to remember that extending the Lautenberg amendment will not increase the number of refugees allowed from the countries included in the law. Refugee admissions are set each year by the administration in consultation with Congress. The credible basis standard is not irrafutable, and it is still up to the INS interviewer to make the decision of whether or not to grant refugee status to these individuals.

7. Hugh G. Mullane. "Political Asylum: Determining Standards of Review." GEORGETOWN IMMIGRATION LAW JOURNAL, Vol. 6: 1993, pp. 87-88. The refugee act of 1980 provides statu-

tory protections for persons fleeing from persecution. The Refugee Act defines a refugee and authorizes the Attorney General to grant asylum to all individuals who qualify as refugees. The regulations implementing Section 208 of the INA provide three procedures for an alien to apply for asylum. An individual granted asylum is eligible for permanent residence status in the United States after one year. A person may also apply for withholding of deportation, which, if obtained, precludes the government from returning the alien to her home country. An application for asylum requires the Government to consider the individual for withholding of deportation.

The quantum of proof necessary to establish an asylum claim differs from the amount of proof required for withholding of deportation. An individual must show a well-founded fear of persecution in order to be granted asylum. The standard of proof for withholding deportation is a clear probability of persecution. The Supreme Court has interpreted the standard of proof in an asylum claim to be an easier standard to meet.

The Attorney General implements his statutory authority through Immigration Judges (IJ) and the Board of Immigration Appeals (BIA or Board). The IJ conducts the deportation hearing and makes the initial determination on all matters raised at the hearing, including asylum and withholding of deportation requests. These decisions are subject to review by the BIA and are reviewable by the circuit courts.

8. Jean-Pierre Benoit and Lewis A. Kornhauser. "Unsafe Havens." THE UNIVERSITY OF CHICAGO LAW REVIEW, Vol. 59, no. 4: Fall 1992, p. 1439. Several classes of immigrants are not subject to the numerical limitations. For our purposes, four are of particular importance: (a) refugee status, for which aliens outside the United States may apply at selected locations; (b) withholding of deportation, for which aliens within or at the borders of the United States may apply; (c) asylum status, for which aliens within or at the borders of the United States may apply; and (d) temporary protected status, which the Attorney General may designate on a country-by-country basis. These provisions impose different substantive and procedural requirements on applicants; they also offer different benefits. Moreover, the relation of these provisions of domestic law to the provisions of the 1967 Protocol are complex.

9. COMMITTEE ON GOVERNMENT OPERATIONS, SECOND REPORT. "The Immigration and Naturalization Service: Overwhelmed and Unprepared for the Future." August 4, 1993, Y1.1/8:103-216. Responsibility for implementing these laws resides primarily at the Immigration and Naturalization Service (INS), Department of Justice. INS facilitates the entry into the United States of persons legally admissible as visitors and immigrants. It is also responsible for preventing the unlawful entry and employment of those who are not eligible for admission. It must apprehend and remove those who reside in the United States unlawfully while, at the same time, grant assistance to those who are eligible for benefits under the Immigration and Nationality Act. The Department of State is responsible for screening and issuing visas to individuals from abroad who have legitimate reasons for entering the United States. Obviously, how effectively INS is managed is central to the successful implementation of policies established by Congress.

10. Frank Trejo. "Rethinking Immigration." DALLAS MORNING NEWS, January 2, 1994, p. 1A. According to the INS, more than 800,000 legal immigrants entered the country last year. In addition, more than 100,000 refugees were allowed in and thousands were granted political asylum.

11. A.M. Rosenthal. "On My Mind; Fear of Compassion." NEW YORK TIMES, June 25, 1993, Editorial p. A31. In any case, immigration creates national wealth, not national burden. It does add government costs in some places—which Washington wrongly shoves off on cities and states.

About 90,000 to 100,000 other foreigners arrive every year to ask for asylum as refugees—people who fear death, imprisonment or torture if returned. Must prove their cases.

12. A.M. Rosenthal. "On My Mind; Fear of Compassion." NEW YORK TIMES, June 25, 1993, Editorial p. A31. About 800,000 legal immigrants enter America annually. Sometime, lying in a hospital emergency room, look up at a Philippine nurse bringing relief. Decide whether the U.S. needs fewer immigrants or more.

About three million foreigners live illegally in the U.S., many of them Mexicans who saw no moral reason why they should not go from their poor country to seek work in a rich country across a historically recent border. We can stop this by helping the neighbor become somewhat less poor, or saying our house is your house. Otherwise—argue with America's lusty history, which made its borders too big to patrol.

13. Barbara Yarnold. REFUGEES WITHOUT REFUGE: FORMATION AND FAILED IMPLEMENTATION OF U.S. POLITICAL ASYLUM POLICY IN THE 1980'S, University Press: Lanham, Maryland, 1990, p. 105. Also interesting is the fact that most asylum-related appeals to the BIA during the period in question involve aliens from Central American countries (particularly persons from El Salvador and Nicaragua), Cubans from the "Mariel Boatlift," and aliens from Haiti. About 67% (259) of the asylum-related appeals brought to the BIA from 1980-1987 involved aliens from El Salvador (53 appeals), Honduras (1

appeal), Guatemala (6 appeals), Nicaragua (13 appeals), Cuba (97 appeals), and Haiti (89 appeals). This may be attributed to two factors: first, the proximity of these aliens to the U.S. which allows them to emigrate to the U.S. with relative ease and low cost when compared to aliens from Europe, Asia, Africa, and other locations distant from the U.S. The fact that large numbers of aliens from El Salvador, Honduras, Guatemala, Nicaragua, Cuba, and Haiti enter the U.S. each year accounts for the high percentage of asylum applications filed by these aliens. For example, during the period of 1982-1985, the INS took action (approved or denied) on 69,177 asylum applications filed by persons from 137 countries worldwide. These six countries accounted for 37,191, or 54% of the total asylum applications adjudicated by the INS during the period 1983-1985.

14.   Eduardo Arboleda and Ian Hoy. "The Convention Refugee Definition in the West: Disharmony of Interpretation and Application." INTERNATIONAL JOURNAL OF REFUGEE LAW, Vol. 15: 1993, p. 80. Considerable caution is required in comparing national acceptance rates of Convention refugees. It is far from straight-forward to obtain accurate and current statistics. Governments are often reluctant to distribute publicly statistics that reflect directly on their treatment of asylum seekers. Some States occasionally provide the number of asylum seekers accepted from a given country of origin, but will not give the overall percentage of acceptances and rejections. This statistical difficulty is further exacerbated because certain countries do not specify how many asylum seekers were denied status, but simply give the figures of those recognized as Convention refugees and those accepted under non-Convention grounds. In the absence of information on the numbers who were unsuccessful on either Con-vention or non-Convention grounds, one could be led to believe that most asylum seekers were accepted.

15.   Arthur C. Helton. "Undocumented Immigrants to Avoid U.S. Services." NEW YORK TIMES, September 1, 1993, p. A18. Policy analysis by anecdote is carried to new heights in "Crackdown Fails to Stem Smuggling of Chinese to U.S." (front page, Aug. 23). After reading the alarming headline, I studied the article to find the factual basis for the assertion on smuggling of Chinese, only to discover to my astonishment that the principal proponents of the position were private lawyers who had accepted more cases for representation and Government officials charged with detecting immigration smuggling.

Often there is little or no useful data available from the immigration bureaucracy. The inability to generate adequate information for management and policy uses has been repeatedly identified as an area needing improvement.

16.   Frank Trejo. "Debate Rages over Economic Benefits of Immigrants; Studies Conflict over Taxes Paid." THE DALLAS MORNING NEWS: NEXUS, January 3, 1994, p. 8A. Frank Sharry, executive director of the National Immigration Forum, emphasized that since most immigrants enter legally, they are in essence "invited" by U.S. immigration policy.

Through these laws, "we're benefiting American companies. We're benefiting American citizens and permanent residents who have family members, and we're benefiting American foreign policy and humanitarian policy by setting better standards of who we accept as refugees," Mr. Sharry said.

17.   THE PROGRESSIVE. "Hold the Wretched Refuse." August 1993, p. 10. Such interference has already become part of American immigration policy. The U.S. Committee for Refugees reports that the Immigration and Naturalization Service has paid Mexican officials to intercept and repatriate refugees from other Latin American countries, before they can make their way north. And the Senate recently appropriated $350,000 to pay the government of Mexico to carry out the same task.

The United States is becoming increasingly aggressive about discouraging immigration. And the contemptuous treatment of refugees is just part of a disturbing larger pattern, as the Clinton Administration backs away from its campaign pledges to defend human rights. Advocates of immigrants' rights who worked on Clinton's transition team voice an outrage that has become commonplace as the Administration shows its true colors on human and civil rights.

18.   Barbara Yarnold. REFUGEES WITHOUT REFUGE: FORMATION AND FAILED IMPLEMENTATION OF U.S. POLITICAL ASYLUM POLICY IN THE 1980'S, University Press: Lanham, Maryland, 1990, p. 23. U.S. immigration policy has been influenced by nativist groups which adopted a "mentality of exclusion" toward non-group members, or immigrants. Early in U.S. history, Protestant religious organizations and nativist organizations sought to bar the entrance of immigrants, many of whom were Roman Catholics and were from Eastern and Southern European countries. Briggs (1984) comments that many of the legal barriers to immigration were adopted for the purpose of excluding undesirable immigrants, namely aliens who were not Anglo-Saxon and were believed to be morally and intellectually inferior. One manifestation of the "mentality of exclusion" is discrimination by group members against those who do not share the characteristics of the group, due to their race or ethnicity, for example. The distinguishing features of non-group members are often used as a justification for their exclusion.

Given the exclusionary mentality of many American religious and civic organizations, it is not surprising to

find that U.S. immigration laws have been explicitly discriminatory, limiting the immigration of Eastern European, Chinese, and Japanese aliens (Morris, 1985; Briggs, 1984). The recent practice of excluding Haitians, Salvadorans, and other non-Europeans may also be attributable to the "mentality of exclusion."

19.   Barbara Yarnold. REFUGEES WITHOUT REFUGE: FORMATION AND FAILED IMPLEMENTATION OF U.S. POLITICAL ASYLUM POLICY IN THE 1980'S, University Press: Lanham, Maryland, 1990, p. 24. What has been referred to as a "mentality of exclusion," Higham (1965) refers to as "nativism." According to Higham, U.S. immigration policy has been the product of a struggle between two countervailing tendencies in this country: a cosmopolitan and democratic ideal of nationality, and nativism, which is a combination of both racism and nationalism. Nativism is based upon a core premise that national problems are externally created, and that measures should be taken to limit the influence of external forces through, for example, limiting immigration to the U.S. of persons who differ from U.S. citizens culturally, politically, linguistically, racially, and religiously.

20.   Barbara Yarnold. REFUGEES WITHOUT REFUGE: FORMATION AND FAILED IMPLEMENTATION OF U.S. POLITICAL ASYLUM POLICY IN THE 1980'S, University Press: Lanham, Maryland, 1990, p. 13. Passage of the Refugee Relief Act of 1953 heralded a major change in U.S. refugee policy, marking the first time that U.S. law explicitly recognized the existence of refugees. The Act allowed for the admission of 28,000 special immigrants, above normal immigration quotas. Half of these were reserved for refugees escaping from Eastern European countries. However, the Act had stringent requirements. Refugees were required to have U.S. citizens as sponsors who would guarantee that refugees would find housing and employment. The federal government also did not support the resettlement effort, leaving this to private individuals and organizations (Loescher and Scanlon, 1986).

21.   Deborah Sontag. "Reneging on Refuge: The Haitian Precedent." THE NEW YORK TIMES: NEXUS, June 27, 1993, p. 1, sec. 4. As part of its effort to crack down on illegal immigration, the Clinton Administration is expected to announce a plan this week to create a kind of night court for aliens, dispensing instant justice for those who arrive without proper documents and request political asylum.

The plan calls for an on-the-spot administrative hearing—and then a quick appeal, if requested—at all ports of entry. It also calls for the speedy deportation of those who do not demonstrate a 'credible fear' of persecution in their home country. Major international airports, especially John F. Kennedy in New York, would have a special staff, while other ports of entry would rely on 'circuit riders' who would go where needed.

The plan, drawn up in response to public outrage over the perceived abuse of the political-asylum system, is expected to be introduced as a compromise bill by Senator Edward M. Kennedy, Democrat of Massa-sachusetts, and Senator Alan K. Simpson, Republican of Wyoming. Mr. Kennedy is chairman of the Judiciary Committee's Immigration and Refugee Affairs Subcommittee, and Mr. Simpson is the ranking Republican.

22.   Gwen Ifill. "President Chooses an Expert to Halt Smuggling of Aliens." NEW YORK TIMES, June 19, 1993, p. 6. The Clinton Administration's new immigration policy, officials said, is expected to include proposals to toughen penalties for smuggling to as much as 20 years in prison, to allow racketeering laws to be applied to smuggling syndicates, to expand the ability of the Government to seize the assets of immigration smugglers and to expedite the admission or deportation of aliens seeking entry into the United States.

23.   Deborah Sontag. "Mexico's Position on Aliens Contradicted by Past Deed." NEW YORK TIMES, July 15, 1993, p. A18. Immigration experts expect that the United States will continue to seek other countries' cooperation in helping to process and repatriate illegal aliens bound for the United States. Indeed, a new Administration policy calls for the interdiction and 'redirection' of boats smuggling aliens.

The Supreme Court ruled recently that Federal and international laws prohibiting the summary return of aliens do not apply to those stopped in international waters or outside the United States. And immigration experts believe that ruling has emboldened the Administration.

Some human-rights advocates are concerned that the Government is pushing the limits of its powers in seizing and redirecting foreign vessels. The United States, through a treaty with the Haitian Government, has permission to interdict only Haitian boats.

24.   A.M. Rosenthal. "On My Mind; the U.S. Smashes a Peril." NEW YORK TIMES, July 20, 1993, Editorial p. A19. But the Clinton Administration has shown that it knows how to put together the power of the United States Navy, the Supreme Court and the Federal bureaucracy to stop this danger: the possibility that refugees from Communist China can get a decent hearing before they are shipped back in handcuffs.

For anybody who still cares about that old sentimental stuff about America being a home for those who flee despotism, that is the meaning of the nasty episode of the three ships intercepted by the Navy in international waters.

The Clinton Administration has decided to get tough about immigration. No more mushy Reagan-Bush era

insistence on following regulations that gave undocumented immigrants landing in the U.S. a full chance to prove they were refugees.

25.   Barbara Yarnold. REFUGEES WITHOUT REFUGE: FORMATION AND FAILED IMPLEMENTATION OF U.S. POLITICAL ASYLUM POLICY IN THE 1980'S, University Press: Lanham, Maryland, 1990, p. 18. Aliens must meet certain "burdens of proof" in applications for asylum and withholding of deportation. Applicants for asylum must establish that they have a "well-founded fear" of persecution. In withholding cases, the standard is more stringent: there must be a "clear probability" that the alien in question will be persecuted. The most serious criticism of these standards relates to their vagueness. Blum (1986) suggests, for example, that a number of issues arise when one attempts to prove eligibility for either type of asylum-related claim:

How much and what kind of evidence the applicant is required to provide, and what criteria the trier of fact and the reviewing court should use in evaluating that evidence… In addition, the courts have examined whether asylum and withholding of deportation applications are governed by the same standard and, if not, what the significant difference is between the two standards (Blum, 1986: 333-334).

Most important is that both standards, a "well-founded fear" and a "clear probability" of persecution, lack clear definitions. [ellipses in original]

26.   Barbara Yarnold. REFUGEES WITHOUT REFUGE: FORMATION AND FAILED IMPLEMENTATION OF U.S. POLITICAL ASYLUM POLICY IN THE 1980'S, University Press: Lanham, Maryland, 1990, p. 17. 1980 was the first year in which asylum was given explicit statutory recognition, with passage of the Refugee Act of 1980. Section 208(a) of the Act allows aliens within the U.S. to apply for asylum, and sets forth the following definition of a "refugee":

…any person who is outside any country of such person's nationality…who is unable to avail himself or herself of the protection of, that country because of persecution or a well-founded fear of persecution on account of race, religion, nationality, membership in a particular social group, or political opinion…(Refugee Act of 1980, section 208(A))

This definition of "refugee" applies to those outside of the U.S. who seek refugee status and to aliens in the U.S. who seek asylum. [ellipses in original]

27.   Barbara Yarnold. REFUGEES WITHOUT REFUGE: FORMATION AND FAILED IMPLEMENTATION OF U.S. POLITICAL ASYLUM POLICY IN THE 1980'S, University Press: Lanham, Maryland, 1990, pp. 15-16. The term "asylum policy" includes policy relating to both political asylum and withholding of deportation, two mechanisms in U.S law which allow "refugees" who are in the U.S. or at a port of entry to remain if they have a well-founded fear of persecution (asylum claims), or if there is a clear probability of persecution if they are deported (withholding of deportation claims). Asylum-related cases and appeals are cases and appeals which involve claims for either asylum or withholding of deportation.

28.   Lawyers Committee for Human Rights Refugee Project. THE NEW INS ASYLUM PROCEDURE: AN INTERIM ASSESSMENT BY PRACTITIONERS; A SURVEY AND REPORT, New York, September 1991, p. 18. A third complaint mentioned by several of those surveyed concerns applicants who are denied asylum on account of restrictive application of criteria. A practitioner in Houston said that some applicants "slip through the cracks." These are individuals who deserve asylum but do not fall into any legal category. "It is hard to show the political angle sometimes." A practitioner from Los Angeles adds, "the whole system is geared to single, educated men with the means to get to the USA, however, most refugees are women with children who cannot get to the USA." A practitioner in San Francisco complains that, "wars, such as in El Salvador, have affected people in ways which do not fit into the present law pertaining to asylum."

29.   Barbara Yarnold. REFUGEES WITHOUT REFUGE: FORMATION AND FAILED IMPLEMENTATION OF U.S. POLITICAL ASYLUM POLICY IN THE 1980'S, University Press: Lanham, Maryland, 1990, pp. 18-19. Hyndman (1986) suggests further that there is no accepted definition of "persecution." She suggests, however, that the determination as to whether an alien has a "well-founded fear" of persecution contains both objective and subjective elements.

Edwards (1983) agrees that the "well-founded fear" standard contains both objective and subjective elements. The subjective component causes a decisionmaker to examine such factors as the statements made by an alien, and the alien's personality and opinions, in an attempt to discover whether the alien has an actual fear of persecution. The objective component, on the other hand, requires an examination of the alien's credibility, and factors such as the following may be considered: the experience of the alien, the experience of friends and relatives of the alien, the laws of the alien's country of origin, and general conditions existing in the alien's country.

30. Lawyers Committee for Human Rights Refugee Project. THE NEW INS ASYLUM PROCEDURE: AN INTERIM ASSESSMENT BY PRACTITIONERS: A SURVEY AND REPORT, New York, September 1991, pp. 17-18. Another widely remarked complaint refers to the mechanics of work authorization. Although the Newark office is reportedly experiencing the majority of problems, complaints were reported from across the nation. A frequently mentioned problem is the difficulty of extending work authorization. A practitioner in Miami reports waiting up to three months just to get an appointment to extend work authorization. Before the new regulations, the waiting period was two to three weeks. One practitioner recommended that work authorizations be granted for twelve-month periods rather than a six-month period. Another urged that "employment authorization should be given immediately." A practitioner in Los Angeles recommended that Asylum Officers be given full jurisdiction over employment authorization.

31. Lawyers Committee for Human Rights Refugee Project. THE NEW INS ASYLUM PROCEDURE: AN INTERIM ASSESSMENT BY PRACTITIONERS: A SURVEY AND REPORT. New York, September 1991, p. 17. Another frequent complaint regards those fleeing war situations. "Individualized persecution versus upheaval in countries is a fine line," according to one practitioner. Another explained, "there should be exemption for civilians escaping civil war. They should not be returned to countries in civil war." Another in Chicago dislikes the "narrow U.N. definition of refugees leaving war." He feels that the great majority do not have political opinions, and persons escaping a war should be considered worthy of protection, even if they are not fleeing due to political opinion.

32. Lawyers Committee for Human Rights Refugee Project. THE NEW INS ASYLUM PROCEDURE: AN INTERIM ASSESSMENT BY PRACTITIONERS: A SURVEY AND REPORT. New York, September 1991, pp. 16-17. There are several complaints regarding current criteria for refugee status. The most frequent complaint pertains to the exclusion of conscientious objectors from refugee protection. A practitioner from New York stated that military deserters and draft evaders "are not given an opportunity to show [a] well-founded fear." Another from Washington D.C. feels war resister exclusions should be eliminated. An Arlington practitioner was of the view that forced recruitment should be enough for asylum.

33. Lawyers Committee for Human Rights Refugee Project. THE NEW INS ASYLUM PROCEDURE: AN INTERIM ASSESSMENT BY PRACTITIONERS: A SURVEY AND REPORT, New York, September 1991, p. 18. A practitioner in Chicago recommended that applicants who have suffered torture should be identified and considered separately from other applicants. In his agency's office, affirmative asylum applicants are sent to a torture treatment center. Thirty to 40 percent of these are found to have post-traumatic stress disorders stemming from their experiences in their home country. This renders them unable to give a credible account of why they left their home country and what happened to them there. They sometimes hide information which would lend support to their case because of fear, paranoia, severe psychological problems, and cultural differences. A protocol should be developed to address this issue and identify people who suffer psychological problems and are unable to recount their experiences.

34. Elizabeth Mary McCormick. "HIV-Infected Haitian Refugees: An Argument Against Expulsion." GEORGETOWN IMMIGRATION LAW JOURNAL, Vol. 7: 1993, p. 164. For example, in the case of aliens seeking political asylum in the United States, the possibility that the alien might be or become dependant upon public support may not be a basis for exclusion. This provision no doubt takes into consideration the political strife, war, poverty, and famine which frequently coincide with an alien's need to flee her home and seek refuge in another country. Under those circumstances, it would be unreasonable to require a refugee to have made financial or employment arrangements which might be expected of an alien coming to the United States as a permanent resident or temporary visitor. In fact, to deny a refugee entry in that case would be to ignore the very circumstances which have conferred that refugee status upon her in the first place.

35. A.M. Rosenthal. "On My Mind; The U.S. Smashes a Peril." NEW YORK TIMES, July 20, 1993, Editorial p. A19. Americans seem to be in an anti-immigration mood. "What, you want a billion Chinese over here and all those, you know, Haitians?" Let's cut through it—the obsessive emphasis on Chinese and Haitians is racism.

President Clinton owes the country a careful report on immigration—advantages as well as costs. Instead the Administration is rushing legislation that could reduce hearings to kangaroo courts presided over by immigration agents, not judges.

36. Barbara Yarnold. REFUGEES WITHOUT REFUGE: FORMATION AND FAILED IMPLEMENTATION OF U.S. POLITICAL ASYLUM POLICY IN THE 1980'S, University Press: Lanham, Maryland, 1990, p. 201. The fact that U.S. law provides no remedy for the vast majority of refugees from Central America has been attested to by many commentators. Among these are members of the sanctuary movement who initially attempted to help Central American refugees through legal immigration channels. Instead,

they found repeated violations of refugees due process rights by the immigration bureaucracy. There are reports that these aliens are often not informed of their right to apply for asylum and withholding. Susan Gzesch, an immigration attorney who inspected detention camps in Texas, suggests:

> The vast majority of Salvadorans are voluntarily returned to their own country by the INS without ever having had the opportunity to apply for political asylum. Many of them return never knowing such an opportunity exists, or if they did know, they were discouraged from applying by INS authorities, who see their primary work as returning undocumented entrants quickly (Golden and McConnell, 1986. p. 41).

37.   Vincent Bonaventura. HOUSE HEARINGS, April 27, 1993, Y4J89/1:103/7. Theoretically, every one with a valid travel document should be able to clear preinspection without incident. However, we are concerned that, as the legislation is now written, a lawful permanent resident could be denied entry on the basis of a single inspector's suspicion that the permanent resident has somehow relinquished status or is otherwise no longer eligible to return to the United States. Similarly, persons carrying a valid visa of any sort can be barred from the United States at the whim of the inspecting officer. The potential for harm is apparent: persons with every equity for returning—a home, U.S. family, future citizenship—can be kept out by a single INS officer, without any protections against error or capriciousness.

38.   Barbara Yarnold. REFUGEES WITHOUT REFUGE: FORMATION AND FAILED IMPLEMENTATION OF U.S. POLITICAL ASYLUM POLICY IN THE 1980'S, University Press: Lanham, Maryland, 1990. The preceding discussion suggests that the BIA, during the period in question, was not an effective "overseer" of asylum-related decisions made by other actors within the immigration bureaucracy. Hence, for example, decisions of immigration judges in these types of cases were rarely overturned, and procedural irregularities were typically over-looked. The BIA is best understood as an integral part of the immigration bureaucracy. "Bureaucratic intransigence" by the BIA leads to quick decisionmaking.

39.   Barbara Yarnold. REFUGEES WITHOUT REFUGE: FORMATION AND FAILED IMPLEMENTATION OF U.S. POLITICAL ASYLUM POLICY IN THE 1980'S, University Press: Lanham, Maryland, 1990, p. 134. An examination of the "merits" of asylum-related appeals to the BIA reveals that the BIA operates in an administrative fashion, bureaucratically reviewing asylum-related appeals, usually in the absence of oral argument, and narrowly applying the Act. Most

aliens who pursued appeals to the BIA, and particularly aliens from "non-hostile" states, were engaging in a practically futile undertaking. Sections 208 and 243(h) of the Act were intentionally narrowly drawn, so that aliens from states which are in the midst of a civil war are not eligible for refugee status. Hence, Haitians could not show that persecution suffered during the Duvalier regime was due to their political opinion, race, religion, membership in a social group, or nationality; Salvadorans could not demonstrate they would be singled out for persecution by either guerrillas or security forces; Cubans had criminal convictions which precluded them from obtaining asylum and withholding.

40.   Barbara Yarnold. REFUGEES WITHOUT REFUGE: FORMATION AND FAILED IMPLEMENTATION OF U.S. POLITICAL ASYLUM POLICY IN THE 1980'S, University Press: Lanham, Maryland, 1990, p. 104. Another procedural shortcut employed by the BIA in asylum-related appeals is to simply adopt the immigration judge's findings of fact, findings of law, and conclusions. For example, an appeal of a Salvadoran was summarily dismissed on October 20, 1982, when the BIA determined the "…immigration judge's conclusion that the respondent failed to establish a likelihood of persecution if he returns to El Salvador is clearly supported by the record."

The dependence of the BIA on immigration judges is demonstrated by the relatively low success rate for aliens in the sample of decisions taken from the BIA's published and unpublished decisions in asylum-related appeals from 1980 to 1987: 12%. Of 387 asylum-related appeals, only 46 were decided in favor of aliens.

Given the extent to which the BIA accepts decisions of immigration judges in asylum-related appeals, the BIA is not properly seen as a separate and independent appellate body in the administrative process, but as an integral part of the immigration bureaucracy, enforcing decisions on asylum-related claims made by the INS and immigration judges. [ellipses in original]

41.   Priscilla Clapp. "The Future of Refugee Policy." IN DEFENSE OF THE ALIEN, Vol. 15: 1993. U.S. refugee admissions law further provides that the annual admissions program will be based on national interest. For the period of the Cold War our struggle against communism has dominated our foreign policy, including the national interests that the U.S. body politic has used to determine the composition of refugee admissions to the United States. Most of our refugee resettlement has focused on groups fleeing communism: whether from the Soviet Union, from Eastern Europe, from Cuba, from Vietnam or from Ethiopia.

This year, for example, despite the end of the Cold War our admissions program is still very much a product of it. We are fulfilling what you might call an historic commitment. Of the 132,000 refugees that we are plan-

ning to admit to the United States this year, the vast majority come from Vietnam and the former Soviet Union. They represent the end—or perhaps more aptly, the last segment—of a refugee program that we have sustained for two decades. In the next three to four years, we hope that conditions will permit these very large Vietnamese and ex-Soviet programs to be brought to a close. Our definition of national interest as it affects refugee admissions will shift naturally to other types of refugees. For example, we are now beginning to resettle some of the refugees who cannot return to Iraq in the aftermath of the Persian Gulf War.

42.   Barbara Yarnold. REFUGEES WITHOUT REFUGE: FORMATION AND FAILED IMPLEMENTATION OF U.S. POLITICAL ASYLUM POLICY IN THE 1980'S, University Press: Lanham, Maryland, 1990, p. 26. There is much support in the literature (Economist, 1986; Preston, 1986) for the proposition that U.S. foreign policy consideration dominate its refugee and asylum policy, even in the post-Refugee Act of 1980 period. However, a question remains as to how these foreign policy objectives are communicated to decisionmakers within the immigration bureaucracy. Loescher and Scanlon (1986) suggest that these foreign policy goals are communicated through advisory opinions issued by the U.S. State Department's Bureau of Human Rights and Humanitarian Affairs (BHRHA) in cases involving asylum and withholding. Preston (1986) also notes the signification, before an INS agent may determine if an alien is eligible for asylum, the application must first be forwarded to the State Department for an advisory opinion. He claims that the advisory opinion is often dispositive of an asylum-related application since: "…many adjudicating officers give great deference to the opinion and rarely rule against its conclusions" (Preston, 1986, p. 91). [ellipses in original]

43.   Austin T. Fragomen, Jr. "Immigration Policy." IN DEFENSE OF THE ALIEN, Vol. 15: 1993, p. 203. Policy ambivalence through political manipulation is even more evident in the refugee and asylee area. Elaboration, particularly to this audience, is unnecessary. The basic policy is clear enough. It is the execution that creates the crises. The law protects persons having a well-founded fear of persecution based upon specified factors and envisions individualized determination. Legitimate legal issues are created through the terminology. For instance, is "well-founded" essentially an objective or subjective standard. However, it is not the existence of such questions that undermines policy. When citizens of one country are summarily granted asylum almost regardless of particular facts and those from another land held to the highest burden of proof, it is not the fault of the policy embodied in the law, but rather its implementation.

44.   Barbara Yarnold. REFUGEES WITHOUT REFUGE: FORMATION AND FAILED IMPLEMENTATION OF U.S. POLITICAL ASYLUM POLICY IN THE 1980'S, University Press: Lanham, Maryland, 1990, pp. 137-138. As seen in Chapter 4, the Refugee Act of 1980 has an objective the elimination of a long-standing hostile country bias in refugee policy. As shown in Chapters 5 and 6, the organizational goals of the immigration bureaucracy (in promoting a "state interest" in favoring aliens from hostile countries) diverged from the goal of the Refugee Act of 1980 of neutralizing refugee admissions. Since the federal courts are generally committed to upholding acts of Congress, the goals of the federal courts in this policy area are compatible with legislative goals (Bardach, 1984). Hence, while the immigration bureaucracy failed to enforce those provisions of the Act which mandated a de-politicization of refugee and asylum admissions and continued post-1980 to favor hostile country aliens, the federal courts were able to implement the neutralization policy.

45.   Barbara Yarnold. REFUGEES WITHOUT REFUGE: FORMATION AND FAILED IMPLEMENTATION OF U.S. POLITICAL ASYLUM POLICY IN THE 1980'S, University Press: Lanham, Maryland, 1990, p. 22. The few appeals brought by aliens from non-hostile countries that were successful, were successfully practically on a random basis. It almost appears that these few wins are entered by the BIA for the purpose of maintaining the impression that aliens may obtain an impartial review of their asylum-related claims by the BIA. The "wins" of aliens from non-hostile countries were often minor victories for the aliens; aliens from non-hostile countries received procedural victories from the BIA, and not substantive relief.

46.   Barbara Yarnold. REFUGEES WITHOUT REFUGE: FORMATION AND FAILED IMPLEMENTATION OF U.S. POLITICAL ASYLUM POLICY IN THE 1980'S, University Press: Lanham, Maryland, 1990, p. 103. The political biases of the BIA in favor of hostile state aliens, are readily apparent when one examines the decisions of the BIA from 1980 to 1987 in cases involving asylum and withholding of deportation. The incidence of "bureaucratic intransigence" by the BIA increases in cases where the person claiming refugee status is from a state that is non-hostile to the U.S.

"Bureaucratic intransigence" by the BIA in cases involving aliens from "friendly states" takes many forms. it may, for example, consist of the BIA's summary dismissal of cases involving asylum and withholding where the BIA fails to consider the merits of a claim. Summary dismissals in such cases may be based upon such trivial considerations as the untimely filing of an appeal by an alien, or an alien's failure to state the reasons for seeking an appeal. For example in an unpublished decision in-

volving a Haitian, the BIA on August 6, 1984, dismissed the alien's asylum-related appeal on the basis that it was untimely filed, stating: "In any event, we have no jurisdiction to entertain the applicant's appeal from the decision of the immigration judge inasmuch as it is untimely."

47.   Barbara Yarnold. REFUGEES WITHOUT REFUGE: FORMATION AND FAILED IMPLEMENTATION OF U.S. POLITICAL ASYLUM POLICY IN THE 1980'S, University Press: Lanham, Maryland, 1990, p. 171. Organizational involvement increases an alien's chances of winning in these appeals. Doctrinal analysis of the appeals in which organizations became involved indicates why organizational participation in these appeals may have led to higher success rates by aliens. Organizational involvement meant, at the very least, that important legal issues were raised in the appeals relating to, for example, the due process rights of excludable and deportable aliens, and whether actors within the immigration bureaucracy abused the rights of aliens who applied for asylum and withholding.

48.   Barbara Yarnold. REFUGEES WITHOUT REFUGE: FORMATION AND FAILED IMPLEMENTATION OF U.S. POLITICAL ASYLUM POLICY IN THE 1980'S, University Press: Lanham, Maryland, 1990, p.172. One promising finding was that the federal courts, in their decisionmaking on asylum-related appeals, departed from the biases of the immigration bureaucracy in favor of hostile state aliens and aliens from Europe. However, instead of engaging in a neutral evaluation of asylum-related appeals, the federal courts injected their own, political biases into the decisionmaking process. The danger is that in responding to the "political force" of partisanship, "judicial constituencies," and interest groups, the federal courts are simultaneously overlooking the merits of individual claims for asylum and withholding of deportation, with the result that refugees genuinely in need of "refuge" within the U.S. fail to find it, at least through the legal system.

If political influences cannot be removed from federal court decisionmaking, then federal court judges, like the other political branches, should be subject to political checks, including the vote.

49.   Barbara Yarnold. REFUGEES WITHOUT REFUGE: FORMATION AND FAILED IMPLEMENTATION OF U.S. POLITICAL ASYLUM POLICY IN THE 1980'S, University Press: Lanham, Maryland, 1990, pp. 171-172. This suggestion coincides with relatively recent observations that the courts, both state and federal, are "politicized," and do not exist in a "political vacuum." In fact, federal court judges are even more linked to their political environment than most citizens, since they have often been partisan activists prior to their appointment. Many federal court judges, prior to

their selection, have held positions as state court judges (who are often selected through partisan elections), administrators, and elected politicians. Hence, it is not altogether surprising that they respond to "political" variables, including: organizational involvement in appeals, the partisan affiliation of the president who appointed them, and their "judicial constituencies," defined as those most directly impacted by judicial decisions.

50.   Barbara Yarnold. REFUGEES WITHOUT REFUGE: FORMATION AND FAILED IMPLEMENTATION OF U.S. POLITICAL ASYLUM POLICY IN THE 1980'S, University Press: Lanham, Maryland, 1990, p. 175. The public interest organizations which participated in asylum-related appeals on the behalf of aliens are all legal services providers. They are located throughout the U.S. and provide legal services to aliens in immigration matters, including assistance with asylum and withholding claims. They tend to represent indigent clients, and either charge no fee for legal representation or charge a nominal fee, which may cover the costs of, for example, filing an application for asylum with the INS. Hence, these legal services organizations are properly classified as public interest groups since they seek to make a collective benefit, no-fee or low-fee legal representation, available to non-group members, namely the aliens they represent.

51.   Barbara Yarnold. REFUGEES WITHOUT REFUGE: FORMATION AND FAILED IMPLEMENTATION OF U.S. POLITICAL ASYLUM POLICY IN THE 1980'S, University Press: Lanham, Maryland, 1990, p. 146. Critics of the *Knauff-Mezei* doctrine, however, who focus upon the Supreme Court's analysis of whether excludable aliens are "persons," miss the mark. The refusal of the Supreme Court to extend due process review to the immigration bureaucracy when excludable aliens are involved is due to the "political" nature of the issues that are raised, and to the fact that decisions in this area fall into the orbit of U.S. foreign policy.

That the immigration bureaucracy's treatment of excludable aliens is highly politicized is well-documented in previous chapters: the INS, the State Department, immigration judges, and the BIA favor applicants for asylum and refugee status from "hostile" states. Given that all of these decisionmakers rely, to varying degrees, on the recommendations of the State Department, it is not surprising that the Supreme Court has been unwilling to engage in extensive due process review of decisions of the immigration bureaucracy which impact excludable aliens.

52.   Barbara Yarnold. REFUGEES WITHOUT REFUGE: FORMATION AND FAILED IMPLEMENTATION OF U.S. POLITICAL ASYLUM POLICY IN THE 1980'S, University Press: Lanham,

Maryland, 1990, p. 146. The *Knauff-Mezei* doctrine, however, which persists to the present, provides that excludable aliens are entitled to no due process protection aside from that which an agency provides to them. The rationale for this standard in light of *Yick Wo* is that excludable aliens are not "persons" within the meaning of the due process clause, which is rather surprising since even corporations have been recognized as such. Critics are also quick to point out that many excludable aliens are within the boundaries of the U.S. and, hence, fall within the scope of the due process clause under the standard set forth in *Yick Wo*. Excludable aliens have been found to be "persons" for the purposes of the equal protection clause, *Plyler v. Doe*, 457 U.S. 202 (1982).

53.   David A. Martin. "Asylum Case Law: How the New Regulations Can Help." IN DEFENSE OF THE ALIEN, Vol. 14: 1992, p. 137. To its great credit and contrary to some predictions, the BIA after *Cardoza Fonseca* moved strongly in this humane direction. In *Matter of Pula* the Board overruled a highly restrictive precedent so as to make asylum more nearly automatic for those who satisfy the threshold requirement of a "well-founded fear of persecution." Thus, in most asylum cases today, one need never reach the "clear probability" issue. If the applicant meets the more generous asylum standard, she will almost surely gain a favorable exercise of discretion. Thus, she will be granted asylum and perforce be protected against return. If she fails to satisfy that easier standard, *a fortiori* she does not qualify for *nonrefoulement* or withholding under § 243(h). The operative standard for nearly all cases, then, is simply "well-founded fear." Recognizing this reality, most people can ignore whatever worries *Stevic* once instilled; *Stevic* simply is not very important as long as adjudicative eyes focus on § 208 and its more generous standard, "well-founded fear."

54.   Barbara Yarnold. REFUGEES WITHOUT REFUGE: FORMATION AND FAILED IMPLEMENTATION OF U.S. POLITICAL ASYLUM POLICY IN THE 1980'S, University Press: Lanham, Maryland, 1990, p. 193. The hypothesis that the direct representation of aliens is significantly related to success by these organizations is not supported. Direct representation of aliens in asylum-related appeals to the BIA and the federal courts leads to only a .27 standard deviation increase in the cumulative normal probability function. This variable is not statistically significant.

55.   Barbara Yarnold. REFUGEES WITHOUT REFUGE: FORMATION AND FAILED IMPLEMENTATION OF U.S. POLITICAL ASYLUM POLICY IN THE 1980'S, University Press: Lanham, Maryland, 1990, p. 137. The federal courts function very differently than agencies, such as the INS, the State Department, and the BIA. The federal courts are independent bodies, outside of the immigration bureaucracy. The courts often review the "merits" of an asylum-related appeal in a "rights conscious" fashion. They attempt to preserve their independence from other branches and their unique position as "overseer" of the actions of the other branches of government.

56.   Barbara Yarnold. REFUGEES WITHOUT REFUGE: FORMATION AND FAILED IMPLEMENTATION OF U.S. POLITICAL ASYLUM POLICY IN THE 1980'S, University Press: Lanham, Maryland, 1990, p. 194. Almost all of the organizational representatives suggested that they are aware of a bias in the immigration bureaucracy's handling of asylum-related claims, in favor of hostile state aliens. In spite of their awareness of this "political" obstacle to gaining asylum-related relief, such as asylum or withholding of deportation, representatives of these groups appear committed to their chosen course of action, namely assisting aliens in asylum-related appeals to the BIA and the federal courts through legal channels.

57.   Barbara Yarnold. REFUGEES WITHOUT REFUGE: FORMATION AND FAILED IMPLEMENTATION OF U.S. POLITICAL ASYLUM POLICY IN THE 1980'S, University Press: Lanham, Maryland, 1990, p. 176. "State interests" in limiting immigration flows and favoring hostile state aliens thus led to a countermobilization of public interest groups, such as the ones examined here, which seek to protect the interests of immigrants and, more specifically, refugees and asylees.

58.   Barbara Yarnold. REFUGEES WITHOUT REFUGE: FORMATION AND FAILED IMPLEMENTATION OF U.S. POLITICAL ASYLUM POLICY IN THE 1980'S, University Press: Lanham, Maryland, 1990, p. 201. The impetus to a social movement is collective disaffection with positive law. Hence, the sanctuary movement originated in the frustration of many individuals and groups in the U.S. with the failure of U.S. immigration laws to provide refuge to Central Americans fleeing from deteriorating conditions in El Salvador and Guatemala. Both countries were torn by civil war, and those who sought shelter in the U.S. often came with reports of serious human rights abuses, including torture and murder, usually at the hands of government operatives. Refugees from Central America are able, pursuant to U.S. law, to apply for either political asylum or withholding of deportation on the basis that they have a well-founded fear of persecution or there is a clear probability that they will be persecuted in their countries of origin. However, as shown in Chapter 5 and 6, the immigration bureaucracy favors in refugee and asylum admissions aliens fleeing from hostile countries. Since both of the Central American countries mentioned—El Salvador and Guatemala—maintain cordial re-

lations with the U.S., refugees from these countries are not likely to be successful applicants for asylum or withholding.

59.   David A. Martin. "Asylum Case Law: How the New Regulations Can Help." IN DEFENSE OF THE ALIEN, Vol. 14: 1992, p. 133. The "clear probability of persecution" standard sounds quite severe, and I share the widely held view that it is too narrow a standard to redeem this nation's heritage as a refuge for the persecuted. But an understandable, probably even a defensible, impulse lies behind any effort to frame the governing standards in somewhat restrictive terms. The refugee provisions of statutory and treaty law were not intended to create a broad right of relocation whenever human rights abuses appear or conditions are otherwise difficult in the country of origin, however sympathetic the individual's situation might then be. No legislature in enacting asylum provisions, and no executive branch in signing the governing refugee treaties, intended to make political asylum so expansive that it would overshadow ordinary immigration controls. Moreover, whenever decision-makers begin to perceive that asylum risks that result (as they did, sometimes in panicky fashion, in most Western countries in the late 1970s and early 1980s), they commence to tailor case law and other measures to rein in their country's exposure.

60.   Michel Moussalli. "Prospects for Refugee Protection in the 1990's." IN DEFENSE OF THE ALIEN, Vol. 15: 1993, p. 131. One form of refoulement is putting up barriers to access which impede refugees in flight and prevent them from seeking asylum. Barriers can be as brutal as pushing boats back out to sea or as bureaucratic as imposing sanctions on airline carriers who transport asylum seekers without the proper documents.

Asylum seekers who have been able to enter a country of asylum are often in danger of having their human rights violated. Their physical security is often at risk; some refugees have been subjected to armed attacks or forcible recruitment into government or rebel forces. Detention is also a concern; many asylum seekers, including children, are detained under harsh conditions for long periods of time.

61.   Vincent Bonaventura. HOUSE HEARINGS. April 27, 1993, Y4.J89/1:103/7. Commendably, the legislation anticipates refugee protection and limits preinspection stations to countries that "maintain practices and procedures" that are in accord with the Refugee Convention and Protocol.

While well intended, this ambiguous limitation could result in providing little genuine protection. Although it is a delicate subject from a foreign policy perspective, there are many nations which are signatories to international human rights instruments who do not in actuality comply with them. The Convention and Protocol are no exception, and there are signatory states from which the United States has accepted refugees in the past.

We do appreciate that the loose language of this provision is probably intended to provide some leeway on which countries to establish preinspection stations; "maintains practices and procedures" does convey a functional, and not just rhetorical, commitment to refugee protection. However, the Refugee Act of 1980 was designed to eliminate the politicization of our asylum program, and perhaps a similar approach should be taken here and an objective limitation imposed. We very much favor the provision that appeared in the bill approved by the House last year that would limit placement of preinspection stations to countries from which the United States has not admitted a refugee or asylee in the preceding three years (although we would encourage Congress to consider lengthening that time period). In this way, we can be assured that the preinspection sites will be more "safer" and that their selection will not be swayed by the political expediences at the time a site is established.

62.   J. Michael Cavosie. "Defending the Golden Door: The Persistence of Ad Hoc and Ideological Decision Making in U.S. Refugee Law." INDIANA LAW JOURNAL, Vol. 67: 1992, p. 438. Such a provision ultimately may have the effect of chilling the favorable exercise of the discretion to grant asylum. But such an argument seems tenuous, because it assumes that these decision makers can portend fundamental changes in an applicant's home country. Otherwise, arbitrary denial will be subject to reversal. Furthermore, even assuming a chilling effect, the refugee who is denied asylum is no worse off than an asylee whose status is later revoked. Since the refugee in the first instance will still qualify for withholding of deportation, both will be repatriated when the circumstances change in their home country. At least the withholdee will know all along that her status is strictly temporary.

63.   Karen Bower. "Recognizing Violence Against Women as Persecution on the Basis of Membership in a Particular Social Group." GEORGETOWN IMMIGRATION LAW JOURNAL, Vol. 7: 1993, p. 205. It is inappropriate for the judicial branch to narrow the broad Congressional definition of refugee. The breadth of statutory definitions such as 'refugee' is for the legislature to determine, especially in the area of immigration which involves foreign policy considerations. It is further inappropriate for the courts to limit asylum eligibility, a benefit created by Congress, in deference to the INS, an arm of the executive branch. Furthermore, to the extent that courts should establish clear and "administrable interpretations," the confusing and contradictory standards made in ad hoc decisions to nar-

row asylum eligibility have failed to provide consistent and applicable results.

64. Bennett J. Lee. "The Immigration and Naturalization Service: In Search of the Necessary Efficiency." GEORGETOWN IMMIGRATION LAW JOURNAL, Vol. 6: 1992, p. 528. Over the past decade the INS has become increasingly decentralized through regional offices functioning autonomously from INS Headquarters in Washington, D.C. This was due, in large part, to INS leadership's reluctance to challenge any of the four regional commissioners. This segmentation has resulted in INS policy being implemented in an inconsistent fashion.

Decentralization has resulted in INS' employment sanctions policy being implemented erratically. For example, an employer in the INS' Western Region had incurred violations for six workers and was fined $2,000, which INS settled for $1,500. However, an employer in the Southern Region, with the exact same violations, was fined only $600, which INS settled for $100. Aside from the fairness problems endemic in this kind of incongruity, the rights of employers and, inevitably, immigrant employees, are affected as well, because penalties are not predictable or grounded in any systematic procedure.

Regionalization also impairs the Border Patrols daily operations. Prior to the reorganization plan, the Border Patrol was divided into twenty-one "sectors" among the four regions. Each sector's daily operations were controlled by one sector chief who answers to the regional commissioner. However, within each region were district offices which covered multiple sectors. Each district office was responsible for conducting investigations, adjudications, inspections, detention and deportation proceedings.

65. Bennett J. Lee. "The Immigration and Naturalization Service: In Search of the Necessary Efficiency." GEORGETOWN IMMIGRATION LAW JOURNAL, Vol. 6: 1992, pp. 522-523. The enforcement division is divided into two main parts: the Border Patrol and the Investigations Division. Theoretically, the two arms perform separate yet complementary functions. Originally, the Investigations arm was established to conduct criminal investigations involving smuggling across the borders and crimes committed by illegal entrants. Meanwhile, the Border Patrol's historical function has been to interdict illegal entrants at or near the border. Because of an increasingly complex enforcement environment and a lack of initiative by INS management to delineate clearly each enforcement branch's responsibilities, neither branch is utilizing its resources in an efficient manner.

66. Bennett J. Lee. "The Immigration and Naturalization Service: In Search of the Necessary Effi-

ciency." GEORGETOWN IMMIGRATION LAW JOURNAL, Vol. 6: 1992, p. 523. Through legislation over the past decade, the INS has been asked to assume a broad yet complex enforcement burden. In 1986, the Immigration Reform and Control Act (IRCA) was passed, requiring the Service to enforce the Act's employer sanction provisions by investigating employer hiring practices. Moreover, IRCA also requires the Border Patrol to investigate drug and alien smuggling operations. Clearly, these duties are inherently investigative and accordingly, should be reserved for the Investigations Division and not the Border Patrol officers. In practice, however, the Service has called upon its Border Patrol to execute the bulk of these investigatory duties. To make matters worse, the Investigation Division agents are forced to perform what are, essentially, administrative tasks. Because the INS has not clearly outlined the functions of each enforcement arm, there is waste of resources and duplication of duties.

67. COMMITTEE ON GOVERNMENT OPERATIONS, SECOND REPORT. "The Immigration and Naturalization Service: Overwhelmed and Unprepared for the Future." August 4, 1993, Y1.1/8:103-216. The Immigration and Naturalization Service (within the Department of Justice) is the principal agency responsible for facilitating the entry into the United States of persons legally admissable and for preventing the unlawful entry and employment of those who are not admissable. Since its creation, INS has faced ever changing and growing demands. Over the past decade, the INS budget has grown but INS has failed to provide enforcement and service programs adequate to serve growing demands. Constituent groups are unhappy with the quality of services provided, efforts to patrol the border are considered by many to be unsuccessful, and government auditors have issued a variety of reports identifying serious management inefficiencies throughout the agency.

68. Bennett J. Lee. "The Immigration and Naturalization Service: In Search of the Necessary Efficiency." GEORGETOWN IMMIGRATION LAW JOURNAL, Vol. 6: 1992, pp. 521-522. Basically, INS serves two functions. First, as an enforcement agency, its task is to keep undocumented aliens from entering the United States. On the other hand, as a service agency, its purpose is to facilitate the legal immigration of aliens into this country. The GAO correctly observed that these two objectives create divergent organizational objectives, and, thus it is difficult to devise and implement a consistent and cohesive policy.

69. COMMITTEE ON GOVERNMENT OPERATIONS, SECOND REPORT. "The Immigration and Naturalization Service: Overwhelmed and Unprepared for the Future." August 4, 1993, Y1.1/8:103-216. Some of the witnesses have concluded that the en-

forcement and service functions of the Immigration and Naturalization Service are so incompatible and the management problems so great that serious consideration should be given to its reorganization. As Mr. Wray explained: "...the two main units within INS—enforcement and service—have quite different, almost opposite, organizational objectives. One unit is charged with keeping aliens from illegally entering the country; the other unit is responsible for facilitating their legal entry." Or, in the words of former Commissioner Castillo, it is "an agency that's torn in several directions." [ellipses in original]

70.   COMMITTEE ON GOVERNMENT OPERA-
        TIONS, SECOND REPORT. "The Immigration and Naturalization Service: Overwhelmed and Unprepared for the Future." August 4, 1993, Y1.1/8:103-216. Similarly, INS has serious problems in the management of information. INS decisionmaking and programs are flawed because the lack of "methods to collect information, to sort it, to analyze to verify it." INS has also failed to comply with Federal requirements for protecting information contained in computer systems. As a result, important program and enforcement information is risk for destruction, alteration, and theft.

71.   COMMITTEE ON GOVERNMENT OPERA-
        TIONS, SECOND REPORT. "The Immigration and Naturalization Service: Overwhelmed and Unprepared for the Future." August 4, 1993, Y1.1/8:103-216. Information management is another area plagued with long-standing problems. Because of the lack of resources and planning for information systems, INS managers and field officials do not have information that is reliable and timely to carry out its responsibilities. GAO testified that INS must begin with the basics to "define its information needs." GAO's findings are consistent with those of the inspector general, who said that the INS "lacks methods to collect information, to sort it, to analyze it, to verify it." As he explained: "...when you have inaccurate, inadequate, or late information, how do you make important decisions and make priority decisions?" (He also told the subcommittee that INS has over 100 unique automated systems supporting every aspect of INS' mission. INS spent $300 million in 3 years for automated systems and plans to spend more money on systems that perform duplicate functions.) [ellipses in original]

72.   Bennett J. Lee. "The Immigration and Natural-
        ization Service: In Search of the Necessary Efficiency." GEORGETOWN IMMIGRATION LAW JOURNAL, Vol. 6: 1992, pp. 533-534. The problem with the current system is that one body receives, controls and accounts for inspection fee revenues, and with over $183 million in inspection user fee revenues in 1991, this is an awesome task for one body. Receiver-

ship and physical management of the funds should always be separate from accounting and book-keeping for such funds. With an accounting system lacking these internal checks, there is a running threat of fraud and theft, not to mention inadvertent mismanagement.

73.   COMMITTEE ON GOVERNMENT OPERA-
        TIONS, SECOND REPORT. "The Immigration and Naturalization Service: Overwhelmed and Unprepared for the Future." August 4, 1993, Y1.1/8:103-216. INS also has serious weaknesses in money management. The INS budget consists of approximately $1.042 billion in appropriated funds and $586 million in fees charged for services. Audit reports have repeatedly identified profound problems in the management of both appropriated funds and the fee accounts: accounting systems are inadequate, internal controls lacking, and the information used by management in making spending decisions is flawed. Deficiencies in money management affect the ability of the agency to carry out its program responsibilities. Constituent groups are frustrated that while the fees charged for services are increasing, they do not see visible improvements in the quality of services. The inspector general believes that with improved cost accounting, more fees could be collected. While the INS has devoted attention to correcting problems, its accounting problems are deep-seated and will require years to solve. Therefore, both short term and long term remedies are needed.

74.   COMMITTEE ON GOVERNMENT OPERA-
        TIONS, SECOND REPORT. "The Immigration and Naturalization Service: Overwhelmed and Unprepared for the Future." August 4, 1993, Y1.1/8:103-216. Members of the public shared the auditors' concerns about the financial state of affairs at INS. In their view, financial problems have undermined the ability of the agency to carry out its program responsibilities. Of particular concern is the collection, accounting for, and use of fees charged for the services utilized by constituency groups. Ms. Muñoz testified that the National Council of La Raza believes the collection of fees to pay for services is appropriate, however: "[t]he problem is that it is not clear that the fee generated in the Examination Fees Account are, in fact, used to provide services and to adjudicate applications." She continued:

> ...INS has never been able to be clear about how it establishes the fees that it does and where that money goes exactly. And yet in the last several years, INS has raised fees by as much as 100 percent in some cases.
>
> We are talking about funds that are paid into the U.S. by...hard-working people to whom this money doesn't necessarily come easily. It is one thing to ask these people to pay so that their ap-

plications can be adjudicated quickly and efficiently. it is another thing to transfer those funds into Enforcement, while at the same time they are waiting very long periods of time to reunite with their family members.

The American Immigration Lawyers Association shared NCLR's concerns that fees were going up, and there is "no empirical evidence that services are being improved at all." [ellipses in original]

75.   Bennett J. Lee. "The Immigration and Naturalization Service: In Search of the Necessary Efficiency." GEORGETOWN IMMIGRATION LAW JOURNAL, Vol. 6: 1992, p. 532. The Service does not have adequate control over its financial resources. This was the conclusion reached by the GAO in its January 1991 report where it outlined three problem areas within INS' fiscal management: (1) an outmoded accounting system, (2) weak internal controls, and (3) poor management over the financial resources. These deficiencies have become even more obvious, as the INS' budget has more than tripled since fiscal year 1980. Furthermore, INS requested more than $1.1 billion in appropriations for fiscal year 1993, with total available resources exceeding $1.5 billion. Therefore, the INS projects that approximately $400 million will be generated from its fee accounts.

76.   COMMITTEE ON GOVERNMENT OPERATIONS, SECOND REPORT. "The Immigration and Naturalization Service: Overwhelmed and Unprepared for the Future." August 4, 1993, Y1.1/8:103-216. The administrative infrastructure of INS is inadequate to support its vital programs. INS is confronted with serious personnel problems. Its staffing for important programs, such as patrolling the border and hearing claims of asylum, is inadequate, despite a 150 percent growth in its budget since 1981. For those staff it has hired, it has been delinquent in insuring that they are adequately screened and supervised. INS was characterized as "often indifferent" to training. it has suffered from deficiencies in training of personnel who perform accounting, procurement, adjudication and security functions as well as failures in fire arms training. Serious questions have been raised about the sufficiency of investigations into allegations of misconduct by INS personnel—in particular, Border Patrol personnel who are often accused of abusive behavior. When misconduct or inadequate performance is identified and documented, INS discipline is "spotty." Witnesses testified that some INS personnel lack a basic sense of civility and courtesy in dealing with the public.

77.   COMMITTEE ON GOVERNMENT OPERATIONS, SECOND REPORT. "The Immigration and Naturalization Service: Overwhelmed and Un-

prepared for the Future." August 4, 1993, Y1.1/8:103-216. Congress has partially responded to the asylum problem by creating a corps of asylum adjudicators; but Mr. Wilson testified that "in the absence of clerks to open mail, respond to inquiries, and perform other clerical and administrative functions, we understand that these asylum officers spend much precious time engaged in nonadjudicatory activities." Inadequate staffing is impeding resolution of infrastructure problems. According to a DOJ staff study, INS is significantly understaffed in the administrative area, a situation expected to have an adverse impact on reforms in areas such as financial and information management. (These are discussed in subsections 2 and 3, infra.)

78.   Bennett J. Lee. "The Immigration and Naturalization Service: In Search of the Necessary Efficiency." GEORGETOWN IMMIGRATION LAW JOURNAL, Vol. 6: 1992, pp. 527-528. Furthermore, enforcement programs will have to meet the challenge presented by increasingly deft drug trafficking operations and the growing number of undocumented aliens entering the United States. Compounding these pressures are the complexities added by a growing body of immigration related law, most significantly the Immigration Act of 1990. As the Border Patrol and Investigations Division stand today, the INS will not be able to meet these challenges and it will fall further behind in striving to accomplish its goals.

79.   Bennett J. Lee. "The Immigration and Naturalization Service: In Search of the Necessary Efficiency." GEORGETOWN IMMIGRATION LAW JOURNAL, Vol. 6: 1992, pp. 523-524 This shift to the interior has several effects. Because resources are limited and interior Border Patrol ranks are swelling, many of the border stations are understaffed. Thus, due to personnel mismanagement, the Border Patrol cannot adequately execute its historical duty of guarding the nation's borders, especially that along the southwest.

80.   COMMITTEE ON GOVERNMENT OPERATIONS, SECOND REPORT. "The Immigration and Naturalization Service: Overwhelmed and Unprepared for the Future." August 4, 1993, Y1.1/8:103-216. Unfortunately, INS has not done a good job. As reflected in this report, people are unhappy with the quality of both the enforcement and service functions performed by the agency. In addition, despite the enactment of the 1986 law to stop illegal immigration, the undocumented population in this country is estimated to be 3.3 million. (Data regarding the number of undocumented aliens in the United States is very inadequate.) Constituency groups are frustrated because of backlogs and inordinate delays in the delivery of services to those who enter the country in accordance with Federal law. In addition, in recent years, government audi-

tors have issued numerous reports identifying management inefficiencies throughout INS. Their findings have been so consistently negative and the problems so pervasive that in the 1992 Department of Justice annual report required under the Federal Managers Financial Integrity Act of 1982, the Immigration and Naturalization Service was identified as the Department's No. 1 "high risk" area.

81. Bennett J. Lee. "The Immigration and Naturalization Service: In Search of the Necessary Efficiency." GEORGETOWN IMMIGRATION LAW JOURNAL, Vol. 6: 1992, p. 543. Perhaps of greatest concern is the financial management problem. If immigration programs are to fund themselves, as Congress intended, then a complete overhaul of the INS' accounting system is required. However, no substantive changes have been implemented as of this writing. Aside from not being able to simply monitor expenses and revenues, the INS is indirectly penalizing immigrants seeking crucial INS services through charging exorbitant fees. If immigrants cannot be effectively served by the INS, the entire viability of the agency must be questioned. Finally, if these problems cannot be reconciled perhaps Congress should consider bifurcating the INS' operations into an enforcement division and a separate bureau for adjudications and naturalization. Until the INS can demonstrate competence in managing its own affairs, its future must remain in question.

82. COMMITTEE ON GOVERNMENT OPERATIONS, SECOND REPORT. "The Immigration and Naturalization Service: Overwhelmed and Unprepared for the Future." August 4, 1993, Y1.1/8:103-216. While fundamental change will take years, we believe that there are actions which can be taken on a short term basis that would show positive improvements in INS performance. Short term change is necessary, not only to improve the quality of services and programs, but to help improve agency morale and enhance its credibility with the American public and the Congress.

To accomplish change, INS must waste no more time in implementing reforms. Its leadership must be knowledgeable, aggressive, and have a clear vision of its purpose. INS personnel must be held accountable for failures in implementing change.

With regard to proposals for extensive restructuring of the service, the committee shares the concerns expressed by witnesses that any efforts to implement such proposals could be distracting to the task of correcting management deficiencies.

The committee recognizes that there are forces outside of the control of the INS which affect its ability to do its job and that the task of controlling the borders of the United States is overwhelming. But while the task is daunting, nevertheless the committee believes that INS can, and must do, a much better job. With creativity, energy, commitment, and competence, significant improvements can be made.

83. Bennett J. Lee. "The Immigration and Naturalization Service: In Search of the Necessary Efficiency." GEORGETOWN IMMIGRATION LAW JOURNAL, Vol. 6: 1992, p. 526. This team treatment fails to solve the fundamental problem confronting the enforcement units. Both the GAO and the Carlson Commission emphasized the need for the INS to delineate the functions of the Border Patrol so that they are distinct from the duties of the Investigation Division. Only with this change can the duplication of duties be avoided and roles be executed efficiently.

84. Bennett J. Lee. "The Immigration and Naturalization Service: In Search of the Necessary Efficiency." GEORGETOWN IMMIGRATION LAW JOURNAL, Vol. 6: 1992, p. 531. Those involved with the INS' daily operations have little confidence in the reorganization plan's efforts to centralize. In a report to the House of Representatives, the Surveys and Investigations Staff found, "[a]greement was almost unanimous among field officials that Headquarter's program management lacks the necessary knowledge of local situations to properly manage field activities on a day-to-day basis. Furthermore, the field officials do not believe the reorganization plan has been thoughtfully conceived. For example, although the Associate Commissioner for Management has control over the regions, the Border Patrol and districts do not report directly to this officer. Thus, if a district needed more investigators, it would need to contact its regional administrator, who would then apprise the Associate Commissioner for Management of the requests. From there, the Associate Commissioner must contact the Associate Commissioner for Human Resources and Administration, who then contacts the appropriate managers within that division. Realistically, with all the new layers of management created by the centralization plan, efficient and timely deployment of replacement personnel seldom will be achieved.

85. Bennett J. Lee. "The Immigration and Naturalization Service: In Search of the Necessary Efficiency." GEORGETOWN IMMIGRATION LAW JOURNAL, Vol. 6: 1992, pp. 530-531. INS efforts to centralize run directly contrary to the recommendations of the Carlson Commission and the sentiments of the district offices. The Carlson Commission concluded, "The [INS] is simply too large, too complex, and too geographically dispersed to be effectively managed from Washington."

86. Bennett J. Lee. "The Immigration and Naturalization Service: In Search of the Necessary Efficiency." GEORGETOWN IMMIGRATION LAW

JOURNAL, Vol. 6: 1992, p. 527. The GAO takes this recommendation a step further. In addition to defining Border Patrol and Investigation division duties more clearly, William Gadsby has suggested that enforcement functions be controlled district by district. In other words, all enforcement functions would be centralized under a single official within each geographic area. The rationale behind this approach is that enforcement activities can be most effective on a regional level, especially given the fact that the INS often works with local authorities and authorities from other agencies. The potential problem, however, is that the INS has encountered the problems associated with partitioning operations by district or region. Partitioning operations by district could only work if INS headquarters in Washington, D.C., maintained strict supervision to ensure implementation of a uniform enforcement policy. Whatever the solution, the INS has not taken adequate measures to ensure the efficient and consistent application of its enforcement policy.

87.   Vincent Bonaventura. HOUSE HEARINGS.
        April 27, 1993, Y4J89/1:103/7, p. 226. While we are deeply concerned about the existence of certain administrative problems and the need for significant structural and operational reform inside the asylum program, we are nonetheless reluctant to label them as irreparable failings. Rather, the program simply needs reform and improvement based on its experience.

We believe that the challenges facing the Asylum Branch are for the most part the product of inadequate support and the inevitable consequences of program development. These problems can be cured with a little commitment and attention from both the Department of Justice and the public. Every indication lately has suggested that this commitment and attention would be forthcoming from INS, and we are optimistic that meaningful administrative reform can take place.

We therefore do not believe that legislative solutions in the area of general administrative operations would be appropriate at this time. We would ask that Congress provide the nongovernmental community and the INS opportunity to explore and test solutions and that Congress set a deadline for reform and revisit the subject of asylum adjudication reform in a few months to assess its progress.

88.   Vincent Bonaventura. HOUSE HEARINGS.
        April 27, 1993, Y4J89/1:103/7, pp. 225-226. We believe that, based on the experience of the first years of the current asylum program, the problem with keeping pace with incoming cases can be overcome. A comprehensive review of INS asylum procedures, practices, and regulations would identify a number of opportunities to streamline the process based on real examples and real experiences. For instance, installation of data processing systems in all Asylum Offices, transferring non-asylum clerical work to other examinations personnel, removing asylum staff from the preparation and issuance of employment authorization documents, eliminating Asylum Officer responsibility to prepare and issue deportation orders to show cause, eliminating mandatory BHRHA opinion letters in all cases, permitting summary approval of deserving cases, and rationalizing the complementary roles of the INS and the INS asylum function of the EOIR immigration judges would all serve to greatly speed up, increase capacity, and reduce the cost of the current asylum program.

89.   Vincent Bonaventura. HOUSE HEARINGS.
        April 27, 1993, Y4J89/1:103/7. Reforms that can accomplish these goals are a redefinition of inspection, to clearly allow the use of electronic passenger manifest and other forms of scrutiny as the basis for the admission of passengers. Expanded use of machine readable data from passports as the basis for government recordkeeping functions to preinspections can free inspectors from time-consuming clerical tasks.

Expansion of the INS preinspection program to additional overseas sites can reduce the burden placed on domestic arrival holds. Making the visa waiver program permanent will encourage a high-level tourism from major source countries.

Earmarking INS user fee legislation will ensure that revenues are spent on passenger inspection and facilitation initiatives, and mandate that U.S. citizens are given expedited treatment by INS. Directing INS to make a more proactive role will prevent illegal travelers from reaching the United States.

Fostering a cooperative effort with the air carriers and other Federal agencies with information on international travelers, would facilitate the prevention of known hostiles or falsely documented travelers from boarding U.S. bound carriers. Providing better training of personnel and official notification of document design changes, as well as positive rewards for carrier's compliance, are also needed to ensure these issues are addressed.

In summary, we must move quickly to assure that another important sector of the American economy is not eroded by competition from other nations. Failure to adjust to the norms in place elsewhere for welcoming tourists and business travelers, cannot be compensated for in other ways. Entry formalities must be efficient or the market will simply go elsewhere.

90.   COMMITTEE ON GOVERNMENT OPERA-
        TIONS, SECOND REPORT. "The Immigration and Naturalization Service: Overwhelmed and Unprepared for the Future." August 4, 1993, Y1.1/8:103-216. He believes that addressing the backlog problem would also solve a second problem, work authorizations:

        …an affirmative applicant for asylum—that is, someone who is not in proceedings for either ex-

clusion or deportation—may apply for an employment authorization document if the decision in the case takes more than 90 days and the applicant can prove to the satisfaction of the authorities that the application is not frivolous.

…The problem is with the adjudication of these cases within the 90 to 120 day period which was originally contemplated under the law. If the law…were to provide the resources to the Service for it to perform these functions, these claims would, and I believe could, be adjudicated within the 90- to 120-day period. The case would be over, the individual would have no need to seek employment, and a decision up or down would be made about political asylum. [ellipses in original]

91.   Laurie E. Elkstrand. *Alien Smuggling*. HEARING BEFORE THE SUBCOMMITTEE ON INTERNATIONAL LAW, IMMIGRATION, AND REFUGEES OF THE COMMITTEE ON THE JUDICIARY. United States House of Representatives, Y4.J89/1:103/9, June 30, 1993, p. 39. In removing illegal aliens from the country, INS is confronted with the almost impossible task of trying to locate and remove those aliens it believes should not remain here. INS does not have sufficient resources to detain the millions of aliens who are subject to detention or who have been ordered deported. Consequently, aliens INS apprehends are generally released pending the resolution of their deportation hearing. Our past work indicated that some aliens who were released did not appear for their hearings. INS did not have sufficient resources to reapprehend them.

92.   Ranee K.L. Punjabi. "The Global Refugee Crisis: A Search for Solutions." CALIFORNIA WESTERN INTERNATIONAL LAW JOURNAL, Vol. 21, no. 2: 1990-1991, p. 263. The first premise would be to agree that "since refugees are a global problem, the search for solutions must also be global." The second equally important premise would be to ensure that any solution enhances the system of human rights and is in accord with its principles. This opinion has attempted to show that restrictive legislative measures, temporary stop-gap approaches, and attempts to deflect refugees to other countries do not stop the refugee flows or ameliorate conditions for those who are already refugees.

93.   Rosemarie Rogers. "The Future of Refugee Flows and Policies." INTERNATIONAL MIGRATION REVIEW, Vol. 26, no. 4: Winter 1992, p. 1122. Widgren estimates that after a final negative decision, about 15-25 percent of the rejected applicants return to their home countries, either voluntarily or through deportation, and that the other 75-85 percent remain illegally in the country in which they had submitted their claim or in a neighboring country.

94.   Laurie E. Elkstrand. *Alien Smuggling*. HEARING BEFORE THE SUBCOMMITTEE ON INTERNATIONAL LAW, IMMIGRATION, AND REFUGEES OF THE COMMITTEE ON THE JUDICIARY. United States House of Representatives, Y4.J89/1:103/9, June 30, 1993, p. 42. INS believes that detention is a deterrent to the flow of illegal aliens entering the country. It reported some success in temporarily reducing the flow of illegal entry in three specific situations, as the Texas example shows. However, the resources needed for such detention projects cannot be sustained nationwide or for extended periods of time because of budget constraints. Further, INS' planned expansion of its detention capacity is small in relation to the number of illegal aliens who are subject to detention.

95.   Laurie E. Elkstrand. *Alien Smuggling*. HEARING BEFORE THE SUBCOMMITTEE ON INTERNATIONAL LAW, IMMIGRATION, AND REFUGEES OF THE COMMITTEE ON THE JUDICIARY. United States House of Representatives, Y4.J89/1:103/9, June 30, 1993, p. 30. As the last two components indicate, the administration's plan to combat alien smuggling by organized crime syndicates focuses on interdicting smuggled aliens when possible and, when not able to interdict, detaining aliens arriving by boat and expediting their cases. We support the administration's effort to interdict illegal aliens before they can arrive here as a means to deter smuggling. For those who are not interdicted, if the plan is to be effective, our work has shown that problems relating to alien detention and removal will have to be addressed. The plan presently does not address these issues.

As indicated, the administration's plan calls for detaining most of the aliens who enter in conjunction with criminal smuggling activities and expediting their cases. For INS to detain these aliens even for a relatively short period of time, it will have to release other aliens or obtain additional detention resources.

96.   Robert Rubin. HOUSE HEARINGS, April 27, 1993, Y4J89/1:103/7. The APSO (Asylum Pre-screening Officers) program, providing for release of those asylum applicants with credible claims who are unlikely to abscond and do not pose a threat to community, is an important step in the right direction. Unfortunately, it operates on a very limited basis; it should be expanded so that all *bona fide* asylum applicants are not subject to detention. Successful implementation of the APSO program will allow for the diversion of substantial resources from detention into the asylum system.

97.   Gene McNary. HOUSE HEARINGS, April 27, 1993, Y4J89/1:103/7. Once the frivolous claims are weeded out, including those where the applicant flew in from a country where he or she could have claimed asylum or where country conditions in the coun-

try of origin were not such that a claim of persecution could in any way be justified, then the numbers of persons who present a credible claim and enter into the asylum system will be manageable and the detention space required substantially reduced.

98.   COMMITTEE ON GOVERNMENT OPERA-
        TIONS, SECOND REPORT. "The Immi-
gration and Naturalization Service: Overwhelmed
and Unprepared for the Future." August 4, 1993,
Y1.1/8:103-216. Subcommittee members were particularly interested in a related problem, the case in which an individual boards an airplane bound for the United States, then seeks entry without appropriate documents by making a claim for asylum. (He or she may either have obtained fraudulent documents and/or may discard them along the way.) The General Accounting Office recommended preventing aliens from entering the country in the first place by placing greater emphasis on the "preclearance process overseas." The inspector general suggested that the problem could be addressed if "INS had a proper communications system when a person boards in London with the proper visa, that would be relayed through, say, JFK in New York, and so that would preclude, or eliminate the factor of people destroying documents on board."

99.   Vincent Bonaventura. HOUSE HEARINGS,
        April 27, 1993, Y4J89/1:103/7, p. 272. For
this reason, the benefits of the preinspection would not be compromised by the inclusion of certain safeguards that were built into last year's approved preinspection legislation. Presumably, preinspection will "scare off" a significant percentage of persons who are not entitled to enter the United States and the extra effort it would take to acquire access to an immigration judge still more. If anything, preinspection may naturally distill the group of persons seeking review to a very small handful whose persistence may very well indicate *de facto* a case worthy of review.

100.   Laurie E. Elkstrand. *Alien Smuggling*. HEAR-
        ING BEFORE THE SUBCOMMITTEE ON
INTERNATIONAL LAW, IMMIGRATION, AND
REFUGEES OF THE COMMITTEE ON THE JUDI-
CIARY, United States House of Representatives,
Y4.J89/1:103/9, June 30, 1993, p. 36. Immigration policy and international relations affect INS' ability to prevent the arrival or entry of illegal aliens. The key to controlling the illegal entry of aliens is to prevent their initial arrival. Once they arrive, their removal is very difficult due to the combination of
—the aliens' use of the relief provisions of the Immigration and Nationality Act, such as applying for asylum, to avoid or delay their deportation;

—INS' limited detention space, which has led it to release most aliens, even though they may not appear for their deportation or exclusion hearings; and
—the limited consequences to the aliens for their failure to appear at their deportation hearings.

101.   Vincent Bonaventura. HOUSE HEARINGS,
        April 27, 1993, Y4J89/1:03/7, p. 268. We
similarly support the proposal to make the visa waiver program a permanent fixture in U.S. immigration law. Thus far, it appears to us that the visa waiver pilot program has been successful at eliminating unnecessary visa processing and has greatly facilitated international travel between the United States and countries with low incidence of visa fraud. Making the program permanent seems only logical at this juncture.

While the concern is still somewhat academic, we do want to remind the Subcommittee that the exclusion and deportation provisions in the visa waiver program could work some unfortunate results insofar as no review exists for such determinations. It is possible for an alien to be mistakenly denied admission or for an international traveler to innocently attempt to enter thinking a visa was not necessary. The Subcommittee should seriously consider the importance of providing some degree of supervisory or administrative review.

We must voice some concern for the restrictive language with regard to refugees under the visa waiver program. While it is vital that any visa waiver program be streamline, we must be careful neither to contradict our obligations to protect refugees nor be unmindful that a legitimate refugee may not have any choice in the method of escape. The visa waiver program should not have more demanding standards than any other program when it comes to asylum-seekers.

102.   James Ward. HOUSE HEARINGS, April 27,
        1993, Y4J89/1:03/7. The disruptions which
would result would be immense; losses of earnings in the travel and tourism industries and foreign relations complications with countries all of which are our friends and international partners. Worst of all, these results would be to no purpose. Allowing the program to expire and the visa requirement to be re-imposed would meet no identified need, solve no identified problem, eliminate no identified threat.

103.   James Ward. HOUSE HEARINGS, April 27,
        1993, Y4J89/1:03/7. Some may continue to
take a cautious approach to this matter, preferring to extend the program for another limited period rather than making it permanent. The Department sees no need for, or benefit from, such an approach. Extending the program for a limited period would simply postpone the inevitable day of reckoning, raising the possibility of the problems we have outlined on the new expiration date rather than on September 30 next year. The Department

believes that five years is long enough to assess the benefits of the program and its problems. The benefits are clear; the problems are not there. The program should be made permanent now and we should turn our attention to the problems we do have.

104.   James Ward. HOUSE HEARINGS, April 27, 1993, Y4J89/1:03/7. The program is currently scheduled to expire on September 30, 1994. If that day comes without action to prolong the life of the program, the Department and our tourist industry (this country's largest single source of foreign currency earnings) will face a serious crisis. The millions of short-term visitors who come to this country annually from the qualifying countries would suddenly be faced again with the requirement of obtaining a visa to do so. The Department would be faced with the impossible task of re-establishing huge nonimmigrant visa operations in places such as Tokyo, London, Paris, Rome, major cities throughout Germany and elsewhere, without the resources to do so and without the prospect of obtaining them.

105.   James Ward. HOUSE HEARINGS, April 27, 1993, Y4J89/1:03/7. H.R. 1153 includes a proposal to make the VWPP permanent. This proposal is identical with one introduced in the last Congress—also by Cong. Schumer—but not acted upon. The Department strongly supported last year's proposal and supports it equally as strongly now. The VWPP has been a success. First, from an enforcement standpoint, there is no evidence that waiving the visa requirement for these short-term visitors from the carefully selected countries has resulted in any meaningful incidence of abuse of our immigration laws. Second, there is nothing to raise a suspicion that the program has created internal security or other law enforcement problems. Third, the program has facilitated tourist travel to the United States and allowed its continuing expansion without hindrance.

106.   "Clinton Asylum Plan Won't Ease Backlog." THE ORLANDO SENTINEL, March 14, 1994, p. A6, NEXUS. The Clinton administration's plan to overhaul and expand the political asylum system would streamline processing of new applications but still leave as many as 1 million asylum-seekers frozen in a backlog for years. The plan, expected to be formally unveiled this month, would double the number of officials hearing cases and partially pay for the increased staff by charging applicants a $150 fee. Other measures would sharply curtail asylum-seekers' access to work authorization that is now routinely issued to almost all applicants. But officials concede that even under rosy projections, it could take a decade to deal with the backlog of people awaiting a decision on their request to be allowed to stay in the United States. As many as 10,000 new cases are currently added to the backlog each month

because the government does not have enough officials to determine whether they are deserving.

107.   Tim Weiner. "Pleas for Asylum Inundate System for Immigration." NEW YORK TIMES, April 25, 1993. Barely two years after it was altered to abolish harsh and arbitrary procedures, the American system of political asylum cannot cope with the growing crowds of people at the nation's gates, immigration officials say.

Nationwide, more than 250,000 foreigners are waiting in line to see one of only 150 asylum officers. Some have been waiting for years. All say they fear persecution at home, and immigration officials estimate that tens of thousands really are running for their lives. Under the law, most are allowed into the United States immediately, physically on free soil, but legally in limbo.

Because of the backup, half have no hope of a hearing in the foreseeable future and thus no resolution of their cases.

108.   "The United States of Asylum." NEW YORK TIMES, September 19, 1993, Sect. 6, p. 56. Still, the numbers are rising rapidly, and if the asylum apparatus is a reflection of the way Americans think about it, it is a subject we find difficult to think about at all. From 1968 to 1975 the United States averaged only 200 applicants per year. The startling rise in applications since—130,000 are expected this year—has until recently been met with bureaucratic paralysis. A ballyhooed asylum corps of 150 specially trained officers (Germany has 3,000; Sweden, 800) inherited a backlog of 114,000 cases the day they started work in 1991. There is now a backlog of 300,000 cases.

109.   Rosemarie Rogers. "The Future of Refugee Flows and Policies." INTERNATIONAL MIGRATION REVIEW, Vol. 26, no. 4: Winter 1992, p. 1122. Tables 2 and 3 show the increases in the numbers of asylum applications in Europe and North America between 1983 and 1991. In Europe most of the numbers have risen further in 1992; Germany, the most impacted country, is expected to report close to 500,000 applications for the year. At the same time as the number of applications has increased, recognition rates have fallen. In 1991, the percentage of asylum applications adjudicated in the first instance that were recognized under the 1951 Convention ranged from 21 percent in the United Kingdom to less than one percent in Finland, with intermediate proportions of 20 percent in France, 13 percent in Austria, 10 percent in the Netherlands, 7 percent in Germany, 5 percent in Sweden, and 3 percent in Switzerland (Intergovernmental Consultations 1992: Table 3).

110.   COMMITTEE ON GOVERNMENT OPERATIONS, SECOND REPORT. "The Immi gra-

tion and Naturalization Service: Overwhelmed and Unprepared for the Future." August 4, 1993, Y1.1/8:103-216. "Personnel are INS' most important resource" according to the IG. Unfortunately, it is also in the area of personnel that some of the most serious problems exist.

Despite staffing increases since fiscal year 1981, INS if fundamentally understaffed for its job. As a result, important programs have suffered. Mr. Wray of the GAO observed "…we've effectively lost control of the southwest border, and I think there are tremendous shortages in staff on the part of the Border Patrol down there." Mr. Richard Wilson, representing the American Bar Association, testified that abuses in asylum adjudication (which allowed the accused CIA killer to stay in the United States) are the direct result of a backlog due to inadequate staffing:

> The most appropriate solution for deterring frivolous cases is to allocate sufficient funding and personnel to ensure prompt asylum adjudications followed by institution of deportation proceedings for ineligible applicants. If applicants were to receive fair decisions within 90 days of application, as intended…the volume of asylum applications would, no doubt, decrease. [ellipses in original]

111.   Vincent Bonaventura. HOUSE HEARINGS, April 27, 1993, Y4J89/1:03/7. Full operations of the INS program were not achieved for some time, and there is now little more than a year's worth of experience with the new program. The program continues to struggle. Adequate funding and resources remain elusive, and the Asylum Branch is still wrestling with its place within the greater structure of INS. Asylum as a program within INS has been the victim of interdepartmental struggles within INS, especially where questions of resource allocation are concerned. In the internal jockeying for funds and resources, the Asylum Branch often gets short shrift. For example, Asylum Officers is being saddled in some regions with clerical duties that detract from the amount of casework they can do—performing data entry, issuing employment authorization documents, orders to show cause, etc.

112.   Deborah Sontag. "Reneging on Refuge: The Haitian Precedent." THE NEW YORK TIMES: NEXUS, June 27, 1993, p. 1, sec. 4. But the bill does not address—and could temporarily worsen—the nemesis of the political-asylum system: a growing backlog, now at 300,000 cases. Rather, the bill focuses on what the public perceives to be the system's primary flaw: exploitation of the asylum system as a way to enter the country by air or by sea, receive working papers and stay for years while claims are processed and appealed.

Following both the grounding off Queens of the Golden Venture freighter loaded with Chinese asylum seekers and the disclosure that a suspect in the World Trade Center bombing had fraudulently entered the country by claiming political asylum, abuse of the asylum system has grown to symbolize a lack of American control over its own borders—although most undocumented migrants slip in across the nation's land borders, where 1.1 million illegal aliens were caught last year.

In addition, only a fraction of asylum seekers make their request when they were caught at an airport or other port of entry; most enter legally and overstay visas, or cross the borders undetected. Only 14,000 immigrants sought asylum at airports last year; about 104,000 immigrants applied for asylum once they were safely in the country.

"This bill gets at a sliver of the problem," said a senior Senate aide involved in immigration. "To us, it's like a boil that needs lancing."

113.   PR NEWSWIRE ASSOCIATION, INC.
"Administration's Statements on 'Elements of Asylum' Undercut Prospects of Serious Reform, Says FAIR." NEXUS, March 7, 1994.
1. "Anyone, from anywhere, at any time, regardless of manner of entry or immigration status, may apply for asylum in the United States."
Comment: This policy is exactly why our asylum laws are routinely abused. The Clinton administration continues to refuse to set even the most minimal standards for applying for protection. Civil courts demand that a plaintiff show some evidence of a legitimate grievance before they will consider a case. If that minimal threshold is not met, civil courts will throw the case out. Yet when it comes to political asylum, the administration seems intent on inviting frivolous claims. Aliens seeking to get around our immigration policies know that they can achieve entry to the United States by filing an asylum claim that they know has no merit. This claim will allow them an opportunity to enter the U.S. and then simply disappear.

114.   Arthur C. Helton. "Uncontrolled Right of Entry Poses a Threat." THE NATIONAL LAW JOURNAL, May 3, 1993, p. 16. The hearing delays are themselves a magnet. From fewer than 5,000 applications a year in 1980, asylum claims have exploded to more than 100,000 a year and are growing. The system was never designed to copy with a caseload of this size. It now takes a year and a half to obtain a hearing, in itself an inducement to fraud. Work authorization and complete liberty are provided in the interim. Since most who come here do so to work, many never even show up for a hearing, and there is no criminal sanction for failure to appear.

Consider the case of Amir Ahmal Kanzi, the Pakistani who orchestrated a pending political asylum claim

while he allegedly planned and murdered the two CIA employees last January. He could purchase property, marry an American citizen and could probably have used most state-administered welfare programs even before his hearing came up.

115. Stein. HOUSE HEARINGS, April 27, 1993. Y4J89/1:03/7. The hearing delays are themselves a magnet. From less than 5,000 applications a year in 1980, asylum claims have exploded to over 100,000 a year and are growing. The system was never designed to cope with a caseload of this size. It now takes a year and a half to obtain a hearing, in itself an inducement to fraud. Work authorization and complete liberty are provided in the interim. Since most who come here do so to work, many never even show up for a hearing. Yet, unlike the criminal proceeding, there are no separate penalties for Failure to Appear.

116. "The United States of Asylum." NEW YORK TIMES, Sect. 6, p. 56. Those awaiting adjudication are not deportable and, in most cases, are given a work authorization. This means that the backlog itself now attracts spurious claims. Apply for asylum in the United States, it is known, and you can pretty much plan to stay. Depending on where you enter the byzantine process, if you are denied, up to four appeals are possible. Some cases have been pending for 12 years.

117. Tom Clark. "Human Rights and Expulsion: Giving Content to the Concept of Asylum." INTERNATIONAL JOURNAL OF REFUGEE LAW, Vol. 4, no. 2: 1992. Administrative decision-making, without discrimination, can thus lead to positive determinations on asylum. The relatively independent bodies used by several countries to make decisions on refugee status come close to what is required, and if they respond to the majority of applicants, offer States a cost-effective process. Relatively swift procedures on clear criteria do not in general attract a large number of manifestly unfounded applicants. If the consequence of the decision is the expulsion of the person, however, then more stringent procedural safeguards are needed. Canada and the United States have different answers to these procedural questions.

118. Robert Rubin. HOUSE HEARINGS, April 27, 1993, Y4J89/1:03/7. One is, that we can end indiscriminate detention policies that result in detaining every asylum-seeker without regard to the merits of their asylum claim. The APSO program, the prescreening program, is a good step in the right direction. Again, it is woefully underfunded, and really only handles a matter of a few hundred cases.

In the present state, it is not the answer. Instead what we do is that we end up detaining, of course, bona fide asylum-seekers, because it is so indiscriminate. Those moneys that we could save from the indiscriminate detention policy could be shifted into the asylum program, and I think it would be an important source of funds, and I think that it ought to be increased.

Finally, I see no reason—when we are talking about special appropriations for building larger detention facilities, which in certain instances may be appropriate, that for what I am told is probably no more than maybe $15 million—that we couldn't seek a direct appropriation so that we could deal with some of the backlog issues in asylum and the asylum process that do lead to abuse and that do lead to delay.

119. Robert Rubin. HOUSE HEARINGS, April 27, 1993, Y4J89/1:03/7. Much of the problem can be traced to a lack of funding for the new Asylum Officer corp that has produced a debilitating backlog of cases. The Congress should commit itself to providing adequate funding for the new asylum system as the most effective method of expediting the process. In so doing, we address delay and abuse but not trample upon the rights of *bona fide* asylum applicants.

120. Deborah Sontag. "Reneging on Refuge: The Haitian Precedent." THE NEW YORK TIMES: NEXUS, June 27, 1993, p. 1, sec. 4. Had the plan been in place when the Coast Guard intercepted three boats carrying 659 undocumented Chinese in the Pacific two weeks ago, the Clinton Administration might have avoided embarrassment and diplomatic tensions with Mexico, which was asked to deport the immigrants.

Instead of keeping the Chinese aboard the cramped ships while their fate was negotiated with Mexico, the Administration could have brought them to San Diego and processed their asylum claims in just days.

121. COMMITTEE ON GOVERNMENT OPERATIONS, SECOND REPORT. "The Immigration and Naturalization Service: Overwhelmed and Unprepared for the Future." August 4, 1993, Y1.1/8:103-216. Mr. Wilson forcefully argued, on behalf of the American Bar Association, against several proposals currently pending in Congress.

It is the view of the American Bar Association that it is not appropriate for the reform of the Immigration Service to adopt those proposals now pending before Congress which would allow officials either to make foreign determinations of asylum or for officials of the Customs Service or the Immigration Service to make on-the-spot decision regarding exclusion as these individuals arrive at ports of entry.

A legitimate refugee is one who has a well-founded fear of persecution in his or her country of origin due to a political opinion, nationality, religion, social group membership, or race. These in-

dividuals arrive in great stress; most of them speak no English; they have no knowledge of the law and may not even have knowledge of their right to political asylum.

Those officers who would be dealing with these cases do not have the knowledge of the law or of the quickly changing political situations in the countries from which these individuals come— which require a great deal of sophistication with regard to the current conditions—which may justify flight from those countries.

122.   Robert Rubin. HOUSE HEARINGS, April 27, 1993, Y4J89/1:03/7, p. 162. Second, persons seeking to abuse the asylum process are individuals without any claim of political persecution. They are not concerned with the substantive standard governing grants of asylum. A more burdensome standard, therefore, does nothing to discourage them from applying because they only want to submit an application and then abscond. Consequently, the more restrictive standard will only punish persons with well-founded fears of persecution who are unable to demonstrate that it is more likely than not that they will be persecuted.

123.   Arthur C. Helton. "Uncontrolled Right of Entry Poses a Threat." THE NATIONAL LAW JOURNAL, May 3, 1993, p. 16. There has been a recent proposal to establish pre-inspection facilities at airports abroad. But such an approach, relying upon the cooperation of the foreign government, could have the effect of creating an impenetrable exit barrier for genuine refugees. At a minimum, such facilities should not be established in countries that violate the fundamental human rights of individuals or that produce refugees. Nor should they be set up in countries of transit that fail to respect the rights of refugees to receive protection.

124.   Robert Rubin. HOUSE HEARINGS, April 27, 1993, Y4J89/1:03/7. Quite simply, overseas refugee processing is not a viable alternative for many *bona fide* refugees who have no choice but to use fraudulent documents to escape the country of persecution. Indeed, those persons with the strongest claims of persecution will be known to governmental authorities; it is ludicrous to require them to obtain exit visas from their persecutors.

125.   Ari Weitzhandler. "Temporary Protected Status: The Congressional Response to the Plight of Salvadoran Aliens." UNIVERSITY OF COLORADO LAW REVIEW, Vol 64: 1993, pp. 271-272. Two additional factors contributed to the registration fee problems. Many applicants were hesitant to request a fee waiver for fear that such a request would provide grounds for denial of future applications for permanent residency status on the basis of being a "public charge." Addition-

ally, for those who overcame this fear, the standards the INS employed for determining eligibility for waiver were initially quite stringent. After an injunction arising from a class action suit, the INS was forced to change its eligibility standards.

126.   Vincent Bonaventura. HOUSE HEARINGS, April 27, 1993, Y4J89/1:03/7, p. 263. It is critical that we not become preoccupied with the means of escape—whether it be misdocumentation or the employment of alien smugglers. The means of escape should not become the litmus test for legitimacy. To do so would deny the reality that persons often *must* use fraudulent documents to escape persecution or rely on unsavory characters to flee for safety. Seldom can persons fleeing for life or freedom obtain valid travel documents from their persecutors; seldom can they be choosy about whose help they rely upon. For many refugees, their avenue out is not selected by them, but for them, by their circumstances, and a refugee may very well have to falsify a passport or innocently follow a smuggler's instructions to destroy a travel document in the course of escape.

127.   Robert Rubin. HOUSE HEARINGS, April 27, 1993, Y4J89/1:03/7. A recent empirical study revealed that bureaucratic inefficiencies were the principal cause for delay in adjudicating asylum claims. Anker, "Determining Asylum Claims in the United States," International Journal of Refugee Law 252 (1990). The study concluded that "[t]he longest cause for delay in the entire process was the EOIR's difficulty in readily producing transcripts for appeals; the unavailability of these transcripts caused average delays of twenty-two months after the immigration judge had rendered a decision." *Id.* at 259. With regard to delay caused by the asylum applicant, the study showed that "[i]n less than one per cent of the continued cases were those continuances attributable to the lawyer's or the applicant's failure to appear." *Id.*

128.   Michel Moussalli. "Prospects for Refugee Protection in the 1990's." IN DEFENSE OF THE ALIEN, Vol. 15: 1993, p. 128. Protecting those who cannot turn to their government for protection is a legal and moral obligation that the international community has imposed upon itself, but it is an obligation which has become increasingly burdensome. The essence of the problem is that increasing numbers of people are in need of protection in a world where the political objectives of many countries of asylum no longer coincide with their humanitarian obligations.

The number of people forced to leave their homes continues to grow at an alarming rate, providing dramatic evidence of continuing widespread violations of international human rights law and humanitarian law by far too many states. The worldwide refugee population

now stands at approximately 17 million and shows no signs of leveling off.

129.   Priscilla Clapp. "The Future of Refugee Policy." IN DEFENSE OF THE ALIEN, Vol. 15: 1993, p. 108. Finally, there are also on the negative side of the ledger some disturbing long-term trends that do not augur well for refugee and migration problems. First, world population is growing very rapidly, some might argue it is out of control. By the year 2025, the population will have nearly doubled. Resources are already strained by this growth in the poorest parts of the world. Economic development is not keeping up with population growth. Ecological erosion is accelerating. And all these pressures together—population, poverty, ecological deterioration, human rights abuses and bad government—are causing migration on a larger and larger scale. There are not effective international strategies in sight to deal with the root causes of migration, and this is something that the international community, as well as individual governments, must focus on seriously and with urgency.

130.   Priscilla Clapp. "The Future of Refugee Policy." IN DEFENSE OF THE ALIEN, Vol. 15: 1993, p. 107. Unfortunately, there is also a negative side to the ledger. Ethnic conflicts are breaking out not only in Europe, but also in many other parts of the world. Yugoslavia is suffering the vilest of ethnic battles, even beyond imagination. This kind of ethnic warfare threatens to spread throughout the territory of the former Soviet Union, where many different ethnic groups are comingled. We are seeing the tragic flight of a specific ethnic group from Burma into Bangladesh. Nasty tribal and religious rivalries are reigniting all over Africa, especially in the Horn.

The end of the Cold War also has brought us a new form of threat and new types of warfare. We saw that in the Persian Gulf last year. Let us hope this does not become a model for the future. It will be a challenge to the international community and the UN to hold in check the ambitions of regional strongmen and bullies now that the tension of the East-West conflict no longer serves that function. But we must expect that other regional strongmen will seek to test the limits of their power in their own regions and beyond. With each new conflict and each new power contest, there will continue to be more groups of displaced persons, migrants and refugees.

131.   Myron Weiner. "Introduction: Security, Stability and International Migration." INTERNATIONAL MIGRATION AND SECURITY (As originally published in *International Security*. Vol. 17, no. 3: Winter 1992/93.), 1993, p. 2. First, international migration shows no sign of abating. Indeed, with the end of the Cold War there has been a resurgence of violent secessionist movements that create refugee flows, while barriers to exit from the former Soviet Union and Eastern Europe have been lifted. The breakup of empires and countries into smaller units has created minorities who now feel insecure. Vast differentials in income and employment opportunities among countries persist, providing the push and pull that motivate economic migrants. Environmental degradation, droughts, floods, famines, and civil conflicts compel people to flee across international borders. And new global networks of communication and transportation provide individuals with information and opportunities for migration.

132.   Eduardo Arboleda and Ian Hoy. "The Convention Refugee Definition in the West: Disharmony of Interpretation and Application." INTERNATIONAL JOURNAL OF REFUGEE LAW, Vol. 15: 1993, p. 74. The current situation has also polarized governments and advocacy groups. Western governments point out that the majority of immigrants are fleeing poverty and harsh economic situations back home, that most are not fleeing persecution in the sense of the 1951 Convention, and that most applicants are using (and therefore 'abusing' refugee determination systems to gain a legal status.

The governments' observations are not without validity. However, the numerous and varied causes of the migratory influxes and the limited alternatives facing those migrating can no longer be explained or viewed simplistically. The equation is now far too complex, and governments need to understand and consider the roots of migratory pressures. Moreover, they need to combine their domestic interest in controlling the numbers of those seeking entrance with a sensible but humanitarian approach in dealing with asylum seekers.

133.   Reginald T. Appleyard. INTERNATIONAL MIGRATION: A CHALLENGE FOR THE NINETIES, 1991, p. 82. Given economic and political conditions in many parts of the South, refugee migration as a result of processes described by Zolberg, *et al*.., could not be avoided even during early stages of the new development strategy. The conditions for their manifestation have already been created in many places, and spin-off from the development strategy would be too late to prevent the worsening of some refugee situations and the creation of others. Yet there is little doubt that in the long run the development approach offers real promise for restraining refugee flows and reducing broader emigration pressures.

134.   Sergio Diaz-Briquets and Sidney Weintraub. MIGRATION IMPACTS OF TRADE AND FOREIGN INVESTMENT: MEXICO AND CARIBBEAN BASIN COUNTRIES, Series on Development and International Migration in Mexico, Central America, and the Caribbean Basin. Vol. 3: 1991, p. xii.

Although research conclusions in the specific areas are discussed in each volume, some overall findings merit emphasis. The most important is the one already stated: that no viable alternative to economic development seems to exist that would significantly reduce undocumented immigration into the United States. It is hardly original to state that as a country becomes better developed, the economic pressure to emigrate is likely to be reduced. Historically, the development thesis has been demonstrated, particularly in Western Europe where countries of emigration became lands of immigration. Western Europe is now coping with its own undocumented, or unwanted, immigrants. Ireland, which has not enjoyed as much sustained growth as other countries in Western Europe, is still a country from which people emigrate. We observed, over time, that domestic economic well-being in European countries overcame the strength of networks in perpetuating outward migration.

135. Stein. HOUSE HEARINGS, April 27, 1993, Y4J89/1:03/7, p. 303. This powerful demographic force will explode in an unprecedented wave of human migration in the 21st century as tens of millions of persons seek economic opportunity and escape from environmental disaster. The patterns have just begun to emerge and will grow with intensity in the decades to come.

In much of the less developed world, we have witnessed the flight from rural to urban areas over the past two generations. Those in the countryside are moving—voting with their feet—in response to poor and declining living conditions. Pushed from the countryside and pulled by the cities' bright lights and economic opportunities—real or imagined—tens of millions have elected to crowd into teeming metropolitan areas. Mexico City, for example, with 3.5 million people as recently as 1950, now holds around 18 million. What we have witnessed to date is only the tip of the iceberg. The UN estimates that between 1987 and 2025, the urban population of the Third world (hopefully no longer "Third"), will have grown by 2.75 billion people, twice the amount that we added during the period from 1950 to 1987.

136. Stein. HOUSE HEARINGS, April 27, 1993, Y4J89/1:03/7, p. 302. Rapid world population growth is placing untenable immigration pressures on the United States. In the world's less developed regions, this growth is accompanied by the development of modern communications and transportation technology. This facilitates international migration pressures unprecedented in human history.

And it will only get worse—dramatically worse. The United Nations estimates that 90 million people are now added to the population of the planet each year. Within the next decade, more people will be added than there were in the entire world in 1800 (in fact, when Thomas Paine wrote "prepare in time an asylum for mankind," in his famous 1775 essay *Common Sense*, world population was far less than one billion, and barely above the level it had averaged for most of human history.) Just two generations ago, global population was 2.5 billion. During 1993, we will reach the 5.5 billion mark, and the UN estimates that we will exceed 10 billion in the next century before population growth levels off.

137. Myron Weiner. "Introduction: Security, Stability and International Migration." INTERNATIONAL MIGRATION AND SECURITY (As originally published in *International Security*. Vol. 17, no. 3. Winter 1992/93.), 1993, p. 2. Third, it is necessary to note that while the news media have focused on South/North migration and East/West migration, this focus is narrow and misleading. The movement of migrant workers from North Africa to Western Europe, migration from Asia and Latin America to the United States and Canada, and the increase in the number of people from the Third World and Eastern Europe claiming refugee status in the West represent simply one dimension of the global flows. Only a fraction of the world's seventeen million refugees are in the advanced industrial countries and only a small portion of global migration has flowed to Western Europe (where migrants total 5 percent of the population) or to the United States. Most of the movement has been from one developing country to another; the world's largest refugee flows have been in Africa, South Asia, Southeast Asia and most recently in the Persian Gulf.

138. Michel Moussalli. "Prospects for Refugee Protection in the 1990's." IN DEFENSE OF THE ALIEN, Vol. 15: 1993, p. 128. Numbers alone are not the problem. Equally troubling is the conclusion on the part of many governments that their humanitarian and political interests are no longer in conjunction. At least part of the motivation for refugee protection efforts in past decades was ideological. Governments of the West were happy to receive persons escaping communist domination: their humanitarian and political concerns were in perfect harmony. Now, however, refugees are more often fleeing ethnic conflict or human rights violations committed by a variety of governments, and they are more likely to be coming from a continent other than Europe. Humanitarian generosity is no longer seen to confer political advantage, and some governments are, therefore, trying to evade the obligations which they have undertaken and regain their unfettered discretion to deal with refugees.

139. Carolyn Davis. "People's Problems Not a World Apart: Editorial." THE PLAIN DEALER, December 19, 1993, Final Edition, *NEXUS*. More and more countries are closing their doors to refugees, often in response to economic pressures that

are leaving citizens of those countries frustrated and looking for someone to blame. The bolts are not only locked tight, but some governments are blocking the roads that run up to the driveways that lead to those national doors. In other words, they are sending back asylum-seekers before they ever get within national borders. Such is the case with U.S. treatment of Haitian refugees.

140.　　Arthur C. Helton. "Refugees and Human Rights." IN DEFENSE OF THE ALIEN, Vol. 15: 1993, p. 143. There is a crisis in refugee protection quite apart from the magnitude of the situation. The demise of the Cold War has changed the context in which refugee protection is addressed. Governments, particularly those of Western developed countries such as the United States, are increasingly treating those once considered to be part of refugee movements as unauthorized migrants. Foreign policy ceases to be a motivating force to assist and protect refugees. Instead, budgetary constraints have come to the fore, and efforts have followed to privatize both assistance and protection. The informing principle thus changes from an ideological perspective to migration management. Today, most asylum seekers are considered economic migrants from less developed countries.

141.　　Eduardo Arboleda and Ian Hoy. "The Convention Refugee Definition in the West: Disharmony of Interpretation and Application." INTERNATIONAL JOURNAL OF REFUGEE LAW, Vol. 15: 1993, p. 73. In Europe, however, the situation is quite different. Despite their multicultural composition and years of reliance on migrant labor, European countries insist that they are not 'immigration nations'. Today's population movements are seen as a relatively new phenomenon for them, and where assumptions of shared ethnicity and nationality have precariously bound nations, the new migrations from the third world are seen as a threat to national unity. As Doris Meissner has noted,

> Europeans are reacting as much to the changes immigration has already thrust upon their societies as they are to the prospect of additional newcomers... From an economic standpoint, there is a good case for immigration. However, economic factors are but one part of the equation. Strong counterpressures pervade European thinking on social, political, and cultural grounds. They have been virulently expressed by France's Jean Marie Le Pen. Although his a similar rightist parties in Austria, Belgium and Italy are not mainstream political movements, they raise a basic question about national identity—in effect, 'Who are we?' [ellipses in original]

142.　　Rosemarie Rogers. "The Future of Refugee Flows and Policies." INTERNATIONAL MI-

GRATION REVIEW, Vol. 26, no. 4: Winter 1992, p. 1138. There is a growing antiforeigner sentiment in Western Europe and perhaps in a milder way in the United States (*see* Sontag, 1992). The physical violence against foreigners, especially in Germany, is particularly alarming. Although opposition to foreign migrants by extremist groups is not a new phenomenon in post-World War II Europe (in some countries the movements go back to the 1960s; *see* Harris, 1990), opinion surveys demonstrate a change from the past with respect to the salience of the migrant issue among countries' general populations (*see* Rogers, 1992).

　　Messina (1990) has shown that the opposition to foreigners by extremist groups and parties in Western European countries has had the effect of shifting the discourse of the mainstream parties to the right.

143.　　Michel Moussalli. "Prospects for Refugee Protection in the 1990's." IN DEFENSE OF THE ALIEN, Vol. 15: 1993, p. 130. Linked to the problem of returning refugees is the situation of internally displaced persons. UNHCR's work with returnees has shown that many of their problems are shared by the internally displaced. In addition, many refugees become internally displaced persons when they go back to their countries, as happened in northern Iraq. Effective protection of internally displaced persons is a key factor in the prevention of refugee flows and in ensuring the success of voluntary repatriation and reintegration of refugees. Providing protection and assistance to people inside their own countries who are caught up in conflict or fragile security situations is an extremely complicated task. I will mention just three of the issues which must be addressed. First, there is an urgent need to define a mandate for international protection and assistance to the internally displaced. UNHCR does not have a general mandate to operate in countries of origin. It is able to do so only in the context of repatriation or on an ad hoc basis in response to a specific request by the Secretary-General or the General Assembly, such as in Vietnam and Sri Lanka. The International Committee of the Red Cross has a right of initiative in situations of international armed conflict, but is powerless to act in internal situations until serious disturbances become internal armed conflict. In any event, humanitarian law principles are too often ignored by the parties to a conflict, with the result that noncombatants must flee for their lives.

144.　　Arthur C. Helton. "Uncontrolled Right of Entry Poses a Threat." THE NATIONAL LAW JOURNAL, May 3, 1993, p. 16. All this stands in stark contrast to the alien who seeks to apply as a refugee from outside the United States. Currently there are some 18 million officially designated "refugees" under the auspices of the United Nations high commissioner for refugees. Refugees are admitted through multilateral resettlement agencies and are provided federal resettlement

assistance through a formal consultation process that allocates slots to regions where refugees are located worldwide. These people have no elaborate process guarantees, no right to counsel and no right to appeal.

145.   Stein. HOUSE HEARINGS, April 27, 1993, Y4J89/1:03/7, p. 305. All this stands in stark contrast to the alien who seeks to apply as a refugee from outside the United States. Currently there are some 18 million officially-designated "refugees" under the auspices of the United Nations High Commissioner for Refugees. Refugees are admitted through multilateral resettlement agencies, and are provided federal resettlement assistance through a formal consultation process allocating slots to regions where refugees are located worldwide. Refugee applicants have no elaborate process guarantees, no right to counsel and no right to appeal. Such inconsistent treatment between asylum-seeker and refugee applicant invites abuse.

146.   Priscilla Clapp. "The Future of Refugee Policy." IN DEFENSE OF THE ALIEN, Vol. 15: 1993, pp. 107-108. If the good news is the end of the Cold War has empowered the UN politically to deal with these situations, the bad news is that the UN does not have the resources to meet all the challenges it will confront in this complex period. Thus we find ourselves scrambling to find the money for peacekeeping, in order to effectuate the repatriations and the resettlements that have been negotiated at the political level. Governments are learning that peacekeeping is extremely expensive and they are not yet ready to commit to the levels of expenditure that will be required.

147.   Michel Moussalli. "Prospects for Refugee Protection in the 1990's." IN DEFENSE OF THE ALIEN, Vol. 15: 1993, p. 129. New responses are called for in order to preserve the institution of asylum and in order to take the necessary next steps toward protecting a more broadly defined category of refugees and internally displaced persons. Although the end of the Cold War removed one motivation for refugee protection efforts, it also has created new opportunities for multilateral cooperation on refugee, migration and humanitarian affairs, with an emphasis on a global, solutions-oriented approach. In this context, increasing attention is being paid to the need for prevention of the circumstances which force people to flee.

148.   Rosemarie Rogers. "The Future of Refugee Flows and Policies." INTERNATIONAL MIGRATION REVIEW, Vol. 26, no. 4: Winter 1992, p. 1124. At the same time as we are dealing with staggeringly high numbers of refugees and externally and internally displaced worldwide, with the potential of new conflicts that may create yet more and with increased migration pressures generally, there exist also unprecedented

opportunities to create new norms and institutional relationships, to revise old policies better to respond to the challenges concerning the situation of forced migrants today, and to experiment with new measures. In a recent address dealing with the situation in Europe, the current UN High Commissioner for Refugees called for "courage to face the challenge fairly and squarely, vision to build a strategy which goes beyond national interests and short-term political consideration, and political will to pursue such a strategy" (Ogata 1992b:3). Her words apply equally to the global refugee situation. Courage is indeed demanded from policy-makers and from the populations in whose name they act and whose support they need.

149.   Eduardo Arboleda and Ian Hoy. "The Convention Refugee Definition in the West: Disharmony of Interpretation and Application." INTERNATIONAL JOURNAL OF REFUGEE LAW, Vol. 15: 1993, p. 67. The problem is accentuated by a legal lacuna in international refugee law, whereby protection is not prescribed for all those in need of it. Many asylum seekers today may not fit strictly within the parameters of the Convention refugee definition, but do merit international protection in accordance with Article 33 of the 1951 Convention, primarily because of situations of generalized violence that prevail in their countries of origin.

To fill the void, various States have implemented different, relatively ad hoc, procedures to provide protection to a wider group of asylum seekers. The United States, for example, has implemented a 'temporary protection' scheme for certain nationalities considered to be generally vulnerable. Some European States grant 'de facto' and/or 'humanitarian' legal status to asylum seekers who are not considered to meet their respective definitions of a Convention refugee, but who cannot or should not be returned to their countries of origin. The distinction between Convention refugees and de facto and humanitarian refugees, however, is not at all clear.

150.   Eduardo Arboleda and Ian Hoy. "The Convention Refugee Definition in the West: Disharmony of Interpretation and Application." INTERNATIONAL JOURNAL OF REFUGEE LAW, Vol. 15: 1993, p. 66. The application of the Convention refugee definition in the developed world is inadequate. This is largely due to the divergent interpretations of the terminology of the definition, among and even within States. This divergence of interpretation is evident in the manner in which certain specific concepts of international refugee law are understood, such as refugees in civil war situations, State complicity and imputed political opinion. The result is uneven and inconsistent application of the Convention refugee definition.

151.   Eduardo Arboleda and Ian Hoy. "The Convention Refugee Definition in the West: Dishar-

mony of Interpretation and Application." INTERNA-TIONAL JOURNAL OF REFUGEE LAW, Vol. 15: 1993, p. 82. The lack of uniformity in applying the Convention refugee definition is partially the result of States' very wide latitude with respect to how they structure their refugee determination procedures. Indeed, the diverse acceptance rates between Western States are directly related to procedural differences inherent in their respective determination systems; there are nearly as many procedural frameworks as there are signatory countries.

152.   Eduardo Arboleda and Ian Hoy. "The Convention Refugee Definition in the West: Disharmony of Interpretation and Application." INTERNA-TIONAL JOURNAL OF REFUGEE LAW, Vol. 15: 1993, pp. 80-81. Different annual acceptance rates for asylum seekers in Western countries do not necessarily establish that there are also divergent interpretation of the Convention refugee definition, but they may be said to raise this presumption. On the one hand, there is a great variety of nationalities of asylum seekers in the receiving States of the West. On the other hand, however, if there are great disparities in acceptance rates between States, this at least gives the appearance that the States in question are interpreting and applying the Convention refugee definition in an inconsistent manner. This is particularly true where divergent acceptance rates between States remain relatively consistent from year to year. For example, according to one source, the overall Convention refugee acceptance rates in Western States during 1991 varied from lows of approximately 3% and 5% in Switzerland and Sweden, respectively, to approximately 21% in the United Kingdom, and up to the highest figure of 69% in Canada. In the last few years, these variations in recognition have been remarkably consistent.

Comparing acceptance rates of asylum seekers coming from the same countries of origin during similar time periods provides further direct evidence of divergent application. A few comparisons, particularly among States that do not provide non-Convention categories of protection, illustrate the lack of consistency in implementation. For instance, in 1989 Germany accepted less than 1% of Sri Lankan asylum seekers as Convention refugees, while Switzerland accepted approximately 5%. In 1990, the acceptance rates for Sri Lankans in both States rose to approximately 1% and 6%, respectively. At the other end of the spectrum, France accepted approximately 64% and 55% of Sri Lankan asylum seekers during the same period. Canada was by far the most generous, accepting approximately 96% and 90% of Sri Lankan asylum seekers.

The same trend manifests itself for other nationalities. For example, in 1989 and 1990, Switzerland and Germany accepted between 0% and 2% of Lebanese asylum seekers, and Canada approximately 89% and 80% during the same period. In 1990 Germany accepted approxi-

mately 11% of Somalis as Convention refugees; Canada, 93%. The disparity is still more evident in comparing the United States and Canada. In 1990, the United States accepted a very small number of Salvadoran and Guatemalan asylum seekers—somewhere between 3% and 15%. In the same year, Canada accepted a much higher percentage: approximately 78% of Salvadorans and 80% of Guatemalan asylum seekers.

153.   Eduardo Arboleda and Ian Hoy. "The Convention Refugee Definition in the West: Disharmony of Interpretation and Application." INTERNA-TIONAL JOURNAL OF REFUGEE LAW, Vol. 15: 1993, pp. 79-80. The Convention refugee definition creates a near-universal base in international law for the determination of refugee status, yet it has resulted in significantly different acceptance rates in Western countries. The one common factor shared by these rates is their downward trend during the past decade. Restrictive interpretations are increasingly evident, and many countries that used to interpret persecution broadly no longer do so. In consequence asylum seekers who once were accepted as Convention refugees may now be denied refugee status though their individual circumstances are identical.

154.   Eduardo Arboleda and Ian Hoy. "The Convention Refugee Definition in the West: Disharmony of Interpretation and Application." INTERNA-TIONAL JOURNAL OF REFUGEE LAW, Vol. 15: 1993, p. 76. In resolving the problem of who is a Convention refugee in Western countries, a two-fold approach is called for. First, more specific criteria must be developed, in order to eliminate the ambiguities of the Convention definition as far as possible. Second, and most importantly, the Convention definition must be applied uniformly. Lacking such uniformity of application, the Convention definition is fast becoming over-legalistic, mired in juridical abstraction, removed from the reality facing refugees, and subject to the vagaries of national interest. Both steps are inter-dependent, thought the second is predicated on the implementation of the first.

Discussion of the issue of asylum in the West often skirts this indispensable starting point. Unless the problems of definition and application are resolved, both the Convention refugee definition and international asylum law may become so manipulated in the domestic arena, that they will lose their relevance. This indeed is cause for concern, for despite the many criticisms levelled against it, the 1951 Convention and its refugee definition continue to be of vital importance in providing a legal foundation for the protection of refugees worldwide.

155.   Eduardo Arboleda and Ian Hoy. "The Convention Refugee Definition in the West: Dishar-

mony of Interpretation and Application." INTERNATIONAL JOURNAL OF REFUGEE LAW, Vol. 15: 1993, p. 89. Establishing an infrastructure that will define a Convention refugee more objectively strengthens the legitimacy of international refugee law. Greater definitional harmonization through negotiation will ameliorate the situation, but not necessarily bring about uniformity of application, given the differences in administrative, judicial and quasi-judicial procedures. In time, however, it can be expected that negotiations between States will gradually reduce the procedural differences.

156.   Eduardo Arboleda and Ian Hoy. "The Convention Refugee Definition in the West: Disharmony of Interpretation and Application." INTERNATIONAL JOURNAL OF REFUGEE LAW, Vol. 15: 1993, p. 79. A refugee definition that is more precise will not alone ensure its own uniform application, even though it is the crucial first step to achieving such uniformity. It is also essential in helping fill the legal lacuna of international refugee law by better defining its parameters. This, in turn, paves the way for less ambiguous and more specific definitions of 'humanitarian' or 'de facto' status.

In addition, agreement on a more precise definition by Western States would ameliorate a number of other serious problems, including the substantial variations in acceptance rates among States; the overlegalization of many refugee determination procedures; and the diverging perceptions of evolving concepts of refugee law, the importance of which was not foreseen by the drafters of the 1951 Convention.

157.   Eduardo Arboleda and Ian Hoy. "The Convention Refugee Definition in the West: Disharmony of Interpretation and Application." INTERNATIONAL JOURNAL OF REFUGEE LAW, Vol. 15: 1993, pp. 89-90. International migration and refugee flows are not going to disappear. It makes more sense, therefore, to define a workable Convention refugee definition that will allow States to manage their asylum flows within a humanitarian context, develop notions and practices of harmonization, and formulate concrete responses to those falling outside the ambit of refugee law.

158.   Tom Clark. "Human Rights and Expulsion: Giving Context to the Concept of Asylum." INTERNATIONAL JOURNAL OF REFUGEE LAW, Vol. 4, no. 2: 1992. Clarifying the definition of refugee used to grant asylum in an unrestrictive manner would make it easier for States to meet procedural obligations and easier to transfer persons to other participating States with safety and dignity. Martin notes the daunting task for a State which seeks to apply case-by-case examination to the complex range of situations in civil wars, and argues in favour of limiting the use of the

refugee definition. However, greater agreement on the use of the definition and a simplified test would be an advantage for the State concerned about the progressive realization of human rights. Moreover, States should not object to including in their policy and practice on asylum those persons who, for the most part, they do not expel anyway. The clarification should take into account those whose non-derogable rights would be at risk upon return and those facing return to a State at war, unable or unwilling to uphold their basic rights.

159.   Eduardo Arboleda and Ian Hoy. "The Convention Refugee Definition in the West: Disharmony of Interpretation and Application." INTERNATIONAL JOURNAL OF REFUGEE LAW, Vol. 15: 1993, pp. 74-75. In light of the radical changes that have recently occurred throughout the world and the migratory pressures that these changes have engendered, the refugee problem can no longer be viewed in a vacuum. Moreover, the refugee problem itself…is multi-faceted and cannot be resolved in isolation from the major political and economic challenges facing the international community. Governments have a legitimate interest in protecting the safety and stability of their respective societies; however, they also have an obligation to uphold the traditions of asylum and humanitarianism. Assisting those in need of international protection will indeed pose a major humanitarian challenge to both governments and advocates, particularly in Europe where, as one author puts it, 'the issue has become one of the most incendiary on the domestic agenda.' [ellipses in original]

160.   Michel Moussalli. "Prospects for Refugee Protection in the 1990's." IN DEFENSE OF THE ALIEN, Vol. 15: 1993, p. 129. A new challenge for the international community is to devise methods, where appropriate, to meet the security and protection needs of individuals prior to departure so that they will not have to flee. In-country protection may very well be feasible in certain situations, provided that it is fully consonant with international human rights standards and that guarantees for protection are present. The human rights which must be upheld include the right of individuals to leave their own country to seek and enjoy asylum elsewhere, or to return voluntarily, and not to be compelled to remain in a territory where their life, liberty or physical integrity is threatened.

The international community should focus on the countries of origin not only in terms of prevention, but also in terms of solutions. The most feasible and desirable solution for most refugees is to return home voluntarily in safety and dignity. Obviously, this can take place only when the root causes of flight are removed or at least greatly lessened. There is an increasing recognition that states have a responsibility not to force their citizens to flee and to allow for the return of those who found it necessary to do so.

161.   Ranee K.L. Panjabi. "The Global Refugee
         Crisis: A Search for Solutions." CALIFORNIA
WESTERN INTERNATIONAL LAW JOURNAL, Vol.
21, no. 2: 1990-1991, p. 247. International solutions
must be found to alleviate the misery of the millions of
displaced refugees in the world today. Currently, fifteen
million men, women, and children are uprooted from
their homes and find themselves in an alien, often hostile environment, as unwelcome guests in a foreign
country, and as international charity claimants suffering
a loss of personal dignity and often losing all hope of
ever returning to their homes. If the world does not act
with urgency to deal fairly with this crisis, the sheer
magnitude of numbers involved could make any future
solution impossible.

162.   Ranee K.L. Panjabi. "The Global Refugee
         Crisis: A Search for Solutions." CALIFORNIA
WESTERN INTERNATIONAL LAW JOURNAL, Vol.
21, no. 2: 1990-1991, p. 258. If there is likely to be little enthusiasm for a solution that will cost a great deal,
is there any area where viable solutions might be possible? Jean-Pierre Hocké, United National High Commissioner for Refugees, has called for a solution which
would place the refugee problem in the "context of an international strategy which addresses all of the relevant
factors." Hocké proposes that refugee law should encompass "the refugee problem as a whole…as a victim-ori-
ented approach." He believes that the refugee problem
must no longer be a peripheral issue but that it should
be "brought into the mainstream of international concern" so that countries of origin can also become involved in the search for solutions. "The humanitarian
objectives and the political will of governments to seek
out the root causes of refugee movement must converge.
States must be ready to take a collective and reasonable
approach to all refugee problems."

It is possible that such an approach, provided it is
combined with a genuine desire to implement the proposals, might produce dramatic solutions and some
strengthening of the institutional framework to implement those proposals; action which could alleviate the
misery of millions. Whether or not the political will exists or can be generated remains to be seen. Collective
concern and collective action have been dramatically
demonstrated in recent months in the Persian Gulf crisis.
The same collective will and a fraction of that international expenditure could resolve the refugee crisis. Unfortunately, the collective will to display the arts of war
seem to be easier to formulate than the collective will to
implement the arts of peace. [ellipses in original]

163.   Richard Schifter. "Enhancing Our Human
         Rights Effort." INTERNATIONAL LAW AND
POLITICS, Vol. 24: 1992, p. 1295. But world leaders
are busy people, who do not have a great deal of time for
reflection and theoretical analysis. The case that can be
made to them on the merits needs to be presented to
them also as politically advantageous. That is why I
would hope that members of Congress involved in contacts with G-7 parliamentarians will reach out to these
colleagues in efforts to persuade them of the validity of
the points I have just made. And I would hope that the
NGOs will reach out to NGOs in the G-7 countries with
similar messages. For, notwithstanding the institutional
problems to which I adverted earlier, in this age, the information age, ideas can more easily transcend borders
than ever before. Although we may have lost our position of economic preeminence, we remain the recognized
leader of the democratic world. Our words and our example command attention. The inherent logic of our position, if well presented at all relevant levels, offers us a
chance of prevailing. We should take that chance. We
should insist that a concerted effort to support the cause
of human rights worldwide become an integral part of
the programs adopted by the Group of Seven.

164.   Richard Schifter. "Enhancing Our Human
         Rights Effort." INTERNATIONAL LAW AND
POLITICS, Vol. 24: 1992, p. 1289. The inadequacy of
the U.N. system in dealing with human rights issues is
only one of the problems which I discovered in the years
in which I was directly involved in the international human rights efforts of the U.S. government. Another important problem I would like to address tonight is posed
by the need to persuade the other industrial democracies
to integrate human rights concerns fully into their foreign policy considerations.

I would not want to suggest that the government of
the United States accords primacy to human rights concerns in all instances of foreign policy formulation. Nor
would I suggest that we react consistently and effectively
to all reports of human rights abuse. But I am prepared
to tell you that the United States is more seriously and
effectively engaged in international human rights matters
than any other country. Furthermore, I believe that at
this juncture in history the most useful activity in which
human rights advocates could engage to enhance the effectiveness of our own human rights policy is to encourage their counterparts in other industrial democracies to
urge their governments to infuse human rights concerns
more effectively into foreign policy. Thereafter, all of
us, working together, could get the U.N. system to improve the quality of its human rights work.

165.   Robert Rubin. HOUSE HEARINGS, April 27,
         1993, Y4J89/1:103/7, p. 157. A nation's self-
identity is integrally related to its response to those who
seek to become members of its citizenry. Particularly
when those seeking entry are persons fleeing persecution, our ability to be a moral compass in this complex
world is dramatically impacted by how we respond.

166. David A. Martin. "Strategies for a Resistant World: Human Rights Initiatives and the Need for Alternatives to Refugee Interdiction." CORNELL INTERNATIONAL LAW JOURNAL, Vol. 26: 1993, p. 754. Still, the picture is not wholly bleak. In absolute terms, record high numbers of people are being shielded from immediate return. The world community has rallied, despite the grumbling, to spend more than ever on care and maintenance of asylum seekers and refugees. And perhaps some unintended benefits are possible as an outgrowth of the new public resistance and anxiety. These public reactions might—just might—help lift refugee policy debates out of some well-worn ruts. They could force the serious consideration of novel responses to the threats and needs that uproot people from their homes. Additionally, they might expose long-submerged humanitarian weaknesses in classical refugee law, especially its "exilic bias," which has obscured the possibilities and responsibilities for supporting human rights improvements in the home country.

167. Rosemarie Rogers. "The Future of Refugee Flows and Policies." INTERNATIONAL MIGRATION REVIEW, Vol. 26, no. 4: Winter 1992, p. 1113. Second, today countries are redefining their conceptions of national security. The new conceptions go beyond military threats to countries' borders or threats to particular regimes, to include broader concerns such as the populations' quality of life or whether governments are able to preserve their full range of policy choices in all issues area (see for example, Ullmann, 1983). In this context, matters pertaining to voluntary and forced migrants are increasingly regarded as security issues and are now at the top of many countries' policy agendas. One need only recall governments' concerns about the rising numbers of illegal migrants and asylum seekers in Western Europe today, as well as the challenges presented by the violence perpetrated against foreigners by various groups in a number of European host countries.

168. David A. Martin. "Strategies for a Resistant World: Human Rights Initiatives and the Need for Alternatives to Refugee Interdiction." CORNELL INTERNATIONAL LAW JOURNAL, Vol. 26: 1993, p. 765. With the conceptual barriers lowered, the world community is gradually gaining experience with novel techniques meant to improve the situation at home. For example, international election observers are now routinely deployed to help monitor, and perhaps ultimately to help legitimize, election contests in countries where democracy is new or newly restored. This precedent has now been expanded to include sending teams of international human rights monitors even when no election is in the offing. And some are beginning to recognize the potential for human rights protection that may go hand-in-hand with a more traditional humanitarian assistance presence.

169. Rosemarie Rogers. "The Future of Refugee Flows and Policies." INTERNATIONAL MIGRATION REVIEW, Vol. 26, no. 4: Winter 1992, p 1113. Among recent important changes in the international system is a renewed emphasis on human rights. Today, the UN is willing to scrutinize the human rights records of a wide range of countries, and there is in general a greater readiness to question a country's right to do as it will with its citizens—a readiness to put limits on sovereignty. Strong actions may be undertaken to avert new forced migrations or to protect and assist populations that were displaced within their home countries. This new policy stance represents an important change: from a reactive one, when the international community was essentially waiting until refugees reached an asylum country (where they would then be protected and assisted), or an inactive one (with respect to many of the internally displaced), to a more proactive stance in which the focus is quite explicitly on the countries of origin.

170. Priscilla Clapp. "The Future of Refugee Policy." IN DEFENSE OF THE ALIEN, Vol. 15: 1993. Another positive feature of the end of the Cold War has been the political empowerment of the United Nations to deal with humanitarian and refugee crises. One might say that the UN may have been the child of World War II, but it was the victim of the Cold War. During this period, it was nearly impossible to get the Security Council together on any significant issue. We were caught in what the United States and Soviet Union came to describe as a "zero sum game," in which a gain for one side was a loss for the other and vice versa. However, when it is added up, it always equals zero.

We are no longer living in a "zero sum" world, and we can now work productively with those who were formerly our rivals. This has revolutionized the role of the UN in dealing with humanitarian and political situations, including those involving refugees, potential refugees and large migrations. We have witnessed this already in the case of Iraq; we have witnessed it in the other cases I have just enumerated, and we are now beginning to witness it in Cambodia. There will be many more to come.

171. Michel Moussalli. "Prospects for Refugee Protection in the 1990's." IN DEFENSE OF THE ALIEN, Vol. 15: 1993, p. 129. The international community, through UNHCR and other bodies of the UN, is actively investigating the new possibilities for protection activities in countries of origin as a complement to the more traditional role in countries of asylum. Prevention must take into account the causes of displacement: armed conflict, violations of human rights and poverty. The lesson of the outpouring from Albania to Italy last year is that political and legal reform is not enough to keep people at home if they have no economic prospects. The potential for development aid to

reduce migratory pressures must be investigated more fully. Other prevention-oriented activities include human rights monitoring; providing advisory services, especially on legislative and administrative structures for protecting human rights; ensuring that people in countries of origin have realistic information on their prospects for immigration and for asylum; promoting mediation as a means of conflict resolution; and encouraging tolerance for diversity and respect for human rights and the rule of law, generally, and for the rights of minorities in particular.

172.   David A. Martin. "Strategies for a Resistant World: Human Rights Initiatives and the Need for Alternatives to Refugee Interdiction." CORNELL INTERNATIONAL LAW JOURNAL, Vol. 26: 1993, p. 764. But the new activism, once loosed, proved to have a wider reach. Shortly after the Gulf War's end, Saddam's efforts to crush internal rebellion touched off such an outpouring of global sympathy for his victims, particularly the Kurds in the north, that global action was demanded. Few of the usual legal objections were heard when the coalition forces joined in creating a safe haven in northern Iraq in April 1991. More objections surfaced recently when the United States sought to use the arguable authority of the earlier Security Council resolutions to enforce a no-fly zone in the south of Iraq. Nevertheless, the whole experience has transformed "humanitarian intervention" from an obscure and rather wistful topic for professors of international human rights into a buzzword for the op-ed pages.

World action of this sort is now an available option for responding to a host of troubling post-Cold War international crises. President Bush, of all people, helped prove that humanitarian intervention has wider application than simply in circumstances where the target nation once committed classic cross-border aggression. Bush was an unlikely candidate for this role; his great reluctance to aid the Kurds through any use of U.S. military power had been obvious in the bitter spring of 1991. Nevertheless, in his final major foreign initiative, Bush proposed a surprising humanitarian foray into Somalia in December 1992, to end starvation and restore a modicum of order. Significantly, he worked this time to assure that the action received express UN sanction under the Security Council's Chapter VII powers.

173.   Rosemarie Rogers. "The Future of Refugee Flows and Policies." INTERNATIONAL MIGRATION REVIEW, Vol. 26, no. 4: Winter 1992, p. 1126. Significant changes are occurring in how the international community views state sovereignty. There is less willingness to permit states to claim that certain issues are strictly internal matters, with the corollary of greater willingness to intervene. Intervention may take several forms and may occur in a variety of spheres or for a variety of reasons, not all related to human rights

abuses or issues of forced migration (other issues, for example, might concern adherence to arms control agreements or environmental protection; *see* Lyons and Mastanduno, 1992:4-5).

Intervention can be preceded by active diplomacy, by pressures on a country through threats or positive inducements to change certain policies, by public condemnation of certain behaviors, or by economic sanctions, and can itself range from flooding a country with human rights monitors to, finally, military measures. The world community's willingness to intervene militarily to protect and assist forced migrants and to prevent the creation of still larger numbers has been illustrated in this decade by the intervention in the Liberian civil war by the Economic Community of West African States (ECOWAS), in Iraq by a multilateral force led by the United States to protect the Kurdish and Shiite populations through the creation of safety zones in the north and the south of the country, in the former Yugoslavia by UN peacekeeping forces, and in Somalia, again by a multilateral force led by the United States.

174.   Rosemarie Rogers. "The Future of Refugee Flows and Policies." INTERNATIONAL MIGRATION REVIEW, Vol. 26, no. 4: Winter 1992, p. 1116. A set of important actors assisting forced migrants are nongovernmental organizations (NGOs), whether indigenous to the country in which they work or headquartered elsewhere. NGOs act as "implementing partners" to UNHCR and individual governments, and/or undertake independent activities, which in many instances are funded by private contributions. NGO personnel are often the most knowledgeable about problems (including protection problems) of refugees or the internally displaced, since they are closest to the affected populations. International NGOs can be particularly important for the protection of forced migrants; they can "blow the whistle" on human rights violations, and thus their presence in itself often acts as a restraining force.

175.   Rosemarie Rogers. "The Future of Refugee Flows and Policies." INTERNATIONAL MIGRATION REVIEW, Vol. 26, no. 4: Winter 1992, p. 1133. The Comprehensive Plan of Action (CPA) was formulated in Southeast Asia in 1988-1989, when the number of arrivals of boat people from Vietnam was increasing rapidly. It is a complex instrument, developed by the asylum countries, other major countries in the region, the resettlement countries, and, importantly, Vietnam—the major refugee-sending country, which until then had been quite isolated. The plan succeeded in preserving the asylum system in the region, in return for agreement on a number of measures that assuaged the asylum countries' security concerns: resettlement of long-stayers in refugee camps, the commitment to continue the Orderly Departure Program (which was seen as an emigration program), the establishment of a refugee

determination procedure (heretofore absent) in ASEAN countries, and—the most contentious issue—the agreement on the part of most participants that screened-out asylum seekers would henceforth be returned to Vietnam, forcibly if necessary (*see* Jambor, 1992; Knowles, 1989). Not only did the plan succeed in upholding principles of humanitarianism, but it seems to have eased political tensions among former enemies—ASEAN and Vietnam—and has led to increased economic exchanges.

176.   Priscilla Clapp. "The Future of Refugee Policy." IN DEFENSE OF THE ALIEN, Vol. 15: 1993, p. 111. As we face more and more of these complex mass migrations, we will undoubtedly see additional efforts to organize comprehensive solutions embodying the principles that guided the CPA. Among these, I would enumerate: the principles of first asylum, internationally endorsed (UNHCR) screening for refugees, third country resettlement for refugees, and repatriation for nonrefugees. A comprehensive solution must by definition embrace the sending country, as well as the countries of first asylum and resettlement, so that repatriation can be carried out in safety and dignity, with adequate reception, monitoring and reintegration assistance.

177.   Michel Moussalli. "Prospects for Refugee Protection in the 1990's." IN DEFENSE OF THE ALIEN, Vol. 15: 1993, p. 13. The basic goal for refugee and migration policy must be to maintain the availability of asylum for refugees and to uphold the humane treatment of nonrefugees within a framework which clearly distinguishes between the two groups. This requires several initiatives: first, immigration possibilities should be made available in Western Europe, as they are in the United States and Australia, so that people have an opportunity to immigrate legally and will be less likely to resort to asylum procedures for entry. This would have the added benefit for states of rationalizing their formal labor market policies to reflect the contributions of foreign workers.

Second, claims for asylum should be dealt with fairly and expeditiously. Third, a liberal asylum policy should be maintained for all those in need of protection, even if only for a temporary period. Fourth, public information activities should be enhanced to improve understanding of refugee issues. Political and moral leaders should confront racist and antiforeigner sentiments, especially among young people. Finally, a humane set of principles for the orderly and safe return of people who do not need international protection should be developed. The experience with the Vietnamese under the Comprehensive Plan of Action will provide valuable lessons in this regard.

178.   Eduardo Arboleda and Ian Hoy. "The Convention Refugee Definition in the West:

Disharmony of Interpretation and Application." INTERNATIONAL JOURNAL OF REFUGEE LAW, Vol. 15: 1993, pp. 71-72. Today, the refugee problem is more complex than ever, and the last decades have seen unprecedented changes in both the kind and scale of refugee movements. International migration is now increasingly multi-dimensional and inter-related, generated by wars, including civil wars, human rights deprivations, natural calamities and poverty. While the causes of some international migrations and refugee movements can still be isolated, most are the result of diverse and inextricably entwined factors.

179.   Tom Clark. "Human Rights and Expulsion: Giving Content to the Concept of Asylum." INTERNATIONAL JOURNAL OF REFUGEE LAW, Vol. 4, no. 2: 1992, p. 195. It is not clear, however, that a State is invariably obliged to allow the entry of a person forcibly returned or expelled, even if the person is a national. If the receiving State is willing but unable to guarantee the most basic human rights of a returning national, that state's human rights obligations would be breached by receiving the person. There is thus a basis for denying entry. Looked at another way, if the sending State is not following the principles and policies of the UN in expelling the person, the receiving State has a basis for not allowing admission. Perhaps for these reasons, there is some evidence that return of significant numbers of nationals requires a specific international agreement. Under the UN Comprehensive Plan of Action, Viet Nam at first gave notice that it would only accept back those nationals who voluntarily returned or who did not object to being returned. In 1991, with an agreement to provide some financial assistance, Vietnam agreed to take back Vietnamese nationals who did not volunteer to return from Hong Kong.

180.   J. Michael Cavosie. "Defending the Golden Door: The Persistence of Ad Hoc and Ideological Decision Making in U.S. Refugee Law." INDIANA LAW JOURNAL, Vol. 67: 1992. Asylum, in its contemporary context, is understood as "the protection a state may afford to an individual by letting him or her enter the territory of the state and allowing him of her to remain." Although the concept of asylum is an ancient one, there is no right to asylum in contemporary international law, nor is the right embodied in international treaties or the Convention. Rather, the right of asylum must be seen as the right of the state, as a sovereign entity, to grant asylum at its discretion.

181.   J. Michael Cavosie. "Defending the Golden Door: The Persistence of Ad Hoc and Ideological Decision Making in U.S. Refugee Law." INDIANA LAW JOURNAL, Vol. 67: 1992, pp. 417-418. Article 33 of the Convention—"Prohibition of Expulsion or return ('Refoulement')"—is the keystone of the refugee's

rights. The principle of nonrefoulement dictates that a state may not return a refugee within its borders, either legally *or* illegally, to her home country to face political persecution. This is an established principle of international law, codified by the Convention.

Note, however, that while article 33 delineates the right not to be returned, it does not grant any right to remain in the country of refuge. Accordingly, a Contracting State may, consistent with the Convention, remove the refugee to another country willing to accept and protect her. In either instance, the refugee is guaranteed safe haven from the persecution of her home country, the overriding goal of the article.

182.   Suzanne Gluck. "Intercepting Refugees at Sea: An Analysis of the United States' Legal and Moral Obligations." FORDHAM LAW REVIEW, Vol. 16: 1993, p. 865. The desperate plight of refugees seeking sanctuary in the United States raises critical legal and humanitarian issues. While the United States is under no legal obligation to grant asylum, even to refugees fleeing persecution, humanitarian concerns demand protection for victims of persecution. Accordingly, the international community has granted refugees the right of *nonrefoulement*, the most fundamental principle of refugee protection.

183.   Rosemarie Rogers. "The Future of Refugee Flows and Policies." INTERNATIONAL MIGRATION REVIEW, Vol. 26, no. 4: Winter 1992, p. 1129. However, the political and economic obstacles proved to be larger than expected: not all operations were initiated, and others resulted in fewer returns than had been projected. Returnees must be both safe and able to establish a new livelihood in the area to which they return; otherwise they will become tomorrow's internally displaced or again refugees. The challenges to be overcome to make returns successful are truly daunting.

184.   Rosemarie Rogers. "The Future of Refugee Flows and Policies." INTERNATIONAL MIGRATION REVIEW, Vol. 26, no. 4: Winter 1992, pp. 1129-1130. For one, refugees often return to countries or areas in which peace is still fragile, if it has been reached at all. The Zimbabwes and the Namibias are the exceptions, the El Salvadors of 1990 and the Cambodias of 1992 are the rule. This raises issues of timing of repatriation programs and of protection of the refugees after their return. On the one hand, opportunities for repatriation should not be missed (sometimes the refugees themselves decide that it is time to return even while the international community still has serious concerns about safety); on the other hand, the potential returnees should not be pressured to return to unsafe conditions (which sometimes happens for political reasons). The fact that there may be protection needs after the refugees' return has been recognized, and UNHCR's mandate has been

expanded accordingly. It now almost routinely performs a monitoring function in the home country for one or even two years after a group's return. The presence of such monitors can contribute to building a stronger peace.

A second major condition for returns to be viable is the reconstruction of devastated home regions or countries. Refugees frequently return to areas where land mines are abundant and much of the infrastructure has been destroyed. Some of the necessary rebuilding must occur immediately. In Nicaragua, UNHCR developed the concept of "Quick Impact Projects" (QIPs)—highly specific, relatively low-cost development projects (for example, the building or repair of wells, bridges, roads or schools) which are planned by the affected community and are generally implemented by local NGOs over a period of months. Such projects are now being undertaken also in Cambodia. However, far greater reconstruction needs must be met over the long term. The need for removing land mines alone represents a formidable challenge.

Third, for refugees returning to rural areas the issue of available land is paramount. Whether it is a question of land reform, of settling old claims, or of assigning other available land to the returnees, without this issue settled many refugees will not be able to start a new life. In the currently ongoing repatriation of Cambodians from the Thai border camps, it was not possible to implement the original plan of supplying every refugee family that chose this option with two hectares of agricultural land: "…it was back to the drawing board almost as soon as repatriation began" (Guest, 1992:25). Refugees can still choose land (among other options such as a housing plot and a housing kit; a professional tool kit; or strictly cash), "but they will have to wait until land becomes available." UNHCR deserves to be criticized for lack of more realistic planning(*see* also Robinson 1992), and some also have criticized it for rushing the returns unduly for political reasons.

Fourth, there is a multiplicity of issues concerning human resources and needs. Refugees returning to agriculture have often lacked the opportunity to use their skills for years or even decades. Their children may have known no other life than that in refugee camps. Another issue is the physical and mental health of the returnees. They will need adequate medical attention, and not all will be able to provide for themselves. A study of the population in the Thai-Cambodian border camps (Mollica *et al.*, 1991) allows some predictions of potential mental health difficulties. Until the mid-1980s, specific protection and assistance issues concerning single women and female heads of households had been almost completely neglected in policy planning concerning asylum; they are now coming to the fore with respect to the repatriation process (*see* Martin, 1992; Women's Commission for Refugee Women and Children, 1992).

Finally, the repatriations have highlighted a number of organizational issues that must be addressed. In particular, they have shown that there is a gap between humanitarian work on behalf of refugees on the one hand and necessary development work on the other. Furthermore, it is now increasingly taken for granted that efforts aimed at helping returning refugees reintegrate successfully into their communities must be broadened to benefit all populations who return—refugees, externally displaced and internally displaced—as well as the local populations who have never moved. [ellipses in original]

185.   Michel Moussalli. "Prospects for Refugee Protection in the 1990's." IN DEFENSE OF THE ALIEN, Vol. 15: 1993, pp. 129-130. Possibilities for voluntary repatriation have been created by the resolution of conflicts in South Africa, Angola, El Salvador and Cambodia. However, guaranteeing the safety of the returnees is a major challenge. The problems range from the practical—how to find and remove the thousands of land mines in Cambodia so that returning refugees can farm their fields—to the political—how to protect returnees from reprisals in the form of harassment, arbitrary detention and disappearances, often carried out precisely because they are returning refugees. Monitoring of guarantees for the safety of returning refugees is a crucial part of protection, especially when returnees are going home to an area which is still subject to disturbances or tensions. Nor is mere presence enough: monitoring also implies active intervention with the authorities in case of violations.

Successful repatriation also requires that the refugees be reintegrated into national economies which often have been devastated by war. Unless returning refugees can be made part of national reconstruction, the durability of repatriation as a solution is at risk.

186.   J. Michael Cavosie. "Defending the Golden Door: The Persistence of Ad Hoc and Ideological Decision Making in U.S. Refugee Law." INDIANA LAW JOURNAL, Vol. 67: 1992, pp. 419-420. Care should be taken, however, to avoid revoking the status based on ephemeral or cosmetic changes in the refugee's country. The U.N. Refugee Handbook notes that "[a] mere—possible transitory—change in facts surrounding the individual refugee's fear, which does not entail such major changes of circumstances" should not result in the loss of refugee status. In other words, the refugee should not be compelled to justify his status upon each shift in the prevailing political winds of his country, for this would undermine the very sense of security for which he initially sought international aid.

Continued protection may occasionally be warranted even in light of a fundamental change in circumstances: The second paragraph of article 1(C)(5)—although explicitly addressing only statutory refugees—may also apply to Convention refugees. It specifies that the change-of-circumstances doctrine shall not apply to a refugee "who is able to invoke compelling reasons arising out of previous persecution for refusing to avail himself of the protection of the country of nationality." This exception contemplates particularly atrocious forms of persecution not easily forgotten by the refugee, and Goodwin-Gill argues that it should be liberally applied since refugees frequently suffer ongoing distress as a result of their persecution. At a minimum, the provision seems to preclude a blanket revocation of status and to insist upon individual reevaluations of that status whenever fundamental changes have occurred.

187.   Rosemarie Rogers. "The Future of Refugee Flows and Policies." INTERNATIONAL MIGRATION REVIEW, Vol. 26, no. 4: Winter 1992, p. 1131. The option of resettling refugees from countries of first asylum to third countries is a costly and scarce resource. Troeller (1991:568-569) reports that in 1990 only ten countries formally announced refugee resettlement quotas. The United States, Canada, Australia, New Zealand and six countries in Western Europe (four Nordic countries, the Netherlands and Switzerland) made 156,800 resettlement places available Several other Western European countries (including France, the United Kingdom and Germany) also resettle refugees, but do not announce annual quotas.

188.   Rosemarie Rogers. "The Future of Refugee Flows and Policies." INTERNATIONAL MIGRATION REVIEW, Vol. 26, no. 4: Winter 1992. UNHCR argues for offering the scarce resettlement slots to refugees who have the greatest protection needs. Such needs arise from situations in which the asylum country demands resettlement, the refugee's safety in the asylum country is in jeopardy, where there are special needs for family reunification, or if refugees belong to particularly vulnerable groups such as difficult medical cases, survivors of torture or other forms of violence, or women-at-risk (*see* UNHCR, 1991a).

189.   Rosemarie Rogers. "The Future of Refugee Flows and Policies." INTERNATIONAL MIGRATION REVIEW, Vol. 26, no. 4: Winter 1992, p. 1129. So great are today's expectations of large-scale returns that UNHCR has declared the 1990s the "decade of repatriation" (*see* Ogata, 1992a). At the beginning of 1992, UNHCR anticipated repatriation operations for 21 countries, involving 3 million expected returnees, at a projected cost of U.S.$405.5 million (*Refugees*, 1992:9, 10).

190.   Priscilla Clapp. "The Future of Refugee Policy." IN DEFENSE OF THE ALIEN, Vol. 15: 1993, p. 208. On the positive side of the ledger, the end of the Cold War has given us the opportunity to resettle a number of long-standing conflicts. It is probably

not unfair to say that the majority of the world's refugee populations, which our assistance sustains today, were spawned by East-West conflict and the expansion of communism throughout the world: in the Soviet Union and Eastern Europe, in Indochina and Afghanistan, the Horn of Africa, Angola and in Central America. The list is long. The number of refugees under international care is very high—some 16 million.

As political settlements have been forged, people have started to go home. Repatriation has now become a major durable solution, where is was only a hope in the past. In the preceding year, there have been large repatriations in Angola, Namibia, Nicaragua and Iraq. In the coming year, we hope to see large new repatriations in Cambodia, Afghanistan, Ethiopia and Eritrea, Southwest Africa and Vietnam. We have the opportunity before us to reduce the world's refugee population by one-third or more.

191.   Rosemarie Rogers. "The Future of Refugee Flows and Policies." INTERNATIONAL MIGRATION REVIEW, Vol. 26, no. 4: Winter 1992, pp. 1138-1139. At the same time there is the need, in Western Europe and in the United States, to deal differently with mass flows of people who flee turmoil in their own countries: a need for options of temporary asylum based on group determinations. The magnet effect of the wealthy countries must not be minimized. There is ample reason for concern that temporary asylum may not turn out to be temporary after all, given the time it may take to rebuild security in the origin countries (during which the asylees become integrated into the host society), the possibility that a feeling of trust cannot be restored at all (a not unlikely outcome for Muslims from Bosnia), and the economic attraction of the Western industrialized countries. But where the affected populations' protection needs are overwhelming, a positive response is needed. Recent events suggest the urgency of a search for comprehensive strategies, including seeking asylum options as close to the asylees' homes as possible, through effective burden-sharing, and addressing the root causes of the flows.

192.   Amnesty International. REASONABLE FEAR: HUMAN RIGHTS AND UNITED STATES REFUGEE POLICY, Amnesty International USA: New York, March 1990, p. 8. A government's policy of detaining asylum seekers who have entered the country may also constitute a human rights concern. In accordance with international human rights standards, governments are obliged to demonstrate legitimate reasons for detaining an asylum seeker in prisons, closed camps, or similar facilities for physical restriction. Governments must also provide people they have detained with a prompt and fair hearing before an authority who is competent and impartial. Under international norms, all detainees are entitled to prompt information in a language

they understand about the reasons for detention. This information must relate to an individual's particular case and must be provided in sufficient detail for asylum seekers to exercise their right to judicial challenge of their detention.

193.   Amnesty International. REASONABLE FEAR: HUMAN RIGHTS AND UNITED STATES REFUGEE POLICY, Amnesty International USA: New York, March 1990, p. 7. Governments have a responsibility for ensuring that asylum seekers are not penalized for attempting to flee from human rights violations. The protection of refugees is a necessary component of all governments' obligations to prevent human rights abuses. Even in situations of mass refugee flight, all asylum seekers must be afforded their fundamental rights. Discrimination against asylum seekers because of their ethnic origin, race, language, or political or religious beliefs contravenes human rights standards.

194.   Amnesty International. REASONABLE FEAR: HUMAN RIGHTS AND UNITED STATES REFUGEE POLICY, Amnesty International USA: New York, March 1990, p. 7. The Universal Declaration of Human Rights articulates principles crucial to the treatment of refugees. This seminal human rights statement was proclaimed without dissent by the United Nations General Assembly in 1948, as the horrors of World War II unfolded before the international community. Every United Nations member state is obliged to maintain the principles enshrined in the Declaration, which include:
- No one shall be subjected to arbitrary arrest, detention or exile. (Article 9)
- Everyone has the right to freedom of movement and residence within the borders of each state. (Article 13.1)
- Everyone has the right to leave any country, including his own, and to return to his country. (Article 13.2)
- Everyone has the right to seek and enjoy in other countries asylum from persecution. (Article 14.1)

All governments clearly are entitled to control access to their territory, and restrictive measures are justified for the legitimate purposes of immigration control. International human rights norms, however, distinguish between asylum seekers and illegal immigrants. Governments have special obligations to asylum seekers, including those who have entered the country without official authorization. These norms specify that under no circumstances should a government expel asylum seekers to a country where they risk violations of basic human rights.

195.   Amnesty International. REASONABLE FEAR: HUMAN RIGHTS AND UNITED STATES REFUGEE POLICY, Amnesty International USA: New York, March 1990, p. 4. United States authorities have

forced thousands of Guatemalans, Haitians, and Salvadorans to return to a homeland strafed with patterns of gross human rights violations. Haitians have been interdicted at sea. A large number of others have been denied asylum after formal hearings of their cases. These people have been excluded from the promise enshrined in the Statue of Liberty by restriction of their right to apply for asylum and by the bias against them in the asylum determination process.

196.   Amnesty International. REASONABLE FEAR: HUMAN RIGHTS AND UNITED STATES REFUGEE POLICY, Amnesty International USA: New York, March 1990, p. 7. Restriction or obstruction of any asylum seeker's flight is also incompatible with human rights norms if he or she is seeking safety from risk of imprisonment for the peaceful exercise of human rights or from risk of torture, "disappearance," or execution. No government's refugee policies should prevent a person from exercising the right to seek and obtain asylum which the Universal Declaration of Human Rights guarantees.

197.   Tom Clark. "Human Rights and Expulsion: Giving Content to the Concept of Asylum." INTERNATIONAL JOURNAL OF REFUGEE LAW, Vol. 4, no. 2: 1992, pp. 144-145. States have no explicit international authorization to expel persons to another State against their wishes. The individual has an unambiguous declared human right to return to his or her country of nationality, and a State has an implicit right to expel a national to their country of citizenship, inherent in the general concept of sovereignty. However, 'sovereignty does not signify unbridled freedom, but rather is an attribute of equality between States and is subject to the duty to comply faithfully with international obligations.' Limits or prohibitions on expulsion have been set by international agreement. The clearest is the prohibition on expelling a person to a country where their life or freedom may be threatened. There are also limits on a receiving State's right to deny entry.

198.   Jack Donnelly. INTERNATIONAL HUMAN RIGHTS, Westview Press: Boulder, 1993, p. 26. It is also often argued that there is a qualitative difference between "negative" civil and political rights and "positive" economic and social rights. Negative rights require only the forbearance of others to be realized. Violating a negative right thus involves actively causing harm, a sin of commission. Positive rights require that others provide active support. Violating a positive right involves only failing to provide assistance, a (presumably lesser) sin of omission.

199.   Jack Donnelly. INTERNATIONAL HUMAN RIGHTS, Westview Press: Boulder, 1993, p. 27. The moral basis of the positive-negative distinction is also questionable. Does it really make a moral difference if one kills someone through neglect or by positive action? What if the neglect is knowing and willful? Consider, for example, leaving an injured man to die; refusing to implement relatively inexpensive health care or nutrition programs for needy and malnourished children; or the fact that a black infant in the United States is twice as likely to die as a white infant. The central moral issue, I would suggest, is the destructive impact on lives, not the means used to achieve it.

200.   Jack Donnelly. INTERNATIONAL HUMAN RIGHTS, Westview Press: Boulder, 1993, p. 26. All human rights, however, require both positive action and restraint by the state if they are to be effectively implemented. Some rights, of course, are relatively positive and others are relatively negative. But even this distinction does not correspond to that between civil and political and economic and social rights.

201.   Jack Donnelly. INTERNATIONAL HUMAN RIGHTS, Westview Press: Boulder, 1993, pp. 36-37. Internationally recognized human rights represent a good first approximation of the guarantees necessary for a life of dignity in the contemporary world of modern states and modern markets. In all countries of the world, the unchecked power of the modern state threatens individuals, families, groups, and communities alike. Likewise, national and international economic markets, whether free or controlled, threaten human dignity in all countries of the contemporary world. The Universal Declaration and the Covenants provide a generally sound approach to protecting human dignity against these threats. For example, it is difficult to imagine defensible arguments in the contemporary world to deny rights to life, liberty, security of the person, or protection against slavery, arbitrary arrest, racial discrimination, and torture. The rights to food, health care, work, and social insurance are equally basic to any plausible conception of equal human dignity.

202.   Jack Donnelly. INTERNATIONAL HUMAN RIGHTS, Westview Press: Boulder, 1993, pp. 24-25. Despite the absence of philosophical consensus, there is, as we saw in the preceding chapter, an international *political* consensus on the list of rights in the Universal Declaration of Human Rights and the International Human Rights Covenants (see Table 1.1 and the Appendix). This consensus can also draw theoretical support from the fact that it can be derived from a plausible and attractive philosophical account, namely, the requirement that the state treat each person with equal concern and respect. Consider the Universal Declaration of Human Rights.

One must be recognized as a person (Universal Declaration, Article 6) in order to be treated with any sort of concern or respect. Personal rights to nationality and to

recognition before the law, along with rights to life and to protection against slavery, torture, and other inhuman or degrading practices can be seen as legal and political prerequisites to recognition and thus respect (Articles 3, 4, 5, 15). Rights to equal protection of the laws and protection against racial, sexual, and other forms of discrimination are essential to *equal* respect (Articles 1, 2, 7).

Equal respect for all persons will be at most a hollow formality without personal autonomy, the freedom to choose and act on one's own ideas of the good life. Freedoms of speech, conscience, religion, and association, along with the right to privacy, guarantee a private sphere of personal autonomy (Articles 12, 18-20). The rights to education and to participate in the cultural life of the community provide a social dimension to the idea of personal autonomy (Articles 26, 27). The rights to vote and to freedom of speech, press, assembly, and association guarantee political autonomy (Articles 18-21).

Rights to food, health care, and social insurance (Article 25) are also needed to make equal concern and respect a practical reality rather than a mere formal possibility. The right to work is a right to economic participation very similar to the right to political participation (Article 23). A (limited) right to property may also be justified in such terms (Article 17).

Finally, the special threat to personal security and equality posed by the modern state requires legal rights to constrain the state and its functionaries. These include rights to be presumed innocent until proven guilty, due process, fair and public hearings before an independent tribunal, and protection from arbitrary arrest, detention, or exile. (Articles 8-11). Anything less would mean that the state may treat citizens with differential concern or respect.

203.　　Joan A. Pisarchik. "A Rawlsian Analysis of the Immigration Act of 1990." GEORGETOWN IMMIGRATION LAW JOURNAL, Vol. 6: 1993, p. 729. Under liberal theory, the rights of an individual are independent of his or her identity as a member of a particular community or nation. Our policies, however, differentiate among would-be immigrants largely on the basis of group identity or nationality. Identity thus becomes the greatest barrier to immigration, one that can be overcome only by a showing of special skill or some other desirable trait which makes the immigrant acceptable despite his or her nationality. If, as Rawls contents, "social justice is the principle of rational prudence applied to an aggregative conception of the welfare of the group," and can be applied globally, then United States immigration policies traditionally have been illiberal, drawing distinctions among potential immigrants based solely on nationality or special skills possessed. United States policy admits those people deemed to be best for United States interest. The total global good may be increased by the addition of talented and skilled immigrants to the United States. However, this policy dispropor-

tionately benefits the United States and maintains the status quo for those who are worst off. This may be the correct result under utilitarian theory, but it fails to take into account any distinctions between persons.

204.　　Joan A. Pisarchik. "A Rawlsian Analysis of the Immigration Act of 1990." GEORGETOWN IMMIGRATION LAW JOURNAL, Vol. 6: 1993, pp. 743-744. This policy is illiberal because it defines people and their rights in geographic terms. Within each region, people are subdivided by education and work experience or training; the acceptability and amounts are defined according to Western standards. This is contrary to liberal thought which considers political boundaries to be morally arbitrary and illegitimate when they are used to protect certain privileged groups while denying others access to a better life. Geography is the final hurdle for those who are otherwise qualified. It enables policymakers in the United States to tailor carefully the racial and ethnic mix of immigrants, while ensuring that they are ready to contribute to the economy of the United States upon admission.

Under a Rawlsian analysis, the 1990 Act keeps immigration subservient to the whims of sovereigns. Freedom of movement between countries remains something less than a basic liberty or even an issue of fair equal opportunity. The 1990 Act is another instance of guarding the economy and standard of living from the perceived threat and fear of an influx of immigrants.

In order to comport with the difference principle, those who are the most disadvantaged would have to be made better off than under any other feasible plan. In this respect, the regional construct of the 1990 Act may be one of the harshest provisions. It does nothing to further the interests of those who are the worst off. It is not difficult to conceive of numerous other ways in which regional boundaries could have been drawn to promote the interests of the poorest people, who are unable to qualify for visas under current law. The lottery has the same effect through its careful enunciation of those who are permitted to participate. The denial of participation to the worst off reinforces their position and maintains the status quo.

205.　　Joan A. Pisarchik. "A Rawlsian Analysis of the Immigration Act of 1990." GEORGETOWN IMMIGRATION LAW JOURNAL, Vol. 6: 1993, pp. 730-731. United States policies, however, have jealously guarded domestic economic well-being against a potential influx of those who could have the effect of lowering our standard of living. Currently, preference visas are awarded to those who are highly educated or skilled, such as scientists and professionals. There is no corresponding visa allocation for persons with less education or a low level of skill. This reflects our desire to recruit only those with superior intellects or skills, while excluding those whom we view as a threat to the economic well-

being of our working-class. As a result, equal access for all is impossible, due to these requirements.

Rawls' difference principle views the unequal distribution of primary goods, "things that every rational man is presumed to want," such as rights or wealth, as acceptable only if those who are in the worst position are made better off than under any other feasible plan. Some of these primary goods need not be scarce, although the use of artificial constructs, such as political boundaries and visas, have served to make them scarce.

If visas may be viewed as primary goods, tied to the job market, among other things, then under the difference principle visas would be issued to alleviate the suffering of the greatest number of the most disadvantaged. In theory, some liberties are given up for economic and social gains. However, through the use of boundaries, restrictions, and requirements developed by governments as tools of exclusion, not only have liberties been relinquished, but there has been no corresponding economic or social gain on a global scale.

Additionally, immigration policies affect the distribution of income, presumably with the income of new aliens increasing while the income of citizens decreases. However, would-be immigrants are generally those who are worst off because they have the fewest social and economic rights. They are the recipients of unequal treatment and such inequality is allowable in a Rawlsian framework only if everyone in society benefits, and particularly if the least advantaged members of society benefit. Current immigration policy keeps those who are most disadvantaged in the same position, while guarding the rights of the privileged. The drawing of political boundaries prevents both global free movement as a basic liberty and the chance to gain fair equal opportunity.

206.   Joan A. Pisarchik. "A Rawlsian Analysis of the Immigration Act of 1990." GEORGETOWN IMMIGRATION LAW JOURNAL, Vol. 6: 1993, pp. 729-730. In a Rawlsian framework, two different principles are initially available for ordering society. Basic rights can be assigned unequally, or social and economic inequalities can be accepted, but only "if they result in compensating benefits for everyone, and in particular for the least advantaged members of society." Similarly, on a global scale, nations may attempt to alleviate inequality with respect to unequal distribution of resources and unequal levels of economic development by migration. This allows for three possible justifications for freedom of movement: basic liberty; fair equal opportunity; and the difference principle.

A basic liberty, garnering the greatest protection, is that of internal movement. Under a Rawlsian system, it can be restricted only when it impinges on another basic liberty. Economic considerations and the preservation of the income level of citizens do not qualify as basic liberties. However, exclusion is often justified by economic considerations, such as concern that immigrants will take jobs away from citizens and drive down wages, thereby lowering the standard of living. It would be difficult to imagine a scenario in which a basic liberty or civil right was trampled on by movement of persons into and out of a country. Global migration, however, is not viewed by policymakers as similar to internal movement. Instead, national boundaries, which some argue are morally arbitrary, have become significant in the denial of global freedom of movement because they serve to maintain privileges for an elite group.

If movement is not a basic liberty, perhaps it may be justified as fair equal opportunity. This means that everyone has the equal right of access to a desirable social position, based on one's qualifications. It assumes that the "distribution of natural assets [to] those…[of] the same level of talent and ability…should have the same prospects of success regardless of their initial place in the social system." The main reason that people desire to move is to improve their condition or career prospects, thus linking social and geographical mobility. This equal right of access, like a basic liberty, cannot be overcome by economic considerations. [ellipses in original]

207.   Joan A. Pisarchik. "A Rawlsian Analysis of the Immigration Act of 1990." GEORGETOWN IMMIGRATION LAW JOURNAL, Vol. 6: 1993, p. 728. This notion is in direct contrast to the ideas of thinkers, such as John Rawls, who distinguish between the claims of liberty and right on the one hand and the desirability of increasing aggregate social welfare on the other; and that we give a certain priority, if not absolute weight to the former. Each member of society is thought to have an inviolability founded on justice…which even the welfare of everyone else cannot override…. Therefore in a just society the basic liberties are taken for granted and the rights secured by justice are not subject to political bargaining.

Rawls believes that the "first virtue of social institutions" is justice. If laws or institutions are unjust, they should be changed or abolished. Rawls does not presuppose that all people will have equal rights. However, those who disagree about which conception of justice is correct may still agree that an aspect of justice is the lack of "arbitrary distinctions…between persons in the assigning of basic rights and duties."

His "conception of social justice… provid[es] …a standard whereby the distributive aspects of the basic structure of society are to be assessed." What rational people would choose, behind a veil of ignorance, as equal liberty will become the principles of justice. If rational people viewed themselves as equals, presumably they

would not agree to a principle which may require lesser life prospects for some simply for the sake of a greater sum of advantages enjoyed by others…

No one has a reason to acquiesce in an enduring loss for himself in order to bring about a greater net balance of satisfaction. [ellipses in original]

208.   THE NATION. "Watching Rights." January 24, 1994, p. 79. The advent of the Clinton Administration aroused great hopes among proponents of human rights. It was not only his campaign statements; it was also appointments of such reliable human rights advocates as John Shattuck, now Assistant Secretary of State for Human Rights and Humanitarian Affairs. This seemed a sign that a concern with rights would weigh heavily in the Administration's foreign policy.

Yet as demonstrated by the public reprimand of Shattuck for advocating a review of the policy of repatriation of Haitians, the Clinton Administration is a supporter of human rights except when it has some other interest that it considers more important. That concern with rights will not always prevail is hardly surprising; what is cause for dismay is how many other interests take precedence.

209.   Jack Donnelly. INTERNATIONAL HUMAN RIGHTS, Westview Press: Boulder, 1993, p. 159. The prospects for a sustained U.S. effort, however, are not bright. Both public attention and U.S. foreign policy have typically lurched from crisis to crisis, separated by long stretches of neglect. Consider, for example, the dramatic swings in U.S. policy toward Central America over the past four decades or the tendency for Sub-Saharan Africa to be in the news only when there is a coup, famine, or civil war. In the absence of dramatic short-term successes, the risks of lapsing into disinterest are great. Hard economic times at home further deflect attention. None of the candidates in the 1992 presidential election had much to say about human rights, and few people in the public or the media criticized this.

210.   Jack Donnelly. INTERNATIONAL HUMAN RIGHTS, Westview Press: Boulder, 1993, pp. 133-134. Internationally, the end of the cold war has eliminated the principal U.S. rationale for supporting repressive regimes. The demise of the Soviet Union has eliminated the postwar world's other major supporter of rights-abusive regimes. But a variety of rationales for antihumanitarian intervention remains. Furthermore, there is no necessary connection between a decline in foreign policy actions that harm human rights abroad and the development of positive international human rights policies. For all the changes of recent years, international human rights policies in the 1990s, especially in their positive dimensions, are likely to look very much like those of the late 1970s and 1980s.

211.   J. Michael Cavosie. "Defending the Golden Door: The Persistence of Ad Hoc and Ideological Decision Making in U.S. Refugee Law." INDIANA LAW JOURNAL, Vol. 67: 1992, p. 436. On a more fundamental level, and perhaps more importantly, such a practice cheapens the United States' commitment to human rights. President Bush recently wrote:

Ever since the first Europeans came to this country in search of freedom and opportunity, America has been viewed as a safe haven and a source of hope for millions of people around the globe. We take tremendous pride in our leading efforts to assist refugees, and we continue to cherish the great and generous spirit embodied by our magnificent Statue of Liberty. As Emma Lazarus wrote in her timeless sonnet to the famed Mother of Exiles, "from her beacon-hand glows worldwide welcome."

These are grand and, to a large extent, true words. Yet, in allowing ideology to creep into refugee considerations, the United States undermines them. For at its most elementary level, refugee law reflects the noblest of humanitarian instincts: to help those who need it. Ideology simply has no part in these determinations; it is as irrelevant as the color of a refugee's eyes.

The use of ideology is frequently rationalized by arguing that since far more aliens apply for refugee status than can possibly be admitted such an additional selection criterion is necessary to narrow their numbers. For example, consider this statement by Representative Morrison:

The people who can come here are a trickle (compared to those who want to come). Therefore, there is an impossible picking and choosing. By the very nature of things, there has to be a reason for why we take a particular person. And that gives rise to politics, not in a corrupt sense, but in a sense of identifying American interests.

However, an ideological criterion is purely arbitrary and has nothing to do with discerning who is *worthy* of protection. "American interests" are not the issue; humanitarian interests are. If a limited criterion is necessary, then at the very least it should be tied to humanitarian, not political, considerations.

212.   HUMAN RIGHTS AND U.S. FOREIGN POLICY; REPORT AND RECOMMENDATION, Lawyers Committee for Human Rights: New York, 1992, p. 45. So long as the U.S. rejects economic, social and cultural rights and fails to become a party to the major international treaties, it will remain unable to realize its potential to influence human rights activities at the international level. Moreover, in doing so, it has given other countries the opportunity to shift attention from their human rights records to the U.S.'s unwillingness to embrace the same international standards at home.

213. Jack Donnelly. INTERNATIONAL HUMAN
RIGHTS, Westview Press: Boulder, 1993, p.
80. Reporting as an implementation technique thus functions primarily through the goodwill and good intentions of reporting states. The obvious limitations of such a process simply reflect the basic problem of international action on behalf of human rights in a world of sovereign states. Each state has almost exclusive responsibility for implementing human rights in its own territory. The human rights practices of all states are (in principle) subject to scrutiny in the commission on Human Rights. Many states have accepted additional scrutiny by becoming parties to the Covenants and other human rights treaties. But actual implementation is up to states. Supervisory bodies must thus struggle to make the most of the opportunities for influence available during the review of reports.

214. Jack Donnelly. INTERNATIONAL HUMAN
RIGHTS, Westview Press: Boulder, 1993, p.
158. Real support, however, will require more than just words of encouragement and a reprogramming of already-appointed aid. It will require a willingness to pay for further international human rights achievements. No state, and certainly not the United States, seems willing to make the sizable financial investment required. Even forgiving past debt, let alone providing substantial new resources, seems more than most countries are willing to do. Simply retaining U.S. foreign aid at its already pitifully low levels will require substantial work.

215. Jack Donnelly. INTERNATIONAL HUMAN
RIGHTS, Westview Press: Boulder, 1993, p.
66. The limitations of the procedure, however, are no less noteworthy. Most major human rights violators, not surprisingly, have elected not to be covered. This is the overriding problem of treaty-based enforcement mechanisms. Obligations apply only to parties to the treaty, and states are free to choose not to accept these obligations. The stronger the monitoring and implementation procedures, the fewer the states that are willing to be covered. The optional protocol thus presents a striking example of the typical trade-off between the scope and the strength of international procedures.

216. Jack Donnelly. INTERNATIONAL HUMAN
RIGHTS, Westview Press: Boulder, 1993, p.
64. Here, however, we come face-to-face with the problem of political bias in the UN system, for until recently, public action was largely limited to the pariah regimes of South Africa, Israel, and Chile. Although all three countries richly merited international condemnation, comparable violations elsewhere have not received comparable—or in some cases any—scrutiny or action.
In both South Africa and the Occupied Territories, human rights violations of special concern to the Third World have been linked to regional political struggles.

The resulting politics is thus easily understood. But the case of the third pariah, Chile, did not even raise issues of racism or colonialism. Furthermore, comparable violations in neighboring Argentina and Uruguay went unaddressed. And barbaric regimes in Africa and Asia, such as that of Pol Pot in Cambodia, the Amin and (second) Obote governments in Uganda, and the Mengistu regime in Ethiopia, were never even the subject of a GA human rights resolution.

217. Jack Donnelly. INTERNATIONAL HUMAN
RIGHTS, Westview Press: Boulder, 1993,
p. 81. There has also been an increased interest in alternatives to treaty reporting systems. It seems unlikely, though, that real international monitoring can be achieved through any politically acceptable alternative. For example, special rapporteurs and working groups, which gather their own information from a variety of sources, seem to have fallen into disfavor among most Third World states, largely because of their relative independence from political control. Likewise, proposals for a high commissioner for human rights, which have surfaced periodically for more than a quarter century, have received only limited support. For all their drawbacks, reporting schemes seem to be the best that is politically possible.

218. Jack Donnelly. INTERNATIONAL HUMAN
RIGHTS, Westview Press: Boulder, 1993, p.
81. If a state lacks the skills or the resources required for a conscientious review of its practices, reporting is an empty formality, even if the government is well intentioned. The impact of reporting systems thus could be significantly improved by linking them to a system of technical and financial support. Although many states would not avail themselves of such help, at least some would. (Countries that have recently undergone a change of government would be particularly promising candidates.) But given the financial problems of the UN system and the tendency not to support human rights projects through traditional channels of development assistance, such changes are unlikely. Substantially less than 1 percent of the UN budget is devoted to human rights work.

219. Jack Donnelly. INTERNATIONAL HUMAN
RIGHTS, Westview Press: Boulder, 1993, p.
158. This would seem to be one area in which external assistance could have a significant positive impact. Although foreign actors can usually play only a supporting role in establishing rights-protective regimes, at crucial turning points, and in the stage of democratic consolidation, the right kind of external support can indeed make a difference. For example, foreign technical and financial assistance can in many cases not only directly improve the enjoyment of economic and social rights but also indirectly strengthen new governments, whose legitimacy

is likely to be enhanced by demonstrated economic efficacy. Such assistance is also attractive because it is likely to avoid changes of intervention.

220.   Jack Donnelly. INTERNATIONAL HUMAN RIGHTS, Westview Press: Boulder, 1993, pp. 80-81. There is thus a paradox at the root of international monitoring procedures. They are likely to be most effective in improving national human rights practices where they are in some sense least needed; that is, where human rights records are relatively good (or less bad). Recalcitrant states usually can violate human rights with impunity. But the fact that international reporting schemes are unlikely to have much impact in such cases does not make them worthless. A country with a relatively good (or less bad) record may still violate human rights. A victim of human rights violations in such a country is likely to receive little solace from knowing that there are people who are treated worse elsewhere. Any victim who is helped is a victory for international action, wherever that person resides.

221.   Jack Donnelly. INTERNATIONAL HUMAN RIGHTS, Westview Press: Boulder, 1993, p. 19. If all human beings have them simply because they are human, human rights are held equally by all. And because being human cannot be renounced, lost or forfeited, human rights are inalienable. Even the cruelest torturer and the most debased victim are still human beings. In practice, not all people *enjoy* all their human rights, let along enjoy them equally. Nonetheless, all human beings *have* the same human rights and hold them equally and inalienably.

222.   Jack Donnelly. INTERNATIONAL HUMAN RIGHTS, Westview Press: Boulder, 1993, p. 21. Human rights are a special type of right. In their most fundamental sense, they are paramount moral rights. In the preceding chapter we saw that human rights are also recognized in international law. Most countries also recognize many of these rights in their national constitution, legislation, or legal practice. As a result, the same "thing"—for example, food, protection against discrimination, or freedom of association—often is guaranteed by several different types of rights.

223.   Jack Donnelly. INTERNATIONAL HUMAN RIGHTS, Westview Press: Boulder, 1993, p. 160. Continued commitment will be easier if we can clarify and highlight the moral fundamentals underlying international human rights policy. U.S. policy must recapture—or, perhaps, capture for the first time—a clear sense of the meaning and importance of the international struggle for human rights. It is not (and never has been) equivalent to the struggle against communism, which is but one model of systematic human rights violations. Human rights are about guaranteeing, through the insti-

tution of equal and inalienable rights for all persons, the conditions necessary for a life of dignity in the contemporary world. They are universal rights. Systematic violations therefore demand our concern and condemnation, wherever they occur.

224.   Richard Schifter. "Enhancing Our Human Rights Effort." INTERNATIONAL LAW AND POLITICS, Vol. 24: 1992, p. 1294. To reach this goal it will be necessary to persuade the heads of government of the G-7 to put teeth into human rights pronouncements. The case which can be made to them is that as we look at the world today democracy and respect for human rights are closely linked to peaceful behavior and support for international tranquility. These world leaders are well aware of the fact that the global economy is not a place where we play a zero-sum game. They know that, to use John Kennedy's felicitous phrase, a rising tide raises all boats. And they should know that democracies, respectful of human rights, focus on improving their economies and tend not to threaten their neighbors, while the same cannot be said of nondemocratic regimes that violate human rights. These violators have been and continue to be a threat to world stability.

225.   HUMAN RIGHTS AND U.S. FOREIGN POLICY; REPORT AND RECOMMENDATION. Lawyers Committee for Human Rights. New York. 1992, p. 3. It is in the U.S. national interest for human rights issues to be afforded a higher priority and given greater attention in the foreign policy decision making process. Stable governments which respect fundamental rights make the best allies. Governments that allow freedom of association and freedom to participate in the political process are less likely to be governments that go to war or create international disorder. Governments that uphold the rule of law and have independent legal institutions are more likely to be reliable economic partners. Governments that encourage an independent press and which are publicly accountable to their own people are more likely to attend to the material needs of their citizens and less likely to generate large refugee populations, or require substantial economic assistance.

226.   Richard Schifter. "Enhancing Our Human Rights Effort." INTERNATIONAL LAW AND POLITICS, Vol. 24: 1992, p. 1295. The case if Iraq offers another example of a country guilty of human rights violations being also a threat to world peace. A case can thus be made to the G-7 leadership that combating human rights violations is not only a moral activity; it also serves to advance the cause of international tranquility.

227.   Jack Donnelly. INTERNATIONAL HUMAN RIGHTS, Westview Press: Boulder, 1993, pp. 21-22. The language of human rights is fundamentally

that of the oppressed or dispossessed. The principal use of human rights claims is to challenge or seek to alter legal or political practices. Claims of human rights thus aim to be self-liquidating. To assert one's human rights is to attempt to change political structures and practices in ways that will make it no longer necessary to claim those rights (as human rights). For example, the struggle for human rights in South Africa has been a struggle to change South African laws and practices so that average South Africans would no longer need to claim human rights. Rather, they would be able to turn to the South African legislature, courts, or bureaucracy should they be denied, for example, equal protection of the laws, political participation, or health care.

228.   Jack Donnelly. INTERNATIONAL HUMAN RIGHTS, Westview Press: Boulder, 1993, p. 38. Such an argument does not imply wanton cultural imperialism. In fact, the Western legacy of imperialism demands that we show special caution and sensitivity when dealing with fundamentally clashing cultural values. Caution, however, must not be confused with inaction. Even if we are not entitled to impose our values on others, they are our own values. Sometimes they may demand that we act on them even in the absence of agreement by others. And if the values of others are particularly objectionable—consider, for example, societies in which it is traditional to kill the first-born child if it is female, or the deeply rooted tradition of anti-Semitism in the West—even strong social sanctions may deserve neither respect nor toleration.

229.   Barbara Yarnold. REFUGEES WITHOUT REFUGE: FORMATION AND FAILED IMPLEMENTATION OF U.S. POLITICAL ASYLUM POLICY IN THE 1980'S, University Press: Lanham, Maryland, 1990, p. 197. Throughout history, there has been a tension between man's adherence to either positive law or natural law. A common reason for conflict among men and nations has been that one participant in the conflict enacted a written norm or customary practice, or relied upon conventional law in undertaking certain actions, with unjust results. In spite of the argument that the actor's activities conformed with "conventional" or "positive" law, consisting of prevailing laws, norms, or practices, these activities seemed to violate a higher "moral" law, or man's innate "natural law" precepts, which originates either from man's ability to reason or from revelations from God.

230.   Jack Donnelly. INTERNATIONAL HUMAN RIGHTS, Westview Press: Boulder, 1993, p. 21. Those who seek to ground human rights in a scientific theory of human nature usually speak of basic human needs. Unfortunately, any list of needs that can make a plausible claim to be scientifically (empirically) established provides a clearly inadequate list of human

rights: life, food, protection against cruel or inhuman treatment, and not much else. Whether because of contingent failings in our current scientific procedures or knowledge, or because science is in principle incapable of providing an appropriate theory of human nature, few specific human rights can be grounded in the psychological, physiological, and biochemical sciences. We have human rights not to what we need for health but to what we need for human dignity.

231.   Jack Donnelly. INTERNATIONAL HUMAN RIGHTS, Westview Press: Boulder, 1993, p. 22. Unfortunately, no philosophical theory of human nature has ever achieved widespread acceptance. Consensus is no measure of truth. Without it, however, any particular theory—and any international action based on it—is vulnerable to attack. The problem is even more severe when we consider that many moral theories, and their underlying theories of human nature, deny the very existence of human rights.

232.   Jack Donnelly. INTERNATIONAL HUMAN RIGHTS, Westview Press: Boulder, 1993, p. 138. The moral interdependence underlying human rights, however, is not a tangible part of daily life for most Americans (nor for most ordinary citizens elsewhere). Furthermore, other states are not directly harmed by a government's failure to respect human rights. The moral sensibilities of foreign citizens and leaders may be offended, but human rights violations rarely cause direct or material harm to foreigners. Therefore, the incentives to retaliate are largely intangible—which in practice usually means low.

233.   Jack Donnelly. INTERNATIONAL HUMAN RIGHTS, Westview Press: Boulder, 1993, p. 157. The focus on economics is also important because of the American tendency to think that once a free election has been held, the human rights situation is under control. Even if we ignore the cases in which the elected government does not in fact control the country, in many countries economic, social, and cultural rights remain unaddressed. These human rights are intrinsically important, although many Americans persist in disparaging them. Furthermore, a country's performance on economic, social, and cultural rights can have an important impact on the fate of civil and political rights. Consider the rise of neo-Nazi violence in Germany, which ominously links ethnic conflict and economic dislocation. And when market reforms take place in an environment of economic crisis and failure, the threat to human rights is likely to be especially severe.

234.   Jack Donnelly. INTERNATIONAL HUMAN RIGHTS, Westview Press: Boulder, 1993, p. 158. Opposing systematic human rights violations is no longer enough. As we have already seen, ending old

forms of abuse is only a first step on the way to protecting human rights. Unfortunately, there is no evidence that the new human rights needs and opportunities of the 1990s are being seriously explored, let alone exploited, by the United States, the Europeans, or the international community.

235. Jack Donnelly. INTERNATIONAL HUMAN RIGHTS, Westview Press: Boulder, 1993, p. 152. The collapse of the old order has also unleashed or created new threats to human rights, most notably nationalism. Internationally recognized human rights rest on the idea that individuals, simply because they are human beings, not only have certain basic rights but also have (and ought to enjoy) these rights equally. Aggressive, exclusive nationalism challenges the notion of equality that lies at the root of international human rights norms.

236. Nancy Kelly. "Gender-Related Persecution: Assessing the Asylum Claims of Women." CORNELL INTERNATIONAL LAW JOURNAL, Vol. 26: 1933, p. 627. However, women are much less likely than men to be found to meet the eligibility criteria for refugee status because of the absence of explicit recognition of gender-based persecution, and because of the social and political context in which the claims of women are adjudicated. The problem is twofold. First, the definition of "refugee" contained in the Convention does not specify name gender as one of the bases upon which protection can be granted. Second, in applying the refugee definition, adjudicators have traditionally neglected to incorporate the gender-related claims of women in the interpretation of the grounds already enumerated in the Convention.

237. Karen Bower. "Recognizing Violence Against Women as Persecution on the Basis of Membership in a Particular Social Group." GEORGETOWN IMMIGRATION LAW JOURNAL, Vol. 7: 1993, p. 173. Violence against women, in various forms, is pervasive worldwide. Although the United States allegedly protects and welcomes those who are persecuted throughout the world, current U.S. asylum law fails to recognize gender-based violence that involves government participation or complicity as "gender persecution" of a distinct "social group," namely women, sufficient to warrant the grant of asylum. Acceptance of women as a social group subject to "gender persecution" would acknowledge and be consistent with the remedial purpose of asylum, and would provide refuge to asylum applicants with valid claims of persecution on a non-discriminatory basis.

238. Karen Bower. "Recognizing Violence Against Women as Persecution on the Basis of Membership in a Particular Social Group." GEORGETOWN IMMIGRATION LAW JOURNAL, Vol. 7: 1993, p.

175. Although the presence of gender-based violence distinguishes women's experiences from those of men, women are currently not recognized as a distinct "social group" for the purposes of the U.S. asylum law. Therefore, even if a woman can prove that she is the victim of gender persecution, she is often unable to prove that it is "on account of" one of the five enumerated reasons. Women who are victimized on account of race, religion, political opinion or nationality may be granted asylum, while women who are victimized because of their gender currently have no such recourse. Recognition of women as a social group would entitle women with valid claims of persecution to the same protection afforded to individuals persecuted for other prohibited reasons.

239. Amnesty International. REASONABLE FEAR: HUMAN RIGHTS AND UNITED STATES REFUGEE POLICY, Amnesty International USA: New York, March 1990, p. 6. A majority of adults who flee their countries are women, according to the Office of the United Nations High Commissioner for Refugees. Of the people who cross borders into some countries, 90 percent are women and children. In addition to fleeing for reasons of persecution, war, or civil strife, the UNHCR recognized in 1985 that many women flee because they suffer severe discrimination solely on the basis of their sex. In some cases, government authorities tolerate or condone local populations' harsh or inhuman treatment of women.

A common misconception about refugees is the location in which most of them seek asylum. Some 18 million people fled from their homes during 1988, according to the United States Committee for Refugees. Less than 2.5 million of these people sought protection in the developed nations of Western Europe and North America. The vast majority of them fled to developing countries.

240. Nancy Kelly. "Gender-Related Persecution: Assessing the Asylum Claims of Women." CORNELL INTERNATIONAL LAW JOURNAL, Vol. 26: 1993, pp. 625-627. The majority of the world's refugees are female. Women as a group are often the first victims of political, economic and social repression. This is in part because of laws and social mores which dictate gender-specific behavior and treatment. In addition, in societies facing economic, social and political upheaval, women are often left alone to care for children or elderly family members, and thus become the most exposed to violent attack during wars or ethnic crises. Women forced to flee their countries as refugees face continuing gender-related abuse including sexual harassment, rape, and torture by pirates, smugglers, border guards, camp administrators, and employers. Until recently, however, the asylum claims of women refugees have largely gone unaddressed under both the 1951 Convention Relating to the Status of Refugees and United States Immigration and Nationality Act. The definition

of "refugee" incorporated into the Convention is gender-neutral, making no distinction between male and female applicants.

241.   Ranee K.L. Panjabi. "The Global Refugee Crisis: A Search for Solutions." CALIFORNIA WESTERN INTERNATIONAL LAW JOURNAL, Vol. 21, no. 2: 1990-1991, pp. 252-253. Geneviève Camus-Jacques asserts that "refugee women are a forgotten majority." While numerically, indications are that women and girls dominate today's refugee groups, this numerical superiority is not reflected in a proportionate influence exerted by women in refugee camps which are still male-dominated. As refugees, women face specific problems, difficulties that cry out for urgent solutions. First, the "feminization of global migrations" has forced women to become heads of households in traditional societies which normally reject such a role for women. Frequently, the women and children are all that is left of the family unit, especially as adult males tend to be prime targets for government or terrorist violence. Camus-Jacques explains that "[r]efugee women encounter specific problems regarding protection, assistance, and participation in decision-making. The safety factor was brought to world attention by the news stories about the plight of Vietnamese boat people, particularly women at the hands of pirates. The UNHCR estimates that between 1980 and 1984 at least 2,400 women were raped by pirates.

242.   Pamela Goldberg. "Anyplace but Home: Asylum in the United States for Women Fleeing Intimate Violence." CORNELL INTERNATIONAL LAW JOURNAL, Vol. 26: 1993, p. 584. Intimate violence includes conduct such as taking the life of a woman, physical and mental harm, forcing a women to perform sexual or other acts against her will, confining a woman to the home, and repeated verbal and emotional abuse. At a minimum, any of this conduct, virtually de facto, constitutes serious violations of internationally recognized human rights. At the same time, it can be argued that the acquiescence of the state in the perpetration of these acts itself raises the physical and emotional torment of a battered woman to the level of human rights violations and, as such, constitutes persecution. The international recognition of intimate violence as a human rights violation strongly supports the argument that these acts of violence constitute persecution in the asylum law context, and that protection from these violations must be recognized under U.S. asylum law.

243.   Pamela Goldberg. "Anyplace but Home: Asylum in the United States for Women Fleeing Intimate Violence." CORNELL INTERNATIONAL LAW JOURNAL, Vol. 26: 1993, p. 603. Alternatively, the use of violence to maintain a woman in sex-stereotyped roles is persecution on account of her political

opinion because the man's acts are a form of political repression, designed to repress her from "expressing" her political opinion of not accepting the traditional expected role of a woman. If we look at resisting intimate violence, or at intimate violence itself, as a form of punishment for resisting "stereotypical role restrictions, then we see the man's behavior as identical to what the "totalitarian state" does to political dissidents. As discussed, this conduct is expressly outlawed by customary international law as well as by international treaties such as the Convention Against Torture and the International Covenant on Civil and Political Rights. As such, men are carrying out the wishes of the state in a kind of "parallel state." That is, the "home" functions as a microcosm of the state. The state allows the home to exist under a separate dominion or authority that mirrors or parallels that of the state. In allowing this, the state implicitly endorses the act and therefore has culpability. This argument takes intimate violence out of the realm of the "private sphere" and brings it into the "public sphere" because it has to do with repression of political expression.

244.   Pamela Goldberg. "Anyplace but Home: Asylum in the United States for Women Fleeing Intimate Violence." CORNELL INTERNATIONAL LAW JOURNAL, Vol. 26: 1993, pp. 575-576. To establish the objective basis of this fear, in an elaboration of the "reasonable person similarly situated " test mentioned above, a person must be able to show that the fear has "some basis in the reality of the circumstances [and not] mere irrational apprehension." In the case of battered women, this can be done in several ways. Expert testimony can be presented to show that the woman's testimony of what transpired, both the abuser's treatment of her and her response to it, is consistent with current understanding of battering. Expert testimony also can be presented on post-traumatic stress disorder (PTSD), verifying that her reactions and psychological state are consistent with that disorder. This expert could assert that as with other situations of extreme stress and/or violence such as traditionally recognized forms of torture, battering in the intimate sphere can, due to the nature of the acts, likewise induce a state of PTSD.

245.   Pamela Goldberg. "Anyplace but Home: Asylum in the United States for Women Fleeing Intimate Violence." CORNELL INTERNATIONAL LAW JOURNAL, Vol. 26: 1993, p. 598. The refusal to submit to the domination of her batterer is a characteristic she should not, as a matter of conscience of the highest order, be required to change. It is the unequivocal and active refusal to submit to male domination, ultimately by fleeing, in addition to her efforts to obtain protection from state authorities or the failure of the state to provide any such protection for her, that identify her and single her out for persecution by the government. The

government seeks to uphold the male dominant culture by withholding its protection from members of this social group while extending it to other segments of society.

246.   Karen Bower. "Recognizing Violence Against Women as Persecution on the Basis of Membership in a Particular Social Group." GEORGETOWN IMMIGRATION LAW JOURNAL, Vol. 7: 1993, pp. 202-203. Moreover, the requirement that asylum applicants prove they are individually targeted for persecution is directly contradictory to the standard that asylum applicants demonstrate a reasonable fear of persecution. In INS v. Cardoza-Fonseca, the Supreme Court held that unlike withholding of deportation, which requires a demonstration that it is "more likely than not that the alien would be subject to persecution" if returned to her country of origin, the granting of asylum only requires that the alien demonstrate that she has a "well-founded fear of persecution." The "well-founded fear" standard contemplates a mere showing of likelihood of persecution, while the more stringent "more likely than not" standard requires showing a fifty percent or greater probability of persecution. Requiring proof that one would be "singled out" for persecution is tantamount to applying the higher "more likely than not" standard to asylum applicants. As such, the singled out requirement is improper and inappropriate.

Moreover, it is also directly contrary to the language in both the Handbook and the fourth prong enunciated in Sanchez-Trujillo, which provide that special circumstances may exist where mere membership can be a sufficient ground to fear persecution and proof of being singled out is not necessary. Such circumstances may exist where a demographic or statistical group, such as women, is specifically targeted for persecution, transforming that group into a social group. Countrywide, gender persecution could be such a special circumstance where mere membership is enough.

Commentators have suggested that requiring applicants to prove they are singled out is particularly inappropriate when applied to the social group category since "denial of asylum to those at risk on account of collective persecution allows despotic regimes to eliminate members of the collectively persecuted group one by one until none remain. Indeed, victims of genocide would thus fall outside the scope of so restricted a definition of refugee."

247.   Pamela Goldberg. "Anyplace but Home: Asylum in the United States for Women Fleeing Intimate Violence." CORNELL INTERNATIONAL LAW JOURNAL, Vol. 26: 1993, p. 588. Where a government imposes no criminal sanctions for any but the most heinous or lethal assaults by men on female intimates, or when it systematically refuses to afford women the protections that exist under the law, it is abandoning its function of protecting women from the violent assaults of their male intimates. This failure on the part of the state to impose penal sanctions for the physical and mental abuse of women by male intimates brings intimate violence into the arena of human rights violations. As such, these failures are acts of persecution, accomplished with the acquiescence, if not overt complicity, of the state.

248.   Pamela Goldberg. "Anyplace but Home: Asylum in the United States for Women Fleeing Intimate Violence." CORNELL INTERNATIONAL LAW JOURNAL, Vol. 26: 1993, p. 591. The Refugee Act of 1980 offers no guidance as to what constitutes a particular social group, nor do the implementing regulations discuss the term. The legislative history of the Act is also silent on the inclusion of this particular term. Commentators on the U.S. statute have argued for an expansive interpretation of the social group category. At least some of these commentators take the position that a study of the travaux preparatoires of the Convention and Protocol upon which the Refugee Act is based, supports the view that the social group category was meant to be a kind of catch-all category to protect those legitimately fearing persecution but unable to fit their claims into one of the other four grounds.

249.   Pamela Goldberg. "Anyplace but Home: Asylum in the United States for Women Fleeing Intimate Violence." CORNELL INTERNATIONAL LAW JOURNAL, Vol. 26: 1993, pp. 590-591. The preeminent scholar on international refugee law, Atle Grahl-Madsen, is among those who have commented on the meaning of the term "social group" contained in the Refugee Convention. He propounds that the social group category is meant to be broader than the other categories and that, in fact, it was added to the Convention definition to protect against persecution that would arise from unforseeable circumstances. Another commentator has asserted that the social group concept "possesses an element of open-endedness which states, in their discretion, could expand in favor of a variety of different classes susceptible to persecution.

Notably, leading commentator James Hathaway asserts unequivocally that gender, though not one of the five Convention grounds for protection, "is properly within the ambit of the social group category." He further states the "[g]ender-based groups are clear examples of social subsets defined by an innate and immutable characteristic." He concludes his comments on gender as a social group category by refuting the criticism that "gender-defined social groups" constitute too broad a spectrum; "adherence to the ejusdem generis principle defeats such concerns, since race, nationality, religion, and even political opinion are also traits which are shared by large numbers of people."

250. Karen Bower. "Recognizing Violence Against Women as Persecution on the Basis of Membership in a Particular Social Group." GEORGETOWN IMMIGRATION LAW JOURNAL, Vol. 7: 1993, pp. 187-188. Especially with infibulation, the woman must be cut open in order to have intercourse and give birth. There are many serious short-term health problems related to genital mutilation, including hemorrhage, septicemia, shock, blood loss, accute infection and death. The long-term health problems include chronic infection, urinary tract complications, kidney infections, menstrual difficulties, difficulty urinating, infertility, and painful intercourse and childbirth. In Somalia "[v]iolence in the form of female circumcision is still commonplace. It is performed in state-run hospitals. Pharaonic circumcision [infibulation] (the most extreme and dangerous form of genital mutilation) is widely practiced"

251. Linda Cipriani. "Gender and Persecution: Protecting Women Under International Refugee Law." GEORGETOWN IMMIGRATION LAW JOURNAL, Vol. 7: 1993, p. 526. Considering the conditions under which the surgery is performed, it is not surprising that genital mutilation causes many health complications and in some cases even death. The severe pain of the procedure and the lack of sterile conditions under which it is performed can lead to shock, infection, and death. Doctors in the Sudan estimate that one-third of all girls die in areas where antibiotics are not used. Death due to female genital mutilation contributes to the infant mortality rates. Countries practicing female circumcision and infibulation tend to have the highest infant mortality rates in the world. Long term complications are also various, especially with infibulation. They range from chronic infection and excruciating pain to menstrual difficulty and sterility. With infibulation, there often is a build up of scar tissue which sometimes becomes so severe that walking is impaired. This scar tissue presents a danger to future children as it blocks oxygen to the baby during birth which can result in brain damage or death of the child. In addition, reinjury occurs on the wedding night, when an infibulated woman is opened up either through intercourse or with a knife.

252. Nancy Kelly. "Gender-Related Persecution: Assessing the Asylum Claims of Women." CORNELL INTERNATIONAL LAW JOURNAL, Vol. 26: 1993, pp. 673-674. The evaluation of gender-related persecution claims also requires a rethinking of the *procedures* followed by advocates and adjudicators in developing and presenting the cases of refugee women. The United States asylum adjudication system contains no provisions which acknowledge the particular needs of women asylum applicants. As a result, numerous problems inherent in the system, which go unaddressed, combine to deny women access to protection. The UN-HCR has recommended a number of measures to improve access to protection for women. These measures include: providing women access to independent adjudication of their cases; instituting gender-sensitive procedures for interviewing women applicants; providing training regarding the nature of relationships between female and male family members within the applicant's culture; and familiarizing adjudicators with status and experiences of women in the country from which the applicant has fled. While these guidelines do not address all of the problems faced by women asylum applicants, incorporation of these recommendations into domestic asylum: adjudication procedures would greatly help in opening the process to women applicants.

253. Linda Cipriani. "Gender and Persecution: Protecting Women Under International Refugee Law." GEORGETOWN IMMIGRATION LAW JOURNAL, Vol. 7: 1993, pp. 535-536. One method of granting refugee status to persecuted women is to consider them a "social group" within the meaning of the Convention. In October of 1985, the UNHCR'S Subcommittee of the Whole on International Protection considered a Note on the International Protection of Refugee Women. It acknowledged that there were a number of cases in which women sought asylum pursuant to the Convention due to the treatment of women in their country. States were asked to consider the resolution of the European Parliament in 1984 and adopt its conclusions.

254. Linda Cipriani. "Gender and Persecution: Protecting Women Under International Refugee Law." GEORGETOWN IMMIGRATION LAW JOURNAL, Vol. 7: 1993, p. 538. A third method of enabling women to achieve refugee status is to expand the definition of a refugee to include anyone having a well-founded fear of persecution because of gender. If the Convention recognized persecution because of gender, individual women who opposed the rules and traditions of their society and were persecuted because of it would be protected. Women would then just have to prove that they were persecuted because they were women and would not have to show they were members of a social group of persecuted women with common beliefs and practices.

255. Karen Bower. "Recognizing Violence Against Women as Persecution on the Basis of Membership in a Particular Social Group." GEORGETOWN IMMIGRATION LAW JOURNAL, Vol. 7: 1993, p. 206. Failure to adequately protect women through use of these discriminatory practices must stop. Recognizing a human rights approach to defining persecution, and acknowledging that protected categories are not exhaustive, but rather a framework for evaluating asylum claims, broad and flexible enough to include women as a social group, will afford women urgently needed protection and will comply with the humanitarian and remedial pur-

poses of asylum. It is therefore essential that the United States recognize gender-based violence as persecution on account of membership in a particular social group.

256.   Nancy Kelly. "Gender-Related Persecution: Assessing the Asylum Claims of Women." CORNELL INTERNATIONAL LAW JOURNAL, Vol. 26: 1993, p. 674. Fundamentally, it includes a legal recognition of the harm women experience and the illegitimacy of governmental indifference to women's suffering. In addition, advocates and adjudicators must reevaluate the manner in which the claims of women are investigated and presented to insure that these claims become a more accurate reflection of women's reality. This includes the institution of procedures to insure that women have a meaningful opportunity to present their cases and education of advocates and adjudicators regarding the nature of persecution of women, both with regard to the overall political and social framework in which it occurs and in relation to the specific factual situations of particular countries.

257.   Pamela Goldberg. "Anyplace but Home: Asylum in the United States for Women Fleeing Intimate Violence." CORNELL INTERNATIONAL LAW JOURNAL, Vol. 26: 1993, pp. 603-604. When a woman's human rights are violated, she is as entitled as any man to protection and redress. The human rights community is already awakening to the fact that battered women deserve protection under human rights doctrine. The law must recognize what society propounds. It is time U.S. laws embrace advances being made by the UNHCR, in Canada, and in the international human rights community generally. Providing protection for women seeking refuge from intimate violence under U.S. asylum laws is an essential step toward furthering the human rights of women.

258.   Karen Bower. "Recognizing Violence Against Women as Persecution on the Basis of Membership in a Particular Social Group." GEORGETOWN IMMIGRATION LAW JOURNAL, Vol. 7: 1993, pp. 205-206. Moreover, the fear of opening the floodgates is unjustified. Recognizing violence against women as persecution on the basis of social group membership would not automatically flood the United States with asylum applicants. Applicants must still meet other eligibility criteria and demonstrate a well-founded fear of persecution and a lack of protection from the country of origin. Furthermore, the grant of asylum is discretionary, and may be denied even if eligibility criteria are met.

To mitigate the floodgates concern, the accepted forms of persecution can be narrowly tailored while still recognizing the goal of protection. Asylum applicants must already demonstrate that the state participates in the persecution through persecutory laws or is complicit in the persecution through inaction. To prove a claim of

gender persecution, women must demonstrate that they have no other form of relief or protection other than asylum. For example, where a woman comes from a country where the government does not investigate, prosecute or provide any protection from sexual assault or domestic abuse, coerced prostitution or genital mutilation and such abuse is pervasive, asylum relief is appropriate. On the other hand, asylum would be inappropriate for women whose countries of origin have an accessible and appropriate enforced mechanism for addressing the alleged wrongs, without fear of retaliation. Given the high standards that applicants must meet to prove eligibility for asylum, any concern about opening the floodgates is misplaced.

259.   Linda Cipriani. "Gender and Persecution: Protecting Women Under International Refugee Law." GEORGETOWN IMMIGRATION LAW JOURNAL, Vol. 7: 1993, p. 545. One problem that potentially arises from any expansion of the definition of refugee is how to absorb the influx of claimants caused by the new provision. In a world that is already overburdened with those fleeing not only persecution but war and natural disaster, this is clearly an important concern. A definition that includes persecution based on one's sex would probably not result in a flood of refugees. First, many women in the countries described herein may not feel that their cultures, religions, or legal systems persecute them. Second, others who feel that they do face some persecution may not be willing to leave their country, family, or friends because of it. Third, women who do feel that they are victims of persecution may already be seeking refugee status by attempting to base their claim on one of the provisions already in the treaties, such as persecution because of their political opinion or religion. Adding gender as one more ground for refugee protection, therefore, would ensure protection for those women who truly believe their society was persecuting them and would not encourage those women who would not normally seek refugee status in this manner. In addition, the international community would be fulfilling its commitment to protect women from human rights abuses.

260.   Pamela Goldberg. "Anyplace but Home: Asylum in the United States for Women Fleeing Intimate Violence." CORNELL INTERNATIONAL LAW JOURNAL, Vol. 26: 1993, p. 580. Recent developments in the international human rights theater have brought the issue of violence against women into sharper focus. International law has been interpreted to protect a woman from violence perpetrated against her by someone with whom she has or had an intimate relationship, such as marriage. Moreover, consistent with this understanding, there has been an urging by feminists and women's rights advocates throughout the international human rights community for the inter-governmental or-

ganizations (IGOs) to develop effective means of protection from violence against women in all its forms. IGOs have begun to respond to these demands.

261.   Nancy Kelly. "Gender-Related Persecution: Assessing the Asylum Claims of Women." CORNELL INTERNATIONAL LAW JOURNAL, Vol. 26: 1993, pp. 633-644. Advocates and adjudicators are also increasingly attempting to address the particular nature of gender-related claims. In 1991, the UNHCR issued its *Guidelines on the Protection of Refugee Women* which recognize the particular circumstances of women refugees which may form the basis of a persecution claim, and set out procedures to conduct meaningful evaluations of women's claims. The Canadian Immigration and Refugee Board has also recently developed guidelines for the evaluation of gender-related persecution claims. In addition, courts and administrative bodies in a number of countries have granted protection to women fleeing gender-related persecution. Although the United States has no regulations or guidelines specifically addressing the needs of female asylum seekers and there is little published United States case law in this area, advocates are increasingly presenting the cases of their female clients with an emphasis on gender. A number of cases are pending before the United States courts, the Immigration and Naturalization Service, and the Executive Office for Immigration Review.

262.   Nancy Kelly. "Gender-Related Persecution: Assessing the Asylum Claims of Women." CORNELL INTERNATIONAL LAW JOURNAL, Vol. 26: 1993, pp. 630-633. Despite the relative neglect of gender-related claims in the interpretation of refugee law, there are many encouraging recent developments legitimizing the factual basis for women's claims and the necessity for gender-specific protocols in asylum law. Increasingly, human rights groups and others have focused their attention on gender-specific human rights abuses and human rights abuses imposed on women because of their gender. While they have directed much of this effort toward documenting conditions experienced by women during their flight and in the country of first asylum, attention is lately being directed toward abuses inflicted upon women in the home country. Human Rights groups have documented widespread sexual abuse of women in detention for numerous reasons, including as punishment for political activity, community organizing and simple social independence. They have also documented the systematic failure of governments to protect women from non-governmental actors such as family members and employers. The most graphic example of gender-based persecution being brought to international attention at this time is the systematic rape and sexual abuse of Muslim and Croat women by Serbian soldiers in Bosnia-Herzogovina. Significantly, both the popular media and human-rights groups have recognized that the treatment of women in Bosnia-Herzogovina occurs within a political context. The rape of women there has been characterized not simply as the actions of renegade soldiers, but as a weapon of war—a calculated move that is part of a larger scheme of "ethnic cleansing" of Muslims and other non-Serbs from Bosnia.

263.   Jacqueline R. Castel. "Rape, Sexual Assault and the Meaning of Persecution." INTERNATIONAL JOURNAL OF REFUGEE LAW, Vol. 4, no. 2: 1992, p. 263. It was argued above that rape should constitute persecution within the refugee definition when it is inflicted by the State as a form of torture, when there is no system of redress against the attacker, and when the woman would put her life in danger by alerting the authorities. However, the ability of women to make successful claims will be limited by a number of factors. If the State connection requirement is interpreted to mean that the State must be the persecuting agent, only women who are sexually assaulted by a State actor who is functioning in his official capacity will be eligible. If 'social group' is defined as membership in a group whose activities are perceived as a threat to the State, it is not likely that women will succeed in categorizing themselves as a social group since the rationale for such a categorization would be predicated on women's powerlessness. Thus, women who could not identify themselves with a politically active family member or household, which would qualify as a perceived threat to the State under the social group category, would be required to base their claim for refugee status on political opinion or one of the other enumerated grounds. Unless the woman making the claim is active in politics or in a religious, racial or nationalist group, she is not likely to qualify. Many women refugees are reluctant to speak openly about being sexually assaulted. It is very traumatic for women to relive these experiences, particularly in front of men, whether they be family members or strangers. In many societies, it is strictly taboo to speak about anything concerning sex. Also, due to cultural conditioning, many women are afraid that if the authorities in the country in which they seek asylum are informed that they have been sexually assaulted or have endured other sexual indignities, they will be regarded as 'dirty' and unfit.

As noted in an Amnesty International document on human rights violations against women,

> Rape sometimes appears to be used as a form of torture because those responsible realize that their victims may be constrained from revealing what has occurred after their release from custody. The same associated with rape can be a strong inducement to silence.

It is not uncommon for women who have been sexually abused to leave out facts that may be material to their claim.

Even if women who have fled their countries because of rape, or other forms of sexual violence, are willing to reveal their stories, they often have trouble substantiating them. A claimant's account is generally considered in light of background information on the country in question. However, few refugee documentation centres have information on the position of women in a given country, on the incidence of sexual violence in that country, and on the consequences of returning to the country in question for a woman in the claimant's alleged position. In the absence of reliable information on these matters, the woman's story may not appear credible.

Other factors mitigate against the credibility of the woman's story. When rape is alleged, there is generally no physical evidence. A pervasive sexist and racist mythology also surrounds rape, which includes stereotypes such as: 'good girls don't get raped'; women whose behaviour can be described as seductive or provocative want to be raped; forced intercourse between parties who know each other or in situations where extreme violence is not used is not real rape; women who fail to forcibly resist are not raped; women lie about being raped for revenge, to protect their reputation, and out of jealousy. These stereotypes can be expected to undermine the credibility of the complainant's contention that she was sexually assaulted and/or has a well-founded fear of being sexually assaulted if she returns to her home country. When the rape survivor is a woman of colour, the likelihood that she will be disbelieved is intensified.

264. Linda Cipriani. "Gender and Persecution: Protecting Women Under International Refugee Law." GEORGETOWN IMMIGRATION LAW JOURNAL, Vol. 7: 1993. The sexual abuse of some of these women has been especially severe as they have been repeatedly raped until they become pregnant. These women are only released during the last stages of pregnancy after it is too late to have an abortion. Their captors tell them to take good care of the child and to raise a Serbian soldier-hero. The rape and subsequent pregnancy have an especially harsh impact on Muslim women because of the importance Islam puts on the virginity of women. Officials of Bosnia-Herzegovina fear tens of thousands of rapes have been carried out on Muslim and Croatian women. The reports of rape are so extensive that some analysts think it is systematic.

Although the conditions endured by these women are extreme and some forms of the abuse may be particular to the ethnic conflict that now divides the region, they do highlight some of the security problems all women refugees face. Women who flee gender-based persecution are especially susceptible to these problems. These women will probably continue to face other abuse from those men who still wish to impose cultural, religious, or social customs on them. They will be especially vulnerable because, unlike many women refugees who come with husbands or other family members, they will probably come to the country of refuge alone or with only their children.

265. Ranee K.L. Panjabi. "The Global Refugee Crisis: A Search for Solutions." CALIFORNIA WESTERN INTERNATIONAL LAW JOURNAL, Vol. 21, no. 2: 1990-1991, p. 253. Women are not even safe in refugee camps. The general chaos which precedes and accompanies refugee flows makes women and young girls particularly vulnerable. Violence is not the only problem. Discrimination in food distribution can lead to undernourishment for women. Health problems, stress, lack of free time to acquire skills for employment, the burden of caring for children in an alien environment where even language may become a major obstacle—these are briefly the plight and ordeal of refugee women.

266. Suzanne B. Goldberg. "Give Me Liberty or Give Me Death: Political Asylum and the Global Persecution of Lesbians and Gay Men." CORNELL INTERNATIONAL LAW JOURNAL, Vol. 26: 1993, p. 607. So long as an applicant *"establishes a well-founded fear of persecution"* based on at least one of the five designated categories, he or she is eligible for asylum. Although "membership in a particular social group" is the classification that most closely describes those persecuted because of their sexual orientation, neither the INA nor the related regulations define the category precisely.

267. Shannon Minter. "Sodomy and Public Morality Offenses under U.S. Immigration Law: Penalizing Lesbian and Gay Identity." CORNELL INTERNATIONAL LAW JOURNAL, Vol. 26: 1993, p. 783. Two provisions in the current INA are used to exclude and deport individuals for consensual homosexual conduct and expression: the "crimes involving moral turpitude" exclusion, and the requirement that an alien prove "good moral character" in order to become a citizen or to qualify for certain benefits such as voluntary departure. An alien convicted of a crime of moral turpitude (or who admits to acts constituting such an offense) can be excluded or deported under the crimes involving moral turpitude provision. Conviction of a crime involving moral turpitude automatically bars a finding of good moral character. Neither of these provisions explicitly singles out homosexual sexual activity as such. It is only because the INS and most courts interpret sodomy and public morality offenses as crimes of moral turpitude that these provisions have a disparate impact on lesbians and gay men.

268. Shannon Minter. "Sodomy and Public Morality Offenses under U.S. Immigration Law: Penalizing Lesbian and Gay Identity." CORNELL INTERNATIONAL LAW JOURNAL, Vol. 26: 1993, p. 810.

Ironically, however, the INS and many U.S. courts persist in recognizing discriminatory convictions under public morality statutes as crimes of moral turpitude. Because the INS and the courts have not reevaluated their irrational and anachronistic interpretations of these provisions, individuals who have ever been convicted of or who admit to a public same-gender sex offense, including those who may be seeking refuge from homophobic persecution in their country of origin, may be precluded from visiting or immigrating to the United States under the provision for crimes involving moral turpitude, or barred from citizenship under the good moral character requirement.

269.   Shannon Minter. "Sodomy and Public Morality Offenses under U.S. Immigration Law: Penalizing Lesbian and Gay Identity." CORNELL INTERNATIONAL LAW JOURNAL, Vol. 26: 1993, pp. 772-773. The elimination of the provision used to exclude lesbians and gay men significantly redressed the homophobic bias of U.S. immigration law. Even after the 1990 Act, however, lesbians and gay men convicted of sodomy or of a public morality offense are at risk of exclusion or deportation under the "crimes involving moral turpitude" exclusion, and may be denied citizenship under the "good moral character" requirement. Both within the United States and internationally, lesbians and gay men are prosecuted under sodomy and public morality statutes which are often used to target lesbians and gay men by penalizing the expression of lesbian and gay identity, especially when that expression is deemed "public." Public expressions of heterosexual identity are not similarly policed or criminalized. Although the 1990 Act eliminated the rationale for doing so, the Immigration and Naturalization Service (INS) and the courts continue to exercise their discretion to use these statutes to exclude and deport gays and lesbians from the country, and to deny them citizenship and other benefits and privileges.

270.   Shannon Minter. "Sodomy and Public Morality Offenses under U.S. Immigration Law: Penalizing Lesbian and Gay Identity." CORNELL INTERNATIONAL LAW JOURNAL, Vol. 26: 1993, pp. 782-783. Both for pragmatic and for principled reasons, the 1990 Act eliminated the provision that had been used to exclude lesbians and gay men. There is currently no language in the statute that excludes or provides for the deportation of aliens based on lesbian or gay sexual orientation. The 1990 Act did not, however, explicitly provide new guidelines or standards about how to interpret or apply the crimes involving moral turpitude exclusion or the good moral character requirement. As before the 1990 Act, the INS and the courts retain nearly unfettered discretion as to how to interpret these provisions. As a result, although the U.S. immigration law no longer explicitly discriminates on the basis of lesbian or gay identity alone, the INS and the courts have not reevaluated

their old policy of interpreting these provisions in a manner that singles out lesbians and gay men for disparate treatment.

271.   Shannon Minter. "Sodomy and Public Morality Offenses under U.S. Immigration Law: Penalizing Lesbian and Gay Identity." CORNELL INTERNATIONAL LAW JOURNAL, Vol. 26: 1993, p. 818. The most effective way to challenge the discriminatory impact of public morality offenses on lesbians and gay men under U.S. immigration law is to extend the argument used in *Nemetz* to exempt private sodomy from the good moral character analysis. That argument combined the "uniform rule of naturalization" requirement with an appeal to Congress' intent with regard to private sexual behavior in the immigration statute. The 1990 Act clarified Congress' intention to eliminate discrimination against homosexuals in immigration. The 1990 Act was also consistent with court decisions and legislative amendments that increasingly exempted consensual sexual behavior from the scrutiny of the immigration law. It appears that Congress did not intend for consensual homosexual behavior, even when criminalized by state or national law, to affect an alien's treatment under the immigration law.

Currently, conviction or admission of same-gender public morality offenses triggers the crimes involving moral turpitude exclusion, and can also be used to negate a finding of good moral character. This state of affairs violates Congress' intent in the 1990 Act. The inconsistency among state and national laws regulating public same-gender activity and in enforcement from state to state and nation to nation also violates the requirement of geographic uniformity in the federal immigration law. Together, these violations of Congressional intent and of the uniformity requirement create a strong argument against the use of consensual sodomy and public sex offenses for immigration purposes.

272.   Ellen Vagelos. "The Social Group That Dare Not Speak Its Name: Should Homosexuals Constitute a Particular Social Group for Purposes of Obtaining Refugee Status? Comment on *RE: INSUDI*." FORDHAM INTERNATIONAL LAW JOURNAL, Vol. 17: 1993, pp. 257-258. Claiming persecution on account of membership in a particular social group, homosexuals from numerous countries are currently applying to the United States for asylum, refugee status or for the suspension of deportation. One BIA decision and one Immigration Judge's decision recognize homosexuals as members of a particular social group. These decisions, however, are not binding on other Immigration Judges, other panels of the BIA, or the federal courts.

273.   Suzanne B. Goldberg. "Give Me Liberty or Give Me Death: Political Asylum and the Global Persecution of Lesbians and Gay Men." COR-

NELL INTERNATIONAL LAW JOURNAL, Vol. 26: 1993, p. 623. As the political world order continues to shift, lesbian women and gay men enter increasingly into the ranks of refugees pressing for asylum. Tatiana exemplifies members of this class of women and men who experience and fear severe treatment imposed by their governments because they are lesbian or gay. The extreme official persecution perpetrated against lesbian women and gay men underscores the need to respond to women such as Tatiana and to protect this group of refugees.

As members of "a particular social group," lesbian and gay nationals of countries with threatening laws and practices should be eligible for asylum under the United States Immigration and Nationality Act standards. The discussion of Tatiana's case illustrates that being lesbian or gay is fundamental to human identity and, as such, should be recognized as a characteristic that individuals should not be required to change according to the dictates of the government in power. Claims such as Tatiana's will become increasingly common as the body of information documenting persecution grows and as advocates press these claims on behalf of lesbian women and gay men who must leave their home countries in order to survive.

274.   Suzanne B. Goldberg. "Give Me Liberty or Give Me Death: Political Asylum and the Global Persecution of Lesbians and Gay Men." CORNELL INTERNATIONAL LAW JOURNAL, Vol. 26: 1993, pp. 615-616. A long and tortured history of institutionalized discrimination against lesbian women and gay men sadly attests to the differential treatment of this minority group. Sanctioned police assault and brutality are among the most dangerous manifestations of official targeting of lesbians and gay men. In still other instances, gay men and lesbians face harsh criminal liability, and in some cases the death penalty, for engaging in consensual sexual relationships, for identifying themselves as lesbian or gay, or for asserting basic civil rights.

Pervasive negative stereotypes fuel the discriminatory treatment of lesbian and gay people as a group, most of which relate to sex role characteristics. Additional stereotypes characterize gay men "as mentally ill, promiscuous, lonely, insecure, and likely to be child molesters, while lesbians have been described as aggressive and hostile toward men." Relying on these stereotypes as well as anti-gay religious doctrine and other sources, many governments and societies endorse discrimination against, and sometimes persecution of, lesbian and gay members of society. The Romanian laws and policies which threaten Tatiana exemplify this reliance.

275.   Suzanne B. Goldberg. "Give Me Liberty or Give Me Death: Political Asylum and the Global Persecution of Lesbians and Gay Men." COR-

NELL INTERNATIONAL LAW JOURNAL, Vol. 26: 1993, pp. 605-606. In a time marked by dramatic global change, women and men persecuted because they are lesbian or gay form part of the growing pool of international refugees. Their persecution takes the form of police harassment and assault, involuntary institutionalization and electroshock and drug "treatments," punishment under laws that impose extreme penalties including death for consensual lesbian or gay sexual relations, murder by paramilitary death squads, and government inaction in response to criminal assaults against lesbians and gay men. The survival of these women and men, like the survival of all refugees, depends on obtaining asylum outside the home country. Yet, to date there have been few published decisions internationally and only one in the United States that grant asylum to people in these situations.

276.   Shannon Minter. "Sodomy and Public Morality Offenses under U.S. Immigration Law: Penalizing Lesbian and Gay Identity." CORNELL INTERNATIONAL LAW JOURNAL, Vol. 26: 1993, pp. 803-804. Worldwide, at least 67 countries criminalize sex between men, and at least 27 criminalize sex between women. Some of these countries follow the U.S. pattern and retain sodomy laws on the books but rarely investigate or prosecute violations. In many countries, however, laws criminalizing lesbian and gay sex are rigorously enforced, and the punishments imposed are extremely severe, ranging from the death penalty to imprisonment and involuntary psychiatric treatment. Laws against homosexuality tend to be most severe in African, Asian, Middle Eastern, and Oceanic countries. Most European states have decriminalized private consensual sodomy, with the exception of Ireland, Cyprus, Lithuania, Romania, and the former Yugoslavian republics of Bosnia, Macedonia, and Serbia. In Latin America, the legal status of homosexuality varies widely from country to country.

277.   Ellen Vagelos. "The Social Group That Dare Not Speak Its Name: Should Homosexuals Constitute a Particular Social Group for Purposes of Obtaining Refugee Status? Comment on *RE: INSUDI*." FORDHAM INTERNATIONAL LAW JOURNAL, Vol. 17: 1993, p. 276. Holding that homosexuals constitute a particular social group is consistent with BIA and federal court precedent, and treatment of homosexuals by the federal government. Thus far the definition of a particular social group has not been applied to its full potential. The stage is set for homosexuals to be recognized in the United States as a particular social group and thereby obtain refugee status. The BIA and Federal Courts should adopt the reasoning in *Re: Insudi* and hold that homosexuals constitute a particular social group.

278. Suzanne B. Goldberg. "Give Me Liberty or Give Me Death: Political Asylum and the Global Persecution of Lesbians and Gay Men." CORNELL INTERNATIONAL LAW JOURNAL, Vol. 26: 1993, pp. 612-613. Whether currently or historically, people who identify themselves as, or are perceived to be, lesbian or gay experience unique and sometimes oppressive treatment both by the state and by society. As a population sharing the fundamental characteristic of minority sexual orientation, lesbians and gay men have long been treated as a distinct and particular social group.

279. Suzanne B. Goldberg. "Give Me Liberty or Give Me Death: Political Asylum and the Global Persecution of Lesbians and Gay Men." CORNELL INTERNATIONAL LAW JOURNAL, Vol. 26: 1993, p. 614. In addition, like race, ethnicity, religion, and political opinion, sexual orientation cannot be altered or renounced according to the dictates of a government in power. Regardless of whether sexual orientation has a genetic origin, lesbian women and gay men cannot disassociate themselves from the basis of their persecution. To that extent, sexual orientation is indeed immutable.

280. Suzanne B. Goldberg. "Give Me Liberty or Give Me Death: Political Asylum and the Global Persecution of Lesbians and Gay Men." CORNELL INTERNATIONAL LAW JOURNAL, Vol. 26: 1993, p. 613. Much popular confusion surrounds the nature and origin of sexual orientation. Social scientists and psychologists, however, are careful to distinguish sexual orientation—the erotic and/or affectional attraction to members of the same or opposite gender—from biological sex, general identity, and social sex role.

The term "sexual orientation" itself encompasses several aspects of human identity and activity: 1) sexual conduct with partners of a particular gender; 2) enduring psychological attraction to partners of a particular gender; and 3) private identity based on sexual orientation (thinking of oneself as lesbian, gay, bisexual or heterosexual). In addition, one may claim or be assigned a public identity based on sexual orientation, and identify with a community based on sexual orientation.

As is evident from this last, sexual orientation refers to much more than sexual behavior. Being lesbian or gay forms part of a person's identity and involves more than simple engaging in sexual conduct with persons of the same gender. Tatiana, for example, identifies herself as a lesbian, socializes with other lesbian women, and collects information and publications about lesbians in all parts of the world. Her identity as a lesbian does not depend on being in a relationship with another women, any more than a woman's identity as a heterosexual depends on being in a relationship with a man.

Most social and behavioral scientists believe that sexual orientation—whether heterosexual, lesbian or gay—is fundamental to human identity and highly resistant to change.

281. Ellen Vagelos. "The Social Group That Dare Not Speak Its Name: Should Homosexuals Constitute a Particular Social Group for Purposes of Obtaining Refugee Status? Comment on *RE: INSUDI*." FORDHAM INTERNATIONAL LAW JOURNAL, Vol. 17: 1993, pp. 256-257. The minority decisions that characterize homosexuality as immutable argue that homosexuals cannot change their sexual orientation without immense difficulty. Furthermore, a district court judge in *Jantz v. Muci* pointed out that the circuit court decisions finding that homosexuality is behavioral fail to cite any scientific or medical authority supporting such conclusions. In contrast, this district court cited a number of scientific articles concluding that sexual orientation generally cannot be changed. Thus, the court held that homosexuality is immutable.

282. Ellen Vagelos. "The Social Group That Dare Not Speak Its Name: Should Homosexuals Constitute a Particular Social Group for Purposes of Obtaining Refugee Status? Comment on *RE: INSUDI*." FORDHAM INTERNATIONAL LAW JOURNAL, Vol. 17: 1993, p. 276. If homosexuals are held to constitute a particular social group, the United States will not be obliged to open its doors as a haven for all homosexuals. Each person who applies for asylum must satisfy the other requirements set out by the definition of "refugee" in the Refugee Act of 1980. Therefore, neither the courts nor the BIA should reject homosexuals' claims of persecution on account of membership in a particular social group for fear of a flood of these refugees.

283. Shannon Minter. "Sodomy and Public Morality Offenses under U.S. Immigration Law: Penalizing Lesbian and Gay Identity." CORNELL INTERNATIONAL LAW JOURNAL, Vol. 26: 1993, p. 807. Despite its inconsistencies, however, the Wolfenden perspective on the public expression of lesbian and gay identity has profoundly influenced the repeal of sodomy laws in Canada, the United States, Europe, and Latin America. In practical terms, the effect of the Wolfenden strategy in states and countries that have adopted it has been to increase dramatically police surveillance, harassment, and prosecution of lesbians and gay men under public morality statutes. In the four years after England abolished its sodomy law in 1967, prosecutions for homosexual offenses increased by 160 percent. A similar increase in police surveillance and prosecution resulted when Canada decriminalized sodomy in 1969, and when Northern Ireland abolished its sodomy laws in 1982.

284. Shannon Minter. "Sodomy and Public Morality Offenses under U.S. Immigration Law: Penaliz-

ing Lesbian and Gay Identity." CORNELL INTERNATIONAL LAW JOURNAL, Vol. 26: 1993, pp. 806-807. Public lewdness, solicitation and other public morality statutes are the primary tools through which this strategy of containment is enforced. These statutes are "invoked against sexual expression—including loitering, flirtation, solicitation, and actual sexual encounters—outside the home. While such laws do not [usually] refer to gay sex specifically, they are enforced almost exclusively against people perceived to be gay." Similarly, although the official rationale behind these statutes is the need to protect the public against offensive or annoying behavior, they are actually enforced against conduct that is public in name only, and that is almost always discovered only through undercover police activity or hidden video surveillance. As Arthur Warner has pointed out:

the very methods which have to be employed by the police to apprehend persons for homosexual soliciting is proof of the inoffensiveness of the conduct…these are certainly not the methods customarily required to apprehend persons whose conduct is alleged to be so open and blatant that it constitutes an affront to public decency. [ellipses in original]

285.   Ellen Vagelos. "The Social Group That Dare Not Speak Its Name: Should Homosexuals Constitute a Particular Social Group for Purposes of Obtaining Refugee Status? Comment on *RE: INSUDI*." FORDHAM INTERNATIONAL LAW JOURNAL, Vol. 17: 1993, pp. 273-274. Although the Supreme Court denied a constitutional challenge to sodomy statutes in *Bowers v. Hardwick*, the decision focused on homosexual conduct rather than status. In *Bowers v. Hardwick*, the Supreme Court held that statutes prohibiting sodomy are Constitutional. Such statutes prohibit homosexual conduct. In contrast, homosexuals seeking asylum in the United States claim that their countries of origin persecute them on account of their status as homosexuals. The Supreme Court, in fact, has held that statutes criminalizing status, such as drug addiction, are unconstitutional. Therefore, *Bowers* does not undermine a policy to protect homosexuals from persecution on account of their status as homosexuals.

286.   Shannon Minter. "Sodomy and Public Morality Offenses under U.S. Immigration Law: Penalizing Lesbian and Gay Identity." CORNELL INTERNATIONAL LAW JOURNAL, Vol. 26: 1993, p. 782. Sponsors and supporters of the 1990 Act and of the legislative proposals that preceded it also articulated more principled reasons for getting rid of the exclusion. They hoped that the removal of the categorical exclusion would place lesbians and gay men on an equal footing with their heterosexual counterparts and eliminate the

pressure on lesbians and gay men to conceal their sexual orientation. As Senator Cranston argued in 1985, the "inconsistent enforcement discriminates against the openly homosexual person and those who appear homosexual even though they may not be, and may reward those who choose to hide their homosexuality." Cranston also criticized "the unwise and harshly discriminatory underlying law, which attempts to use private sexual orientation as a criterion for judging who does and who does not qualify for admission to the United States," and argued that the new legislation would "end a form of discrimination which has no valid scientific or medical basis and which violates traditional American respect for the privacy and dignity of an individual." In 1988, the House Committee on the Judiciary agreed that "the continued existence of this ground for exclusion in the statute is an affront to basic notions of privacy…The Committee strongly supports the notion that a person's sexual orientation should be a private matter, and that homosexuality should no longer have any relevance to immigration." The House Report accompanying the 1990 Act specified that "in order to make it clear that the United States does not view personal decisions about sexual orientation as a danger to other people in our society, the bill repeals the 'sexual deviation' exclusion ground."

287.   Shannon Minter. "Sodomy and Public Morality Offenses under U.S. Immigration Law: Penalizing Lesbian and Gay Identity." CORNELL INTERNATIONAL LAW JOURNAL, Vol. 26: 1993, pp. 771-772. Until 1990, the United States was the only country in the world with an explicit policy of excluding visitors and potential immigrants because of their sexual orientation. Although the word "homosexual" has never appeared in U.S. immigration law, from 1952 to 1990 most U.S. courts interpreted the provision excluding persons "afflicted with a psychopathic personality" to require the exclusion of any person identified as homosexual or who engaged in homosexual acts. Countless individuals have been excluded at the border, deported, or denied naturalization under this provision. After years of lobbying by openly gay Congressperson Barney Frank and others, and in the wake of increasingly tangled litigation challenging the exclusion of lesbians and gay men, Congress eliminated the "psychopathic personality" exclusion in 1990 as part of a general reform of the old exclusion grounds. Under the 1990 Act, lesbians and gay men are no longer automatically barred from entering or immigrating to the United States.

288.   Pamela Goldberg. "Anyplace but Home: Asylum in the United States for Women Fleeing Intimate Violence." CORNELL INTERNATIONAL LAW JOURNAL, Vol. 26: 1993, p. 622. Several courts around the world have granted asylum to lesbians and gay men persecuted on the basis of their sexual orienta-

tion. Concluding that lesbians and gay men constitute a social group, these courts granted refuge from persecution to applicants who either experienced physical assault by government officials or faced the threat of capital punishment for consensual lesbian and gay sexual relationships in their country of origin.

289.   Shannon Minter. "Sodomy and Public Morality Offenses under U.S. Immigration Law: Penalizing Lesbian and Gay Identity." CORNELL INTERNATIONAL LAW JOURNAL, Vol. 26: 1993, p. 809. As this overview demonstrates, governments worldwide use public morality laws to force lesbians and gay men to conceal their sexual orientation, to stigmatize and discourage homosexuality, and to punish political dissent and social nonconformity. In recent years, the European Court of Human Rights, the Council of Europe, the United Nations (U.N.), and other international human rights organizations have increasingly recognized and condemned this worldwide harassment and abuse. In 1993, two lesbian and gay human rights groups, the New York-based Human Rights Watch and the Brussels-based International Lesbian and Gay Association were granted formal recognition by the Economic and Social Council, the U.N. body responsible for monitoring violations of international human rights agreements. The U.N. Human Rights Commission has shown an increasing willingness to recognize the claims of lesbian and gay men, and Amnesty International now recognizes lesbians and gay men imprisoned under sodomy and public morality statutes as prisoners of conscience. A growing number of countries, including the United States, have granted political asylum to lesbians and gay men persecuted in their country of origin.

290.   Ellen Vagelos. "The Social Group That Dare Not Speak Its Name: Should Homosexuals Constitute a Particular Social Group for Purposes of Obtaining Refugee Status? Comment on *RE: INSUDI*." FORDHAM INTERNATIONAL LAW JOURNAL, Vol. 17: 1993, pp. 271-272. The U.S. government's current treatment of homosexuals, however, demonstrates a more favorable attitude toward homosexuals. The U.S. government, while still recognizing homosexuals as a group, is beginning to recognize that homosexuals have been unjustifiably discriminated against. President Clinton's recent efforts to repeal the ban against homosexuals in the military, for example, reflects the administration's recognition that the government no longer should persecute this group. The repeal of the exclusionary policies toward homosexuals in immigration also reflects a more favorable attitude towards homosexuals. In addition, the Hate Crime Statistics Act's includes homosexuals. This law reflects an understanding that homosexuals are potential victims of discrimination and therefore need protection.

291.   Harold Hongju Koh. "The Human Face of the Haitian Interdiction Program." VIRGINIA JOURNAL OF INTERNATIONAL LAW, Vol. 33: 1993, p. 486. Our second case, the "non-return case, began in May 1992, when the Bush administration changed course yet again and decided that henceforth it would simply return all Haitians coming form Haiti by boat directly to Haiti without any screening whatsoever. In effect, the Bush administration made a blanket determination that none of the fleeing Haitians were political refugees, thereby dispensing with the legally required individualized determination as to whether or not the people were political refugees or economic migrants. Following that decision, the administration quite literally began to take fleeing Haitians back to the people who were persecuting them.

292.   Elaine Sciolino. "Clinton says US will continue ban on Haitian exodus." NEW YORK TIMES, January 15, 1994, page A1. Saying that he feared a mass exodus of Haitians unless he acted, President-elect Bill Clinton announced today that he would at least temporarily abandon a campaign pledge and would continue the Bush Administration's policy of forcibly returning Haitians who try to emigrate to the United States.

It was Mr. Clinton who helped create the expectation of an exodus from Haiti when he condemned the Bush Administration for a "cruel policy of returning Haitian refugees to a brutal dictatorship without an asylum hearing."

293.   Barbara Yarnold. REFUGEES WITHOUT REFUGE: FORMATION AND FAILED IMPLEMENTATION OF U.S. POLITICAL ASYLUM IN THE 1980'S, University Press: Lanham, Maryland, 1990, p. 111. The review of Haitian asylum-related appeals to the BIA during the period 1980-1987, may be summarized as follows:

(1) Haitians involved in asylum-related appeals to the BIA have difficulty establishing that their actual or feared persecution is due to their race, nationality, religion, political opinion, or membership in a particular social group. Since both section 208(a) (asylum) and section 243(h) of the Act (withholding) require a demonstration of a nexus between persecution and the enumerated categories, Haitians are not likely to obtain relief and win asylum-related appeals unless they are able to change their arguments to conform with the requirements of the Act. Of 89 Haitian appeals to the BIA during this period, aliens were successful in only 6 appeals, or 7% of the total. The BIA decided in favor of aliens in 12% of all asylum-related appeals, so Haitians had a poor record in these appeals, in spite of the fact that they had higher than average organizational participation; the mean organizational participation in these appeals was 16%

and 25% of the Haitian appeals had organizational involvement.

(2) Alternately, it might be argued that the Haitian asylum-related appeals are not representative of "the merits" of most Haitian claims for asylum and withholding. Haitians who have been able to establish a link between persecution and the enumerated categories have been granted asylum or withholding at lower administrative levels and hence, the appeals heard by the BIA are those which tend to be "weak" on the merits. However, this argument is unpersuasive, given that the INS, from 1983-1985, approved 13% of all asylum applications, and asylum applicants from Haiti obtained only 2.4% approval.

294.   Deborah Sontag. "Reneging on Refuge: The Haitian Precedent." NEW YORK TIMES, June 17, 1993. Sect. 4, p. 1. In the Haitian case, the Supreme Court overturned a lower court ruling that forcible repatriation violated both the Immigration and Nationality Act and the United Nations Protocol Relating to the Status of Refugees, an international treaty. In a narrowly cast decision, Justice John Paul Stevens wrote that while forced repatriation may violate the spirit of the laws, it does not violate their letter, which he said do not explicitly protect refugees outside a nation's borders or on the high seas.

He added that the drafters of refugee laws may not have contemplated 'that any nation would gather fleeing refugees and return them to the one country they had desperately sought to escape.' Advocates point out that the Haitians would not be outside the borders if the Government did not take to the seas to find them.

295.   THE PROGRESSIVE. "Hold the Wretched Refuse." August 1993, p. 10. These racist and alarmist stories are in sync with the message from Washington. The most appalling news on U.S. immigration policy came in June, when the Supreme Court upheld the Clinton Administration's practice of intercepting and returning Haitian refugees shortly after they set sail for the United States. It was a particularly despicable piece of legalistic maneuvering that sustained the Court's eight-to-one decision.

Justice John Paul Stevens, writing for the majority, reasoned that Federal law and international protocol prohibiting forced repatriation of refugees do not apply in international waters even though, he conceded, forced repatriation might "violate the spirit" of international law, and the law's authors "may not have contemplated that any nation would gather fleeing refugees and return them to the one country they had desperately sought to escape."

296.   FDCH CONGRESSIONAL TESTIMONY (Lexis/Nexis), March 8, 1994. At the time of this writing, the Clinton administration was considering

lending its support for a tougher UN embargo, proposed by France, similar to the U.S.'s own current bilateral embargo that would encompass all items except humanitarian fuel, food, medicine, and some industrial traffic. The U.S. is also urging other countries to cancel or reject requests for visas of more than 500 military officers, with visa cancellations extended to officers' families if the military refuses to yield. The U.S. reportedly plans to allow the sanctions against Haiti to take their toll and force the de facto leaders back to the negotiating table or to honor previous obligations under the Governors Island Accord. 26 With U.S. support for Aristide clearly deteriorating, and its efforts to "broaden" the cabinet and include "moderate" members of the armed forces in any political settlement escalating, the likelihood that future negotiations will emphasize respect for human rights is remote.

297.   FDCH CONGRESSIONAL TESTIMONY (Lexis/Nexis), March 8, 1994, pp. 12-13. Instead of insisting that the protection of human rights of Haitians be a fundamental component of any political solution in Haiti, the Clinton administration deliberately ignored the issue of human rights throughout the Governors Island negotiations and after. The Administration sacrificed accountability for human rights abuses for the hope of achieving a quick political settlement, and supported an indiscriminate and inhumane policy of forcibly repatriating Haitians fleeing well-documented persecution. While the Administration took some actions against the de facto leaders following the collapse of the Governors Island Accord, those actions were undermined by its record of granting innumerable concessions to the human rights abusers in power in Port-au-Prince who chose to ignore the Accord's provisions. Now, with its credibility seriously undermined, the Administration is left with few options to facilitate the restoration of democracy in Haiti.

298.   David A. Martin. "Strategies for a Resistant World: Human Rights Initiatives and the Need for Alternatives to Refugee Interdiction." CORNELL INTERNATIONAL LAW JOURNAL, Vol. 26: 1993, pp. 769-770. In-country refugee processing, touted by the Bush Administration (and more recently by Clinton's) as an alternative mode of protection for Haitians, is not wholly plausible as an avenue of protection, particularly for those who should be the principal objects of our concern—those who are the most clearly threatened, those who are unmistakably viewed by the regime as dangerous opponents. Even if processing expands to locations outside of Port-au-Prince, no applicant can have confidence in his or her ability to make it safely into and out of the facility, and then the country. These risks are compounded when the process is as slow and bureaucratic as the early rounds of processing in Haiti reportedly have been. *See Clinton Continues Summary Return*

of Haitians; U.S. Lawyers Investigate In-Country Processing, REFUGEE REPORTS, Jan. 29, 1993, at 1.

This analysis also touches upon another central objection to interdiction, at least in the extreme form now applied to Haiti. Interdiction with immediate return, even when coupled with other human rights initiatives, blots out intermediate avenues of protection (those purchased by the individuals involved at the initial price of contriving a self-help escape), even for the most gravely threatened. However important human rights initiatives and in-country processing may be, they do not deal with "the meantime," as Bill Frelick so aptly phrases the matter in his contribution to this volume: "[Human rights initiatives] cannot be the sum total of a refugee policy. A refugee policy is about what to do in the meantime, how to protect and assist people outside their country while the country of origin is still dangerous." Bill Frelick, *Haitian Boat Interdiction and Return: First Asylum and First Principles of Refugee Protection*, CORNELL INT'L L.J. 675 (1993).

299.   FDCH CONGRESSIONAL TESTIMONY (Lexis/Nexis), March 8, 1994, p. 16. The ICP program has been criticized by Human Rights Watch/ Americas, the National Coalition for Haitian Refugees, and by others as seriously flawed and inappropriately applied in Haiti. In no other instance is ICP seen as a viable substitute for the internationally recognized right to flee one's country and seek refuge. The program is incapable of protecting applicants, and the information supplied by them in support of their asylum claims. Numerous cases of persecution of applicants to the program have been documented. Moreover, case adjudication is biased against applicants and the State Department's consistently inaccurate assessment of the human rights situation is infused into the program at all levels.

300.   FDCH CONGRESSIONAL TESTIMONY (Lexis/Nexis), March 8, 1994, p. 18. During a fact-finding trip to Haiti in mid-February, however, Human Rights Watch/Americas and the National Coalition for Haitian Refugees found that the ICP program was more restrictive and unresponsive to the severity of the refugee crisis. Moreover, forced repatriations to the Port-au-Prince pier have become increasingly dangerous since the October retreat of the Harlan County, with human rights monitors and journalists barred from the dock. In addition, repatriates identified as "high priority" for expedited asylum interviews by U.S. Embassy personnel prior to disembarkation have been arrested at the pier and detained for several days.

301.   Jennifer Kaylin. "Yale Law School Team Takes on an Alumnus." THE NEW YORK TIMES: NEXUS, April 11, 1993, p. 6. Sec. 13 (Connecticut Weekly Desk) Such tactics have only strengthened the resolve of Mr. Koh and his students, who say they believe that the treatment of the Haitians is the most egregious United States human rights violation since Japanese-Americans were interred in concentration camps in California and boatloads of Jews fleeing the Nazis were turned away and sent back to their deaths. 'Our tax dollars are being used to return refugees to torture and death, or to hold them in filthy concentration camps, where families are separated, some for as long as 15 months,' Mr. Koh said. 'It's heartbreaking.'

302.   Harold Hongju Koh. "The Human Face of the Haitian Interdiction Program." VIRGINIA JOURNAL OF INTERNATIONAL LAW, Vol. 33: 1993, p. 484. Following the overthrow of the Aristide government in November 1991, when the exodus from Haiti reached unprecedented levels, the Bush administration changed this policy in two significant respects. First, instead of allowing "screened-in" Haitians to enter and remain in the United States for asylum hearings, the Immigration and Naturalization Service started to hold those Haitians at Guantanamo Naval Base, Cuba, where they were kept incommunicado behind barbed wire. There the refugees endured inadequate medical care and squalid living conditions for months on end.

303.   Deborah Sontag. "Reneging on Refuge: The Haitian Precedent." NEW YORK TIMES, June 17, 1993, Sect 4, p. 1. And so last week, when the Supreme Court, in an 8-1 decision, upheld the Haitian repatriation policy, immigration experts could not help but wonder: Will this ruling by one of the most influential courts in the world set a tempting precedent, particularly for developing nations? If the United States, with the imprimatur of its highest court, appears to put the protection of its borders above its responsibilities under international law, will others be enticed to follow suit?

'I think it introduces a very destructive precedent at the international level,' said Arthur Helton, immigration expert for the Lawyers Committee for International Human Rights. 'The U.S. will be seen in some eyes as a virtual outlaw, and others will take the decision as an invitation to use brutal forms of refugee control.'

Reverberations might be felt, Mr. Helton said, by Tajik Muslim refugees in Afghanistan, Bosnians in Western Europe, and Vietnamese boat people in Thailand, Malaysia and the Philippines, among others.

304.   Deborah Sontag. "Reneging on Refuge: The Haitian Precedent." NEW YORK TIMES, June 17, 1993, Sect 4, p. 1. When the Supreme Court last week upheld the forcible repatriation of Haitians intercepted at sea, human rights advocates cringed with the dread that their work of three decades was coming unraveled.

Since World War II, they had fought to pass international and Federal laws establishing the obligation of nations to provide haven for political refugees. The broad notion of refugee protection was based on the principle

of *non-refoulement*, that no refugees should be forcibly returned to a place where they could suffer persecution. (Refouler is French for 'to force back.')

Under international law, non-refoulement is not a policy preference; it's a legal requirement. But with anti-immigrant sentiment on the rise while increasing numbers of Asians, Africans and Eastern Europeans flee their homelands, many nations have been tempted to defy humanitarian obligations and shut their gates. It is a global dilemma, the ambivalence of nations that, on principle, feel compassion for displaced people but practically fear the burden of accommodating them.

305. Deborah Sontag. "On-the-Spot Hearings for Aliens Are Considered." NEW YORK TIMES, July 22, 1993, p. A14. Last week, the United Nations High Commissioner for Refugees issued a strong rebuke of the Supreme Court decision as a "major setback to modern international refugee law." And the human rights commission of the Organization for American States urged President Clinton—who during the campaign had called Mr. Bush's repatriation policy cruel and illegal—to abandon the program.

"Even though the courts have ruled that Clinton no longer has to accept Haitians fleeing by sea, the fact of the matter is, he can if he wants to," said Cheryl Little, a lawyer with Florida Rural Legal Services. "It's his moral prerogative."

306. Elizabeth Mary McCormick. "HIV-Infected Haitian Refugees: An Argument Against Expulsion." GEORGETOWN IMMIGRATION LAW JOURNAL, Vol. 7: 1993, p. 150. Therefore, in formulating its response to this crisis, the new Administration will undoubtedly consider the message its actions will send to those who may perceive that response as directly implicating them: minority groups; families unable to afford health care; the unemployed or underemployed; and people living with HIV or AIDS in the United States. Moreover, President Clinton cannot ignore the message he sends to the international community regarding the United States' willingness to accept refugees generally and those with the HIV infection in particular. He must be careful to acknowledge that the HIV and refugee crises are international crises from which the United States cannot effectively protect itself through a policy of blanket exclusion. Rather, the United States must acknowledge its role in an international endeavor to combat AIDS and provide humanitarian relief to refugees.

307. Suzanne Gluck. "Intercepting Refugees at Sea: An Analysis of the United States' Legal and Moral Obligations." FORDHAM LAW REVIEW, Vol. 16: 1993, p. 866. The United States affirmed its commitment to observe *non-refoulement* by embodying the principle in section 243(h) of the Immigration and Nationality Act ("INA"). The United States' obligation ex-

tends to those aliens who satisfy the criteria for refugee status. That is, the United States is required to protect those aliens who possess individual, well-founded fears of persecution on account of their race, religion, nationality, social group, or political opinion. Yet the United States' current policy of interdicting and repatriating Haitian nationals on board vessels on the high seas, without screening for refugees, violates this basic tenet.

308. Deborah Sontag. "Reneging on Refuge: The Haitian Precedent." NEW YORK TIMES, June 17, 1993, Sect 4, p. 1. In May 1992, the United States began to stop Haitians at sea and, without allowing them to claim political asylum, return them to a military government that the nation does not officially recognize. Until 1991, when Italy forcibly returned Albanians, no nation that signed a 1951 refugee treaty—which was born of guilt after the treatment of Jews fleeing the Nazis—had sent potential refugees home without any screening.

309. J. Michael Cavosie. "Defending the Golden Door: The Persistence of Ad Hoc and Ideological Decision Making in U.S. Refugee Law." INDIANA LAW JOURNAL, Vol. 67: 1992, pp. 436-437. Furthermore, at least when applied to justify the double-standard refugee definition of the Foreign Operations Act, such an argument assumes what it seeks to prove. Select Soviet groups receive the benefit of a relaxed standard, so that argument goes, because there has to be some way to choose from among the overwhelming number of refugees needing protection. But this begs the question, for it presupposes that those groups were entitled to protection in the first place. The fact that denial rates were high when the normal refugee standard was applied indicates that such an assumption is questionable at best.

Accordingly, the refugee standard should be consistently and even-handedly applied to all applicants irrespective of their country of nationality. Only by doing so can the United States meet its humanitarian and international law obligations.

310. FDCH CONGRESSIONAL TESTIMONY (Lexis/Nexis), March 8, 1994, pp. 16-17. In addition to violating international law regarding the prohibition of refoulement, 15 as well as numerous other principles of refugee protection, the U.S. policy of forcibly repatriating Haitian refugees undermines the Administration's ability to condemn human rights violations committed by the de facto leaders because it might justify its repatriation policy by contending that those fleeing are not suffering from widespread political violence. The result is a tacit agreement between the U.S. and the de facto leaders, that the refugees do not warrant attention or protection as long as each side benefits by ignoring their plight.

311.   David A. Martin. "Strategies for a Resistant
            World: Human Rights Initiatives and the Need
for Alternatives to Refugee Interdiction." CORNELL
INTERNATIONAL LAW JOURNAL, Vol. 26: 1993,
p. 768. Refugee flows have been important not only because of the way they have triggered a conceptual break-
through, breaching the artificial walls of sovereignty that
once pretended that oppression inside a country was no
one else's business. They have been important for another, far more pragmatic reason. Asylum seekers, even
if their claims ultimately fall short of the legal standards
for winning full political asylum, have served a vital
signalling function. Their arrival in significant numbers
forces the media, the public, and the political elite in the
receiving state to take notice of the poverty or abuses in
the home state that may have triggered the flow. Beyond
this, a desire to reduce the burdens and expenses associated with asylum claims—including adjudication costs,
care and maintenance, and friction with the local population—can feed into efforts to bring relief or find solutions in the home country. The objective is to reduce future migration, or to encourage voluntary returns, or
perhaps only to make more palatable the forced return of
those whose claims are rejected by the asylum adjudication system, because the home state's situation is becoming demonstrably better. All these factors amount to
"'selfish' national interest reasons" for human rights policy, to use a phrase introduced by Richard Bilder in
1974. Selfish reasons may be troubling, but they are
better than no reasons at all, and they are probably more
effective than reasons built solely on altruistic appeals.

312.   David A. Martin. "Strategies for a Resistant
            World: Human Rights Initiatives and the Need
for Alternatives to Refugee Interdiction." CORNELL
INTERNATIONAL LAW JOURNAL, Vol. 26: 1993,
pp. 768-769. In the 1980s, these processes were evident
in the United States regarding Central American asylum
seekers, and in Europe for Sri Lankan Tamils. Human
rights abuses in the home countries stayed on the policy
agenda, in major part because of the receiving states
struggles with the challenges posed by large numbers of
asylum seekers. This effect occurred even though most
of those claimants were ultimately deemed not to fit the
Convention refugee definition. A similar process also
unfolded for Haitians from the time of the first post-coup
outflow in October 1991 until May 1992, when President Bush's order brought an abrupt and near-total halt to
further outflows. The Supreme Court's preliminary approval of Bush's harsh action, however (when it stayed
the Second Circuit's injunction), dropped Haiti to a low-
priority issue—a status it maintained throughout the
presidential election campaign. If inertia pulls President
Clinton into keeping Haitian interdiction in place indefinitely, we may well see a similar draining of interest and
priority from efforts to reinstate a democratic government in Haiti.

313.   David A. Martin. "Strategies for a Resistant
            World: Human Rights Initiatives and the Need
for Alternatives to Refugee Interdiction." CORNELL
INTERNATIONAL LAW JOURNAL, Vol. 26: 1993,
p. 770. Such a strategy is admittedly counter-intuitive. It
asks that we help give the domestic asylum system a
better capacity to say "no," so that the executive branch
can be coaxed into ending an interdiction policy that basically just says "no" indiscriminately, at some point far
from our borders, our media, and our courts. Such a
paradoxical achievement may be essential, however, if
refugee flows are still to play the signalling and inducement role they have developed in recent years. Comfortable nations may need this ongoing stimulus if they are
to use the new international legal regime to its maximum advantage, by pressing hard—even sometimes
through multilateral intervention—for human rights improvements at the source.

314.   David A. Martin. "Strategies for a Resistant
            World: Human Rights Initiatives and the Need
for Alternatives to Refugee Interdiction." CORNELL
INTERNATIONAL LAW JOURNAL, Vol. 26: 1993,
pp. 769-770. Here is where the increasingly sophisticated proliferation of barriers to the arrival of asylum
seekers may pose its greatest threat. If U.S. interdiction
teaches the world that insulation from a refugee flow can
be achieved unilaterally without having to address the
underlying causes, much of the fire may go out of humanitarian efforts and human rights diplomacy. Hence it
is important to remove interdiction as a policy tool, not
only because of its impact on the threatened individuals
who might seek to escape—though that is clearly a worthy reason that should not be lost from view. Removing
that option is also vital in order to keep the pressure on
neighboring countries to go to the source, so that they
have immediate reasons to push for constructive change
inside the country whose misgovernment, oppression, or
other severe suffering sends people across the frontiers.

315.   Elizabeth Mary McCormick. "HIV-Infected
            Haitian Refugees: An Argument Against Ex-
pulsion." GEORGETOWN IMMIGRATION LAW
JOURNAL, Vol. 7: 1993, p. 162. The exclusion policy
has also been criticized because it perpetuates a false notion that HIV comes from other countries—from foreigners and that by excluding those foreigners the United
States could protect itself from the spread of AIDS. Such
a policy not only endangers the public health by creating
misinformation about the risks and means of transmission of the virus in the United States, but also encourages prejudice and discrimination against people living
with HIV, aliens and United States citizens alike. Given
the high rates of infection in countries with black and
hispanic populations, and the overall prevalence of HIV
among homosexuals, it seems especially likely that a
policy of exclusion for HIV could be enforced in a way

which arbitrarily discriminates against aliens on the basis of race or sexual orientation.

316.   Elizabeth Mary McCormick. "HIV-Infected Haitian Refugees: An Argument Against Expulsion." GEORGETOWN IMMIGRATION LAW JOURNAL, Vol. 7: 1993, p. 156. Economic necessity fosters another practice which has been viewed as a factor in the transmission of AIDS throughout the general population in Haiti. Due to very limited access to health care providers in impoverished communities, particularly in rural areas, untrained and uncertified practitioners, known as *piqurists*, are widespread and popular. *Piqurists* dispense penicillin, vitamins and other drugs via intramuscular injection, sometimes reusing unsterilized needles. Five to six percent of the AIDS cases in Haiti are believed to have been transmitted through such injections.

317.   Elizabeth Mary McCormick. "HIV-Infected Haitian Refugees: An Argument Against Expulsion." GEORGETOWN IMMIGRATION LAW JOURNAL, Vol. 7: 1993, p. 162. The HIV exclusion policy defies not only the recommendation of United States health authorities, but also disregards the opinions of international health organizations regarding this "global" crisis. The World Health Organization has labeled AIDS a pandemic and has called for a global response to the virus which includes among its priorities: "opposing discrimination and stigmatization as irrational and unethical responses to HIV-infected persons, which endanger public health" and "fighting complacency and denial so that countries everywhere face and fight the AIDS pandemic in a spirit of realism and solidarity." Rather than be guided by these priorities, the Administration has acted in an irrational attempt to rid the United States of the AIDS virus by insulating itself from foreign carriers of the disease. This policy has no doubt cost the United States the respect of those in the international health community struggling against this global catastrophe. More importantly, though, until the United States reconsiders its decision to exclude aliens infected with HIV and, instead, cooperates in the international effort to contain the spread of the virus worldwide, many lives and valuable resources will be wasted in this isolated and vain endeavor.

318.   Elizabeth Mary McCormick. "HIV-Infected Haitian Refugees: An Argument Against Expulsion." GEORGETOWN IMMIGRATION LAW JOURNAL, Vol. 7: 1993, p. 171. The United States has used this exclusion policy to deny entry to 222 HIV-infected Haitians whose circumstances have left them without alternatives. To ignore their right to seek asylum because they are infected with HIV is to say that their infection has somehow condemned them to persecution. Such a policy not only contravenes the clear purposes of the Refugee Act of 1980, but displays a blatant cynicism about Haitian asylum claims in general. These Haitians became political pawns during an election year when the United States economy and health care system were central issues. In its decision to exclude them, the Bush Administration, preying upon fears and ignorance about the transmission of HIV, made false promises to the American people which placed the public health at greater risk. If President Clinton fails to reverse this policy, he will deny these Haitians their right to seek protection from dangers which are far more real and deadly than any they could pose to the United States.

319.   Jean-Pierre Benoit and Lewis A. Kornhauser. "Unsafe Havens." THE UNIVERSITY OF CHICAGO LAW REVIEW, Vol. 59, no. 4: Fall 1992, pp. 459-460. According to the model outlined in Part I, unreliable screening of Haitians by the United States will discourage political refugees more than economic refugees if Haiti's treatment of repatriated citizens meets two conditions. First, political refugees must face an increased threat of persecution upon their return. Second, if economic refugees are persecuted on their return, the increased risk to them must be less than the increased risk of persecution to repatriated political refugees.

320.   David Martin. "Interdiction, Intervention, and the New Frontiers of Refugee Law and Policy." VIRGINIA JOURNAL OF INTERNATIONAL LAW, Vol. 33: 1993, p. 481. Indeed, the Clinton administration will have to face these questions soon. it will come under a good deal of pressure to revoke the Kennebunkport Order early in Clinton's term. Simply ending interdiction without more, however, is not enough; that change would leave us with a politically unsustainable policy. Just what else the Clinton team can devise as alternatives will provide a crucial early test of the new administration. One may hope for resolute reforms to streamline and energize the regular asylum adjudication system, coupled with reinvigorated efforts, including international guarantees, to restore democracy and safeguard human rights inside Haiti.

321.   Ari Weitzhandler. "Temporary Protected Status: The Congressional response to the Plight of Salvadoran Aliens." UNIVERSITY OF COLORADO LAW REVIEW, Vol. 64: 1993, pp. 274-275. In the end, evaluation is principally a matter of perspective. For refugees desiring only temporary haven from El Salvador or countries designated by the Attorney General, TPS will probably represent an acceptable solution. However, refugees from countries which the Attorney General refuses to designate will continue to face the problems of political bias that characterized EVD. By codifying the discretionary designation practices of EVD, TPS practically ensures that future conflicts between the executive and legislative branches will continue to arise.

322. FDCH CONGRESSIONAL TESTIMONY (Lexis/Nexis), March 8, 1994, p. 17. The Administration's efforts to defend its repatriation policy have become increasingly embarrassing to the White House and State Department. At a December 8 briefing by Assistant Secretary of State for Human Rights and Humanitarian Affairs John Shattuck, he replied to a reporter's question about the refugee policy by stating, "In the future when that restoration of democracy occurs, the policy of interdiction and the grave difficulties that I think that poses for issues of asylum, will no longer be the applicable policy." Two days later, Shattuck was asked whether the U.S. policy conformed with either the spirit or letter of the International Covenant on Civil and Political Rights, to which he responded, "The U.S. is committed to considering the asylum applications of all who make them in Haiti, and it—to the extent that that commitment is fulfilled, and I believe it is, then the United States is acting consistent with the covenant in question. But this is not an easy issue and it is not an issue that will be resolved until democracy returns to Haiti.

323. Elizabeth Mary McCormick. "HIV-Infected Haitian Refugees: An Argument Against Expulsion." GEORGETOWN IMMIGRATION LAW JOURNAL, Vol. 7: 1993, p. 163. The debate surrounding the Administration's policy of exclusion has to a great extent centered around the admission of HIV-infected aliens seeking to enter the United States as temporary visitors or permanent residents. Nevertheless, this policy has distinct and important implications for political refugees, aliens whose circumstances provide them with few, if any, alternatives if denied entry to the United States.

324. Larry Rohter. "U.S. Lets 400 Haitians in Florida." NEW YORK TIMES, April 23, 1994, p. A4. As if to underline the Administration's continued commitment to the policy, State Department and Coast Guard officials announced that a group of 15 Haitians were forcibly returned to their country today. Their vessel was halted by a Coast Guard cutter in the Windward Passage, between Haiti and Cuba, on Thursday night.

325. Larry Rohter. "U.S. Lets 400 Haitians in Florida." NEW YORK TIMES, April 23, 1994, p. A4. Miami, April 22—A group of 406 Haitians crammed aboard a wooden freighter off the Florida coast were brought ashore here today by the Coast Guard, immediately making them eligible to seek political asylum. The Clinton Administration denied that the rescue represented a change in its policy of forced repatriation of Haitian refugees.

326. Larry Rohter. "U.S. Lets 400 Haitians in Florida." NEW YORK TIMES, April 23, 1994, p. A4. Mr. Lake said the Administration would press the United Nations to turn the trade embargo on Haiti, which now covers fuel and arms, into a comprehensive embargo that covers everything but fuel and medicine. The Administration also promised to step up pressure on the Dominican Republic to stop oil smuggling across its border with Haiti.

327. Elizabeth Mary McCormick. "HIV-Infected Haitian Refugees: An Argument Against Expulsion." GEORGETOWN IMMIGRATION LAW JOURNAL, Vol. 7: 1993, pp. 164-165. Similar considerations were likely to have been important to Congress' determination that refugees with an otherwise excludable medical condition might still be admissable "for humanitarian purposes, to assure family unity, or when it is otherwise in the public interest." In light of the nature of their flight and their lack of viable alternatives under frequently life-threatening circumstances, to exclude refugees on health related grounds would contradict the protective intent of United States and international asylum Law. Congress clearly intended to remove obstacles to the entrance of refugees, giving priority over all to their claims of persecution. Therefore, particularly where a medical condition has been determined to pose no risk to the public welfare of the United States, as in the case with HIV, it would seem unconscionable to deny entry and, subsequently, access to health care, to an otherwise admissible political refugee.

328. Elizabeth Mary McCormick. "HIV-Infected Haitian Refugees: An Argument Against Expulsion." GEORGETOWN IMMIGRATION LAW JOURNAL, Vol. 7: 1993, p. 165. A discussion of current United States refugee policy will reveal that the exclusion of HIV-infected refugees is contrary to the humanitarian purpose of the Refugee Act. In the case of these Haitians, not only should established refugee policy prevent them from being excluded, but the economic and public health arguments against their admission should also fail in view of the negligible actual threat they pose to those interests. Particularly, in light of the preceding discussion of the Haiti-AIDS myth and the HHS recommendations not to exclude HIV-infected aliens, the Administration's refusal to admit these Haitians will be revealed as essentially misguided, if not motivated purely by politics and prejudice. Rather than focusing on their status as refugees, United States policy decisions regarding the Haitians have focused instead on HIV status. In particular, in its refusal to provide them access to counsel, the Administration has used the Haitians' HIV infection as a basis for denying them rights and privileges that any other refugee would enjoy. Such actions clearly contravene the spirit of the refugee

provisions of the INA and strongly suggest that other considerations motivate the Administration's policy decisions in this area.

329. Larry Rohter. "U.S. Lets 400 Haitians in Florida." NEW YORK TIMES, April 23, 1994, p. A4. "It would be good news for Haitians because they are dying," said one political analyst, who asked for anonymity. "They are suffering from the embargo and repression."

330. Suzanne Gluck. "Intercepting Refugees at Sea: An Analysis of the United States' Legal and Moral Obligations." FORDHAM LAW REVIEW, Vol. 16: 1993, p. 888. Another option is for the United States simply to resume the policy of screening for refugees—those with a well-founded fear of persecution—on board Coast Guard vessels or at the United States naval base at Guantanamo Bay, Cuba, as was the practice from 1981 until the executive order of May 1992. Although this approach would be an improvement over the Bush Administration's policy, the shipboard interviews, nevertheless, are an inadequate screening device.

331. Deborah Sontag. "Reneging on Refuge: The Haitian Precedent." NEW YORK TIMES, June 17, 1993, Sect 4, p. 1. Some legal scholars see the opinion as narrow because the only refugees now stopped outside United States borders are Haitians, who are interdicted in international waters by American agents. The United States has a formal interdiction treaty only with Haiti, and so cannot stop vessels belonging to other nations.

332. Brunson McKinley. "US Policy on Haitian Boat People." IN DEFENSE OF THE ALIEN, Vol. 15, 1993, p. 135. Our immigration laws dictate who can legally enter the United States. Haitians are major beneficiaries in all categories.

Three quarters of a million Haitians—one out of every ten—already live here. In the past ten years, 140,000 Haitians have legally settled in the United States—our fifth largest immigrant group. Despite Cuba's much larger population, more Haitians immigrate to the United States than Cubans—96,000 to 76,000 in the last five years. Haitians are good citizens and good immigrants.

333. Brunson McKinley. "US Policy on Haitian Boat People." IN DEFENSE OF THE ALIEN, Vol. 15, 1993, p. 136. The best hope of addressing the plight of the Haitian boat people remains the restoration of democratic government in Haiti. The U.S. government worked hard to help President Aristide and has spared no effort to reverse the results of the coup. The Protocol of February 23, negotiated by Haitians with the help of the OAS, calls for the return of President Aristide, the creation of a new government of national consensus and the dispatch to Haiti of an OAS civilian mission. We still consider the Protocol the key to a political solution in Haiti.

334. Larry Rohter. "U.S. Lets 400 Haitians in Florida." NEW YORK TIMES, April 23, 1994, p. A4. during a photo session in the Oval Office today, President Clinton defended the current policy, inherited from the Bush Administration, calling it "the appropriate thing to do." Mr. Clinton said "the whole purpose of the return policy is primarily to deter people from risking their lives" in incidents like today's, adding that "hundreds of people have already drowned trying to come here."

335. Larry Rohter. "U.S. Lets 400 Haitians in Florida." NEW YORK TIMES, April 23, 1994, p. A4. Port-Au-Prince, Haiti, April 22—Haitians said today that if the American decision to allow passengers ashore from a crowded vessel was broadened to cover all refugee-filled boats then thousands of people would try to reach the United States.

Battered by an embargo imposed by the United Nations and fearsome of the increasingly harsh campaign of violence by the ruling military, poor Haitians would seize on a policy change to escape their homeland, analysts and human rights workers agreed.

336. John J. Glisch. "Few Boats Test U.S. Operation around Haiti." ORLANDO SENTINEL TRIBUNE, February 13, 1993, p. B1. A naval operation off Haiti designed to stop a flood of refugees from sailing to Florida is working so well that few if any Haitians are running the gauntlet of warships.

That was the assessment Friday from U.S. Coast Guard officials and crew members of the Coast Guard cutter Confidence, which returned home to Port Canaveral after 39 days of front-line duty in the armada.

"From our standpoint, it's an unheralded success," said Cmdr. James Underwood, the Confidence's captain. "Our presence is definitely a factor. They're broadcasting it around the country and it has discouraged people.

The Coast Guard sent the Confidence and 21 other ships on Jan. 15 to encircle the impoverished Caribbean nation for fear that tens of thousands of Haitians were ready to head to South Florida.

337. Michael Teitelbaum. "Political Tides, Haitian Waves." NEW YORK TIMES, February 2, 1993, p. A19. Perhaps one in five Haitians have already escaped the Western Hemisphere's poorest country and now live in the U.S., Dominican Republic or Bahamas. Hundreds of thousands of the 6.5 million people left in Haiti would depart if they could find a country to admit them.

338.   Mike Clary. "Secret Plan Prepares for Influx of Refugees into U.S." LOS ANGELES TIMES, September 25, 1993, p. A12. what is also driving ordinary Haitians to flee is a sense that the United Nations embargo against Haiti will hurt them the most.

In the past, Haitians used to say they were fleeing for fear of their lives; now many readily admit they will be leaving because of economic hardship.

Prices in Haiti have skyrocketed. In just a few days, gasoline prices went to $3.70, from $1.50, and the price of rice quadrupled. Unemployment is spreading rapidly; every day, young men here sit idly under the verandas and play cards to pass the time.

339.   Michael Teitelbaum. "Political Tides, Haitian Waves." NEW YORK TIMES, February 2, 1993, p. A19. The President-elect faced his first foreign and domestic crisis: the prospect of a flotilla arriving in Florida around Inauguration Day. President Aristide, asked to exhort his countrymen to stay home, did so by radio, but those waiting to leave were undeterred. At that point, Mr. Clinton embraced George Bush's policy of repatriating the boat people. His well-intentioned promise had been made impossible to honor. A disorderly mass migration would have politically savaged his Administration before it had begun to settle in. Public support for all refugee programs would have been weakened, while thousands might have perished at sea, unseen.

This experience reminds us that millions of desperate people are willing to undergo great danger and suffering to escape their circumstances. American actions that encourage them to migrate will continue to lead to large-scale responses. Too often our Government seems blind to the effects of its policies.

340.   Ari Weitzhandler. "Temporary Protected Status: The Congressional response to the Plight of Salvadoran Aliens." UNIVERSITY OF COLORADO LAW REVIEW, Vol. 64: 1993, pp. 249-250. Whether relevant or not, political considerations can and do enter into asylum adjudications. Applicants from countries with which the United States maintains friendly relations have frequently encountered an uphill struggle in establishing the requisite fear of persecution needed for a successful asylum application. Throughout the 1980s, refugees from the conflict in El Salvador fell prey to this situation. After years of debate, Congress addressed the Salvadoran refugee issue in the Immigration Act of 1990 (the Act). Among the sweeping reforms included within the Act were provisions providing safe haven for Salvadoran aliens within the United States, as well as a statutory framework for providing similar status to nationals of other countries embroiled in conflict. Although the program this framework established, Temporary Protected Status (TPS), represents an improvement over past practices, the problems of political bias that it failed to address will likely limit its effectiveness.

341.   Barbara Yarnold. REFUGEES WITHOUT REFUGE: FORMATION AND FAILED IMPLEMENTATION OF U.S. POLITICAL ASYLUM POLICY IN THE 1980'S, University Press: Lanham, Maryland, 1990, p. 202. These commentators also suggest that a lack of information about background conditions in these countries—El Salvador and Guatemala—keeps the U.S. public uninformed of conditions in which Central American refugees, deported to their countries of origin, are forced to live. Hence, public opinion in the U.S. has not risen to the level of opposing the immigration bureaucracy with respect to its treatments of these refugees, and public pressure is not likely to force policy changes in this area. Further, both the public and policy makers in the U.S. are, according to these authors, intentionally misinformed about conditions in El Salvador, Guatemala, and Honduras, since government reports suggest human rights abuses in these countries are declining as these countries engage in democratization when conditions have either remained the same or deteriorated.

342.   Amnesty International. REASONABLE FEAR: HUMAN RIGHTS AND UNITED STATES REFUGEE POLICY, Amnesty International USA: New York, March 1990, p. 16. Death threats and summary killings continue to rend lives in a broad cross-section of Guatemalan society. Yet many Guatemalans who requested asylum in the United States from abuses in their homeland were turned away. United States statistics support evidence of bias. According to Immigration and Naturalization Service statistics, the United States Government denied 3,325 applications for asylum filled by Guatemalan nationals during Fiscal 1989. The government approved 67 applications during that period—that is, less than 2 percent.

343.   Amnesty International. REASONABLE FEAR: HUMAN RIGHTS AND UNITED STATES REFUGEE POLICY, Amnesty International USA: New York, March 1990, p. 5. Human rights violations have escalated during recent years in Guatemala. Hundreds of people have been executed extrajudicially or have "disappeared." Civil patrols organized and directed by military personnel are reportedly responsible for large numbers of these abuses.

"Death squads" in Guatemala are often composed of armed men in plain clothes who use vehicles with darkened windows and no license plates. Citizens have been abducted, beaten, and killed by unidentified "death squad" assailants. Significant evidence also points to increased abuses by the military against people considered to be critical of the government or "subversive." Government procedures for investigating human rights abuses have proved ineffective, and many of the same governmental officials and structures have remained through successive administrations.

Numerous people living in areas of conflict between government forces and armed opposition groups have been abducted. Some have "disappeared" following abduction. The mutilated bodies of others have been found on streets or in ravines.

344.   Amnesty International. REASONABLE FEAR: HUMAN RIGHTS AND UNITED STATES REFUGEE POLICY, Amnesty International USA: New York, March 1990, p. 5. Citizens of El Salvador live in a country where so-called death squads are responsible for abductions, "disappearances," and politically motivated killings. Although compelling evidence indicates that the death squads are composed of police and military personnel operating in plain clothes, government officials claim an inability to control their operations. In some cases, the authorities apparently condone or encourage the killings.

Former political prisoners, trade unionists, human rights activists, and families and colleagues of anyone falling within these groups are at risk of becoming "death squad" targets or victims of other abuses. Unidentified gunmen kill, and the government takes little action to investigate the murders or to curb the violence.

Many hundreds of Salvadorans have "disappeared" in recent years, often after abduction by hooded gunmen or apparent detention by government agents. The torture of people held in government custody has also been widely reported. In addition, armed opposition groups have reportedly abducted and killed civilians suspected of supporting or collaborating with government authorities.

345.   Ari Weitzhandler. "Temporary Protected Status: The Congressional response to the Plight of Salvadoran Aliens." UNIVERSITY OF COLORADO LAW REVIEW, Vol. 64: 1993, p. 252. Two factors contributed significantly to the denial rate: the characterization of Salvadoran nationals as economic migrants, and the Reagan and Bush Administrations' foreign policy toward El Salvador. Although a fair number of Salvadorans may have come to the United States in search of greener economic pastures, it seems unlikely, given the conditions within El Salvador, that such a small percentage of asylum applications constituted bona fide claims. Evidenced that the largest migrations of Salvadorans to the United States coincided with the most intense periods of conflict in El Salvador belies this characterization. The massive migration of Salvadorans to Honduras and Guatemala, countries whose economies were no better than El Salvador's, casts further doubt upon the characterization.

346.   Barbara Yarnold. REFUGEES WITHOUT REFUGE: FORMATION AND FAILED IMPLEMENTATION OF U.S. POLITICAL ASYLUM POLICY IN THE 1980'S, University Press: Lanham, Maryland, 1990, p. 214. Although these efforts have not yet had a significant impact upon U.S. policy with respect to the governments of El Salvador and Guatemala, or upon its refugee policy for aliens from these countries, the fact that the number of religious and secular organizations which provide sanctuary to Central American refugees, an illegal act, has increased from 30 in 1982 to 448 by December, 1987 indicates that core ideas of the sanctuary movement have been adopted by certain segments of American society. Most important is the fact that the concept of sanctuary has gained the support of religious leaders from the largest religious organizations in the U.S. (including Baptist, Brethren, Disciples of Christ, Episcopalian, Jewish, New Jewish Agenda, Lutheran, Mennonite, Methodist, Presbyterian, Quaker, Roman Catholic, United Church of Christ, Unitarian Universalist, and other Protestant, and Ecumenical), since religious leaders have an existing communications system through which they may spread the ideas of the movement to their congregations and, hence, the public (McFarland, 1983). If the public comes to support a more even-handed application of the laws relating to refugees and asylees from these countries, "political entrepreneurs" may attempt to garner electoral support through adopting the policy platform of the movement.

347.   Ranee K.L. Panjabi. "The Global Refugee Crisis: A Search for Solutions." CALIFORNIA WESTERN INTERNATIONAL LAW JOURNAL, Vol. 21, no. 2: 1990-1991, p. 262. The popularity of the sanctuary movement is indicative of the fact that in the United States, at the popular level, there is considerable concern over the refugee crisis. If this wellspring of popular compassion can be channelled constructively into public debate on a mass sale about the refugee crisis, the ensuing weight of public opinion could have a dramatic effect on the government of the world's greatest democracy. The formulation of cohesive concrete remedies and the will to implement them could be the result of such a public debate across the nation. Given the international influence of the United States, this debate could have a considerable impact on other democratic States like Canada and the United Kingdom. A dedicated commitment by the West to resolving this crisis may well generate positive response among Third World nations who host approximately ninety percent of the world's refugees. Those nations desperately need a resolution of this problem.

348.   Barbara Yarnold. REFUGEES WITHOUT REFUGE: FORMATION AND FAILED IMPLEMENTATION OF U.S. POLITICAL ASYLUM POLICY IN THE 1980'S, University Press: Lanham, Maryland, 1990, p. 215. However, one feature of the sanctuary movement which distinguishes it from other social movements and gives it an added measure of "survivability" is that it is, for the most part, church-based, and thus has a constant source of organizational

support. Other social movements, such as the consumer protection movement, tended to wane as public attention came to focus upon other policy issues and movement groups began to see their supply of funds diminish. In contrast, religious groups that dominate the sanctuary movement have a constant source of support from members of their congregations who contribute to the support of the religious organizations, and not specifically to support sanctuary movement goals. Leaders of these religious groups may continue to press for the goals of the sanctuary movement even after public support for the movement dissipates. Hence, the sanctuary movement is likely to have a semi-perpetual existence, losing impetus not due to a lack of financial and organizational support, but due to a loss of interest on the part of religious leaders.

349.   Barbara Yarnold. REFUGEES WITHOUT REFUGE: FORMATION AND FAILED IMPLEMENTATION OF U.S. POLITICAL ASYLUM POLICY IN THE 1980'S, University Press: Lanham, Maryland, 1990, p. 214. One of the most important mechanisms through which the ideas of a social movement, including the sanctuary movement, are communicated to other sectors of society is the media. Members of religious fringe groups which support the sanctuary movement made use of the media as a communications tool, through contacting members of the press whenever an affiliate organization offered sanctuary to refugees, and through press coverage of trials of those active in the movement.

350.   Barbara Yarnold. REFUGEES WITHOUT REFUGE: FORMATION AND FAILED IMPLEMENTATION OF U.S. POLITICAL ASYLUM POLICY IN THE 1980'S, University Press: Lanham, Maryland, 1990, p. 225. Countervailing power produced by social movements tends to decrease when social movements wane, and public support for the movement and movement organizations diminishes. However, the sanctuary movement is unusual in that countervailing power is not likely to wane even if public support for sanctuary diminishes. This is due to the fact that the sanctuary movement is largely the product of religious groups which have independent financial and organizational resources necessary to sustain the movement even in the absence of popular support.

351.   Barbara Yarnold. REFUGEES WITHOUT REFUGE: FORMATION AND FAILED IMPLEMENTATION OF U.S. POLITICAL ASYLUM POLICY IN THE 1980'S, University Press: Lanham, Maryland, 1990, p. 204. One of the most significant "links" between social movements and interest groups is that interest groups may act as a "communications network" for social movements, facilitating the communication of major ideas of social movements in a way that may legitimize movements, bring public pressure for policy changes to the fore, attract entrepreneurial politicians who adopt all or part of the social movements platform, and effect policy change (McFarland, 1983; Freeman, 1975). Thus, social movements are dependent upon organized interests; the failure of interest groups to communicate any of the ideas of a social movement may result in the failure of the movement to cause any significant policy change.

352.   Ari Weitzhandler. "Temporary Protected Status: The Congressional response to the Plight of Salvadoran Aliens." UNIVERSITY OF COLORADO LAW REVIEW, Vol. 64: 1993, pp. 273-274. As a replacement for Extended Voluntary Departure, Temporary Protected Status may well be a moderately successful program. By providing a clear statutory basis for the Attorney General's exercise of discretion, Congress has placed its stamp of approval on the concept of safe haven and thereby encouraged the protection of imperiled alien nationals. The TPS notice provisions also constitute a distinct improvement over EVD, replacing a haphazard approach with a reasonable and comprehensive system.

353.   Rosemarie Rogers. "The Future of Refugee Flows and Policies." INTERNATIONAL MIGRATION REVIEW, Vol. 26, no. 4: Winter 1992, pp. 1133-1134. The most successful intergovernmental effort to solve a regional refugee problem is currently taking place in Central America. At the 1989 International Conference on Central American Refugees (CIREFCA), seven governments came together to seek permanent solutions for an estimated 2 million persons who were displaced in the region as of 1987. In addition, the needs of affected local populations are also being taken into account.

One key to CIREFCA's success is the fact that it builds on a regional peace initiative. A second important aspect is its integrated approach: its concern with all affected populations. Third, it offers forced migrants not only the option of a safe return, but also that of local integration for those who wish to remain in the host countries. Finally, it recognizes the need to combine repatriation with short- and long-term development efforts. In this context, CIREFCA has helped to identify problems in the transition from humanitarian aid to development.

354.   Stanley Mark. ALIEN SMUGGLING, Hearing before the Subcommittee on International Law, Immigration, and Refugees of the Committee on the Judiciary, United States House of Representatives, (Y4,J89/1:103/9) June 30, 1993, p. 143. The substandard wages and working conditions for slave labor serve as the fertile ground for the continued growth of the slave trade. To stop the slave trade, we must end the inhuman working conditions, long hours, and violations of the minimum wage and other labor laws endured by

working people regardless of their legal status. Criminal prosecution and international cooperation must be part of a total enforcement package but only full labor law enforcement will remove the financial incentive for employers to hire indentured servants or undocumented aliens. In addition, the repeal employer sanctions must be considered since this law has benefitted and facilitated the slave trade by cutting off any hope for indentured servants trying to leave their masters for a new employer.

355.   Stanley Mark. ALIEN SMUGGLING, Hearing before the Subcommittee on International Law, Immigration, and Refugees of the Committee on the Judiciary, United States House of Representatives, (Y4.J89/1:103/9) June 30, 1993, p. 141. However, the Clinton Administration's proposed plan of action fails to include, as a fundamental part of its total enforcement package, the full and vigorous enforcement of labor laws that would eliminate slave-like working conditions and minimum wage violations that serve as fertile ground upon which the slave trade of indentured servants has grown during the last two years. Any long term structural response (to the issues raised by alien smuggling as well other related immigrant rights issues) must incorporate an Asian American perspective which is currently missing on the Commission on Legal Immigration Reform mandated to review and recommend changes in immigration policy and law.

356.   Chris Sale. ALIEN SMUGGLING, Hearing before the Subcommittee on International Law, Immigration, and Refugees of the Committee on the Judiciary, United States House of Representatives, (Y4.J89/1:103/9) June 30, 1993, p. 60. Alien smugglers comprise an international criminal network including recruiters, suppliers, transporters and guides, fraudulent document vendors, and safehouse operators. Smugglers and their associated criminal gangs subject their human cargo to deplorable conditions while enroute to the U.S., and deliver them into a life of indentured servitude, torture, fear, and extortion. Smugglers also exploit the laws of the United States and international maritime law to evade detection. Among the many crimes associated with alien smuggling are: kidnapping, rape, murder, holding smuggled aliens as hostages for ransom, coerced prostitution, narcotics and firearms trafficking, extortion, and public corruption.

357.   Chris Sale. ALIEN SMUGGLING, Hearing before the Subcommittee on International Law, Immigration, and Refugees of the Committee on the Judiciary, United States House of Representatives, (Y4.J89/1:103/9) June 30, 1993, pp. 61-62. Aliens smuggled on ships are often transferred to small crafts in international waters for transport from the "mother ship" to the mainland of the U.S. This allows the smugglers

to circumvent laws regulating vessels within territorial waters. Investigations have revealed that these smuggling operations are carried out by organized crime members and/or associates.

There are dire humanitarian implications, including loss of life, in many alien smuggling ventures. The aliens are often subjected to brutal and life threatening conditions.

358.   Romano L. Mazzoli. ALIEN SMUGGLING, Hearing before the Subcommittee on International Law, Immigration, and Refugees of the Committee on the Judiciary, United States House of Representatives, (Y4.J89/1:103/9) June 30, 1993, p. 58. In addition to generating illicit proceeds, criminal organizations use alien smuggling to bring in their associates and others who might not otherwise qualify for legal entry into the United States. These aliens may be brought here to work for criminal groups involving narcotics trafficking, racketeering, vice and extortion.

More importantly, smuggled aliens without previous criminal orientation represent a labor pool for the criminal organizations when they are unable to repay their smuggling fees and become vulnerable to coercion, which may also occur when aliens are extorted for more than they agreed upon for smuggling fees.

359.   Romano L. Mazzoli. ALIEN SMUGGLING, Hearing before the Subcommittee on International Law, Immigration, and Refugees of the Committee on the Judiciary, United States House of Representatives, (Y4.J89/1:103/9) June 30, 1993, p. 58. Smuggled Chinese aliens in particular constitute an underground community subject to control of criminal groups. This population is a group whose background is unknown, whom we will never be able to accurately identify. In addition, alien smuggling and immigration fraud are perpetrated by organized crime groups with members representing numerous other nationalities. Many of these groups are involved in drug trafficking.

360.   Laurie E. Elkstrand. ALIEN SMUGGLING, Hearing before the Subcommittee on International Law, Immigration, and Refugees of the Committee on the Judiciary, United States House of Representatives, (Y4.J89/1:103/9) June 30, 1993, p.30. Finally, while focusing on stopping alien smuggling on board ships, the plan does not seem to address other, perhaps more active areas of alien smuggling such as that along the Southwest border. Therefore, the plan does not provide a comprehensive strategy for dealing with alien smuggling.

Effective resolution of smuggling and other illegal alien issues will require Congress and the administration to deal with the general issues of how best to control our borders and remove aliens who are here illegally. Complex and sensitive issues relating to our relationships

with other nations, humanitarian concerns related to equitable treatment of aliens, and difficult budgetary tradeoffs are all part of the equation in resolving illegal alien issues.

361.   Romano L. Mazzoli. ALIEN SMUGGLING,
          Hearing before the Subcommittee on International Law, Immigration, and Refugees of the Committee on the Judiciary, United States House of Representatives, (Y4.J89/1:103/9) June 30, 1993, p. 45. We have seen everything from the Rose Garden statement to all of the press releases, but I haven't seen much of anything implemented. We don't really get much information about what is going to be happening first, what sequence of events, how many dollars they are going to spend. We could draft one of these statements sitting around this table, but to pull it together, as you have pointed out, is very much more difficult. First of all, it doesn't talk—at least the President hasn't—about the southwest border, and if you are talking about that, I think a lot of the Chinese that wind up in the districts represented by the gentlewomen who were here earlier are coming across the Mexican border.

362.   Merle Molin. "From China to America, via
          Moscow." NEW YORK TIMES, August 25, 1993, Editorial page A15. It's well known that illegal Chinese immigrants are being smuggled into the United States by boat, by air and over land. What is still virtually unknown is that a number of the estimated 100,000 Chinese being smuggled here each year are routed first through Moscow. If the U.S. ever hopes to stop this flow, it must develop a comprehensive international policy to thwart the smuggling closer to its source.

363.   Merle Molin. "From China to America, via
          Moscow." NEW YORK TIMES, August 25, 1993, Editorial page A15. Russian authorities are willing, even eager, to cooperate with American officials. But the U.S. response has been tepid. True, the Federal Bureau of Investigation recently sent over one agent to assist Russian authorities in their incipient efforts to combat organized crime.

     But more assistance is needed if the U.S. is not to become swamped with Chinese asylum seekers and illegals who, if they do make it, live among us as frightened, indentured servants.

364.   Eugene M. Iwanciw. CONGRESSIONAL
          RECORD—Senate, February 1, 1994, p. S466. It is our understanding that the law will be expiring this year. With the demise of the Soviet Union there have been tremendous changes since the original passage of the "Lautenberg Amendment." Many of the nations which replaced the Soviet Union are striving to establish democratic institutions and policies to protect human rights and minorities. However, the region is

still in transition and there remains a great deal of instability in the area.

     In Ukraine, the government has pursued an exemplary policy toward minorities. there is no evidence of persecution of any ethnic or religious minority. However, we remain concerned about those Ukrainian Catholic and Ukrainian Orthodox believers living in other nations which emerged from the Soviet Union and which have not adopted the same protection of minorities which Ukraine has. For this reason, we support any effort to extend the provisions of the "Lautenberg Amendment" until such time as the institutions required to guarantee religious and minority rights are firmly established in all the newly independent nations of the former Soviet Union.

365.   Martin Kesselhaut. CONGRESSIONAL
          RECORD—Senate, February 1, 1994, p. S466. The post-cold war era in the former Soviet Union is characterized by precarious economic, social and political instability, lack of effective authority and social order and the backlash unleashed toward the non-native populations. the recent elections in Russia are an example of the negative trends in the region where people are seeking solutions by turning to the extremes of the right and the left. Anti-Semitism has surfaced to the point where it is now an accepted form of political rhetoric. We are concerned that the social grievances that led to this outcome in Russia are even more profound in Ukraine. Experts predict further division and civil conflict and the deepening of ultra-nationalist sentiment in addition to the actual and ongoing civil conflicts that are existent in many areas of the region.

366.   Senator Frank Lautenberg. CONGRESSIONAL
          RECORD—Senate, February 1, 1994, p. S465. The law, which now is set to expire at the end of this fiscal year, lowers the evidentiary standard required to qualify for refugee status for Jews and Evangelical Christians from the former Soviet Union, certain Ukrainians, and certain categories of Vietnamese, Laotians, or Cambodians. Once a refugee applicant proves he or she is a member of one of these groups, he or she only has to provide a "credible basis for concern" about the possibility of persecution. Refugee applicants normally must prove a well-founded fear of persecution.

     The law has had a real and positive impact on refugee adjudication. This liberalized standard is still necessary because conditions for the persecuted groups in the former Soviet Union and Indochina still exist, and in some cases, have worsened.

367.   Senator Feinstein. CONGRESSIONAL
          RECORD—Senate, February 1, 1994, p. S467. As was evidenced by the Russian elections last December, Communists and ultranationalists fared surprisingly well. The now infamous Vladimir Zhiri-

novsky—and his ironically named Liberal Democratic Party—scored a major victory, receiving 23 percent of the popular vote. Together with the Communists, the hard-liners in Russia almost took control of the parliament, with a total of 43 percent of the vote.

Zhirinovsky, who some dub "the Russian Hitler," has aspirations of becoming president of Russia. He has talked about sending 300,000 troops into Germany, blockading Japan, and taking back Alaska. All this on top of his antisemitic rhetoric.

The Lautenberg amendment is important because it will provide an extension of existing law through the next Russian elections in 1996. We must all remember that Hitler was first elected with only 18 percent of the vote, and then rose to power a few years later.

368.   Senator Frank Lautenberg. CONGRESSIONAL RECORD—Senate, February 1, 1994, p. S465. This law is working as intended in the former Soviet Union. It has replaced an arbitrary and slow process of refugee adjudication in the former Soviet Union with a stable, consistent, and fair process. It has meant that people already terrorized by longstanding hatred and persecution in their native lands are not further traumatized by a system that does not recognize their historical suffering, or makes arbitrary distinctions among people who have suffered similar fates.

In light of the current election and nagging questions about stability in the republics of the former Soviet Union, it would be unwise to let the law expire at this tie.

369.   J. Michael Cavosie. "Defending the Golden Door: The Persistence of Ad Hoc and Ideological Decision Making in U.S. Refugee Law." INDIANA LAW JOURNAL, Vol. 67: 1992, p. 431. 182. B. Yarnold, United States Refugee and Asylum Policy: Factors that Impact Legislative, Administrative and Judicial Decisions 118 (1988) (citations omitted). For her doctoral dissertation, Yarnold conducted an exhaustive statistical study of post-1980 refugee and asylum policy. She concluded that, at least through 1985, decision makers "were overwhelmingly influenced by one variable: whether an alien is from a 'hostile' country of origin, defined as a country with a communist, socialist, or leftist form of government."

370.   J. Michael Cavosie. "Defending the Golden Door: The Persistence of Ad Hoc and Ideological Decision Making in U.S. Refugee Law." INDIANA LAW JOURNAL, Vol. 67: 1992, pp. 431-432. Congress seemingly abandoned its commitment to a nondiscriminatory refugee standard with the passage of the Foreign Operations Act. A provision in that bill resurrected a double standard in refugee determinations.

After the enactment of the Refugee Act of 1980, aliens seeking refugee status had to prove an individual-

ized well-founded fear of persecution. Section 599(D) of the Foreign Operations Act, however, establishes a different standard for some aliens:

> In the case of an alien who is within a category of aliens established under subsection (b), the alien may establish, for purposes of admission as a refugee under section 207 of the Immigration and Nationality Act, that the alien has a well-founded fear of persecution on account of race, religion, nationality, membership in a particular social group, or political opinion by asserting such a fear and asserting a *credible basis for concern about the possibility of such persecution.*

This section applies to Soviet Jews or Evangelical Christians, those active in the Ukrainian Catholic Church or Ukrainian Orthodox Church, and selected Vietnamese, Laotians, and Cambodians. As the italicized clause indicates, a credible fear of persecution—instead of a well-founded fear—suffices to qualify these persons as refugees.

This legislation was clearly intended to bestow preferential treatment. The distinction between the "well-founded fear" standard and the "credible basis for concern" standard is apparent in the conference report on the bill: A "credible basis of concern" is established if the alien asserts that a "similarly situated individual in his or her geographic locale" has been persecuted or the alien has "knowledge, either from having read of or heard of [persecution] as affecting persons in the same category residing elsewhere in the home country." The results speak for themselves: denial rates dropped from a high of more than 30% to less than 10%.

371.   J. Michael Cavosie. "Defending the Golden Door: The Persistence of Ad Hoc and Ideological Decision Making in U.S. Refugee Law." INDIANA LAW JOURNAL, Vol. 67: 1992, pp. 435-436. My first recommendation is that the United States should refrain from manipulating its refugee law—as in, for example, selectively relaxing refugee standards—to accommodate certain groups for ideological reasons. Such a practice violates article 3 of the Convention, which dictates that "[t]he Contracting States shall apply the provisions of this Convention to refugees without discrimination as to…country of origin." Granting special consideration to aliens from hostile countries, especially when it appears that they may not even qualify as refugees, certainly constitutes discrimination based on nationality. The problem is exacerbated by the fact that refugee levels are subject to numerical ceilings. Granting special status to less deserving aliens may ultimately have the indefensible effect of excluding deserving aliens. [ellipses in original]

372.   Senator Simpson. CONGRESSIONAL RECORD—Senate, February 1, 1994,

p. S740. This amendment causes us to lock ourselves in to act on behalf of specified groups—powerful specified groups—resulting in multiyear commitments on their behalf, creating what is known as a "pipeline." This effectively restricts our refugee program in its ability to respond flexibly to the fast-changing patterns of human rights violations in Eastern and Central Europe.

373. Senator Simpson. CONGRESSIONAL RECORD—Senate, February 1, 1994, p. S470. Is there really a justification for designating some groups and not others as category groups? Should certain categories of Bosnians be included? Certain categories of Haitians? Why should we designate some groups and not others? The answer is we should not designate any groups. That is why, with Senator Kennedy's good tutelage and efforts and skill—and he will not be able to participate in this debate; that is the way this works, too, when you get to an issue like this—we changed our refugee laws in 1980, to take the politics, the pressure, the ideology, the parole use, which was so misused, to take it out of the refugee program so that we can offer refuge to those persons truly fleeing political persecution and who are of special humanitarian concern to the United States.

374. Senator Simpson. CONGRESSIONAL RECORD—Senate, February 1, 1994, p. S470. What this well-intended amendment does is it creates a bottleneck in refugee processing for the former Soviet Union. Hundreds of thousands of persons from the Lautenberg category groups have joined the queue for the 40,000 to 50,000 resettlement places per year from the former Soviet Union. This has caused a backup in processing. It makes it extremely difficult for these non-category members, persons who do not get this special treatment provided by the Lautenberg amendment, to be considered for U.S. resettlement. An Armenian/Azerbaijani family of mixed ethnicity, for example, is at a great disadvantage here, without question.

375. Senator Simpson. CONGRESSIONAL RECORD—Senate, February 1, 1994, p. S470. The sad part of it is—and this amendment will pass like a dose of salts; that is the way it works in this place—this amendment has essentially turned a very fine refugee program into an immigrant program, an immigration program, with one important exception, and do not miss this: The beneficiaries under this program are then resettled in the United States at taxpayers' expense, although they come to join family members in the United States, for the most part, they are not subject to the "public charge exclusion."

376. Senator Simpson. CONGRESSIONAL RECORD—Senate, February 1, 1994, p. S469. Debate about who is a political refugee and

who is an economic migrant has proceeded vigorously in recent years, but very little is said about the slide of U.S. refugee policy into pure politics, just as illustrated by this amendment by my friend from New Jersey. And I respect Frank Lautenberg thoroughly. He and I have worked together on many issues. The pressures he has on this amendment are total. I have watched it over the years.

Under our Refugee Act and under the United Nations Convention and Protocol, a refugee is a person with a well-founded fear of persecution on account of race, religion, nationality, membership in a particular social group, or political opinion. This is a refugee. The way we determine refugees is on a case-by-case basis, which is the only sane and sensible way to determine who is a refugee. That is why Senator Kennedy did yeoman's work in 1980 on the Refugee Act, new legislation, with which I assisted. But under this amendment, any member of a group or category covered can establish eligibility as a refugee just by being a member of the group without any case-by-case determination. They do that by "asserting"—this is the word, asserting—a well-founded fear of persecution and asserting a credible basis for concern about the possibility of persecution.

In other words, admission to the United States as a refugee is made then on the basis of two assertions that do not in themselves involve any test of credibility at all. Every other refugee applicant to this country is required to establish his or her eligibility. But those who benefit from this amendment need only "assert" a claim. Accordingly, once an individual is asserting that he or she is a member of a covered class and asserts that he or she has been persecuted or has a fear of persecution, then that person is deemed to be a refugee.

377. Senator Simon. CONGRESSIONAL RECORD—Senate, February 1, 1994, p. S467. Mr. President, Senator Lautenberg has summarized this well, but let me just add a word or two.

First of all, all we are doing is asking for the extension of existing law. We are not increasing numbers; we are not changing anything like that. Both the State Department and INS have indicated informally they have no objection to this extension of the law.

378. Senator Lautenberg. CONGRESSIONAL RECORD—Senate, February 1, 1994, p. S469. All applicants for refugee status, excepting only those covered by this amendment, go through a case-by-case interview process to determine whether or not a well-founded fear of persecution exists. The applicant has the burden of establishing that well-founded fear of persecution, as it should be. This is not a new thing here.

379. Senator Lautenberg. CONGRESSIONAL RECORD—Senate, February 1, 1994,

p. S469. It is now anomalous, to say the least, to include such category groups as current members of the Ukrainian Catholic or Ukrainian Orthodox Church. The 1994 Human Rights World Watch Report does not even include an entry on the Ukraine. The 1993 Amnesty International report mentions only "one known prisoner of conscience, a conscientious objector to military service." The Amnesty International report said, "A civilian alternative to military service was open only to religious beliefs." In other words, the only prisoner of conscience in the Ukraine is in prison because of a lack of religious affiliation. I point all this out only to show how unnecessary this amendment is and the violence that it does to the integrity of the Refugee Act of 1980, where we would do these things on a case-by-case basis.

380.   Deborah Sontag. "Waiting for a Rudder at INS"
        NEW YORK TIMES, June 13, 1993, p. 43.
To be fair, few recent Presidents have rushed to fill the top I.N.S. job upon assuming office. But the immigration issue carries a distinct urgency now. From the outset of his Presidency, when Mr. Clinton risked having his inaugural celebration disturbed by an exodus of Haitian boat people, one major problem after another has presented itself: Zoe Baird's hiring of illegal immigrants, the revelation of a World Trade Center bombing suspect's entry into the country by claiming political asylum, the Golden Venture, and last week's judicial order closing the detention camp for H.I.V.-positive Haitians in Guantanamo, Cuba.

381.   Deborah Sontag. "Waiting for a Rudder at INS"
        NEW YORK TIMES, June 13, 1993, p. 43.
After the World Trade Center bombing and again after the grounding of the Golden Venture, Mr. Slattery seized the moment to make public appearances railing against the humanitarian leniencies of the asylum system. While advocates for immigrants have long criticized the Immigration and Naturalization Service for its backlogged system, Mr. Slattery and other officials turned the tables, blaming the supposedly crafty immigrants who stormed the gates.

382.   Myron Weiner. "Introduction: Security,
        Stability and International Migration." INTERNATIONAL MIGRATION AND SECURITY (As originally published in *International Security*, Vol. 17, no. 3. Winter 1992/93.), 1993, p. 2. Second, more people want to leave their countries than there are countries willing or capable of accepting them. the reluctance of states to open their borders to all who wish to enter is only partly a concern over economic effects. The constraints are as likely to be political, resting upon a concern that an influx of people belonging to another ethnic community may generate xenophobic sentiments, conflicts between natives and migrants, and the growth of anti-migrant right-wing parties.

383.   Eduardo Arboleda and Ian Hoy. "The Convention Refugee Definition in the West: Disharmony of Interpretation and Application." INTERNATIONAL JOURNAL OF REFUGEE LAW, Vol. 15: 1993, p. 73. Most migration involves people who move within their own countries. A smaller number move across national boundaries within the third world, and a relatively minor percentage go to the developed countries of the West. Albeit a small percentage, the numbers coming to the West are large and the phenomenon is growing; so to is the feeling of paranoia within these countries.

Many of those moving from the third world to the West arrive illegally or with false documentation. Frequently racially, ethnically or religiously distinct from the majority of people in western societies, the new arrivals are causing concern, if not panic, in countries like Canada, the United States of America and Australia, traditionally countries of immigration.

384.   Frank Trejo. "Rethinking Immigration."
        DALLAS MORNING NEWS, January 2, 1994, p. 1A. Many immigrants and their supporters express concern that the anti-immigrant sentiment and statements sometimes do not differentiate between illegal and legal immigrants.

385.   Ira Mehlman. "The Issue is Immigration;
        Increasing Opposition to Current US Immigration Policy that does not Control Numbers of Immigrants Entering the US." NATIONAL REVIEW, November 29, 1993, p. 26. At the root of the growing concern about immigration is the public's sense that their country is being dramatically transformed without their consent. This concern cannot be addressed merely by cracking down on illegal immigration. Legal immigrants have essentially the same economic, social, and cultural impact as illegal ones, and legal immigration accounts for a much higher percentage of the influx.

386.   NEW YORK TIMES, September 19, 1993.
        "The United States of Asylum." Sect. 6, p. 56. Asylum is much in the news because the average citizen lumps it together with all forms of immigration, and in these recession-plagued times, the pendulum is making a swing toward intolerance of immigrants. It is one more component of the fear that we've 'lost control of our borders.'

In contrast to many European countries, however, asylum here adds only a sliver to overall numbers of immigrants. A hundred thousand people applied for asylum in the last fiscal year (the approval rate is about 30 percent), compared with almost a million who immigrated legally in other Government programs.

387.   Deborah Sontag. "Reneging on Refuge: The
        Haitian Precedent." NEW YORK TIMES, June

17, 1993, Sect 4, p. 1. Once, the United States criticized Hong Kong for returning Vietnamese boat people without properly screening them. But the American mood has gradually grown more hostile to immigrants, as the latest New York Times/CBS News Poll indicates, and critics believe the decision reflects that.

"With this Supreme Court decision, the United States has abdicated its role as the champion of refugee rights," said Bill Frelick, senior policy analyst with the U.S. Committee for Refugees. "Instead, we are now showing leadership in the post-cold-war movement to see ourselves as the victims of refugees and so treat them like trash."

Political refugees have lost Washington allies.

"Asylum policy was always driven by cold war politics, with some refugees prized as the enemies of our enemies who were voting with their feet," said Frank Sharry, executive director of the National Immigration, Refugee and Citizenship Forum. "Now that no refugees are seen as strategic assets in geopolitical confrontation, they all have become solely a headache."

388.   Seth Mydans. "Poll Finds Tide of Immigration Brings Hostility." NEW YORK TIMES, June 27, 1993, p. A1. The tightening economy also seems to be a major reason for the increasing anti-immigration sentiment in the new poll, which was conducted Monday through Thursday and questioned 1,363 adults nationwide. The poll has a margin of sampling error of plus or minus three percentage points. The participants in the 1986 poll and last week's poll were asked, "Do you think that, in general, the United States should welcome immigrants who come here with very little to try to make a success of their lives, or are conditions here today too hard for this to be practical?"

In the new poll, only 32 percent said the country should welcome immigrants, while 60 percent said this was not practical because of hard conditions.

In 1986, when the same question was asked at a time when economic conditions were better, 43 percent said the country should welcome immigrants, approximately equal to the 45 percent who said it was not practical because of hard conditions.

"If we had a robust economy, even a sustained high level of immigration would not create much controversy," said Arthur C. Helton, director of the Refugee Project of the Lawyers Committee for Human Rights. "I think if you look at the development of immigration policy, the impact on the work place would emerge as a decisive factor."

389.   Barbara Yarnold. REFUGEES WITHOUT REFUGE: FORMATION AND FAILED IMPLEMENTATION OF U.S. POLITICAL ASYLUM POLICY IN THE 1980'S, University Press: Lanham, Maryland, 1990, pp. 21-22. In each of the examples, immigration increased during periods when local or na-

tional unemployment rates in the U.S. were low. At some point, the unemployment rate began to climb, either due to an increase in the labor supply caused by immigration flows, or due to an unrelated decrease in the supply of jobs. Increases in the unemployment rate were followed by changes in public policy which tended to curb immigration flows. This suggests that policy makers in the U.S. are aware of unemployment rates, and take steps to curb immigration flows in order to decrease domestic unemployment rates.

390.   Seth Mydans. "Poll Finds Tide of Immigration Brings Hostility." NEW YORK TIMES, June 27, 1993, p. A1. Shifts in public attitudes seem to parallel changes in economic conditions. In 1965, the nation's unemployment rate fell to just over 4 percent, as compared with the 6.9 percent reported for last May, and the economic growth rate then was 5.6 percent, as compared with this year's forecast of 3.1 percent, a prediction that may be scaled back.

According to the Immigration and Naturalization Service, 8.9 million people have immigrated legally into the United States over the past decade, and an estimated 3 million more have slipped into the country illegally. Immigration experts say the numbers approach those of the great wave of European immigration at the turn of the century and are the highest since comprehensive immigration laws were enacted in 1924.

"What people are reacting to now is the reality of the past 20 to 25 years," said Ira Mehlman, a spokesman for the Federation for American Immigration Reform, a lobbying group that seeks to reduce immigration. "There are unprecedented levels of immigration and the numbers are growing, and the American people are saying, 'Enough is enough.'"

391.   Seth Mydans. "Poll Finds Tide of Immigration Brings Hostility." NEW YORK TIMES, June 27, 1993, p. A1. Mr. Mehlman said he was concerned that a backlash against immigration could lead to increased acts of violence against immigrants, like those that have swept Germany. But the new poll shows that while many Americans may be ready to slam the country's door on immigrants, they remain unwilling to be personally rude to them.

Asked what would happen "if some of today's new immigrants moved into your neighborhood," 67 percent of respondents in the poll said the newcomers "would be welcomed." In 1968, 68 percent offered a similar welcome.

392.   Myron Weiner. "Introduction: Security, Stability and International Migration." INTERNATIONAL MIGRATION AND SECURITY (As originally published in *International Security,* Vol. 17, no. 3. Winter 1992/93.), 1993, p. 11. Conflicts create refugees, but refugees can also create conflicts. An inter-

national conflict arises when a country classifies individuals as refugees with a well-founded fear of persecution, thereby accusing and condemning their country of origin for engaging in persecution. The mere granting of asylum can create an antagonistic relationship. Thus, the January 1990 debate in Congress over whether Chinese students should be permitted to remain in the United States because of the persecutions in China was regarded by the Peoples' Republic of China as "interference" in its internal affairs. President Bush was prepared to permit graduating students and other Chinese in the United States to remain by extending their visas, but not to grant asylum, while many Congressmen wanted to grant formal asylum status in order to condemn China. Moreover, to classify individuals as refugees with a well-founded fear of persecution is also to acknowledge that they have a moral (as distinct from a political) right to oppose their country's regime.

393.   Myron Weiner. "Introduction: Security, Stability and International Migration." INTERNATIONAL MIGRATION AND SECURITY (As originally published in *International Security,* Vol. 17, no. 3. Winter 1992/93.), 1993, p. 11. Moreover, democratic regimes generally allow their refugees to speak out against the regime of their country of origin, allow them access to the media, and permit them to send information and money back home in support of the opposition. The host country's decision to grant refugee status thus often creates an adversary relationship with the country that produces the refugees. The receiving country may have no such intent, but even where its motives are humanitarian the mere granting of asylum can be sufficient to create an antagonistic relationship. In the most famous asylum episode in this century, Iranian revolutionaries took violent exception to the U.S. decision to permit the shah of Iran to enter the US. for medical reasons; many Iranians regarded it as a form of asylum and used it as an occasion for taking American hostages.

394.   Representative Elton Gallegly. HOUSE HEARINGS, April 27, 1993, Y4J89/1:03/7. The recent bombing at the World Trade Center and the random shootings outside the CIA are among the tragedies that have ensued as a consequence of our lax policy regarding illegal aliens and aliens claiming asylum. Taken together with the mounting statistics involving the millions of aliens who are allowed to enter our country illegally each year, adding to the financial burden of our states and local governments, who steal jobs, services and benefits from our poor and needy citizens and legal immigrants and their families, these recent stories of criminal atrocities committed by illegal aliens show clearly that our immigration policies must be reexamined and revised. Judging from the correspondence I have received from my own constituents and from citizens all over this country, as a consequence of the package of bills I have introduced to address this problem, and based on the polls and surveys I have read taken among all representative groups throughout the United States, the American people are demanding action by the Congress and this Administration.

395.   Vincent Bonaventura. HOUSE HEARINGS, April 27, 1993, Y4J89/1:03/7, p. 262. The solution lies in prompt adjudication. If the problems at the airports stem from exploitation of asylum processing, then accelerate adjudications in ways that do not undermine existing protections for legitimate asylum-seekers. First, identify and summarily reject frivolous asylum claims. Second, remove the window of opportunity by eliminating the protracted delay between the time a person applies for asylum and the time INS (and EOIR) finally adjudicate a claim. Third, institute a reasonable and consistent detention and release policy that would detain only those cases where there is a threat to the public security or a high risk that the alien will abscond.

396.   Vincent Bonaventura. HOUSE HEARINGS, April 27, 1993, Y4J89/1:03/7. The picture, though serious, is not really so bleak. To begin with, asylum is not a security threat. The connection made between asylum and recent criminal acts is irrational and ungrounded. Also, while there are some serious problems with how asylum is now handled in this country, those problems are manageable when approached in a thoughtful and precise manner. If broken down into its respective components and properly analyzed and improved, the asylum program can be entirely workable and its shortcomings can be remedied.

397.   William Sposato. "FBI Ex-Chief Sees More Terrorism on US Soil." NEXUS, March 8, 1994. The February 26 1993 blast, which prosecutors called the worst terrorist attack on U.S. soil, killed six people and injured more than a thousand and caused millions of dollars' worth of damage.

Fox said the problem is U.S. immigration policy that allowed thousands of Muslim extremists into the country, including radical fundamentalist followers of Sheik Omar Abdel-Rahman, who preaches violent revolution in his native Egypt.

He criticized laws that have made it easy for anyone arriving in the United States to stay while seeking political asylum.

398.   Barbara Yarnold. REFUGEES WITHOUT REFUGE: FORMATION AND FAILED IMPLEMENTATION OF U.S. POLITICAL ASYLUM POLICY IN THE 1980'S, University Press: Lanham, Maryland, 1990, p. 14. The expansion of the President's role in refugee admissions through use of the parole authority coincided with a diminution in Congressional authority in this area. In 1975, Congress attempted to re-

assert itself. It brought refugees into the normal preference system (as seventh-preference aliens) and eliminated the "national origins" system. Simultaneously, a clear "double standard" appeared in U.S. refugee policy. While Cubans, for example, were freely allowed into the U.S., Haitians were turned away. Unlike Cubans, Haitians were not fleeing from a hostile regime, but from a dictatorship that maintained cordial relations with the U.S. (Loescher and Scanlon, 1986). The bias in favor of aliens fleeing from "hostile" countries was codified in the Immigration and Nationality Act of 1965 which specifically defines a "refugee" as one who is fleeing from a Communist country or a country in the Middle-East (Loescher and Scanlon, 1986).

399.   Deborah Sontag. "Mexico's Position on Aliens Contradicted by Past Deeds." NEW YORK TIMES, July 15, 1993, p. A18. Mexico has never signed the international treaty. And advocates for refugees charge that the Mexican Government, which has historically prided itself on an open-arms policy toward refugees, has recently treated many potential applicants for asylum, particularly Central Americans, summarily, even abusively.

Moreover, these advocates have been alarmed by the agreement between the United States and Mexico. "We have been paying—and continue to pay—for the deportations from a country that doesn't show any respect for the basic human rights of refugees," said Bill Frelick, senior policy analyst with the United States Committee for Refugees, an advocacy group based in Washington.

400.   Deborah Sontag. "Mexico's Position on Aliens Contradicted by Past Deeds." NEW YORK TIMES, July 15, 1993, p. A18. The quiet but rocky arrangement between the United States and Mexico was noisily thrust into the open in the last week. Mexican officials learned from American newspapers, rather than through diplomatic overtures, that the United States wanted them to accept and then deport 659 Chinese who had been intercepted at sea by the United States Coast Guard and escorted to within 60 miles of Ensenada.

It was a breach of protocol, and Mexican officials publicly took offense, defending their country's sovereignty.

"Of all the countries to ask to do this, Mexico must be the least appropriate," a senior Mexican Foreign Ministry official said. "I don't think it is Mexico's place, nor do I think anybody reasonably expects Mexico to become an arm of the U.S. immigration service."

401.   Deborah Sontag. "Mexico's Position on Aliens Contradicted by Past Deeds." NEW YORK TIMES, July 15, 1993, p. A18. Despite its recent declarations that Mexico will never act as an agent of American immigration policy, the Mexican Government has for years been quietly deported undocumented aliens heading to the United States.

For at least the last three years, Congress has appropriated $350,000 a year to pay Mexico for its costs in deporting residents of third countries passing through Mexico on the way to the United States.

CHAPTER III

TAKING CONTROL OF IMMIGRATION REGULATIONS

Resolved: That the United States government should substantially decrease immigration to the United States.

Immigration reform has for many years been a significant issue in some regional areas of the United States, such as the South and the West, and it promises to become a full-blown national issue soon. An August 9, 1993, poll conducted by *Newsweek* found that 60 percent of all Americans saw immigration as being too high. In areas such as California, where illegal immigration from Mexico is substantial, almost 90 percent of citizens describe illegal immigration as a moderate or major problem. Responding to public anger over illegal immigration, President Bill Clinton announced a tougher stand on immigration on July 27, 1993, when he said: "We must say no to illegal immigration so we can continue to say yes to legal immigration." While Clinton was delivering his address, someone thought they heard Attorney General Janet Reno mumble, "Give those people air."

Many people feel that immigration levels are too high and must be curtailed. Leon Bouvier, an adjunct professor of demography at the Tulane School of Public Health, projects that at least 15 million immigrants will arrive in the United States during the 1990s. According to Bouvier, this influx will continue unabated until at least the year 2020. There are a number of circumstances which influence migration. Some of them are "pull" factors—incentives available in America which lure foreigners to this country. These can include things such as the promise of employment, good working conditions, and freedom. Immigrants may also be influenced by reasons known as "push" factors—conditions in their home country which encourage them to leave. These can include poor living conditions, lack of social services, overcrowding, a poor economic climate, and political persecution.

It is generally assumed that immigration, especially illegal immigration, is out of control. However, there are several scholars who contend that immigration levels are not that significant. Statistics based on the number of people that the Border Patrol apprehends can be flawed, because many illegal aliens go into the United States for only a short time, usually to find seasonal employment. Many illegal aliens return to their families in their home country. In the near future, if the North American Free Trade Agreement (NAFTA) improves the economic situation in Mexico, fewer people there may want to leave.

There are several impact areas that debaters will discuss this year, and there is evidence in this chapter for the pros and cons on each of them. These include the economic, social, cultural, political, and environmental impacts of immigration.

Debaters will have to familiarize themselves with economic issues in order to competently discuss immigration reform. Opponents of liberal immigration policies contend that all forms of immigration have a negative economic effect on the United States. A recent study conducted by Rice University economics professor Donald L. Huddle found that even after taxes, immigrants will be a net cost of $668.5 billion over the decade. According to Huddle, illegal immigrants will cost U.S. taxpayers over $186 billion. Immigrants can consume vast amounts of social services: some obtain welfare; immigrant mothers obtain aid when they give birth to children in the United States; a U.S. Supreme Court decision has mandated that the children of illegal aliens must receive public education; many immigrants receive free health care by using the emergency services of hospitals; and society pays for the cost of incarceration when deviant aliens commit crimes. The impact of immigration is especially significant to local and state governments—they pick up most of the costs of immigration, while the federal government accrues many of the advantages of immigration, such as tax revenue.

One of the most repeated affirmative arguments is that immigrants compete with natives for jobs. This is especially true of disadvantaged minority groups, who must compete with illegal aliens for low-skilled jobs. Economist Vernon Briggs, Jr. of Cornell University has said that the lower end of the labor pool is victimized by immigration. John Tanton, the founder of the Federation for American Immigration Reform, has stated that vast pools of cheap immigrant labor have driven down wages in many U.S. metropolitan areas.

Proponents of immigration argue that immigrants do not cause unemployment. Kevin McCarthy and R. Burciaga Valdez of the RAND Corporation found that in California in the 1980s, the effect of immigrants on wages was insignificant. Further studies, such as the one conducted by Thomas Muller of the Urban Institute, have confirmed this. In fact, many economists feel that immigration is a boon to the American economy. Two of the most prominent advocates of this position are Julian L. Simon, a professor of business economics at the University of Maryland, and Ben Wattenberg, a scholar at the American Enterprise Institute. They believe that immigrants promote economic growth because they pay taxes, take jobs that Americans do not want, and start new businesses. They also feel that immigrants have the ingenuity and drive to tackle new challenges.

One of the major arguments in favor of immigration is that it helps to save the Social Security system. Many economists warn that the Social Security system will collapse under the weight of the baby boom generation. Since native birth rates are so low, future Social Security will have to be paid for through higher taxes or increased deficit spending, which risks financial ruin. New immigrants could provide the tax base necessary to avoid these hard choices. However, opponents of immigration rebut that immigrants will someday grow old, which means the problem is only postponed. Furthermore, many immigrants are now beginning to bring in their immediate families, including older parents, which places more burdens on American social services.

There are several social impacts to immigration. One of the most serious is the threat of increased crime. For the U.S. population as a whole, the incarceration rate in federal and state prisons is 233 per 100,000 persons. Among illegal aliens, the incarceration rate is three times the U.S. average. Since 1980 there has been a 600 percent increase in alien inmates. Many illegal aliens are involved in the drug trade, taking advantage of the porous border between the United States and Mexico to smuggle in drugs. Sometimes peddlers and drug rings make illegal aliens smuggle drugs in to America in return for "safe" passage across the border. A growing number of illegal aliens are being recruited by drug rings in this country to sell narcotics on the street.

Advocates of immigration contend that newcomers come to America looking for employment, not for something to steal. Economist Stephen Moore of the congressional Joint Economic Committee found that urban crime rates do not rise with the influx of illegal aliens. The 10 cities with the lowest rate of violent crime have the same percentage of foreigners as the 10 cities with the highest rate. All too often, immigrants are the victims, not the perpetrators, of crime. Civil rights activists fear that anti-immigrant rhetoric will only fuel hatred and distrust. They contend that the immigrant attacks by neo-fascists in Germany will be repeated in America if immigrants are blamed for society's social and economic ills.

Some people fear that immigrants will contribute to the spread of deadly diseases, such as AIDS. This was one of the reasons that Congress refused to allow some Haitian refugees into this country. AIDS can have profound social, economic, and political consequences, since its victims are the young, productive members of society. Some even fear that AIDS could mutate into an airborne virus, threatening millions. However, almost every health authority confirms that restrictions or bans on HIV-positive immigrants does nothing to actually slow the spread of the disease. If anything, such a policy heightens fear and misunderstanding about the disease, making attempts at health education more difficult.

There are also several cultural impacts to immigration reform. One of the fears of immigration opponents is that rapid demographic change will exacerbate ethnic tensions. Another concern is that immigrants will refuse or be unable to adapt to their new surroundings and be unable to assimilate into American culture. This could lead to calls for a Quebec-like separatism, or for more pressures for multicultural education in American schools. Opponents of immigration contend that this will endanger national unity, leading to a situation, such as the one described by Richard Lamm and Gary Imhoff, where "America's culture and national identity are threatened by massive levels of legal and illegal immigration."

Each wave of immigration has been accompanied by fears that the immigrants would not blend into American culture, say proponents of immigration, and each time the immigrants have gotten along well. Immigrants are predisposed to the American way of life—they come to this country because they are dissatisfied with where they are living. They also want to succeed economically in America. To do this, they and their families need to adopt the language and the culture of their new home. Although some first-generation immigrants are uncomfortable with English, their children usually learn it quickly and use it extensively, if not exclusively. As for ideas of separatism, most scholars familiar with immigrants say this is not a possibility. Most Hispanic groups, for example, denounce separatism.

Immigration creates a host of political concerns. With the recent bombing of the World Trade Center, one of the most publicized of these fears is terrorism. Some scholars believe that the lack of border enforcement makes it easy for terrorists to slip into the United States. Terrorism has always been a favorite impact scenario among debaters, especially the possibility of nuclear terrorism. Negative debaters are likely to contend that the reforms instituted after the World Trade Center bombing are enough to thwart terrorist attacks, and that the advantages of immigration outweigh the minuscule risk of terrorism.

The "brain drain" and "safety valve" arguments are likely to be popular affirmative case scenarios this year. This argument says that with immigration, dissatisfied citizens of a foreign country have an outlet for their frustrations. If they do not like their home country, they can leave and come to America. However, if they had stayed, they would have been the people encouraging economic reforms and leading political revolutions in their home country. Immigration thus indirectly encourages the continuation of the status quo. According to John Vinson, the president of the American Immigration Control Foundation, "By giving these foreigners an easy way out, we weaken reform efforts in other countries."

Proponents of immigration are not too concerned about this argument. The "brain drain" scenario assumes that these immigrants would foment political change in their home countries, which is not guaranteed. At least in America, they have the opportunity to develop their skills and talents. This benefits the U.S. economy, and an immigrant who reaches a position of authority here in the U.S. might stand a better chance of influencing and encouraging political change in their former country.

The realm of politics offers the negative some important disadvantages on the immigration topic. One of them is the "modeling" disadvantage. This argument states that other countries will copy our human rights and immigration policies. America is generally perceived as a "land of immigrants" and as a beacon of freedom to the oppressed peoples of the world. If the United States were to adopt restrictive immigration policies, there could be severe political consequences. Other countries might copy us and adopt similar laws, preventing refugees from entering their borders. Some countries might perceive America as hypocritical, and refuse to support our international humanitarian efforts.

Another disadvantage against restrictive immigration policies is the political damage such legislation would create for our relations with Mexico. The Mexican government might backlash against any attempts to police the border, and refuse to support the United States politically. This could mean an end to the NAFTA agreement, the discontinuation of drug enforcement, and so on.

Finally, there are environmental consequences of immigration. Immigration has been a major contributor to population growth in the United States. According to Leon Bouvier, the United States population could reach 333 million by 2020 and 388 million in 2050. About half of that population growth would be due to immigrants and their descendants who arrive after 1990. Once here, immigrants tend to have higher birth rates than natives. This is because immigrants tend to idealize the birth rates of their home country, which usually are higher than American birth rates.

High population growth in America is generally worse for the environment than the same amount of growth in developing countries, because Americans consume so many resources. Although immigrants are not likely to consume as much resources as natives, eventually their families will settle into American habits and customs, which need to be fueled by a lot of oil. At any rate, their resource consumption will be much higher than if they had stayed in their home country.

Immigration can also fuel Third World population growth. One of the reasons is that immigrants send some of their earnings back to families in their home countries, and this helps to support larger families. And, according to some scholars, liberal immigration policies help retard the acceptance of birth control, since the U.S. provides a safety valve for high population.

Immigration advocates contend that environmental problems are the result of a variety of factors, and cannot be blamed on immigration. Julian Simon in particular denounces the population argument against immigration. He states that natural resources are more plentiful now than they ever have been, and that immigration actually encourages the technical knowledge that helps to solve environmental problems.

The immigration topic offers debaters a multitude of advantages and disadvantages to choose from. The index of evidence and the cards in the following pages provide support for both sides of these issues. Debaters should be prepared to encounter any of them in a debate round, since most of them apply generically to all of the proposed solutions to the immigration problem.

CHAPTER III

OUTLINE

I. THE FEDERAL GOVERNMENT SHOULD SUBSTANTIALLY DECREASE IMMIGRATION TO THE UNITED STATES.

A. IMMIGRATION IS OUT OF CONTROL
1. Immigration is increasing. (1-4)
2. Millions enter illegally. (5-6)
3. U.S. being invaded by immigrants. (7-8)
4. Latino immigrants increasing. (9-10)
5. High immigration will persist. (11)
6. Many illegal aliens in California. (12-13)
7. Immigration higher than expected. (14-16)
8. Illegal aliens eventually get through. (17)
9. Only U.S. accepts such large numbers. (18)
10. Millions want to come. (19)
11. Millions will be added to U.S. population. (20-21)
12. Apprehensions are increasing. (22-23)
13. Border Patrol is outnumbered. (24-27)
14. High wages attract immigrants. (28)
15. Family reunification increases immigration. (29-30)
16. Poor Mexican economy spurs immigration. (31-36)
17. Overpopulation causes immigration. (37-45)
18. Economic problems lead to immigration (46-47)
19. Political strife increases immigration. (48-49)
20. Environmental problems cause immigration. (50)
21. Welfare benefits attract immigrants. (51)
22. Many factors contribute to immigration. (52-53)
23. Many ways to get in. (54-55)
24. Immigrants will not return to home countries. (56)
25. Legalizing aliens increases immigration. (57)

B. IMMIGRATION HURTS THE AMERICAN ECONOMY.
1. Most immigrants are unskilled. (58-62)
2. Immigrant skill level is declining. (63)
3. Most immigrants live in poverty. (64-66)
4. Immigrants consume social services. (67-72)
5. Immigration decreases wages. (73)
6. Entrenches underclass. (74-75)
7. Curbing immigration would save the U.S. billions. (76-83)
8. Immigrants do not pay much in taxes. (84-86)
9. Studies verify that aliens consume resources. (87-88)
10. Immigration causes fiscal disaster in some states. (89-95)
11. Immigration lowers the standard of living. (96)
12. Decreases economic productivity. (97)
13. Immigration encourages a low-wage economy. (98-100)
14. Low-wage economy cannot compete. (101-102)
15. Low-wage economy leads to protectionism. (103)
16. Protectionism causes world catastrophe. (104)
17. Labor shortage is a myth. (105-107)
18. Japan proves economic growth possible without immigration. (108)
19. U.S. growth declining despite immigration. (109)
20. Long-term negative forecasts unreliable. (110-111)
21. Immigration discourages skill training. (112)
22. Immigration trades off with other priorities. (113-114)
23. Immigration increases costs in many ways. (115-116)
24. Impact is national in scope. (117)

F. IMMIGRATION CAUSES UNEMPLOYMENT.
1. Immigrants compete with Americans for jobs. (118-122)
2. Immigrants depress wages. (123)
3. Unskilled immigrants compete with natives for jobs. (124-129)
4. Immigrants compete with African Americans for jobs. (130-138)
5. Immigrants hurt disadvantaged groups. (139)
6. New immigrants displace older immigrants. (140-141)
7. Immigration hurts American productivity. (142-146)
8. Studies prove immigration causes joblessness. (147-149)
9. Jobs would improve if no immigration. (150)
10. Garment industry remained low-tech because of immigrants. (151)
11. Immigration does not save jobs from imports. (152)
12. Negative unemployment data is deceptive. (153)
13. Immigrants hurt native employment opportunities. (154-156)
14. Immigration encourages worker exploitation by employers. (157-158)
15. Immigrant jobs are outmoded. (159)
16. Unemployment caused by immigrants leads to social breakdown. (160-162)

160

17. Cities with high immigration have high unemployment. (163)

D. IMMIGRANTS CONSUME WELFARE AND OTHER SOCIAL SERVICES
1. Immigrant welfare use is increasing. (164-167)
2. Immigrants use more welfare than natives. (168-170)
3. Welfare is a magnet that attracts immigrants. (171-173)
4. Immigrants are costly to social services. (174-175)
5. Immigrants abuse AFDC payments. (176-177)
6. RAND study proves drain on social services. (178)
7. Immigrants get welfare despite "fear of detection." (179)
8. Must set limits to welfare use. (180-181)
9. Immigrant welfare abuse threatens collapse of welfare system. (182)
10. Immigrants consume education budgets. (183-190)
11. Free education is a big draw for immigrants. (191)
12. Immigrants cause California education crisis. (192-193)
13. Immmigrants compete with natives for scarce education resources. (194-195)
14. Many immigrants are illiterate. (196-198)
15. Bilingual programs are expensive. (199-200)
16. Voters will backlash against education because of immigrants. (201)
17. U.S. educational system cannot accommodate illegal aliens. (202-206)
18. Immigrants consume health care budgets. (207-211)
19. Health care is a magnet for immigrants. (212-213) .
20. Illegal mothers give birth at U.S. taxpayer expense. (214-216)
21. Immigrants spread diseases. (217-220)

E. IMMIGRANTS ARE NOT NEEDED TO "SAVE" THE SOCIAL SECURITY SYSTEM.
1. No Social Security crisis—a growing economy will solve. (221-223)
2. Dependency ration will not be high. (224-225)
3. Elderly can work longer. (226)
4. Plenty of time to adjust. (227)
5. Immigration will not solve. (228)
6. Turn: immigration hurts economy, which hurts Social Security. (229-233)
7. Turn: immigration equals an older population. (234)
8. Turn: immigrants bring in older relatives. (235)
9. Turn: use of fake documents imperils Social Security system. (236)

10. Turn: immigrants will backlash against Social Security. (237)

F. IMMIGRATION DESTROYS THE ENVIRONMENT.
1. Immigrants increase U.S. population. (238-246)
2. Immigrants are key to U.S. population growth. (247-250)
3. Immigration makes U.S. population growth endless. (251-253)
4. Population models accurate. (254)
5. Census Bureau underestimates immigrant growth. (255)
6. Native fertility will remain low. (256-259)
7. Immigrant fertility rates are soaring. (260-265)
8. U.S. carrying capacity is exceeded. (266-267)
9. Figures underestimate impact of immigration. (268)
10. Slight increase in fertility equals massive population. (269)
11. U.S. population growth especially bad. (270-271)
12. Liberal immigration policy encourages Third World population growth. (272-275)
13. Immigration will not ease Third World overpopulation. (276)
14. Population growth threatens quality of life. (277-279)
15. Population growth causes worldwide suffering. (280-286)
16. Population crisis getting worse. (287-288)
17. Population growth causes global warming. (289-290)
18. High population decreases prosperity. (291)
19. Not immoral to decrease population. (292-293)
20. Population is the world's number one issue. (294-296)
21. Immigration control key to decreasing population. (297-298)

G. IMMIGRATION DESTROYS AMERICAN CULTURE.
1. Immigrants do not assimilate well into American society. (299-301)
2. Immigrants not encouraged to adopt American values. (302)
3. Immigration creates cultural conflicts. (303-305)
4. Assimilation only possible on small scale. (306)
5. U.S. becoming non-white too rapidly. (307-309)
6. Immigration causes social breakdown. (310-316)
7. Immigration leads to defiance against U.S. (317)

8. Immigration leads to separation. (318-320)
9. Immigration causes ethnic tensions. (321-323)
10. Diversity inhibits ability to control population growth. (324)
11. Immigration destroys American civilization. (325-327)
12. Cultural disunity leads to dictatorship. (328-330)
13. Leads to a feuding nation. (331)
14. Increases rich-poor gap. (332)

H. IMMIGRATION HAS NEGATIVE POLITICAL CONSEQUENCES.
1. Illegal immigration threatens legal immigration. (333-341)
2. Immigration prevents political reform abroad. (342-347)
3. Modeling is non-unique. (348)
4. Immigration decreases sovereignty. (349-350)
5. Immigration threatens democracy. (351-352)
6. Immigration is worst post-Cold War threat. (353)
7. Immigration encourages Mexican radicalism. (354)
8. Immigration encourages terrorism. (355-361)
9. Leads to foreign policy shift away from Europe/Israel. (362)
10. Decreases ability to aid Third World. (363)
11. Public wants restrictions on immigration. (364-369)
12. Immigration is a defining political issue. (370-374)

I. IMMIGRATION LEADS TO CRIME
1. Immigrants cause increased crime. (375-380)
2. U.S. is vulnerable to alien crime. (381-384)
3. Failure to assimilate leads to crime. (385)
4. Many aliens are violent, career criminals. (386-387)
5. Immigration leads to ethnic gangs. (388-393)
6. Immigration bolsters organized crime. (394)
7. Empirically, Cuban immigrants became criminals. (395-396)
8. Immigration causes riots. (397)
9. Many immigrants involved in Los Angeles riots. (398-400)
10. Illegal illiteracy fosters crime. (401)
11. Illegal youths commit crime. (402)
12. L.A. County study proves illegals are criminals. (403)
13. Aliens have higher incarceration rate. (404-408)
14. Alien criminals burden prison system. (409-414)

15. Money spent on alien crime diverted from other law enforcement. (415)
16. Illegal immigration encourages lawlessness. (416-421)
17. Immigration forces natives to commit crime. (422-423)
18. Immigration contributes to drug problem. (424-426)
19. Illegals smuggle drugs into America. (427-432)
20. Cocaine smuggled by aliens. (433)
21. Foreigners responsible for drug problem. (434-435)
22. Mexico is a major drug gateway. (436-437)

II. THE FEDERAL GOVERNMENT SHOULD NOT SUBSTANTIALLY DECREASE IMMIGRATION TO THE UNITED STATES.

A. IMMIGRATION IS NOT A CRISIS.
1. Historically, immigration at an all-time low. (438-439)
2. Immigration is not significant. (440-441)
3. Immigration is decreasing. (442-443)
4. Most immigrants do not travel to U.S. (444-445)
5. Net illegal immigration is zero. (446)
6. Mexicans only 25% of immigration (447)
7. White House estimate shows low immigration. (448)
8. Many immigrants go back. (449-450)
9. Immigration is sound policy. (451)
10. U.S. not overwhelmed by illegal immigration. (452)
11. Immigration low compared to past. (453)

B. IMMIGRATION BENEFITS THE U.S. ECONOMY.
1. Immigrants are skilled workers. (454-461)
2. Regardless of skill, immigrants benefit economy. (462)
3. Immigrants are hard-working, innovative. (463-469)
4. Immigration increases productivity. (470-475)
5. Immigrants pay more taxes than natives. (476-484)
6. Young immigrants productive. (485)
7. Immigration decreases the deficit. (486)
8. Immigrants not a drain on economy. (487-488)
9. Immigrants not poor. (489-491)
10. Immigrants educate themselves quickly. (492)
11. Immigrants take jobs natives won't. (493)
12. Empirically, immigration saves U.S. industry. (494-495)
13. Historically, immigrants benefit economy. (496)
14. Immigrants provide needed labor. (497-499)
15. Long term benefits outweigh. (500)

16. Immigrants increase wages. (501)
17. Economists agree immigration boosts economy. (502)
18. Americans starve without immigrants. (503)
19. Anti-immigrant arguments are racist. (504-506)
20. L.A. County study overstates cost. (507-509)
21. L.A. County study ignores benefits of immigration. (510-515)
22. L.A. County study actually proves immigration good. (516-517)
23. L.A. County study indicted by Urban Institute. (518-519)

C. IMMIGRATION DOES NOT CAUSE UNEMPLOYMENT.
1. Immigration does not cause unemployment. (520-524)
2. Immigrants create jobs. (525-532)
3. Immigrants increase native productivity. (533)
4. Immigrants push natives into better jobs. (534-535)
5. Immigrants do not depress wages. (536-541)
6. Immigrants do not displace low-skilled workers. (542-544)
7. Simon study shows no unemployment. (545)
8. Immigrants take undesirable jobs. (546-547)
9. Immigrants not an underclass. (548)
10. Immigrants pay taxes. (549)
11. Job creation offsets losses. (550-551)
12. No effect on native employment. (552-554)
13. Other factors cause unemployment. (555-557)
14. No studies prove unemployment. (558-560)
15. Discrimination against immigrants causes unemployment. (561)

D. IMMIGRANTS DO NOT ABUSE WELFARE AND SOCIAL SERVICE SYSTEMS.
1. Immigrants do not burden welfare system. (562-565)
2. Immigrants less dependent than natives. (566-569)
3. Welfare not a magnet. (570)
4. Immigrants are net gain to economy. (571)
5. Wages increase where immigrants settle. (572)
6. Immigrants use less welfare than refugees. (573)
7. Welfare costs decreasing. (574)
8. Mechanisms exist to thwart abuse. (575)
9. Immigrants will get less welfare in future. (576)

10. Immigrants pay for education, health care. (577)
11. Must provide education. (578-580)
12. All education is an investment. (581)
13. Immigrants do not abuse health care services. (582-584)
14. Immigrants are healthy—don't use much health care. (585)
15. Health care prevents diseases. (586-587)
16. Health care is an investment. (588)
17. Immigrants not an AIDS risk. (589)

E. IMMIGRATION SAVES THE SOCIAL SECURITY SYSTEM.
1. Social Security crisis looms. (590-593)
2. Baby boomers will be a burden. (594-597)
3. Promises will be curtailed. (598)
4. Financial disaster impends. (599-600)
5. Social Security problems cause racial tension. (601)
6. Social Security problems cause intergenerational conflict. (602-603)
7. Not enough natives to pay for Social Security. (604-605)
8. Immigrants do not use much Social Security. (606)
9. Immigrants save Social Security system. (607-614)
10. Immigration only way to cover for Social Security. (615-616)

F. IMMIGRATION DOES NOT HARM ENVIRONMENT.
1. Population decreasing despite immigration. (617-618)
2. Population is not a crisis. (619)
3. Immigrants not to blame for environmental harms. (620-622)
4. Immigrants help save the environment. (623)
5. Free market solves for environmental woes. (624-625)
6. Population models not accurate. (626)
7. Population increases wealth. (627-628)
8. Anti-immigrant population arguments encourage racism. (629)
9. Population control leads to eugenics. (630)

G. IMMIGRATION DOES NOT THREATEN AMERICAN CULTURE.
1. Immigrants assimilate well into American society. (631-633)
2. Immigrants want to join mainstream. (634)
3. Historically, immigrants adapt. (635)
4. Current immigrants are better than those in past. (636)
5. Immigrants are patriotic. (637)
6. No separatist threat. (638-639)
7. Immigrants want to learn English. (640-641)
8. Immigrants learn English quickly. (642-646)

9. Immigrant children adapt quickly. (647)
10. America needs diversity. (648)
11. Media exaggerates impacts. (649)
12. Anti-immigrant rhetoric is racist. (650-651)

H. IMMIGRATION DOES NOT CAUSE CRIME.
1. Immigrants not responsible for crime. (652)
2. Immigrants not responsible for riots. (653)
3. Anti-immigrant rhetoric leads to vigilante attacks. (654-657)
4. Drug enforcement not possible. (658)

CHAPTER III

EVIDENCE

1. Michael D'Antonio. "Apocalypse Soon." LOS ANGELES TIMES MAGAZINE, August 29, 1993, p. 20. The available statistics do suggest that immigration is on the rise worldwide. According to the U.S. Committee for Refugees, a private, nonpartisan organization the worldwide refugee population has climbed steadily, from fewer than 8 million in 1983 to more than 17.5 million today.

2. Rodman D. Griffen. "Illegal Immigration." CONGRESSIONAL QUARTERLY RESEARCHER, April 24, 1992, p. 374. Anxiety about the economy and illegal immigration has created a false perception that the United States is closing the door on immigrants. In fact, the 1990 Immigration Act expanded immigration by 40 percent above previous levels, already the most generous in the world.

3. Daniel James. "Bar the Door." NEW YORK TIMES, July 25, 1992, p. 21. By Sept. 30, well over one million people will have crossed the Mexican border into the U.S. illegally in the past 12 months. Illegal aliens, mainly from Mexico and Central America, have arrived at the same rate annually since 1989, the Immigration and Naturalization Service says—and the trend is upward.

4. Leon F. Bouvier. PEACEFUL INVASIONS: IMMIGRATION AND CHANGING AMERICA, 1992, p. 31. Demographers Long and McMillen, analyzing Census statistics and critiquing the Census Bureau's projections, estimate that "actual levels of [illegal immigration] may have been such that total net immigration is closer to 750,000." Another study has calculated that legal immigration alone may reach 900,000 by 1995. These two estimates were based on the pre-1990 immigration law. The GAO estimates an increase of about 200,000 in annual legal immigration after passage of the 1990 legislation.

5. Senator Barbara Boxer. CONGRESSIONAL RECORD, October 15, 1993, p. S13540. Just look at the statistics. Every night of the week, the San Diego Border Patrol unit apprehends up to 2,000 illegal immigrants, and an estimated 3 million people illegally cross the United States-Mexico border each year. Between 200,000 and 300,000 of these entrants become permanent inhabitants. By some estimates, California is home to approximately 1.3 million illegal immigrants, more than 50 percent of all the undocumented immigrants living in America.

6. Ken Silverstein. "The Labor Debate." SCHOLASTIC UPDATE, November 19, 1993, p. 16. An estimated 1 million immigrants became legal citizens last year. But hundreds of thousands more secretly crossed the border—joining some 3 million "illegals" already living here.

7. William F. Jasper. "Illegal Immigration Is a Crisis." IMMIGRATION: OPPOSING VIEWPOINTS, 1990, p. 158. Invasion. That's what we are witnessing: an ongoing invasion that has been escalating for over a decade. Each day, at hundreds of points along our southern border, thousands of people from countries all over the world are entering the United States illegally. Most will enter along the U.S.-Mexican border. Some will be smuggled across in secret compartments in some of the thousands of vehicles that cross the border each day. Others will enter using forged documents. Still others will fly into this country on student or tourist visas and never leave. The vast majority, however, will simply walk in, wade in, or float in. Their chances of escaping apprehension are quite good. The U.S. Border Patrol is, in some cases, too short on men and resources even to give chase.

8. William F. Jasper. "Illegal Immigration Is a Crisis." IMMIGRATION: OPPOSING VIEWPOINTS, 1990, p. 159. Even if we go with the most conservative estimates of "only" three to six million, we're still talking about an invasion in numbers potentially greater than the total manpower of the Soviet armed forces (5.9 million) and greater than the population count of most of our individual states.

9. Fernando Torres-Gil. "Separating Myth From Reality." THE CALIFORNIA-MEXICO CONNECTION, 1993, p. 165. During the 1980s, Latinos increased their share of California's population by 69.2 percent. According to the 1990 census, nearly one-third of southern California's population and one-fourth of the state's population comprises Latinos. Although precise immigration figures from Mexico and Latin America are unavailable, estimates show that more than half of the people moving to California are from other countries, and Mexico is the largest single source. California and Los Angeles have become the new Ellis Island, replacing New York City as the primary destination of immigrants and refugees.

10. Daniel James. ILLEGAL IMMIGRATION: AN UNFOLDING CRISIS, 1991, p. 8. The problem will probably become acute in the remaining years of this century and first years of the next, for the trend is toward a decided increase in the flow of Mexicans into this country illegally. Three million or more illegals, the great majority of them Mexicans, are expected to enter during the 1990s—and that is a conservative estimate, since more than one million of them were apprehended in 1990 alone. A still larger number of Mexicans is likely to cross the border illegally between 2000 and 2010.

11. Daniel James. ILLEGAL IMMIGRATION: AN UNFOLDING CRISIS, 1991, p. 47. Most immigration experts seem to agree that the trend is to-

ward higher immigration, in general, overwhelmingly from Mexico but also from Central America, and that it will persist throughout the rest of the century. Sidney Weintraub, who is well known for his sympathetic attitude toward Mexico's problems, particularly immigration, collaborated with Chandler Stolp in a study which "sought to project Mexican economic migration to the United States to the year 2000." They concluded that "...it would be unwise to anticipate an easing of immigration pressure over this period regardless of the international economic setting." [ellipses in original]

12.   John Tanton and Wayne Lutton. "Welfare Costs For Immigrants." THE SOCIAL CONTRACT, Fall 1992, p. 10. The state experienced an estimated net increase of 1 million illegal aliens during the 1980s. Of that figure, 85 percent of them are Hispanic; another 10 percent are Asian. For scale: combining these three numbers comes to 2.8 million, or more than ten percent of California's 1980 population of 24 million.

13.   Dianne Feinstein. "We Can Get a Grip on Our Borders." LOS ANGELES TIMES, June 16, 1993, p. A11. In Los Angeles County alone, there are an estimated 700,000 illegal residents. Added to this the fact that 3,000 to 5,000 people attempt to cross the Mexico-California border each night—and at least half of them succeed.

14.   Barry Edmonston. "Discussion." DEMOGRAPHY AND RETIREMENT, 1993, p. 61. Immigration has been somewhat higher than current projections assume. Over 2 million aliens were legalized under the general amnesty conditions of the 1986 Immigration Reform and Control Act (IRCA). In addition, about a million and a half aliens sought legalization under the provisions of IRCA concerning special agricultural workers. Our research at the Urban Institute suggests that slightly over one million of those applying as agricultural workers will eventually be granted legal residence. Finally, the recently enacted Immigration Act of 1990 provided legal residence, under special conditions, for about one-half million refugees residing in the United States.

15.   Bob Sutcliffe. "Immigration and the World Economy." CREATING A NEW WORLD ECONOMY, 1993, p. 105. The demand of people from the Third World to migrate to developed countries is immense and growing. And, on present trends, it will grow even faster. It is so strong that many people are prepared to take incredible risks in order to cross borders illegally.

16.   Barry Edmonston. "Discussion." DEMOGRAPHY AND RETIREMENT, 1993, p. 61. In the last year, however, there appears to be a turnaround in the flow of illegal immigrants and it now appears uncertain whether IRCA will achieve its principal goal of stopping the entry of undocumented immigration. Illegal immigrant flows are apparently back to the levels that were witnessed in the mid-1980s, during the years before the enactment of IRCA.

17.   Richard Rothstein. "Immigration Dilemmas." DISSENT, Fall 1993, p. 455. We now have over three thousand federal agents patrolling two thousand miles of the U.S.-Mexican land border, also with little success. Last year, the border patrol intercepted 1.2 million would-be immigrants from Mexico, but since there is no point to incarcerating them (or jail space to do so), nearly all are sent back to try again; 100,000 to 600,000 a year evade capture. So if the intercepted ones keep trying, the odds are increasingly in their favor.

18.   Leon F. Bouvier. PEACEFUL INVASIONS: IMMIGRATION AND CHANGING AMERICA, 1992, p. 2. The United States accepted more than 9 million immigrants during the 1980s. In contrast to its major European and Asian trading partners, the United States is the only major nation accepting large numbers of newcomers.

19.   Leon F. Bouvier. PEACEFUL INVASIONS: IMMIGRATION AND CHANGING AMERICA, 1992, p. 46. If a recent poll of residents of Mexico taken by the *Los Angeles Times* is any indicator, that number could be large. More than 4.7 million Mexican citizens believe they are very likely to move north in the next year; 1.3 million would go to California. Much of this is "wishful thinking" on the part of the respondents. Yet, it serves as an indicator of the strong desire on the part of millions of people to emigrate to the United States.

20.   John Vinson. IMMIGRATION OUT OF CONTROL, 1992, p. 29. If the current rate of immigration continues, adding between 1.2 and 1.6 million permanent residents a year, the United States will add almost 100 million people to its current population of approximately 250 million within the next 50 years.

21.   Daniel James. "Bar the Door." NEW YORK TIMES, July 25, 1992, p. 21. A Tulane University demographer, Leon Bouvier, projects that at least 15 million immigrants, including illegals, will arrive during the 1990's. The influx, he projects, will continue unabated until at least the year 2020. Thus we can expect perhaps 30 million or more newcomers in the first two decades of the 21st century. That will make the immigration wave, which began in 1965, the longest and biggest ever, adding 61 million people to the population.

22.   Rodman D. Griffen. "Illegal Immigration." CONGRESSIONAL QUARTERLY RESEARCHER, April 24, 1992, p. 363. The number of people caught at the U.S.-Mexican border dropped sharply from 1986 to 1989, after IRCA legalized more than 3 million aliens already living here. But apprehensions have increased dramatically in the past two years. More than 1 million people were intercepted last year, and apprehensions were up 15 percent in the first quarter of this year, leading many observers to claim, once again, that our borders are out of control.

23.   Daniel James. "Bar the Door." NEW YORK TIMES, July 25, 1992, p. 21. Up to five mil-

lion people are living in the U.S. without legal immigration papers. About 700,000 immigrants enter each year legally.

24.   Senator Barbara Boxer. CONGRESSIONAL RECORD, October 15, 1993, p. S13540. We know that our Border Patrol officers are spread too thin. In California, we only have 200 Border Patrol agents patrolling the 200-mile border at any given time. As of September 18, nationally we had 3,993 Border Patrol officers; 1,247 of these officers were assigned to California.

25.   Daniel James. ILLEGAL IMMIGRATION: AN UNFOLDING CRISIS, 1991, pp. 64-65. But there are only 3,857 Border Patrol personnel, out of a grand total of 4,324, who are assigned to patrol the 9 Southwest sectors along 2,000 miles of border and they must cope with an upsurge in illegal crossings into the United States estimated at 3 to 5 million—some Border Patrol agents put the total at 10 million—annually. In fact, the Border Patrol has 9 percent fewer agents than it did in 1988, according to a GAO study dated March 1991. And of those assigned to the Southwest border only 800 are on duty at any one time.

26.   Daniel James. ILLEGAL IMMIGRATION: AN UNFOLDING CRISIS, 1991, p. 65. "Further, the proportion of total Border Patrol agent time devoted to border control activities decreased from 71 percent to 60 percent from 1986 to 1990," continues the GAO study. Yet alien apprehensions, the GAO found, "were 23 percent higher than in fiscal year 1989." The skimpy Border Patrol is far outnumbered by the aliens who attempt to steal across the Río Grande daily.

27.   Phil Sudo. "The Golden Door." SCHOLASTIC UPDATE, November 19, 1993, p. 3. Fueled by a concern that the country is stretched beyond its capacity to assimilate more newcomers, Americans are asking some fundamental questions about immigration. Even people who are pro-immigration agree that this nation has lost control of its borders, that it no longer knows how many immigrants are entering the country. U.S. immigration policy is in disarray, and some states like California and New York find their social services overburdened.

28.   David W. Stewart. IMMIGRATION AND EDUCATION, 1993, p. 15. These immigrants, often motivated by imported television programs showing a way of life that they perceive will never be possible in their homeland, seek economic opportunity in the United States. If they tend to enter life at the bottom in the United States, even this is generally superior to what they left behind. The economy in Southern California, for example, produces wages that are five to ten times what can be expected almost anywhere below the Rio Grande.

29.   Tom Morgenthau. "America: Still a Melting Pot?" NEWSWEEK, August 9, 1993, p. 21. Kinship to U.S. citizens, known as the "family-reunifi-

cation policy," has become the overwhelming favorite of visa seekers and the primary reason the pattern of immigration has shifted so hugely to the Third World. It was never intended to be: given the fact that most immigration to the United States had always been from Europe, those who voted for the act of 1965 generally assumed that family-reunification visas would be used by Europeans.

30.   David W. Stewart. IMMIGRATION AND EDUCATION, 1993, p. 15. In the absence of restrictive immigration policies that are enforced, massive immigration flows are inevitable to the wealthy United States from countries where poverty levels are very high. Once the flow begins from almost any nation, it is sure to increase as first-comers establish themselves and family reunification provisions of current immigration law take effect.

31.   Leon F. Bouvier. PEACEFUL INVASIONS: IMMIGRATION AND CHANGING AMERICA, 1992, p. 49. In the absence of major and unforeseen social and economic changes, conditions in Mexico point to heavy incentives for migration northward: a dizzying growth in the younger population most prone to migration; the availability of jobs to only half to three-quarters of those entering the labor force, and the declining economic appeal of available jobs compared to possible alternatives in the United States as the peso's value continues to fall. "An appreciation of the social nature of immigration...suggests that Mexican migration to the United States will persist and that it will be more difficult and costly to control than many Americans believe." [ellipses in original]

32.   Daniel James. ILLEGAL IMMIGRATION: AN UNFOLDING CRISIS, 1991, p. 116. The major factor that sustains illegal migration will continue to be Mexico's population growth—despite a lower rate than a decade ago—and the even more rapid expansion of its working age population. The "pull" factor of jobs in the United States is basically secondary; what is primary is the "push" of poverty and massive unemployment/underemployment in Mexico that drives people north regardless of the availability of jobs in the United States.

33.   Daniel James. ILLEGAL IMMIGRATION: AN UNFOLDING CRISIS, 1991, p. 117. Mexico's economy shows signs of improvement after a decade of crisis, but it has not risen much above the level of stagnation caused by the crisis. Although economic growth rates are positive, they are only slightly above the population rate of increase. Worst of all, the reduction by about half in the standard of living that the average Mexican enjoyed in 1982, when the crisis broke out, has not been restored.

34.   Rodman D. Griffen. "Illegal Immigration." CONGRESSIONAL QUARTERLY RESEARCHER, April 24, 1992, p. 373. Furthermore, the underlying economic reasons for the immigration flow have not changed on either side of the border. In Mexico,

inflation has dropped sharply, and economic growth is up to 4 percent a year after nearly a decade of crisis. Yet 44 million Mexicans still qualify as impoverished, underemployment stands at 40 percent and real wages are at about what they were in 1980.

35. Leon F. Bouvier. PEACEFUL INVASIONS: IMMIGRATION AND CHANGING AMERICA, 1992, p. 49. To some degree, Mexican migration has acquired a dynamic of its own. Yet long term migration pressures will depend greatly on the health of the Mexican economy, as well as the quality of Mexico's political life and its success in improving the distribution of income.

36. Daniel James. ILLEGAL IMMIGRATION: AN UNFOLDING CRISIS, 1991, p. 47. Weintraub, using projections made by the Mexican Government's Department of Programming and Budget, calculated that Mexico's economically active population by the year 2000 would total between 35 and 40 million. It presently stands at about 30 million. He doubts seriously that Mexico can supply jobs for an estimated "oversupply" of 5.6 million or more workers. The pressure to emigrate to El Norte, he again concludes, "is unlikely to abate for at least the rest of this century."

37. Michael D'Antonio. "Apocalypse Soon." LOS ANGELES TIMES MAGAZINE, August 29, 1993, p. 20. Dan Stein, director of FAIR, the Federation for American Immigration Reform, says that overpopulation in the developing world "will lead to explosive immigration pressure between now and the year 2020." Stein is especially critical of immigration regulations that have led to a steady increase in the numbers of immigrants since 1965. "A huge wave of immigration is going on now," he notes, "a wave that appears to have no end."

38. Michael D'Antonio. "Apocalypse Soon." LOS ANGELES TIMES MAGAZINE, August 29, 1993, p. 20. "Today, Mexico is producing on the order of 2 million or 3 million people a year that try and get into the United States," [Henry] Kendall [MIT physics professor] says. "Mexico's growth rate, while it's not out of control, is still pretty damn large. They are going from 88 million people now to 125 million people in about 15 years. Mexico's got deep pollution and environmental problems. Their agricultural base is not in great shape. With all that, there will be at least a doubling of the flow [of illegal immigrants] in five or 10 years."

39. Leon F. Bouvier. PEACEFUL INVASIONS: IMMIGRATION AND CHANGING AMERICA, 1992, p. 44. Given this high fertility, developing countries have young populations with a tremendous momentum for growth. Even though fertility levels are falling in some places, many developing countries could double their populations over the next 30 to 50 years. Nigeria is expected to grow from 115 million to 274 million between 1990 and 2020. Iran could increase from 54 to 130 million. Egypt could grow to 103 million

from 55 million today. And so the story goes in developing country after developing country.

40. Leon F. Bouvier. PEACEFUL INVASIONS: IMMIGRATION AND CHANGING AMERICA, 1992, p. 43. The enormous potential for future immigration to the United States is directly related to the demographic situation in the Third World. Rapid population growth in developing countries will play an important role in determining how many people will want to enter the United States in future years.

41. Leon F. Bouvier. PEACEFUL INVASIONS: IMMIGRATION AND CHANGING AMERICA, 1992, pp. 48-49. As Mexico moves into the nineties the number of new entrants into the workforce each year will grow to more than 900,000 and surpass 1 million by the end of the century. The nation's labor force will have risen from 14 million in 1970 to 40 million in 2000, an increase of 180 percent! After the turn of the century, the labor force will continue to grow by more than one million a year until 2010 when the changing age distribution resulting from lower fertility will lower the pace of growth.

42. Leon F. Bouvier. PEACEFUL INVASIONS: IMMIGRATION AND CHANGING AMERICA, 1992, p. 47. Dramatic increases in the number and proportion of children and young adults are the first shock waves of a population explosion that began some two decades earlier. Their impact will be felt for years to come. Even with sharply reduced fertility, the *number* of Mexican births will rise simply because the *number* of women of reproductive age will be larger.

43. David W. Stewart. IMMIGRATION AND EDUCATION, 1993, p. 14. Mexico, its extreme poverty fueled by overpopulation, is filled with desperate would-be immigrants. The same conditions exist in Haiti and in many other poor nations in Central and South America, Asia, and Africa. Jobs for the rapidly increasing numbers of young people in these nations are in very short supply—a serious problem given their rapid rates of population expansion. Dr. Antonio Golini, a demographer at Rome's Institute of Population Research, estimates that the eligible labor force in less developed countries will grow by 733 million in the next twenty years, fifteen times more than in developed countries.

44. Hobart Rowen. "Overpopulation Remains World's Defining Crisis." WASHINGTON POST, April 4, 1993, p. H5. The population trap arising from fertility rates in Mexico will keep illegal migration to the United States high, no matter what NAFTA does to boost economic growth in Mexico.

45. Leon F. Bouvier. PEACEFUL INVASIONS: IMMIGRATION AND CHANGING AMERICA, 1992, p.45. The number of young adults is disproportionately large in most developing countries because of previous high fertility and declining child mortality. That generation not only produces more babies. That

generation looks for employment. That generation is restless and easily moved to violence in the absence of any improvement in quality of life. That generation is increasingly aware of the "good life" elsewhere. That generation is most likely to cross international borders looking for a share in that "good life."

46.   George J. Borjas. FRIENDS OR
       STRANGERS: THE IMPACT OF IMMI-
GRANTS ON THE U.S. ECONOMY, 1990, p. 22.
Nevertheless, the United States can influence economic conditions abroad through such economic policies as import restrictions, foreign aid, and debt repayment subsidies, as well as through its participation in the programs of the World Bank and the International Monetary Fund. These economic policies, which are often ignored in discussions of immigration policy, partly determine the attractiveness of America's offer in the immigration market and the role immigrants play in the United States.

47.   Leon F. Bouvier. PEACEFUL INVASIONS:
       IMMIGRATION AND CHANGING AMER-
ICA, 1992, pp. 49-50. The situation in Mexico appears grim. Yet the same trends are underway for a host of other countries which are traditional sources of migration to the United States: Philippines, Jamaica, El Salvador, Dominican Republic, and so on. Strong pressure for emigration is gradually building up in these developing countries. Other such countries are also experiencing the same kind of demographic and economic problems with a resulting emigration to western European countries as well as to Canada, Australia, and the United States.

48.   Barry Edmonston. "Discussion."
       DEMOGRAPHY AND RETIREMENT, 1993,
p. 63. Second, we can anticipate that the U.S. population will experience at least one major refugee flow during the next decade or so. Although one cannot name the country, the United States experienced four or five major refugee flows during the past forty years. It is likely therefore that one major country in the world will witness major civil violence that provokes widespread refugee movements to the United States. This will markedly affect the numbers of immigrants to the United States.

49.   David W. Stewart. IMMIGRATION AND
       EDUCATION, 1993, pp. 14-15. Unrest stemming from political, ethnic, or religious strife is the second major immigration trigger. Many persons have arrived as refugees from such war-wracked nations as Vietnam, Afghanistan, and Ethiopia. Still others are fleeing the ethnic and religious hatreds of the Middle East and eastern Europe. An estimated 25 percent of the entire population of the war-torn and desperately poor Central American nation of El Salvador has immigrated to the United States, Canada, Mexico, or other Central American countries.

50.   Michael D'Antonio. "Apocalypse Soon." LOS
       ANGELES TIMES MAGAZINE, August 29,
1993, p. 20. Political chaos and environmental problems also have made life so hard that tens of thousands have tried to emigrate to the United States. Many have lost their lives making the passage to Florida in small boats. Others have tried to use official channels, applying for admittance as political refugees. According to the U.S. Immigration and Naturalization Service, more than 35,000 Haitians sought asylum in the United States in just the last six months of 1992.

51.   Representative Gallegly, Fact Sheet on Illegal
       Immigration, April 9, 1993, quoted in CON-
GRESSIONAL RECORD, July 1, 1993, H4437. As ABC-TV's "20/20" documented in early 1992, a growing part of the illegal alien problem stems from pregnant women coming to the U.S. solely to give birth here, which automatically makes the child of an illegal alien a U.S. citizen. These children are eligible for a full array of welfare benefits, and when he or she turns 21, he or she can petition to bring his or her entire family to the U.S. as legal residents.

52.   Leon F. Bouvier. PEACEFUL INVASIONS:
       IMMIGRATION AND CHANGING AMER-
ICA, 1992, p. 49. The heavy migration from Mexico since the 1970s may be only the leading edge of a far larger wave of migrants who will sojourn or settle in the United States over the next few decades. Many of the demographic, social, and economic factors driving this wave are already at work. Major lures are the presence in the United States of large Mexican communities, village and ethnic networks to provide jobs and support to the migrants, and certain American industries that have accepted dependence on Mexican workers.

53.   Susan Forbes Martin. "U.S. Immigration
       Policy: Challenges for the 1990s." NATIONAL
STRATEGY REPORTER, Fall 1993, p. 5. The technological revolution continues to make the world a smaller place. With an expanding global communications infrastructure—including telephones, fax machines, computer networks, and enhanced transportation systems—movement is encouraged. The result has been increased migration throughout the world.

54.   Bill Turque, et. al. "Why Our Borders Are Out
       of Control." NEWSWEEK, August 9, 1993,
p. 25. While the United States seeks new ways to thwart gate-crashers, about half of all illegal immigrants walk unchallenged through the front door. Fraudulent passports and visas, questionable claims of asylum and bureaucratic bungling, help tens of thousands reach American soil and stay indefinitely.

55.   Virginia D. Abernethy. POPULATION
       POLITICS, 1993, p. 263. Airports are points
of illegal entry second only to the land border with Mexico. The number caught at U.S. airports with fraudulent or no papers doubled, to 43,580, between fiscal years 1987 and 1990. The San Diego airport was a favored port of entry until a detention center was enlarged so that would-be immigrants without papers could be held pending a hearing. New York City's Kennedy Airport (JFK) replaced San Diego as the place to walk off a plane into

the United States when word got around that its detention center had space for just 190 detainees.

56.   Tracy Wilkinson. "Will Democracy's Growth Stanch Migrant Flow, Even Prompt a Return?" LOS ANGELES TIMES, October 18, 1993, p. A11. Where there is some measure of stability and greater chance for economic recovery, there is less reason for citizens to stay away. But where unrest and poverty are overwhelming, or where the changes seem more fleeting than permanent, there is little incentive to return.

57.   Daniel James. ILLEGAL IMMIGRATION: AN UNFOLDING CRISIS, 1991, p. 103. Legalizing more illegals will hardly contribute to resolving or even alleviating the basic problem of how to stem the flow of those who cross the border daily. Nor does it address the more vexing problem that follows illegal migration: How to enable the assimilatory process to absorb new millions of immigrants when there is no "time-out," no interregnum? Above all, the legalization of successive waves of illegal immigrants would amount to a *rolling amnesty*, as it were; it would represent an open invitation to endless millions of persons to cross the border at will, in the secure knowledge that eventually America would legalize their status. Obviously, this would vastly expand the indigestible mass of illegals in our midst and ultimately lead to an untenable situation.

58.   Donald Huddle and David Simcox. "Red Ink from Abroad." THE WORLD AND I, January 1994, p. 383. Once heralded as a font of vitality and enrichment, since 1970 immigration has increasingly meant mass importation of the poor and unskilled. The cost of public assistance and services to immigrants has skyrocketed as immigration has swelled in the last twenty years. By 1990 new legal immigrants were twice as likely as the native-born to be below the government-designated poverty level.

59.   George J. Borjas. FRIENDS OR STRANGERS: THE IMPACT OF IMMIGRANTS ON THE U.S. ECONOMY, 1990, pp. 18-19. The essence of the empirical evidence summarized here is that because of changes in U.S. immigration policy and because of changing economic and political conditions both here and abroad, the United States is currently attracting relatively unskilled immigrants. For the most part, these immigrants have little chance of attaining economic parity with natives during their lifetimes. Although these immigrants do not greatly affect the earnings and employment opportunities of natives, they may have an even greater long-run economic impact because of their relatively high poverty rates and propensities for participation in the welfare system and because national income and tax revenues are substantially lower than they would have been in the United States had attracted a more skilled immigrant flow. In short, the United States is losing the international competition for skilled workers to other host countries such as Australia and Canada, and this fact imposes costs on the American economy.

60.   Donald Huddle and David Simcox. "Red Ink from Abroad." THE WORLD AND I, January 1994, p. 393. While earnings for some may increase with longer experience in the United States, many of the current wave of newcomers, lacking even a high school education, will be unlikely to escape low-wage, unstable, dead-end jobs. The dilemma for U. S. fiscal policy is that immigration brings in successively larger waves of low-skilled people faster than earlier waves can acclimate and improve their earnings.

61.   George J. Borjas. FRIENDS OR STRANGERS: THE IMPACT OF IMMIGRANTS ON THE U.S. ECONOMY, 1990, pp. 20-21. The fact that the new immigrants are less skilled than the old is responsible for a significant reduction in the potential national income of the United States. If the persons who migrated between 1975 and 1979 had been as skilled as those who came in the early 1960s, national income would be at least $6 billion higher in every single year of the immigrants' working life. The accumulation of these losses over time, combined with the continuing entry of unskilled immigrant flows, implies that the long-run reduction in national income and the corresponding losses in tax revenues may be substantial. There are large economic costs associated with America's poor performance in the immigration market.

62.   Peter Brimelow. Response to Simon, Borjas, Wattenberg, Stein, and Bartley. NATIONAL REVIEW, February 1, 1993, p. 34. Just as economic growth is caused by ideas, not raw labor, so U.S. preeminence in the world is based on the quality, not the quantity, of its population. Unskilled immigration can't help much. And, by causing economic distortion and social stress, it may actually hurt.

63.   George J. Borjas. FRIENDS OR STRANGERS: THE IMPACT OF IMMIGRANTS ON THE U.S. ECONOMY, 1990, p. 20. The skills of immigrants entering the United States have declined during the past few decades. More recent immigrant waves have relatively less schooling, lower earnings, lower labor force participation rates, and higher poverty rates than earlier waves had at similar stages of their assimilation into the country. Therefore, the nature of the skill sorting generated by the immigration market has deteriorated substantially in recent years.

64.   Donald L. Huddle. "A Growing Burden." NEW YORK TIMES, September 3, 1993, p. A23. According to 1990 Census data, the poverty rate of immigrants is 42.8 percent higher than that of the native-born. On average, immigrant households receive 44.2 percent more public assistance dollars than do native households.

65.   Daniel James. ILLEGAL IMMIGRATION: AN UNFOLDING CRISIS, 1991, p. 42. Confirming these experiences, Lief Jensen found in 1988 that the foreign born, according to U.S. Census data, were 56 percent more likely than natives to be in poverty, 25

percent more likely to receive public assistance and to have an average per capita income from public assistance 13.6 percent higher than natives.

66.   Donald Huddle and David Simcox. "Red Ink from Abroad." THE WORLD AND I, January 1994, p. 381. Immigration, once heralded as a font of vitality and enrichment, since 1970 has increasingly meant mass importation of the poor and unskilled. by 1990, new legal immigrants were twice as likely to be below the U.S. government's poverty level as were the native-born.

67.   Representative Gallegly, Fact Sheet on Illegal Immigration, April 9, 1993, quoted in CONGRESSIONAL RECORD, July 1, 1993, p. H4436. Nationwide, the Center for Immigration Studies estimates that illegal aliens cost the taxpayers this year more than $6 billion in direct benefits, a total that excludes social Security, Medicare, food stamps and unemployment compensation, or the extra costs for police, fire, courts, parks and transportation services.

68.   Virginia D. Abernethy. POPULATION POLITICS, 1993, pp. 237-238. An unintentionally favored category of illegal immigrants is women who give birth in the United States. Their children, automatically U.S. citizens, cannot be deported, and reluctance to separate families effectively means that the mother gets to stay, too. As citizens, the children are entitled to AFDC payments. The 1991 bill for this category of recipients was $125 million in Los Angeles County alone. Indeed, children born to women who are in the United States illegally account for 25 percent of the welfare caseload in California. And California accounts for 26 percent of welfare payments in the United States.

69.   Annelise Anderson. "What Should Our Immigration Policy Be?" THE WORLD AND I, January 1994, p. 367. The state of California has estimated that illegal immigrants and their children, who are citizens if born in the United States, cost the state $2.9 billion a year. Most of the expense is probably for education, although health care may also loom large; the figure includes welfare and law enforcement as well.

70.   Dianne Feinstein. CONGRESSIONAL RECORD, June 30, 1993, S8277. Last year, the State and localities of California spent $1.7 billion to pay for the educational, medical, and correctional costs associated with undocumented persons.

71.   John Tanton and Wayne Lutton. "Welfare Costs For Immigrants." THE SOCIAL CONTRACT, Fall 1992, p. 10. One-third of all refugees admitted by the U.S. settle in California. Of all refugees, 90 percent begin receiving public aid within the first four months of their residency.

72.   Virginia D. Abernethy. POPULATION POLITICS, 1993, p. 237. Wherever concentrations of immigrants—most of whom are designated minorities—are found, significant public monies are used or requested for services. In St. Paul, Minnesota, for example, members of the Hmong tribe from Southeast Asia take up a significant portion of public housing, police time (on account of wife abuse), and educational funds. In Montgomery County, North Carolina, 25 percent of the health department's 6,000-person caseload can be traced to Mexicans.

73.   Virginia D. Abernethy. POPULATION POLITICS, 1993, pp. 215-216. The impact is still more sever in the high-school-dropout sector, where immigration and the trade imbalance together raised the 1988 effective supply of labor by 28 percent for men and 31 percent for women. The large labor supply, these economists say, is sufficient to account for up to half of the 10-percentage-point decline in the relative weekly wage of unskilled labor.

74.   Leon F. Bouvier. PEACEFUL INVASIONS: IMMIGRATION AND CHANGING AMERICA, 1992, p. 3. The availability of immigrants keeps private business from experimenting with effective ways to integrate the underclass into the work force. Employers who depend on immigrants have been much less innovative in finding new workers or new ways to get work done. Instead of permitting such employers to maintain the status quo, a tight labor market in the 1990s may provide a unique opportunity for private businesses to help lift people out of poverty and into the mainstream of American society.

75.   Leon F. Bouvier. PEACEFUL INVASIONS: IMMIGRATION AND CHANGING AMERICA, 1992, pp. 2-3. First, the presence of newcomers in large numbers makes it impossible to deal with America's indigenous poor in compassionate and effective ways. The United States has a large, and growing, number of people, especially in the inner cities, with weak ties to the labor market but strong links to welfare programs, crime, and drugs. There are also significant numbers of immigrants in many of these cities. These immigrants gain a foothold in the labor market and then they preserve the status quo because they do not complain about inferior wages or working conditions. As long as eager immigrants are available, private employers are not going to make the difficult and costly adjustments needed to employ the American underclass. Instead, they continue to operate their sweatshops and complain about the unwillingness of Americans with welfare and other options to be enthusiastic seamstresses or hotel maids alongside the immigrants.

76.   Donald L. Huddle. "A Growing Burden." NEW YORK TIMES, September 3, 1993, p. A23. And these costs are projected to rise, assuming that laws and their enforcement don't change. Our estimate is that 11.1 million immigrants, legal and illegal, will enter the country in the next decade. The bill for supporting all immigrants and the American workers they displace for those 10 years will total $951.7 billion. We estimated that the immigrants will pay $283.2 billion in taxes.

Thus there will be a net cost to U.S. taxpayers of $668.5 billion over the decade. Legal immigrants will account for almost three-quarters of the total cost; illegal aliens will account for $186.4 billion.

77.   Donald L. Huddle. "A Growing Burden." NEW YORK TIMES, September 3, 1993, p. A23. Curbing illegal immigration could save $186 billion by 2002. Stricter control of the border, enforcement of sanctions against employers who hire illegals and better programs to screen immigrant welfare applications could help stem the flow.

78.   Virginia D. Abernethy. POPULATION POLITICS, 1993, p. 236. U.S. Rep. Elton Gallegly (R-Calif.) states that in 1990, Los Angeles County spent $276.7 million in services to *illegal* aliens—representing a 34 percent increase from the previous year. Statewide, Gov. Pete Wilson's preliminary estimate was that immigration—illegal, legal, and refugees—accounted for $1 billion of California's projected $13 billion 1991-1992 budget deficit.

79.   Mary H. Cooper. "Immigration Reform." CONGRESSIONAL QUARTERLY RESEARCHER, September 24, 1993, pp. 846-847. On the national level, the most widely cited study of the problem concluded that the 19.3 million immigrants who have settled in the United States since 1970 have received a total of $22.3 billion more in public services than they have paid in taxes. The study's author, Donald Huddle, an economics professor at Rice University, predicts that those costs will skyrocket with the expected arrival of 11.1 million new legal and illegal immigrants over the next 10 years. He estimates that taxpayers would save $22 billion each year over the decade if immigration were halted.

80.   John Vinson. IMMIGRATION OUT OF CONTROL, 1992, p. 26. And through a series of administrative rulings and court decisions, illegal immigrants are entitled to benefits and services. According to a 1991 CIS study, these payments amount to a minimum of $4.6 billion a year. But when all factors, such as costs from the displacement of American workers (in welfare and unemployment benefits), are added in, the annual burden may be as high as $35 billion.

81.   Donald Huddle and David Simcox. "Red Ink from Abroad." THE WORLD AND I, January 1994, p. 393. By putting an end to the public assistance, education, and displacement costs of just the illegal immigrants, the public would save $186 billion by 2002.

82.   Donald Huddle and David Simcox. "Red Ink from Abroad." THE WORLD AND I, January 1994, p. 393. No major legislative changes are needed, however to be more vigilant toward illegal immigration and more prudent in making humanitarian admissions. Such measures alone could reduce costs by scores of billions between now and 2002.

83.   Monique Miller. Letter. WASHINGTON POST, January 13, 1994, p. A26. While reforming the welfare system to reduce certain entitlements available to immigrants already in this country would save money, by far the greatest costs (a projected $668.5 billion net, after subtracting taxes that immigrants pay) and potential savings to the taxpayer are related to the 11.1 million legal and illegal immigrants projected to enter the United States during the next 10 years under current immigration policy.

84.   Daniel James. ILLEGAL IMMIGRATION: AN UNFOLDING CRISIS, 1991, p. 43. It is argued, by those who believe that illegal immigration carries little or no cost to the U.S. taxpayer, that illegals pay the taxes that fund the costs of public services to them. A major study in 1985 of Mexican aliens in Southern California, many of them illegal, analyzed extensively their contributions in state and local taxes and compared them to the total costs of state and local services they obtained. The study, done by Thomas Muller and Thomas J. Espenshade, found that Mexican immigrant households received $2,200 more in state and local services, including education, than they paid in taxes.

85.   Daniel James. ILLEGAL IMMIGRATION: AN UNFOLDING CRISIS, 1991, p. 43. Further, the indications are that tax compliance among illegals is lower than for the general population. North and Houston's 1976 survey of illegal alien workers shows that 22.7 percent of them did not have Social Security taxes withheld, 26.8 percent did not have federal income tax withheld, and 68.5 percent did not file federal income tax returns.

86.   Daniel James. ILLEGAL IMMIGRATION: AN UNFOLDING CRISIS, 1991, p. 43. Given the poor economic circumstances of illegal aliens generally, it is hard to see how their taxpaying ability could match, much less exceed the costs of services rendered to them. A person's capacity to pay taxes depends ultimately on his earnings ability. Illegal aliens are concentrated in low-wage, unstable occupations and tend to work fewer hours a year than the population as a whole. Obviously, low wages mean a low state and local income tax liability.

87.   John Tanton and Wayne Lutton. "Welfare Costs For Immigrants." THE SOCIAL CONTRACT, Fall 1992, p.11. Richard Dixon, chief Administrative Officer for Los Angeles County, issued a report on April 22, 1991, outlining the impact that illegal immigration is having in their jurisdiction. Said Dixon, "The Federal government's inability to control our nation's borders has resulted in an ever growing impact on the County; the estimated net cost to the County of services provided to undocumented aliens has grown from $207.2 million in 1989-90 to $276.2 million in 1990-91."

88.   Virginia D. Abernethy. POPULATION POLITICS, 1993, p. 236. A subsequent report on illegal immigration (Rea and Parker, 1992) prepared for the California Auditor General's office estimates that

undocumented immigrants residing in San Diego County in 1992 accounted for 9 percent of the total population and a vastly greater percentage of the county's health, justice system, education, and welfare costs. "Using the San Diego data, the Auditor General extrapolated that illegal aliens statewide generate a net cost to state and local governments of 'approximately $3 billion' per year" (Walters, 1992).

89.   Harold Gilliam. "Bursting At The Seams." THE SOCIAL CONTRACT, Summer 1993, p. 263. As a result of immigration, the state's population has been increasing at the rate of 700,000 a year, equivalent to 10 more San Franciscoes every decade. This is one of the biggest migrations in history, and if it continues, the state is likely to go broke and suffer a steadily declining standard of living.

90.   John Tanton and Wayne Lutton. "Welfare Costs For Immigrants." THE SOCIAL CONTRACT, Fall 1992, p. 10. California faces a $14 billion state budget deficit as the costs of education, medical care, welfare, and crime escalate. Governor Pete Wilson has pointed out that each category has been significantly inflated by the heavy flow of immigrants—both legal and illegal—into the state. Speaking of the state's recent immigrants, Wilson said, "We have consumers of expensive services, and they continue to grow.... There is a limit to our ability to absorb immigrant populations."

91.   Frank Padavan. Letter. NEW YORK TIMES, January 26, 1994, p. A14. More than 20 percent of all immigrants in the United States reside in New York State. That share should rise. Nearly 100,000 immigrants, including 45,000 who are undocumented, come to this state annually. While meeting the needs of legal immigrants is difficult because of meager Federal support, providing services for an illegal alien population estimated at 490,000, for whom the Federal Government provides virtually no reimbursement, is Herculean.

92.   Susan Forbes Martin. "U.S. Immigration Policy: Challenges for the 1990s." NATIONAL STRATEGY REPORTER, Fall 1993, p. 5. States with large concentrations of foreign born feel overly burdened by federal immigration policies mandated without accompanying federal support. 78% of the foreign born live in five states: California, New York, Hawaii, Florida, and New Jersey. California, with 22% of its residents among the foreign born, feels particularly overwhelmed by the costs of services mandated by federal law.

93.   Annelise Anderson. "What Should Our Immigration Policy Be?" THE WORLD AND I, January 1994, p. 367. Despite long-term benefits, the short-term costs of immigrants—for example, of illegal immigrants who get emergency medical services, including hospitalization for childbirth, and of those operating with fraudulent documents—have hit some states particularly hard. Six states—California, New York, Texas, Florida, Illinois, and New Jersey—are home to 60-70

percent of immigrants, legal and probably illegal as well. These states are big, with about 40 percent of the U.S. population but are disproportionately hard hit by expenses for education and medical care.

94.   Michael D. Weiss. "Sisyphean Policy: Borders and Bureaucracies." THE WORLD AND I, January 1994, p. 376. The federal government has retained exclusive power over immigration, deportation, customs, and international relations. It is, however, insulated from the results of its failure because most of the social programs that illegal immigrants place demands on, such as schools, welfare, jails, public hospitals, and emergency medical care, are financed at the state, county, or city level.

95.   Rodman D. Griffen. "Illegal Immigration." CONGRESSIONAL QUARTERLY RESEARCHER, April 24, 1992, p. 365. In Los Angeles County, illegal immigrants—mostly from Mexico—generated almost $3 billion in assorted tax revenues during 1990-91, according to a recent study. But the bulk of those funds—$1.7 billion—went to Washington in the form of income tax and Social Security levies. Related county costs—mostly in health and child care, jails and other justice-type expenses associated with the immigrant population—outpaced local tax inputs by nearly 3 to 1.

96.   Michael D'Antonio. "Apocalypse Soon." LOS ANGELES TIMES MAGAZINE, August 29, 1993, p. 20. In recent years, immigrants have settled mainly in California, Texas, Illinois, New York and Florida. In certain locales, "schools are already overcrowded, and there's increased demand for social services" Stein says. By expanding the labor pool, immigrants also push down wages, he says. "If you don't intervene, the pressure won't stop until the standard of living here equals Bangladesh."

97.   John Vinson. IMMIGRATION OUT OF CONTROL, 1992, p. 24. Among the other economic costs: availability of cheap immigrant labor weakens the incentive of business to automate and develop other labor-saving technology—a real liability as we face competition from countries like Japan. Also, without cheap labor, marginal businesses dependent on these workers would fold and free up capital for more productive enterprises.

98.   Leon F. Bouvier. PEACEFUL INVASIONS: IMMIGRATION AND CHANGING AMERICA, 1992, p. 60. Second, the availability of many unskilled immigrants encourages low-wage and low-tech industries to expand, when the United States should be developing a high-tech economy to compete in the global marketplace. The major challenge posed by labor market trends is a looming mismatch between workers and jobs: tomorrow's work force will be more disadvantaged, but new jobs will require workers to have more skills. To avoid a labor market nightmare of workers not qualified for the jobs that are available, the United States should increase its investment in education and training

its citizens and reduce admissions of immigrant workers who face difficulty in succeeding in an ever-more sophisticated economy.

99.　　Rodman D. Griffen. "Illegal Immigration." CONGRESSIONAL QUARTERLY RESEARCHER, April 24, 1992, p. 365. The larger issue concerns how undocumented workers affect the structure of the economy—making it more service-oriented and labor-intensive. Illegal immigration has almost certainly postponed greater mechanization, particularly in agriculture and manufacturing, which may be essential for U.S. industries if they are to compete in the global economy.

100.　　Lawrence Harrison. "Those Huddled Unskilled Masses." THE SOCIAL CONTRACT, Summer 1992, pp. 222-223. In fact, the United States now emphasizes relatively cheap labor—a good part of it available because of immigration—much as Third World countries do. Aside from the retreat from the objective of a rising standard of living implicit in it, cheap labor encourages investors to use labor-intensive means of production, and that means slow or no technological advance and further slippage in our competitive position. The resulting slow overall growth of the economy has meant lower federal, state and local revenues.

101.　　Leon F. Bouvier. PEACEFUL INVASIONS: IMMIGRATION AND CHANGING AMERICA, 1992, p. 3. Although large numbers of unskilled immigrants may help American businesses to hold down wages and thus prices in order to remain competitive, a low-wage and low-price strategy cannot succeed in the global economy. Developing countries are becoming more adept at producing goods, such as garments and agricultural products, that are currently made in the United States by immigrant workers. Consequently, even wages which are low by United States standards are not low enough to compete with Chinese seamstresses or Chilean farm workers.

102.　　Lawrence Harrison. "Those Huddled Unskilled Masses." THE SOCIAL CONTRACT, Summer 1992, p. 222. The loss of competitive advantage of many U.S. products in recent decades is importantly the consequence of the slow growth of labor productivity. This is partly the result of low levels of U.S. research, development and investment compared with our principal competitors, Japan and Germany. But it is also the consequence of a labor force relatively unskilled by comparison with Japan's and Germany's—a labor force whose real income has been declining while the incomes of Japanese and German workers have been increasing. American wages are no longer the highest in the world.

103.　　Leon F. Bouvier. PEACEFUL INVASIONS: IMMIGRATION AND CHANGING AMERICA, 1992, p. 3. Industries which rely on immigrant workers are often slow to innovate, and when developing countries ship similar products produced at even lower wages to the United States, these American businesses often turn protectionist. The result is familiar. The American industry which "needed" immigrant workers to

survive and ensure, for example, that grapes do not cost $2 per pound soon complains that cheaper foreign grapes threaten the survival of the American grape industry and asks for restrictions on imports. This in turn drives up consumer prices.

104.　　Leonard Silk. "Head Off a Trade War." NEW YORK TIMES, February 4, 1993, p. A23. Expansion by the industrial countries is crucial to nourish growth in the rest of the world—and provide markets and resources to prevent the economic and political disasters threatening the third world and ex-Soviet empire. Flirting with protectionism is flirting with a world catastrophe.

105.　　Virginia D. Abernethy. POPULATION POLITICS, 1993, p. 218. No economic consideration justifies present U.S. immigration policy. America is not now, and never since the closing of the frontier has been, threatened by insufficient labor. Labor shortage is a myth promulgated by those who want fresh immigration as a source of cheap labor, as a way to consolidate political power by increasing the representation of their ethnic group, or out of a misguided humanitarian motive. Labor shortage is simply a convenient assertion. In fact, not even skilled labor is in short supply.

106.　　Virginia D. Abernethy. POPULATION POLITICS, 1993, pp. 214-215. Begin, however, with a fact: We live in a world of too much labor. The world's working-age population is expected to grow by 700 million persons during the 1990s, creating a need for 400 million new jobs. The United States cannot change that reality, but it can mitigate the effect at home. Rapid growth in the U.S. labor force is a principal factor that keeps real wages from rising. The result—many Americans unable to make a living wage—left two-thirds of the middle class worse off at the end of the 1980s than when the decade began, and America's poor stymied before getting a foot on the first rung of the employment ladder.

107.　　Michael S. Teitelbaum. "New Polemics on Immigration." THE SOCIAL CONTRACT, Spring 1992, p. 182. While the advocates assert that there are (or soon will be) significant 'labor shortages,' labor economists overwhelmingly reject such claims. They point not to overall 'shortages' of workers but to mismatches between the skills needed by some growing occupations and the outputs of the troubled U.S. education system, coupled with unwillingness by some employers to offer market wages and benefits to would-be American employees.

108.　　Peter Brimelow. "Time to Rethink Immigration?" NATIONAL REVIEW, June 22, 1992, p. 39. Despite its population of only 125 million and virtually no immigration at all, Japan has grown into the second-largest economy on earth. the Japanese seem to have been able to substitute capital for labor, in the shape of factory robots. And they have apparently steadily reconfigured their economy, concentrating on high value-added production, exporting low-skilled jobs

to factories in nearby cheap-labor countries rather than importing the low-skilled labor to Japan.

109.   Lawrence Harrison. "Those Huddled Unskilled Masses." THE SOCIAL CONTRACT, Summer 1992, p. 222. High levels of immigration, legal and illegal, have not produced the positive economic results that growth-minded advocates have expected. For four decades, we have accepted vastly more immigrants than any other advanced country. Yet despite the big start the U.S. economy enjoyed after World War II, our average performance measured over the last 40 years has been among the worst of the developed nations, roughly comparable to Britain's.

110.   Leon F. Bouvier. PEACEFUL INVASIONS: IMMIGRATION AND CHANGING AMER-ICA, 1992, p. 31. Long-term trends could be called "scenario builders." These describe a future that could be a plausible outcome of current trends, but not the only possible outcome. Their value lies in alerting policy makers to what might happen, but the other side of the same coin is the high degree of uncertainty attached to the outcomes they foresee. They are especially vulnerable because of the requirement that they make assumptions that hold over a long period of time: for if there is one universal in projections, it is the constancy of change—underlying trends will change, usually in unforeseen ways.

111.   Michael J. Piore. "Give Me Your Skilled." (Review of *The Economic Consequences of Immigration* by Julian L. Simon) NEW LEADER, May 14, 1990, p. 27. The difficulty comes with the second generation. Children of the newcomers inevitably develop a native perspective on the labor market, and tend to reject the menial jobs held by their parents. In their quest for upward mobility the either edge native minority-group members out of higher status job slots, or else join the growing pool of the discontented trapped in urban ghettos, unable to meet their aspirations and disappointed in the American dream.

112.   Vernon M. Briggs. "Political Confrontation with Economic Reality: Mass Immigration in the Postindustrial Age," in ELEPHANTS IN THE VOLKSWAGEN, 1992, p. 83. As to immigration, the current pattern of mass immigration of primarily unskilled people is a direct threat to the nation's well-being. We do require the immigration of certain skills and professional expertise, but not in such numbers as to discourage our national effort to produce professionals and skilled workers in those categories.

113.   Donald Huddle and David Simcox. "Red Ink from Abroad." THE WORLD AND I, January 1994, p. 392. Clearly, the current and prospective costs of education and public assistance for immigrants and those they displace is a massive diversion of public resources from alternative investments with greater potential return. Hardest hit by the state and local shares of these costs are California, New York, Texas, Florida,

New Jersey, and Illinois, where nearly 80 percent of immigrants settle.

114.   Donald Huddle and David Simcox. "Red Ink from Abroad." THE WORLD AND I, January 1994, p. 392. To put these costs in perspective here are some possible alternative public uses of the $668.5 billion that immigration will cost in the next ten years:
• The Clinton administration's five-year deficit-reduction target of $496 billion could be more than met.
• Complete coverage of premiums under President Clinton's health plan could be provided for 12.2 million low-income American families for ten years.
• Some 2.7 million public works and service jobs could be created and maintained over a decade with the expenditures projected to 2002.
• If the projected outlays were used as tax credits for business investment, more than 7.6 million private-sector jobs could be created and maintained.

115.   Donald Huddle and David Simcox. "Red Ink from Abroad." THE WORLD AND I, January 1994, p. 391. Environmental costs that accompany population growth, such as for compliance with clean air and cleanwater acts, preservation of wetlands, and toxic waste disposal. One example of such costs is the uncompensated environmental and resource costs of operating motor vehicles. The projected driving costs for all legal and illegal immigrants for the next ten years, which are not included in this study, total $144.7 billion in 1993 dollars.

116.   Donald Huddle and David Simcox. "Red Ink from Abroad." THE WORLD AND I, January 1994, p. 391. While the federal government contributes only $200 million to bilingual education's nearly $3.5 billion total cost, federal proposals to increase spending on bilingual programs and English as a second language could mandate significantly more spending on those programs by state and local education agencies. The White House has gotten congressional assent to expand earned-income tax credit subsidies to additional low-income households, which would carry a total cost to the Treasury of nearly $30 billion a year in tax expenditures and cash grants by the end of the decade, nearly $2 billion of which would go to immigrants.

117.   Barbara McCarthy. "Memo from the San Diego Border." THE SOCIAL CONTRACT, Spring 1993, p. 176. It is geography, of course, that causes California to bear a disproportionate share of these costs. Yet, to a lesser extent, every part of the country is affected. The impact of uncontrolled illegal immigration falls on other border states, especially Texas. Florida has its own problems, and such cities as Detroit, Chicago, Denver and Kansas City have experienced problems with illegal alien activity and the high costs involved. When the federal government picks up any of these bills, it is felt by all of the taxpayers.

118.   John Vinson. IMMIGRATION OUT OF CONTROL, 1992, p. 23. Many immigrants compete with disadvantaged Americans for these jobs.

This compounds the problems of "tired, huddled, masses" of underclass citizens in our cities. And because of the extra competition for jobs, employers can afford to cut back on wages and working conditions.

119. Arturio Santamaria Gomez. "The Porous U.S.-Mexico Border." THE NATION, October 25, 1993, p. 460. Today, with U.S. unemployment hovering officially around 7 percent (and in reality much higher), the hiring of undocumented immigrants continues unabated. It has actually increased in sectors such as agriculture, construction, domestic service, small industry and food service. In addition, in cities like New York and Los Angeles, a large part of the informal economy is made up of undocumented immigrants.

120. Daniel James. ILLEGAL IMMIGRATION: AN UNFOLDING CRISIS, 1991, p. 49. In agriculture, the continued availability of new immigrant workers weakens the demand for domestic workers and established immigrants. Farm workers outnumber available jobs by nearly two to one. Some farmers hire as many as ten times the number of workers needed, simply to maintain one complete harvest crew.

121. Leon F. Bouvier. PEACEFUL INVASIONS: IMMIGRATION AND CHANGING AMERICA, 1992, p. 80. Case studies of such immigration networks demonstrate how quickly certain jobs become the property of immigrants. In Los Angeles, many of the unionized Black janitors who once cleaned high-rise office buildings were displaced by Mexican immigrants over a five-year period in the early 1980s. This displacement occurred quickly and indirectly: according to a GAO report, the number of unionized Black janitors in Los Angeles county fell from 2,500 in 1977 to 600 in 1985, even though janitorial employment rose 50 percent because of a building boom. The reason for this displacement of unionized Black janitors in an expanding service industry is that competing janitorial services which employed recent immigrants offered to clean buildings for 25 to 35 percent less because they paid their immigrant workers up to two-thirds less than prevailing union wages.

122. Leon F. Bouvier. PEACEFUL INVASIONS: IMMIGRATION AND CHANGING AMERICA, 1992, p. 77. However, immigration policies are not generally connected to employment policies: the United States recently legalized 3 million immigrants who, on average, had less than a high school education while at the same time a series of reports sounded the alarm that, within a decade, the number of jobs for persons with less than a high school education will shrink.

123. Daniel James. ILLEGAL IMMIGRATION: AN UNFOLDING CRISIS, 1991, p. 48. Studies show that the unchecked growth of illegal immigration into the United States could threaten the equilibrium of the labor market in certain major urban areas. The presence in any area of substantial numbers of illegals is usually accompanied by depressed wages, particularly in the vicinity of the border. They are willing and able to

work for the minimum wage or less, and since they fear detection by the authorities they are unlikely to blow the whistle on unscrupulous employers who refuse to pay more. They have a competitive edge over U.S. or legal foreign workers because, in many cases, they are unmarried or have dependents in Mexico who support costs and expectations are lower.

124. Vernon M. Briggs. "Political Confrontation with Economic Reality: Mass Immigration in the Postindustrial Age," in ELEPHANTS IN THE VOLKSWAGEN, 1992, p. 81. The postindustrial economy of the United States is facing the real prospect of serious shortages of qualified labor. It does not have a shortage of actual or potential workers: No advanced industrial nation that has twenty-three million illiterate adults (some say the figure is now twenty-seven million) and another forty million adults who are marginally literate need have any fear about a shortage of unskilled workers in its foreseeable future.

125. Susan Forbes Martin. "U.S. Immigration Policy: Challenges for the 1990s." NATIONAL STRATEGY REPORTER, Fall 1993, p. 4. Other economists argue, however, that immigrants displace US workers, particularly those with equivalent skills or training. They believe that immigrant workers depress wages and undermine working conditions. They also argue that disadvantaged minorities in the United States are particularly hurt by the continuing entry of immigrants who compete with them for scarce jobs.

126. Leon F. Bouvier. PEACEFUL INVASIONS: IMMIGRATION AND CHANGING AMERICA, 1992, p. 103. Suppose net immigration rises to 1.5 million annually, a level higher than the almost one million per year of the 1980s but still a lower immigrant proportion of the population than the United States had in the early 1900s. At such high immigration levels, the labor force would jump from 127 million in 1990 to 175 million in 2020 and 218 million in 2050. If the immigrant composition is unchanged, most of the almost 100 million new workers added over the next two generations would be unskilled immigrants.

127. Leon F. Bouvier. PEACEFUL INVASIONS: IMMIGRATION AND CHANGING AMERICA, 1992, p. 82. Furthermore, international competition and seasonality cause periodic layoffs, contributing to unemployment and pleas for tariffs and quotas against imports. Unskilled immigrants often want to escape from such jobs and industries, but many are trapped by their lack of English and other skills. If technological breakthroughs, international competition, or a recession lead to widespread layoffs, these unskilled immigrant workers may find few opportunities for upward mobility or even lateral transitions. They risk becoming a lost generation which is used to squeeze a few extra years of production and profits from declining sectors until imports, technology, or changing consumer tastes finally eliminate their jobs.

128.	Leon F. Bouvier. PEACEFUL INVASIONS: IMMIGRATION AND CHANGING AMERICA, 1992, p. 83. The expansion of the low-tech economy because immigrant workers are available makes the United States vulnerable to twin mismatches: the mismatch which occurs when immigrant workers are displaced from low-tech jobs and cannot find re-employment in the shrinking low-tech economy, and the mismatch which results from the preference of expanding businesses for unskilled immigrants rather than disadvantaged American workers. Both mismatches threaten to frustrate a generation of immigrant and disadvantaged American workers and aggravate the problem or retraining them to avoid a widening skills gap in the twenty-first century.

129.	Vernon M. Briggs. "Political Confrontation with Economic Reality: Mass Immigration in the Postindustrial Age." in ELEPHANTS IN THE VOLKSWAGEN, 1992, p. 81. The vast preponderance of the illegal immigrants and refugees of the 1980s have had very few skills, little formal education, and limited (if any) literacy in English.

130.	Frank Morris. "Re: Legal Immigration Reform." THE SOCIAL CONTRACT, Summer 1991, p. 189. There is little basis for repeated assurances that African-Americans have not been harmed by heavy immigration of the less-skilled during the past two decades. Many of the immigrants compete directly with blacks in the same labor markets and occupations, and have become substitutes for black workers more often than they have become complements.

131.	Frank Morris. "Re: Legal Immigration Reform." THE SOCIAL CONTRACT, Summer 1991, p. 188. This remarkable growth of the immigrant population is most intense in areas where African-Americans have a major presence and have important interests. Much of the increase in the foreign-born population is concentrated in relatively few major metropolitan areas where sizable African-American populations now reside. A quarter of the growth of the nation's labor force now comes from immigration, while immigrants' share of the public school population has increased even more rapidly.

132.	Mary H. Cooper. "Immigration Reform." CONGRESSIONAL QUARTERLY RESEARCHER, September 24, 1993, p. 848. In the opinion of Briggs, however, immigration's effect on employment is profound, especially for low-skilled black Americans, many of whom live in the same urban areas as recent immigrants. (See map, p. 844.) "The labor-force participation rate [the employment rate] for black youths in New York City is almost 40 points off the national average," he says. "I think it's basically because of direct competition with illegal immigrants for entry-level jobs."

133.	Otis Graham, Jr. and Roy Beck. "Immigration's Impact on Inner City Blacks." THE SOCIAL CONTRACT, Summer 1992, p. 215. Adding insult to the black L.A. residents is that they must contend not only with traditional white racism but with intense discrimination through what Philip Martin of the University of California at Davis calls ethnic networking. Recent immigrants achieve positions of authority within a business and begin to recruit relatives, friends and acquaintances from their country of origin. Wages and working conditions stagnate or decline in the firm.

134.	Frank Morris. "Re: Legal Immigration Reform." THE SOCIAL CONTRACT, Summer 1991, p. 189. Studies claiming to show insignificant change in rates of African-American unemployment or labor force participation fail to take into account employment opportunities closed to black Americans who might otherwise migrate to metropolitan labor markets increasingly impacted by immigration.

135.	Frank Morris. "Re: Legal Immigration Reform." THE SOCIAL CONTRACT, Summer 1991, p. 189. The pervasive effects of ethnic-network recruiting and the spread of non-English languages in the workplace has, in effect, locked many blacks out of occupations where they once predominated. Heavy immigration is affecting the mobility of black workers and altering migration patterns within the United States. The rate of African-American migration to Los Angeles and other major urban areas in California has slowed markedly in the past two decades.

136.	Mary H. Cooper. "Immigration Reform." CONGRESSIONAL QUARTERLY RESEARCHER, September 24, 1993, p. 844. Some labor experts decry immigration's impact on job opportunities for native-born Americans, especially black Americans, who tend to live in the same urban areas as most recent immigrants—areas hard hit by unemployment. "I feel deeply that we may not be able to help the black population very much through public policy," says Vernon Briggs, a labor economist at Cornell University, "but we certainly shouldn't have policies that hurt them. I think current immigration policy is really hurtful in terms of competition for available dollars in urban areas, for education, housing, human services and access to jobs—especially entry-level jobs."

137.	Frank Morris. "Re: Legal Immigration Reform." THE SOCIAL CONTRACT, Summer 1991, p. 189. About half of last year's nearly 900,000 legal and illegal immigrants, refugees, asylees and parolees can be expected to enter the labor market. Some 40 to 45 percent of them will settle in six major metropolitan statistical areas (MSAs): New York, Los Angeles, Miami, Chicago, Houston and San Francisco-Oakland. Some 5.6 million black Americans, nearly one-fifth of the nation's black population, now live and work in those six MSAs. Perhaps millions more would consider migrating to those cities from high unemployment areas if the job prospects for black Americans were brighter.

138.	Frank Morris. "Re: Legal Immigration Reform." THE SOCIAL CONTRACT, Sum-

mer 1991, p. 189. Many of the 1989 immigrants, like those in earlier years of the decade, will be forced by their limited skills to seek employment in occupations in which African-Americans are already over-represented: building services and maintenance, construction, apparel- and other light manufacturing, non-professional health care jobs, and hotel and restaurant work. African-Americans in these occupations understandably would be particularly skeptical about claims of "labor shortages." These fields of work are among those where the stagnation of real wages for the less skilled is greatest, where unemployment is significantly higher than the national average, and where the period of unemployment after displacement or layoff tends to be longer than normal.

139. Vernon M. Briggs. "Political Confrontation with Economic Reality: Mass Immigration in the Postindustrial Age." in ELEPHANTS IN THE VOLKSWAGEN, 1992, p. 81. Unfortunately, many of the nation's citizens who are in the underclass are also in these same employment sectors. A disproportionately high number of these citizens are minorities, women, and youth. As these citizen groups are growing in both absolute numbers and percentages, the logic of national survival would say that they should have the first claim on the nation's available jobs. The last thing they need is more competition from immigrants for the limited number of existing jobs and for the scarce opportunities for training and education.

140. George J. Borjas. FRIENDS OR STRANGERS: THE IMPACT OF IMMIGRANTS ON THE U.S. ECONOMY, 1990, p. 19. Immigrants do, however, have a significant effect on the earnings and employment opportunities of foreign-born persons already residing in the United States. A 10-percent increase in the number of immigrants decreases the wage of foreign-born persons by at least 2 percent.

141. Virginia D. Abernethy. POPULATION POLITICS, 1993, pp. 216-217. Earlier immigrants also lose, even when an influx is their own ethnic group. Estrada (1990) attributes unemployment among established Hispanics to new arrivals who undercut wages, that is, will work for less and with fewer benefits. He writes, "Whatever the impact on other segments of society, there can be little doubt that the massive influx into the Hispanic community since the late 1960s has undermined U.S. Hispanics in the labor market, as well as in access to social services and affordable housing."

142. Leon F. Bouvier. PEACEFUL INVASIONS: IMMIGRATION AND CHANGING AMERICA, 1992, p. 102. Suppose, for example, that net immigration remained at its 1980s level of 750,000 annually. Within 30 years, the labor force would be 24 percent larger, and most of the additional new workers would be traditionally disadvantaged workers. This means that continued workforce growth—and the 1990 legislation will expand net immigration to perhaps 950,000 per year—will aggravate the challenge of raising productivity and integrating disadvantaged workers

into the workforce. It makes more sense to begin to solve persisting workforce and productivity challenges at the lower levels of immigration recommended in the early 1980s than to endorse the higher levels that the U.S. Congress has recently approved.

143. Leon F. Bouvier. PEACEFUL INVASIONS: IMMIGRATION AND CHANGING AMERICA, 1992, p. 94. As former Secretary of Labor F. Ray Marshall noted in his dissent to the Final Report of the U.S. Select Commission on Immigration and Refugee Policy, "Additional supplies of low-skilled alien workers with Third World wage and employment expectations cannot only lead employers to prefer such workers, it can also lead to outmoded labor-intensive production processes, to the detriment of U.S. productivity."

144. Leon F. Bouvier. PEACEFUL INVASIONS: IMMIGRATION AND CHANGING AMERICA, 1992, p. 94. Unskilled immigrants and low wages are a double-edged sword affecting economic growth. Unskilled immigrants can lower wages and increase profits, but if workers are readily available, firms are discouraged from buying machinery which raises productivity. Low wages, uncertain economic prospects, and high interest rates discouraged productivity-increasing investment in the 1980s despite high profits. Low wages and high interest rates encourage many firms to hire easily laid-off workers instead of committing themselves to buying equipment which must be paid for whether it operates or not. The availability of immigrant workers helps to explain why parts of the American economy remained labor-intensive in the 1980s despite calls for business to raise labor productivity to compete successfully in the global economy.

145. Leon F. Bouvier. PEACEFUL INVASIONS: IMMIGRATION AND CHANGING AMERICA, 1992, p. 94. Unskilled immigrants keep wages low and increase profits, but these extra profits do not often turn into productivity-increasing business investment. When wages rise in industrial countries, employers have an incentive to invest in productivity-increasing machinery, increasing worker productivity and lowering consumer prices. Higher profits enable business to make productivity-increasing investments, but the availability of low-wage labor deprives entrepreneurs of the incentive to make such investments.

146. Leon F. Bouvier. PEACEFUL INVASIONS: IMMIGRATION AND CHANGING AMERICA, 1992, pp. 103-104. The labor market and economy do not need large numbers of unskilled immigrants to prosper; such immigrants are more likely to hurt rather than to help both American workers and economic growth in the twenty-first century. Immigration levels should be reduced to satisfy the humanitarian, economic, foreign policy, and other goals of immigration in an open society.

147. John Vinson. IMMIGRATION OUT OF CONTROL, 1992, p. 24. In 1990, the Washington-based Center for Immigration Studies (CIS) did a

study which further suggests a link between immigration and unemployment, particularly for the large-city poor. The study found that nine of the top twelve cities for immigration had unemployment rates higher than the national average.

148.   John Vinson. IMMIGRATION OUT OF CONTROL, 1992, p. 24. Professor Donald Huddle of Rice University has found that illegals often take good-paying jobs in the construction industry. From his research, Huddle concludes that for every 100 illegals in the work force, 65 Americans will be put out of work. Former Labor Secretary Marshall estimated in 1980 that sharp reductions of illegal immigration would reduce U.S. unemployment substantially.

149.   Ken Silverstein. "The Labor Debate." SCHOLASTIC UPDATE, November 19, 1993, p. 17. Still, critics of current immigration policy say these workers are taking entry-level jobs away from the U.S. citizens who need them most: the poor, minorities, and women. Other analysts contend that even more jobs are lost when well-paid factory workers are replaced by illegal immigrants working in low-paying sweatshops. One study estimates that 3.5 million American workers have lost their jobs as a result of illegal immigration over the last decade.

150.   Virginia D. Abernethy. POPULATION POLITICS, 1993, p. 217. Jobs are systematically downgraded by labor competition so that the nostrum, "There are some jobs that Americans won't do," becomes a self-fulfilling prophecy. Bring in fresh third-world labor and, indeed, the wage, benefit, and safety conditions to which jobs devolve attract neither native-born Americans nor established immigrants. Whitmire (1992) sums up: "A surge in immigration guarantees that the less skilled service-sector jobs remain low paid."

151.   Leon F. Bouvier. PEACEFUL INVASIONS: IMMIGRATION AND CHANGING AMERICA, 1992, p. 83. Low-tech garment employment expanded in part because immigrant workers were available; this industry probably would not have expanded without immigrants. It is thus correct to say that the availability of immigrants permitted the low-tech garment industry to expand, creating jobs in the United States. However, without such immigrant workers, a high-tech garment industry might have emerged which employed American rather than immigrant workers. The availability of immigrant workers pushed the garment economy along a losing low-tech rather than a winning high-tech trajectory. The low-tech garment industry can buy a few extra years of survival, but this temporary survival will not help the United States to employ its disadvantaged workers nor will it help the U.S. economy to become more competitive.

152.   Leon F. Bouvier. PEACEFUL INVASIONS: IMMIGRATION AND CHANGING AMERICA, 1992, p. 105. Recognizing that immigrant workers will for a time work at wages low enough to compete with imports, some have suggested that the United

States should continue to import unskilled workers in order to avoid pleas from business for tariffs, quotas, and other protections from imports. However, low-wage immigrants will not be enough to help sunset industries. Many of the industries clamoring for protection from imports, such as shoes and apparel, already employ large numbers of unskilled immigrants. A policy of importing workers to avoid inevitable adjustments is often self-defeating. Helping an industry to survive without making adjustments usually guarantees that there will be vulnerable jobs and businesses asking for protection in the future.

153.   Leon F. Bouvier. PEACEFUL INVASIONS: IMMIGRATION AND CHANGING AMERICA, 1992, p. 77. These common sense arguments against unskilled immigration are often obscured in the sometimes emotional arguments for more immigrants. Immigration advocates argue that unskilled immigrants cannot be hurting American workers because unemployment rates in the southwestern cities which have the most immigrants are as low or lower than rates in eastern and midwestern cities with few immigrants. Such a static comparison of unemployment rates ignores the fact that the southwestern cities which used to attract unskilled Americans are now sending, for example, Blacks from Los Angeles to Atlanta. Unskilled immigrants often drive unskilled Americans from immigration areas such as Los Angeles, and the underclass which remains tends to drop out of the labor force, making the low unemployment rate deceptive.

154.   Rodman D. Griffen. "Illegal Immigration." CONGRESSIONAL QUARTERLY RESEARCHER, April 24, 1992, p. 365. Moreover, expanding the nation's gross domestic product on the backs of low-paid workers may not be morally just or economically sound. Billions of dollars' worth of wages are sent out of our economy. And hard-won benefits to American workers—the minimum wage, an eight-hour work day, pensions—are undermined by the enormous underground economy.

155.   Donald L. Huddle. Letter. NEW YORK TIMES, January 26, 1994, p. A14. As Richard Bean of the University of Texas recently showed, slow growth areas are particularly prone to labor displacement. As in California during the 1990's, many native born, according to Randy Filer in a National Bureau of Economic Research study, end up fleeing the region to avoid job losses and falling wage levels.

156.   Leon F. Bouvier. PEACEFUL INVASIONS: IMMIGRATION AND CHANGING AMERICA, 1992, p. 80. Once the immigrant network is established, unskilled Americans tend to be bypassed in the scramble for jobs. An ethnic foreman favors the people he knows best, and the language of the work place becomes Spanish or Tagalog. The Americans who show up feel out of place and soon quit, reinforcing the employer's belief that Americans don't want low-wage jobs anyway. The jobs become less and less attractive because the isolated immigrants do not demand and employers do

not offer the wage and working condition improvements that are occurring in other labor markets. In this way, the American workers who used to be recruited for low-wage jobs find themselves excluded from them by immigrants.

157.	Daniel James. ILLEGAL IMMIGRATION: AN UNFOLDING CRISIS, 1991, p. 52. Exploitation of illegal immigrants by unscrupulous U.S. employers, which has proceeded apace ever since illegal immigration became common in the 1920s, has only exacerbated competition for jobs. The very status of being undocumented makes an immigrant vulnerable to exploitation. Employers in agriculture, industry, or the service sector are naturally prone to use illegal immigrants as a source of cheap labor who often perform menial work—e.g., dishwashing—that native-born or legal alien workers are not willing to at the depressed wages and conditions that prevail.

158.	Leon F. Bouvier. PEACEFUL INVASIONS: IMMIGRATION AND CHANGING AMERICA, 1992, p. 74. They settle in poor neighborhoods, seek unskilled jobs, and often have an easier time finding such jobs than poor Americans. employers sometimes prefer to hire the immigrants: even though they may not speak English, the newcomers are likely to be grateful for what to them is a high wage job. The American workers who are available for such unskilled jobs, by contrast, are likely to be dissatisfied with the low wages and lack of advancement opportunities.

159.	Leon F. Bouvier. PEACEFUL INVASIONS: IMMIGRATION AND CHANGING AMERICA, 1992, p. 105. What would happen if the jobs which depend on the availability of unskilled immigrants disappeared? All inevitable adjustments are costly, but policies which promote necessary economic adjustments are in the nation's best long-term interest. Blacksmiths argued correctly that the automobile would eliminate their jobs, but Americans would be much poorer today if the nation had remained a horse and buggy economy to protect blacksmiths.

160.	Virginia D. Abernethy. POPULATION POLITICS, 1993, p. 224. Considering both U.S. competitiveness in international markets and the outlook for labor, the present situation is untenable. The social fabric is in jeopardy in part because, at the socio-economic bottom, discouraged workers do not search for work at all. Limited job opportunities distort incentives straight through developmental milestones: Why stay in school? Why apply oneself? Why not get pregnant? Rationally, welfare and criminal activities including drug-dealing *do* offer better opportunity.

161.	Dianne Feinstein. CONGRESSIONAL RECORD, June 30, 1993, S8276. In California, 1.3 million Californians are out of work, jobs are hard to find, every classroom is overcrowded, crime abounds, and affordable housing is virtually non-existent.

It is in this atmosphere that newcomers must compete with residents for jobs, education, health care, and housing. Tension, competition, fear, and anxiety are the inevitable result when the numbers of newcomers are great and the opportunities are few.

162.	Garrett Hardin. LIVING WITHIN LIMITS, 1993, p. 288. A prime danger to continued national survival is uncontrolled immigration, which unquestionably increases unemployment. Long continued unemployment produces social disorder. If it were true (as some journalists maintain) that immigration actually increased employment, then we would do well to invite all the world's two billion wretchedly poor to come into our country. No advocate of immigration has yet had the nerve to suggest that we do this, so we should take with a bucket of salt all claims that immigration has no adverse effect on employment.

163.	Virginia D. Abernethy. POPULATION POLITICS, 1993, p. 217. American voters— and businesses that pay into unemployment compensation funds—might take note that every area which is highly impacted by immigration has unemployment rates substantially higher than the nation at large. Dade County, Fla., had a December, 1991, unemployment figure of 9.5 percent at the same time that unemployment was 7.1 percent for the country at large. In 1980, one of four Miami residents fell below the federal poverty line; by 1990, after steady Haitian immigration and the 120,000 of the Mariel boatload from Cuba, it was one in three!

164.	John Tanton and Wayne Lutton. "Welfare Costs For Immigrants." THE SOCIAL CONTRACT, Fall 1992, p. 6. At one time, factual information about the effects of immigrants on our social welfare system was hard to come by, but now we have an impressive body of knowledge relating to this field. In summary: immigrants who have come to the United States since 1965 are generally less well-educated and have fewer job skills and poorer language abilities than immigrants of earlier eras. It is hardly surprising to discover that these newer immigrants are more likely to use welfare than their predecessors.

165.	George J. Borjas. Reply to an Article by Peter Brimelow. NATIONAL REVIEW, February 1, 1993, p. 29. My book documented that more recent immigrant waves are less skilled than earlier waves. Consequently, current immigration policy has an important fiscal impact. I've estimated that welfare expenditures on immigrants are $1 to $3 billion more per year than the immigrant contribution to the welfare system.

166.	Michael S. Teitelbaum. "New Polemics on Immigration." THE SOCIAL CONTRACT, Spring 1992, p. 182. Immigrants to the United States during the 1960s and 1970s did reasonably well, in terms of both economic well-being and modest dependence on the welfare system. But the much larger numbers of immigrants entering the more complex economic circumstances of the 1980s have not prospered, and welfare

dependence has increased. Moreover, some nationalities fare well as U.S. immigrants, while others suffer, for reasons no one really understands.

167. Daniel James. ILLEGAL IMMIGRATION: AN UNFOLDING CRISIS, 1991, p. 42. In 1990, the welfare rolls in 49 states increased, due to the recession and the efforts of state governments to supply the needy with food, cash, and medical care. One reason for the welfare increase was, "changes in the immigration law [which] allowed more non-citizens onto the welfare rolls, an especially important factor in California and the Southwest."

168. Donald Huddle and David Simcox. "Red Ink from Abroad." THE WORLD AND I, January 1994, p. 387. Average individual cost of public assistance for illegal aliens in 1992 was $2,103, while per capita tax payments were only $519. This $1,584 deficit for direct services is due to dramatically higher poverty rates, lower tax compliance, and a relatively high propensity to use public assistance programs and services not barred to them.

169. Donald Huddle and David Simcox. "Red Ink from Abroad." THE WORLD AND I, January 1994, p. 386. In 1992, the 4.8 million illegal aliens settled in the United States consumed $10.1 billion in assistance and services while paying an estimated $2.5 billion in taxes (see table 3). More than 70 percent of the $10.1 billion in outlays were for public education, county health and welfare services, and criminal justice.

170. John Tanton and Wayne Lutton. "Welfare Costs For Immigrants." THE SOCIAL CONTRACT, Fall 1992, p. 7. Welfare participation rates differ among immigrants. Those coming from less-developed countries and possessing skills that do not meet the requirements of a high-tech economy are much more likely to use welfare than are skilled immigrants from industrialized nations. The most recent census figures indicate that 29.3 percent of Vietnamese immigrants were on welfare, 25.8 percent of those from the Dominican Republic, 18 percent from Cuba, 12.4 percent from Mexico, all the way down to 4 percent from Denmark and 3.9 percent from Switzerland.

171. George J. Borjas. Reply to an Article by Peter Brimelow. NATIONAL REVIEW, February 1, 1993, p. 29. The financial benefits received by U.S. welfare recipients greatly exceed the per-capita incomes of many source countries. Our income-redistribution policies, which tax the skilled and subsidize the less skilled, distort the incentives of potential migrants (the skilled want to stay behind, the unskilled want to come); reduce the work incentives of immigrants in the U.S.; and diminish the incentives of immigrants who fail in the U.S. to return home (why go back when the safety net here is cushier than opportunities elsewhere?).

172. John Tanton and Wayne Lutton. "Welfare Costs For Immigrants." THE SOCIAL CONTRACT, Fall 1992, p. 6. The United States has become a "welfare magnet" to people around the world. Benefits granted by federal, state, and local agencies are often far higher than typical wage scales in many countries of origin.

173. Lawrence Harrison. "Those Huddled Unskilled Masses." THE SOCIAL CONTRACT, Summer 1992, p. 223. Massachusetts consequently became a magnet for immigrants. Between 1980 and 1990, the Hispanic population more than doubled to 288,000, while the Asian population almost tripled to 143,000. The treatment of immigrants did not become a really hot issue until the sharp downturn in the state's economy and the resulting budget crisis. Now there can be no question that immigrants compete with needy citizens for drastically-reduced public services.

174. David W. Stewart. IMMIGRATION AND EDUCATION, 1993, p. 227. The United States has not been, and should not be, a refuge just for the world's elite. Still, it is an undisputed fact that relatively uneducated immigrants are much more costly to the nation in terms of services required than are more highly educated individuals. It also takes them much longer to make the adjustment to this country and to enter its national life.

175. Donald L. Huddle. "A Growing Burden." NEW YORK TIMES, September 3, 1993, p. A23. Public assistance costs in 1992 at the county, state and national levels were $42.5 billion for the 19.3 million legal and illegal immigrants who have settled in the U.S. since 1970. These are net costs, after deducting the $20.2 billion in taxes paid by immigrants and including the $11.9 billion for public assistance for the 2.1 million displaced U.S.-born workers. The biggest expense was for primary and secondary public education, followed by Medicaid.

176. William F. Jasper. "Illegal Immigration Is a Crisis." IMMIGRATION: OPPOSING VIEWPOINTS, 1990, p. 162. A study conducted in 1986 by the Chief Administrative Office of Los Angeles County determined that services to illegal aliens were costing county taxpayers $172.8 million per year. That total did not include the tax dollars paid to the sixty thousand citizen children in Los Angeles County who receive federal Aid to Families with Dependent Children. These are children (allegedly) born in the United States to illegal aliens. Under current law, being born here is sufficient for citizenship.... [ellipses in original]

177. Tom Bethell. "Immigration, Si; Welfare, No." AMERICAN SPECTATOR, November 1993, p. 19. And the fastest growing component of Aid for Families with Dependent Children, the main welfare program, goes to the offspring of illegals who give birth in U.S. hospitals; the children become U.S. citizens. As the guardians, their mothers get the welfare checks. At that point they are "empowered" with victim status, and no doubt grievance tribunals and government-paid attorneys.

178.   Donald L. Huddle. Letter. NEW YORK
          TIMES, January 26, 1994, p. A14. For example, the Rand Corporation, hardly a nativist anti-immigrant group, found that each permanent Mexican immigrant in California had a public service deficit of more than $1,000 annually in 1982.

179.   Donald Huddle and David Simcox. "Red Ink
          from Abroad." THE WORLD AND I, January 1994, p. 393. A final, baffling argument of these researchers and other immigrant advocacy groups is that illegal aliens do not use much public assistance, because they are "afraid of detection." Major benefits to illegal immigrants such as free public education, school feeding, public housing, the earned-income tax credit, and AFDC and food stamps for their U.S.-born children are protected by law and regulation. Established civic and church groups work with illegal immigrants to secure these benefits. Moreover, a costly program such as prison confinement requires no application by the recipient.

180.   Monique Miller. Letter. WASHINGTON
          POST, January 13, 1994, p. A26. Real savings gained from reforming the welfare system must not only be viewed in terms of the difficult choices available in cutting entitlements to those already receiving benefits but in terms of the comparatively easier choice of setting reasonable limits to the number of new immigrants our welfare system can support before they are legally accepted into this country.

181.   Donald Huddle and David Simcox. "Red Ink
          from Abroad." THE WORLD AND I, January 1994, p. 382. A quarter of all immigrants now enter illegally, thus avoiding any legally required test of their solvency or ability to become self-supporting. Some of the most costly forms of public services, such as free public education, are not considered public assistance under the law. The Supreme Court has guaranteed free public schooling to illegal immigrants.

182.   Daniel James. ILLEGAL IMMIGRATION: AN
          UNFOLDING CRISIS, 1991, p. 46. The U.S. Government has constructed an extensive and costly social and economic safety net, over the past half-century, for the less fortunate members of the national community whose interests it exists to serve. Illegal immigration may threaten the viability and solvency of that safety net and the concept of community underlying it. The primary obligation of the nation-state is to its legitimate citizens and legal residents. The concept of community becomes hollow if outsiders can enter it in defiance of its laws and regulations, and swiftly gain entitlements to its benefits. The very viability of the U.S. welfare system is threatened when resources for the neediest are diluted by the claims of outsiders, and taxpayers conclude that the number of potential claimants is not limited by national boundaries.

183.   Representative Gallegly, Fact Sheet on Illegal
          Immigration, April 9, 1993, quoted in CONGRESSIONAL RECORD, July 1, 1993, H4436. In California, the state Auditor General estimates it costs state and local governments a new $3 billion each year to provide services to illegal aliens. The Department of Education estimates that fully 17 percent of California's public elementary and high school students—866,000—are the children of illegal and non-citizen immigrants. This costs the state and local school districts some $3.6 billion a year. And the Department of Health Services estimates that it costs the taxpayers $918 million for health and welfare benefits for immigrants.

184.   Virginia D. Abernethy. POPULATION
          POLITICS, 1993, p. 235. Illegal immigrants absorb additional sums, more difficult to trace. The Center for Immigration Studies (CIS) estimates, however, that $5.4 billion of 1990 expenditures on thirteen major federal and state programs can be traced to illegal aliens. Public education (K-12) is the largest expense category attributable to illegal aliens: The CIS (1991) estimates that kindergarten through high school plus Headstart accounted for over $2.5 billion in 1990: "Other major programs used by illegal aliens are uncompensated medical care in public hospitals ($963.5 million), criminal justice and corrections ($831 million), and Medicaid ($665.3 million)."

185.   John Tanton and Wayne Lutton. "Welfare Costs
          For Immigrants." THE SOCIAL CONTRACT, Fall 1992, p. 12. The cost to Texas taxpayers of educating the children of illegal aliens is heavy and rising. A 1990 Texas news survey determined that illegal aliens were costing schools in the Texas border area as much as $26 million.

186.   David W. Stewart. IMMIGRATION AND
          EDUCATION, 1993, p. 204. The Center for Immigrations Studies in 1991 estimated that the total cost of federal and state services to illegal aliens in 1990 was $5.4 billion. Of this, the largest sector was that for K-12 public education, which at $2.1 billion represented 39 percent of the total; approximately 93 percent of this amount was expended by state and local sources. These figures are based on an estimated illegally resident population of 4.2 million and do not include expenses for those previously illegal aliens redefined as legal under amnesty provisions of the Immigration Reform and Control Act.

187.   David W. Stewart. IMMIGRATION AND
          EDUCATION, 1993, p. 204. Education is by far the largest tax-supported service used by illegal immigrants, according to a study in 1984 by the Lyndon B. Johnson School of Public Affairs at the University of Texas. At a Senate hearing that same year, Raul Besteiro, superintendent of schools in hard-hit Brownsville, Texas, outlined the high costs to his system of accommodating the large numbers of illegal immigrant children. Among these costs was $2,160,000 for rapid construction of classroom space.

188.   David W. Stewart. IMMIGRATION AND
          EDUCATION, 1993, p. 214. A recent study of Mexican immigration to the United States suggests that

these new residents probably receive more in educational and certain other tax-supported services than they pay; their relatively low incomes and large families contribute to this result. Other studies also show that state and local expenditures for education substantially exceeding tax revenues derived from immigrants.

189.   Virginia D. Abernethy. POPULATION POLITICS, 1993, p. 238. Another especially entitled category is school-age children. A U.S. Supreme Court ruling requires the states to educate all children regardless of legal or illegal status. In Florida, the influx of illegal immigrants adds about $100 million annually to the education budget. In Dallas, Texas, 2,000 to 2,500 *additional* non-English-speaking children enroll in the public schools each year. In 1987 (long ago in terms of the rapid rise in numbers), 90 percent of the 600,000-plus non-English-speaking children in California had been born outside of the United States.

190.   John Tanton and Wayne Lutton. "Welfare Costs For Immigrants." THE SOCIAL CONTRACT, Fall 1992, p. 11. According to Michael Antonovich, chairman of the Los Angeles County Board of Supervisors, Los Angeles County and its county and city school districts are currently paying an estimated $1.16 billion every year for services provided to illegal aliens. This burden substantially contributed to the Los Angeles Unified School District's 1991 $274 million deficit.

191.   David W. Stewart. IMMIGRATION AND EDUCATION, 1993, p. 27. The educational opportunities of the United States in no small measure are a drawing card for today's immigrants. Examples are not hard to find in interviews with immigrants. "I didn't see any way to send the kids to school," reported one Haitian father awaiting deportation at the U.S. naval base at Guantanamo Bay, Cuba, in 1992. "I see that when kids go to school, at least you won't be pulling a cart in the road like an animal," he continued. A Korean immigrant put the case a bit differently: "At home, Koreans have to fight for an education. They see America just giving this stuff away."

192.   John Tanton and Wayne Lutton. "Welfare Costs For Immigrants." THE SOCIAL CONTRACT, Fall 1992, p. 11. Illegal alien children comprise almost 7 percent of the state's total school population. Their education is costing Californians nearly $2 billion a year.

193.   William F. Jasper. "Illegal Immigration Is a Crisis." IMMIGRATION: OPPOSING VIEWPOINTS, 1990, p. 162. Los Angeles public schools are bursting at the seams and are going on year-round rotating class schedules to accommodate the tremendous numbers of children of illegal aliens, refugees, and immigrants who have settled there in recent years. The cost to the county and city school districts for services provided to undocumented aliens is estimated at close to $570 million.

194.   David W. Stewart. IMMIGRATION AND EDUCATION, 1993, p. 227. Competition for education resources is one of the hidden, but real, issues involving immigration and education. Immigration policy can cruelly, if unintentionally, impair the educational and training climate for the native-born. Native-born schoolchildren suffer if the school district decides to cut out art, music, or mediated instruction in order to employ bilingual teachers or aides.

195.   John Vinson. IMMIGRATION OUT OF CONTROL, 1992, p. 26. The children of illegals, under a 1982 Supreme Court decision, have the right to education at U.S. taxpayers' expense. They and the children of many legal immigrants must receive remedial instruction and bilingual education. The costs of these programs divert money from the education of American pupils at a time when many of our schools are failing to turn out graduates who can meet the demands of a high-tech economy.

196.   David W. Stewart. IMMIGRATION AND EDUCATION, 1993, p. 26. There are links between illiteracy and immigration—especially illegal immigration to the United States. The U.S. Department of Education's *Update on Adult Illiteracy* (illiteracy being defined as inability to read at all, or reading below the fourth-grade level) reports that 37 percent of all persons considered to be illiterate in the U.S. speak a language other than English at home. Of these non-English-speaking residents, 82 percent were born outside the United States, with only 14 percent of this group being literate in their home language.

197.   David W. Stewart. IMMIGRATION AND EDUCATION, 1993, p. 26. The states ranking first, second, third, fourth, and fifth, respectively, in population of illiterate adults 20 years of age and older are the high-immigration receiving states of California, New York, Texas, Illinois, and Florida. New Jersey, the other major receiver of immigrants, ranks eighth among all states. Texas and New York share the highest levels of illiteracy (16 percent each); Florida is at 15 percent, and California, New Jersey, and Illinois share a 14 percent level.

198.   David W. Stewart. IMMIGRATION AND EDUCATION, 1993, p. 26. Hispanic immigrants in particular often arrive without the most basic literacy skills. Of all Hispanics living in the United States, 56 percent are functionally illiterate in English according to a report released in 1990 by the National Council of La Raza. This disadvantage is a source of concern for their advocates in this country. In a statement before a congressional committee reviewing issues bearing on immigration and education, Congressman Edward Roybal (D-California) cited statistics compiled by the National Association of Latino Elected and Appointed Officials (NALEO). These indicated that 20 percent of all illiterate adults are immigrants who had come to the United States within the prior six years. Also, according to NALEO, "only 23 percent of Mexican immigrants have a reading ability in English."

199. John Tanton and Wayne Lutton. "Welfare Costs For Immigrants." THE SOCIAL CONTRACT, Fall 1992, p. 11. Under current law, most alien children—whether their parents are here legally or illegally—must be taught in their native language in programs that cost, on average, $6600 per student annually, versus $4000 per student per year to educate children who are fluent in English. Nearly 100 languages are now spoken in California schools. And bilingual teachers receive bonuses of up to $5000.

200. John Tanton and Wayne Lutton. "Welfare Costs For Immigrants." THE SOCIAL CONTRACT, Fall 1992, p. 13. As *The Christian Science Monitor reported* in its issue of May 18, 1992, "After Spanish, the most commonly spoken languages at the schools are Chinese, Urdu, and Bengali. Every notice is sent home in Spanish and English, even report cards. Translators are present at all parent-teacher conferences." Immigrant language programs are costing New York City taxpayers $130.6 million every year.

201. Leon F. Bouvier. PEACEFUL INVASIONS: IMMIGRATION AND CHANGING AMERICA, 1992, p. 174. Immigration and demographic trends may limit the resources available just to maintain, let alone improve, the educational system in the future. Strong support for public education has traditionally been taken for granted in American politics, but that automatic support is eroding. There are many reasons why voters in many states are less inclined to support higher taxes for education. However, demographic trends also threaten more erosion of support for educational funding. The demographic cause of the decline in support for educational funding is the divergence between students and voters. Anglo students will become a minority of all students after 2030, but Anglos will remain a majority of the voting population even as their share of the population shrinks. As these voters grow older, they may be more inclined to use limited tax dollars for public safety and health care programs rather than for education.

202. Virginia D. Abernethy. POPULATION POLITICS, 1993, p. 238. Limiting the discussion to population growth, consider this: The United States is entering another cycle where the schools are not large enough to accommodate all the children. Temporary outbuildings are being pressed back into service. building out will mean bond issues for construction and more teachers. If immigration into California increases in the 1990s as projected, one elementary school would have to be built every day of every year for the next thirty years to keep up with the demand! The alternative is much larger class size.

203. Harold Gilliam. "Bursting At The Seams." THE SOCIAL CONTRACT, Summer 1993, p. 263. But quality education does not seem possible if schools are swamped by illegal immigrants coming across the borders and being smuggled from overseas by the boatload at the rate of about 100,000 a year. And there are twice that many incoming *legal* immigrants.

204. John Tanton and Wayne Lutton. "Welfare Costs For Immigrants." THE SOCIAL CONTRACT, Fall 1992, p. 11. As Ted Hilton, director of the San Diego-based Coalition for Immigration Law Enforcement, observed, "Without this [additional educational] financial burden, California could substantially reduce its current budget deficit…and improve the quality of education of all its lawful residents—including impoverished African-Americans and other minorities, and also legal immigrants—if we didn't have to educate unlawful residents as well." [ellipses in original]

205. James Scheuer, "A Disappointing Outcome." THE SOCIAL CONTRACT, Summer 1992, p. 204. Immigration is a controversial issue in the United States. With legal and illegal entries now surpassing one million every year, there is growing concern that such numbers may be too high for the welfare of all Americans. Our absorptive capacity is being stretched beyond its limits. It is increasingly difficult to provide the proper education to additional millions of immigrants for the demands of the 21st century when we are failing to educate our own population.

206. John Tanton and Wayne Lutton. "Welfare Costs For Immigrants." THE SOCIAL CONTRACT, Fall 1992, p. 13. Over the past three years, New York City public schools have enrolled 120,000 children from 167 countries. Often illiterate in their native languages, New York City has cut back on the number of regular teachers, while trying to fill vacancies for bilingual instructors, often imported for this purpose.

207. Dianne Feinstein. CONGRESSIONAL RECORD, June 30, 1993. S8277. The Federal Government spent an additional $377 million of its share of medical costs. That is a total of almost $2.1 billion in California alone. Put in another perspective, Mr. President, 10 percent, or $308 million, of Los Angeles County's entire budget goes to the cost of undocumented individuals.

208. William F. Jasper. "Illegal Immigration Is a Crisis." IMMIGRATION: OPPOSING VIEWPOINTS, 1990, p. 162. County hospitals and health delivery systems have been particularly hard hit. Jackson Memorial Hospital in Florida's Dade County provides health services to thousands of refugees and illegal aliens. Besides receiving the bulk of the 150,000 Cuban refugees from Mariel in 1980, Dade County is host to 50,000 to 75,000 illegal aliens from Nicaragua, and many thousands more from Haiti, Jamaica, El Salvador, Mexico, and elsewhere. After receiving reimbursement from the Federal Government, Jackson Memorial is still looking at an $8-10 million shortfall for unpaid services rendered to illegal aliens…. [ellipses in original]

209. Virginia D. Abernethy. POPULATION POLITICS, 1993, p. 275. About two-thirds of births in the Los Angeles County Hospital are to women who are in the United States illegally. The children, as American citizens, are entitled to the full range

of social, health-care, and welfare benefits. AFDC for the *citizen children of illegals* costs Los Angeles County taxpayers $250 million annually.

210. John Tanton and Wayne Lutton. "Welfare Costs For Immigrants." THE SOCIAL CONTRACT, Fall 1992, p. 7. Uncompensated medical care provided to illegal aliens at publicly-supported hospitals follows education as the most costly burden to U.S. taxpayers. The average cost to taxpayers is $4700 *per admission* (*Estimated Annual Costs of Major Federal and State Services to Illegal Aliens*, Center for Immigration Studies).

211. John Vinson. IMMIGRATION OUT OF CONTROL, 1992, p. 26. In 1991, California paid $395 million in health benefits for illegal aliens. Much of this total was for pregnancies. These are among the benefits that illegals are legally entitled to receive. In Los Angeles County, the net cost to the county for services to illegal aliens was $276 million in 1990. Children born to them automatically became American citizens, and have the same entitlement to welfare benefits as other citizens. The state estimates that, by 1993, benefits for these children will amount to 25 percent of the state's entire welfare budget. According to Robert Kuziara, assistant division chief of finance for Los Angeles County, services for illegal aliens are a subsidy taxpayers are paying for the local businessmen who profit from cheap immigrants' labor.

212. Virginia D. Abernethy. POPULATION POLITICS, 1993, p. 236. All told, "Almost a third of current [California] residents migrated here within the last 10 years, many from foreign countries and without substantial resources" write Chase and Dolan (1992). They expect that in the "coming year," illegal aliens will account for an additional 315,000 beneficiaries of state Medicaid assistance, increasing the roll by 25 percent.

213. Donald Huddle and David Simcox. "Red Ink from Abroad." THE WORLD AND I, January 1994, pp. 391-392. The Clinton administration's plan for universal health coverage would cause formidable increases in cost for medical care for immigrants, a larger percentage of whom tend to be uninsured. Unless carefully administered, universal health care itself could become a magnet for additional highly dependent migrants. The White House has stated that the plan would be open to only citizens and legal residents. As in the past, court decisions could overrule the government's exclusion of illegal aliens. At this time there is no mechanism for barring health-care coverage to more than a million illegal aliens who work using false documents.

214. Virginia D. Abernethy. POPULATION POLITICS, 1993, p. 239. Health care for persons illegally in the United States is unexpectedly high, considering the youth of most illegal migrants, because women routinely use public hospitals for delivery. Taxpayers pay for this, although the hospital is not technically compensated by Medicaid. A Texas hospital was

close to bankruptcy due to the numbers arriving for obstetrics care; the flood was reduced to a trickle when admitting clerks dressed in green uniforms resembling those worn by Immigration and Naturalization Service (INS) personnel.

215. Rodman D. Griffen. "Illegal Immigration." CONGRESSIONAL QUARTERLY RESEARCHER, April 24, 1992, p. 365. Los Angeles officials say that children born to illegal immigrants now account for more than 65 percent of all births at county-run hospitals, costing taxpayers $28 million a year. Federal welfare payments to U.S.-born children of illegal immigrants residing in Los Angeles County approach $250 million annually.

216. Alan C. Nelson. "A Governor's Brave Stand on Illegal Aliens." NEW YORK TIMES, August 23, 1993, p. A15. Two-thirds of the births in Los Angeles County Hospital are to illegal aliens. The mother applies for welfare, knowing the child is eligible, and lives off the grant. Twenty-three percent of the Los Angeles County welfare load consists of children of illegal migrants, the fastest-growing group of welfare dependents.

217. John Vinson. IMMIGRATION OUT OF CONTROL, 1992, p. 28. And unlike the days of Ellis Island, we have huge numbers of illegal aliens who enter our country with no health screening at all. Some are bringing in the dreaded HIV (AIDS) virus. Among the Haitian illegals who were apprehended by the Coast Guard in 1991 and taken to the U.S. naval facility at Guantanamo, Cuba, five percent tested positive for AIDS.

These diseases are a direct danger to American citizens. On top of this problem, many immigrants make demands of our health care systems which reduce the resources and quality of care available for Americans.

218. William F. Jasper. "Illegal Immigration Is a Crisis." IMMIGRATION: OPPOSING VIEWPOINTS, 1990, p. 163. Of course, many immigrants are already infected with serious diseases before they arrive here. Applicants for immigration who come through legal channels receive only a cursory health examination: illegal aliens receive no inspection whatsoever. The upsurge of tuberculosis and leprosy cases in recent years is almost completely attributable to our resident alien population.

219. William F. Jasper. "Illegal Immigration Is a Crisis." IMMIGRATION: OPPOSING VIEWPOINTS, 1990, pp. 162-163. A visible effect of our uncontrolled immigration is what is increasingly referred to as the "Third World colonization" of the United States. Large sections of major U.S. cities now resemble Mexico City, San Salvador, Bombay, and Calcutta—with tens of thousands of people living in cardboard and tin shanties, or sleeping in the streets. California, which has been especially hard hit by the recent immigration waves, has been christened by *Time* magazine as our first "Third World state." Many of our small towns and rural areas have also been severely impacted. Several

thousand migrant farm workers live in settlements without sanitation or potable water, in conditions that breed sickness and disease.

220. Paul Kennedy. PREPARING FOR THE TWENTY-FIRST CENTURY, 1993, p. 41. More recently, concern has been expressed that illegal immigration into (for example) the United States is responsible for outbreaks of old and new diseases— cholera, measles, AIDS—which place a further strain upon the health-care system as well as provoking new resentments against migrants.

221. Anna M. Rappaport and Sylvester J. Schieber. "Overview." DEMOGRAPHY AND RETIREMENT, 1993, p. 3. The future of our economy is extremely important, determining what effect the aging of the baby boom will have on our ability to sustain our existing retirement institutions. Policies that encourage the growth of the economy during the remaining working lives of the baby boomers will lighten the load that future workers will have to bear during the baby boomers' retirement years.

222. Eric R. Kingson and Edward D. Berkowitz. SOCIAL SECURITY AND MEDICARE, 1993, p. 105. Additionally, experts generally expect that the economy will, over the long run, expand slowly, at perhaps an average of 1.5 percent to 2.0 percent per year after adjusting for inflation. This means that after adjusting for inflation, the income available per person—what economists call real per capita gross domestic product— would double in roughly every forty to fifty years, thereby enabling workers of the future to pay higher taxes, if necessary, while simultaneously enjoying considerably higher standards of living. Consequently, barring unforeseen disasters, the economy of the future seems likely to be able to support a mix of private and public efforts to meet the needs of all age groups.

223. James H. Schulz. THE ECONOMICS OF AGING, 1992, p. 266. Certainly the days of cheap social security, like the days of cheap gasoline, are gone forever. We will have to do some very hard thinking and some belt-tightening. But there is no rational justification for the hysteria that is being promoted today by some people who are attacking social security and raising the specter of the aged burden in an aging society. As we point out elsewhere (Schulz et al., 1991), even moderate rates of real economic growth will enable us to substantially increase real capita support of nonworkers without increasing substantially (if at all) the burden on the workers of the future.

224. Eric R. Kingson and Edward D. Berkowitz. SOCIAL SECURITY AND MEDICARE, 1993, p. 105. Because the proportion of the population under 18 is projected to decline, *never at any time during the next 65 years is the overall dependency ratio projected to exceed the levels it attained in 1964*. Even from 2030 through 2050, the total dependency ratio is projected to be below (about 78:100) what it was during the 1960s (e.g., 83:1000 in 1965) when most of the baby boomers were children. While the composition of governmental and private expenditures for younger and older Americans is quite different, careful analysis of all the facts surrounding dependency ratios do not support the gloomy view that changing demographics will overwhelm the nation's ability to meet the retirement needs of future generations.

225. James H. Schulz. THE ECONOMICS OF AGING, 1992, p. 9. As pointed out by Cowgill (1981), "from a demographic standpoint such fears are not warranted. The analysis on which they are based is one-sided and misleading." Cowgill points out that most modernized countries of the world, all with relatively aged populations, have quite low dependency loads, much *lower than developing nations*. As we show below, historically *total* dependency ratios in the United States have been declining, and projections indicate that they are likely to continue to decline until around the year 2010.

226. Eric R. Kingson and Edward D. Berkowitz. SOCIAL SECURITY AND MEDICARE, 1993, p. 105. Also, interpreting the changing demography of society in very pessimistic terms fails to recognize that some among today's elderly work and that policies can, if needed, be developed to encourage healthy older people to work longer and employers to retain them longer.

227. Eric R. Kingson and Edward D. Berkowitz. SOCIAL SECURITY AND MEDICARE, 1993, p. 105. As previously discussed, under the intermediate assumptions used to forecast the financial status of Social Security, the program is able to meet benefit payments through 2036, and there is plenty of lead time to deal with any problems that may occur.

228. Anna M. Rappaport and Sylvester J. Schieber. "Overview." DEMOGRAPHY AND RETIREMENT, 1993, p. 3. As the generations behind the baby boom begin their careers, the labor force's growth rate is projected to stabilize because there will be a smaller pool of potential workers to draw from. The smaller population of younger people available to staff the work force may be augmented by increased numbers of immigrant workers, by greater percentages of women in the work force, and by extended working careers of increased numbers of older workers. These changes are not forecasted to solve the problem, however.

229. John Vinson. IMMIGRATION OUT OF CONTROL, 1992, p. 41. Ignoring Japan, and its example that prosperity doesn't depend on cheap labor, Simon and company commonly try to make points with another issue: Social Security and retirement. They claim that the aging population of native-born Americans will need an influx of young immigrant workers to provide them Social Security in retirement.

This argument has numerous flaws. the ability of Americans to provide themselves Social Security and retirement depends on the general health of our economy. As Borjas and other researchers have shown, massive

Third World immigration today is taking more from our economy than it gives.

230.   Rich Thomas and Andrew Murr. "The Economic Cost of Immigration." NEWS-WEEK, August 9, 1993, p. 19. Donald Huddle, an immigration expert at Rice University, recently calculated that the 19.3 million legal, illegal and amnestied aliens accepted into the United States since 1970 utilized $50.8 billion worth of government services last year. They paid $20.2 billion in taxes. So the net burden on native-born taxpayers was $30.6 billion—a social-welfare cost per immigrant of $1,585. Huddle projects these immigrants will cost taxpayers another $50 billion a year on average over the next 10 years.

231.   Rich Thomas and Andrew Murr. "The Economic Cost of Immigration." NEWS-WEEK, August 9, 1993, p. 19. A decline in the skills of new immigrants helps to explain these numbers. Ninety percent of current immigrants arrive from Third World countries with income and social-service levels one tenth or even one twentieth those of the United States'. Their education levels relative to those of native-born Americans are steadily declining.

232.   Rich Thomas and Andrew Murr. "The Economic Cost of Immigration." NEWS-WEEK, August 9, 1993, p. 18. In the last great decade of immigration, 1900 to 1910, public education and a little public health were the only services provided to those migrating to New York and other Northeastern cities. One third of the new immigrants simply failed and moved back home. Today dozens of welfare programs—from food stamps to unemployment compensation—cushion failure and attract immigrants who might otherwise stay home.

233.   Rich Thomas and Andrew Murr. "The Economic Cost of Immigration." NEWS-WEEK, August 9, 1993, p. 19. George Borjas of the University of California, San Diego, says that in 1970 the average immigrant actually earned 3 percent more than a native-born American but by 1990 was earning 16 percent less. "Each year the percentage is heading downward," says Borjas. What's more, welfare dependency has steadily climbed and is now above that of native-borns. In 1990, 7.7 percent of native Californians received public assistance vs. 10.4 percent of new immigrants.

234.   Barry Edmonston. "Discussion." DEMOGRAPHY AND RETIREMENT, 1993, p. 62. The long-term impact of a steady stream of migration, which may seem counter-intuitive, is to make the population older. This occurs because the immigrants age—as do residents of the population—but immigrants enter the population at ages greater than zero. Hence, a constant number of immigrants, with a fixed age and sex distribution, produces an older population in the long-run.

235.   John Vinson. IMMIGRATION OUT OF CONTROL, 1992, p. 41. One interesting point

in relation to Social Security is that, with the family re-unification emphasis of our laws, any immigrants are bringing in older relatives. As a consequence, the average age of legal immigrants is not, contrary to Simon's claim, much less than that of native-born Americans.

236.   Daniel James. ILLEGAL IMMIGRATION: AN UNFOLDING CRISIS, 1991, pp. 33-34. In many jobs, however, the law requires that he have a Social Security number in order to work in the United States. Usually, the illegal immigrant will therefore either use someone else's valid Social Security number or obtain a false one. In so doing, he commits fraud and at the same time violates the Social Security law. The illegal alien's use of a false Social Security card in a range of official and unofficial transactions compounds the original violation. Besides, such practices, multiplied on an astronomical scale given the volume of illegal immigrants using fake Social Security documents, tend to confuse the records of the Social Security Administration. Those records are relied upon for accuracy by millions of American citizens and permanent resident aliens, who will someday expect to receive Social Security pensions.

237.   John Vinson. IMMIGRATION OUT OF CONTROL, 1992, p. 41. A further point to consider is whether large numbers of barely assimilated immigrants would feel obligated to support an older generation of native-born Americans. As citizens with the right to vote, these recent immigrants might well decide to keep their money.

238.   Lawrence Harrison. "Those Huddled Unskilled Masses." THE SOCIAL CONTRACT, Summer 1992, p. 222. During the past forty years, America outpaced all other developed countries in population growth. Immigration, legal and illegal, has been a major contributor to that growth. Since 1950, 20 million people have immigrated legally. No one knows how many have entered illegally. Estimates range from 5 million to 8 million. In the wake of liberalizing legislation in 1990, upwards of 1 million immigrants are now entering annually.

239.   Virginia D. Abernethy. POPULATION POLITICS, 1993, p. 207. Newcomers daily become a larger share of the whole demographic picture. For example, direct legal immigration accounts for 28 percent of California's population growth, and two-thirds of the 800,000 people a year who come to California are foreign-born. Some are illegal. Some move to California after spending time in other states. This progression is particularly evident among refugees (mostly Vietnamese, Cambodian, and Russian) because they often do not choose their first destination and, due to refugees' automatic entitlement, are attracted to California for its generous health and welfare benefits.

240.   Harold Gilliam. "Bursting At The Seams." THE SOCIAL CONTRACT, Summer 1993, p. 264. Among non-immigrant Californians, the average birthrate in the past decade has been near the replacement

level—two children per couple. Immigrants tend to have much larger families, running in some groups close to double that number.

241.   David W. Stewart. IMMIGRATION AND EDUCATION, 1993, p. 15. Four states—California, Arizona, New Mexico, and Texas—line the U.S.-Mexican border. Some idea of the force of immigration pressures from Mexico can be sensed from the disproportionate increases in population in these states beginning as early as the 1970s. Between the 1970 and 1980 census reports, population growth in these border states was 23 percent, more than twice the national average during the same period. The concurrent 40 percent increase in the population of the 25 border counties was almost four times the national rate. Immigration was a substantial contributor to this surge, according to a U.S. Department of Labor study issued in 1989.

242.   Michael S. Teitelbaum. "New Polemics on Immigration." THE SOCIAL CONTRACT, Spring 1992, p. 183. Similarly, the advocates emphasize that the percentage of foreign-born in the United States is lower than it was earlier in this century, but neglect to mention the equally true fact that immigration today accounts for a higher percentage of U.S. population increase—at least 30 percent nationwide, and much more in urban areas—than it has since perhaps colonial times.

243.   Population-Environment Balance, Position Paper, April 1991, quoted in CONGRESSIONAL QUARTERLY RESEARCHER, April 24, 1992, p. 377. The United States cannot afford to continue to allow the rapid population growth we are experiencing, largely due to immigration. Approximately 2.7 million foreign-born job seekers will enter the U.S. labor market between 1991 and 1995, according to estimates by the Center for Immigration Studies.

244.   Jack A. Meyer and Rosemary Kern. "Economic and Social Implications of Demographic Change," in DEMOGRAPHIC CHANGE AND THE AMERICAN FUTURE, 1990, pp. 126-127. Given this relatively flat growth in the indigenous population, immigrants constitute an increasing proportion of population growth. For example, 11 percent of the population growth in the United States between 1955 and 1959 was attributed to immigration. In 1980-85, however, 28 percent of the population growth was accounted for by immigration.

245.   David E. Simcox. "Sustainable Immigration: Learning to Saying No," in ELEPHANTS IN THE VOLKSWAGEN, 1992, p. 168. Even allowing for emigration, immigration under current law and practice directly accounts for 32 percent of national population growth, and the proportion is rising. The 1990 Census is expected to show that the foreign-born population has grown from 4.7 percent in 1970 to 8.5 percent in 1990. fears of labor shortages—although the U.S. 1990 unemployment rate of 5.8 percent was twice that of Japan—led Congress to approve expansions of immigration of both temporary and permanent workers in the 1990 legislation. Under that act, net annual legal and illegal immigration will climb to about 1.1 million by 1995, or more than 44 percent of population growth. Two to three million aliens amnestied under the 1986 law will convert to permanent status in the early 1990s, further swelling the permanent population as they bring their families to this country.

246.   Robin Abcarian. "Immigration Talk Borders on Environmental Dramatics." LOS ANGELES TIMES, November 10, 1993, p. E1. In 1950, U.S. population was 150 million. Today it is about 260 million. If the growth rate continues, the population will double by the middle of the next century. Immigration accounts for less than half of U.S. population growth. the great majority of immigrants—75%—are here legally.

247.   John Tanton and Wayne Lutton. "Welfare Costs For Immigrants." THE SOCIAL CONTRACT, Fall 1992, p. 7. Since 1970, U.S. immigration policies are responsible for an increase in our population of more than 27 million. Immigrants and their children—because of their high fertility rates—account for more than half of U.S. population growth since 1970. They are likely to contribute two-thirds of the anticipated increase through the remainder of the 1990s, according to demographer Leon Bouvier of Tulane University.

248.   Virginia D. Abernethy. POPULATION POLITICS, 1993, p. 220. The 1990 legislation increased legal immigration by 40 percent. The flows of regular immigrants plus refugees and asylees now combine for a total of about 1 million arrivals annually. Permanent settlers who immigrate illegally add 400,000 to 1 million more. Against this total, approximately 160,000 persons voluntarily leave the United States each year. Thus, a net of at least 1,300,000 new settlers come each year intending to stay. This mass movement across borders has increased in every year since 1965. The Center for Immigration Studies (1992) estimates that 1972-1992 immigrants, including their descendants, account for half of the U.S. population growth during this period.

249.   Peter Brimelow. "Time to Rethink Immigration?" NATIONAL REVIEW, June 22, 1992, p. 44. Yet the single biggest problem for the environment is the fact that the U.S. population, quite unusually in the developed world, is still growing quickly. Immigration is currently an unusually large factor in U.S. population growth.

250.   Virginia D. Abernethy. POPULATION POLITICS, 1993, pp. 259-260. Government data released in January, 1991, suggest that legal and illegal immigration will propel the United States population to 400 million by the year 2080. This is the middle projection within an array of possibilities. The Urban Institute (1992) has arrived at substantially the same figures by assuming a fertility decline to 1.9 children per woman and immigration stabilizing at under 1 million

per year—highly conservative assumptions. The Urban Institute model projects 440 million people by 2090.

251.   James Scheuer, "A Disappointing Outcome." THE SOCIAL CONTRACT, Summer 1992, p. 204. With rising fertility rates and a continuing increase in immigration, legal and illegal, there is no end in sight to population growth in the United States.

252.   Leon F. Bouvier. PEACEFUL INVASIONS: IMMIGRATION AND CHANGING AMERICA, 1992, p. 127. If current demographic trends are maintained, there will be 388 million Americans in the year 2050. With slight increases in fertility and immigration, there could be 454 million Americans in the year 2050. Looking farther into the future, the range of possibilities becomes even more dramatic: the same scenario that produces 454 million Americans in 2050 leads to 900 million Americans by 2120.

253.   Barry Edmonston. "Discussion." DEMOGRAPHY AND RETIREMENT, 1993, p. 57. With annual net immigration of 900,000 to 950,000, the total U.S. population of 249 million in 1990 will top 400 million in 2070 and reach about 432 million in 2090. Thus, the current level of net immigration assumed in these projections suggests considerable population growth for the next hundred years.

254.   Anna M. Rappaport and Sylvester J. Schieber. "Overview," DEMOGRAPHY AND RETIREMENT, 1993, p. 4. If our future birth rates, death rates, and immigration and emigration rates mirrored those we are currently experiencing, our demographic projections would prove to be extremely reliable previews of the future. The science of demographic calculation is sufficiently well developed that the models give us reliable answers.

255.   Barry Edmonston. "Discussion." DEMOGRAPHY AND RETIREMENT, 1993, p. 67. The fertility of immigrants is assumed to adjust instantaneously to the fertility level of comparable ethnic or racial groups in the United States. This underestimates for many ethnic groups the higher fertility of immigrants that persists for one or two generations after entering the United States. This underestimate of fertility levels is probably strongest for the Mexican-origin population and for selected refugee groups, including those immigrants originating in Southeast Asia. These groups will likely grow at faster rates than estimated by Bureau of the Census forecasts.

256.   Virginia D. Abernethy. POPULATION POLITICS, 1993, p. 210. Not optimism, but loss of optimism brings down fertility. The history of U.S. fertility since 1960 confirms it. Just like Irish have to farm peat bogs and Indonesians scratching a living from eroded mountain slopes, native-born Americans started to seriously limit family size precisely when the average person's economic prospects began to stagnate. Fertility among native-born Americans of every race and ethnic group will stay low so long as events threaten to make them poorer.

257.   Virginia D. Abernethy. POPULATION POLITICS, 1993, p. 272. Replacement-level immigration, an equitable complement to replacement-level fertility, is at present about 160,000 immigrants a year because that is the estimated number of persons who annually leave the United States. All-inclusive, replacement-level immigration is a political objective urged by a number of Americans. Regular immigrants, asylees, refugees, and an estimated illegal number totaling no more than 160,000 persons a year would put the United States on the path toward population stabilization.

258.   Virginia D. Abernethy. POPULATION POLITICS, 1993, p. 262. Since U.S. fertility is right at replacement level, the population would stop growing in about forty years were it not for immigration. Immigration into the United States is about six or seven times greater than the number required to replace those who voluntarily leave.

259.   Virginia D. Abernethy. POPULATION POLITICS, 1993, p. 206. To take just two signs of a falling median standard of living: A smaller proportion of Americans owned their own home in 1990 than in 1950, and the disparity between rich and poor appears to be increasing. Young people and less-educated families bear the heaviest burden from competition for entry-level jobs, but the middle class is also struggling to protect its economic position. Thus, native-born Americans are unlikely to shift to a much larger family size in the foreseeable future.

260.   Virginia D. Abernethy. POPULATION POLITICS, 1993, p. 210. To summarize, total U.S. fertility was 2.0 births per woman in 1989. It was 2.1 in 1990. It fell in 1991 in response to recession. Births in the foreseeable future are expected to reflect the presence of immigrants from third-world countries, the larger family-size ideals they bring, and the higher fertility enabled by opportunity in the United States.

261.   Virginia D. Abernethy. POPULATION POLITICS, 1993, p. 209. Immigrants tend to bear children at the rate idealized in their country of origin and facilitated by the jobs, health care, subsidized housing, and welfare benefits in the United States. One should take into account that, where native-born Americans see deterioration in the standard of living, most newcomers perceive themselves as much better off than before. Relative to their previous experience, immigrants find opportunity in the United States. Despite the poor housing and sweatshop ghettos developing in Southern California, Texas border towns, Florida, and major metropolitan centers, conditions are usually better than in the third world. Opportunity acts as an enabling factor in immigrant fertility: Life in the United States presents a golden time to have a baby. Immigration allows families to realize the family size they had wanted all along

but could not afford. And the baby is an American citizen!

262.   Leon F. Bouvier. PEACEFUL INVASIONS: IMMIGRATION AND CHANGING AMERICA, 1992, p. 136. Furthermore it is quite possible that a portion of the very recent increase in fertility may reflect the changing ethnic proportions of the population. As long as these ethnic shares continue to grow, overall fertility will rise. As long as the fertility of minority groups surpasses that of the current majority population, the growing numbers in the minorities will raise the nation's overall fertility.

263.   Virginia D. Abernethy. POPULATION POLITICS, 1993, p. 209. All told, Hispanics (particularly of Mexican and Central American origin) have disproportionately high fertility and are also the most rapidly growing ethnic group in America on account of immigration. In California, their number grows 40 percent faster than the state average. Their representation in the U.S. population as a whole almost doubled, to 10 percent, between 1980 and 1990. The Hispanic proportion of total population is growing rapidly and will quickly surpass the black minority if present immigration policy continues in force.

264.   Virginia D. Abernethy. POPULATION POLITICS, 1993, p. 208. Demographers Laurie E. Banks and Joseph J. Salvo stated in a paper presented at the 1990 meeting of the Population Association of America that "For areas where native fertility is generally low, an influx of immigrants can have a major impact on the future population. Population projections for such areas must cope with both population growth due to immigration itself as well as the higher fertility of many foreign-born persons.... An analysis of fertility differentials by nativity, race and Hispanic origin indicate that, foreign-born women have higher total fertility rates than native-born women regardless of race and Hispanic origin." [ellipses in original]

265.   Virginia D. Abernethy. POPULATION POLITICS, 1993, p. 209. Immigration also drives a worrisome upsurge in teenage pregnancy: "In California, Hispanic girls accounted for 75 percent of the increase in teen births between 1986 and 1989." Similar increases in births among Hispanic teens are seen in other southwestern border states, and "experts now say this growing birthrate is largely responsible for the surprising increase in national figures" (The Teen Pregnancy Boom, 1992).

266.   Virginia D. Abernethy. POPULATION POLITICS, 1993, p. 253. Now for the bad news. Depletion of soil, water, and fuel at a much faster rate than any of these can be replenished suggests that the carrying capacity of the United States already has been exceeded. David and Marcia Pimentel (1991) of the College of Agriculture and Life Sciences, Cornell University, take these three factors into account to estimate that, at a standard of living only slightly lower than is enjoyed today, the sustainable population size for the

United States is less than half its present number. Beyond this, we abuse the carrying capacity and should expect sudden shocks that will massively drive down the standard of living.

267.   Lawrence Harrison. "Those Huddled Unskilled Masses." THE SOCIAL CONTRACT, Summer 1992, p. 223. We are a society imbued with Emma Lazarus' words on the Statue of Liberty: "Give me your tired, your poor, your huddled masses yearning to breathe free." When the statue was dedicated 105 years ago, some 60 million people lived in the United States; the frontier was still open, and an open immigration policy clearly suited our needs. Today, our population is more than four times greater, the frontier is long gone, and population growth is a principal contributor to the environment that so preoccupies us.

268.   David E. Simcox. "Sustainable Immigration: Learning to Saying No," in ELEPHANTS IN THE VOLKSWAGEN, 1992, p. 170. Census data and immigration statistics understate the degree of population growth due to entries from abroad. The Census count disregards such categories as foreign students, long-staying temporary workers, and most illegal and commuter aliens—categories that add another million the U.S. population on any given day. Furthermore, many of these immigrants have children, and their children have children, swelling the population base.

269.   Leon F. Bouvier. PEACEFUL INVASIONS: IMMIGRATION AND CHANGING AMERICA, 1992, p. 136. According to recent Census Bureau projections, the difference between fertility remaining constant at 1.8 and fertility gradually rising to 2.2 by 2050 (while holding mortality and migration constant) amounts to over 63 million by that year! A very slight increase in fertility yields massive increases in population size decades later. Given these numbers, it would appear that any end to population growth in the United States is nowhere in sight so long as immigration levels remain high.

270.   Michael D'Antonio. "Apocalypse Soon." LOS ANGELES TIMES MAGAZINE, August 29, 1993, p. 52. People born in undeveloped countries actually put less pressure on the planet because they use fewer resources and cause less pollution, says Miranda. A baby born in the United States, he says, uses five times more energy and other resources—and also generates more tons of waste in a lifetime.
[Miranda—Armindo Miranda, senior population analyst at the United Nations]

271.   Leon F. Bouvier. PEACEFUL INVASIONS: IMMIGRATION AND CHANGING AMERICA, 1992, p. 135. Because the average consumption of Americans far exceeds that of any other country, any increase in the number of Americans has a disproportionate negative effect. According to Norman Myers:

The one billion people at the top of the pile generally do not feature high population rates, but such are their materialist lifestyles—many of them, for

instance, consume 100 times as much commercial energy as do most Bangladeshis, Ethiopians, and Bolivians—that in certain respects the additional 1.75 million Americans each year may well do as much damage to the biosphere as the 85 million additional Third Worlders.

272.   Garrett Hardin. LIVING WITHIN LIMITS, 1993, p. 283. Not to be forgotten are the remittance payments sent home by emigrants. Indians, Pakistanis, and Africans work in the oil fields of the Arabian peninsula, sending much of their wages home to their families. Emigrant men generally manage to visit home a time or two during the year, thus seeing to it that more babies justify their remittances. Mexicans migrating to the United States generally follow the same pattern. The end result is that some of the wealth produced in rich countries finances population expansion in poor countries. Since most poor countries are already suffering from deforestation, soil exhaustion, and other consequences of overpopulation, the end result of the emigration-and-remittance system is a further degradation of natural resources. A generous immigration policy in rich countries prolongs the reign of poverty in poor.

273.   Population-Environment Balance, Position Paper, April 1991, quoted in CONGRESSIONAL QUARTERLY RESEARCHER, April 24, 1992, p. 377. We are being unethical and unjust to our own people and to those from other countries by allowing excessive immigration and thus refusing to confront directly the carrying-capacity problem. Allowing high levels of immigration sends these countries the wrong signal, the signal that their high emigration and high birth rates can continue because the U.S. will provide a safety valve.

274.   Virginia D. Abernethy. POPULATION POLITICS, 1993, p. 295. We have shown that more children are wanted when parents think that opportunity is expanding. Thus, foreign aid and liberal U.S. immigration policies may retard acceptance of birth control. The harm is probably proportional to how much our policies lead the third world to discount signs of economic, social, or environmental limits. At the least, one concludes that the humanitarian case is flawed. Belief in abundance somewhere neutralizes local signs of limits. Perceiving poverty as a distributional problem that can be resolved by emigrating or by appeals to equity, people may not be motivated to plan realistically.

275.   John Vinson. IMMIGRATION OUT OF CONTROL, 1992, p. 30. In fact, it might even encourage high foreign birthrates, by giving foreigners the impression that we can absorb their excess numbers. It is noteworthy that populations in Germany, Italy, and other European countries grew rapidly during the 19th century, even as they were sending millions of immigrants to the United States.

276.   John Vinson. IMMIGRATION OUT OF CONTROL, 1992, p. 30. As for admitting more immigrants to relieve density elsewhere, there is no reason to think that such use of America as a population safety valve would relieve overpopulation. With the world adding nearly one billion people every decade, even the most generous U.S. immigration policy would not significantly ease population pressure abroad.

277.   Leon F. Bouvier. PEACEFUL INVASIONS: IMMIGRATION AND CHANGING AMERICA, 1992, pp. 4-5. The nation's infrastructure is already deteriorating; rapid population growth exacerbates this deterioration by increasing the burden on roads and water systems and creating demands for schools and other types of public investment. Americans are concerned about environmental issues, about air and water quality, and while population growth is not necessarily the major cause of environmental problems, more people are certainly an accomplice. Quality of life can improve more without population growth. Given the built-in momentum for further growth, a population of 320 or 330 million is manageable and attainable if immigration is drastically curtailed. Growth beyond such levels would pose significant problems for the nation's environment and infrastructure.

278.   Virginia D. Abernethy. POPULATION POLITICS, 1993, p. 213. The majority lose from population growth because of its effect on wages, benefits, workplace safety, and educational opportunity. The poor lose still more because the public health care and social services on which they depend are stretched thinner. That happens even while taxpayers cough up more and more to try to maintain quality services. All lose eventually because no sector escapes rising taxes and environmental degradation. Writes Olsen (1989), "While U.S. industry generally applauds increased immigration, some critics say it keeps wages and benefits unfairly low for American workers while environmentalists charge immigration is lowering the quality of American life."

279.   George F. Kennan. "U.S. Overpopulation Deprives the Planet of a Helpful Civilization." THE SOCIAL CONTRACT, Spring 1993, p. 193. There will be those who will say, "Oh, it is our duty to receive as many as possible of these people and to share our prosperity with them, as we have so long been doing." But suppose there are limits to our capacity to absorb. Suppose the effect of such a policy is to create, in the end, conditions within this country no better than those of the places the masses of immigrants have left: the same poverty, the same distress.

280.   Michael D'Antonio. "Apocalypse Soon." LOS ANGELES TIMES MAGAZINE, August 29, 1993, p. 19. If nothing is done, these problems will converge in the next 50 years and plunge the world into terrible suffering, Kendall says. He describes a level of pain—starvation, disease, anarchy, a scarred landscape— more horrific than anything humanity has seen before. As he speaks, it is easy to imagine hungry people piled atop each other in Third World countries where the rivers are polluted and green valleys have become desert.

[Kendall—Henry Kendall, Nobel Prize-winning MIT physics professor]

281.   Hobart Rowen. "Overpopulation Remains World's Defining Crisis." WASHINGTON POST, April 4, 1993, p. H5. "As Earth adds to its total population by nearly 95,000,000 people each year, the pressure upon environments and resources grows greater, the pace of illegal immigration quickens, and entire societies in the developing world collapse under the strain," Kennedy said in a Financial Times article.
[Kennedy—Yale history professor Paul Kennedy]

282.   Harold Gilliam. "Bursting At The Seams." THE SOCIAL CONTRACT, Summer 1993, p. 263. Yet no one in authority has been able to confront publicly the fact that population growth, in this state as well as on the planet, cannot go on forever. It will come to an end either by conscious control or by catastrophe.

283.   Michael D'Antonio. "Apocalypse Soon." LOS ANGELES TIMES MAGAZINE, August 29, 1993, p. 19. Last year, the National Academy of Sciences and Britain's Royal Society issued a rare joint statement on the dangerous trends in population and environmental degradation. The campaign gained further momentum last November, when the Union of Concerned Scientists published a "World Scientists' Warning to Humanity" on the same topics. Signed by more than 1,500 experts, including 104 Nobel Prize winners, this document warns that humanity faces "spirals of environmental decline, poverty and unrest leading to social, economic and environmental decline."

284.   John Vinson. IMMIGRATION OUT OF CONTROL, 1992, p. 29. Environment covers many topics related to the quality of life. It can refer to the presence or absence of overcrowding and pollution. It can also refer to adequate supplies of crucial resources for society, such as farmland and drinkable water; or it can refer to the health of the biological systems—the ecology—which sustain all life. The rate of immigration we allow today has a negative effect on all of these things, not only in the United States, but throughout the world.

285.   John Vinson. IMMIGRATION OUT OF CONTROL, 1992, p. 31. According to one estimate, each person added to our population consumes almost one acre for development. Not all of the land so used would be suitable for farming, but a large share of it is. Much of our good farmland is near cities, and many of these urban areas are spreading out. One reason is the nonstop inflow of immigrants. The highly productive Central Valley of California produces the nation's largest harvests of 40 different crops. During the past 13 years, development, spurred by population growth, has covered 200,000 acres of this valley.

286.   Michael D'Antonio. "Apocalypse Soon." LOS ANGELES TIMES MAGAZINE, August 29, 1993, p. 19. Deforestation and pollution threaten agriculture worldwide. About 11% of the planet's "vegetated surface"—an area the size of China and India combined—is already damaged.

287.   Hobart Rowen. "Overpopulation Remains World's Defining Crisis." WASHINGTON POST, April 4, 1993, p. H5. The global population crisis promises to get worse instead of better. Many poor countries are unable (lack of funds) or unwilling (pressures from religious groups) to provide modern birth control information and devices to women. Most of the additional 95 million people born each year will therefore be born in the most impoverished countries in the world.

288.   Michael D'Antonio. "Apocalypse Soon." LOS ANGELES TIMES MAGAZINE, August 29, 1993, p. 19. The Earth's population is growing by nearly 900 million every year. Today's total of about 5.5 billion is expected to grow to about 10 billion by 2050. Most of the increase will occur where hunger and poverty are already widespread.

289.   Michael D'Antonio. "Apocalypse Soon." LOS ANGELES TIMES MAGAZINE, August 29, 1993, p. 20. As more and more people crowd the planet, they produce more of the "greenhouse gases" that can cause global warming, and they strain ecological resources such as tropical forests and water supplies.

290.   Leon F. Bouvier. PEACEFUL INVASIONS: IMMIGRATION AND CHANGING AMERICA, 1992, p. 129. Although population growth is more rapid in developing nations, per capita energy use in the United States is so large that even a small rate increase of population growth in the United States results in large increases in energy uses—and hence, production of greenhouse gases.

    Not only would the United States benefit directly from a stabilization of its own population, but people throughout the world would benefit through reduced United States production of greenhouse gases.

291.   Peter Brimelow. Response to Simon, Borjas, Wattenberg, Stein, and Bartley. NATIONAL REVIEW, February 1, 1993, p. 34. This brings me to a more fundamental disagreement with Mr. Wattenberg. He thinks the U.S. population must keep growing. I think a stable population is just fine, so long as its skills keep improving. The very facts Mr. Wattenberg cites mutiny against his thesis. India and China are not more important than the United States. And anyway, with the collapse of the Soviet Union, the United States is now the third most populous country in the world.

292.   John Vinson. IMMIGRATION OUT OF CONTROL, 1992, p. 35. If we seek to help the world by never closing our gates, we will end up helping no one. True morality, as wise and good people have always known, must begin with humility—the honest recognition of one's limitations. The same applies to nations. America is not God, and we cannot save the world. To think that we can is an unrighteous conceit.

293.   Virginia D. Abernethy. POPULATION
        POLITICS, 1993, p. 281. Enforcement of immigration law must be weighed against infringement on the privacy rights of citizens. But without enforcement at some point, citizens go on losing jobs, most people's real income falls, energy security becomes a bitter joke, the environment suffers, the carrying capacity is exceeded, and Americans lose cherished values along with their privacy right.

294.   Hobart Rowen. "Overpopulation Remains
        World's Defining Crisis." WASHINGTON POST, April 4, 1993, p. H5. Increasingly, the political leaders of the richer nations, panicked by the threat of invasion by hordes of poor immigrants, are being forced to pay some attention. Count Otto Lambsdorff, chairman of the Free Democratic Party of Germany, said in Washington last week: "Population growth is the number one problem of the world."

295.   Michael D'Antonio. "Apocalypse Soon." LOS
        ANGELES TIMES MAGAZINE, August 29, 1993, p. 19. Indeed, now that the Cold War and the threat of nuclear annihilation have receded, overpopulation may replace the atom bomb in our collective nightmares.

296.   Hobart Rowen. "Overpopulation Remains
        World's Defining Crisis." WASHINGTON POST, April 4, 1993, p. H1. The daily grist of global news can be depressing: war in the former Yugoslavia, the steady economic collapse of Russia and other states of the former Soviet empire and a deteriorating peace process in the Middle East.

    Added to the negative mix are the more mundane economic troubles of the so-called "developed" nations in the Americas, Europe and Asia, which seem to enjoy trade wars when shooting wars—after a period of exhaustion—are put aside.

    But all of these problems pale beside the overwhelming issue of our times, one that politicians won't face head on: excessive population that is devastating the environment and triggering an explosive, uncontrolled, illegal migration of poor people seeking food, shelter and jobs.

297.   Virginia D. Abernethy. POPULATION
        POLITICS, 1993, pp. 271-272. Environmentalists might take note, as well, that more people simply mean more who pollute and consume. Growing population pressure inexorably strengthens the hand of those who argue for sacrificing environmental values in order to provide jobs, housing, drinking water, and more roads. Immigration control is a fundamental element of population stabilization and conservation.

298.   Paul Kennedy. PREPARING FOR THE
        TWENTY-FIRST CENTURY, 1993, p. 45. These push factors in the overpopulated developing world are compounded by the pull factor of population decline in the more developed societies. Today, as in the past, "billions of peasants and ex-peasants…are ready and eager to move into places vacated by wealthier, urbanized

populations." As the better-off families of the northern hemisphere individually decide that having only one or at the most two children is sufficient, they may not recognize that they are in a small way vacating future space (that is, jobs, parts of inner cities, shares of population, shares of market preferences) to faster-growing ethnic groups both inside and outside their national boundaries. But that, in fact, is what they are doing. [ellipses in original]

299.   John Vinson. IMMIGRATION OUT OF
        CONTROL, 1992, p. 15. Dr. David Hayes-Bautista, head of the Chicano Studies Research Center at the University of California at Los Angeles, has found that Mexican immigrants are less likely than past immigrants to assimilate to American culture.

    Previous immigrants, he notes, felt stronger pressure to conform because they generally were cut off from their homelands by an ocean and poor communications. This is not the case today with Mexicans and other Latin immigrants. Says Hayes-Bautista, "We could come back in one hundred years and the Latinos will not have assimilated in the classic sense."

300.   Robert N. Hopkins. "Third World Immigrants
        Cannot Adapt to the U.S." IMMIGRATION: OPPOSING VIEWPOINTS, 1990, p. 238. It is quite clear that it is no longer realistic to assume that this vast and growing number of immigrants, who also prove to be more prolific in child-bearing than the native white American population, are likely to comply with the cultural ideal of conformity to "Old American" ideals and institutions.

301.   Susan Forbes Martin. "U.S. Immigration
        Policy: Challenges for the 1990s." NATIONAL STRATEGY REPORTER, Fall 1993, p. 5. Immigration to the United States is more diverse than ever before. According to a 1993 Census Bureau study, today it takes 19 nationalities to account for 2/3 of the total foreign born. In 1900 the top three nationalities alone equaled 2/3 of all foreign born. There is a growing concern about the capacity to absorb people from countries that previously did not have a history of immigration to the United States.

302.   Robert N. Hopkins. "Third World Immigrants
        Cannot Adapt to the U.S." IMMIGRATION: OPPOSING VIEWPOINTS, 1990, p. 239. Today the government deliberately gives no recognition to race or ethnicity, except to advance the interests of minority ethnic and racial groups, which are thereby encouraged to maintain their own identity and to avoid being absorbed into the "Old American" tradition so readily accepted by most earlier immigrants of European origin.

303.   Leon F. Bouvier. PEACEFUL INVASIONS:
        IMMIGRATION AND CHANGING AMERICA, 1992, p. 184. Immigration is closely intertwined with problems of cultural maintenance. this has been an issue throughout human history and has caused many, sometimes bloody, conflicts. With the emergence of

nation-states and their clearer geographic boundaries, this issue becomes even more threatening.

304. John Vinson. IMMIGRATION OUT OF CONTROL, 1992, p. 23. Without teamwork, new ideas won't necessarily help the economy. If we don't share at least some values and goals, it will be hard to agree on what ideas we want to use and how to apply them. Also, if we cannot agree, the energies of immigrants will end up clashing, instead of contributing to common success.

305. Leon F. Bouvier. PEACEFUL INVASIONS: IMMIGRATION AND CHANGING AMERICA, 1992, pp. 184-185. Whenever the immigrant group refuses to adapt to the dominant culture, conflicts can emerge. This is especially true when the number of such immigrants is relatively large and comes from a single source. Whenever the host group refuses to allow the newcomers to participate in the activities of the society, cultural conflicts can emerge.

306. Thomas Fleming. "Immigrants Threaten American Culture." IMMIGRATION: OPPOSING VIEWPOINTS, 1990, p. 70. Part of the problem is a question of numbers. Talented immigrants are, for the most part, highly assimilable, but mass migrations are disruptive and threaten social cohesion. Between 1976 and 1986, the number of immigrants from Africa doubled, while the numbers from Asia, Mexico, and Haiti all quadrupled. (Haiti, by the way, was on the low side for the Caribbean: Jamaica was up 700 percent). The big winner, however, was India, whose stock rose an impressive 2,000 percent.

307. Paul Kennedy. PREPARING FOR THE TWENTY-FIRST CENTURY. 1993, p. 312. Meanwhile, the ethnic composition of the United States is also changing. Although the forecasts are subject to amendment—many earlier predictions of the future population of the United States have tended to be notoriously inaccurate—demographers are reasonably confident that the white, Caucasian segment will continue to shrink. This is partly due to the expectation of further large-scale immigration, both legal and illegal, chiefly from Latin America and Asia; as "have-not" families stream to "have" societies, America is seen as the most desirable *and* accessible destination to many migrants.

308. Barry Edmonston. "Discussion." DEMOGRAPHY AND RETIREMENT,1993, p. 57. The United States in on the eve of substantial shifts in the racial/ethnic composition of the population. These changes will occur as a response to new patterns of immigration that have evolved during the last thirty years. Current immigrants are predominantly Asian and Hispanic, with some Black immigrants from Caribbean and Africa and some White immigrants from Canada, Europe, and Oceania. Present immigrants are different from the overwhelmingly European movements of the nineteenth and early twentieth centuries.

309. Barry Edmonston. "Discussion." DEMOGRAPHY AND RETIREMENT, 1993, p. 57. Asians and Hispanics will experience substantial growth during the next century. The Asians population will grow from 7 million in 1990 to 60 million in 2090, increasing its proportionate share from 3 percent in 1990 to 14 percent in 2090. Hispanics will increase from 22 million in 1990 to 108 million in 2090, a gain from 9 to 25 percent in the period. Both Asians and Hispanics would be larger groups than Blacks by 2090, although the Hispanic population will be a larger numerical group than Blacks by about 2010.

310. Garrett Hardin. LIVING WITHIN LIMITS, 1993, p. 289. The waves of immigration into the United States during the first decades of the twentieth century were bearable because both residents and immigrants agreed that the newcomers should adopt the language and the ways of the residents as rapidly as possible. The process was called "assimilation." Today, however, assimilation is out of favor: *diversity* is the magic word. "Ethnic pride" causes some minorities to resist assimilation. We can all rejoice when ethnic pride results in the descendants of immigrants becoming genuinely bicultural. But in recent years self-appointed leaders of immigrants have interpreted ethnic pride to mean *ethnic intolerance*—of the ways of the majority. This new development bodes ill for future peace in America.

311. Rodman D. Griffen. "Illegal Immigration." CONGRESSIONAL QUARTERLY RESEARCHER, April 24, 1992, p. 363. But Americans are nearing the breaking point. The United States accepts 700,000 immigrants legally each year, more than the rest of the world put together. Many wonder how many more the country could absorb without causing a social breakdown. According to a poll conducted by the Gallup Organization last month, two-thirds of Americans want greater restrictions placed on immigration.

312. Peter Brimelow. "Time to Rethink Immigration?" NATIONAL REVIEW, June 22, 1992, p. 40. Third World populations are very large and their wage levels very low—Mexican wages are a tenth of those north of the border, and Mexico is relatively advanced. So calculations of the market-clearing wage in a U.S. with open borders necessarily imply that it must be level. This arrangement might optimize global economic utility. But it can hardly improve American social harmony.

313. Thomas Fleming. "Immigrants Threaten American Culture." IMMIGRATION: OPPOSING VIEWPOINTS, 1990, pp. 71-72. First of all, we need to put an end to the mass migrations to the US. It was the *Völkerwanderungen* of the Germans and Huns that brought the Roman Empire down, and we shall be in even worse straits if we fail to control our Southern border and do not adopt a more hard-nosed approach to refugees fleeing the political turmoil, high population growth, and economic chaos of the Third World.

314.   Robert N. Hopkins. "Third World Immigrants
         Cannot Adapt to the U.S." IMMIGRATION:
OPPOSING VIEWPOINTS, 1990, p. 241. After even a
cursory survey of the Third World, anyone can see that
only a foolish ethnocentrism can account for the fond belief of many Americans that their political heritage—
imperfectly received in the past by immigrants from nations having cultures closely related to that of the nation's founders—will in the future transform and overwhelm all that is alien. Such a universal constant cannot
anywhere be found in the records of political history.

315.   Daniel James. ILLEGAL IMMIGRATION: AN
         UNFOLDING CRISIS, 1991, p. 8. Unless a
solution satisfactory to all parties concerned is reached
soon, not only could bilateral relations suffer a sever
setback but U.S. society as a whole could become torn
by schisms. The Southwest is particularly susceptible,
due to the exponential rise in its Hispanic population of
predominantly Mexican origin, but major northern states
are not much less vulnerable. In New York, for example,
the Hispanic population increased by an astonishing
33.4 percent between 1980 and 1990. Now second to the
blacks as the state's biggest minority, it could conceivably overtake them if black growth remains about where
it is—15.9 percent—as projected, while Hispanics grow
at the present or a higher rate. The likelihood is that
Hispanics will again leap forward in number by the year
2000, as a result of the continued "push" from south of
the border and their high rate of population growth.

316.   Leon F. Bouvier. PEACEFUL INVASIONS:
         IMMIGRATION AND CHANGING AMER-
ICA, 1992, p. 190. By limiting immigration, the nation
will at least have a better chance at achieving the goals
of a true national community inhabited by individuals
proud to be American, but equally aware of its shortcomings and its role in the global economy of which we are
all members. This can only take place if these selected
immigrants, and other minorities, are accepted by the
majority as full members of the community and themselves express a sincere desire to join this community.

317.   Daniel James. ILLEGAL IMMIGRATION: AN
         UNFOLDING CRISIS, 1991, p. 35. The threat
of illegal immigration to the U.S. legal system also encourages violence and defiance towards U.S. officials and
agencies—such as the INS, Drug Enforcement Administration, Customs Service, and local police—particularly
in Mexico-U.S. border areas.

318.   Thomas Fleming. "Immigrants Threaten
         American Culture." IMMIGRATION: OPPOS-
ING VIEWPOINTS. 1990, p. 71. If we refuse to control
immigration, our options are severely limited. The least
unattractive solution would be to implement the federal
principle on a state and regional level, recognizing Hispanics and Orientals, in states where they form a majority, as the dominant group—much as the French are
given special status in Quebec. (We must not imitate the
disastrous Canadian policy of nationwide bilingualism.)
Descendants of the old settlers that fought and won the
land from Mexico will be quite rightly indignant with

what many Mexicans are already calling the Reconquest,
and we shall probably have far more trouble than Canada
in adjusting to a multicultural situation. Perhaps after a
century or two we can evolve into a safely neutered society of consumers—like Switzerland. It is just as likely
to be a bloodbath.

319.   Daniel James. ILLEGAL IMMIGRATION: AN
         UNFOLDING CRISIS, 1991, p. 102. The high
growth in illegal immigration from Mexico retards further the relatively slow rate of assimilation of the Mexican-American community in general. This could also
contribute, unwittingly, to the germination of separatist
ideas. Since they cannot legally become eligible for
membership in the general society, or even in the mainstream Mexican-American community, the illegals con-
fine themselves to existing enclaves which are already
outside normal society, and that makes for separateness
if not separatism.

320.   Lawrence Auster. THE PATH TO NATIONAL
         SUICIDE. 1990, pp. 48-49. The decisive fac-
tor, ignored by almost everyone in our sentimental land,
is the sheer force of numbers. The United States has
shown that is has the capacity to absorb a certain number of ethnic minorities into its existing cultural forms.
The minorities, so long as there remains a majority culture that believes in itself, have powerful incentives to
accept the legitimacy of the prevailing culture even as
they add their own variety to it. But as they continue to
grow in numbers relative to the whole population, a
point of critical mass is reached. The new groups begin
to assert an independent peoplehood, and the existing society comes to be seen as illegitimate and oppressive;
what was once (granting its flaws) applauded as the most
beneficent society in the history of the world, is suddenly, as though by a magician's curse, transformed into
an evil racist power.

321.   Paul Kennedy. PREPARING FOR THE
         TWENTY-FIRST CENTURY, 1993, p. 313.
Demographic change can also exacerbate ethnic tensions,
as between African-Americans and Hispanic-Americans
(over jobs), or Asian-Americans and African-Americans
(over educational access), as well as stimulate the racial
worries of poor whites. Over the longer term, the gray-
ing/browning tendency may be setting up a massive contest over welfare and entitlement priorities between predominantly Caucasian retirees and predominately non-
white children, mothers, and unemployed, each with its
vocal advocacy organizations.

322.   John Vinson. IMMIGRATION OUT OF
         CONTROL, 1992, p. 15. Thus, if history is
any guide, the assimilation of current immigrants will
be much more difficult. Their numbers will also tend to
weaken the existing goodwill and trust among our native
racial groups by changing their relative positions in society, a situation certain to bring insecurity, mistrust,
and even hostility.

323.   Robert N. Hopkins. "Third World Immigrants
         Cannot Adapt to the U.S." IMMIGRATION:

OPPOSING VIEWPOINTS, 1990, pp. 238-239. Indeed, recent legislation has affirmed the right of illegal immigrants who have been permitted to stay in the U.S. under the amnesty provisions to benefit from Affirmative Action programs, which is thus unfair to the American blacks and American Indians who were originally targeted to benefit from such programs in light of past disadvantages.

324. Garrett Hardin. LIVING WITHIN LIMITS, 1993, p. 290. It cannot be too often repeated that an extravagantly multicultural nation is poorly positioned to compete with nations that have not succumbed to the siren call for more "diversity." Think of Japan. In facing the real dangers of overpopulation following World War II, Japan showed that she could achieve a unanimity of purpose that is hard to imagine in a multicultural nation. Whatever measures may be required to tame population growth, their difficulty will increase strictly in proportion to the amount of diversity in the population. In a multicultural nation patriotism withers under the onslaught of internal competition between ethnic groups. The nation is then less favorably positioned to deal with external competition. Everyone within the multiethnic nation suffers.

325. Lawrence Auster. THE PATH TO NATIONAL SUICIDE, 1990, p. 53. The argument presented in these pages is that the combined forces of open immigration and multiculturalism constitute a mortal threat to American civilization. At a time when unprecedented ethnic diversity makes the affirmation of a common American culture more important than ever, we are, under the pressure of that diversity, abandoning the very idea of a common culture.

326. Lawrence Auster. THE PATH TO NATIONAL SUICIDE, 1990, pp. 54-55. But for a culture to deny its own "false" legitimacy, as America is now called upon to do, does not create a society free of false legitimacy; it simply means creating a vacuum of legitimacy—and thus a vacuum of power—into which other cultures, replete with their own "imperialistic lies," will move. Training Hispanic and other immigrant children in American public schools to have their primary loyalty to their native cultures is not to create a new kind of bicultural, cosmopolitan citizenry; it is to systematically downgrade our national culture while raising the status and power of other cultures.

327. Lawrence Auster. THE PATH TO NATIONAL SUICIDE, 1990, p. 51. As suggested earlier, pro-immigration conservatives and liberals deal with the looming threat to national cohesion by imagining that it doesn't exist; America, they believe, has an infinite capacity for the assimilation of diverse peoples. This astounding conceit can be made credible only at a great cost—that is, by flattening our idea of American society to the most superficial image of consumerism and pop culture. American culture is thus made equally accessible to all—and equally *meaningless*.

328. Thomas Fleming. "Immigrants Threaten American Culture." IMMIGRATION: OPPOSING VIEWPOINTS. 1990, p. 71. A far less attractive scenario than either Switzerland or tribal civil war Nigerian style would be a forced Americanization on the grand scale. It didn't work all that well the last time we tried it, when Catholics were hectored and bullied out of the officially Protestant public schools, and considering the sort of people who run the federal bureaucracy today, we will in effect be writing the death sentence on republican self-government. Only an empire, with a vast machinery of manipulation (including some form of state religion) could succeed in creating order out of such a Babel, and the best we could hope for would be either a military *junta* or a fascist welfare state—Sweden with a führer.

329. John Vinson. IMMIGRATION OUT OF CONTROL, 1992, pp. 20-21. If the people of America lose common ties, the government will have to step in (or will want to step in) and become the tie that binds us together. This could lay the pathway to dictatorship. The Founding Fathers of this country firmly believed that our freedom required a population with common outlooks and values. This, as noted in Chapter 1, is why they wanted the United States to be cautious about accepting large numbers of immigrants.

Immigrants came to America seeking freedom. It would be sadly ironic if immigration destroyed that liberty for everyone.

330. John Vinson. IMMIGRATION OUT OF CONTROL, 1992, p. 22. But the United States, as we saw in the last chapter, is risking its freedoms on an uncharted voyage to multiculturalism. In a climate of distrust, confusion, and hostility—where cooperation must be enforced by government—freedom and prosperity will decline and fall together.

331. Leon F. Bouvier. PEACEFUL INVASIONS: IMMIGRATION AND CHANGING AMERICA, 1992, p. 60. Third, while it is true that earlier immigrants did eventually adapt to American society, adaptation occurred only after considerable hostility between the new immigrants and the resident population. Furthermore, this successful adaptation occurred in large part because immigration was drastically curtailed for some three decades, beginning in the late 1920s. This is not the case today. Continued high levels of immigration could result in a drastically different, and feuding, kind of nation in the twenty-first century.

332. Otis Graham, Jr. and Roy Beck. "Immigration's Impact on Inner City Blacks." THE SOCIAL CONTRACT, Summer 1992, p. 215. We should not have to rediscover that immigration in large numbers widens the divide between wealth and poverty, storing up social dynamite. This country has a long and sad history of allowing the massive importation of low-skilled foreign workers to displace African Americans, though most black contemporary leaders have lost or renounced the ability to speak about this difficult reality.

333. Dianne Feinstein. CONGRESSIONAL RECORD, June 30, 1993, p. S8276. I am deeply concerned about the consequences of these rising tensions. I believe that we can avoid a serious backlash against all immigrants if we take strong action now to restrict illegal immigration and to protect legal immigration.

334. Mary H. Cooper. "Immigration Reform." CONGRESSIONAL QUARTERLY RESEARCHER, September 24, 1993, p. 845. Moreover, says Charles Wheeler, directing attorney of the National Immigration Law Center, a Los Angeles group that aids legal immigrants, "a certain national hysteria has built up to a level where people are seeing both lawful and undocumented immigrants somehow as the enemy. We are afraid that this is going to lead to some draconian laws that will ultimately hurt the U.S. interest and also the interests of immigrants here in the United States."

335. Dianne Feinstein. "We Can Get a Grip on Our Borders." LOS ANGELES TIMES, June 16, 1993, p. A11. These hard facts could lead, I fear, to a serious backlash against all immigrants if strong and prudent federal policies to protect our border are not put in place.

336. Dianne Feinstein. "We Can Get a Grip on Our Borders." LOS ANGELES TIMES, June 16, 1993, p. A11. The words chiseled into the Statue of Liberty—"huddled masses," "breathe free," "golden door"— vividly come to mind today. If we allow the meaning of these words to be eroded by hate and prejudice, the American dream will be shattered. If we stand tall and institute a fair immigration policy, we can maintain the dream of legal immigration for countless generations to come.

337. Joel Kotkin. "Is Fascism Back in Fashion?" WASHINGTON POST, January 2, 1994, p. C4. The immigration issue especially needs candid confrontation. The decades-long reluctance of Western politicians to take control over the immigration of newcomers, many of them entering illegally, has, indeed, placed enormous social and financial burdens on parts of their nations—such as the south of France, the suburbs of Paris and Brussels, the Ruhr Valley of Germany, parts of Northern Italy, southern California, south Florida, and Texas. That neglect has now fostered a backlash that threatens to result in outright bans on immigration throughout the Euro-American world.

338. Elton Gallegly. Letter. WALL STREET JOURNAL, December 6, 1993, p. A15. We are a nation of immigrants, and I support legal immigration. In fact, we have the world's most generous legal immigration policy, admitting more legal immigrants each year than all of the other nations of the world combined. But in order to preserve the national consensus on legal immigration, the U.S. must quickly act to solve the growing crisis caused by virtually unchecked illegal immigration.

339. Senator Barbara Boxer, CONGRESSIONAL RECORD, October 15, 1993, p. S13540. But, at the same time, we realize that there could be a tremendous backlash against legal immigration if we do not stem this flow of illegal immigrants into our country.

340. Daniel James. ILLEGAL IMMIGRATION: AN UNFOLDING CRISIS, 1991, p. 32. The illegals traffic, among its other evils, does an injustice to the more than two million persons on our immigrant visa waiting lists at U.S. embassies overseas, including the more than 20 percent who are Mexicans. Silvestre Reyes, the Chief U.S. Border Patrol Agent in McAllen, Texas, put it succinctly in a newspaper interview in which he said, "the country that fails to control its borders will fail to control its history."

341. Daniel James. ILLEGAL IMMIGRATION: AN UNFOLDING CRISIS, 1991, p. 32. In practically every case, adult illegal immigrants are conscious of the fact that they have knowingly violated U.S. law, but do so because they know that they would be ineligible for a normal immigrant visa, or because they do not wish to go through the lengthy wait than an immigrant visa would entail. (For Mexicans, it may take up to nine, and as many as a dozen years for some family preference categories.) The ease with which illegal immigrants are able to enter the United States by simply walking undetected across the border mocks our immigrant visa issuance system.

342. John Vinson. IMMIGRATION OUT OF CONTROL, 1992, p. 48. In the last analysis, each country is responsible for its own liberty. If foreigners do not like their governments, it is their responsibility to stay and change them. By giving these foreigners an easy way out, we weaken reform efforts in other countries.

343. Virginia D. Abernethy. POPULATION POLITICS, 1993, p. 295. A further important political consequence of a liberal immigration and refugee policy should also concern us. The possibility of simply leaving a bad situation undercuts pressure for internal reform. The most energetic people, who are most likely to initiate change, may choose emigration if that option is easy; whereas they might otherwise engage constructively with conditions in their country of birth. Thus, emigration is a safety valve for excess population and retards change both because it fosters belief in expanding opportunity and because it lets a nation's dissident elements *out*.

344. John Vinson. IMMIGRATION OUT OF CONTROL, 1992, p. 36. National boundaries maximize responsibility and the incentive for nations to solve poverty and other problems. If a poor country believes that it can indefinitely export its poor people, it will have little motivation to make the difficult decisions and adjustments necessary to put its house in order.

345. Population-Environment Balance, Position Paper, April 1991, quoted in CONGRESSIONAL QUARTERLY RESEARCHER, April 24, 1992, p. 377. Emigration does not provide a net benefit for the country from which immigrants come, either. It is often the politically dissatisfied or economically unfulfilled who decide to leave....These dissatisfied people...are often the most motivated and best able to rectify the problems of their own societies. [ellipses in original]

346. Virginia D. Abernethy. POPULATION POLITICS, 1993, p. 295. Irrational governments have often tried to keep people even against their will: Fossilized political theory equates more people with more clout. But events in Eastern Europe and the former USSR reveal the effect of containing population, including dissidents, within their own country. People who are dissatisfied energize, lead, and structure internal reform.

347. John Vinson. IMMIGRATION OUT OF CONTROL, 1992, p. 36. With immigration to the United States as a safety valve for poverty and discontent, the Mexican people have not had to come to grips with the attitudes and practices that have held back their progress. Those Mexicans arriving in the United States will have little incentive to change their values, either, if their growing numbers prevent assimilation.

348. Bob Sutcliffe. "Immigration and the World Economy." CREATING A NEW WORLD ECONOMY, 1993, p. 93. The United States likes to present a liberal international image, though this is partly hypocritical. It publicly opposed British forcible repatriation of Vietnamese "boat people" from Hong Kong in 1990, and yet it forcibly repatriates around one million illegal immigrants a year. It has condemned the Soviet Union for restricting the emigration of Jews, and yet in 1990 it increased its restrictions on the immigration of Jews from the USSR. It has the largest number of people infected with the HIV virus, and yet is has imposed harsh restrictions on the immigration of infected people. These contradictions are some of the things that keep immigration regulations a leading issue in United States politics.

349. Michael S. Teitelbaum. "New Polemics on Immigration." THE SOCIAL CONTRACT, Spring 1992, p. 183. No sovereignty is possible for a nation with "open borders." If Kuwait had followed such advice over the past decade, there would have been no need for an Iraqi invasion, as Kuwait would have been overwhelmed long ago by immigrants from its largest neighbor.

350. Daniel James. ILLEGAL IMMIGRATION: AN UNFOLDING CRISIS, 1991, p. 9. Yet they already constitute a threat to our very sovereignty. For if, by definition, the movement of people from one nation to another without the latter's consent is a violation of its fundamental laws, that constitutes a breach of its sovereignty. The 159 members of the United Nations recognize that every sovereign nation-state has the right to guard and protect its borders, and the right, above all, to determine who shall be permitted to enter and reside within its national territory.

351. John Vinson. IMMIGRATION OUT OF CONTROL, 1992, p. 60. The essence of democracy is the right of citizens to make the laws that govern their society, including immigration laws. If we do not enforce the limits we set on immigration with a secure border, we are admitting, both to ourselves and to the world. a terrible truth—namely, that the laws we democratically enact mean nothing. If we admit this, then we might as well admit that our democracy and our nation are well on their way to dying.

352. Peter Brimelow. Response to Simon, Borjas, Wattenberg, Stein, and Bartley. NATIONAL REVIEW, February 1, 1993, p. 33. *My June 22 article demonstrated that U.S. immigration policy since the 1965 reforms has been a grand accident. The resulting influx has been vastly larger, more unskilled, and more overwhelmingly Third World than was ever envisioned. There is no positive economic rationale for this influx—essentially because labor is far less important than innovation as a factor of production. But if continued it must have radical political consequences, displacing and dissolving the American nation as it had evolved by 1965.*

353. Dan Stein. Reply to an Article by Peter Brimelow. NATIONAL REVIEW, February 1, 1993, p. 32. "Post-history" presents us with a whole new set of challenges. More and more, people across the political spectrum are recognizing human migration as one of those thorny issues that stand between us and post-historical bliss. Waves of desperate migrants seeking relieve from hunger, poverty, or tribal warfare may prove to be a more formidable challenge to the West than Soviet missiles or tanks.

354. Daniel James. ILLEGAL IMMIGRATION: AN UNFOLDING CRISIS, 1991, p. 103. Finally, if the crisis in Mexico continues and especially if economic conditions worsen, that will drive additional millions of Mexicans into the United States illegally, and intensify the twin problems of high population concentration and low assimilation rate. It is not impossible that among the new arrivals will arise forces which demand radical solutions to their plight, and enlist in their cause the illegal alien underclass and even legal Mexican residents and perhaps some Mexican-American citizens. Caught between economic failure in Mexico and inability to make headway in the United States, frustrated illegals might resort to confrontational tactics and even violence to obtain redress.

355. Daniel James. ILLEGAL IMMIGRATION: AN UNFOLDING CRISIS, 1991, p. 106. The ebbs and flows of world affairs are not, however, the only factor to consider in evaluating whether, or to what degree, the security of the United States may be vulnerable to attack. Its long, porous borders to the north and south of-

fer a permanent invitation to terrorists, or others who may have reason to seek its destruction or dismemberment. That is especially true of its southern flank, where it co-exists with a country, and beyond it a continent, which suffer from most of the ills of semi- or under-developed societies, and in which many kinds of subversive forces continue to flourish.

356.   Daniel James. ILLEGAL IMMIGRATION: AN
         UNFOLDING CRISIS, 1991, pp. 111-112.
Terrorists or subversives might take advantage of the "loose security" that reigns at the border, in at least three ways:

1. They could slip across the Río Grande to carry out hit-and-run attacks against Americans or American property.

2. They could opt for quietly establishing safehouses in the country, looking more to future than present objectives. The Soviets, and before them the Nazis, proved adept at establishing safehouses in strategic locations and putting them to good use. These can be used to raise funds, build support groups, or even store weapons—all important tools for the conduct of terrorist or covert political operations within the United States or in other countries nearby not excluding Mexico itself.

3. They would almost certainly seek to utilize the large communities of illegal aliens already in the United States, particularly those who might feel isolated or perceive cultural, racial, religious, or economic discrimination against them. They could be turned into sympathetic or supportive subcultures to obtain political or logistical support for their movements, or to suppress dissenters in their midst.

357.   Jeffrey H. Birnbaum. "Clinton Administration
         Gearing Up for Effort to Strengthen Barriers to
Illegal Immigrants." WALL STREET JOURNAL, June 29, 1993, p. A20. Fears about illegal immigration have been heightened recently with the arrests of fundamentalist Muslims linked to the World Trade Center bombing and, to a number of planned terrorist acts, even though most of those arrested entered the U.S. illegally.

358.   David G. Savage. "Temporary Visas Used to
         Stay in U.S. Indefinitely." LOS ANGELES
TIMES, March 8, 1993, p. A1. The World Trade Center bombing and the recent shooting outside the CIA point up a surprising laxity in U.S. immigration laws that permit foreigners to enter this country on a temporary visa and to stay indefinitely—with virtually no chance of getting caught.

359.   Rep. Bereuter. CONGRESSIONAL RECORD.
         July 1, 1993, p. H4430. We want to be open to legal immigrants, but I want to tell my colleagues, and particularly the members of the Judiciary Committee, that if we do not take some of the actions that the INS has been crying for these many years now, if we don't give them the legal tools and resources to reduce the numbers of people who are coming in here illegally or by devious and fraudulent abuse of our processes, some coming with ill intent in their hearts, if we do not take some steps to begin to shut the door on abuses of politi-

cal asylum, then we are going to have terrorist events in this country that will shake the foundations of our constituencies.

360.   Ken Silverstein. "The Labor Debate."
         SCHOLASTIC UPDATE, November 19, 1993, p. 16. The growing public outcry against immigration stems partly from concern about crime: illegal immigrants account for one in every five inmates at federal prisons. Fears were also fanned earlier this year when six immigrants—several of them illegal—were arrested as suspects in the terrorist bombing of New York City's World Trade Center.

361.   Daniel James. ILLEGAL IMMIGRATION: AN
         UNFOLDING CRISIS, 1991, p. 115. A similar patter could show up in Mexico if that country's government is unable to resolve its decade-long crisis. In the event, Mexicans who are fed up with bad conditions at home could, in an effort to draw worldwide attention to their plight, perpetrate acts of terror against American nationals in Mexico and/or American lives and property on U.S. territory. The sheer size of the illegal flow would make it extraordinarily difficult for Mexico's security agencies to halt such acts, even did they possess the political will to do so. U.S. agencies, chronically undermanned, would be helpless.

362.   Paul Kennedy. PREPARING FOR THE
         TWENTY-FIRST CENTURY, 1993, pp. 313-314. Simply because the regional electoral balances (e.g., share of seats in the House of Representatives) do, over time, reflect population change, there is likely to be a further shift in voting power from the North and East to the South and West, from Caucasian to non-Caucasian districts, from Europe/Israel-centered issues to Hispanic/Pacific concerns. The executive, judiciary, and legislative branches, at present with a mere sprinkling of normal, nonwhite members, will find it difficult to halt their metamorphosis into bodies containing many more women and minorities. Schools and colleges, already grappling with the demands to teach both "multiculturalism" and "Western civilization," may come under further social and cultural pressures as the demographic tide advances.

363.   George F. Kennan. "U.S. Overpopulation
         Deprives the Planet of a Helpful Civilization."
THE SOCIAL CONTRACT, Spring 1993, p. 193. What we shp. A11 then have accomplished is not to have appreciably improved conditions in the Third World (for even the maximum numbers we could conceivably take would be only a drop from the bucket of the planet's overpopulation) but to make this country itself a part of the Third World (as certain parts of it already are), thus depriving the planet of one of the few great regions that might have continued, as it now does, to be helpful to much of the remainder of the world by its relatively high standard of civilization, by its quality as example, by its ability to shed insight on the problems of the others and to help them find their answers to their own problems.

364. Representative Gallegly, Fact Sheet on Illegal Immigration, April 9, 1993, quoted in CONGRESSIONAL RECORD, July 1, 1993, H4436. Illegal immigration into the United States is a growing crisis that is causing widespread problems across the entire nation. The recent examples of Zoe Baird, and the bombing of the World Trade Center, show that illegal immigrants are not just a problem in California or the Southwest— and the public outrage that grew out of these instances are further proof that the American people overwhelmingly support actions to finally regain control over our borders.

365. Dianne Klien. "Majority in State Are Fed Up With Illegal Immigration." LOS ANGELES TIMES, September 19, 1993, p. A1. "Anti-immigrant feeling is definitely up," said Times Poll director John Brennan, who conducted the survey among 1,162 California residents from Sept. 10-13. "The bottom line is, people believe immigration is the third-largest problem facing California."

366. Ken Silverstein. "The Labor Debate." SCHOLASTIC UPDATE, November 19, 1993, p. 16. This nation accepts more foreigners than the rest of the world combined. But polls show that 60 percent of p. A11 Americans favor drastically curbing immigration.

367. Mary H. Cooper. "Immigration Reform." CONGRESSIONAL QUARTERLY RESEARCHER, September 24, 1993, p. 843. According to a recent *New York Times*/CBS News poll, 61 percent of Americans want a decrease in current immigration levels, up from 49 percent in 1986. Only a third said the country should welcome new immigrants, while 60 percent said such a policy was not feasible because of economic conditions.

368. Tom Morgenthau. "America: Still a Melting Pot?" NEWSWEEK, August 9, 1993, p. 18. The latest *Newsweek* poll reveals the public's sharply shifting attitudes. Fully 60 percent of all Americans see current levels of immigration as bad; 59 percent think immigration in the past was good. Fifty-nine percent also say "many" immigrants wind up on welfare, and only 20 percent think America is still a melting pot.

369. David W. Stewart. IMMIGRATION AND EDUCATION, 1993, p. 215. Nearly every survey over the past several decades indicates that the majority of the public does not endorse an increase in legal levels of immigration. A national poll conducted by the Roper Organization and released in June 1990 showed that 77 percent of all those surveyed held this opinion; Hispanic-Americans (74 percent) and black Americans (78 percent) shared the majority view. Some 67 percent of those polled stated that they believed the level of legal immigration should be reduced.

370. Michael D. Weiss. "Sisyphean Policy: Borders and Bureaucracies." THE WORLD AND I, January 1994, p. 371. Illegal immigration is rapidly emerging as one of the "hot-button" issues of the nineties. Though once regarded as a strictly regional issue, events have thrust it into the center of the national debate. The bombing of the World Trade Center, the beaching of a shipload of illegal Chinese immigrants within sight of the Statue of Liberty, the interception of similar ships off of Mexico, the increased number of Cuban defectors fleeing to Florida, the continuing influx of Haitian refugees, and a persistent economic recession have brought the immigration debate to a level unknown since the Chinese Exclusion Act (1882).

371. Dick Kirschten. "Catch-Up Ball." NATIONAL JOURNAL, August 7, 1993, F376, p. 1976. But suddenly, things have changed. Reports of terrorist plots and alien-smuggling rings combined with high unemployment appear to have inflamed public opinion. When her firm, Mellman•Lazarus•Lake Inc., conducted two dozen focus groups around the country in June, Lake said she was startled by the results. "I can't believe how intense the immigration issue is," she said in an interview. "It's agenda-setting."

372. Fred Barnes. "No Entry." NEW REPUBLIC, November 8, 1993, p. 12. The Wilson effect did not go unnoticed, as Republicans sensed a new wedge issue. "This is a defining issue for many Americans because it spells out a difference between the two parties," says Representative Lamar Smith of Texas, chairman of the House GOP's task force on immigration. Smith points to recent House votes in which a majority of Democrats opposed adding more Border Patrol agents and requiring National Service officials to report illegal aliens. "These votes show Republicans put American workers and taxpayers ahead of the interests of illegal aliens, and with Democrats it's the reverse," says Smith.

373. Fred Barnes. "No Entry." NEW REPUBLIC, November 8, 1993, pp. 10-12. As the debate heated up this year, Republicans quickly leapfrogged routine Democratic proposals to toughen border interdiction of illegals. Republican Governor Pete Wilson of California called for the elimination of all education, medical and welfare benefits for illegal aliens, claiming that these are a "magnetic lure" to immigrants. He also advocated killing another lure, automatic citizenship for children born here to parents who have come illegally. The result: Wilson experienced his first jump in popularity in more than two years. In a *Los Angeles Times* poll, his approval rose from 30 percent to 37 percent and his disapproval dropped from 59 percent to 45 percent.

374. Tom Morgenthau. "America: Still a Melting Pot?" NEWSWEEK, August 9, 1993, p. 19. On Capitol Hill, the revival of an issue that many had thought dead is shaking both political parties, and Democrats such as Sen. Dianne Feinstein of California are scrambling to neutralize nativist backlash.

375. Michael S. Teitelbaum. "New Polemics on Immigration." THE SOCIAL CONTRACT, Spring 1992, p. 182. Most immigrants and refugees are

235

law-abiding and hardworking, as the advocates emphasize. but even those of us who support generous immigrant and refugee admissions must admit with dismay that some immigrants and refugees have played leading roles in the destructive rise of the drug trade and violent crime in cities such as New York, Washington, Miami, and Los Angeles.

376.   William F. Jasper. "Illegal Immigration Is a Crisis." IMMIGRATION: OPPOSING VIEWPOINTS, 1990, p. 163. The alien influx has also contributed greatly to our spiraling crime statistics. Most illegal aliens are not criminally inclined, and, other than violating our immigration laws, do not engage in illegal activities, But when we're dealing with millions of aliens, it does not take a large percentage to add up to a sizable criminal element.

377.   Palmer Stacy and Wayne Lutton. "Illegal Immigrants Cause Crime." IMMIGRATION; OPPOSING VIEWPOINTS, San Diego: Greenhaven Press, 1990, p. 95. In years past our elected representatives passed laws to keep criminals out and then enforced those laws. Today the laws are still on the books but our leaders have lost the will to enforce them. There is scarcely a community in America that has gone untouched by alien-related crime—a crime-wave which will continue to worsen unless strong action is taken.

378.   John Tanton and Wayne Lutton. "Immigration and Crime." THE SOCIAL CONTRACT, SPRING 1993, p. 165. Orange Police Chief Merrill Duncan disclosed during a press conference in April 1992 that the 12 percent increase in crime from the previous year in that city is the result of a "tremendous influx of illegal aliens." He added that, "most crime suspects are illegals."

379.   Daniel James. ILLEGAL IMMIGRATION: AN UNFOLDING CRISIS, 1991, p. 63. The truly frightening aspect of the illegal immigration across our southern border is that it tends to foster violence. For some years, even before the recent resurgence in illegal crossings, the increase in violence and the threat of it along the border have been such as to alarm law-abiding residents of the region.

380.   Rodman D. Griffen. "Illegal Immigration." CONGRESSIONAL QUARTERLY RESEARCHER, April 24, 1992, p. 375. According to the INS and other enforcement officials, crimes committed by illegal aliens are skyrocketing, fueled in part, critics say, by an unwieldy and impractical deportation process. Los Angeles and other cities say between 15 percent and 30 percent of the major crimes reported each year may be attributable to illegal aliens. At present, nearly 20 percent of the inmates in federal prisons are illegal aliens."

381.   Palmer Stacy and Wayne Lutton. "Illegal Immigrants Cause Crime." IMMIGRATION; OPPOSING VIEWPOINTS, San Diego: Greenhaven Press, 1990. pp. 93-94. Many illegals engage in crime as soon as they are across the border. Charles Perez, INS

director from the El Paso, Texas, area, says half of that city's downtown crime is related to illegal immigration. In Houston, more than 30 percent of the city's murders involve illegal aliens. And Denver Police chief Art Dill notes that illegals who cannot quickly find work "steal to survive."

382.   Palmer Stacy and Wayne Lutton. "Illegal Immigrants Cause Crime." IMMIGRATION; OPPOSING VIEWPOINTS, San Diego: Greenhaven Press, 1990. p. 91. One of the consequences of ceasing to enforce sensible immigration controls has been the wave of alien-related crime that has struck our nation from coast to coast. Our immigration laws prohibit the entry of criminals and ex-convicts, the mentally ill, persons likely to become welfare charges, prostitutes and procurers and other undesirable individuals. Despite the intent of these laws, politicians have allowed thousands of dangerous criminals and perverts to enter our country.

383.   John Tanton and Wayne Lutton. "Immigration and Crime." THE SOCIAL CONTRACT, Spring 1993, p. 167. The alien-related crime that plagues this country is one of the consequences of failure to enact and enforce sensible immigration controls. The problem posed by alien criminals is not new. Since the early days of the Republic, foreign criminal elements have viewed this as a "land of opportunity."

384.   William F. Jasper. "Illegal Immigration Is a Crisis." IMMIGRATION: OPPOSING VIEWPOINTS, 1990, p. 163.
• Illegal aliens are involved in one-third of the rapes and murders and one-fourth of the burglaries in San Diego County.
• Aliens account for over half of the homicides in Orange County.
• Aliens are responsible for about 90 percent of the narcotics traffic in the city of Santa Ana, and 80 percent of the same in Fullerton.

385.   John Vinson. IMMIGRATION OUT OF CONTROL, 1992, p. 28. With high immigration rates making assimilation difficult, and limited economic prospects for many immigrants, we face more crime on top of the highest crime rate in the Western world. The cost of lawlessness to our economy is difficult to calculate, but it is certainly high. Incalculable is the loss of the "domestic tranquillity" which the Constitution states as a primary reason for the American union.

386.   John Vinson. IMMIGRATION OUT OF CONTROL, 1992, p. 27. Growing numbers of illegal aliens who cross the Mexican border come from big cities in Mexico and Central America. Many are streetwise, and carry the influence of slum life. Border Patrol spokesman Ted Swofford noted in 1990 that "We see increasingly more of the criminal element [crossing the border], not just people coming over here to get a job. These people tend to be more violent."

387.   John Vinson. IMMIGRATION OUT OF CONTROL, 1992, p. 27. Today, as noted in

chapter two, at least a quarter to even as many as 45 percent of all immigrants enter illegally. Literally, their first action in America is to break our laws. And they continue breaking laws to stay here, such as using fake identity papers to get jobs and welfare. Most illegals are poor and, being illegal, they do not feel part of society. Not surprisingly, some take up crime as a career.

388.   John Tanton and Wayne Lutton. "Immigration and Crime." THE SOCIAL CONTRACT, Spring 1993, p. 165. Gang activity is no longer limited to the traditional areas of immigrant settlement. As new immigrants have migrated to the Midwest, America's heartland has come to experience the ethnic violence that plagues the East and West Coasts, Florida, and the Southwest. In Chicago, the police are doing battle against not only black and Hispanic gangs, but Assyrians, Chinese, Cambodians, Vietnamese, Filipinos, and Greeks.

389.   John Tanton and Wayne Lutton. "Immigration and Crime." THE SOCIAL CONTRACT, Spring 1993, pp. 159-160. Since the mid 1980s, major crime operations have not only come to be directed by foreign nationals, but staffed by them as well, instead of employing American agents. An INS report titled, *The Newest Criminals: The Emergence of Non-Traditional Organized Ethnic Crime Groups and INS's Role in Combating Them*, says that many of the ethnic criminal organizations exist in their native countries and simply expand into the United States. Said David Leroy, chief of domestic intelligence for the U.S. Drug Enforcement Administration, "Ethnic gangs appear to be *the* new trend in crime."

390.   Palmer Stacy and Wayne Lutton. "Illegal Immigrants Cause Crime." IMMIGRATION; OPPOSING VIEWPOINTS, San Diego: Greenhaven Press, 1990, p. 94. Mexican gangs have already made large sections of East Los Angeles unsafe for law-abiding Americans, and the problem is bound to get worse as more illegals enter southern California from Mexico. As the Urban Institute explains in its study, *The Fourth Wave: California's Newest Immigrants*, "Youth gangs unquestionably pose a problem. Since the mid-1970s violent gang warfare resulting from drug usage and dealing have become common in the barrios and public housing projects."

391.   John Tanton and Wayne Lutton. "Immigration and Crime." THE SOCIAL CONTRACT, Spring 1993, pp. 165-166. As bad as the situation is now, the problems created in the U.S. by our new immigrant street gangs are bound to become much worse in the future if corrective measures are not quickly enacted and strictly enforced.

392.   Representative Gallegly, Fact Sheet on Illegal Immigration, April 9, 1993, quoted in CONGRESSIONAL RECORD, July 1, 1993, H4437. Law enforcement authorities agree that there are some 23,000 members of two gangs in Los Angeles who are illegal aliens—gangs responsible for more than 100 murders.

393.   John Tanton and Wayne Lutton. "Immigration and Crime." THE SOCIAL CONTRACT, Spring 1993, p. 165. This gang culture belies the media-created image of immigrants as "model citizens." For example, in California, as reported by *The New York Times*, "the simmering ethnic stew not that is Los Angeles seems to favor youth gang activity. Gangs of almost every nationality flourish: Samoan, Filipino, Salvadoran, Mexican, Korean, Vietnamese. Experts estimate there are about 600 gangs…" Law enforcement officials put the current number of members for these gangs at over 100,000. In nearby Long Beach, a war between Cambodian and Hispanic gangs has been raging for over two years. [ellipses in original]

394.   John Vinson. IMMIGRATION OUT OF CONTROL, 1992, p. 27. Legal and illegal immigration is giving organized crime a new lease on life in the United States. Just as law enforcement was bringing the Mafia and other old-time syndicates under control, the nation, especially in the larger cities, has witnessed the rise of ethnic mobs that draw most of their recruits from new arrivals.

395.   Palmer Stacy and Wayne Lutton. "Illegal Immigrants Cause Crime." IMMIGRATION; OPPOSING VIEWPOINTS, San Diego: Greenhaven Press, 1990, p. 91. The 1980 Cuban and Haitian invasion of southern Florida turned what was an alien crime *problem* into an alien crime *crisis*. After the Carter Administration made it clear that no action would be taken to halt the illegal flood of "refugees" from Mariel Harbor, Castro seized the opportunity to rid his island of some of the dregs of the Cuban population and proceeded to empty his prisons and insane asylums. As many as 40,000 hardcore criminals and sex deviates were welcomed by Jimmy Carter with "an open heart and open arms."

396.   Palmer Stacy and Wayne Lutton. "Illegal Immigrants Cause Crime." IMMIGRATION; OPPOSING VIEWPOINTS, San Diego: Greenhaven Press, 1990, p. 91. Bullets and knives were soon entering the hearts of other Americans, such as Lieutenant Jan Brinkers of the New York City Housing Police, murdered May 4, 1981, by Cuban "boat people." According to a shocking *New York* magazine article entitled "Los Bandidos Take the Town: Castro's Outcasts Shoot Up New York," some 2,000 Cuban gunmen prowl New York City, where they commit "thousands of shootings, robberies, and rapes."

397.   John Vinson. IMMIGRATION OUT OF CONTROL, 1992, p. 16. In 1991, the nation's capital witnessed two days of riots by illegal aliens from El Salvador, who caused considerable property damage and even burned police cars. The disturbance received nationwide press coverage. News commentators cited disagreements brought about by cultural differences as a major source of tension, along with the difficulty the immigrants had obtaining employment in a depressed economy. Some commentators speculated that similar

disorders could take place in other cities with large numbers of illegals.

398.   John Vinson. IMMIGRATION OUT OF
          CONTROL, 1992, p. 17. Blacks, however, did
not make up the majority of rioters. Approximately half
of those arrested for rioting were Hispanics, most of
whom came from neighborhoods with large concentrations of recent immigrants. Many of those arrested were
illegal aliens.

399.   John Vinson. IMMIGRATION OUT OF
          CONTROL, 1992, p. 17. Korean immigrants
were a major target of black hostility during the riots.
Cultural differences between blacks and Koreans caused
great misunderstanding. Large-scale immigration from
Korea slowed Korean assimilation.

400.   John Vinson. IMMIGRATION OUT OF
          CONTROL, 1992, p. 17. These tensions
played a part in the Los Angeles riots of 1992. Although
much of the media tried to portray this violence as a conflict between black and white citizens, immigration was
the major underlying cause. As a consequence of massive
immigration, blacks in Los Angeles have lost political
clout and economic opportunities. This has been a significant source of anger and frustration in the black
community.

401.   Vernon M. Briggs. "Political Confrontation
          with Economic Reality: Mass Immigration in
the Postindustrial Age." in ELEPHANTS IN THE
VOLKSWAGEN, 1992, pp. 81-82. Immigration is a
contributing factor to the growth of adult illiteracy in
this nation. As a consequence, immigration, by adding
to the surplus of illiterate job seekers, is serving to diminish the limited chances of many poorly prepared citizens to find jobs or to improve their employability. It is
not surprising therefore, that the underground economy,
with its culture of drugs, crime, and gangs, is thriving in
many of the nation's urban centers.

402.   Barbara McCarthy. "Memo from the San Diego
          Border." THE SOCIAL CONTRACT, Spring
1993, p. 176. Illegal alien minors in California who
have broken not only federal law by illegal entry, but
state penal codes, are being held in California Youth Authority facilities at a cost of $31,000 per youngster, for a
total cost of $20,150,000 in FY 1991.

403.   Barbara McCarthy. "Memo from the San Diego
          Border." THE SOCIAL CONTRACT, Spring
1993, p. 176. A Los Angeles County study found that at
least 11 percent of the criminals in their county jails are
illegal, deportable aliens with a cost to taxpayers of
some $75.1 million per year.

404.   John Tanton and Wayne Lutton. "Immigration
          and Crime." THE SOCIAL CONTRACT,
Spring 1993, p. 159. For the U.S. population as a
whole, the incarceration rate in federal and state prisons
is 233 per 100,000 persons. Among illegal aliens, the
incarceration rate is three times the U.S. average. Since

1980 there has been a 600 percent increase in alien inmates, principally for drug-related offenses. Over the past
five years, an average of more than 72,000 aliens have
been arrested annually on drug charges.

405.   John Tanton and Wayne Lutton. "Immigration
          and Crime." THE SOCIAL CONTRACT,
Spring 1993, p. 164. A study commissioned by the San
Diego Association of Governments found that one in
four jail inmates acknowledged being in this country illegp. A11y. Judges estimate that up to 35 percent of the
felony cases in Superior Court involve illegals. A 1990
check in felony disposition court discovered that 41 percent of the defendants had immigration "holds"—on
completion of sentence, they would be released to the
INS for detention.

406.   John Tanton and Wayne Lutton. "Immigration
          and Crime." THE SOCIAL CONTRACT,
Spring 1993, p. 164. As a test, Orange County Superior
Court Judge David O. Carter invited the INS
(Immigration and Naturalization Service) into his courtroom to help identify criminal aliens and develop deportation cases against them. Judge Carter informed the
House Judiciary Committee that "the results are staggering.…My criminal calendar is 36 percent illegal felons."
[ellipses in original]

407.   John Tanton and Wayne Lutton. "Immigration
          and Crime." THE SOCIAL CONTRACT,
Spring 1993, p. 165. Twelve percent of the nearly
58,000 inmates in New York's state correctional system
are foreign-born (either illegal aliens or legally admitted
aliens who have committed crimes). The Governor's office reports it costs taxpayers $27,000 per alien, per
year, to house these criminals, or about $183 million
annually. Nearly half of the foreign-born inmates in New
York come from Caribbean nations.

408.   John Tanton and Wayne Lutton. "Immigration
          and Crime." THE SOCIAL CONTRACT,
Spring 1993, p. 165. In the Texas state prison system,
only 4.3 percent of the inmates are foreign-born. But
this is because, as *The Dallas Morning News* pointed
out in its February 2, 1992 issue, "the state in effect
uses municipal and county jails to house some of its
prisoners. In the largest jail on the Texas-Mexico border,
the county facility at El Paso, the percentage of criminal
aliens ranges from 10 to 15 percent of the inmate population. Of the federal inmates in Texas, 36 percent are
foreign-born."

409.   John Vinson. IMMIGRATION OUT OF
          CONTROL, 1992, p. 27. In San Diego
County, California, 12 percent of felony crimes are
committed by illegal aliens. In Los Angeles County, 11
percent of jail inmates are illegal aliens. Nationwide, illegals cost the criminal justice system a total of $800
million a year.

410.   Representative Gallegly, Fact Sheet on
          Illegal Immigration, April 9, 1993, quoted in
CONGRESSIONAL RECORD, July 1, 1993, p.

H4436. A growing number of illegal aliens are involved in criminal activity. A 1990 study found that some 22,000 deportable aliens are incarcerated in L.A. county's jails—more than 18 percent of the jail population. this costs the county $75 million a year, what a report termed "an unnecessary burden on the local justice system" Statewide, the Department of Corrections spends $250 million to imprison 13,000 illegal aliens convicted of felonies.

411.   John Tanton and Wayne Lutton. "Immigration and Crime." THE SOCIAL CONTRACT, Spring 1993, p. 164. The California Attorney General reports that approximately 16,000 illegal alien felons are incarcerated in state prisons. Every year it costs California taxpayers $350 million to keep these criminal aliens behind bars.

412.   John Tanton and Wayne Lutton. "Immigration and Crime." THE SOCIAL CONTRACT, Spring 1993, p. 165. On April 27, 1992, the state of New York filed a suit against the Federal Government, demanding that it start taking custody of thousands of illegal aliens currently incarcerated in state prisons. The suit charges that the Federal Government is responsible for taking charge of these inmates and launching deportation proceedings against them. But too often, the U.S. Justice Department fails to do that. Once convicts serve their terms, the state is forced to simply release them onto the streets, where they are often arrested for new crimes.

413.   Dianne Feinstein. "We Can Get a Grip on Our Borders." LOS ANGELES TIMES, June 16, 1993, p. A11. A study for the Board of Supervisors found that 11% of the nearly 18,000 Los Angeles County jail inmates were deportable illegal residents. Another study showed that of those deported once they are released from prison, a shocking 80% return to commit another serious crime.

414.   John Tanton and Wayne Lutton. "Immigration and Crime." THE SOCIAL CONTRACT, Spring 1993, p. 164. State and local governments in California spend more than $500 million a year to arrest, try and imprison illegal aliens who commit serious crimes, according to a California state Senate report issued on March 23, 1993.

415.   Mario Cuomo. Letter to Senator Bob Graham, quoted in CONGRESSIONAL RECORD, November 16, 1993, S15758. New York State and others are proud to serve as gateways for the nation, but we cannot shoulder the resultant burdens alone. The costs of undocumented alien felons are of particular concern, especially as they drain precious state resources from other crime-fighting efforts and beneficial programs for our residents.

416.   Daniel James. ILLEGAL IMMIGRATION: AN UNFOLDING CRISIS, 1991, p.33. The violation of U.S. immigration law inherent in crossing the border surreptitiously is not the only threat that illegal immigration poses to the American legal system. Indeed, illegal immigration invites, and appears to foster, violations of U.S. legislation in a multitude of fields. Living a life beyond the law logically encourages a culture of lawlessness.

417.   Daniel James. ILLEGAL IMMIGRATION: AN UNFOLDING CRISIS, 1991, p. 34. Illegal male immigrants between 18 and 25 are also apt to violate the U.S. Selective Service law by not registering. In many instances, illegal aliens violate housing codes by, for example, crowding more immigrants into apartments or houses in immigrant neighborhoods than local codes allow. Illegal aliens, by virtue of their status and avoidance of contact with the authorities, also present a standing invitation to their employers (whether U.S. citizens, permanent resident aliens, or illegal immigrants themselves) to violate U.S. health and safety, wage and hour, and labor laws.

418.   Daniel James. ILLEGAL IMMIGRATION: AN UNFOLDING CRISIS, 1991, p. 34. Because it is imperative for them to remain inconspicuous and out of sight of the authorities, illegal aliens often end up violating various other laws. Many of them insist, for example, on being paid in cash in order to avoid having to pay U.S. income taxes or file U.S. income tax returns—a practice which unscrupulous American employers may be only too willing to countenance.

419.   Palmer Stacy and Wayne Lutton. "Illegal Immigrants Cause Crime." IMMIGRATION; OPPOSING VIEWPOINTS, San Diego: Greenhaven Press, 1990, p. 93. Gangs of Mexicans have repeatedly attacked Border Patrol officers with rocks and guns near the border. The Border Patrol has been forced to obtain some special armored vans—nicknamed "War Wagons"—in which to conduct border watches.

420.   Mary H. Cooper. "Immigration Reform." CONGRESSIONAL QUARTERLY RESEARCHER, September 24, 1993, p. 843.
• Two CIA employees were shot and killed as they sat in their cars outside CIA headquarters near Washington, D.C. Police said the suspect was a Pakistani national living in the United States illegally. While here, he managed to get a job, a driver's license—and the gun he allegedly used in the crime.

421.   Daniel James. ILLEGAL IMMIGRATION: AN UNFOLDING CRISIS, 1991, p. 30. The rapid expansion of illegal immigration into the United States is a threat to the integrity of its legal system in general. By its very nature, illegal immigration constitutes a violation of the U.S. immigration legislation, and contributes to a growing sub-culture of lawlessness in which a host of federal, state, and locals laws and ordinances are regularly violated.

422.   Leon F. Bouvier. PEACEFUL INVASIONS: IMMIGRATION AND CHANGING AMERICA, 1992, p. 3. The availability of immigrant workers has several effects: Immigrants make it unnecessary to

improve "bad jobs," which soon become even less attractive. As these immigrant jobs slip further behind mainstream expectations, welfare and crime become preferred alternatives for unskilled Americans.

423.   John Vinson. IMMIGRATION OUT OF
          CONTROL, 1992, p. 24. Even at the lowest wages and working conditions, there still aren't enough jobs for arriving immigrants. This is particularly true in times of recession, such as the economic slowdown of the early nineties. Lack of jobs was one reason for the May 1991 illegal alien riots in Washington, D.C., and the 1992 Los Angeles riots.

424.   Palmer Stacy and Wayne Lutton. "Illegal
          Immigrants Cause Crime." IMMIGRATION; OPPOSING VIEWPOINTS, San Diego: Greenhaven Press, 1990, p. 93. The millions of illegal aliens flooding our country by land, sea and air clearly have little respect for our laws—their very presence shows that. Many bring illegal drugs with them as they come. Immigration and Naturalization Service Commissioner Alan C. Nelson said in 1986 that 28% of the persons arrested for drug possession by the Border Patrol are illegal aliens.

425.   Dianne Feinstein. CONGRESSIONAL
          RECORD, June 30, 1993, S8277. The consequences of lax border enforcement have other serious dimensions. In 1990, along California's southern border, the INS, Customs, DEA, working together in Operation Alliance seized nearly 400,000 pounds of marijuana with a minimum street value of $1.2 billion, and 34,000 pounds of cocaine, conservatively valued at $326 million on California streets.

426.   William F. Jasper. "Illegal Immigration Is a
          Crisis." IMMIGRATION: OPPOSING VIEWPOINTS, 1990, p. 164. Our uncontrolled borders are an open invitation to the international drug cartels to flood the American markets with their deadly wares. And they have done just that. Our backroads, our interstates, and our airways in the Southwest have become cocaine corridors and heroin highways, transporting billions of dollars worth of narcotics transshipped through Mexico. The Border Patrol accounts for 70 percent of the drug interdiction on our southern border, even though that is not their primary responsibility....

427.   Barbara McCarthy. "Memo from the San Diego
          Border." THE SOCIAL CONTRACT, Spring 1993, p. 175. Others are involved in much larger drug transactions and will attempt to drive a large load across the border and make a substantial profit. Many have done this successfully, using their vehicles to knock down an old fence or to drive through the gap left by a previous dealer.

428.   Daniel James. ILLEGAL IMMIGRATION: AN
          UNFOLDING CRISIS, 1991, p. 68. Illegal immigration into the United States has become a vital instrument used by both Mexican and Colombian drug smugglers to infiltrate increasing quantities of narcotics

into this country, at a time when both the Mexican and U.S. governments are cooperating closely to win the drug war. In recent years, ever larger amounts of cocaine are being transported from Colombia to Mexico, then transshipped across the border; these are in addition to traditional Mexican-produced drugs, such as heroin and marijuana, which enter the United States directly from Mexico. Increasingly, cocaine is being moved into the United States by illegal aliens.

429.   Barbara McCarthy. "Memo from the San Diego
          Border." THE SOCIAL CONTRACT, Spring 1993, p. 175. Some illegals enter this country with direct intent to commit crimes. Close to the border area, auto theft is a favored activity. The vehicles tend to be either sold to chop shops on this side of the border, or taken south and sold as is. Many illegals are involved in the drug traffic. Substantial numbers will body-carry a few pounds of marijuana or cocaine to be delivered north of the border. They do this for their smugglers who will accept it as payment for guiding them across the border.

430.   Daniel James. ILLEGAL IMMIGRATION: AN
          UNFOLDING CRISIS, 1991, p. 69. Organized drug rings are using illegal immigrants to carry drugs into the United States more frequently. There is also substantial evidence that drug dealers and drug rings operating inside the United States seek out illegal immigrants already here and recruit them for their operations in this country. Though the number of illegal immigrants involved in drug trafficking constitute a small minority of all illegal aliens, they represent a significant problem nonetheless.

431.   Daniel James. ILLEGAL IMMIGRATION: AN
          UNFOLDING CRISIS, 1991, p. 69. In testimony before the Western Hemisphere Affairs Subcommittee of the Senate Foreign Relations Committee on May 13, 1986, William von Raab, then Commissioner of the U.S. Customs Service, declared that "our Southwest border has become a serious problem of crisis proportions with respect to the trafficking of narcotics across it."

432.   Palmer Stacy and Wayne Lutton. "Illegal
          Immigrants Cause Crime." IMMIGRATION; OPPOSING VIEWPOINTS, San Diego: Greenhaven Press, 1990, p. 93. In an affidavit filed in the U.S. District Court in Portland, Oregon, In a 1986 heroin case, Neil Van Horn, a federal Drug Enforcement Administration agent, said, "I know that in and around the Portland metropolitan area, upper-level distributors often use illegal immigrants to transport heroin or other controlled substances into the United States from Mexico....The illegal immigrants are then used to protect or distribute the heroin or other contraband substances and in that manner obtain their livelihood. Oftentimes, if arrested, they only action taken is deportation back to Mexico." [ellipses in original]

433.   Daniel James. ILLEGAL IMMIGRATION: AN
          UNFOLDING CRISIS, 1991, p. 71. Cocaine smuggling has been increasing at a very rapid rate since

the Colombian drug cartels began to use Mexico as a trampoline. The DEA estimates that an average of three-quarters of a ton of cocaine a day is entering the United States through Brownsville, Texas, the *Washington Post* reported. It noted that the drug is transported in all sorts of ways, hidden in produce, equipment, cattle trucks, or simply, on human bodies.

434.   John Tanton and Wayne Lutton. "Immigration and Crime." THE SOCIAL CONTRACT, Spring 1993, p. 166. The international dimension of the drug trade in America highlights the failure of past policies to protect the nation's interest. Federal officials concede that foreign nationals not only are responsible for producing virtually all of the drugs consumed in the U.S., but are in charge of nearly all of the distribution.

435.   William F. Jasper. "Illegal Immigration Is a Crisis." IMMIGRATION: OPPOSING VIEWPOINTS, 1990, p. 164. During 1987, the INS's Western Regional Office (covering California, Nevada, Hawaii, and Arizona) deported then thousand illegal aliens for criminal activities, and most of them were serious felony offenses. Half of these cases were drug-related.

436.   Daniel James. ILLEGAL IMMIGRATION: AN UNFOLDING CRISIS, 1991, p. 68. In its *International Control Strategy Report,* issued in March 1991, the State Department's Bureau of International Narcotics Matters revealed:

Mexico continues to produce about one-third of the heroin and 70 percent of the marijuana imported into the U.S. The [United States Government] estimates that over half the cocaine which entered the U.S. in 1990 transitted Mexico.

The most alarming fact in the State Department's report is that "over half the cocaine which entered the U.S. in 1990 transitted Mexico." It reflected an increase of nearly 60 percent in the amount of cocaine coming into the United States from Mexico the year before.

437.   John Tanton and Wayne Lutton. "Immigration and Crime." THE SOCIAL CONTRACT, Spring 1993, p. 166. Florida remains a major hub for their North American operations. The drug trade has pumped billions of dollars in to the Sunshine State's economy. But as Florida, which sits astride the major air and trade routes from South America, has come under increasing surveillance by law enforcement, our porous border with Mexico has become the path favored by foreign suppliers. As one Colombian drug dealer told a Miami-based colleague, "Come to California. It's the promised land."

438.   National Council of La Raza. "Third World Immigrants Are Adapting to the U.S." IMMIGRATION: OPPOSING VIEWPOINTS, 1990, p. 230. Another cause for fear has been the seemingly large number of immigrants in recent years. In fact, there are proportionately few foreign-born people in the United States now than during almost any earlier period in our history. Between 1860 and 1920, for example, the foreign-born never dropped below 13% of the total population. In 1980, the figure was 6.2%.

439.   Julian L. Simon. "Immigrants and Alien Workers." JOURNAL OF LABOR RESEARCH, Winter 1992, p. 74. The volume of immigration as a *proportion* of the population (see Figure 1) is a more appropriate measure of economic effects than are absolute numbers. Immigrants who arrived between 1901 and 1910 constituted 9.6 percent of the population; between 1961 and 1970 immigrants constituted only 1.6 percent. The recent flow is less than one-sixth as heavy as it was in the earlier period.

440.   Julian L. Simon. "Immigrants and Alien Workers." JOURNAL OF LABOR RESEARCH, Winter 1992, p. 75. The National Research Council, in a recent study paid for by the Immigration and Naturalization Service, estimated that the number of illegal aliens is between 2 and 4 million. This new estimate is even lower than the Census Bureau estimate, making the double-digit figures of the INS and the anti-immigration organizations seem even more preposterous. The illegal immigrant scare no longer serves as an effective red herring for the anti-immigration advocates.

441.   Julian L. Simon. "The case for greatly increased immigration." PUBLIC INTEREST, Winter 1991, p. 91. Between 1901 and 1910 immigrants arrived at the yearly rate of 10.4 per thousand U.S. population, whereas between 1981 and 1987 the rate was only 2.5 percent of the population. So the recent flow is less than a fourth as heavy as it was in that earlier period. Australia and Canada admit three times that many immigrants as a proportion of their population.

442.   Julian L. Simon. "Immigrants Help the U.S. Economy." IMMIGRATION: OPPOSING VIEWPOINTS, San Diego: Greenhaven Press, 1990, p. 83. A solid body of research has now shown that the actual number of illegals at its peak in the early 1980s was perhaps 3 million, many of whom were only transitory workers. The million-plus number of persons who registered for the amnesty of 1987-88 verifies that the total was and is nowhere near the huge numbers that were bandied about when the 1986 Simpson-Mazzoli law was passed.

443.   Julian L. Simon. POPULATION MATTERS: PEOPLE, RESOURCES, ENVIRONMENT, AND IMMIGRATION, 1990, pp. 264-265. Leonard Chapman, then the commissioner of the Immigration and Naturalization Service, first scared us in the 1970s with an estimate that up to 12 million people were illegally in this country. It was just a guess, but now ingenious statisticians using a variety of methods report that the total number of illegals is almost certainly below 6 million, and may be only 3.5 to 5 million. Furthermore, the number of illegals in the country overstates the number of Mexicans who intend to remain permanently, leaving perhaps 1.3 million Mexican illegals—certainly

not a large number by any economic test, and far less than the scare figures promulgated earlier.

444.   Michael D'Antonio. "Apocalypse Soon." LOS ANGELES TIMES MAGAZINE, August 29, 1993, p. 20. But while industrialized countries may be bracing for an onslaught, it has yet to materialize. It turns out that most of the world's refugees do not travel from one continent to the next. Instead, hungry Third World people travel to neighboring underdeveloped states in search of relief. Tom Argent, a policy analyst for the committee, says that poorer countries bear the real brunt of refugees, who migrate en masse and can seriously overburden resources.

445.   Julian L. Simon. "Immigrants Help the U.S. Economy." IMMIGRATION: OPPOSING VIEWPOINTS, San Diego: Greenhaven Press, 1990, p. 82. Even in absolute numbers, total immigration is nowhere near its volume in those years when U.S. Population was less than half of what it now is.

The foreign-born population is only about 6% now— less than the proportion in such countries as Britain, France, and West Germany, and vastly lower than in Australia and Canada. The U.S. is not at present a "country of immigrants"—it is a country of the descendants of immigrants.

446.   Julian L. Simon. POPULATION MATTERS: PEOPLE, RESOURCES, ENVIRONMENT, AND IMMIGRATION, 1990, p.265. Based on all the evidence available up to 1980, a crack team of demographers at the Census Bureau estimated that net illegal immigration is only 200,000 to 250,000 per year— much less than the 500,000 to 1 million that the Immigration and Naturalization Service still tells us are entering each year. And the following also could be said: This June, a National Research Council study lowered the estimate to zero—yes, zero. That is, on the basis of the most recent and best evidence, no net illegal immigration has occurred since 1977. The council says there are 2 million to 4 million illegal aliens, a far cry from INS's inflammatory estimates of 12 million or more.

447.   National Council of La Raza. "Third World Immigrants Are Adapting to the U.S." IMMIGRATION: OPPOSING VIEWPOINTS. 1990, p. 230. Mexicans today constitute about 13 to 14% of legal immigrants and perhaps 50% of undocumented entrants; even if the largest estimates are used, Mexicans probably constitute less than 25% of total immigrants today. The actual proportion of immigrants is far lower if we exclude the large number of Mexican entrants who do not plan to stay in the United States permanently.

448.   James Flanigan. "Blaming Immigrants Won't Solve Economic Woes." LOS ANGELES TIMES, August 15, 1993, p. D1. The Clinton White House recently estimated that 3 million people live here illegally, from many nations—China, Mexico, Ireland, Nigeria, India—and in many parts of the country. That's less than half the widespread estimates used by immigra-

tion critics, that more than 6 million illegals live in America.

449.   James Flanigan. "Blaming Immigrants Won't Solve Economic Woes." LOS ANGELES TIMES, August 15, 1993, p. D1. To begin with, estimates vary incredibly about how big a "problem" illegal immigration is. The U.S. Immigration and Naturalization Service estimates that 300,000 people enter the country illegally each year, but don't remain here. Illegal aliens go back and forth between Mexico and the United States, says the INS.

450.   Rodman D. Griffen. "Illegal Immigration." CONGRESSIONAL QUARTERLY RESEARCHER, April 24, 1992, p. 374. More than 3 million people illegally cross the U.S.-Mexican border each year. The common assumption is that they all stay but, in reality, more than nine out of 10 don't. Experts say only 200,000 to 300,000 become permanent inhabitants each year.

451.   Mary H. Cooper. "Immigration Reform." CONGRESSIONAL QUARTERLY RESEARCHER, September 24, 1993, p. 849. But according to Sharry of the National Immigration Forum and other supporters of U.S. policies, the reforms enacted since 1980 work to everyone's benefit. "Immigrants come here for three main reasons," says Sharry. "To join close family members from whom they've been separated, because they have skills for jobs that Americans can't fill and if they are refugees, who are considered to be of special interest to the United States. So when people say our immigration policy is out of control and irrational and that we're being overwhelmed, I say we let in people who want to come because of family, freedom and work."

452.   Mary H. Cooper. "Immigration Reform." CONGRESSIONAL QUARTERLY RESEARCHER, September 24, 1993, pp. 844-845. "We already have a rational immigration policy,' says Frank Sharry, executive director of the National Immigration Forum, which supports generous immigration and refugee policies. "It's just been distorted in recent months by the dramatic events and a fair amount of manipulation of public opinion by the media. The message is that it's out of control, that we're being overrun by Chinese boat people, Haitians and Mexicans." In fact, Sharry says, of the approximately 1 million people who enter the United States each year to stay, 700,000 are legal immigrants, 125,000 are admitted as refugees and 250,000 enter illegally. "The assumption that we're being overwhelmed by illegal immigration is wrong."

453.   Ben J. Wattenberg and Karl Zinsmeister. "The U.S. Should Encourage Immigration." IMMIGRATION: OPPOSING VIEWPOINTS, San Diego: Greenhaven Press, 1990, p. 114. The first thing to be said about current immigrant flows to this country is that in historical terms they are fairly moderate. While the actual number of foreign citizens now entering the U.S. may seem high—about 650,000 per year, counting

legals, illegals, and refugees, and subtracting out-migration—it amounts all in all to an annual increase in the population of only about one-fifth of 1 percent. At the turn of the century, by contrast, when immigration was at its height, it increased the U.S. population by about 1 percent per year.

454.   Stephen Chapman. "Immigrant myths and the recurrent urge to exclude." CHICAGO TRIBUNE, July 25, 1993, sec. 4, p. 3. It's a populist myth that only blue-collar workers face competition from foreigners: In recent years, those admitted from abroad have been more likely than Americans to have college degrees and managerial or professional skills. Asians, who made up 43 percent of those accepted in the 1980s, have been described by one authority as "the most highly skilled of any immigrant group we've ever had." Ivy Leaguers, beware.

455.   Arturio Santamaria Gomez. "The Porous U.S.-Mexico Border." THE NATION, October 25, 1993, p. 461. By 1991 the Valley of Mexico, including Mexico City, had become the biggest source of undocumented workers in the United States. The new wave of migration to the north is made up of people who, by and large, are better educated and more cosmopolitan than in the past. It includes a large number of professionals and technicians whom the Mexican job market has not been able to absorb.

456.   Tom Morgenthau. "America: Still a Melting Pot?" NEWSWEEK, August 9, 1993, pp. 20-21. Looking around the world, "one can't find the natural forces that will bring down the flow," says Harvard University sociologist Nathan Glazer. "The first impact of prosperity will be to increase it. Look at China. These people don't come from the backward areas, they come from the progressive parts. As they learn how to run a business, they say to themselves, 'Why not go to the United States and do even better?'"

457.   Julian L. Simon. "Immigrants Help the U.S. Economy." IMMIGRATION: OPPOSING VIEWPOINTS, San Diego: Greenhaven Press, 1990, p. 82. First- and second-generation children do astonishingly well ins school—at Boston's 17 public high schools, 13 of the 1989 valedictorians were immigrants or the children of immigrants. They win an astonishing proportion of scholastic prizes—22 of 40 Westinghouse Science Talent Search finalists in [a] recent contest, according to the American Enterprise Institute's Karl Zinsmeister and Ben Wattenberg.

458.   Julian L. Simon. "Immigrants Help the U.S. Economy." IMMIGRATION: OPPOSING VIEWPOINTS, San Diego: Greenhaven Press, 1990, p. 81. *Immigrants are typically as well-educated and occupationpally skilled as natives.* [This was true even a century ago.] New arrivals bring valuable technical knowledge with them, and the proportion with post-graduate education is far higher than the average of the native labor force. Immigrants who arrived between 1970 and 1980 were 50% more likely than natives to have post-

graduate education; immigrants from Asia were 2-1/2 times more likely to have post-graduate education than natives.

459.   George J. Borjas. FRIENDS OR STRANGERS: THE IMPACT OF IMMIGRANTS ON THE U.S. ECONOMY, 1990, pp. 21-22. Because only a fixed number of visas is available, allocating a large fraction of these visas to relatives of U.S. residents implies that many highly skilled applicants cannot enter the United States simply because they lack these family ties. But the empirical evidence indicates that persons who migrate as part of a family unit are more skilled than single or unattached immigrants.

460.   James Shenfield. "New Blood." (Review of *The Economic Consequences of Immigration* by Julian L. Simon) NATIONAL REVIEW, September 3, 1990, p. 42. Skilled immigrants are in short supply. And it has been predicted that by the year 2000 more than half of all new workers in the labor force will be from minorities; half of their numbers will be immigrants."

461.   Ruben G. Rumbaut. "Passages to America." AMERICA AT CENTURY'S END, 1991, p. 235. For example, we have already mentioned the disproportionate impact of immigrant engineers in U.S. universities. Given the continuing decline of enrollments in advanced engineering training among the native-born, the proportion of the foreign-born in these fields has grown rapidly. By 1987 over half of all assistant professors of engineering under thirty-five years of age in U.S. universities were foreign-born, and it is estimated that by 1992 over 75 percent of all engineering professors in the United States will be foreign-born. Already one out of every three engineers with a doctorate working in U.S. industry today is an immigrant.

462.   Julian L. Simon. "Immigrants Help the U.S. Economy." IMMIGRATION: OPPOSING VIEWPOINTS, San Diego: Greenhaven Press, 1990, p. 81. Of course, people at all levels of skill and education benefit the economy. And the total number of immigrants is the most important issue. An overall increase in immigration is the best way to boost the crucial stock of talented scientists, inventors, engineers, and managers who will improve U.S. competitiveness.

463.   Rich Thomas and Andrew Murr. "The Economic Cost of Immigration." NEWSWEEK, August 9, 1993, p. 18. Immigration has ranked with corn and cars as a mainstay of American economic growth. The traditional theory is simple: energetic workers increase the supply of goods and services with their labor, and increase the demand for other goods and services by spending their wages. A benign circle of growth uncurls as a widening variety of workers create rising riches for each other.

464.   Anthony Lewis. "The Politics of Nativism." NEW YORK TIMES, January 14, 1994, p. A29. The historic American pattern of striving immi-

grants building the economy also continues. Here in San Jose, the big city of Silicon Valley, Vietnamese are about 10 percent of the population. Vietnamese businesses are thriving, and many a high school valedictorian is of Vietnamese origin.

465.   Julian L. Simon. POPULATION MATTERS: PEOPLE, RESOURCES, ENVIRONMENT, AND IMMIGRATION, 1990, p. 266. The central economic fact now—as it has been throughout U.S. history—is that, in contrast to the rapidly aging U.S. population, immigrants tend to arrive in their 20s and 30s, when they are physically and mentally vigorous and in the prime of their work life. On average, they have about as much education as do natives, and did so even at the turn of the century. Immigrants also tend to be unusually self-reliant and innovative: they have the courage and the belief in themselves that is necessary for the awesome challenge of changing one's culture and language.

466.   Tom Bethell. "Immigration, Si; Welfare, No." AMERICAN SPECTATOR, November 1993, p. 19. Meanwhile I'm trying to understand the illogical position of such anti-immigrant conservatives as Pat Buchanan. He looks back to the United States of the 1950s, in which he grew up, and sees the huge decline that has taken place. I have no disagreement there. But his conclusion is a non-sequitur: Keep out the foreigners! Why? The American decline has been an indigenous, not an externally driven phenomenon; precipitated by inheritors, not newcomers. The best hope of pulling out of the nose-dive is to bring in lots of new people who have never been anywhere near Choate, Groton, or Harvard Yard. It's the people whose parents were rich enough to give them sports cars for graduation who are the most likely source of decline.

467.   Julian L. Simon. POPULATION MATTERS: PEOPLE, RESOURCES, ENVIRONMENT, AND IMMIGRATION, 1990, p. 287. Perhaps the greatest contribution of immigrants is the push they give to this country's vitality and growth. They contribute to the vitality of our institutions because they tend to be more intellectually vigorous as well as harder-working than natives.

468.   Julian L. Simon. "Immigrants and Alien Workers." JOURNAL OF LABOR RESEARCH, Winter 1992, p. 73. There are many hard-working and skilled people all over the world who are ready and willing to supply their labor to fill the demand for workers in the United States. Labor shortage solved! And, as bonuses, additional people would receive the blessings of life in the United States; the standard of living for American citizens would go up; the competitive position of the United States relative to the rest of the world would improve; and the image of the nation would gain from the connections of the new immigrants with their relatives back home.

469.   Alan W. Bock. "Illegal Immigration Should Be Legalized." IMMIGRATION: OPPOSING

VIEWPOINTS, 1990, p. 179. Even in such hard times, however, only a minority choose to emigrate. They tend to be a special type—unusually restless, resourceful, adaptable, and ambitious. Such people, as U.S. history records, tend to add dynamism and entrepreneurial zeal to the land they choose as a destination.

470.   Julian L. Simon. "The case for greatly increased immigration." PUBLIC INTEREST, Winter 1991, pp. 98-99. Most important in the long run is the boost that immigrants give to productivity. Though hard to pin down statistically, the beneficial impact of immigration upon productivity is likely to dwarf all other effects after these additional workers and consumers have been in the country a few years. some of the productivity increase comes from immigrants working in industries and laboratories that are at the forefront of world technology. We benefit along with others from the contribution to world productivity in, say, genetic engineering that immigrants could not make in their home countries. More immigrants mean more workers, who will think up productivity-enhancing ideas.

471.   Julian L. Simon. POPULATION MATTERS: PEOPLE, RESOURCES, ENVIRONMENT, AND IMMIGRATION, 1990, p. 274. Lastly, and what is likely the most important long-run effect of immigrants: The impact on productivity of these additional workers and consumers is likely to dwarf all else after a few years in the country. Some productivity increase arises from immigrants working in industries and laboratories here that are at the forefront of world technique. We benefit along with others from the contribution to world productivity in, say, genetic engineering and so forth that immigrants would not be able to make in their home countries.

472.   Julian L. Simon. "Immigrants and Alien Workers." JOURNAL OF LABOR RESEARCH, Winter 1992, p. 78. The number of immigrants now coming to the United States is proportionally only a fraction of the number that came in earlier years, and there is nothing in those numbers to suggest a difficult absorption burden. Immigrants, both legal and illegal, more than pay for the services they use with the taxes they pay, leaving a considerable net surplus that benefits American citizens. Immigrants raise productivity and do not cause an observable amount of unemployment of citizens. Admitting far more immigrants into the country than the law now allows would have positive effects on the incomes of citizens, and would enhance the continuing vitality of the United States.

473.   Julian L. Simon. POPULATION MATTERS: PEOPLE, RESOURCES, ENVIRONMENT, AND IMMIGRATION, 1990, p. 287. But the benefits of variety go beyond consumer and esthetic pleasures. Variety is a key ingredient of invention. Immigrants also stimulate natives to produce more and be more innovative as the natives attempt to keep up with the new competition. And we should not forget that just as the movement of people in earlier times was crucial in transmitting ideas, it is important today.

474. Julian L. Simon. "The case for greatly increased immigration." PUBLIC INTEREST, Winter 1991, p. 94. Nowadays, however, the most important capital is human capital—education and skills, which people own themselves and carry with them—rather than capitalist-supplied physical capital. The bugaboo of production capital has been laid to rest by the experience of the years since World War II, which taught economists that, aside from the shortest-run considerations, physical capital does not pose a major constraint to economic growth. It is human capital that is far more important in a country's development. And immigrants supply their own human capital.

475. Ben J. Wattenberg and Karl Zinsmeister. "The U.S. Should Encourage Immigration." IMMIGRATION: OPPOSING VIEWPOINTS, San Diego: Greenhaven Press, 1990, p. 120. Immigration can energize whole communities with a new entrepreneurial spirit, keeping us robust and growing as a nation. At a time when the idea of competitiveness has become a national fixation, it can bolster our competitiveness and help us retain our position as the common denominator of the international trade web.

476. Ken Silverstein. "The Labor Debate." SCHOLASTIC UPDATE, November 19, 1993, p. 17. Economists also note that illegal immigrants not only pay sales tax on purchases, but—because they often use fake documents to obtain employment—have Social Security and federal income taxes withheld from their paychecks. Few dare file for a refund, so that money remains in government coffers.

477. Julian L. Simon. POPULATION MATTERS: PEOPLE, RESOURCES, ENVIRONMENT, AND IMMIGRATION, 1990, p. 274. In sum, immigrants benefit natives through the public coffers by using less than their share of services and paying more than their share of taxes. They cover the additional public capital needed on their account through the debt service on past investments. In the long run, lower-paid workers will not suffer from the new immigrants because immigrants' occupations and educations cover the income spectrum.

478. Ben J. Wattenberg and Karl Zinsmeister. "The U.S. Should Encourage Immigration." IMMIGRATION: OPPOSING VIEWPOINTS, San Diego: Greenhaven Press, 1990, p. 116. What is more, within eleven to sixteen years of coming to America the average immigrant is earning as much as, or more than, the average native-born worker. Immigrant *families*, who typically have more working members, outstrip native families in income in as little as three to five years. In this way, immigrants become above-average tax*payers*. Viewed strictly in terms of fiscal flows and social-welfare budgets, then, immigrants tend to represent a good deal for the nation.

479. Julian L. Simon. "The case for greatly increased immigration." PUBLIC INTEREST, Winter 1991, p. 98. There are two main reason why today's

immigrants make net contributions to the public coffers. First, far from being tired, huddled masses, immigrants tend to come when they are young, strong, and vibrant, at the start of their work lives. For example, perhaps 46 percent of immigrants are in the prime labor-force ages of twenty to thirty-nine, compared with perhaps 26 percent of natives. And only 4 percent of immigrants are aged sixty or over, compared with about 15 percent of natives. Second, many immigrants are well educated and have well-paying skills that produce hefty tax contributions.

480. Julian L. Simon. "The case for greatly increased immigration." PUBLIC INTEREST, Winter 1991, p. 99. An economist always owes the reader a cost-benefit assessment for policy analysis. So I combined the most important elements pertaining to legal immigrants with a simple macroeconomic model, making reasonable assumptions where necessary. The net effect is slightly negative for the early years, but four or five years later the net effect turns positive and large. And when we tote up future costs and benefits, the rate of "investment" return from immigrants to the citizen public is about 20 percent per annum—a good return for any portfolio.

481. Julian L. Simon. "Immigrants and Alien Workers." JOURNAL OF LABOR RESEARCH, Winter 1992, pp. 75-76. Immigrants also pay *more* than their share of taxes. Within three to five years, immigrant-family earnings reach and surpass those of the average American family. Tax and welfare data computed together indicate that immigrants contribute to the public coffers an average of about $1,300 per year. The main reason why immigrants make net contributions is that they tend to come to the United States when they are young and strong and at the start of their work lives. They are not poor, huddled masses.

482. Larry Rohter. "Revisiting Immigration and the Open-Door Policy." NEW YORK TIMES, September 19, 1993, Sec. 4, p. 4. In fact, a 1991 study by the Federal Reserve Bank of New York found that the male immigrant "faces on average significantly higher rates of average taxation than do natives." Julian Simon, author of "The Economic Consequences of Immigration" calculates that during their first three decades in the country, immigrant families typically pay more taxes than their native counterparts and on average contribute about $2,500 a year more in taxes than they obtain in public services.

483. Anthony Lewis. "The politics of Nativism." NEW YORK TIMES, January 14, 1994, p. A29. In fact, most economists believe that immigrants benefit, not burden, the economy. Julian L. Simon of the University of Maryland, writing in The Wall Street Journal last year, showed that immigrants do not reduce others' jobs and that the average immigrant family pays $2,500 more in taxes annually than it receives in public services.

484.   Julian L. Simon. POPULATION MATTERS: PEOPLE, RESOURCES, ENVIRONMENT, AND IMMIGRATION, 1990, p. 265. Immigrants also pay more than their share of taxes. Within three to five years, immigrant-family earnings reach and pass those of the average American family. The tax and welfare data together indicate that, on balance, immigrants contribute to the public coffers an average of $1300 or more each year that family is in the United States.

485.   Blayne Cutler. "Wanted: More Irving Berlins." (Review of *The Economic Consequences of Immigration* by Julian L. Simon) AMERICAN DEMOGRAPHICS, June 1990, p. 12. When immigrants come to this country, they are younger than the average American. Their average educational attainment is equal to or greater than the national average. Most often, immigrants arrive just as they enter their prime earning years. Nearly one-third of Asians who came to the U.S. between 1970 and 1980 were aged 25 to 34, compared with just 16 percent of all Americans in 1980.

486.   Ben J. Wattenberg. Reply to an Article by Peter Brimelow. NATIONAL REVIEW, February 1, 1993, p. 32. Additional moderate demographic growth, via immigration, is good for America for a variety of reasons, including deficit reduction—to aid native-born young workers in paying off fixed costs like defense, debt, and, for several generations, Social Security.

487.   Julian L. Simon. "Immigrants Help the U.S. Economy." IMMIGRATION: OPPOSING VIEWPOINTS, San Diego: Greenhaven Press, 1990, p. 81. *Immigrants do not rip off natives by over-using welfare services.* Immigrants typically arrive when they are young and healthy. Hence new immigrant families use fewer welfare services than do average native families because immigrants do not receive expensive Social Security and other aid to the aged. And immigrant families pay more taxes than do native families. Therefore, immigrants contribute more to the public coffers in taxes than they draw out in welfare services. Every year, an average immigrant family puts about $2,500 into the pockets of natives from this excess of taxes over public costs.

488.   Julian L. Simon. "Immigrants Help the U.S. Economy." IMMIGRATION: OPPOSING VIEWPOINTS, San Diego: Greenhaven Press, 1990, pp. 81-82. *Immigrants demonstrate desirable economic traits.* Compared to natives, immigrants save more, apply more effort during working hours, have twice as great a propensity to be self-employed (according to Teresa Sullivan of the University of Texas), have higher rates of participation in the labor force and are unusually self-reliant and innovative. Immigrants contribute important new productivity-enhancing ideas to industry and science, and they win Nobel prizes.

489.   Penny Loeb, et. al. "To Make a Nation." *U.S. News and World Report*, 4 Oct 1993, p. 52. Time proves a great leveler for many immigrants. According the *U.S. News* analysis, only 20 percent of the immigrants who arrived in the United States between 1980 and 1990 earned more than $22,419 a year, the average income of U.S. citizens between ages 25 and 54. Of those immigrants who arrived before 1980, however, most now earn only $2,000 less than the U.S. average.

490.   Penny Loeb, et. al. "To Make a Nation." *U.S. News and World Report*, 4 Oct 1993, p. 49. While only 20 percent of recent immigrants boast incomes higher than the average U.S. citizen, they catch up. After a decade in this country, immigrants, on average, took home salaries comparable to those of nonimmigrant Americans.

491.   Ben J. Wattenberg and Karl Zinsmeister. "The U.S. Should Encourage Immigration." IMMIGRATION: OPPOSING VIEWPOINTS, San Diego: Greenhaven Press, 1990, p. 120. Researchers at San Diego State University report that "immigrants and refugees to the U.S.—whether from Asia, Europe, or Latin America—are systematically outperforming all native-born American students in grade-point averages despite…English-language handicaps." Beyond the specific contributions made by such people, we may also consider the salutary shock effect their presence in our schools could have on young native-born Americans.

492.   Julian L. Simon. POPULATION MATTERS: PEOPLE, RESOURCES, ENVIRONMENT, AND IMMIGRATION, 1990, p. 285. Moreover, the period during which the immigrants' inferior informally learned skills—related to language and lack of experience with communications technology—detract from productivity appears fairly short. In perhaps two to five years, immigrants pick up the informal learning and then forge ahead of natives. The average immigrant worker comes to have higher earnings than the average American worker after a few years, due in large part to his or her youth and high level of education.

493.   Ben J. Wattenberg and Karl Zinsmeister. "The U.S. Should Encourage Immigration." IMMIGRATION: OPPOSING VIEWPOINTS, San Diego: Greenhaven Press, 1990, p. 119. With the harassment's of crime and the low spending habits of the residents, only long hours of unpleasant work can make inner-city businesses succeed. And in Anacostia, as in many other places, it is largely immigrants who are opening establishments in the commercial desert. It is easy to downplay the significance of their contribution, and their motive is not altruism. But for residents who can buy milk and newspapers and hay-fever pills at 2 A.M. where before there was nothing, they make a significant addition to the quality of life…. [ellipses in original]

494.   Alan W. Bock. "Illegal Immigration Should Be Legalized." IMMIGRATION: OPPOSING VIEWPOINTS, 1990, p. 179. It is likely, in fact, that illegal immigration has contributed to economic dynamism and even kept a number of domestic industries from moving overseas. The garment industry in New York, the garment and furniture industries in Southern California, and electronic assembly in Silicon Valley, to

name a few, would have all but disappeared or have moved to Hong Kong or Korea if not for immigrants, legal and illegal, willing to work for relatively low wages. Those industries also employ native-born Americans, but often in higher-paying management or skilled support positions. If a magic wand could be waved to send all the illegals back where they came from in an instant, the economic effects on many industries could be devastating.

495.   Alan W. Bock. "Illegal Immigration Should Be Legalized." IMMIGRATION: OPPOSING VIEWPOINTS, 1990, p. 179. Most areas with a large illegal population, including Houston and Dallas before the collapse of oil prices, have had generally higher wage levels and lower unemployment levels than the country as a whole during the "illegal invasion." That could be a tautological statement. Why would illegals go where there weren't any jobs available? But if immigration really wrecked an area's economy, some deterioration would be obvious.

496.   James Fallows. "Immigrants Do Not Threaten American Culture." IMMIGRATION: OPPOSING VIEWPOINTS, San Diego: Greenhaven Press, 1990, p. 75. The economic evidence about immigration is open and shut. Immigrants are disproportionately entrepreneurial, determined, and adaptable, and through history they have strengthened the economy of whatever society they join. John Higham, of Johns Hopkins University, probably the leading historian of American immigration, has argued that immigrants strengthened American capitalism during its rocky periods at the turn of the century, and that they add crucial flexibility today. "At the simplest level one notes the prominence of the foreign-born among American inventors and also entrepreneurs and technicians in new, high-risk industries such as textile manufacturing in the early nineteenth century, investment banking in mid-century, and movie-making in the early twentieth century," Higham told a congressional committee in 1986.

497.   Bob Sutcliffe. "Immigration and the World Economy." CREATING A NEW WORLD ECONOMY 1993, p. 93. Immigrant workers furnish the labor force in three areas of the economy. First, they fill various professional posts, such as doctors and engineers, in which the number of qualified U.S. personnel is insufficient to meet the demand. Second, they occupy a disproportionate number of the rapidly expanding low-paid service jobs that have grown alongside the high-paid financial and other services in the major cities (Sassen 1988:ch. 3). The sharp growth of inequality in income distribution in the United States is in part a reflection of this development. And third, immigrants have been a major constituent of the great expansion of low-paid manufacturing jobs in the Southwest in areas such as clothing and electronics.

498.   Ben J. Wattenberg and Karl Zinsmeister. "The U.S. Should Encourage Immigration." IMMIGRATION: OPPOSING VIEWPOINTS, San Diego: Greenhaven Press, 1990, p. 118. Many, though not all,

economists believe we may be entering an era of long-term labor deficit. Business cycles may rise and fall, they maintain, but the long-term trend will probably be one of too few qualified workers for the positions available. From mid-1985 to 1990, eleven million new jobs opened up while the total working-age population grew by only five million. If that squeezing trend continues, it will become harder and harder for employers to fill positions.... [ellipses in original]

499.   Julian L. Simon. "Immigrants Help the U.S. Economy." IMMIGRATION: OPPOSING VIEWPOINTS. . San Diego: Greenhaven Press, 1990, p. 83. *Immigrants increase the flexibility of the economy.* Newcomers are unusually mobile both geographically and occupationally even after they arrive. Hence they mitigate the tight labor markets that the U.S. is beginning to experience.

500.   Rich Thomas and Andrew Murr. "The Economic Cost of Immigration." NEWSWEEK, August 9, 1993, p. 18. "The short-term costs of immigration today are much higher," says Michael Boskin, formerly chief economist to George Bush, "but in the long run, immigrants are still great news for our economy."

501.   Bob Sutcliffe. "Immigration and the World Economy." CREATING A NEW WORLD ECONOMY, 1993, p. 104. Even if unskilled immigrants read to work for relatively low pay may exert a depressing effect on wages in some sectors, this effect at present is diminished or eliminated because existing immigration as a whole has a stronger tendency to raise wages by raising demand.

502.   Alan W. Bock. "Illegal Immigration Should Be Legalized." IMMIGRATION: OPPOSING VIEWPOINTS, 1990, pp. 179-180. There is a virtual consensus among those who have studied the phenomenon in any depth—from the Urban Institute to the Rand Corporation to dozens of academic economists to the president's own Council of Economic Advisers—that immigrants, legal and illegal, are a boon to the economy, and that the boon would be greater if they were all legal.

503.   Pete Hamill. "Illegal Immigration Is Not a Crisis." IMMIGRATION: OPPOSING VIEWPOINTS, 1990, p. 169. The energy of the Mexican immigrant, his capacity for work, has become essential to this country. While Mexicans, legal and illegal, work in fields, wash dishes, grind away in sweatshops, clean bedpans, and mow lawns (and fix transmissions, polish wood, build bookcases), millions of American citizens would rather sit on stoops and wait for welfare checks. If every Mexican in this country went home next week, Americans would starve. The lettuce on your plate in that restaurant got there because a Mexican bent low in the sun and pulled it from the earth.

504.   Anthony Lewis. "The Politics of Nativism." NEW YORK TIMES, January 14, 1994,

p. A29. "Some people genuinely worry about the problem of too many immigrants in a stagnant economy," Prof. Bill O. Hing, an immigration expert at the Stanford Law School, says. "But for most, economics is a diversion. Underneath it is a race."

505.　Anthony Lewis. "The Politics of Nativism." NEW YORK TIMES, January 14, 1994, p. A29. But facts are being overwhelmed by the emotions of fear and hatred. And politicians are running with those feelings much the same way they used to with anti-Communism.

506.　Alan W. Bock. "Illegal Immigration Should Be Legalized." IMMIGRATION: OPPOSING VIEWPOINTS, 1990, p. 177. In fact, though, most objections to immigration are based on myths and unfounded fears. Most of the substantive problems associated with immigration are caused by attempts to restrict immigration or by a welfare system out of control.

507.　Mary H. Cooper. "Immigration Reform." CONGRESSIONAL QUARTERLY RESEARCHER, September 24, 1993, p. 847. But for every report pointing to the high costs of immigration, there exists equally compelling data that contradict their results. According to a recent Urban Institute report, for example, the Los Angeles county study overstated the costs to the local government of immigration by as much as $137 million. Another Los Angeles County study concluded that wen calculations include federal taxes and services, immigrants were found to have *contributed* $1.85 billion more than they cost in 1991-92.

508.　Rebecca L. Clark and Jeffrey S. Passel. "Studies Are Deceptive." NEW YORK TIMES, September 3, 1993, p. A23. The cost of services provided to recent legal immigrants in Los Angeles has been overestimated. For some social service programs, the Los Angeles County report mistakenly computed the costs for recent legal immigrants by using the costs for *all* legal immigrants. As a result, the report overestimated the costs of recent immigrants by one-third.

509.　Greg Miller. "Immigrants Costs Overstated, Study Finds." LOS ANGELES TIMES, September 3, 1993, p. B1. A pivotal study of immigration in Los Angeles County inflated the costs and undercounted the contributions of legal and illegal immigrants to local government, according to a report issued Thursday by the Urban Institute.

510.　Greg Miller. "Immigrants Costs Overstated, Study Finds." LOS ANGELES TIMES, September 3, 1993, p. B4. The Urban Institute report said that, by focusing on recent immigrants, the Los Angeles study overlooked the contributions of long-term immigrants, those who entered the country before 1980.

511.　Greg Miller. "Immigrants Costs Overstated, Study Finds." LOS ANGELES TIMES, September 3, 1993, p. B4. "Once you've let people stay in the country for about 10 years they start paying a lot

more in taxes," said Rebecca L. Clark, Passel's research partner. "ALL of the focus in recent studies has been on recent immigrants, which fosters the mistaken impression that problems they face the first few years they come to the country last indefinitely."

512.　Larry Rohter. "Revisiting Immigration and the Open-Door Policy." NEW YORK TIMES, September 19, 1993, Sec. 4, p. 4. Immigration advocacy groups and scholars have been critical of the study and its methodology, however. For instance, the study defined immigrants as the 2.3 million people who had arrived, legally or illegally, since 1980, and lumped earlier arrivals with the rest of the population. research has shown, however, that "the longer immigrants are in the country, the more they contribute to the economy," and the more prosperous they become, Mr. De Freitas said.

513.　Julian L. Simon. "The Nativists are Wrong." WALL STREET JOURNAL, August 4, 1993, p. A8. The L.A. study has another shortcoming: It considers only those immigrants who arrived after 1980. It lumps earlier immigrants—those who make the largest tax contributions—into the same category as natives. This group of earlier immigrants is particularly productive and puts a great deal more into the system than it takes out. The report is further flawed because it gives no apparent source for crucial income estimates.

514.　Rebecca L. Clark and Jeffrey S. Passel. "Studies Are Deceptive." NEW YORK TIMES, September 3, 1993, p. A23. The Los Angeles government report is probably correct in concluding that immigrants get more in services from the county than they contribute in county taxes. But this is also the case for natives. The study is incomplete because it fails to include all sources of revenue and omits indirect economic benefits from immigrants' consumer spending and businesses.

515.　Julian L. Simon. "The Nativists are Wrong." WALL STREET JOURNAL, August 4, 1993, p. A8. The L. A. County report calculated immigrant-related revenues to the county of $139 million vs. costs of $947 million. This is misleading. If only because it reveals more about our system of taxation and distribution than about immigrants. The federal government receives most of taxes immigrants pay, while local communities cough up most of their welfare and immigration costs. But even if the numbers were correct, they imply that total taxes paid by this group—$4.3 billion in federal, state and local taxes—are quadruple their local costs.

516.　Julian L. Simon. "The Nativists are Wrong." WALL STREET JOURNAL, August 4, 1993, p. A8. Anti-immigration activists claim that the Los Angeles County report showed that immigrants take more than they put into our system. In fact, the report didn't say that. The report stated that recent immigrants "generate 18 times more revenue to the federal government, nine times more revenue to the state of California, and about two and one-half times more revenue to other

local government entities than to the County of Los Angeles.

517. Larry Rohter. "Revisiting Immigration and the Open-Door Policy." NEW YORK TIMES, September 19, 1993, Sec. 4, p. 4. Still, even under the narrow definition used by the Los Angeles authorities, a closer look at the study finds inconsistencies, including data showing the county's immigrants gave more than they took. The county study concluded that immigrants paid $4.3 billion in taxes in 1991, but used only $2.5 billion in public services—a net contribution of $1.8 billion to government.

518. Greg Miller. "Immigrants Costs Overstated, Study Finds." LOS ANGELES TIMES, September 3, 1993, pp. B1, B4. After reviewing the study, the Urban Institute concluded that the Los Angeles study's cost estimate is as much as $140 million too high because it attributes to recent immigrants the costs of county health and public social services used by all legal immigrants. Similarly, the county study's revenue figure for federal, state and local taxes is $848 million too low because it did not take into account additional revenue sources, the Urban Institute said.

519. Julian L. Simon. "The Nativists are Wrong." WALL STREET JOURNAL, August 4, 1993, p. A8. In another study, immigrants in Los Angeles County were studied by Rebecca Clark and Jeffrey Passel of the Urban Institute, They, too, estimated tax revenues from recent immigrants and reached a far different conclusion. They found that this group pays more property taxes, more FICA, more unemployment insurance, and more federal and state income taxes than the L.A. County study said they did.

520. Penny Loeb, et. al. "To Make a Nation." *U.S. News and World Report*, 4 Oct 1993, p. 52. Perhaps the most common fear voiced about immigrants is that they take jobs from Americans; the fear is largely unfounded. Of the 500 occupation categories studied in its computer analysis, *U.S. News* documented only 6 percent in which new immigrants held 10 percent or more of the jobs.

521. George J. Borjas. FRIENDS OR STRANGERS: THE IMPACT OF IMMIGRANTS ON THE U.S. ECONOMY, 1990, p. 84. There is, therefore, no compelling theoretical rationale to support the assertion that natives refuse to work in certain types of jobs, and that immigrants are somehow crowded into these jobs. The conjecture that natives and immigrants do not interact in the labor market, like the one that immigrants displace natives from their jobs on a one-to-one basis, depends on arbitrary assumptions about the operations of the labor and immigration markets. Moreover, neither of these propositions is supported by any empirical evidence.

522. Julian L. Simon. "Immigrants Help the U.S. Economy." IMMIGRATION: OPPOSING VIEWPOINTS, San Diego: Greenhaven Press, 1990,

p. 81. *Immigrants do not cause native unemployment, even among low-paid and minority groups.* A spate of recent studies, using a variety of methods, have shown that the bogey of "displacement" of natives does not exist. New entrants take jobs, but they also make jobs. And the jobs they create with their purchasing power, and with the new businesses which they start up, are at least as numerous as the jobs which immigrants fill.

523. Julian L. Simon. "The Nativists are Wrong." WALL STREET JOURNAL, August 4, 1993, p. A8.
• Using 1980 Census data, Gregory De Freitas of Hofstra University showed that Hispanic immigrants, many of them illegal, had no discernible negative effect on unemployment.

524. Julian L. Simon. "The Nativists are Wrong." WALL STREET JOURNAL, August 4, 1993, p. A8. *My economic analyses and those of others during the past 15 years convince me that immigrants do not abuse the welfare system, nor do they steal jobs from native-born Americans.*

525. Julian L. Simon. POPULATION MATTERS: PEOPLE, RESOURCES, ENVIRONMENT, AND IMMIGRATION, 1990, p. 284. Immigrants not only create new jobs indirectly with their spending, they do so directly with the new businesses that they are more likely than natives to start. A Canadian government survey, which should also describe U.S. experience, found that almost 5 percent—ninety-one of 1746 males and 291 single females—had started their own businesses within their first three years in Canada. Not only did they employ themselves, they employed others too, "creating" a total of 606 jobs. Thus roughly 30 percent as many new jobs were created as were held by immigrants.

526. Ben J. Wattenberg and Karl Zinsmeister. "The U.S. Should Encourage Immigration." IMMIGRATION: OPPOSING VIEWPOINTS, San Diego: Greenhaven Press, 1990, p. 117.

Immigrants and Jobs
Immigrants seem generally to complement rather than compete with native workers. They often fill manual or specialized jobs for which domestic workers are in short supply. They sometimes attract minimum-wage industries which would otherwise have located elsewhere. They stimulate activity in the service economy. They start new businesses. As anyone who has lived in a neighborhood with such businesses can attest, these enterprises are largely original: far from driving someone else from a job, many immigrant entrepreneurs carve a narrow foothold for themselves out of the rubble of empty buildings and unserved needs.

527. Larry Rohter. "Revisiting Immigration and the Open-Door Policy." NEW YORK TIMES, September 19, 1993, Sec. 4, p. 4. Immigrants, said Gregory De Freitas, an economist and immigration expert at Hofstra University in New York, "help expand the demand for labor and increase the number of jobs,

which tends to outweigh any negative effects they may have."

528.   Rodman D. Griffen. "Illegal Immigration." CONGRESSIONAL QUARTERLY RESEARCHER, April 24, 1992, p. 365. Though few economists would deny that immigrant competition hurts low-skilled American workers, Lawrence Fuchs, former executive director of the U.S. Select Commission on Immigration and Refugee Policy and currently a professor at Brandeis University, says his research convinced him that illegal aliens "probably create more jobs than they take away." Douglas Massey, a sociologist at the University of Chicago, agrees. "Without illegal immigrants," he says, "many U.S. factories would go offshore. The garment industry in East Los Angeles…would be in Taiwan or Mexico." [ellipses in original]

529.   George J. Borjas. FRIENDS OR STRANGERS: THE IMPACT OF IMMIGRANTS ON THE U.S. ECONOMY, 1990, p. 85. If the two groups are complements in production, an increase in the number of immigrants raises the productivity of natives, which makes natives more valuable to employers and increases the demand for native labor. Because employers are now competing for native workers, native wages rise. Moreover, some natives who previously did not find it profitable who work see the higher wage rate as an additional incentive to enter the labor market, hence native employment also increases.

530.   Ruben G. Rumbaut. "Passages to America." AMERICA AT CENTURY'S END, 1991, p. 237. Rather than take jobs away, entrepreneurial immigrants often create them. For example, among Koreans in Los Angeles in 1980, a recent study found that 22.5 percent were self-employed (compared to 8.5 percent of the local labor force), and they in turn employed another 40 percent of Korean workers in their businesses. The 4,266 Korean-owned firms thus accounted for two-thirds of all employed Koreans in the Los Angeles metropolitan area.

531.   Julian L. Simon. POPULATION MATTERS: PEOPLE, RESOURCES, ENVIRONMENT, AND IMMIGRATION, 1990, p. 283. No research has shown noticeable unemployment caused by immigrants, either in the United States as a whole or in particular areas of high immigration. One reason is that Potential immigrants have considerable awareness of labor-market conditions here and tend not to come if their skills are in small demand. Also, immigrants tend to have a variety of skills and do not affect only a few industries. At the same time, immigrants increase the demand for labor across the range of occupations; they consume goods and services as well as produce them. In the long run, they create as many jobs with their spending as they themselves occupy.

532.   Julian L. Simon. POPULATION MATTERS: PEOPLE, RESOURCES, ENVIRONMENT, AND IMMIGRATION, 1990, p. 276. The income im-migrants earn increase the demand for goods and for workers to produce them, which in turn produces more income and more new jobs. This continues until the economy approaches a new equilibrium, with the same rate of unemployment as before.

533.   George J. Borjas. FRIENDS OR STRANGERS: THE IMPACT OF IMMIGRANTS ON THE U.S. ECONOMY, 1990, pp. 84-85. It is possible, however, that immigrants and natives are not interchangeable types of workers, but that they complement each other in the production process. For instance, some immigrant groups may be relatively unskilled and have a comparative advantage in agricultural production. This frees the more skilled native work force to perform tasks that make better use of their human capital. The presence of immigrants increases native productivity because natives can now specialize in tasks in which they too have a comparative advantage.

534.   Ruben G. Rumbaut. "Passages to America." AMERICA AT CENTURY'S END, 1991, p. 236. An influx of new immigrant labor also has the effect of pushing up domestic workers to better supervisory or administrative jobs that may otherwise disappear or go abroad in the absence of a supply of immigrant manual labor. Less-skilled immigrants, paralleling the pattern noted above for FMG professionals, typically move into manual labor markets deserted by native-born workers, who shift into preferred non-manual jobs.

535.   Alan W. Bock. "Illegal Immigration Should Be Legalized." IMMIGRATION: OPPOSING VIEWPOINTS, 1990, p. 179. A surprising illustration of this principle was witnessed when economists of the Urban Institute studied Mexican immigration in Southern California. Wage levels for black people were higher in Los Angeles, which has experienced a great deal of illegal immigration from Mexico, than in San Francisco, which had experienced hardly any. Their conclusion: Illegals, rather than displacing native-born workers, were pushing them up into better jobs.

536.   George J. Borjas. FRIENDS OR STRANGERS: THE IMPACT OF IMMIGRANTS ON THE U.S. ECONOMY, 1990, p. 90. A 10-percent increase in the size of the Mexican illegal-alien population reduces the earnings of Mexican-American men by .1 percent; does not change the earnings of black men; reduces the earnings of other men by .1 percent; and increases the earnings of women by .2 percent. There is no evidence, therefore, to suggest that illegal immigration had a significant adverse impact on the earnings opportunities of any native group, including blacks.

537.   Ruben G. Rumbaut. "Passages to America." AMERICA AT CENTURY'S END. 1991, p. 236. As a rule, the entry of immigrants into the labor market helps to increase native wages as well as productivity and investment, sustain the pace of economic growth, and revive declining sectors, such as light manu-

facturing, construction, and apparel (New York City, Los Angeles, and Miami offer recent examples).

538.   Ben J. Wattenberg and Karl Zinsmeister. "The U.S. Should Encourage Immigration." IMMI-GRATION: OPPOSING VIEWPOINTS, San Diego: Greenhaven Press, 1990. pp. 116-17. Immigration to a given area can be quite compatible with job growth, and even with wage increases. Indeed, one finds little evidence of higher unemployment or of a serious depressive effect on wages even among the most vulnerable native groups—low-skill black workers or American-born Hispanics—when there is rise in the proportion of immigrants in the local labor market.

539.   George J. Borjas. FRIENDS OR STRANGERS: THE IMPACT OF IMMI-GRANTS ON THE U.S. ECONOMY, 1990, pp. 82-83. Alternatively, it could be argued that illegal aliens, who are afraid of being reported to the immigration officials, are easy prey for exploitation and are paid less than the going wage by employers. As I noted in chapter 4, however, illegal aliens have the same wage as legal immigrants once differences in observable demographic characteristics are taken into account. Thus, there is no reason to believe that employers would prefer to hire immigrants over equally qualified natives. In sum, the presumption that immigrants must displace natives rests on a rather peculiar, and erroneous, view of how the immigration and labor markets operate.

540.   George J. Borjas. FRIENDS OR STRANGERS: THE IMPACT OF IMMI-GRANTS ON THE U.S. ECONOMY, 1990, p. 87. Generally, immigrant groups tend to be weak complements with some native groups, and weak substitutes with others. Still, regardless of the particular permutation of groups being compared, the impact of an increase in the supply of immigrants on the wage of any native group remains numerically small.

541.   George J. Borjas. FRIENDS OR STRANGERS: THE IMPACT OF IMMI-GRANTS ON THE U.S. ECONOMY, 1990, p. 89. During the 1950s, the immigration accounted for 17 percent of the growth in the labor force. During the 1970s, however, immigration accounted for perhaps as little as 11 percent, despite the large increase in the number of immigrants entering the country. Therefore, the contribution of immigration to labor force growth was overshadowed by other, much more important demographic changes. Thus, it is not surprising that the labor market hardly reacted to the entry of immigrants and that native earnings opportunities were not greatly affected.

542.   Richard Rothstein. "Immigration Dilemmas." DISSENT, Fall 1993, p. 459. There is also no displacement of native workers in low-wage service jobs, in restaurant kitchens, say, or hotels. It is, of course, theoretically possible that restaurants and hotels could be forced to pay wages high enough to attract American high-school graduates, but if they did so, we'd have many fewer (because much more expensive) vacations

and conventions, not to mention meals away from home.

543.   Julian L. Simon. POPULATION MATTERS: PEOPLE, RESOURCES, ENVIRONMENT, AND IMMIGRATION, 1990, p. 266. Experiments conducted by INS show little, if any, damage to citizens even in the few areas where immigrants—legal and illegal—concentrate: in the restaurant and hotel industries. Most Americans, having better alternatives (including welfare programs), do not accept these jobs on the conditions offered.

544.   Julian L. Simon. POPULATION MATTERS: PEOPLE, RESOURCES, ENVIRONMENT, AND IMMIGRATION, 1990, p. 284. As to special groups of workers, especially low-income earners, the negative effect is probably less than commonly thought, and may be nonexistent. As I've said, legal immigrants arrive with considerable education and skills and enter a wide variety of occupations, hurting no occupation or income level much, even in the short run.

545.   Julian L. Simon. "Immigrants and Alien Workers." JOURNAL OF LABOR RE-SEARCH, Winter 1992, p. 76. Stephen Moore and I, for example, have systematically studied the effects on overall unemployment by looking at the *changes* in unemployment in various cities in the United States. Our finding is that whatever negative effect immigration may have on unemployment, it is too small to observe.

546.   Julian L. Simon. POPULATION MATTERS: PEOPLE, RESOURCES, ENVIRONMENT, AND IMMIGRATION, 1990, p. 283. Even in the few industries where immigrants concentrate, such as the restaurant and hotel industries, they do little harm to native workers. According to various studies, few natives want those jobs, because the work is hard and the pay is low.

547.   Susan Forbes Martin. "U.S. Immigration Policy: Challenges for the 1990s." NATIONAL STRATEGY REPORTER, Fall 1993, p. 4. One school argues that there is a net benefit to the United States. They show that immigrants appear to have little negative impact on the overall US workforce and may, in fact, have a positive effect on the economy through their entrepreneurial activities and their willingness to take jobs that US workers find undesirable.

548.   Bob Sutcliffe. "Immigration and the World Economy." CREATING A NEW WORLD ECONOMY, 1993, p. 103. A second argument used against migration, from the standpoint of development, is that migrants frequently suffer the worst economic conditions and enjoy the fewest rights in the countries to which they migrate and that therefore massive migration is something that should not be encouraged, because it creates a class of underprivileged citizens. But this often paternalistic argument ignores the fact that most of the recent migrants choose to migrate because they believe that migration will improve their material life. And

most migrants try to establish themselves in their new country rather than return home.

549. Julian L. Simon. "The case for greatly increased immigration." PUBLIC INTEREST, Winter 1991, p. 97. Immigrants pay more than their share of taxes. Within three to five years, immigrant-family earnings reach and pass those of the average American family. The tax and welfare data together indicate that, on balance, an immigrant family enriches natives by contributing an average of $1,300 or more per year (in 1975 dollars) to the public coffers during its stay in the U.S. Evaluating the future stream of these contributions as one would a dam or harbor, the present value of an immigrant family—discounted at the risk-free interest rate of 3 percent—adds up to almost two years' earnings for a native family head. This means that the economic activities of an average immigrant family reduce the taxes of a native head of household enough to advance his or her possible date of retirement by two years.

550. Rich Thomas and Andrew Murr. "The Economic Cost of Immigration." NEWS-WEEK, August 9, 1993, p.18. But in normal times, any job loss is ore than offset by the creation of new jobs stemming from the immigrants' own work. The immigrants' new spending creates demand for housing, groceries and other necessities, and their employers invest their expanding profits in new machinery and jobs. "It is called competitive capitalism," says Tony Carnevale of the American Society for Training and Development, "and it works. It's how America got rich."

551. Ruben G. Rumbaut. "Passages to America." AMERICA AT CENTURY'S END, 1991, p. 235. Notwithstanding the relative dispersal of immigrant professionals, they have significant impacts in the sectors within which they are employed. Rather than compete with or take jobs away from the native-born, these groups fill significant national needs for skilled talent and in some respects also serve as a strategic reserve of scarce expertise.

552. George J. Borjas. FRIENDS OR STRANGERS: THE IMPACT OF IMMI-GRANTS ON THE U.S. ECONOMY, 1990, p. 82. Finally, there is no evidence suggesting that immigrant labor is cheaper than equally skilled native labor. Such a wage differential could arise if there were systematic labor market discrimination against foreign-born persons in the United States. The available evidence, however, does not support the assertion that immigrants are systematically discriminated against.

553. George J. Borjas. FRIENDS OR STRANGERS: THE IMPACT OF IMMI-GRANTS ON THE U.S. ECONOMY, 1990, p. 90. Immigrants are likely to have a much more adverse impact on their own earnings than on the earnings of natives. A 10-percent increase in the number of immigrants decreases the earnings of other immigrants by at least 2 percent. In other words, immigrants are more substitutable for themselves than for natives.

554. Larry Rohter. "Revisiting Immigration and the Open-Door Policy." NEW YORK TIMES, September 19, 1993, Sec. 4, p. 4. During the 1980's, average wages for native-born workers hit a plateau, and those of recently arrived immigrants declined slightly. When David Card, an economist at Princeton University, examined the impact of the arrival of 125,000 Cubans in the 1980 Mariel boatlift, which increased Miami's labor force by 7 percent in an overnight expansion rarely seen in recent American history, he found that "the Mariel influx appears to have had virtually no effect on the wages or unemployment rates of less-skilled workers," whether white or black.

555. Bob Sutcliffe. "Immigration and the World Economy." CREATING A NEW WORLD ECONOMY, 1993, p.104. In recent years there has been a vast increase in the mobility of certain kinds of capital. This means that immigration is not necessary for foreign workers to be placed in competition with domestic workers in the same labor market; they are already in competition because some capitalists regard the whole world as their field of operations. If they cannot get the labor they need in the developed countries, they will look elsewhere. In this case (especially true in "footloose," as opposed to "rooted," industries) it is not migration but the mobility of capital that creates the depressing effect on unskilled wages.

556. Julian L. Simon. "The case for greatly increased immigration." PUBLIC INTEREST, Winter 1991, p. 97. Wages are admittedly pushed downward somewhat in industries and localities in which immigrants are concentrated. Barton Smith and Robert Newman of the University of Houston found that adjusted wages are 8 percent lower in the Texas border cities in which the proportion of Mexicans is relatively high. Much of the apparent difference is accounted for by a lower cost of living in the border cities, however.

557. Jaclyn Fierman. "Is Immigration Hurting the U.S.?" FORTUNE , 9 Aug. 1993, p. 78. Still, Harvard economist Richard Freeman attributes about one-third of the gap to the fact that the ranks of willing but poorly educated workers were swelled by immigrants. However, the only sure-fire way to help displaced blue-collar Americans, he says, is through better education and training, not through immigration policy.

558. Ruben G. Rumbaut. "Passages to America." AMERICA AT CENTURY'S END, 1991, p. 236. Concerns about the economic impact of working-class immigrants more often focus on claims that they take jobs away from or depress the wages of native-born workers. Such claims, however, are made in the absence of any evidence that unemployment is caused by immigrants either in the United States as a whole or in areas of high immigrant concentration, or that immigration adversely affects the earnings of either domestic majority or minority groups. To the contrary, recent research studies of both legal and undocumented immigration point to significant net economic benefits accruing to U.S. natives.

559.   Julian L. Simon. POPULATION MATTERS: PEOPLE, RESOURCES, ENVIRONMENT, AND IMMIGRATION, 1990, p. 276. But in the economy as a whole, immigrants not only take jobs, they make jobs. Their income adds to total demand, creating new jobs, and they open businesses that employ natives as well as other immigrants and themselves. Job displacement is mainly a false fear, and rational Americans should not let this fear influence immigration legislation.

560.   Julian L. Simon. POPULATION MATTERS: PEOPLE, RESOURCES, ENVIRONMENT, AND IMMIGRATION, 1990, p. 276. With Stephen Moore, I examined how the rates of immigration into a large number of cities in the United States from 1960 to 1976 related to changes in unemployment rates. We found that no matter how we looked at it, the effect was either very small or nonexistent. While our study has not been examined in detail by colleagues, we believe it contains much more solid evidence on the matter than provided by previous studies that have been cited in the newspapers but also have not been available for scrutiny.

561.   Bob Sutcliffe. "Immigration and the World Economy." CREATING A NEW WORLD ECONOMY, 1993, p. 104. Moreover, discrimination and racism, which bring about the division of workers, have a depressing effect on the bargaining power of labor. If immigrant workers are subjected to racist and xenophobic discrimination within the host society, they will as a consequence have to live at a lower economic level and will have more of a depressive effect on the labor market in general. Sometimes the very sections of the labor movement that have supported immigration controls (in the interests of labor) have at the same time participated in racist and xenophobic practices against immigrants. Their argument can therefore be partially self-fulfilling.

562.   Stephen Chapman. "Immigrant myths and the recurrent urge to exclude." CHICAGO TRIBUNE, July 25, 1993, sec. 4, p. 3. It's widely assumed, for instance, that new arrivals doom Americans to the dole or, at least, push wages down to Dickensian levels. But the evidence is that immigrants create as many jobs as they fill and that they have little impact on the earnings of American workers. Even the expert most often invoked by the closed-borders crowd, University of California at San Diego economist George Borjas, has to concede that immigrants account for a tiny fraction of welfare costs and barely cause a ripple in the labor market.

563.   Julian L. Simon. POPULATION MATTERS: PEOPLE, RESOURCES, ENVIRONMENT, AND IMMIGRATION, 1990, p. 265. In an analysis of Census Bureau data I conducted for the Select Commission on Immigration and Refugee Policy, I found that, aside from social security and Medicare, immigrant families average about the same level of welfare services as do citizens. When programs for the elderly are included, immigrant families use far *less* public funds than do na-

tives. During the first five years in the United States, the average immigrant family receives $1404 (in 1975 dollars) in welfare compared with $2279 received by a native family. The receipts become equal in later years, but when immigrants retire, their own children contribute to their support and so they place no new or delayed burdens upon the tax system.

564.   Julian L. Simon. POPULATION MATTERS: PEOPLE, RESOURCES, ENVIRONMENT, AND IMMIGRATION, 1990, p. 265. Study after study shows that small proportions of illegals use government services: free medical, 5 percent; unemployment insurance, 4; food stamps, 1; welfare payments, 1; child schooling, 4. Illegals are afraid of being caught if they apply for welfare. Practically none receive social security, the costliest service of all, but 77 percent pay social security taxes, and 73 percent have federal taxes withheld.

565.   Frank Sharry. Letter. WASHINGTON POST, January 27, 1994, p. A26. Legal permanent residents may be deported as a public charge if they use public benefits during their first five years in the country. Undocumented immigrants are eligible for few public benefits—among them are emergency medical care under Medicaid and enrollment in the Women, Infants, and Children nutrition program.

566.   Fernando Torres-Gil. "Separating Myth From Reality." THE CALIFORNIA-MEXICO CONNECTION, 1993, p. 172. Another public concern is that Mexican immigrants use welfare programs heavily and contribute to massive public expenditures for social services. Again, the data suggest otherwise. Studies consistently show that Mexican and other immigrant groups use fewer public services, rely more on informal support systems, and are less dependent on welfare income than native families with similar socioeconomic characteristics.

567.   Frank Sharry. Letter. WASHINGTON POST, January 27, 1994, p. A26. A 1990 U.S. Department of Labor survey indicates that immigrant families are less dependent on welfare and receive lower levels of welfare payments than native families. A July 1992 Business Week article shows that immigrants earn $240 billion per year, pay $90 billion per year in taxes—with most of it going into federal coffers—and receive only $5 billion in welfare.

568.   Ruben G. Rumbaut. "Passages to America." AMERICA AT CENTURY'S END, 1991, p. 236. In addition, immigrants, on average, actually pay more taxes than natives, but use much smaller amounts of transfer payments and welfare services (such as aid to families with dependent children [AFDC], supplemental security income, state unemployment compensation, food stamps, Medicare, and Medicaid). It has been estimated that immigrants "catch up" with natives in their use of welfare services only after 16 to 25 years in the United States.

569. Julian L. Simon. "The case for greatly increased immigration." PUBLIC INTEREST, Winter 1991, p. 94. In an analysis of Census Bureau data I found that, side from Social Security and Medicare, about as much money is spent on welfare services and schooling for immigrant families as for citizens. When programs for the elderly are included, immigrant families receive far *less* in public services than natives. During the first five years in the U.S., the average immigrant family receives $1,400 in welfare and schooling (in 1975 dollars), compared with the $2,300 received by the average native family.

570. Mary H. Cooper. "Immigration Reform." CONGRESSIONAL QUARTERLY RESEARCHER, September 24, 1993, p. 874. Wheeler of the National Immigration Law Center also takes issue with Gov. Wilson's anti-immigrant push. "His comments tend to be based on the premise that aliens come to the United States legally and illegally to get on welfare, to deliver babies in hospitals and to put their kids in education," Wheeler says. "Every study and every report and everybody that's ever dealt with immigrants knows that that's not only untrue but almost laughable."

571. Julian L. Simon. "Immigrants and Alien Workers." JOURNAL OF LABOR RESEARCH, Winter 1992, p. 75. The supposed costs that most capture the public's imagination are welfare payments and services, such as schooling. In an analysis of Census Bureau data, I found that, aside from Social Security and Medicare, immigrant families average about the same level of welfare services as do other citizens. When programs for the elderly are included, immigrant families use far *fewer* public services than citizens do. During its first five years in the United States, the average immigrant family receives (in 1975 dollars) $1,400 in welfare, compared with $2,300 received by a nonimmigrant family. Overall several decades, the amounts gradually become equal.

572. Larry Rohter. "Revisiting Immigration and the Open-Door Policy." NEW YORK TIMES, September 19, 1993, Sec. 4, p. 4. Spokesmen of the nativist right see the newcomers swelling the welfare rolls. Disputing them, Jeffrey S. Passel, head of the immigrant research project at the Urban Institute, a research group in Washington, said "places that got immigrants during the 1980's generally did better in terms of wage growth than places that didn't.

573. Rodman D. Griffen. "Illegal Immigration." CONGRESSIONAL QUARTERLY RESEARCHER, April 24, 1992, p. 374. The legal status of immigrants—whether they are refugees, legal immigrants or undocumented—has a major effect on their use of welfare and all public services. Ironically, refugees, who garner the most public sympathy, tend to rely most heavily on welfare and Medicaid. Illegal immigrants are barred from most forms of government assistance and tend to avoid all contact with public officials.

574. Rich Thomas and Andrew Murr. "The Economic Cost of Immigration." NEWSWEEK, August 9, 1993, p. 19. The welfare costs of immigration should dramatically decrease as the California and U.S. economies recover. The long-term benefits of immigrant labor and business enterprise will then be more apparent.

575. Julian L. Simon. "The case for greatly increased immigration." PUBLIC INTEREST, Winter 1991, p. 95. Of course there must be some systematic abuses of the welfare system by immigrants. But our legislative system is capable of devising adequate remedies. Even now there are provisions in the Immigration and Naturalization Act that deny visas to aliens who are "likely to become public charges" and provide for the deportation of immigrants who have within five years after entry become public charges "from causes not affirmatively shown to have arisen after entry."

576. Fernando Torres-Gil. "Separating Myth From Reality." THE CALIFORNIA-MEXICO CONNECTION, 1993, p. 169. Historically, taxpayers have been reluctant to expand social programs for disadvantaged groups in times of budget cuts and economic recession, regardless of ethnicity, race, or immigration status. Given the current shortage of state funding for health and human services, competition between young and old, native-born and immigrant, poor and affluent will increase. Political influence will increasingly determine resource allocations and, in that context, immigrants are likely to lose.

577. Julian L. Simon. "The case for greatly increased immigration." PUBLIC INTEREST, Winter 1991, p. 94. The main real cost that immigration imposes on natives is the extra capital needed for additional schools and hospitals. But this cost turns out to be small relative to benefits, in considerable part because we finance such construction with bond issues, so that we operate largely on a pay-as-you-go basis. Immigrants therefore pay much of their share.

578. Anthony Lewis. "The Politics of Nativism." NEW YORK TIMES, January 14, 1994, A29. The Supreme Court held in 1982 that denying education to illegal aliens was unconstitutional. Even the dissenters, in an opinion by then Chief Justice Warren Burger, said that as a matter of social policy it would be "senseless for an enlightened society to deprive any children...of an elementary education." [ellipses in original]

579. Senator Paul Simon (D-IL), Congressional Record, November 5, 1993, p. S15162. The same on primary and secondary schools. You simply cannot have children running around without going to school and believe that you know we are going to have a healthy society.

580. David W. Stewart. IMMIGRATION AND EDUCATION, 1993, p. 214. A narrow or short-term view of educational expenditures, however, ignores the investment dimension of education. Immedi-

ate financial return should not be the measure that is applied in these instances. Few actions are more costly to society than failure to provide appropriate educational opportunities for *all* of society's members. Dollars invested in education for immigrants and their children now will be repaid many times over in the future.

581.   Fernando Torres-Gil. "Separating Myth From Reality." THE CALIFORNIA-MEXICO CONNECTION, 1993, p. 172. Ultimately, however, the ability of Mexican immigrants to acculturate successfully and to avoid becoming a burden on the health and human service system is contingent upon employment that provides decent wages and employee benefits. The capacity of the California economy to produce such jobs and the willingness of the California electorate to improve the educational system for immigrants and minority populations may have a greater impact on the social conditions of Mexican immigrants and on California society than any social welfare policies.

582.   Fernando Torres-Gil. "Separating Myth From Reality." THE CALIFORNIA-MEXICO CONNECTION, 1993, p. 171. The health of Latino children, measured by pregnancy outcome, prevalence of chronic medical conditions, and birthweight patterns, is also good compared with that of non-Latinos, despite higher poverty rates. As a relatively young and healthy population, Latinos rely on emergency and pregnancy-related services but do not overuse the public health care system.

583.   Fernando Torres-Gil. "Separating Myth From Reality." THE CALIFORNIA-MEXICO CONNECTION, 1993, p. 165. Contrary to popular perceptions, the overall impact of Mexican immigration on health and human services has been manageable. Latinos are relatively healthy, productive, and persevering. But if they do not receive certain basic services that enable them to integrate successfully into California society, their health and social status may decline. Already, Latinos face chronic school dropout rates, rising crime, and other poverty-related problems that add costs to state programs and foster resentment among other groups.

584.   Fernando Torres-Gil. "Separating Myth From Reality." THE CALIFORNIA-MEXICO CONNECTION, 1993, p. 164. Foreign immigrants, who lack political representation and my be perceived as unworthy of access to state-funded programs, will be particularly vulnerable to retrenchments in social services. Since the majority of immigrants in California are Mexican, the perception and handling of this issue will affect relations with the state's most important neighbor.

585.   Fernando Torres-Gil. "Separating Myth From Reality." THE CALIFORNIA-MEXICO CONNECTION, 1993, p. 171. The general perception of the health status of Mexican immigrants is that they are in very poor health and contribute to serious public health problems. In reality, studies on Latino health care suggest that the health status of Mexican Americans, especially in the Southwest, is quite good given their in-

come and education levels. First-generation Mexican immigrants generally have good health practices, including relatively low rates of smoking, drinking, and drug use.

586.   Senator Paul Simon (D-IL), CONGRES SIONAL RECORD, November 5, 1993, p. S15162. Or, take another program, immunization: Measles do not care whether you are here legally or illegally. And if young people who are here illegally are not immunized, everyone is in jeopardy. So I think it makes sense to have some eligibility here.

587.   Senator Murray, CONGRESSIONAL RECORD, November 5, 1993, p. S15167. One, it would be a tremendous public health hazard to many of our communities out there if an outbreak were to occur and children who are in our schools were not vaccinated or taken care of. They would continue to spread the diseases, or the local community would be required to pick up the costs of that public health service.

588.   Fernando Torres-Gil. "Separating Myth From Reality." THE CALIFORNIA-MEXICO CONNECTION, 1993, p. 165. Although immigrants often have problems adjusting to U.S. society, they represent an industrious entrepreneurial, and young work force essential to California's economy. The state's nonminority population is aging, and its fertility rates are dropping. By the year 2000, U.S. labor-force growth will be primarily in minorities (20 percent), immigrants (22 percent), and white females (42 percent); white males will comprise only 16 percent of the working population. Faced with these demographic realities, California has a vital stake in what becomes of immigrants and minorities. Meeting their health and human service needs is a necessary step in securing California's economic future.

589.   Rep. Meek. CONGRESSIONAL RECORD, June 23, 1993, p. H4007. The notion that these Haitians pose a public health threat is a scare tactic that plays to the worst prejudices in our society, directed at people of color and against HIV positive people. HIV and AIDS are not airborne diseases. Nor are they transmitted by casual contact. Officials at the Center for Disease Control have said repeatedly that there is no reason to keep HIV positive people out of the country. These HIV positive Haitians pose less of a public health threat than the millions of untested Americans who unknowingly infect others through high risk practices.

590.   "Baby Boomers May Drain Social Security Funding." STEVENS POINT JOURNAL, April 12, 1994, p. 11. Without intervention, the baby boom generation will drain Social Security's retirement trust fund by 2036, eight years earlier than forecast just last year, a federal report says.

The annual study, released Monday, also warned that Social Security's disability trust fund could go broke in 1995, while Medicare will be able to pay the hospital

costs of the nation's elderly and disabled workers for only seven more years.

591.   Scott Shepard. "As Boomers Get Older, Nation Faces Hard Choice." ATLANTA CONSTITUTION, March 31, 1993, p. E6. By no later than 2006, when the first baby boomers reach age 50, the United States will have to choose between cutting Social Security benefits and increasing taxes, experts say.

592.   Katherine Dowling. "Social Security: A Widening Gap." ATLANTA CONSTITUTION, January 25, 1994. p. A11. So the debt will become worse and worse, not because of pork-barreling, not because of the evil rich or any other flimsy target that politicians blame. The basic problem is that we will have an increasingly older, sicker and more dependent population and an increasingly smaller work base.

593.   Paul Kennedy. PREPARING FOR THE TWENTY-FIRST CENTURY, 1993, p. 312. Over the longer term, however, the most serious consequence will be that the Social Security funds—at present still in surplus, and helping to disguise the true size of the federal deficit—will simply run out, causing a crisis not only in health provisions for the average elderly American, but also in the fiscal system. The politicians then in charge, facing a federal deficit worsened by Social Security losses, will have to make unpleasant choices: slash Social Security provisions *or* other forms of federal spending, or vastly increase taxes upon the relatively smaller proportion of "productive" Americans to pay for the swollen costs of caring for the fast-growing numbers of over-sixty-five-year-olds. The only other alternative would be to risk enormous federal deficits and consequent financial instability.

594.   Katherine Dowling. "Social Security: A Widening Gap." ATLANTA CONSTITUTION, January 25, 1994, p. A11. Whereas in 1900 the senior population numbered 3.1 million, the senior population in 2010—when most baby boomers will begin to hanker for their Social Security checks in large numbers—will be more than 50 million.

595.   Anna M. Rappaport and Sylvester J. Schieber. "Overview." DEMOGRAPHY AND RETIREMENT, 1993, p. 2. As a result of the baby boom, our society has a disproportionately large group of people in the same age group. During 1991, the oldest of the "baby boomers" will turn 45 years of age, and the youngest will turn 27. The aging of the baby boom is extremely important from a retirement policy perspective. During their working lives, baby boomers will comprise an abnormally large group of workers, who can help sustain the living standards of a relatively small existing retire population. During their own retirement, the boomers will comprise an abnormally large group of retirees who must be sustained by a relatively small working population.

596.   Barry Edmonston. "Discussion." DEMOGRAPHY AND RETIREMENT, 1993,

p. 67. The "aging of the United States" will have direct and dramatic impact on programs for the elderly. There will be an increase in the demand for services that reflect the increase in numbers. But the most important impact of the changing age of our population will take place because of sharp increases in the number of older and much older people—those 75 and 85 years of age and older.

597.   Barry Edmonston. "Discussion." DEMOGRAPHY AND RETIREMENT, 1993, p. 67. Females now make up about two-thirds of the older elderly (those over 75 years). The poverty rate for very old women is disproportionately high—nearly twice that of very old males. The plight of very old women, particularly those living alone, is one of the most serious income and health problems among the elderly. The projected expansion of the very old population will prompt additional calls for program reform and will continue pressure on public maintenance programs to meet the needs of this relatively impoverished group.

598.   Scott Shepard. "As Boomers Get Older, Nation Faces Hard Choice." ATLANTA CONSTITUTION, March 31, 1993, p. E6. "It is indisputable that some of Social Security's promises will be broken," said A. Haeworth Robertson, president of the Retirement Policy Institute in Washington.

Already, the government plans to push back the age at which it will pay full retirement benefits. Starting in 2000, the full retirement age of 65 will be increased in periodic steps until it reaches age 67 in 2027.

599.   Dorcas R. Hardy and C. Colburn Hardy. SOCIAL INSECURITY, 1991, p. 30. "The coming Social Security disaster will make the savings and loan fiasco look like child's play," says Walter Williams, a professor of economics at George Mason University. "Here are several realistic scenarios we face: when today's twenty-year-olds retire, they will receive pensions 50 percent less than those of today's Social Security recipients; many others will be excluded from receiving Social Security checks despite having made enormous contributions; if tomorrow's recipients are to receive pensions equal to today's, the 2020 work force will have to pay a 40 percent Social Security tax."

600.   Dorcas R. Hardy and C. Colburn Hardy. SOCIAL INSECURITY, 1991, p.40. The total number of Social Security beneficiaries—the elderly, survivors, and the disabled—is expected to increase from around forty million in 1990 to fifty million in 2010; to sixty-five million in 2020; to seventy-five million in 2030; and to eighty million in 2050.

Expenditures will double every ten years, until we talk about trillions the way we used to talk about billions. Current benefit payments are now $275 billion; they will be $500 billion at the turn of the century, and $20 *trillion* by 2050.

601.   Dorcas R. Hardy and C. Colburn Hardy. SOCIAL INSECURITY, 1991, p. 40.

Racial Overtones

There is also the potential for this conflict between baby boomers and baby busters to take on racial overtones. The reason is that retirees will still be overwhelmingly white, and workers will increasingly belong to various minorities.

602.   James H. Schulz. THE ECONOMICS OF AGING, 1992, p. 8. Many people are concerned about the increased competition that may arise among age groups as each strives for a larger share of the nation's output. For example, improving retirement income by increasing social security often heads the list of demands by the aged segment of the population; in contrast, this is a relatively unimportant priority for younger workers.

603.   Dorcas R. Hardy and C. Colburn Hardy. SOCIAL INSECURITY, 1991, p. 40. Michael J. Boskin is a former Stanford University professor who is now chairman of the president's Council of Economic Advisers. In his 1986 book *Too Many Promises—the Uncertain Future of Social Security*, he painted the potential for economic war between the baby boomers and the baby busters in bleak terms.

> When the baby boom generation retires...hard-pressed workers will certainly resist tax rate increases of 5, 10, or 15 percentage points. The larger elderly population, meanwhile, will push for these tax increases to finance not only existing benefits, but also new ones. A confrontation between workers and retirees will arise (involving trillions of dollars) that will create the greatest polarization along economic lines in our society since the Civil War. [ellipses in original]

604.   Scott Shepard. "As Boomers Get Older, Nation Faces Hard Choice." ATLANTA CONSTITUTION, March 31, 1993, p. E6. In 1950, there were 16 active workers for every Social Security recipient. Today the ratio is 3.3-to-1, and as the huge baby boom generation enters retirement early in the 21st century, the ratio will narrow further. That will shrink the financial base upon which the system rests.

605.   Katherine Dowling. "Social Security: A Widening Gap." ATLANTA CONSTITUTION, January 25, 1994, p. A11. Meanwhile, overall population will have increased to only about four times the number in 1900, meaning that the number of people over 65 is growing at about four to five times the rate of the population in general. And we are producing far fewer children than did our parents and grandparents; Americans aren't quite replacing themselves, whereas the average 1950s mother had at least four children.

606.   Ben J. Wattenberg and Karl Zinsmeister. "The U.S. Should Encourage Immigration." IMMIGRATION: OPPOSING VIEWPOINTS, San Diego: Greenhaven Press, 1990, p. 116. Immigrants tend to be disproportionately young, and as a result they draw very lightly on Social Security and Medicare—by far our largest social programs. Nor do they draw much more

than natives on other kinds of welfare spending, like Aid to Families with Dependent Children, food stamps, and unemployment compensation. In all, immigrants actually consume smaller amounts of public funds than do natives for about their first dozen years in the U.S. After that, levels tend to equalize.

607.   Annelise Anderson. "What Should Our Immigration Policy Be?" THE WORLD AND I, January 1994, p. 366. Immigrants are beneficial to the United States in another way: They are on average younger than the U.S. population, and they have more children. This is important, because the U.S. birthrate hovers around the replacement rate; if it were only slightly lower, the population would eventually begin to decline. But before it did so, the number of people of working age would decline drastically in comparison to the number of people retired, requiring greatly increased taxes to support medical and retirement benefits for the elderly.

608.   Julian L. Simon. "Immigrants Help the U.S. Economy." IMMIGRATION: OPPOSING VIEWPOINTS, San Diego: Greenhaven Press, 1990, p. 83. *Immigration reduces the uncuttable social costs of the elderly.* More and more of the U.S. population is retired, with a smaller proportion of adults in the labor force. New immigrants typically are just entering the prime of their work lives and taxpaying years. Immigration is the best way to lighten the Social Security burden of the aging U.S. population. It also reduces the federal deficit, which would not exist if people still lived the short lives, and had the large number of children, that they did early in the century.

609.   Ruben G. Rumbaut. "Passages to America." AMERICA AT CENTURY'S END, 1991, pp. 236-237. Because of their vulnerable legal status, undocumented immigrants, in particular, are much less likely to use welfare services, and they receive no Social Security income, yet about three-fourths of them pay Social Security and federal income taxes. And because newly arrived immigrants are primarily younger workers rather than elderly persons, by the time they retire and are eligible to collect Social Security (the costliest government program of transfer payments), they have usually already raised children who are contributing to Social Security taxes and thus balancing their parent's receipts.

610.   Paul Kennedy. PREPARING FOR THE TWENTY-FIRST CENTURY, 1993, p. 38. Not all advanced economies are equally affected by the problem of excessively aging populations. In the United States, for example, the continued inflow of immigrants and the relatively high fertility rates of ethnic-minority families mean not only that overall population is expected to grow, but also that the bottom segments of the age-structure pyramid will not drastically narrow.

611.   Julian L. Simon. "The Case for Greatly Increased Immigration." PUBLIC INTEREST, Winter 1991, p.98. Because immigrants arrive in the early prime of their work lives, they ward off a major

looming threat to U.S. economic well-being. This treat is the graying of the population, which means that each working native has an increasing burden of retired dependents to support. In 1900, there were five and one-half people aged twenty-five to fifty-four for each person aged sixty and above, whereas the Census Bureau projects that in the year 2000 the ratio will shrink to two and one-half to one—resulting in a burden that will be more than twice as heavy on workers.

Being predominantly youthful adults, immigrants mitigate this looming problem of more retired natives being supported by fewer workers. Indeed, immigration is the only practical way to alleviate the burden of increasingly dependency that native workers would otherwise feel.

612.   Julian L. Simon. POPULATION MATTERS: PEOPLE, RESOURCES, ENVIRONMENT, AND IMMIGRATION, 1990, p. 282. Contrary to popular opinion, legal immigrants to the United States bestow important economic benefits upon natives. These include a reduced burden of social security taxes without a reduction in benefits, increased productivity, an entrepreneurial shot in the arm to business, and new vitality and cultural diversity.

613.   Julian L. Simon. POPULATION MATTERS: PEOPLE, RESOURCES, ENVIRONMENT, AND IMMIGRATION, 1990, pp. 266-267. On balance, immigrants are far from a drag on the economy. As workers, consumers, entrepreneurs and taxpayers, they invigorate it and contribute healthy economic benefits. By increasing the work force, they also help solve our social-security problem. Immigrants tend to come at the start of their work lives but when they retire and collect social security, they typically have raised children who are then contributing taxes to the system.

614.   Ben J. Wattenberg and Karl Zinsmeister. "The U.S. Should Encourage Immigration." IMMIGRATION: OPPOSING VIEWPOINTS, San Diego: Greenhaven Press, 1990, p. 120. Immigration, then, can bring us significant numbers of bold creators and skilled workers. It can diminish whatever labor shortages may be coming our way. Immigration can keep America from aging precipitously and fill in the demographic holes that may harm our pension and health-care systems.

615.   Richard Rothstein. "Immigration Dilemmas." DISSENT, Fall 1993, p. 459. Ultimately, we can't increase the working-to-retired ratio enough without a lot more immigration. While only 26 percent of the U.S. population is now in the prime working age of twenty to thirty-nine, 46 percent of immigrants are in that age group. Retiring baby boomers need people who contribute more in taxes than they consume in services. Immigration will have to be an increasing part of the solution, not only in the United States, but throughout the industrial world.

616.   Julian L. Simon. "The case for greatly increased immigration." PUBLIC INTEREST, Winter 1991, p. 98. In the public sphere this means that immi-

grants immediately lessen the Social Security burden upon native workers. (The same holds for the defense burden, of course.) And if there is a single factor currently complicating the government's economic policies, it is the size of Social Security payments and other assistance to the aged. Immigration—and the resulting increase in tax payments by immigrants—provides the only way to reduce the federal budget deficit without making painful cuts in valued services.

617.   Samuel H. Preston. "Demographic Change in the United States, 1970-2050." DEMOGRAPHY AND RETIREMENT, 1993. p. 44. Eventually, with fertility, mortality, and migrations rates constant, the population age structure stabilizes and growth rates become constant from year to year. In the meantime, the population growth rate will decline, even in the face of "high" fertility, life expectancy, and immigration, from 1.06% in 1990 to 0.62% in 2050.

618.   Ben J. Wattenberg and Karl Zinsmeister. "The U.S. Should Encourage Immigration." IMMIGRATION: OPPOSING VIEWPOINTS, San Diego: Greenhaven Press, 1990, p. 114. Yet according to medium-variant ("most likely") projections by the Census Bureau, at current levels of birth, mortality, and immigration, the U.S. over the next fifty years will experience relatively slow population growth, then slower growth, then no growth, and then decline. This is due primarily to the fact that, for fifteen years now, fertility rates have been below the replacement level. Even an immigration moderately higher than the current level would still leave us on a slow-growth path toward population stability in the next century.

619.   Michael D'Antonio. LOS ANGELES TIMES MAGAZINE, August 29, 1993. p. 52. It turns out that experts at the United Nations more or less agree with Simon. "It's assumed that world population will stabilize at 11.6 billion people by the end of the 22nd Century," says Armindo Miranda, senior population analyst at the U.N. in New York. Some countries will experience serious problems due to overpopulation, Miranda predicts, but he does not foresee a worldwide crisis. "I am concerned," he adds, "but a catastrophe is not impending."
[Simon—Julian Simon, University of Maryland economist]

620.   Mary H. Cooper. "Immigration Reform." CONGRESSIONAL QUARTERLY RESEARCHER, September 24, 1993, pp. 845-846. Sharry concedes that in theory there is a point beyond which more people will deplete the Earth's natural resources. "But the notion that we're even close to it is preposterous," he says. The real environmental issue in the United States, he says, is overconsumption, not overpopulation. "The United States has 6 percent of the world's population and consumes about 40 percent of its resources. We can't blame that on immigrants."

621.   Ben J. Wattenberg and Karl Zinsmeister. "The U.S. Should Encourage Immigration." IMMI-

GRATION: OPPOSING VIEWPOINTS, San Diego: Greenhaven Press, 1990, p. 116. Similarly, ecological degradation is caused in large measure by what people do or fail to do, not by how many people there are. Within the last two decades, since America began spending significant sums on abatement, pollution has declined even as population has gone up. Recent concern about environmental trends like carbon dioxide build-up and alleged ozone depletion are particularly irrelevant to the immigration question.

622.   Julian L. Simon. "Immigrants and Alien Workers." JOURNAL OF LABOR RESEARCH, Winter 1992, p. 77. Environmental groups argue that natural resources will become increasingly scarce because of immigrants. This is said in total disregard for the fact that natural resources are getting increasingly more available in the U.S., as measured by their prices relative to wages and relative to the Consumer Price Index. Metals and foodstuffs follow the pattern, for example. If there was ever an unsupported economic objection to immigration, it is the fallacy that it depletes natural resources.

623.   Julian L. Simon. "Immigrants Help the U.S. Economy." IMMIGRATION: OPPOSING VIEWPOINTS, San Diego: Greenhaven Press, 1990, p. 82. *Natural resources and the environment are not at risk from immigration.* The long-term trends reveal that our air and water are getting cleaner rather than dirtier, and our supplies of natural resources are becoming more available rather than exhausted, contrary to common belief. Immigration increases the technical knowledge to speed these benign trends.

624.   Sheldon Richman. "Population Means Progress, Not Poverty." WASHINGTON POST, September 1, 1993, p. A23. The population "experts" used to think that India would never be able to feed itself. Then India introduced market incentives to agriculture; it soon became net exporter of food, achieving what billions in foreign aid could not accomplish.

625.   Sheldon Richman. "Population Means Progress, Not Poverty." WASHINGTON POST, September 1, 1993, p. A23. The overriding fact is that wherever markets are allowed to operate, the condition of people improves. And as they become better off, they choose to have fewer children. A falling fertility rate is an effect, not a cause, of development.

626.   Anna M. Rappaport and Sylvester J. Schieber. "Overview." DEMOGRAPHY AND RETIREMENT, 1993, p. 4. Looking into the future generally yields uncertain results. In a world where we cannot precisely predict tomorrow's weather, or next year's economic performance, we should not expect to predict the exact size, composition, and structure of our population 20 or 50 years in the future.

627.   Sheldon Richman. "Population Means Progress, Not Poverty." WASHINGTON POST, September 1, 1993, p. A23. During the Indus-

trial Revolution, Europe and the United States became rich while their populations grew dramatically. More recently, Hong Kong amassed great wealth after World War II as its population grew faster than Britain's in the 19th century and India's in the 20th. And Hong Kong, essentially an island of rock, grew wealthy without natural resources.

628.   Sheldon Richman. "Population Means Progress, Not Poverty." WASHINGTON POST, September 1, 1993, p. A23. If you look at a list of population densities and per capita incomes in different countries, you find that, almost without exception, the richest countries have the highest densities and the poorest have the lowest. Famines occur in Somalia, Ethiopia, and Sudan—countries that are sparsely populated—not in "crowded Hong Kong, Singapore, the Netherlands or New Jersey.

629.   Michael D'Antonio. "Apocalypse Soon." LOS ANGELES TIMES MAGAZINE, August 29, 1993, p. 52. Simon also fears that the dire warnings about population pressures will encourage racist, anti-immigrant sentiment in America. "It's not only morally repugnant," he says, "but it also keeps out the new workers and new thinkers the country will need to maintain its economy."

630.   Michael D'Antonio. "Apocalypse Soon." LOS ANGELES TIMES MAGAZINE, August 29, 1993, p. 54. Ideas such as drastic limits on immigration and cutting the U.S. population by as much as half evoke immediate and vocal opposition. FAIR's agenda for controlling immigration has been opposed by those who see a racial bias in efforts to close the door at a time when Asians and Latinos compose the largest immigrant groups. The connection between population control and anti-immigration efforts is "an unholy alliance that can lead to eugenics," says Vibiana Andrade, director of the immigrant-rights program for the Mexican American Legal Defense and Educational Fund.

631.   Julian L. Simon. "Immigrants Help the U.S. Economy." IMMIGRATION: OPPOSING VIEWPOINTS, San Diego: Greenhaven Press, 1990, p. 83. *Immigrants of all origins assimilate quickly.* In every decade, the "new" immigrants are thought difficult to assimilate, unlike the "old" immigrants. But in each decade—including the 1970s and 1980s—the "new" immigrants have adjusted quickly both economically and culturally. Within a decade or two, immigrants come to earn more than natives with similar educational characteristics.

632.   Fernando Torres-Gil. "Separating Myth From Reality." THE CALIFORNIA-MEXICO CONNECTION, 1993, p. 172. A major public concern regarding Mexican immigrants is that they add to an "underclass" of individuals with high levels of illiteracy, criminal behavior, and welfare dependence. Although most Latinos live in poverty, the Mexican immigrant population is highly diverse and exhibits varying levels of assimilation and acculturation. Generally, the first

generation possesses supportive family relationships, communal values (e.g., assisting fellow immigrants to find work), and a strong work ethic. Despite some decline in positive behaviors as Mexicans become assimilated, Mexican immigrants have historically matched the performance of European immigrants in becoming "mainstream" members of society by the third generation.

633. Fernando Torres-Gil. "Separating Myth From Reality." THE CALIFORNIA-MEXICO CONNECTION, 1993, p. 170. California has always attracted large numbers of immigrants and minorities who have, by and large, become part of mainstream society and contributed to economic and social prosperity.

634. National Council of La Raza. "Third World Immigrants Are Adapting to the U.S." IMMIGRATION: OPPOSING VIEWPOINTS. 1990, p. 232. Nor do Mexican-Americans face anything approaching the religious, linguistic, political, or historical differences which separate English-speaking from French-speaking Canadians. Throughout the United States, Hispanic leaders seek increased opportunities for Hispanics to join the economic mainstream.... [ellipses in original]

635. National Council of La Raza. "Third World Immigrants Are Adapting to the U.S." IMMIGRATION: OPPOSING VIEWPOINTS, 1990, p. 227. Much of the protectionism in American attitudes toward immigration is based on fear of "different" ethnic and nationality groups—people the public believes may not become "real Americans." While a part of this fear and mistrust stems from active racism and nativism, much of it is rooted in ignorance and a lack of historical perspective. The descendants of most of the feared immigrants of the nineteenth century have become the respected mainstream Americans of today. More than a century ago, Germans were a culturally distinct, and therefore a threatening, immigrant group; today, more than one-fifth of all Americans claim some German ancestry.

636. Alan W. Bock. "Illegal Immigration Should Be Legalized." IMMIGRATION: OPPOSING VIEWPOINTS, 1990, p. 181. ALL this is not to say that open immigration will not result in some culture clashes and tensions that will require tolerance, patience, and understanding on the part of the native-born and immigrants alike. But the current wave of immigration is less, as a percentage of total population, than the great wave that this country handled between 1890 and 1910. Today's immigrants also have resources earlier immigrants often lacked: established communities of their countrymen in many American cities to ease the transition, and the more widespread use of English as a lingua franca in many parts of the world.

637. Alan W. Bock. "Illegal Immigration Should Be Legalized." IMMIGRATION: OPPOSING VIEWPOINTS, 1990, p. 181. Most immigrants don't want to overthrow this government; they want to benefit from the opportunities created by its policies. As proof, most immigrants become almost exaggeratedly patriotic. The majority understand the importance of learning English, and even if they never master it fully, take pains to see that their children do.

638. Ruben G. Rumbaut. "Passages to America." AMERICA AT CENTURY'S END, 1991, p. 242. For all the alarm about Quebec-like linguistic separatism in the United States, the 1980 census suggests that this generational pattern remains as strong as in the past. It counted well over 200 million Americans speaking English only, including substantial proportions of the foreign-born. Among new immigrants who had arrived in the United States during 1970-80, 84 percent spoke a language other than English at home, but over half of them (adults as well as children) reported already being able to speak English well.

639. National Council of La Raza. "Third World Immigrants Are Adapting to the U.S." IMMIGRATION: OPPOSING VIEWPOINTS, 1990, p. 232. An often unspoken but very real public fear is that, rather than acculturating, Hispanic immigrants, especially Mexicans, will pursue a goal of separatism, perhaps seeking to reunite the southwestern states with Mexico. Parallels with Quebec are often drawn, but most expert observers believe that the two situations are totally dissimilar. In fact, no national Hispanic organization or leader supports such separatism, and Hispanic groups are unanimous in their advocacy of additional opportunities to learn English.

640. National Council of La Raza. "Third World Immigrants Are Adapting to the U.S." IMMIGRATION: OPPOSING VIEWPOINTS, 1990, p. 232. Recent immigrants also face real obstacles in their quest to learn English. Only a minority of limited-English-proficient children receive special language services in school. Adult literacy programs have been severely reduced because of federal budget cuts, and almost no existing programs are geared to limited-English-proficient adults. There are far too few English as a second language programs for adult immigrants, and the result is that hundreds of thousands of new immigrants who want to learn English find it difficult to do so.

641. Anthony Lewis. "The Politics of Nativism." NEW YORK TIMES, January 14, 1994, p. A29. A frequent claim, for example, is that today's immigrants do not assimilate as readily as those in the past. But English-language courses have long waiting lists.

642. National Council of La Raza. "Third World Immigrants Are Adapting to the U.S." IMMIGRATION: OPPOSING VIEWPOINTS, 1990, p. 231. Historically, immigrants have tended to learn some English but speak their native language better, and their children have typically been bilingual. Their grandchildren, however, have almost always been English-dominant, and the native language has largely disappeared by the fourth generation. A study of the French-speaking

community in the United States indicates that language shifts may be occurring even more rapidly—that children of immigrants generally are English-dominant and use French only occasionally. The research also indicates that this language shift occurs more quickly in the United States than in other countries.

643. National Council of La Raza. "Third World Immigrants Are Adapting to the U.S." IMMIGRATION: OPPOSING VIEWPOINTS, 1990, p. 231. A study by the Rand Corporation found that 90% of the Mexican-American children of immigrants in California were proficient in English, and more than half of their children were monolingual English speakers. The study concluded that "the transition to English begins almost immediately and proceeds very rapidly."

644. National Council of La Raza. "Third World Immigrants Are Adapting to the U.S." IMMIGRATION: OPPOSING VIEWPOINTS, 1990, p. 231. Available information indicates that Hispanics follow the same acculturation process as other immigrants. Several studies have concluded that by the third generation, the vast majority of Hispanic-Americans are English-dominant. Surveys in San Antonio and Los Angeles found that 89% of Mexican-American citizens were bilingual or spoke only English; for those 18 to 25 years of age the figure was 94%.

645. Ruben G. Rumbaut. "Passages to America." AMERICA AT CENTURY'S END, 1991, p. 243. To be sure, immigrant groups vary significantly in their rates of English language ability, reflecting differences in their levels of education and occupation. But even among Spanish speakers, who are considered the most resistant to language shift, the trend toward anglicization is present; the appearance of language loyalty among them (especially Mexicans) is due largely to the effect of continuing high immigration to the United States. For example, a recent study of a large representative sample of Mexican-origin couples in Los Angeles found that among first-generation women, 84 percent used Spanish only at home, 14 percent used both languages, and 2 percent used English only; by the third generation there was a complete reversal, with 4 percent speaking Spanish only at home, 12 percent using both, and 84 percent shifting to English only.

646. Ruben G. Rumbaut. "Passages to America." AMERICA AT CENTURY'S END, 1991, p. 243. English proficiency has always been a key to socioeconomic mobility for immigrants, and to their full participation in their adoptive society. It is worth noting that in the same year that Proposition 63 (the initiative declaring English as the state's official language) passed in California, more than 40,000 immigrants were turned away from ESL classes in the Los Angeles Unified School District alone: the supply of services could not meet the vigorous demand for English training. Indeed, English language dominance is not threatened in the United States today—or for that matter in the world, where it has become already firmly established as the premier international language of commerce, diplomacy,

education, journalism, aviation, technology, and mass culture.

647. Stephen Chapman. "Immigrant Myths and the Recurrent Urge to Exclude." CHICAGO TRIBUNE, July 25, 1993, sec. 4, p. 3. Recent immigrants are often accused of a mulish refusal to assimilate. In fact, while assimilation takes time for immigrants, it's automatic for their kids. Two-thirds of Hispanics born here speak no Spanish or speak it less fluently than English.

648. National Council of La Raza. "Third World Immigrants Are Adapting to the U.S." IMMIGRATION: OPPOSING VIEWPOINTS, 1990, p. 229. The motto of the United States, *E pluribus unum* ("from many, one"), reflects the American confidence that diversity can strengthen unity. In spite of tremendous ethnic and racial variation—or perhaps because of it—Americans are an identifiable people not because of how they look, but because of the political values they share. To "become American" is not to lose all ethnic heritage, but adopt and share certain basic beliefs.

649. National Council of La Raza. "Third World Immigrants Are Adapting to the U.S." IMMIGRATION: OPPOSING VIEWPOINTS, 1990, p. 227. However, today's mad media increase immigrant visibility and therefore may create unwarranted concerns. A century ago, the arrival of immigrants from east Europe was evident primarily in the cities where they settled. Today, the evening news makes Americans in every part of our nation aware of new Indochinese immigrants in California or Cubans in Florida. The short-term visibility of new immigrants with their distinctive language and culture can make native Americans uneasy, but over the long term, the effects of acculturation and time make these immigrants and their children and grandchildren less identifiable and more familiar. We do not notice them because they have become a part of American society.

650. Stephen Chapman. "Immigrant Myths and the Recurrent Urge to Exclude." CHICAGO TRIBUNE, July 25, 1993, sec. 4, p. 3. Some of the opposition to immigration reflects a simple distaste for anything foreign or different, especially if it comes in a yellow, brown or black container.

651. Anthony Lewis. "The Politics of Nativism." NEW YORK TIMES, January 14, 1994, p. A29. People say that immigrants are clannish, live by themselves, don't speak English. ALL of those things were said 100 years ago about Jews and Italians and others whom nativists denounced as "undesirable immigrants." Much of what is going on in California today is old-fashioned nativism or xenophobia.

652. Stephen Chapman. "Immigrant Myths and the Recurrent Urge to Exclude." CHICAGO TRIBUNE, July 25, 1993, sec. 4, p. 3. Economist Stephen Moore of the congressional Joint Economic Committee notes that urban crime rates don't rise with the influx of

the immigrants. The 10 cities with the lowest rate of violent crime have almost exactly the same percentage of foreigners (13.7) as the 10 cities with the highest rate (13.3).

653.   Stephen Chapman. "Immigrant Myths and the Recurrent Urge to Exclude."CHICAGO TRIBUNE, July 25, 1993, sec. 4, p. 3. Rising crime is also supposed to be the fault of foreigners—as when some Hispanics took part in last year's Los Angeles riots. But those Hispanics had plenty of patriotic natives to keep them company.

654.   Michael D'Antonio. "Apocalypse Soon." LOS ANGELES TIMES MAGAZINE, August 29, 1993, p. 54. Such conflicts are already brewing in Western Europe. In Germany, skinheads have killed Turkish immigrants with a firebomb. Attackers have said they were motivated by the belief that the outsiders take away jobs, drain funds from social programs and erode their country's standard of living.

655.   Roberto Martinez. "Illegal Immigrants Are Victims of Crime." IMMIGRATION: OPPOSING VIEWPOINTS, San Diego: Greenhaven Press, 1990, p. 99. The growing number of human rights violations, the use of a popular San Diego radio show to promote anti-immigrant sentiment, the hate calls and threats I receive at my office, the "light up the border" movement (private citizens park their cars, with headlights beamed at the border, to protest the so-called "invasion of Mexicans, drug traffickers and terrorists") all point to the xenophobic atmosphere rising out of baseless claims that migrant workers steal jobs and are causing a national crime wave, clogging our jails and courts.

As the surge of violence illustrates, those fears are being translated into physical attacks on defenseless people whose only crime is being poor, hungry and persecuted.

656.   Gerald F. Seib. "In Tense Times, It's Easy to Hit At Immigrants." WALL STREET JOURNAL, October 27, 1993, p. A18. But there also is mounting evidence that politicians are demonizing aliens to score cheap political points. In doing so, they are playing with fire. One need only look at the ugly anti-immigrant hatred spreading across Europe to get some idea of where nativism can lead.

657.   Jorge A. Bustamente. "Mexico-Bashing: A Case Where Words Can Hurt." LOS ANGELES TIMES, August 13, 1993, p. B7. As a sociologist trained in the United States, I am afraid of the repetition of a pattern: The anti-Mexican rhetoric is raised by a public figure of authority, and soon somebody finds justification in this for taking matters in his own hands and punishing the "enemy."

658.   Pete Hamill. "Illegal Immigration Is Not a Crisis." IMMIGRATION: OPPOSING VIEWPOINTS, 1990, p. 167. No wonder George Bush gave up on interdiction as a tactic in the War on Drugs; there are literally hundreds of Ho Chi Minh trails leading into the United States from the South (and others from Canada, of course, and the sea). On some parts of the Mexican border there is one border patrolman for every twenty-six miles; it doesn't require a smuggling genius to figure out how to get twenty tons of cocaine to a Los Angeles warehouse. To fill in the gaps, to guard all the other U.S. borders, would require millions of armed guards, many billions of dollars.

STOPPING THE FLOW OF IMMIGRANTS

Resolved: That the United States government should substantially strengthen the regulation of immigration to the United States.

The United States has traditionally viewed itself as a nation of immigrants. Underlying this notion is the belief that the individual has the right to emigrate, that within reasonable limits those who desire admission should be allowed to enter the country, and that those who are admitted will be absorbed into an ethnically and racially diverse society. John F. Kennedy eloquently summarizes this tradition when during an address to Congress in 1961 he said:

> From the earliest days of our history, this land has been a refuge for the oppressed, and it is proper that we now, as descendants of refugees and immigrants, continue our long humanitarian tradition of helping those who are forced to flee to maintain their lives as individual, self-sufficient human beings in freedom, self-respect, dignity, and health (Public Papers of the Presidents: JFK, 528).

During the first century of U.S. history, there were no qualitative limitations on immigration in the United States. In 1875, concerned with the quality of arriving immigrants, Congress passed legislation that banned prostitutes, criminals and other "undesirables" from entering the United States. In 1882, "lunatics," "idiots," and "those likely to become public charges" were banned (Morris, 18). As the number of immigrants grew, the ethnic origins of those immigrating spurred Congress to pass a literacy requirement and enact a national origins quota formula. The purpose of this legislation was to prohibit Eastern and Southern Europeans as well as Asians from immigrating to the United States. The Immigration and Nationality Act of 1952 codified the exclusionary elements of prior immigration legislation.

It was not until the passage of the Immigration and Nationality Act of 1965 that the openly biased system of immigrant application and review was rejected. This national origin system was replaced by a system that placed an annual ceiling on immigration and placed a capitation on the number of immigrants on a per-country basis. The 1965 Act placed an emphasis on family unification, which the Congress intended to favor those from Northern and Western Europe. But the 1965 Act unintentionally increased the rate of Hispanic and Asian immigration.

During the late 1970s, Congress created the Select Commission on Immigration and Refugee Policy. The Commission was charged with studying U.S. Immigration and Refugee policy and procedures. The Commission concluded that immigration increases were within the best interests of the nation, but that illegal immigration had to be significantly curtailed. The 1986 Immigration Reform and Control Act was passed to codify the changes recommended to discourage illegal immigration. The mechanisms developed by this Act to control illegal immigration included better reporting and identification of illegal immigrants, employer sanctions for using illegally derived labor and an amnesty period for those who had been living and working in the United States to apply to become citizens.

If the 1986 legislation is viewed as an attempt to control illegal immigration, the Immigration Act of 1990 can be viewed as vehicle for increased legal immigration that is in the national interest. Quantitatively, the 1990 Act increased legal permanent immigration to the U.S. by over thirty-five percent and currently allows up to 700,000 immigrants a year to permanently reside in the United States (Congressional Quarterly, 12/8/90, 4105). This legislation augmented family-sponsored immigration and reaffirmed family unification as the number one priority of U.S. immigration policy. The Act also addressed the shortcomings of past policies by widening the array of skills and ethnic backgrounds of immigrants who can apply to immigrate. By instituting "diversity" guidelines the Act redressed the needs of those who had been excluded under prior immigration legislation.

Much like the National Health Insurance debate, the debate on strengthening regulation on immigration is quantitatively evaluated. The 1990 Act placed a flexible capitation on worldwide immigration to the United States that also restricts admissions from any one country to no more than seven percent of all visas. The Act establishes ceilings on non-refugee admissions and establishes three categories of immigrants: family sponsored immigrants, employment-based immigrants and diversity immigrants. The family based provisions of the Act emphasize the traditional goals of U.S. immigration policies, with priorities for admission allocated in the following manner. First, unmarried sons and daughters of United States citizens. Then, spouses and unmarried sons and daughters of permanent resident aliens are given a higher priority than married sons and daughters of U.S. citizens. The last category is brother and sisters of adult U.S. citizens. The Act also addresses abuses that occur within the family preference system, such as fraudulent marriages and a higher priority for abused families or families that stay in an abusive relationship out of fear of deportation.

Reforms instituted by the Act in the area of employment-based immigration were aimed at streamlining the application process and reducing the backlog for visas that could extend the process over three and a half years. Five categories of employment based visas were created. Priority workers are deemed to be aliens with extraordinary ability, professors and researchers, and executives of multinational corporations. The second employment-based preference is reserved for professionals holding advanced degrees or aliens with exceptional ability. These are individuals in the arts, sciences or business that must have a job offer and be eligible for labor certification. The third preference is available to skilled workers and professionals who hold at least two years of training or experience in a specific occupation. The fourth employment-based preference is certain special immigrants, defined as certain religious ministers, overseas employees of the U.S. government and the Panama Canal and former employees of certain international organizations. Immigrants from Hong Kong were also given a high priority based on the reacquisition of the island nation by the People's Republic of China. A new fifth category was created by the 1990 Act, which allotted visas for foreign investors willing to invest between $500,000 and $3 million in a U.S. business that provides employment for at least ten individuals. The employment creation provision is unprecedented in U.S. immigration law (Congressional Quarterly, 12/8/90, 4105).

U.S. immigration law had traditionally favored those immigrating from Europe. In order to compensate for this inequity, the 1965 Immigration and Nationality Act Amendments moved U.S. immigration policy towards improving the representation of those nations that were not well represented in the ranks of previous immigrants. The 1990 Act carried on the spirit of incorporating diversity in the immigration equation by promoting diversity in four ways. Section 131 creates a permanent diversity program for those countries that have been under-represented in the past. Section 132 targets thirty four nations that have been under under-represented as a result of the numerical limitations imposed by the 1965 legislation. Sections 134 and 135 lifted regulations on certain visas that had diversity implications, but were backlogged or unavailable due to numerical limitations. An example of the type of visa granted under these sections are visas for displaced Tibetans, who reside in India or Nepal. The goals of the 1990 Act were to assist the U.S. economy by increasing employer-based immigration, streamline the application process and reduce the backlog in the family preference categories, while promoting the diversity of nationalities that immigrate to the United States.

The debate on strengthening the regulation of immigration will focus on the Immigration Act of 1990 and its performance since being adopted. Diversity goals often run counter to the petitions of family preference applicants and the lag time for processing applications may not be any more efficient than prior to the implementation of the legislation. Others view the diversity goals as a form of social engineering and object to the subjugation of the principles of universal equal treatment.

Another area of potential affirmative ground is found in the employer-based immigration mandates. The prospects of the U.S. government fine tuning a highly dynamic and fluid economy through immigration is open to many levels of criticism. Fears are that welfare dependency and increased demands on the educational system will trade off with the potential economic productivity gains generated by U.S. immigration policies. Also some will find it contemptible that the U.S. immigration policy specifically targets potential immigrants who are "able-bodied" laborers while ignoring the needs of the disadvantaged, disabled, or seniors who might apply to immigrate.

The organization of this unit is grounded in the economic and social aspects of immigration policies. Exploration of the resolution begins with the economic effects of immigration. Employer-preferenced immigration, unskilled labor trade-off and the impact on wages are discussed in this section. The political aspects of illegal immigration, tighter border controls and the ability of the Immigration and Naturalization Service to manage the system are detailed in the following section. Along with the domestic concerns associated with immigration, the foreign policy implications of immigration and the potential public backlash against perceived impacts of changing the U.S. immigration policy will be discussed in the next section. Any discussion of immigration policies would also require the evaluation of the push-pull effects of U.S. and world economic growth on world migration patterns. An exploration of the methodologies and extrapolations of certain immigration studies round out the coverage of the issues associated with the strengthening of U.S. immigration policies. The final aspects of this exploration of the topic concern the specific populations that make up U.S. immigration applicants. These populations include the skilled and the unskilled laborer; the educated and the uneducated immigrant; or even specific groups like entertainers, athletes and circus performers that apply to immigrate to the United States. Another area of potential argumentation on this resolution would revolve around U.S. refugee and asylee policies. Arguments specific to refugees and asylees may be found under the resolution on the protection of human rights through refugee admission policies.

CHAPTER IV

OUTLINE

I. GENERAL INFORMATION ABOUT IMMIGRATION

  A. POLICY ESTABLISHED BY IMMIGRATION LAWS

    1. IRCA of 1986 described (1-2)

    2. Aspects of the IMMACT of 1990

      a. Allows increased immigration (3-4)

      b. Increased emphasis on skilled immigrants (5-6)

      c. Act increases allotments for the exceptionally talented (7-9)

      d. The act prevents job trade-offs from occurring (10)

      e. Investors are given preference (11)

      f. Ideology is removed as a barrier (12)

      g. Changes in the O and P nonimmigrant status (13)

    3. Nurses are given preference (14-15)

    4. General description of the philosophy behind our laws (16-17)

    5. Future trends in the law

      a. Increased restrictions are coming (18-21)

      b. No restrictions are pending (22-23)

  B. TOPICALITY ISSUES

    1. 1980, 1986, and 1990 Acts are contextually topical (24-25)

    2. Laundry list of topical cases (26-27)

    3. Contextually, immigration includes refugees/asylees (28-31)

    4. Immigration doesn't include refugees/asylees

      a. Immigration isn't migration (32-33)

      b. Policies concerning the groups are distinct (34-37)

      c. Settlement policy proves that they're different (38)

    5. Classification schemes are regulations on immigration (39)

  C. INFORMATION ABOUT IMMIGRATION

    1. We don't know how many illegal immigrants there are (40-43)

    2. Generally, information about immigrants is lacking (44-45)

    3. Reliable studies show immigration numbers (46)

    4. Not need precise information for policy action (47-48)

    5. Immigration will increase in the future (49)

    6. Immigration won't substantially increase to the United States (50)

II. POLITICAL ASPECTS OF IMMIGRATION

  A. THE "IMMIGRATION BACKLASH"

    1. Risk of an immigration backlash is increasing (51-56)

    2. Public opposition to immigration increasing

      a. Generally, opposition to immigration increasing (57-59)

      b. Public wants major crackdown (60-63)

      c. This reflects historical progression, isn't cyclical (64)

      d. Public doesn't support an open door (65)

      e. Public especially opposes illegal immigration (66)

      f. Public hates asylum system abuse (67)

      g. Immigration is a critical political issue (68-69)

    3. Public perception arguments

      a. Generally, the public doesn't understand the facts (70)

      b. They perceive a job trade-off (71-73)

      c. Public doesn't believe arguments for immigration (74-75)

      d. Public uses immigration as a scapegoat (76)

      e. Public doesn't perceive policy failures (77)

      f. Public not perceive refugees (78)

      g. Public perceives refugee system abuse (79)

    4. Impacts to the immigration backlash

      a. Causes overreaction and a crackdown on immigration (80-81)

      b. Causes a cycle of increased immigration and backlash (82)

      c. Risks American xenophobia and racial conflict (83-87)

      d. Causes vigilante actions by public (88)

      e. Asians will be specifically targeted (89)

5. Legal and illegal immigration trade-off: anger over illegal immigration causes legal immigration decreases (90-96)
6. Need quick action to avoid backlash (97-99)
7. No risk of the backlash occurring
   a. No proof of public attitudes (100)
   b. Public opposes hardline policy (101)
   c. Immigration isn't an important issue (102)
   d. Opposition will fade soon (103)
   e. Clinton actions forestall the backlash (104)
   f. Backlash isn't caused by immigration levels (105)
   g. All immigration policies cause a backlash (106)
   h. No real impact to the backlash (107-108)
   i. No risk of xenophobia in the U.S. (109-111)

B. IMMIGRATION AND EXECUTIVE / LEGISLATIVE RELATIONS
   1. Immigration policy causes conflicts
      a. Its always been a major source of conflict (112-113)
      b. Immigration uniquely risks conflict (114)
      c. Different views on immigration makes conflict likely (115)
   2. Immigration policy doesn't cause conflicts
      a. Refugee act of 1980 proves this (116)
      b. Not a key source of conflict anymore (117)
      c. Congress accepts executive role in immigration policy (118)

III. ECONOMIC AFFECTS OF IMMIGRATION

A. ECONOMIC BENEFITS OF IMMIGRATION
   1. Immigration needed to prevent labor shortages
      a. Immigration is key component of labor force (119-120)
      b. Regional shortages still exist (121)
      c. Future shortages will emerge (122)
      d. Alternatives to immigration will fail (123-124)
   2. Immigration increases employment
      a. No displacement effect—consensus agrees (125)
      b. 1980s prove immigration increases employment (126)
      c. LA study proves it increases employment (127)
      d. Entrepreneurship effect increases employment (128)
   3. Immigration generally helps the American economy
      a. Consumers benefit with lower prices (129-139)
      b. Immigration needed for survival of specific industries (131-132)
      c. Prevents the relocation of US industry (133-134)
      d. Generally increases economic growth (135)
   4. Immigration saves social security system (136)

B. ECONOMIC HARMS CAUSED BY IMMIGRATION
   1. Immigration decreases employment
      a. Generally causes job trade-offs (137-138)
      b. Offset gains from economic expansion (139-140)
      c. Studies prove displacement effect (141-142)
      d. Immigration reform needed to increase employment (143-146)
   2. Immigrants not needed for the economy (147-148)
   3. Immigrants not needed to solve labor shortages (149-150)
   4. Free trade arguments don't justify immigration (151-154)

IV. SOCIAL ASPECTS OF IMMIGRATION

A. SOCIAL HARMS OF IMMIGRATION (155)
   1. Immigration drains the public coffers (156)
      a. Immigrants more likely to use welfare
      b. Displacement effect forces Americans onto welfare (157)
      c. New data proves immigration is a net burden (158-159)
      d. RAND study proves immigration taxes government resources (160-161)
      e. New Huddle study proves they're a huge burden (162)
      f. Safety net will be used by new immigrants (163)
   2. Immigrants overload social services
      a. They're eligible for all social services (164)

b. Generally, immigrants worsen problems in social programs (165-166)

c. Immigrants destroy state education systems (167-168)

d. Immigration overloads medical care systems (169)

3. Immigration hurts inner city poor and minorities (170)

   a. Generally, all the benefits they receive trade-off

   b. Immigration decreases wages (1710

      1- Immigration caused a 5% decrease in the 1980s (172)

      2- California proves the wage decrease argument (173-175)

      3- In the future, the problem will worsen (176)

      4- Immigration hurts the non-minimum wage poor (177-178)

   c. Immigration reduces jobs for Americans (179)

      1- Generally, jobs trade-off (180)

      2- Immigrants settle in same areas as the poor (181)

      3- There is direct competition for jobs (182)

      4- Immigrants don't just take jobs Americans don't want (183-184)

      5- Structural changes in the economy will magnify the trade-off

      6- No unskilled labor shortage exists (185)

      7- Must decrease immigration to increase minority employment (186-189)

   d. Redistribution won't solve the harmful effects of immigration (187)

4. No benefits to immigration—new immigrants are less skilled

   a. This is true for legal and illegal immigrants

   b. New immigrants are less educated (190)

   c. New immigrants are more likely to be dependents (191-192)

   d. New immigration laws encourage low-skilled workers (193)

5. Immigration burdens specific regions in the U.S.

   a. Immigration strains coastal regions (194)

b. It imposes large costs on Texas, California, Florida, New York (195-196)

c. Immigration will bankrupt California (197-200)

d. "Aggregate analysis" of effects ignores local impacts (201)

e. Burdens and benefits not equally distributed (202)

      1- States pay for services, federal government gets the taxes (203)

      2- Federal government doesn't pay its fair share back to states (204)

6. Immigration causes "social pathology" problems

   a. Immigrants add to the underclass (205)

   b. It increases the problems of illegitimacy and unemployment (206)

   c. Immigration increases crime (207-208)

   d. It increases gangs (209)

   e. Immigration increases drug trade (210)

7. Immigration increases racial and social tensions (211)

   a. Competition for scarce resources increases tensions (212)

   b. Future trends will increase the severity of competition (213-214)

   c. Risk of social breakdown is significant (215-216)

   d. Risk is linear-—increased immigration increases problems (217-218)

   e. Other nations show the potential impact of ethnic breakdown (219-220)

8. Immigration hurts American culture (221)

   a. Risk exists of rapid ethnic transition

   b. Demographic changes hurt cultural strength

   c. Immigration increases pressure for multiculturalism (222-224)

   d. Cultural unity needed for social stability (223)

   e. Assimilation is no longer possible (225)

   f. Need to decrease immigration to restore ethnic balances (226-227)

9. Immigration generally decreases American quality of life (228)

10. Immigration hurts our national ideals and prestige (229-230)
11. Benefits to immigration are overstated (231)
    a. Benefits happen too long in the future (232)
    b. Cultural benefits of immigration have already been reached (233)

B. IMMIGRATION BRINGS MANY SOCIAL BENEFITS
1. Immigrants add to the public coffers
   a. They're no more of a burden than Americans (234-235)
   b. Studies prove they're net contributors (236-237)
2. Immigrants don't overload social services
   a. Immigrant taxes paid fund American services (238)
   b. Federal redistribution solves shortage (239-240)

3. Immigrants don't hurt the inner city poor
   a. Immigrants don't drive down wages (241)
      1- Wage decreases due to unions, not immigration (241-242)
      2- California disproves these arguments (243)
      3- Cubans prove they don't drive down wages (244)
      4- Decreased immigration won't increase wages (245)
   b. Immigrants don't displace American workers
      1- They're concentrated in only a few industries (246)
      2- No evidence supports displacement claims (247)
      3- INS raids disprove trade-offs (248)
      4- Texas studies prove they only take jobs Americans don't want (249)
      5- Labor markets too complex to have simple trade-offs (250-251)
4. New immigrants don't have less skills (252-253)
5. Local areas working to control immigration burdens
6. Immigrants don't cause "social pathology"
   a. Italians prove these arguments are false (254)

b. Assumes Puerto Rico, not apply to all immigrants (255)
7. Immigrants don't cause cultural fissions
   a. Immigration is only a scapegoat for deeper problems (256)
   b. Immigrants don't push for multiculturalism (257)
   c. Whites are still a significant majority (258)
   d. Assimilation very common among immigrants (259)
   e. Racial status irrelevant to cultural identification (260)
   f. No "Bosnia" in the United States (261)
   g. Immigrants increase American family values (262)
   h. Immigration crackdown hurts culture (263)
   i. Assumes Latin immigrants, ignores Asians (264)

C. METHODOLOGICAL ISSUES IN DETERMINING THE EFFECTS OF IMMIGRATION
1. Knowledge limits on determining these effects exist (265)
2. Studies are contradictory, can't determine what is true (266)
3. No basis for anti-immigration claims (267-270)
4. Indicts to the Huddle study (271-272)
   a. It is the one most quoted by anti-immigration forces (273)
   b. Huddle relied on the LA study for his data (274)
   c. Huddle's numbers are flawed
      1- No one can verify his facts (275)
      2- Because of bias, he omitted important numbers (276)
      3- Huddle admits he underestimated the taxes paid (277)
      4- He overestimated job loss, ignored job gains (278)
   d. His study is an anomaly (279)
      1- All other studies contradict his findings (280)
      2- Other major studies disagree (281)
5. Indicts to the Los Angeles / San Diego studies
   a. Multiple problems with these studies (282-284)
   b. LA study underestimated income earned by immigrants (285)

c. Impact is exaggerated, they make long-term contributions
6. Simon study is flawed
   a. His arguments are logically inconsistent (286)
   b. Recent studies prove his job arguments are flawed (287)
   c. His data is outdated (288)
   d. He doesn't take into account low-skilled immigrants (289-291)
7. Briggs' arguments ignore any contradictory evidence (292)
8. Huddle study is accurate (293-294)
9. Impact of legal and illegal immigrants is different (295)

D. GOVERNMENT RESPONSES TO THE IMMIGRATION BURDEN
   1. Government should act to decrease burdens on local areas (296-297)
   2. Should cut welfare benefits to illegal aliens (298)
   3. Welfare cuts won't decrease illegal immigration (299-300)

E. PHILOSOPHICAL ISSUES OF IMMIGRATION CONTROL (301)
   1. Can make a just immigration policy (302-303)
   2. Lottery doesn't ensure justice (304-305)
   3. Economic considerations exclude the less fortunate (306)
   4. Exclusion violates Rawlsian justice (307-310)
   5. Immigrants don't deserve full rights (311)
   6. Must sacrifice rights to ensure national sovereignty (312)

V. ENVIRONMENTAL EFFECTS OF IMMIGRATION

A. THE WORLD IS PAST THE CARRYING CAPACITY (313-315)

B. IMMIGRATION INCREASES POPULATION PRESSURES
   1. It is the key factor driving US growth (316-318)
   2. Safety valve increases Third World fertility (319-320)
   3. Immigration increases U.S. fertility (321-323)
   4. Immigration more important than fertility (324)

C. POPULATION GROWTH IS HARMFUL
   1. It causes international conflicts (325-327)

2. Population growth destroys the environment (328-329)
3. Immigration destroys American farmland (330-332)
4. US population worse than Third World population (333-335)
5. Impact is linear on the environment (336)
6. Society won't adapt to change consumption patterns (337)

D. IMMIGRATION DOESN'T THREATEN THE ENVIRONMENT
   1. Population increasing around the world (338-339)
   2. Immigration doesn't affect population growth (340-341)
   3. Gloom and doom scenarios are flawed (342-343)
   4. No resource shortages will emerge (343)
   5. Immigration reduces harms of Third World population (344-345)

VI. IMMIGRATION POLICY AND FOREIGN POLICY ISSUES

A. IMMIGRATION GENERALLY AFFECTS US FOREIGN POLICY
   1. It is a key factor in foreign policy decisions (347-349)
   2. WW2 proves it's an important factor (350)
   3. Japan empirically proves this argument (351)

B. IMMIGRATION GENERALLY DOES NOT AFFECT US FOREIGN POLICY
   1. The effects are exaggerated (352)
   2. Empirical examples don't apply to current policy (353)
   3. Assimilation moots the effect of immigration (354)
   4. Immigration backlash prevents policy swing (355)

C. IMMIGRATION POLICY AND US / MEXICAN RELATIONS
   1. Now is an important time to foster relations (356-357)
   2. Unilateral restrictions will impede cooperation (358-360)
   3. Mexico is important to foster US / Latin America ties (361)

D. IMMIGRATION POLICY AND US / LATIN AMERICAN RELATIONS
   1. Now is an important time to foster relations with Latin America (362-366)

2. Immigration makes the United States focus on Latin America (367-369)
3. Unilateral restrictions impede increased cooperation (370-371)
4. Perception of domestic problems in the US blocks ties (372-373
5. Many benefits exist to improved cooperation (374-377)

E. MISCELLANEOUS FOREIGN POLICY ISSUES
1. Recognizing refugees limits our foreign policy (378)
2. Closed border mentality prevents solutions of world problems (379-380)
3. Refugee support needed for international credibility (381)

VII. DEVELOPMENT ISSUES AND IMMIGRATION POLICY

A. DEVELOPMENT AND IMMIGRATION LEVELS
1. Current development model flawed, encourages migration (382-385)
2. Full development needed to reduce migration pressures (386-391)
3. Development won't reduce immigration (392)
4. Development increases immigration by causing sectoral shocks (393-394)

B. NAFTA AND ITS EFFECT ON IMMIGRATION
1. NAFTA will decrease immigration
   a. Generally it will decrease immigration (395-397)
   b. Not need full wage parity to reduce pressures (398-399)
   c. Gains happen quickly, solving short-term turns (400)
2. NAFTA won't solve immigration
   a. NAFTA increases short-term immigration (401-404)
   b. Free trade will decrease Mexican jobs (405-406)
   c. NAFTA won't solve Mexico's problems (407-408)
   d. NAFTA increases inequality which increases long-term pressures (409-410)

C. IMMIGRATION POLICY'S EFFECT ON DEVELOPMENT
1. Immigration acts as a safety valve (411-412)
2. Immigration acts as a safety valve for Mexico (413-416)

3. Immigration reduces the north-south gap (417)
4. Immigration crackdown hurts economy, increasing immigration (418-419)
5. Safety valve model hurts long-term development (420-421)

VIII. SPECIFIC POLICIES TO REGULATE IMMIGRATION

A. NEED A MORATORIUM / STRONG CONTROLS ON LEGAL IMMIGRATION (422-425)
B. NEED LABOR LAW ENFORCEMENT TO DECREASE IMMIGRATION (426-429)
C. CHANGING LAWS TO ALLOW NURSES TO IMMIGRATE (430-431)
D. NEED TO CHANGE THE FEE STRUCTURE OF INS (432)
E. NEED INCREASED EFFICIENCY OF THE NATURALIZATION PROCESS (433-434)
F. NO NEED FOR INCREASED LABOR LAW ENFORCEMENT (435-436)
G. THE CASE FOR AN ECONOMIC-BASED IMMIGRATION POLICY
1. Status quo approach is ad hoc (437-439)
2. We don't use immigration to advance our economic needs (440-441)
3. Barriers to skilled workers exist (442)
4. Advantages to an economic-minded policy
   a. Eliminates encouragement for low-skilled immigration (443-445)
   b. Allows control over the borders (446)
   c. It solves motives for illegal immigration (447)
   d. Need new policy to adapt to structural changes in the economy (448-449)
   e. New policy increases flexibility (450)
   f. Need to coordinate with overall employment policy (451-454)
   g. Australia and Canada prove this approach is successful
5. Legal immigration can offset any labor shortage (457)

H. THE CASE FOR JUDICIAL NATURALIZATION CEREMONIES
1. IMMACT of 1990 eliminated judicial ceremonies (458-460)
2. Judiciary increases dignity and importance of ceremony (461-464)
3. Amending the act to allow a 45-day preference solves (465-469)

298

4. No risk of court clog or delays
    a. 45-day limit solves this problem (470)
    b. No problems with backlog (471)
    c. Delays are due to the INS, not the courts (472-473)
    d. Decreased paperwork requirements solve any delays (474-475)
    e. Decreased de novo appeals reduces delays (476-479)
5. Judicial ceremonies should be mandatory (480-481)
6. Alternatives don't capture the benefits of the judiciary (482)
7. This proposal is unnecessary and undesirable (483-485)

IX. THE UNITED STATES'S ABILITY TO REGULATE IMMIGRATION

A. ISSUES RAISED BY THE IRCA OF 1986
    1. IRCA fails to reduce immigration
        a. It's a continuation of past failures (486-487)
        b. It has failed to reduce immigration (488-489)
        c. INS was underfunded and understaffed to carry out mission (490)
        d. Too many enforcement problems with the legislation (491)
    2. Amnesty provisions of the act
        a. Immigrants not apply for amnesty (492)
        b. Amnesty is very costly (493)
        c. Encourages increased immigration (494)
        d. It decreases illegal immigration (495)
        e. Amnesty isn't excessively costly (496)
    3. Employer sanctions are generally successful
        a. Sanctions generally work
            1- They are important for their symbolic value (497-498)
            2- Post-1986 data proves they have a deterrent effect (499-500)
        b. Reformed sanctions can succeed
            1- Need national ID card to enforce sanctions (501-502)
            2- Can expand on the social security card system (503-504)
            3- Work permits allow for effective enforcement (505)
        c. No problems with discrimination
            1- No evidence proves discrimination occurs (506)
            2- ID system solves motive for discrimination (507-508)
        d. No problems with government abuses or big brother
            1- Similar to card being used in health care reform (509)
            2- Europe has ID cards with no right losses (510)
            3- ID system doesn't risk big brother (511)
    4. Employer sanctions are generally unsuccessful
        a. IRCA failures prove sanctions don't work (512-513)
        b. Other empirical examples prove sanctions fail (514-515)
        c. No evidence proves sanctions' solvency (516)
        d. No enforcement of sanctions by government
            1- Employers can avoid legal liability (517)
            2- Government won't press charges (518)
            3- Judges not uphold penalties (519-520)
            4- The stronger the penalty, the greater the circumvention (521)
        e. No voluntary compliance with the law (522-523)
        f. Never have enough money to have effective sanctions (524)
        g. Sanctions increase discrimination
            1- INS will target employers with large amounts of Hispanics (525)
            2- Employers will treat all Hispanics as illegal aliens (526)
            3- Studies prove that IRCA increased discrimination (527-529)
        h. Sanctions increase alien exploitation
            1- Forces aliens and hiring process underground (530-531)
            2- Decreased job opportunity increases exploitation (532)
            3- Sanctions drive down wages by making aliens a hiring risk (533)
        i. National ID system undesirable
            1- Causes public backlash and uproar (534)

2- Risks abuse by the government (535)

3- Threatens the nation's privacy (536)

B. BORDER CONTROL APPROACH TO CURTAILING IMMIGRATION
  1. INS reforming to improve ability to seal the border (537-540)
  2. Border tax increases INS resources to man the border (541)
  3. Border control will never reduce illegal immigration
     a. Too many barriers to effective control (542)
     b. Border control a utopian dream (543-545)
     c. Patrol has too few staff and resources (546-548)
     d. INS doesn't have adequate tracking capabilities (549)
     e. Court decisions block effective policies (550)
  4. Border control has negative consequences for immigrants
     a. Border fees discriminate against the poor (551)
     b. Border violence against aliens is increasing (552-553)
     c. Even if they are illegal aliens, they still have rights (554)
     d. Funding problems heighten risk of rights violations (555-556)
     e. INS will not have staff to investigate complaints (557-558)
     f. INS will cover up rights violations (559-560)
     g. INS can't reform itself (561-563)
     h. Need external actor to reform the INS, reduce rights violations (564-565)
  5. Major problems with current detention facilities (566-567)
  6. Deportation of illegal aliens needed (568-570)

C. GENERAL ISSUES IN IMMIGRATION CONTROL
  1. Motives for immigration to the US
     a. No evidence provides a coherent explanation (571-572)
     b. Motives are mainly economic (573-574)
     c. Immigrants are fleeing problems at home (575)
     d. America is seen as the promised land of opportunity (576)
  2. Immigration control will never work

a. Society doesn't want real limits, won't allow INS to succeed (577-578)
b. Restrictive policies have always failed (579-581)
c. Nature of a free society blocks controls (582)

  3. INS is an ineffective agency to control illegal immigration
     a. They lack a clear policy mission and coherence (583-584)
     b. Conflicting duties block effective controls (585)
     c. INS has no information management capabilities (586-587)
     d. INS is corrupt (588-589)
     e. INS documents are easy to counterfeit (590-591)
     f. INS is too fragmented, policies not fully implemented (592)
     g. Low morale blocks effectiveness (593-595)
     h. Budget problems limit ability to carry out mandate (596-597)
     i. Even with adequate funding, the INS would still fall short (598)
     j. INS bias blocks it from being an effective agency (599-603)

1.   Barry Chiswick. ILLEGAL ALIENS, Kalamazoo: Upjohn Institute for Employment Research, 1988, p. 3. A compromise legislative package on illegal aliens that had been under discussion for a decade included penalties against employers who knowingly hire illegal aliens (referred to as "employer sanctions"), amnesty (or legalization) for illegal aliens who could prove they were in the U.S. prior to a specified date, and increased resources for INS enforcement activities. Quite unexpectedly, in the closing days of the legislative session, Congress passed and the President signed the Immigration Reform and Control Act of 1986. This is the most sweeping immigration legislation since the 1965 Amendments which abolished the "national origins" quota system. The 1986 Act included employer sanctions, amnesty for illegal aliens who have continuously reside in the U.S. since January 1, 1982, and promises of increased enforcement resources, as well as other less central provisions. The implementation of the employer sanctions and legalization provisions began in the first half of 1987, and it will be some time before it will be possible to ascertain their consequences. Over $2^1/4$ million illegal aliens have received legal status under the various amnesty provisions in the 1986 legislation.

2.   Dan Stein. IMMIGRATION AND NATURALIZATION SERVICE MANAGE-MENT ISSUES, Hrg of the Committee on the Judiciary, House of Representatives, April 24, 1991, p. 177. Although it appears that management restructuring with-in the INS is necessary to a certain extent, such a plan would be a temporary solution to a basic foundational problem: the lack of a national immigration policy. In the past, there was a clearly defined policy toward immi-gration which all branches of government sought to up-hold. This subcommittee, under your leadership, worked closely with the INS and former Commissioner Alan Nelson, to craft a truly historic piece of legislation: the Immigration Reform and Control Act of 1986 (IRCA). Congress and the administration made a firm commit-ment to halt illegal immigration by creating, as the cen-terpiece of IRCA, the employer sanctions provision which prescribes penalties against employers who knowingly hire illegal aliens.

3.   Donald Huddle. "Debate Must Begin with True View of the Costs." HOUSTON CHRONICLE, 8/29/93, p. 1. To make matters much worse, in 1989 as the United States slid into a recession and unemployment escalated, Congress and

President Bush eagerly embraced the Immigration Act of 1990 which increased legal immigration by 40 percent. In 1991 alone, legal migration, including IRCA amnesties, reached 1.8 million. And legal migration flows will remain close to 1 million yearly under current law indefinitely, a total greater than those admitted by the rest of the industrial countries combined.

4.   Klaus Fuchs. "Agenda for Tomorrow." ANNALS OF THE AMERICAN ACADEMY OF POLITICAL SCIENCE, November 1993, p. 170. Finally, in 1990, during a time of extreme economic uncertainty and with the nation about to enter a prolonged recession and war in the Persian Gulf, Congress provided for a slight expansion of family-reunification immigration and almost tripled the number of immigrants chosen for their skills independent of family ties from 54,000, including the immediate families of the principal beneficiaries. Another provision established a safe haven for those already in the United States fleeing civil war and natural disasters and was made applicable immediately to Salvadorans for a minimum of 18 months; this provision has since been renewed. Other pro-immigration measures included an expansion of visas for persons from Hong Kong, establishing a transitional diversity program, and allowing 40,000 visas a year for nationals of 33 countries that had low rates of immigration in recent years.

Under these laws, the total number of persons to be awarded permanent resident status—including refugees and asylees who adjust their status—will average at least 700,000 a year through the rest of the 1990s.

5.   David Williams. IMPLEMENTATION OF THE IMMIGRATION ACT OF 1990, Hrg of the Committee on the Judiciary, House of Representatives, May 15, 1991, pp. 99-100. A. Permanent Employment-Based Immigration. The Act authorizes an increase in the number of employment-based permanent immigrants from 54,000 to 140,000 annually beginning October 1, 1991 in five visa categories of employment-based immigration: (1) Priority Workers; (2) Professionals with Advance Degrees and Aliens of Exceptional Ability; (3) Skilled Workers, Professionals, and Other Workers; (4) Special Immigrants; and (5) Employment Creation. Labor Certifications are required in the categories of Profes-sionals with Advanced Degrees and Aliens of Excep-tional Ability (Preference Group 2), and Skilled Work-ers, Professionals and Other Workers (Preference Group

3). Emphasis is placed on highly skilled positions, with visas for unskilled occupations limited to 10,000.

6.   David Williams. IMPLEMENTATION OF THE IMMIGRATION ACT OF 1990, Hrg of the Committee on the Judiciary, House of Representatives, May 15, 1991, pp. 98-99. The Act represents a major shift in U.S. immigration policy. With respect to immigrant or permanent entry, the Act attempts to achieve a better balance between family reunification and employment-based immigration. This is to make immigration policy more responsive to labor market needs while continuing to protect the interests of U.S. workers. As a result, the new law will significantly increase the total number of visas available for permanent immigration, with most of this increase allocated to higher skilled employment-based immigrants. With respect to nonimmigrants, the Act continues to allow employers to quickly obtain temporary workers when needed, but seeks to balance that needed flexibility with increased protection for U.S. workers in several temporary employment-based categories.

7.   ADMISSION OF O AND P NONIMMI-GRANTS, Hrg of the Committee on the Judiciary, House of Representatives, October 9, 1991, p. 126. A new immigration law establishes a very un-American class system. It says that the more famous you are, the better your chances. Uncle Sam prefers new citizens with prestigious talents, such as symphony orchestra conductors, high-powered multinational corporate executives and scientific wizards.

Designed to lure outstanding professors, scientists, artists and scholars, the US will give first preference to aliens of "extraordinary" ability, which means those with piles of press clippings attesting that everyone already knows who they are. A Nobel Prize, an Academy Award or an Olympic gold medal will do the trick.

8.   Paul Wickham Schmidt. "Business-Related Provisions of the Immigration Act of 1990." IN DEFENSE OF THE ALIEN, Vol. 15: 1993, p. 10. The conference committee report states that a bachelor's degree plus at least five years of progressive experience in the professions should be considered the equivalent of an advanced degree (H.R. Rep. No. 105-955, 101st Cong., 2d. Sess. at 121 (1990) (hereafter "Conference Report")). The INS regulations adopt this definition (8 C.F.R. § 204.5(k)(2)). However, the INS regulations do not permit beneficiaries under the second preference category to substitute professional experience for a bachelor degree (8 C.F.R. § 204.5(k)(2)).

INS regulations state that "exceptional ability" means a degree of expertise significantly above that ordinarily encountered in the sciences, arts or business" (8 C.F.R. § 204.5(k)(2)).

While a labor certification generally is required for the second preference category, the Attorney General is permitted to waive the requirement of a job offer in the United States for an alien of exception ability "when he deems it to be in the national interest" (Act, Revised § 203(b)(B)). In implementing this provision, the INS has declined to define what constitutes "in the national interest" (8 C.F.R. § 204.5(k)(ii)). Consequently, this provision could be the subject of considerable debate and interpretation.

9.   Paul Wickham Schmidt. "Business-Related Provisions of the Immigration Act of 1990." IN DEFENSE OF THE ALIEN, Vol. 15: 1993, p. 8. The first preference is for "priority workers" who are not subject to the labor certification requirement. This category includes aliens with extraordinary ability, outstanding professors and researchers, and certain multinational executives and managers.

Under the INS regulations, aliens with extraordinary ability must demonstrate sustained national or international acclaim through extensive documentation (see 8 C.F.R. § 204.5(h)). This category is intended to be "for that small percentage of individuals who have risen to the very top of their field of endeavor" (H.R. Rep. No. 101-723, 101st Cong., 2d Sess., Pt. 1 at 59 (1990) (hereafter "House Report"); 8 C.F.R. § 204.5(h)(2)).

10.   Aaron Bodin. "Agricultural Labor and the Future of US Immigration Policy." IN DEFENSE OF THE ALIEN, Vol. 15, 1993. The basic criteria for labor certification is that the importation of foreign workers shall not displace workers in the United States or adversely affect their wages and working con-ditions. To meet these criteria, an employer must recruit in the United States for about two months before the work is to begin. A contract must be offered with special wage rates set by the Department of Labor. Housing must be provided without cost and meals at a minimal cost. Work must be guaranteed for three fourths of the contract period, compensation for employment injuries must be assured and, in general, the terms and conditions of employment may not be less than local prevailing practice. If U.S. workers cannot be found in response to this offer, foreign workers may be admitted under the same contract provisions. In addition, any qualified U.S. worker who applies during the first half of the contract period must be hired.

11.   Paul Wickham Schmidt. "Business-Related Provisions of the Immigration Act of 1990."

IN DEFENSE OF THE ALIEN, Vol. 15: 1993, p. 11. The Act also creates a new fifth employment-based preference category, with approximately 10,000 immigrant visas allotted annually, for investors. It should be noted that, as with all the employment-based categories, the 10,000 limit includes dependents of qualifying principals. Therefore, it is likely that substantially fewer than 10,000 principal investors will immigrate annually.

Under prior law, investors had been relegated to the "nonpreference" category which had been unavailable for more than a decade. The investor preference was a controversial provision enacted over opposition from legislators who claimed it amounted to "selling" permanent residence in the United States.

To qualify under this section, a foreign investor must invest at least $1 million in a "new commercial enterprise" that creates full-time employment for at least ten U.S. workers (other than the investor and his or her immediate family). INS regulations define a "new commercial enterprise" as including: the creation of an original business; the purchase of the assets of an existing business and simultaneous or subsequent restructuring or reorganization that results in a new commercial enterprise; or the "substantial expansion" (increase of 40% in net worth or workers) of an existing business (8 C.F.R. § 204.6(h)).

12.   Elizabeth Tamposi. IMPLEMENTATION OF
        THE IMMIGRATION ACT OF 1990, Hrg of
the Committee on the Judiciary, House of Representatives, May 15, 1991, p. 92. The "ideological" grounds have also been substantially revised. The major change relates to membership in or affiliation with communist organizations. Nonimmigrant aliens will cease to be ineligible for this reason as of June 1. Immigrant aliens will still be ineligible for this reason, but in a much more limited way than in the past. Membership of affiliation which was terminated at least two (or, in certain cases, five) years prior to a visa application will not affect their application. In addition, the relief available for immigrants who do not meet the more liberal guidelines is broader than before. The number of immigrant visa applicants who ultimately will be prevented from immigrating for this reason will be much smaller than under the current law.

13.   Gene McNary. ADMISSION OF O AND P
        NONIMMIGRANTS, Hrg of the Committee
on the Judiciary, House of Representatives, October 9, 1991, pp. 14-15. Before commenting on H.R. 3048, I would like to provide you with some background information on the O and P nonimmigrant categories. As you know, IMMACT made a number of significant changes to the immigration laws of the United States. One of the significant changes to the immigration laws of the United States. One of the significant changes

made by IMMACT was the creation of the new O and P nonimmigrant categories. Briefly, the O-1 nonimmigrant classification includes two distinct categories of aliens. First, it includes aliens of extraordinary ability in the arts, sciences, business, athletics and entertainment. Second, the classification includes aliens of extraordinary achievement in motion picture and television industry. This classification is limited to individual aliens, not members of a group.

The P-1 immigrant classification includes athletes, both individually and as part of a group or team, as well as members of entertainment groups. The P-2 classification includes artists and entertainers, both individually and as a member of a group, who are coming to perform in the United States in a reciprocal exchange program. The P-3 classification is limited to artists or entertainers, either individually or as part of a group, who are coming to perform in a program that is culturally unique.

14.   "House Eases Immigration For Foreign
        Nurses." CONGRESSIONAL QUARTERLY,
October 21, 1989. By voice vote, the House Oct. 17 passed a bill (HR 3259) to allow foreign nurses now working in the United States on temporary visas to apply for permanent residence. The measure would also permit more nurses to come to the United States over the next five years.

15.   "House Eases Immigration For Foreign
        Nurses." CONGRESSIONAL QUARTERLY,
October 21, 1989. The bill also creates a five-year pilot program permitting hospitals to recruit licensed nurses from abroad if they attest that they have tried unsuccessfully to recruit and retain U.S. nurses, and that employment of foreign nurses will not "adversely affect the wages and working conditions of registered nurses similarly employed.

16.   Austin T. Fragomen, Jr. "Immigration
        Policy." IN DEFENSE OF THE ALIEN,
Vol. 15: 1993. What is U.S. immigration policy, or perhaps more appropriately, does the United States have an immigration policy? I have pondered this question intermittently since first starting my career as staff counsel to the Subcommittee on International Law, Refugees and Immigration of the House Judiciary Committee.

It is common knowledge that there is no overriding policy which was planned and implemented at a single point in time. However, I would suggest that a policy may be extrapolated from the law. This deductive process results in what at a minimum must be regarded as a de facto policy. I am suggesting that even if there is no comprehensive policy there is a body of law which, taken as a whole, is "the policy."

17.   Austin T. Fragomen, Jr. "Immigration
       Policy." IN DEFENSE OF THE ALIEN,
Vol. 15: 1993, p. 105. Border endorsement is a "given"
in the modern world. Every nation controls its borders
with varying degrees of success. This would seem to be
a noncontroversial policy; however, I would suggest
that the United States has made a purposeful policy
decision to inadequately regulate the flow of
undocumented workers into the country. Allocation of
adequate sources would address this issue were there a
policy commitment. Stopping the influx across the
Mexican border would not be difficult—albeit
expensive. Traditionally, the policy has been to pay lip
service to the severity of the issue but to expand
minimal effort in its resolution. If we further analyze
these various examples, we can reach certain
conclusions about policy. In the immigration and
refugee field, policy is usually expressed reasonably and
even meticulously in the law. Perhaps the derivation is
not a comprehensive study or white paper but the
accretion of ideas over a period of time. At times
specific policies may be controversial or, we may believe, dead wrong. But an identifiable policy exists.
The matter is complicated by the role of the
government, charged with effectuating policy. Ideally,
in the implementation process, policy is honed and
refined. Occasionally, however, a new agenda appears
and policy is undermined. Finally, there are those few
areas where policy is ill-conceived or possibly
purposefully duplicitous. But to posit that there is no
United States immigration policy is erroneous.

18.   Holly Idelson. "Clinton's Immigration
       Changes Aim To Stop Abuses."
CONGRESSIONAL QUARTERLY, July 31, 1993, p.
2061. Amid heightened public anxiety about the cost
and risks of uninvited arrivals, President Clinton on
July 27 called for a series of programs to combat
illegal immigration and terrorism.
    The administration wants new legal tools to stop
fraudulent asylum-seekers at airports and other points
of entry, and to crack down on smugglers who traffic in
illegal aliens. Clinton also seeks $172.5 million in
new spending to beef up immigration control.
    The package got generally favorable reviews on
Capitol Hill as a good start on a large problem.
Political pressure has been building for a crackdown on
illegal immigration, and members from both parties
already were pushing many parts of the administration
plan.

19.   Tony Freemantle. "Anti-Immigrant Sentiment
       Rises." THE HOUSTON CHRONICLE, July
4, 1993, p. A1. Faced with the specter of boats full of
refugees coming aground, President Clinton has ordered
a review of immigration policy that will focus on
keeping illegal immigrants out of the country and on
new ways to deal with requests for asylum, deportation
and refugees.

20.   David Warner. "A Move to Curb Immigrant
       Visas?" NATION'S BUSINESS, February,
1994, p. 65. At a news conference last July, President
Clinton announced efforts to address illegal
immigration, including increased border patrols, and he
pledged that the efforts will not make it tougher for the
immigrant who comes to this country legally, lives by
our laws, gets a job, and pursues the American dream.

21.   David Warner. "A Move to Curb Immigrant
       Visas?" NATION'S BUSINESS, February,
1994, p. 65. But recent Labor Department actions on
H-1B visas suggest that the administration may, in
fact, be clamping down on legal immigration. Labor
Secretary Robert Reich has proposed regulations that
would allow his agency to investigate the validity of a
company's assertion that it needs an H-1B visa when
the firm files a required labor-condition application,
which shows that the company will pay the immigrant
worker the prevailing wage for his or her job category.

22.   "At America's Door." THE ECONOMIST,
       July 24, 1993. Illegal immigration, too, is
scarcely hindered. The border fence with Mexico runs
for a mere 14 miles; immigration officers on the banks
of the Rio Grande sit in their cars as the wetbacks pass
them. Thousands of miles of coast are not patrolled at
all, nor could they be. Campaigns for a national
identity card, the only foolproof way for employers to
tell whether their recruits are legal or not, routinely fell
flat. More effort is going, rightly, towards cracking the
international rings that are smuggling aliens in by the
boatload and selling them into slavery (see page 23).
But beyond that, America has neither the money nor
the will—nor, often, the heart—to keep people out.

23.   Klaus Fuchs. "Agenda for Tomorrow."
       ANNALS OF THE AMERICAN
ACADEMY OF POLITICAL SCIENCE, November
1993, p. 170. Whether or not progress is made in
strengthening measures to curtail illegal migration, the
restrictionists are not likely to have much success in
substantially reducing the scale of legal immigration. It
will be difficult for them to convince Congress to
make such cuts before the Commission on
Immigration Reform submits its final report on 1
September 1997. The only obvious target for reduction
would come from the approximately 465,000 family
reunification immigrants set for annual admissions
beginning in fiscal year 1995. Virtually untouchable
within that category are the immediate relatives of U.S.
citizens—spouses, children, and parents—of whom
237,103 were admitted in fiscal 1991, a number almost
certain to increase by 1995. That leaves as a target the

226,000 numerically restricted visas set aside for all other family reunification preferences, the most vulnerable of which are the preference for the spouses and unmarried children of lawful permanent residents and especially the preference for brothers and sisters of U.S. citizens. The 1990 act sets aside 114,200 visas for the first group, with a minimum of 77 percent allocated to the spouses and minor children of legal permanent residents without regard to per-country ceilings, following the recommendation of the Select Commission. Congress is not likely to vote to prevent hardworking, taxpaying, citizenship-bound permanent resident aliens from having their spouses and minor children join them legally. A stronger case can be made for cutting the maximum 26,226 visas set aside for adult unmarried sons and daughters of resident aliens (subject to country ceilings), based on the argument that such persons, even if unmarried, should wait until their petitioner parents become citizens and should try in the meantime to be admitted as employment-based immigrants. But even if that argument is persuasive to Congress, the reduction in immigration would be tiny.

24. Gene McNary. IMPLEMENTATION OF
THE IMMIGRATION ACT OF 1990, Hrg of the Committee on the Judiciary, House of Representatives, May 15, 1991, p. 76. Together with the Refugee Act of 1980 and the Immigration Reform and Control Act of 1986, the Immigration Act of 1990 made the last decade, in my judgment, the most dynamic and significant in the area of immigration law since the founding of this great republic.

25. Gene McNary. IMPLEMENTATION OF
THE IMMIGRATION ACT OF 1990, Hrg of the Committee on the Judiciary, House of Representatives, May 15, 1991. Mr. McNary. Thank you, Mr. Chairman, members of the subcommittee. Appreciate the opportunity to appear before this subcommittee today to report on the progress that INS is making in the implementation of the Immigration Act of 1990, which we call ImmAct.

On November 29, 1990, the President signed into law the Immigration Act of 1990, landmark legislation which constitutes the most substantial revision of the laws governing legal immigration to the United States since the passage of the Immigration and Nationality Act itself.

26. Michael LeMay. FROM OPEN DOOR TO
DUTCH DOOR, New York: Praeger Press, 1987, p. 15. Several key issues are raised by these numbers and were stressed in the recent debate over immigration policy. At what should be set the overall ceiling on legal immigrants, including immediate relatives and refugees? How broad should be the

amnesty for undocumented aliens? How tough should we attempt to make the enforcement program?

27. Michael LeMay. FROM OPEN DOOR TO
DUTCH DOOR, New York: Praeger Press, 1987, p. 138. Box 5: Reagan's Proposed Immigration Reform Bill.

1.) Amnesty. Aliens living in the U.S. illegally since January 1, 1980 would be permitted to remain, being made eligible for resident-alien status after being here ten years, and would also be free to seek U.S. citizenship (estimated number, 5 million persons).

2.) Guest Workers. A program allowing 50,000 Mexicans annually to come to work temporarily, gradually increasing in numbers over several years until up to hundreds-of-thousands annually.

3.) Employer Sanctions. Employers with more than four employees who "knowingly hire" illegal aliens would be subject to fines for up to $1,000 per violation.

4.) Boat People. Boats carrying Haitians would be intercepted. Detention camps would be established to hold as many as 6,000 people pending hearings on their deportation.

5.) Enforcement. Increase the budget of the INS by 50% and add 1,500 officers to the Border Patrol to enhance enforcement of immigration and labor laws.

6.) Immigration Limits. Allow 610,000 new immigrants to the U.S. annually, with a special preference to persons from Canada and Mexico. (Source: "U.S. Immigration and Refugee Policy," Department of State, Thursday, July 30, 1981. See also "Reagan's Plan for Illegal Aliens—the Impact *U.S. News and World Report*, August 3, 1981: 42-43.)

28. Ellen Kraly. IMMIGRATION AND U.S.
FOREIGN POLICY, San Francisco: Westview Press, 1990, pp. 88-89. Trends in immigration to the United States during the post-World War II period are illustrated in Figure 6.4. Because refugees are included in counts of immigration in the year in which permanent resident status is granted, the strong relationship between immigrant and refugee admissions shown is not surprising. During the first half of the 1950s, refugee migration occurred, along with low levels of immigration, under the restraints of national quotas. Until 1975, nonrefugee immigration to the United States steadily increased. During the 1970s, rather more dramatic swings in immigration developed; these are apparent even after removing the direct effects of refugee admissions.

29. Barry Chiswick. ILLEGAL ALIENS,
Kalamazoo: Upjohn Institute for Employment Research, 1988, p. 22. The basic features of current immigration law, including the changes introduced by the Refugee Act of 1980 and other amendments, are

outlined in table 2-4. The number of immigrants "admitted" to the United States under various categories is shown in table 2-5 for 1984. The worldwide, country and preference category quotas indicated in table 2-4 refer to ceilings on the number of visas issued in a year. The data on immigration refer to the number of persons entering the United States with an immigrant visa or receiving a change in status to permanent resident alien. Immigrant visas need not be used in the fiscal year they are issued, and some are never used.

30.   Vernon M. Briggs. IMMIGRATION POLICY
          AND THE AMERICAN LABOR FORCE,
Baltimore: Johns Hopkins Press, 1984, p. 199. Because only those refugees who were admitted to the United States under the preference system were automatically eligible to become immigrants after a two-year residency period, special legislation was required to grant immigrant status to all those persons who were admitted under the parole authority. The parole authority had originally been intended to apply only to individuals. With the extension of this authority to massive number of refugees, however, individual admission requirements would have caused lengthy waiting periods during which the persons involved would have been in limbo while waiting for a visa slot to open. During such an interval, they could not have worked, and they would not have been eligible for most assistance services. Hence, special legislation was separately enacted for the Hungarians, the Cubans, and the Indochinese, as well as for smaller groups that have not been discussed here. These enactments permitted these groups of refugees to become permanent-resident aliens outside the normal immigration channels.

31.   Vernon M. Briggs. IMMIGRATION POLICY
          AND THE AMERICAN LABOR FORCE,
Baltimore: Johns Hopkins Press, 1984, p. 199. By the end of the 1970s, "a general consensus had developed" that the prevailing provisions of the Immigration Act of 1965 "were totally inadequate as the basis for a fair and coherent refugee policy." Thus, a new bill was drafted in Congress in 1979 that sought to rectify the situation. Testifying in favor of the pending bill, U.S. Coordinator for Refugee Affairs Dick Clark stated:

> Until now we have carried out our refugee programs through what is essentially a patchwork of different programs that evolved in response to specific crises. The resulting framework is inadequate to cope with the refugee problems we face today...The combination of conditional entry and parole procedures has become increasingly cumbersome and inadequate over the years. In both the Administration and Congress we have come to see the need for a comprehensive and long term policy.

The bill that subsequently emerged from Congress was signed into law on March 17, 1980, by President Carter. Known as the Refugee Act of 1980, it constituted a major change in the U.S. immigration system. [ellipses in original]

32.   Vernon M. Briggs. IMMIGRATION POLICY
          AND THE AMERICAN LABOR FORCE,
Baltimore: Johns Hopkins Press, 1984, p. 129. Likewise, the term *immigrant* is not always appropriate. When used accurately, it means that a person is seeking to settle permanently. Some portion of these persons—at least some of those from Mexico—have no such intention. For them the term *migrant* would seem to be more appropriate. In Europe, in fact, the foreign workers who were imported legally from abroad in the 1960s and early 1970s were called migrants because they were viewed as temporary workers, or "guestworkers."

33.   Vernon M. Briggs. IMMIGRATION POLICY
          AND THE AMERICAN LABOR FORCE,
Baltimore: Johns Hopkins Press, 1984, p. 129. In the United States, however, the term *migrant* is used by professional demographers to describe a native person who makes permanent change of residence. That is to say, the term is generally used to describe citizens who move from one part of the United States to another. Someone who moves from New York to Arizona to work or to retire is said to be a migrant, as is one who moves from Puerto Rico to New York City.

34.   Joan Biskupic. "Sizable Boost in Immigration
          OK'd in Compromise Bill." CONGRES-
SIONAL RECORD, October 27, 1990, p. 3608. Under S 358, legal immigration would climb from about 500,000 annually to about 700,000 during each of the first three years of the act. After that, a permanent level of 675,000 would be set.

The totals do not include refugees or people granted asylum because they are fleeing persecution in their own countries. For fiscal 1991, the administration plans to admit 131,000 refugees, most from East Asia and the Soviet Union.

35.   Vernon M. Briggs. IMMIGRATION POLICY
          AND THE AMERICAN LABOR FORCE,
Baltimore: Johns Hopkins Press, 1984, p. 200. Having broadened the definition *refugee*, the critical question for immigration policymakers was how many persons to admit each year under these new terms. After extensive debate on various proposals, Congress repealed the "conditional entry" provisions of the Immigration Act of 1965 (which meant that there would no longer be a seventh preference category). As a result, the ceiling on immigrants was reduced from 290,000 to 270,000 persons. The entry of refugees

since 1980 has been governed by an admissions system that is entirely separate from the preference categories of the nation's immigration statute.

36. Vernon M. Briggs. IMMIGRATION POLICY AND THE AMERICAN LABOR FORCE, Baltimore: Johns Hopkins Press, 1984, p. 225. At the present time, refugee admissions to the United States are not numerically regulated as are all other categories of legal immigrants. Consequently, the president's position is extremely awkward. Given the immense size of the world's refugee populations, he is often under severe political pressure to admit large numbers of refugees to the United States each year. This pressure is exerted by the governments of the countries where the refugees are located. It is also brought to bear by citizens groups that are ethnically similar to the refugee groups and that seek to have these people admitted through channels outside the legal immigration system. Such pressures can contribute to decisions that are politically expedient but that often defy the logic of a regulated immigration system. Accepting the desirability of seeking to accommodate refugees cannot mean that whatever happens is acceptable. If U.S. immigration policy is to have any meaning at all, increases in the number of refugees and asylees admitted will require concurrent modifications in the nation's legal immigration ceilings.

37. Vernon M. Briggs. IMMIGRATION POLICY AND THE AMERICAN LABOR FORCE, Baltimore: Johns Hopkins Press, 1984, p. 245. At the present time there is no limit on the number of refugees admitted or the number of asylees permitted to remain in the United States. The flow of refugees and asylees has increased dramatically in recent years, and, as experience has shown, their numbers can escalate at any given moment. Because there are no fixed refugee ceilings, there is currently no way to force a discussion of priorities. Given the size of world's refugee populations and the paralysis imposed by the U.S. judicial system with respect to asylum procedures, it can be anticipated that refugees and asylees will continue to comprise a substantial portion of the nation's annual immigration flow. If their numbers continue to grow and if their patterns of settlement do not change, they, too, will increasingly affect employment and wage patterns in selected labor markets of the nation.

38. Vernon M. Briggs. IMMIGRATION POLICY AND THE AMERICAN LABOR FORCE, Baltimore: Johns Hopkins Press, 1984, p. 216. Unlike all other legal and illegal immigrants to the United States, refugees and the communities in which they have located have benefited from a series of private and public assistance programs.

39. Gene McNary. ADMISSION OF O AND P NONIMMIGRANTS, Hrg of the Committee on the Judiciary, House of Representatives, May 15, 1991, p. 15. The Service drafted proposed regulations in order to implement the O and P classifications which were published in the *Federal Register* on July 11. The comment period closed on August 12 and the Service is presently in the process of publishing a final rule.

40. Alan C. Miller. "Data Sheds Heat, Little Light, on Immigration Debate." LOS ANGELES TIMES, November 21, 1993, p. 1. The numbers seemed to provide an authoritative foundation for Gallegly's call for a crackdown. But like many of the figures used in the emotionally charged debate over the impact of illegal immigration, they generate more heat than light.

In reality, nobody can prove precisely how many illegal immigrants live in the United States, much less whether they drain more form public funds as recipients of public services than they contribute in economic activity and tax revenues.

41. Frank D. Bean. OPENING AND CLOSING THE DOORS, RAND Corporation Press, 1989, p. 82. Assessing whether illegal immigration into the United States has changed since the passage of IRCA is difficult for at least two reasons. One is that information on the size of the illegal population in the United States has always been hard to acquire. The second is that different types of undocumented migrants exist, each of which may be affected differently by IRCA.

The members of clandestine populations possess incentives not to identify themselves as illegal immigrants in censuses and other surveys. This makes it difficult and costly to identify, sample, interview, and enumerate individual illegal immigrants.

42. Barry Chiswick. ILLEGAL ALIENS, Kalamazoo: Upjohn Institute for Employment Research, 1988, p. 18. Although apprehensions of illegal aliens are easy to measure, these data reflect flows of individuals and INS enforcement policies, rather than the stock of illegal aliens residing in the U.S. It has been difficult to estimate the size and characteristics of the resident illegal alien population. This arises in part because there may be sharp seasonal, cyclical and secular changes in the net flow and hence the stock of illegal aliens. During the "on-season" (the spring, summer and early fall), during peaks in the U.S. business cycle when the economy is closer to full employment, and during periods of economic distress in the sending countries (in particular Mexico), more illegal aliens enter and fewer leave. It is always difficult

to measure the size and characteristics of a fluid population.

43. Frank D. Bean. OPENING AND CLOSING THE DOORS, RAND Corporation Press, 1989, pp. 82-83. Another major reason why it is hard to assess illegal immigration is that there are different kinds of undocumented immigrants. The Immigration and Naturalization Service distinguishes between two kinds of illegal immigrants: (1) persons who enter without any sort of legal visa (called "EWIs" because they "enter without inspection") and (2) persons who enter with legal visas but remain beyond the authorized time limit (called "visa-overstayers"), or persons who violate the terms of their temporary visas by taking a job (for example, persons with tourist visas). Such administrative distinctions are likely to be most useful when they reflect some important dimension of social and economic reality. In this case, the distinctions serve to demarcate reasonably well illegal immigrants who come from Mexico (almost all of whom are EWIs) versus those who come from other countries (almost all of whom are visa-overstayers). EWIs and visa-abusers, however, cannot be operationally differentiated from one another in terms of their reasons for immigrating or their intended duration of residence—distinctions that are important for the formulation of sound immigration policy.

44. Vernon M. Briggs. IMMIGRATION POLICY AND THE AMERICAN LABOR FORCE, Baltimore: Johns Hopkins Press, 1984, p. 7. As for the data that are available, several federal agencies in the course of their activities collect information related to immigration. The two major data sources are the Bureau of the Census of the U.S. Department of Commerce and the U.S. Immigration and Naturalization Service (INS) of the U.S. Department of Justice. The Census Bureau, in its decennial headcount, asks and tabulates questions that distinguish between native and foreign-born persons in the population. Periodically, in conjunction with its *Current Population Survey*, the Census Bureau asks a question pertaining to residential status at some previous point in time. These data, however, have never been fully developed with respect to the data on immigrants. Although various census questions are relevant to the study of immigration, none provides an accurate measure of actual immigration in any given year.

45. Vernon M. Briggs. IMMIGRATION POLICY AND THE AMERICAN LABOR FORCE, Baltimore: Johns Hopkins Press, 1984, pp. 6-7. As will quickly become apparent to anyone who wishes to study the critical effects of immigration on the American population and labor force, the available data are grossly deficient. This inadequacy can be attributed

in part to the long lapse in the relative importance of immigration to the nation between 1924 and 1965. Since 1965, a myriad of international issues and a number of domestic labor market concerns (e.g., the military draft, unemployment among the nation's youth, automation, minority employment patterns, inflation, women in the labor market, poverty, and regional employment shifts) have diverted the attention of policymakers and human resource scholars from the gradual reemergence of immigration as a critical concern. As a result there has been little pressure for better collection and dissemination of immigration data, despite major improvements in most other labor force indicators during this interval. Information on the effects of immigration on the American labor force is the weakest link in the nation's contemporary labor market statistics system.

46. Barry Chiswick. ILLEGAL ALIENS, Kalamazoo: Upjohn Institute for Employment Research, 1988, p. 19. Nonetheless, the studies that have attempted to measure the stock of the illegal alien population are instructive. After reviewing the methodology in several studies, three Census Bureau statisticians (Siegel, Passel and Robinson, 1981) concluded:

> The total number of illegal residents in the United States in some recent year, say 1978, is almost certainly below 6.0 million, and may be substantially less, possibly only 3.5 to 5.0 million...The Mexican component of the illegally resident population is almost certainly less than 3.0 million and may be substantially less, possibly only 1.5 to 2.5 million. The gross movement into the United States of Mexican illegals is considerable, as is reflected in the large numbers of apprehensions made by INS, but this "immigration" is largely offset by a considerable movement in the opposite direction. [ellipses in original]

47. Vernon M. Briggs. IMMIGRATION POLICY AND THE AMERICAN LABOR FORCE, Baltimore: Johns Hopkins Press, 1984, p. 10. Obviously, reliable data are needed, but policy formulation and the selection of topics for social science inquiry cannot depend on the quality of available data. As Charles Keely has testified, "As frequently happens with situations that develop into social issues, concern outruns information." The importance of the subject of immigration dictates that the assessment of trends and the formulation of policy proceed despite the gross inadequacy of available data.

48. Vernon M. Briggs. IMMIGRATION POLICY AND THE AMERICAN LABOR FORCE, Baltimore: Johns Hopkins Press, 1984, p. 10.

Deficiencies in gross data are not unique to the study of illegal immigration. In truth, the lack of reliable and useful data plagues virtually every important area of public policy. Data are either nonexistent or grossly inadequate in such critical areas as unemployment in local labor markets, the health of the population, employment discrimination, mental health, the incidence of crime, the use of narcotics, the degree of environmental degradation, and the size of available energy supplies to the nation. It is an irony of the social sciences that the more important the issue is, the worse the data are. Yet the lack of good data has in no way retarded the initiation of significant policy interventions in these and other critical areas of public concern. It is only with respect to immigration reform that the lack of adequate data has been repeatedly and effectively used to forestall reform efforts.

49.   Tom Morganthau. "America: Still a Melting Pot?" NEWSWEEK, August 9, 1993, p. 16. The second dilemma is worse. There is no particular reason to believe that the current influx of illegals cannot rise from 500,000 a year to 600,000 a year or even beyond. This is conjectural but not necessarily alarmist: as Fuchs says, the word is out. Looking around the world, "one can't find the natural forces that will bring down the flow," says Harvard University sociologist Nathan Glazer. "The first impact of prosperity will be to increase it. Look at China. These people don't come from the backward areas, they come from the progressive parts. As they learn how to run a business, they say to themselves, 'Why not go to the United States and do even better?'"

The same applies to Bangladesh, the Dominican Republic, Mexico or the Philippines. The dynamic, as Fuchs says, is rooted in powerful macroeconomic forces now at work all around the globe—rising birthrates and the conquest of disease, prosperity or the hope of prosperity, even modern telecommunications. (The glittery materialism of American TV shows is now being broadcast everywhere.) Much as Americans tend to regard the new immigrants as poor, uneducated and less skilled, the vast majority are surely enterprising. What they seek is opportunity—the opportunity to hold two jobs that no Americans want, to buy a television set and a beat-up car, to start a family and invest in the next generation. Immigration is for the young: it takes courage, stamina and determination to pull up your roots, say goodbye to all that is dear and familiar, and hit the long and difficult trail to El Norte. Illegal immigration, with all its hazards, is for the truly daring: the Latino men who wait on Los Angeles street corners, hoping for day-work, have faced more risk than most Americans will ever know.

50.   Michael D'Antonio. "Apocalypse Soon." LOS ANGELES TIMES, August 29, 1993, p. 18. The available statistics do suggest that immigration is on the rise worldwide. According to the U.S. Committee for Refugees, a private, nonpartisan organization, the worldwide refugee population has climbed steadily, from fewer than 8 million in 1983 to more than 17.5 million today. But while industrialized countries may be bracing for an onslaught, it has yet to materialize. It turns out that most of the world's refugees do not travel from one continent to the next, Instead, hungry Third World people travel to neighboring underdeveloped states in search of relief. Tom Argent, a policy analyst for the committee, says that poorer countries bear the real brunt of refugees, who migrate en masse and can seriously overburden resources.

51.   "At America's Door." THE ECONOMIST, July 24, 1993, p. 11. They dash across the freeways in San Diego, zig-zagging to avoid the traffic. They labour in long rows in the Michigan fields, keeping their heads down. Shiploads of them, huddled in blankets, arrive on the beach in New York. Open the door of a sweatshop in Los Angeles, a garage in Chicago or a hotel kitchen anywhere, and their faces stare out: tired, wary, slightly defiant. Their language is not English. The laws of the United States are mysterious to them. All they want is to work, earn money and be left alone. But in America in the 1990s, that seems a lot to ask.

Immigration—especially illegal immigration—has many Americans in a panic. After a lull of several decades, figures for new arrivals suddenly shot up in the 1980s. Over those ten years, the United States took in 8.9m legal immigrants and, by most estimates, at least 2m illegal ones. Americans do not always take much notice of that distinction. Because both sorts of immigrants come mainly from Latin America and Asia, and are yellow and brown, they are said to be harder to absorb than the old, invisible, European sort. Because they are relatively unskilled, but willing and full of guile, they are said to take jobs away from the native-born at the lower end of the market; and, in a sluggish economy, those sorts of jobs are scarce anyway.

52.   "They're Coming." THE ECONOMIST, July 24, 1993, p. 23. A debate about America's immigration policy, quietly under way all last year, has come into the open. Facing the prospect of yet more boatloads of shivering Chinese crossing the Pacific, both the administration and some influential congressmen are considering new legislation. In California, the state that feels most hurt by illegal immigration, various ideas to stem the flow are being considered. Meanwhile, in the wake of the arrests of

alleged terrorists in New York last month, most of them foreign nationals, public opinion has become more anti-immigrant than for many years. A recent Gallup poll found 65% of Americans in favour of tighter controls. The young were slightly more tolerant; the South, which until the past 20 years saw very little immigration, was, as ever, the most suspicious of newcomers.

53. Ruth Conniff. "The War on Aliens." THE PROGRESSIVE, October, 1993, p. 22. Newsweek illustrated what it called the "immigration backlash" with a cover depicting the Statue of Liberty up to her nose in a rising tide of boat people. Earlier in the summer, a similar graphic appeared on the cover of the right-wing magazine Chronicles, with a horde of pointy-eared, demonic creatures scaling a wailing Liberty, under the headline Bosnia, U.S.A. Pictures of the Statue of Liberty in distress have rapidly become an op-ed page cliche, as have water metaphors, with so many waves of immigrants flooding, inundating, leaking in, seeping through, and drowning the nation.

In just the last few months, what were once considered right-wing views on immigration—that the United States is being "invaded" by the Third world, that immigrants pose a threat to the American economy and way of life, and that the borders need military fortification—have become part of the accepted wisdom.

54. Aryeh Neier. OPERATIONS OF THE BORDER PATROL, Hrg of the Committee on the Judiciary, House of Representatives, August 5, 1992, p. 209. In recent years anti-immigrant fears have become more charged as U.S. efforts to stop cross-border drug trafficking have been stepped up and the INS has been drafted to play an increasingly larger role in those efforts. The Border Patrol now views the interdiction of drugs and undocumented migrants as virtually synonymous.

55. Tony Freemantle. "Anti-Immigrant Sentiment Rises." THE HOUSTON CHRONICLE, July 4, 1993, p. A1. Legislation aimed primarily at illegal immigrants has been introduced in statehouses across the country and in Congress.

"It's a growing problem that is only going to get bigger unless we do something about it," said U.S. Rep. Tony Beilenson, D-Calif., the author of several anti-immigrant bills.

56. Tom Morganthau. "America: Still a Melting Pot?" NEWSWEEK, August 9, 1993, p. 16. All this—an incendiary mixture of fact, fear and myth—is not making its way into politics. The trend is most obvious in California, where immigration is already a hot-button issue, and it is surfacing in

Washington. Recent events like the World Trade Center bombing, the arrest of Sheik Omar Abdel-Rahman and the grounding of the Golden Venture, an alien-smuggling ship crammed with nearly 300 Chinese emigrants, have revived the 10-year-old controversy about illegal immigration. "We must not—we will not—surrender our borders to those who wish to exploit our history of compassion and justice," Bill Clinton said last week, announcing a $172.5 million proposal to beef up the U.S. Border Patrol and crack down on visa fraud and phony asylum claims. On Capitol Hill, the revival of an issue that many had thought dead is shaking both political parties, and Democrats such as Sen. Dianne Feinstein of California are scrambling to neutralize nativist backlash. "Some of the people who opposed me totally 10 years ago are now saying, 'What's happening to our country? We gotta do something!'" said Republican Sen. Alan Simpson of Wyoming, a perennial advocate of tougher immigration enforcement. "It's ironic beyond belief. Attitudes have shifted dramatically, and it's coming from the citizens."

57. Seth Mydans. "Poll Finds Tide of Immigration Brings Hostility." NEW YORK TIMES, June 27, 1993, p. A1. With both legal and illegal immigration into the United States approaching historic highs, a public reaction against immigration is also growing, the latest New York Times/CBS News Poll shows.

After decades of heavy immigration that has included large numbers of Hispanic laborers and Southeast Asian refugees, and at a time when many Americans are out of work, a large majority of Americans surveyed said they favored a decrease in immigration. Many cited the economy as a factor in their opinion.

58. Larry Rohter. "Debate Rages over Influx of Immigrants." THE DALLAS MORNING NEWS, September 26, 1993, p. 4. Miami—With the immigrant influx at its highest level since the early years of this century and the economy stumbling, U.S. ambivalence about immigration is again painfully obvious.

The masses of tired and poor, whether Mexican, Chinese or Haitian, find themselves less and less welcome in this nation of immigrants, as the chorus of voices calling for further restrictions grows larger and louder.

59. Tom Morganthau. "America: Still a Melting Pot?" NEWSWEEK, August 9, 1993, p. 16. The latest Newsweek Poll reveals the public's sharply shifting attitudes. Fully 60 percent of all Americans see current levels of immigration as bad; 59 percent think immigration in the past was good. Fifty-nine percent also say "many" immigrants wind up on wel-

fare, and only 20 percent think America is still a melting pot.

60.   Henry Ervin. "Illegal Immigration: a Heavy Burden." SAN DIEGO UNION-TRIBUNE, 8/29/93, p. G-3. These changes were enacted at the same time a Roper poll found that 87 percent of Americans believed the United States had a major, or at least some, population problem. Of that group, two-thirds supported reducing legal immigration and more than nine out of 10 supported an "all-out" effort to stop illegal immigration.

61.   Senator Harry Reid. "The Math on Immigration, US Jobs." ROLL CALL, February 7, 1994. Many employers like the glut of labor that immigration provides, and some special interest groups will cry foul if we try to reduce the influx. But the overwhelming majority of Americans, no matter their racial or ethnic background, wholeheartedly endorse lowering immigration levels, especially after more than a decade of record high immigration and unemployment.

On the supply side of the employment equation, Reich has delivered some very encouraging news. It is now up to Congress to regulate that part of the demand side of the equation that is in our power to control by reining in runaway immigration.

62.   Peter Brimelow. "Time to Rethink Immigration?" NATIONAL REVIEW, June 22, 1992, p. 30. The immigration floodgates were opened by accident in 1965. Opinion polls show most Americans want them shut—for example, in a recent poll by FAIR, 84 per cent wanted Congress to take a more active role in decreasing immigration and stopping the entry of illegal aliens. But the elite's reaction is unexpectedly odd: it stands around idly, alternately ignoring the situation, denouncing anyone uncouth enough to mention it, and, most frequently, indulging in romantic rationalizations ("The more the merrier" "Diversity is strength").

63.   "Perspective on Immigration." LOS ANGELES TIMES, April 13, 1994, p. B7. In opinion polls, the majority of Americans, including 78% of Latino Americans, say they support a reduction in immigration, legal as well as illegal. Until our national leaders recognize that our current level of immigration far exceeds this country's carrying capacity, no real remedies to America's problems will be found.

64.   Seth Mydans. "Poll Finds Tide of Immigration Brings Hostility." NEW YORK TIMES, June 27, 1993, p. A1. When asked whether immigration into the United States should be "kept at its present level, increased or decreased," 61 percent of those answering the national telephone survey last week preferred a decrease. That preference is up from a 1986 Times/CBS News poll, when 49 percent favored a decrease.

One of the poll respondents, Dorothy Lepping, a 33-year-old postal worker in East Stroudsburg, Pa., said her opinions had been shaped by the way she had seen immigrants treated in her hometown. "I saw the amount of aid that went out to them and the way that was abused," she said in a telephone interview after the poll. "I feel that our economy is in a bad state and we should take care of our own."

Such sentiments have grown over the decades. When the Gallup Poll posed the same question in 1977, just 42 percent favored a decrease in immigration; in 1965, when a new law ended four decades of low immigration, just 33 percent called for a decrease.

65.   Milton Morris. IMMIGRATION—THE BELEAGUERED BUREAUCRACY, Washington D.C.: The Brookings Institute, 1985, p. 24. Moreover, public opinion surveys since 1946 reveal a remarkably consistent lack of enthusiasm for extensive immigration and suggest much less general commitment to the open door tradition than public officials have assumed.

66.   Milton Morris. IMMIGRATION—THE BELEAGUERED BUREAUCRACY, Washington D.C.: The Brookings Institute, 1985, pp. 24-27. Two features of current public attitudes toward immigration seem especially noteworthy. One is that public opposition to increased immigration is particularly strong with respect to illegal immigration. The other is that usually attitudes toward immigration do not vary greatly across economic or racial lines, even though differences are apparent. The low-income population tends to support reduced immigration and focus on the ill effects of immigrants on the country somewhat more than the high-income population. And although slightly more blacks than whites support reduced legal immigration or are pessimistic about the effects of immigrants, fewer blacks support immediate actions to curb illegal immigration.

67.   Paul Glastris. "Immigration crackdown." U.S. NEWS & WORLD REPORT, June 21, 1993, p. 34. Refugees. America's system of accepting political refugees is a relic of the cold war, when people fleeing Communist persecution were considered strategic assets. That open-door policy didn't swamp the system for the simple reason that Communist regimes let few of their citizens emigrate. Today, most of the 130,000 refugees resettled annually in the United States still come from Vietnam and the former Soviet Union.

Most experts predict that Washington will eventually lift preferences for those nations and ratchet down

the total number of refugees allowed in. What remains to be seen, says Dennis Gallagher of the Refugee Policy Group, a Washington think tank, is how Clinton and Congress will "define who those people are who are still of special interest to the United States."

68.   "A Hot Issue for the '90s." THE SAN FRANCISCO CHRONICLE, June 21, 1993, p. A1. Historically, efforts to curb immigration have collapsed under the weight of democratic traditions that predate the Constitution. But now, a surge of opposition to such dramatic growth is mixing with longstanding anti-foreigner sentiments to fuel a broad anti-immigration movement. Indeed, immigration—legal as well as illegal—is emerging as a defining political issue of the 1990s.

69.   Nathan Glazer. "The Closing Door: is Restrictionism Unthinkable?" THE NEW REPUBLIC, 12/27/93, p. 15. Clearly we are at the beginning of a major debate on immigration. The issue has been raised most immediately in recent months by the immigrants, legal and illegal, now charged with the devastating bombing of the World Trade Center and with planning the bombing of other major New York buildings and New York transportation links; and by the interception of vessels carrying illegal Chinese immigrants approaching New York and California. But the issue is larger than how to control illegal immigration, difficult as this is. Despite the presence of a mass of laws, regulations and court rulings controlling immigration, we are shaky as a polity on the largest questions that have to be answered in determining an immigration policy: What numbers should we admit, of what nations and races, on what basis should we make these decisions, how should we enforce them?

70.   Tony Freemantle. "Anti-Immigrant Sentiment Rises." THE HOUSTON CHRONICLE, July 4, 1993, p. A1. The poll also found that America's attitude toward immigrants is colored by misperception, the most notable of which is that illegal immigrants make up the bulk of all immigrants.

71.   Stanley Mark. ALIEN SMUGGLING, Hearing before the Subcommittee on International Law, Immigration, and Refugees of the Committee on the Judiciary, United States House of Representatives, (Y4.J89/1:103/9) June 30, 1993, p. 144. A recent New York Times/CBS News Poll reported that 61% of the persons surveyed said that they favored decreasing immigration due in large part to the perception that immigrants were taking decent paying jobs away from American workers.

72.   Paul Glastris. "Immigration Crackdown." U.S. NEWS & WORLD REPORT, June 21, 1993, p. 34. That argument has the greatest purchase on politicians. Most Americans intuitively believe that immigrants take jobs from the native-born and drive down wages.

73.   Larry Rohter. "Debate Rages over Influx of Immigrants." THE DALLAS MORNING NEWS, September 26, 1993, p. 4. Most academic and government studies conclude that the presence of immigrants has some overall benefit; few say they harm the economy.

Yet perceptions die hard. Black leaders and labor unions argue that the job market is swamped with cheaply paid workers. Spokesmen of the nativist right see the newcomers swelling the welfare rolls.

74.   David Warner. "A Move to Curb Immigrant Visas?" NATION'S BUSINESS, February, 1994, p. 65. Meanwhile, rising public furor over immigration—particularly illegal immigration—in the face of a slow-growing economy has put pressure on the Clinton administration. Recent public-opinion surveys, including a Gallup Poll, have found that U.S. citizens believe immigrants take jobs from them and use a disproportionate share of social services.

75.   Ira Mehlman. "The Issue is Immigration; Increasing Opposition to Current US Immigration Policy that Does Not Control Numbers of Immigrants Entering the US." NATIONAL REVIEW, November 29, 1993, p. 26. The second part of the Republican strategy—championing the economic argument for high levels of legal immigration—is predicated on selling the American public something they are not interested in buying. Few Americans will be persuaded that the flood of mostly unskilled immigrants in areas like Los Angeles or New York City has been an economic windfall. And, more importantly, Americans see a destruction of their way of life. As George Will put it in his column this July, "America is not just an economy; it is more than an arena for wealth creation. It is a culture."

76.   Milton Morris. IMMIGRATION—THE BELEAGUERED BUREAUCRACY, Washington D.C.: The Brookings Institute, 1985, p. 46. This growing concern about the economic effects of immigration is based in part on the recent increases in immigration (especially in refugee admissions and illegal immigration) and on the rapidly rising cost of the social services that are now available to large segments of the population. As government officials at all levels seek to cope with these higher costs, attention tends to focus on users who might not be eligible. Although immigrants add only a minute share to the escalating costs in all but a few cases, they are a convenient target for complaints.

77.	Milton Morris. IMMIGRATION—THE
	BELEAGUERED BUREAUCRACY, Washington D.C.: The Brookings Institute, 1985, p. 121. Although the public is overwhelmingly opposed to illegal immigration and would like to see it ended or at least sharply curtailed (see table 2-2), many who are concerned with immigration matters tend to ignore the enforcement problems that the INS is facing or appear to be ambivalent about current enforcement policies.

78.	Vernon M. Briggs. IMMIGRATION POLICY
	AND THE AMERICAN LABOR FORCE,
Baltimore: Johns Hopkins Press, 1984, p. 185. The accommodation of refugees and persons seeking political asylum often accounts for a significant portion of the overall flow of immigrants into the United States. The American public, however, tends to view these admissions as humanitarian gestures involving only a few individuals or groups in isolated circumstances.

79.	Vernon M. Briggs. IMMIGRATION POLICY
	AND THE AMERICAN LABOR FORCE,
Baltimore: Johns Hopkins Press, 1984, p. 185. As events since the end of World War II have vividly demonstrated, that perception does not match reality. At times, refugees and asylees have approximated or exceeded the number of persons admitted under the legal immigration system in a given year. Consequently it is necessary to understand that as their numbers have accelerated, so has their influence upon selected U.S. labor markets. It is also widely believed that these admissions provisions are being increasingly abused by people who do not really fear persecution but rather are primarily interested in improving their economic status. to the extent that these provisions are being abused, they serve as a loophole that circumvents the entire U.S. legal immigration system and further undermines the effectiveness of the nation's immigration policy.

80.	Frank Trejo. "Rethinking Immigration."
	DALLAS MORNING NEWS, January 2,
1994, p. 1A. Current immigration proposals range from revamping the backlogged political asylum system to increasing Border Patrol personnel and denying medical, social and educational benefits to illegal immigrants and their children.

	But some also are advocating a drastic reduction in legal immigration or even a moratorium of several years.

	"I suspect we may be at a point where we are witnessing the twilight of the age of innocence when it comes to immigration," said Demetrios Papademetriou, director of the immigration policy program at the Carnegie Endowment for International Peace in Washington, D.C.

81.	Ruth Conniff. "The War on Aliens." THE
	PROGRESSIVE, October, 1993, p. 22. One member of the Clinton Administration, a former advocate himself, told me that public perceptions have had a powerful effect on the Administration's immigration and asylum policy. "If we didn't introduce the legislation that we introduced, they would now be working on the Simpson bill," he says, "and if you don't think our Democratic friends in the Senate read us that message loud and clear, then you don't understand what's going on here.

	The same official, who declined to be identified, seemed tormented by charges that the Administration is bowing to political pressure to adopt a conservative line on immigration.

82.	Milton Morris. IMMIGRATION—THE
	BELEAGUERED BUREAUCRACY, Washington D.C.: The Brookings Institute, 1985, pp. 68-69. Now, however, most developed countries are unwilling or unable to absorb large numbers of immigrant workers because of declining rates of economic growth and growing concern about the social and ecological consequences of such immigration. This is the case particularly in the countries of western Europe, which have sharply curtailed some immigration and the admission of guest workers. Reduced migration opportunities in turn intensify the pressures created by large populations in the developing countries and thus help to impede their social and economic advancement. As U.N. Ambassador Richard E. Benedick recently pointed out to the U.N. Population Commission, not only are current high levels of population growth aggravating already unacceptably high levels of unemployment and underemployment, but the rise of crowded megacities "will bring hitherto unimagined problems and increase the potential for social unrest...Never in human history has there been such a discrepancy between the supply of and the demand for international migration."

83.	"A Hot Issue for the '90s." THE SAN FRAN-
	CISCO CHRONICLE, June 21, 1993, p. A1. But such nationalistic forces are not as far removed as some may think. Right-wing Republican presidential candidate Pat Buchanan, who made Third World immigration a major part of his "America First" campaign, won 37 percent of the vote in last year's New Hampshire primary. He often called for a wide trench across the Mexico-U.S. border and at one point suggested that Virginia could assimilate settlers from England more easily than "Zulus."

	The issue is especially volatile in Southern California, where native-born whites and blacks remain suspicious of Hispanic and Asian newcomers as well as each other. In Los Angeles, fears among whites that they are being pushed out helped lead to the victory by con-

servative businessman Richard Riordan over liberal City Councilman Michael Woo in this month's mayoral election.

84.   Stephen Handelman. "Tight Immigration Hurts Global Stability." TORONTO STAR, January 24, 1993, p. F3. The strict U.S. immigration policies which Baird violated were not specifically focused on household help, but on the vast pool of foreign labor desperately knocking on American doors.

There is similar legislation in most of the Big Seven industrial powers, except for Germany—where the debate over immigration boiled into xenophobic and racist violence.

And there is strong domestic support for those policies, even among ethnic groups, in the United States for instance, whose forebears benefited from the welcome signs hung out the front door by previous generations.

85.   "Conflicting Views of FAIR'S Campaign to Limit Immigration." SAN FRANCISCO CHRONICLE, December 27, 1993, p. A16. By denying certain groups rights to education and health care, as advocated by the Federation for American Immigration Reform (FAIR), we are only creating an environment of ignorance and exploitation and encouraging the spread of diseases.

If we sincerely want to cut down on immigration, both legal and illegal, then we need to stem the tide at its source by encouraging countries we trade with to improve their human rights records and practice humane labor policies.

86.   Charley Reese. "We Should Stop All Immigration Now." THE ORLANDO SENTINEL, July 11, 1993, p. G2. It's my hypothesis that problems produce politics, not the other way around. Whether it was Vladimir Lenin peddling his claptrap in Moscow or Adolf Hitler peddling his in Frankfurt, there would have been no sale if the conditions in both countries had been politically just and economically prosperous. Instead, both countries were in terrible shape and people were desperate. They bought the snake oil.

Americans will buy it, too, if they get desperate. The most decent people can be made bitter. We were lucky in the 1930s; we might not be so lucky in the 1990s.

87.   Ruth Conniff. "The War on Aliens." THE PROGRESSIVE, October, 1993, p 22. But the idea of saving ourselves by building a higher wall around our borders, fortifying it with more guns, and hunting down the "aliens" in our midst is a lost cause. It will not change the global economic and political problems that send people fleeing here from other

countries. And it will certainly not win us a more peaceful society. It is ironic that the anti-immigration groups invoke the example of Yugoslavia. With its divisive rhetoric and undercurrent of racial hate, the anti-immigration movement proposes the very ethnic divisions its members warn about.

88.   Ruth Conniff. "The War on Aliens." THE PROGRESSIVE, October, 1993, p. 22. The ranchers are used to watching illegal immigrants come across their land, and they see it as an example of Government negligence that the border isn't better guarded. "The problem is higher up. The U.S. Government doesn't want to stop the illegals," says Kim Silva, a member of the citizens' group. "They like all the cheap labor coming into the United States."

"The inevitable result is its going to be a border war." says Power. "We're very serious about our sovereignty here and our families. If our government don't do something, by God we will."

89.   Stanley Mark. ALIEN SMUGGLING, Hearing before the Subcommittee on International Law, Immigration, and Refugees of the Committee on the Judiciary, United States House of Representatives, (Y4.J89/1:103/9) June 30, 1993, pp. 143-144. It can be measured by the rising numbers of anti-Asian incidents documented by local and state law enforcement agencies. This recent trend of violence and harassment against Asian Americans has new branches growing from historical roots of exclusionary and discriminatory immigration laws that perpetuated harmful stereotypes. Asian Americans are perceived as "foreigners" regardless of how many generations their families have been in the United States. Instead of acceptance or tolerance, Asian Americans have become too often the scapegoats for the loss of jobs, the trade imbalance, and the economic ills of society. Frequently, Asian Americans are blamed for the problems of those not doing so well and by those who feel threatened by the influx of immigrants from Asia. These nativist attitudes are largely responsible for the current wave of anti-immigrant and anti-Asian violence recognized as a national problem by the United States Commission on Civil Rights.

90.   "A Hot Issue for the '90s." THE SAN FRANCISCO CHRONICLE, June 21, 1993, p. A1. Beilenson, the San Fernando Valley congressman, tries to take a compromise view that supports current levels of legal immigration but seeks tougher controls on illegal immigrants.

If nothing is done about illegal immigration, he says, the resulting backlash could arouse such fears that legal immigration would be imperiled.

91.   Michael LeMay. FROM OPEN DOOR TO
        DUTCH DOOR, New York: Praeger Press,
1987, p. 16. These questions, of course, are all interre-
lated in practical as well as political terms. To be generous on entry requirements it was necessary to emphasize border control. A tough immigration policy also
had to be viewed as compassionate. To avoid cutbacks
on *legal* immigrants and refugees, policymakers had to
enact stronger enforcement measures against *illegals*.
Politically, stronger enforcement measured an amnesty
program, but to make amnesty meaningful required the
prospect of more effective enforcement.

92.   Holly Idelson. "Clinton's Immigration
        Changes Aim To Stop Abuses." CONGRES-
SIONAL QUARTERLY, July 31, 1993, p. 2061.
Clinton, however, predicted a public backlash against
all immigrants if the government does not do more to
block abuses of existing laws. "We must say no to illegal immigration so we can continue to say yes to legal immigration," he said. (Text, p. 2082)

93.   Paul Glastris. "Immigration Crackdown."
        U.S. NEWS & WORLD REPORT, June 21,
1993, p. 34. The spectacle of hordes of illegal immigrants washing up on American beaches—and a federal
government seemingly powerless to stop them—provides groups like the Federation for American Immigration Reform with a chance to advance their larger goal:
an immediate moratorium on all legal immigration.
Proponents of immigration, too, are taking a get-tough
attitude toward illegal immigration, knowing that
Americans will be magnanimous to foreigners only if
they feel the illegal-alien problem is under control.

94.   Gene McNary. "INS Response to Immigration
        Reform." IN DEFENSE OF THE ALIEN,
Vol. 14: 1992, p. 8. Many who still argue for the repeal of employer sanctions do not think illegal immigration is a problem. Some economists, for example,
say that illegal residents and workers are necessary to
our economy. I think the problem is more social than
economic. Illegal aliens may indeed pay more in taxes
than they receive in benefits. They may take jobs that
few others want. But they weaken the legal structure
that supports all immigration into the country. Also,
illegal aliens tend to geographically distribute themselves unevenly, creating more burdens for some states
and cities than for others. Their impact is greater in local communities than in the nation as a whole. They
tip the balance scales.

95.   Paul Glastris. "Immigration Crackdown."
        U.S. NEWS & WORLD REPORT, June 21,
1993, p. 34. At a meeting of his Domestic Policy
Council last week, President Clinton addressed head-on
the sad tale of the Chinese illegal aliens beached off
New York City. "We've got to get out front on this,"
he told aides, and ordered a review of immigration policy involving staffers from agencies as diverse as the
National Security Council and the Department of
Transportation. What most concerns him is that a
backlash against immigrants could sweep the country.
"There is a fear," says a Clinton adviser, "that unless
the administration gets out in front, you'll see what
you did in Germany: a violent reaction against
immigration."

    That fear is well-founded. Just three years ago, when
labor shortages were being predicted, Congress passed
the Immigration Reform Act, which boosted legal immigration levels by 40 percent. Then the economy
tanked, companies shed hundreds of thousands of jobs
and public attitudes toward immigration, never very
positive, grew even more negative. In the most recent
Roper Organization survey on the subject, fully 54
percent of Americans said they think too many immigrants are allowed to enter the country. That mirrors
the growing anti-immigrant sentiment sweeping the
industrial world.

96.   Charley Reese. "We Should Stop All Immi-
        gration Now." THE ORLANDO SENTINEL,
July 11, 1993, p. G2. Better to curb immigration now,
while we can do it calmly, than later, when there is
blood in the streets and there will be political overreac-
tion, the outcome of which no one can predict.

    I am not suddenly seized with a fit of xenophobia—
hatred of foreigners. I'm suggesting if we act now we
can head off xenophobia. We need time to assimilate
the people already here.

97.   Michael D'Antonio. "Apocalypse Soon."
        LOS ANGELES TIMES, August 29, 1993,
p. 18. What America can do, he says, is protect itself
by imposing a temporary moratorium on immigration
and reforming the laws and regulations that determine
how and why many newcomers are admitted each year.
This is necessary, he says, to preserve a high standard
of living and avert the intolerant, even violent backlash
against immigrants that can occur "when people feel
they are losing control of their future. The pressure
forces them into intergroup conflict. It's human
nature."

    Such conflicts are already brewing in Western Eu-
rope. In Germany, skinheads have killed Turkish immigrants with a firebomb. Attackers have said they
were motivated by the belief that the outsiders take
away jobs, drain funds from social programs and erode
their country's standard of living. In recent years, the
number of asylum seekers—who are eligible for free
housing, food, medical care, education and other services—from Eastern Europe has placed a burden on the
German government. With nearly 250,000 asylum
seekers arriving just this year, the Parliament recently

made it easier for the government to send some of them back to their home countries.

98. Vincent Bonaventura. HOUSE HEARINGS, April 27, 1993, Y4J89/1:103/7. These undocumented illegals place a strain on the resources of the inspection services and airport facilities. Aside from the extra cost imposed on INS to deal with this situation, we are concerned about the significant delays in the processing of legitimate air travelers, which is being caused by the lost of INS inspectors' time due to the extent of secondary interviews which must be conducted with the undocumented travelers at the airport.

Furthermore, many of these undocumented travelers are released into the community where they become a drain on the community resources. In addition, as apparently is the case in the World Trade Center bombing, they can pose a significant national security risk.

Legislative reform measures are needed to ensure that a public backlash to the insidious flow of illegal travelers does not result in measures which would impede the flow of the vast majority of the legitimate travelers, who are of no interest to the Federal agencies.

99. Milton Morris. IMMIGRATION—THE BELEAGUERED BUREAUCRACY, Washington D.C.: The Brookings Institute, 1985, p. 121. There are no reliable measures of public opinion on this subject, and thus there are no firm indications of exactly how the public feels about apprehending and expelling aliens.

100. Milton Morris. IMMIGRATION—THE BELEAGUERED BUREAUCRACY, Washington D.C.: The Brookings Institute, 1985. Yet there is no firm evidence that the public has ever enthusiastically shared this sentiment. On the contrary, public attention to immigrants and to immigration policy seems to have been very limited, sporadic, and confined mainly to local or regional concerns. Only small segments of the popu-lation seem to have shown any great interest in immi-gration policy at any particular time, and most have remained largely indifferent even though immigration issues have been hotly debated almost continuously at the national level since 1945.

101. "At America's Door." THE ECONOMIST, July 24, 1993, p. 11. Is America, the land of immigrants, reverting to the nativism of Germany or France? The pressures seem similar. But the panic needs to be put in context. Opposition to immigration is cyclical, usually going hand in hand with unemployment. It has been more extreme before; and numbers, proportionate to population, have been much higher. Nineteenth-century America rose on a flood of immigrant labour, which was welcomed. By the end of the century, as jobs became scarcer, attitudes hardened.

102. Paul Glastris. "Immigration Crackdown." U.S. NEWS & WORLD REPORT, June 21, 1993, p. 34. If Clinton truly wants to forestall an anti-immigrant backlash, he will have to do something rare: argue the case for immigration directly to the voters. "I know of no president who ever went to the American people and explained why we're in the immigration business," laments Demetrios Papademetriou of the Carnegie Endowment for International Peace. The task might not be as quixotic as it sounds. Several recent candidates who tried to run on anti-immigrant themes all lost. The case for a generous immigration policy is compelling even in the midst of economic turmoil. But the American people won't buy it unless they feel that they have control over immigration—not the other way around.

103. Ruth Conniff. "The War on Aliens." THE PROGRESSIVE, October, 1993, p. 22. Part of the backlash against immigrants results from the simple facts of increased worldwide migration, a constricting U.S. economy, and a series of high-profile news stories showing refugees and terrorists coming into the United States. But the current anti-immigration climate also owes a lot to the calculated efforts of conservative individuals and groups.

104. Milton Morris. IMMIGRATION—THE BELEAGUERED BUREAUCRACY, Washington D.C.: The Brookings Institute, 1985, p. 3. The closeness of the House vote and the subsequent collapse of support for the Simpson-Mazzoli bill are not surprising. The fact that the measure came so close to fruition in an election year is perhaps more surprising. Immigration policy has always been extremely controversial, reflecting at once the public's fears about the effects of immigration, deep commitment to the principle of an open country, and the special interests of many employers and ethnic groups to maintain liberal immigration. Even among those who have been convinced about the need for reform to increase the country's control over immigration, there have been widely divergent views about how this should be done.

105. "At America's Door." THE ECONOMIST, July 24, 1993, p. 11. Fortunately, the new nativist polemic does not run deep. Despite much huffing, little restrictive immigration legislation has passed Congress in recent years. Indeed, the most recent change to the law, in 1990, raised the limit for legal immigrants by 40%. The present limit, 700,000 a year, means that America still takes in more legal immigrants than the rest of the world put together.

106. Ira Mehlman. "The Issue is Immigration; Increasing Opposition to Current US Immigration Policy that Does Not Control Numbers of Im-

migrants Entering the US." NATIONAL REVIEW, November 29, 1993, p. 26. Reid's view stands in sharp contrast to those of leading Republicans. "If we were to reduce illegal immigration, there would be less concern about legal immigration," says Congressman Lamar Smith of Texas. He chairs a House Republican task force on illegal immigration, which he calls "a defining issue" between the two parties. He points out that until this year every legislative initiative aimed at excluding illegals from receiving public benefits has come from the GOP.

Though he personally believes that legal immigration levels are too high and has introduced legislation to peg immigration levels to the unemployment rate, Smith does not believe that the political climate favors a reduc-tion. "We just had legal immigration three years ago and it's not ripe to touch again," he says, referring to the Immigration Act of 1990, which increased legal immi-gration by 40 per cent on the dubious premise that the country was facing a labor shortage.

107.   Klaus Fuchs. "Agenda for Tomorrow." ANNALS OF THE AMERICAN ACADEMY OF POLITICAL SCIENCE, November, 1993, p. 170. Unless there is a new surge of xenophobia in the nation generally, immigration from all over the world will continue at high numbers. Except for Pat Buchanan, no major political figure has made the xenophobic argument that newcomers from Asia and Spanish-speaking countries are less capable of becoming Americans than European immigrants were in the past.

108.   Nathan Glazer. IMMIGRATION AND U.S. FOREIGN POLICY, San Francisco: Westview Press, 1990, p. 21. There is little chance of such a consequence today as a result of racism and xenophobia: Elements of racial preference have been struck from our immigration laws and strong domestic legislation bans discrimination. Indeed, even discrimination in favor of citizens will now be legal under the new immigration act.

109.   Donald Huddle. "Debate Must Begin with True View of the Costs." HOUSTON CHRONICLE, 8/29/93, p. 1. Nationwide, 65 percent of Americans favor reductions in immigration. Is this indicative of xenophobia or racism as claimed by some immigrant advocates? I believe not. National polls substantiate that most Americans, including a majority of our minorities, believe that their long-term economic interests are hurt by large-scale immigration. Texas is an example. Large numbers of unskilled immigrants cause much higher educational, medical, border cleanup and welfare costs, while state revenues languish.

110.   Vernon M. Briggs. IMMIGRATION POLICY AND THE AMERICAN LABOR FORCE, Baltimore: Johns Hopkins Press, 1984, p. 5. Historically, many U.S. presidents have differed strongly with the legislative branch over immigration policy. The uses of presidential veto power have been numerous. So have the congressional overrides of vetoes. One would be hard-pressed, in fact, to name any other subject of public policy in which legislative overrides have been so frequent and so far-reaching in their consequences. The executive branch has often sent Congress immigration legislation that was more liberal and humane than the legislative branch was willing to adopt. At other times the end result has been "a stand-off" between the two branches over the appropriateness of immigration reform measures.

111.   Milton Morris. IMMIGRATION—THE BELEAGUERED BUREAUCRACY, Washington D.C.: The Brookings Institute, 1985, pp. 33-34. Probably no other major area of public policy has been the cause of as much conflict between Congress and the executive branch as immigration. Between 1882 and 1952 ten immigration laws were vetoes by six presidents with widely differing styles, perceptions of executive legislative authority, and attitudes about the use of the veto power.

112.   Milton Morris. IMMIGRATION—THE BELEAGUERED BUREAUCRACY, Washington D.C.: The Brookings Institute, 1985, p. 35. To some extent, the executive-legislative conflict over immigration policy is but one facet of a larger ongoing struggle between the two branches for leadership in policymaking. However, other factors too have contributed significantly to the conflict—particularly the profoundly different perspectives of these two institutions with re-gard to immigration issues. The conflict between Con-gress and the executive on the subject of immigration has been at bottom one between domestic and international views of the issue.

113.   Milton Morris. IMMIGRATION—THE BELEAGUERED BUREAUCRACY, Washington D.C.: The Brookings Institute, 1985, pp. 36-37. The predominantly domestic orientation of Congress in immigration matters is consistent with its tendency, noted by many analysts of congressional behavior, to focus on domestic or constituency concerns even in defense or foreign policy matters. Such an orientation is understandable in the light of the local constituency pressures to which members of Congress must respond. When there are strong, clear constituency preferences, an international orientation to immigration could be risky if the resulting policy was inconsistent with those local preferences. Of course, this clash between constituency interests and broader

national or international interests is not peculiar to immigration matters. It is a common occurrence in national policymaking.

114.   Milton Morris. IMMIGRATION—THE BELEAGUERED BUREAUCRACY, Washington D.C.: The Brookings Institute, 1985, p. 43. The refugee bill signed into law by President Jimmy Carter on March 17, 1980, not only reflected the best efforts of the executive branch and Congress, it established a framework for executive-legislative collaboration in making decisions about refugee admissions over and above the annual limit of 50,000 provided for by the law.

115.   Milton Morris. IMMIGRATION—THE BELEAGUERED BUREAUCRACY, Washington D.C.: The Brookings Institute, 1985, pp. 43-44. The differences between the executive branch and Congress over immigration have been narrowed considerably. While Congress now exhibits much greater sensitivity to international aspects of immigration policy, the president has also become more attentive to the domestic effects, especially with respect to refugee decisions. This convergence of views has improved the prospects for well-considered policies. However, it by no means ensures such policies. In virtually every area of immigration policy the issues are so complex and controversial that differences on specifics are inevitable. Furthermore, each branch retains a measure of suspicion about the political intentions of the other. These suspicions were demonstrated in the maneuverings over the Simpson-Mazzoli bill, which the House Speaker once blocked for fear the president planned to veto it in an attempt to win the support of Hispanic voters. Because any decision on the bill would have been controversial and perhaps costly in an election year, neither side wanted to expose itself to blame or to miss any benefits that might accrue from enactment.

116.   Milton Morris. IMMIGRATION—THE BELEAGUERED BUREAUCRACY, Washington D.C.: The Brookings Institute, 1985, p. 42. With the executive's growing influence on immigration policy, something approaching a partnership has developed between the executive branch and Congress. This partnership was solidified by the Refugee Act of 1980. Since the end of World War II the executive branch had urged enactment of refugee legislation that would increase the government's flexibility in responding to demands for refuge. The idea found wide support in Congress but never enough to produce the desired legislation. Thus the parole authority was the sole basis for admitting large numbers of extensive executive-legislative collaboration, provided for a much clearer and more orderly admission and resettlement of refugees.

117.   Ira Mehlman. "The Issue is Immigration; Increasing Opposition to Current US Immigration Policy that Does not Control Numbers of Immigrants Entering the US." NATIONAL REVIEW, November 29, 1993, p. 26. Republican support for high levels of legal immigration may also reflect the growing influence of the pro-life sector of the party. Religiously conservative Republicans who oppose abortion and other forms of family planning are loath to admit that any country, let alone the United States, could be overpopulated. In one of his Nike commercials, Spike Lee celebrates, "The mo' colors, the mo' better." For many Republicans the motto seems to be, "The mo' people, the mo' better."

118.   Ira Mehlman. "The Issue is Immigration; Increasing Opposition to Current US Immigration Policy that Does not Control Numbers of Immigrants Entering the US." NATIONAL REVIEW, November 29, 1993, p. 26. With evidence mounting that immigration is going to be the sort of political issue in the Nineties that welfare fraud and school busing were in previous decades, the Republican leadership—which for more than two decades has prided itself on being in tune with the concerns of the "silent majority"—has recognized that it must take a stand. However, the Republicans have failed to grasp exactly what the new concerns are. Republican leaders have convinced themselves that what really upsets the public is illegal immigration and that, in their confusion, Americans are lumping legal immigrants together with border-crashers. Moreover, many Republicans have bought into the Wall Street Journal argument that immigration is an economic boon. Consequently, the party's approach to immigration has been to couple a get-tough stand on illegal immigration with a dogged insistence that high levels of legal immigration are good for the country.

If the strategy is not rapidly abandoned, Republicans will lose the political high ground on this crucial matter. Controlling illegal immigration is a worthy objective, but illegals account for a fraction of total immigration.

119.   Robert Tucker. IMMIGRATION AND U.S. FOREIGN POLICY, San Francisco: Westview Press, 1990. The United States is in the midst of the second great immigration in its history. In the course of the 1980s, between 8 and 9 million immigrants are expected to enter the United States, whether legally or illegally, a number about 50 percent larger than that of the 1970s and far greater than that of any decade since World War I. Despite recent declines in legal and illegal entries, the expectation is that these numbers will persist and possibly go even higher, notwithstanding a marked public preference for imposing more restrictive limits on immigration. Given the

decline in the nation's birth rate, immigration is likely to become the principal source of labor in a market that may require substantial outside supply if its demands are to be met. More important, however, is the prospect that the population of the countries making up the Caribbean basin will double in the period between 1980 and 2010. The inability of these countries to provide employment for a rapidly expanding work force can only lead to one result: The pressure of those seeking to enter the United States is almost certain to increase.

120.　Vernon M. Briggs. IMMIGRATION POLICY AND THE AMERICAN LABOR FORCE, Baltimore: Johns Hopkins Press, 1984, p. 243. Having discussed the evolution of each of the major components of the nation's immigration policy, it is appropriate to conclude by relating this policy to contemporary labor market trends. As noted earlier, immigration in all its forms has since the 1960s gradually reemerged as a major cause of the growth of the U.S. population and labor force.

121.　David Warner. "A Move to Curb Immigrant Visas?" NATION'S BUSINESS, February, 1994, p. 65. Critics of the bill point out that although the nation's overall unemployment rate may be high—currently about 6.4 percent—it doesn't mean that certain areas of the country or certain occupations aren't experiencing labor shortages.

122.　Sidney Weintraub. THE ILLEGAL ALIEN FROM MEXICO, Austin: University of Texas Press, 1980, pp. 23-24. There are also substantive argu-ments in favor of this position. *The Wall Street Journal*, in an editorial on June 18, 1976, summarized the most significant of these by noting that the supply of illegals "may well be providing the margin of survival for entire sectors of the economy" like restaurants, other small businesses, and both small- and large-scale agriculture, that rely heavily on unskilled labor. Harold Wool, in a report for the Department of Labor, projected the U.S. labor supply to 1985 and concluded that there will be potential shortages for lower-level occupations (Wool, 1976), so that future needs for immigrants (or for labor-saving techniques) may be greater than now exist.

123.　Lincoln Chen. "Living Within Limits." ISSUES IN SCIENCE AND TECHNOL-OGY, December 22, 1993, p. 88. Hardin's approach is simplistic, to say the least. He maintains, for instance, the United States does not need immigrant labor. To address potential U.S. labor shortages, Hardin proposes an extended workweek, postponement of retirement, part-time work for homemakers, and less study and more work for university students. This will not get

houses and offices cleaned, gardens tended, and fruits and vegetables picked, nor will it replace the immigrant scientists and engineers who play a critical role in U.S. universities and businesses.

124.　Ruth Conniff. "The War on Aliens." THE PROGRESSIVE, October, 1993, p. 22. As for arguments about immigrants taking jobs away from Americans, "all of the evidence, both real world and econometric, suggests that there is virtually no displacement of American workers by immigrants," says Papadimitrious. "This is the consensus of the discipline.

While there are temporary displacements in given localities, Papadimitriou explains, there is no trend toward Americans becoming unemployed due to immigrant labor.

125.　Larry Rohter. "Debate Rages over Influx of Immigrants." THE DALLAS MORNING NEWS, September 26, 1993, p. 4. Disputing them, Jeffrey S. Passel, head of the immigrant research project at the Urban Institute, a research group in Washington, said "places that got immigrants during the 1980s generally did better in terms of wage growth than places that didn't."

Immigrants, said Gregory De Freitas, an economist and immigration expert at Hofstra University in New York, "help expand the demand for labor and increase the number of jobs, which tends to outweigh any negative effects they may have.

126.　Michael LeMay. FROM OPEN DOOR TO DUTCH DOOR, New York: Praeger Press, 1987, pp. 133-134. Thomas Muller counters that his study of illegals in Los Angeles shows that they create jobs—an estimated 52,000 in Los Angeles alone, principally as white-collar workers such as teachers, salesclerks, and health-care workers. California's blacks did not suffer an increase in unemployment because of immigration, according to his analysis (*Ibid*). Similarly, a 1986 Rand Corporation study examining the impact of Mexican immigrants on California concluded that up to now it has benefited the state's economy. The study found such immigration had stimulated low wage, labor intensive manufacturing while comparable manufacturing elsewhere across the nation had languished. For example, total manufacturing employment in Los Angeles grew by 13.6 percent between 1970 and 1980, and 28.4 percent statewide compared to a 4.8 percent increase nation-wide. Jobs in the garment and furniture industries, which employ a high percentage of Mexican immigrants, grew by 47 percent during that same period compared to a 7.4 percent drop in jobs in those industries nationwide (McCarthy and Valdez, May, 1986).

127. Larry Rohter. "Debate Rages over Influx of Immigrants." THE DALLAS MORNING NEWS, September 26, 1993, p. 4. One recent study by the Urban Institute concluded that immigrants actually help create more jobs in urban areas than does the native population, especially in the nonmanufacturing sector.

Some other studies show that immigrants are more likely than the rest of the population to be self-employed and start their own businesses.

"The question always seems to be phrased in terms of immigrants taking jobs from Americans, when lots of Americans have jobs, because of the impact of immigrants on the economy," said Mr. De Freitas, who wrote Inequality at Work: Hispanics in the U.S. Labor Force. "Immigrant restaurants and businesses pay taxes, and their workers buy clothes and food and homes in neighborhoods that were formerly dead. There's a multiplier effect, but that doesn't always get captured."

128. Vlae Kershner. "Calculating the Cost of Immigration." THE SAN FRANCISCO CHRONICLE, June 23, 1993, p. A1. Beyond government revenue, immigrants—especially those here legally—have an additional and controversial economic impact. Because they are willing to work for low wages and receive few, if any, benefits, they reduce business costs and consumer prices for goods and services, from table grapes to hotel rooms.

129. Michael LeMay. FROM OPEN DOOR TO DUTCH DOOR, New York: Praeger Press, 1987, p. 133. Virtually all of the experts agree that illegal immigration—as is true for legal immigration as well—is a boon for employers and consumers. Lower labor costs enable business to be more competitive, earn healthier profits, and pass along some of those benefits to the consumer in the form of lower prices.

130. David Warner. "A Move to Curb Immigrant Visas?" NATION'S BUSINESS, February, 1994, p. 65. Employers, Buffenstein says, should let Congress and the administration know that business immigration, whether permanent or temporary, is vital to their ability to compete abroad and ultimately to increase employment at home.

Julian Simon, a business professor at the University of Maryland in College Park and author of *The Economic Consequences of Immigration*, says U.S. business—and the economy—would be hurt by fewer immigrants. According to Simon, restrictions on foreigners mean fewer available workers, fewer taxpayers, and fewer consumers.

131. Richard Rothstein. "Immigration Dilemmas." DISSENT, Fall 1993, p. 459. Important industries (garment manufacturing, for example) could not exist without an immigrant labor supply; no native workers are available or willing to work in these industries even in periods of high unemployment. If natives were willing to work, they would demand wage-and-benefit packages that would certainly make the industries uncompetitive with companies based abroad. Our minimum wage is now so low, however, that lawful employers can survive by paying the minimum to immigrant workers, while sweatshop operators exploit immigrants' vulnerability and collect an additional premium. Because of immigrant seamstresses, an industry exists that supports not only its professional and managerial employees but a variety of upstream workers in computer software, machine tools, textiles, and petrochemicals. In Los Angeles, with mostly undocumented immigrant workers, the garment industry has grown in the last decade, while manufacturing as a whole, and especially garment manufacturing, has declined nationwide.

132. Alan C. Miller. "Data Sheds Heat, Little Light, on Immigration Debate." LOS ANGELES TIMES, November 21, 1993, p. 1. Many illegal immigrants take low-wage personal service jobs as maids, nannies and gardeners, Ong said. Those who work for companies provide a flexible, low-cost labor pool that may keep U.S. firms from relocating overseas.

133. Sherwood Ross. "Experts Applaud Contributions of Illegal Alien Workers." THE REUTER BUSINESS REPORT, March 23, 1993. At the same time, undocumented workers—thought to number between 3 million and 6 million—help U.S. manufacturers fight off competition from low-wage overseas competitors, he argues.

Julian Simon of the University of Maryland agrees. "If you were to roust them (undocumented workers) from textile manufacturing in Los Angeles, they (manufac-turers) would start businesses on the other side of the border." Simon contends such workers, like immigrants, "raise our standard of living, do not take jobs away from natives or increase unemployment and pay more in taxes than they take out.

The experts say it is questionable whether U.S. employers could compete using undocumented workers if they paid them minimum wage or better.

134. Paul Glastris. "Immigration Crackdown." U.S. NEWS & WORLD REPORT, June 21, 1993, p. 34. That does not deny the tremendous value that immigrants, many of them entrepreneurs, bring to the economy. In fact, a hefty proportion of foreigners

entering America have high levels of education and are moving directly into the nation's suburbs and professional classes. "The net effect of immigration is still that it raises the GNP," says Harvard economist Richard Freeman, co-author of the NBER report. The point, says Freeman, is that immigration, like free trade, probably hurts the minority of Americans who directly compete with newcomers, even as it benefits the majority who enjoy, among other things, lower prices on everything from clothes to restaurant meals.

135.   Richard Rothstein. "Immigration Dilemmas." DISSENT, Fall 1993, p. 459. Ultimately, we can't increase the working-to-retired ratio enough without a lot more immigration. While only 26 percent of the U.S. population is now in the prime working age of twenty to thirty-nine, 46 percent of immigrants are in that age group. Retiring baby boomers need people who contribute more in taxes than they consume in services. Immigration will have to be an increasing part of the solution, not only in the United States, but throughout the industrial world.

136.   Vlae Kershner. "Calculating the Cost of Immigration." THE SAN FRANCISCO CHRONICLE, June 23, 1993, p. A1. On the other side, some economists argue that immigrants help ensure the continued solvency of the Social Security system.

Most immigrants move to the United States in their 20s and 30s, so, for many years, they will be paying into the system. Their payments will help build the Social Security trust fund, because unlike natives of the same age, they do not have parents who are collecting benefits.

By the time the immigrant couple retires and collects, the couple typically has raised children who are then contributing Social Security taxes. In this way, there is a one-time benefit to natives," according to free-market economist Julian Simon of the University of Maryland.

The Virginia-based Alexis de Tocqueville Institute found that an increase in legal immigration from the current 810,000 to 1 million a year for the next 25 years would raise Social Security revenue by $70 billion.

137.   Vernon M. Briggs. IMMIGRATION POLICY AND THE AMERICAN LABOR FORCE, Baltimore: Johns Hopkins Press, 1984, p. 165. In the case of the nation's primary labor market (e.g., jobs in construction and manufacturing), there is no debate that the illegal aliens employed in these positions cause worker displacement. Even though citizen workers are readily available, illegal aliens are sometimes regarded as "preferred workers." They are less likely to join unions; to complain about the denial of equal employ-

ment opportunities, safety violations, or sex discrimination; or to make other entitlement demands upon employers. In a 1982 study, which disclosed that illegal immigrants were widely employed in the high-paying construction industry of Houston, Texas, researchers found that foremen and supervisors preferred to hire illegal immigrants over citizen workers because they could easily "extract bribes" in the form of wage kickbacks from them.

138.   Senator Harry Reid. "The Math on Immigration, US Jobs." ROLL CALL, February 7, 1994. Let's look at the numbers: This year we will admit about 825,000 legal immigrants and refugees. Approximately 50 percent of these immigrants enter the labor force immediately. Most of the rest, currently children, will eventually enter as well. That alone accounts for about one-fifth of the expected job growth.

On top of that, the INS issued more than 500,000 "temporary" work authorizations to people contesting their immigration status in the United States last year. More often than not, persons in this category turn out to be permanent additions to our labor force. These two categories combined offset 45 percent of the predicted job creation.

Forty-five percent is a pretty hefty chunk, especially if one considers that we are starting from a point of relatively high unemployment. But it doesn't stop there.

In fiscal year 1992 we also admitted 163,000 nonvisiting people from other countries under the "temporary worker and trainee" category.

Thus, just through legal immigration channels, we are increasing the size of the work force by about 55 percent of the number of new jobs we expect to create.

And this is when our economy is booming. One can imagine the impact when there is no new job creation.

139.   "Letter to the Editor." THE WASHINGTON TIMES, 1/4/93, p. C2. Past economic expansions caused something of a labor shortage, which meant, using classical economic models, that employers had to bid up the price for labor. Thus, the lower end of the labor market benefited from the trickle down. The Reagan job expansion was eaten up by immigrants, and the oversupply of lower-skill labor kept wages depressed. That was why the poor did not advance as expected.

140.   Senator Harry Reid. "The Math on Immigration, US Jobs." ROLL CALL, February 7, 1994. Along with the new year came some encouraging news from Labor Secretary Robert Reich. He said we can expect the creation of about two million new American jobs in 1994, better than any year since the economy slid into recession in the late 1980s.

The bad news is that new immigrants will take most of those newly created jobs. The rate at which the

Immigration and Naturalization Service (INS) is authorizing newcomers to enter the US labor market and its continued failure to prevent unauthorized workers from entering may all but offset the gains Reich is predicting.

141.   Paul Glastris. "Immigration Crackdown."
         U.S. NEWS & WORLD REPORT, June 21, 1993, p. 34. In 1990, legislators anxious to expand immigration had plenty of ammunition from studies done in the 1970s and the 1980s that filed to find any significant evidence of such labor market displacement. More recent research, however, has raised new doubts. A study by the respected National Bureau of Economic Research (NBER) estimates that as much as a third of the decline in the relative earnings of native-born high-school dropouts in the 1980s can be attributed to competition from low-skilled immigrants.

142.   "Perspective on Immigration." LOS ANGELES TIMES, April 13, 1994, p. B7. Almost every week, we hear about thousands of our workers losing their jobs. Yet in 1992, more than 750,000 legal immigrants of working age were admitted to this country. In addition, we admit annually more than 60,000 foreign professionals on extended work visas. Many of these "temporary workers" enter skilled occupations, such as computer programming and engineering, where there have been massive layoffs. If the United States continues with an immigration policy that operates as if we had a labor shortage, how can we expect unemployed Americans and welfare recipients to find jobs? Donald Huddle of Rice University estimates that 2 million American workers were displaced by 1992 as a result of immigration since 1970, at a cost of $11.9 billion paid to U.S. workers in unemployment and other benefits. Huddle also estimates that in 1992 alone, immigrants used services costing $42.5 billion in excess of taxes they paid.

The economy of the past 200 years was mostly labor-intensive. With advances in technology, our economy now requires highly skilled workers to prosper. Yet nearly two-thirds of the legal immigrants entering this country every year are low-skilled. Half of them enter occupations that are disappearing, where they compete mostly with poor minority workers.

143.   Senator Harry Reid. "The Math on Immigration, US Jobs." ROLL CALL, February 7, 1994. The fact is that it doesn't matter how rosy the job creation picture is in the United States. As long as we continue to admit too many immigrants and too many "temporary" workers, while at the same time failing to control illegal immigration, we are spinning our wheels.

The number of new jobs created by our economy is relevant only when viewed in the context of the current unemployment rate and the number of new entrants into the job market.

Two million new jobs, given an official unemployment rate of 6.8 percent (8.2 million jobless), coupled with current immigration policies means, if we are lucky, we might not lose any ground this year.

144.   Senator Harry Reid. "The Math on Immigration, US Jobs." ROLL CALL, February 7, 1994. But no Congress and no Administration can honestly promise to deal with unemployment problems unless it is prepared to limit the number of new job seekers entering the US labor market from other countries. That will require comprehensive reform of our immigration policies leading to lower levels of immigration.

145.   Senator Harry Reid. "The Math on Immigration, US Jobs." ROLL CALL, February 7, 1994. Under the Immigration Stabilization Act that I have introduced, we would roll legal immigration levels back to the historic level of 300,000 a year and make a serious effort to control and reduce illegal immigration.

At these lower levels—which are the historic average for this country—immigrants entering the US work force would offset job growth by about 10 percent, rather than the 60 percent we are likely to see this year. The addition of these new Americans would add to the diversity and strength of our country.

146.   Senator Harry Reid. "The Math on Immigration, US Jobs." ROLL CALL, February 7, 1994. The actual number of new jobs that will be created in 1994, or any other year, depends on a variety of factors, many of which we have little control over. The number of new job seekers entering through immigration channels, however, can be controlled by an act of Congress and a stroke of the President's pen. Moreover, there is no logical reason why we should not cut back.

147.   Peter Brimelow. "Time to Rethink Immigration?" NATIONAL REVIEW, June 22, 1992, p. 30. But Back to the Future makes a more fundamental point: labor is not an absolute. Free economies are infinitely ingenious at finding methods, and machinery, to economize on labor or any other scarce resource.

The implicit assumption behind the economic argument for immigration appears to be something like this:

Labor x Capital = Economic Growth

So, for any given capital stock, any increase in labor (putting aside the question of its quality) will result in at least some increase in output.

This assumption is just wrong. Typically, technical studies that attempt to account for economic growth

find that increases in labor and capital account for at most half and often much less of increases in output. Simon Kuznets's survey of the growth of the West over the last two centuries concluded that increases in labor and physical capital together were responsible for less than 10 per cent of the greatest output surge in human history. The rest seems to be attributable to changes in organization—to technological progress and ideas.

148.   Peter Brimelow. "Time to Rethink Immigration?" NATIONAL REVIEW, June 22, 1992, p. 30. The economic view of labor has influenced the current immigration debate only in one direction: it is triumphantly produced by the pro-immigration side to refute any unwary critic of immigration who assumes that native-born workers must inevitably be displaced. They aren't, necessarily, in aggregate, because the economy adjusts; and because the increase in the factors of production tends to create new opportunities. "Immigrants not only take jobs," writes Julian Simon, "they make jobs."

Maybe. But missing from the current immigration debate is the fact that this effect operates in the other direction too. On the margin, the economy is probably just as capable of getting along with less labor. Within quite wide boundaries, any change in the labor supply can be swamped by the much larger influence of innovation and technological change.

149.   Nathan Glazer. "The Closing Door: is Restrictionism Unthinkable?" THE NEW REPUBLIC, 12/27/93, p. 15. The fulfillment of these ideals does not, however, suggest that there are any moral and ethical imperatives that dictate we have no right to make the decision that the United States, as it stands, with all its faults, is what we prefer to the alternative that would be created by mass immigration. The United States can survive without large numbers of low-skilled workers, and would probably survive, if it was so inclined, without highly trained foreign engineers, doctors, scientists. At the level of the highest skills and talents we will undoubtedly always be happy to welcome immigrants—we did even in the restrictive '30s and '40s. In a world in which masses of people can move, or be moved, too easily beyond their Native borders, we will always need policies to set limits as to what the responsibilities of this country are.

150.   Peter Brimelow. "Time to Rethink Immigration?" NATIONAL REVIEW, June 22, 1992, p. 30. "We need immigrants to meet the looming labor shortage / do the dirty work Americans won't do." This further item from the pro-immigration catechism seems to be particularly resonant for the American conservative movement, deeply influenced by libertarian ideas and open, somewhat, to the concerns of business.

But it has always seemed incongruous, given persistent high levels of unemployment among some American-born groups. Since these groups obviously eat, it would appear that public policy is subsidizing their choosiness about work, thus artificially stimulating the demand for immigrants.

And if there is a looming labor shortage (hotly disputed), it could presumably be countered by natalist policies—encouraging Americans to step up their below-replacement birthrate. Even the current high immigration inflow is exceeded by the 1.6 million abortions in the U.S. each year.

For example, the federal income-tax code could be adjusted to increase the child allowance. In 1950, this provision exempted the equivalent (in 1992 dollars) of $7,800 for each child; now, after inflation, it exempts only $2,100. Or the "marriage penalty"—by which a couple pay more taxes if they marry than if they live together out of wedlock—could be abolished. Or the public-school cartel could be broken up, reducing the crushing costs of educating a child.

151.   Vernon M. Briggs. IMMIGRATION POLICY AND THE AMERICAN LABOR FORCE, Baltimore: Johns Hopkins Press, 1984, pp. 165-166. In the case of full employment it is conceivable that the presence of illegal immigrant workers could provide some aggregate economic benefits to society in the form of higher production due to an additional supply of labor. Under such special circumstances aggregate production costs might even be lower because the increased competition of citizen and alien workers for jobs could reduce overall wage pressures. But all these conceivable benefits would be very limited because most illegal immigrants—especially those from Mexico—are unskilled and poorly educated. There are technological limits to the degree of productivity a society can obtain as a result of simply increasing the supply of workers who have limited human capital endowments. Given the nation's minimum wage laws, there are also limits below which nominal wages cannot legally be reduced even if the supply of labor is artificially increased. Moreover, even under conditions of full employment, the population subgroups that would compete directly with illegal immigrants—youths, women, and minorities—would have to pay a severe price: lower wages and declining labor force participation. These specific costs would have to be balanced against any possible societal benefits.

Talk of the benefits that might accrue to the nation from illegal immigrants in the context of full employment is for the time being purely theoretical. Throughout the 1970s and early 1980s, unemployment rates were consistently high. Moreover, many economists believe that it may not be possible to reduce this rate below 6.0-6.5 percent without triggering unacceptable inflation. In this context a benign attitude toward any

factor that contributes to unemployment among citizen workers cannot be justified.

152.   Peter Brimelow. "Time to Rethink Immigration?" NATIONAL REVIEW, June 22, 1992, p. 30. Contrary to intuition, the theory of the international trade of goods is quite inapplicable to the international movement of persons. There is no immediate large consumer benefit from the movement of persons that is analogous to the international exchange of goods, because the structure of supply is not changed in the two countries as a whole, as it is when trade induces specialization in production...the shifts due to international migration benefit only the migrant. [ellipses in original]

153.   Vernon M. Briggs. IMMIGRATION POLICY AND THE AMERICAN LABOR FORCE, Baltimore: Johns Hopkins Press, 1984, pp. 10-11. The foremost proponent of this perspective in contemporary times has been the "Chicago school of economics," which has long characterized itself as the advocate and perfecter of the free-market philosophy of economics. Yet proponents of Chicago-style economics have consistently and persistently excluded from their laissez-faire precepts the freedom to immigrate. Indeed, Henry Simons—one of the intellectual founders of the Chicago school—took an adamant stand on the subject:

> As regards immigration policies, the less said the better. It may be hoped that world prosperity, increased political security, and ultimate leveling of birth rates may diminish immigration pressures. Wholly free immigration, however, is neither attainable politically nor desirable. To insist that a free trade program is logically or practically incomplete without free migration is either disingenuous or stupid. Free trade may and should raise living standards everywhere... Free immigration would level standards, perhaps without raising them anywhere... not to mention the sociological and political problems of assimilation. Equal treatment in immigration policy, or abandonment of discrimination, should likewise not be held out as purpose or hope. As regards both our export of capital and import of populations, our plans and promises must be disciplined by tough-minded realism and practical sense. [ellipses in original]

154.   Vernon M. Briggs. IMMIGRATION POLICY AND THE AMERICAN LABOR FORCE, Baltimore: Johns Hopkins Press, 1984, p. 11. One would be hard-pressed to find an equivalent example of a major policy issue in which free-market supporters advocated both governmental restriction and overt discrimination as laudable policy goals. Subsequent standard-bearers for the Chicago school of thought have abandoned overt discrimination as a policy rationale. Nevertheless, they have continued to support strongly the need for government restrictions on immigration. As Melvin Reder wrote in 1982: "Free immigration would cause rapid equalization of per capita income across countries accomplished mainly by leveling downward the income of the more affluent. Like Simons and Friedman, I resist this proposal." Reder frankly acknowledges that government efforts to restrict immigration will result in a loss of freedom of opportunity for the individual and that his approval represents an explicit acceptance of reduced worldwide efficiency in the use of human resources. He adds that "[the] intellectual defense of resistance to the implied redistribution of income and possibly of political power requires a quite sharp reformulation of the normative principles of traditional liberalism and the associated goal of an open society."

155.   Donald Huddle. "Debate Must Begin with True View of the Costs." HOUSTON CHRONICLE, 8/29/93, p. 1. California. Gov. Pete Wilson's recent plea for help to President Clinton detailed the disastrous fiscal consequences of large-scale, unregulated illegal immigration to his state. Although immigration policy is exclusively a federal responsibility, all states, like Texas, must pay for many federally mandated medical, educational and social services. As Newsweek magazine recently reported: 10.4 percent of all new immigrants received welfare in 1990, as compared to 7.7 percent of native-born Californians.

156.   Donald L. Huddle. "Letter to the Editor." THE NEW YORK TIMES, January 26, 1994, p. A23. This is not surprising. Data from the 1990 Census show that the poverty rate of post-1970 immigrants is 42 percent higher than that of the native born. An immigrant's probability of receiving public assistance, adjusted by the amount of assistance received, is 44 percent greater than that of the native born. High welfare usage, combined with low earnings (meaning low taxes), means that immigrants must run a public-service deficit that is financed by the native born with low welfare and higher earnings (meaning higher taxes).

157.   Richard Simon. "1992 Cost of Immigrants $18 Billion, Report Says." LOS ANGELES TIMES, November 5, 1993, p. A3. "Some may say, 'You may be getting cheaper tomatoes and strawberries due to illegal immigrants,'" Huddle said, "At the same time, we haven't taken into account a lot of the other costs... national defense, highways... The biggest thing that we haven't taken into account—that probably more than outweighs the benefits—is wage depression." Huddle insists that immigrants depress wages,

thereby forcing working poor people onto public assistance. [ellipses in original]

158. Donald Huddle. "Debate Must Begin with True View of the Costs." HOUSTON CHRONICLE, 8/29/93, p. 1. To determine the truth of how immigrants are affecting the American taxpayer requires a study at the national level. A study of this magnitude and comprehensiveness was made possible for the first time by newly available empirical studies including the just-published 1990 Census and other government reports, additional new research by the auditor general of California and the County of Los Angeles, plus new field research by both myself and academic economists such as George Borjas, David Card, Joseph Altonji, Vernon Briggs and David Simcox.

After one year spent in gathering, studying and analyzing the data, my research group concluded immigrants cost the U.S. taxpayer more than $42.5 billion in 1992 alone, i.e. all legal immigrants arriving in the United States since 1970 plus the total of all illegal and amnestied immigrants residing here in 1992.

The final study is 83 pages in length and includes 23 tables with 22 categories of cost to federal and state governments, plus five categories of assistance costs for American workers displaced from their jobs by immigrant workers. Total gross costs were $62.7 billion, from which were subtracted $20.2 billion in state, federal and local taxes paid by immigrants, resulting in net costs of $42.5 billion in 1992.

159. Donald L. Huddle. "Letter to the Editor." THE NEW YORK TIMES, January 26, 1994, p. A23. Mr. Lewis overlooks other soundly based estimates of public service costs. For example, the Rand Corporation, hardly a nativist anti-immigration group, found that each permanent Mexican immigrant in California had a public service debt of more than $1,000 annually in 1982.

My own recent national study found that the annual after-tax deficit of post-1970 immigrants, both legal and illegal, exceeds $2,000 per immigrant—a total cost of more than $42 billion. Comparatively, the native born had a surplus on public services after taxation.

160. "Headline: New Study Prompts Environmen tal Group to Call for Immigration Moratorium." PR NEWSWIRE, June 3, 1993. The study, commissioned by Carrying Capacity Network, examines net costs for more than 20 categories including education, public assistance and labor displacement. If current immigration law and enforcement policies are not changed, immigration will cost more than $450 billion (in 1993 dollars) over the next decade, according to the study.

161. Leonel Sanchez. "State Immigrants Cost $18.2 Billion in Taxes Last Year, Study Says." SAN DIEGO UNION-TRIBUNE, November 5, 1993, p. A27. Earlier this year, Huddle released a study on the economic impact of immigration nationwide. That study, frequently cited by a Republican task force preparing a broad immigration-reform bill, concluded that legal and undocumented immigrants cost U.S. tax-payers more than $42.5 billion than the immigrants contributed in taxes last year.

162. "Immigration Costs California $18.2 Billion in 1992." PR NEWSWIRE, November 4, 1993. The California study comes on the heels of Huddle's national study, released earlier this year, that found that immigration into the United States will cost U.S. tax-payers over the next 10 years an average of $67 billion annually, after subtracting taxes immigrants pay, unless immigration laws and enforcement policy are changed.

163. William F. Buckley. "Baird and Immigration Laws." DALLAS MORNING NEWS, 1/28/93, p. 19A. Mr. Brimelow defends his thesis with some pretty persuasive arguments. He reminds us, for instance, that the "unimpeachably free-market Gary Becker," on the very day that he received his Nobel Prize for economics, had written for the Wall Street Journal a piece in which he said that contemporary America's massive transfer payments made open immigration impractical. If we are simultaneously committed to helping everyone whose income is below the poverty level, then the redistribution must come from those whose income is above that level.

It is a second's work to acknowledge that since there is only a finite amount of wealth above the poverty level, there cannot be an infinite demand for it below the poverty level. Since nobody knows how many immigrants would come to America if the doors were held wide open, we cannot safely predict that the number that did come would be ingested.

164. Vernon M. Briggs. IMMIGRATION POLICY AND THE AMERICAN LABOR FORCE, Baltimore: Johns Hopkins Press, 1984, p. 180. Another factor that has added to the fears of those who are opposed to amnesty is the potential cost of such a program. Given the disproportionate number of illegal immigrants who are unskilled and poorly educated, it is possible that many among the illegal immigrant population will suddenly become eligible for the broad array of social services that are available to similarly situated citizens. Among these are food stamps, Medicaid, aid for families with dependent children, unemployment compensation, and housing subsidies, to name some of the more prominent entitlement programs. There is already some evidence that there is "substantial use or at-

tempted use" of the existing federal and state income transfer systems by illegal immigrants despite the fact that they are specifically excluded from eligibility for these programs.

165.   "Perspective on Immigration." LOS ANGE
         LES TIMES, April 13, 1994, p. B7. When
the Statue of Liberty was erected in 1886, this country had 60 million people and plenty of resources. Today, the United States has 260 million residents, of whom 37 million are poor, 8.7 million unemployed, more than 35 million without health insurance, hundreds of thousands homeless. We have a $4.5-trillion national debt. Our schools are overcrowded and underfunded and our freeways more congested than ever.

Seeing this nation in distress, the Clinton Administration promises that it will provide health care to all Americans, cut our welfare rolls, put our unemployed back to work, trim our national debt and improve our public schools. Yet how can these goals be achieved without first controlling the population growth in this country?

166.   Donald Huddle. "Debate Must Begin with
         True View of the Costs." HOUSTON CHRONICLE,
8/29/93, p. 1. At the current juncture, some 2 million illegal immigrants and their half-million citizen children in California cost over $5.3 billion annually just for Medi-Cal, criminal incarcerations, education and Aid to Families with Dependent Children. Meanwhile, the state's population is growing at more than 2.2 percent per year, greater than that of either India or Pakistan. This, plus the more than 600,000 annual newcomers, mostly migrant, in California brings a spiraling demand for public services which state revenues are unable to meet.

167.   Senator Harry Reid. "The Math on Immigra-
         tion, US Jobs." ROLL CALL, February 7,
1994. Americans are paying for uncontrolled immi-gration in many ways other than employment opportunities. With our health care and education systems already in crisis, uncontrolled immigration could be the breaking point. Two-thirds of all babies born in Los Angeles County public hospitals last year were born to illegal aliens. California also must build a new school every day just to keep up with its immigration influx. The rest of America should heed California's struggle.

Lax immigration oversight is generating fiscal and social chaos. Illegal aliens, who often pay no taxes, receive welfare, education, free medical care, and other benefits. These social safety nets are in place to boost those in need temporarily, not to entice millions of newcomers. No country could afford to be the world's benevolent caretaker.

In creating the current immigration mess, Congress and successive Administrations have never stopped to consider how we are going to educate all the new children, take care of all the additional sick people, create enough new jobs, build enough housing, or provide the essential services required to sustain annual new populations the size of several states.

168.   Harold Gilliam. "Bursting at the Seams."
         SAN FRANCISCO CHRONICLE, February
21, 1993, p. 7. But quality education does not seem possible if schools are swamped by illegal immigrants coming across the borders and being smuggled from overseas by the boatload at the rate of about 100,000 a year. And there are twice that many incoming legal immigrants.

169.   "Perspective on Immigration." LOS ANGE
         LES TIMES, April 13, 1994, p. B7. The us-
age of welfare by elderly resident aliens, not including naturalized citizens, increased 400% fro 1982 to 1992. In 1992 alone, more than 90,000 legal immigrants age 55 and over entered the United States. if we continue to admit elderly immigrants at this rate, how can we keep our welfare and Medicare rolls from soaring?

170.   Klaus Fuchs. "Agenda for Tomorrow."
         ANNALS OF THE AMERICAN
ACADEMY OF POLITICAL SCIENCE, November 1993, p. 170. Probably the most troublesome of the restrictionists' charges is that immigration is particularly harmful to black and Latino citizens. "The pervasive effects of ethnic network recruiting and the spread of non-English languages in the work place has in effect locked many blacks out of occupations where they once predominated," concluded Frank Morris, the dean of the graduate school at Morgan State. Labor economist Vernon Briggs, Jr., of Cornell University, and demographer Leon F. Bouvier, formerly a vice president of the Population Reference Bureau and a member of the staff of the Select Commission, also argued that American blacks particularly are harmed by mass immigration into the cities of the North and West, where, he maintained, they lose out in competition, not just for jobs and training opportunities but for services and housing, too.

171.   John Judis. "Why Your Wages Keep Falling."
         THE NEW REPUBLIC, February 14, 1994,
p. 26. The trade deficit and immigration didn't help. In 1982 the United States began running massive trade deficits in industrial goods, particularly cars, auto parts and consumer electronics, creating a net loss of American manufacturing jobs. And the influx of unskilled immigrants during the '80s drove down the wages of third-tier workers, particularly in the West. In a 1991 study for the National Bureau of Economic Research, economists George J. Borjas, Richard Freeman and Lawrence Katz (who is now the Labor Department's

chief economist) estimated that from 1980 to 1988, up to half of the 10 percent decline in the wages of high school dropouts was attributable to the trade deficit and the immigration of unskilled labor.

172.   Michael LeMay. FROM OPEN DOOR TO DUTCH DOOR, New York: Praeger Press, 1987, p. 133. The flood of illegal immigrant labor has helped hold down wages in a wide range of lower-level occupations, from computer assembly to sewing clothes. The pay of California's lemon harvest workers, for example, has held steady at about $6.00 per hour since 1980 because of the competition of illegal and non-unionized crews. In 1984, hotel workers in Los Angeles were forced to accept a pay cut from $4.20 to $3.60 per hour because of such competition.

173.   Peter Brimelow. "Time to Rethink Immigration?" NATIONAL REVIEW, June 22, 1992, p. 30. Blacks themselves take a dim view of immigration, according to opinion polls. In the FAIR poll cited above, 83 per cent of blacks thought Congress should curb immigration. But George Borjas found that blacks living in areas of immigrant concentration did not appear to have suffered significantly reduced incomes compared with those elsewhere. The reason, he theorizes, is that during the years in question—the 1970s—the effect of immigration was overwhelmed by the effects of baby-boomers and women entering the lab or market. Now, of course, these factors no longer apply. Additionally, studies of high-immigrant areas may fail to capture a tendency for native-born workers to relocate because of the increased competition. Across the entire country, the wages of native high-school dropouts fell by 10 per cent in the 1980s relative to the wages of more educated workers. Borjas calculates that about a third of that decline is attributable to immigration.

174.   Michael LeMay. FROM OPEN DOOR TO DUTCH DOOR, New York: Praeger Press, 1987, p. 133. David North argues that illegal laborers hurt the poor, benefiting a narrow but powerful and greedy band of interests to the detriment of the large but mostly silent majority (North, 1978 and 1980). Donald Huddle contends that the illegal immigrant impact reaches far higher into the job range. His study of illegal aliens working in the Houston-Galveston area found 53 percent made above $5.00 per hour, and 12 percent over $6.00 per hour; 60 percent were in jobs that were at least semi-skilled occupations, including cement laying, carpentry, and plumbing (*Time*, July 8, 1985: 75).

175.   "Mass Immigration and the National Interest." SOUTHERN ECONOMIC JOURNAL, October 1993, p. 513. The second argument that follows

from the first is that mass immigration impedes the labor market progress of American blacks. This argument undoubtedly has validity. For instance, Briggs stresses the geographic and economic mobility of blacks with the entry of the U.S. into the First World War and the cessation of the third wave of mass immigration. He also notes that recent immigrants tend to settle, and to compete for jobs, in many of the urban areas that also have large black populations.

176.   Peter Brimelow. "Time to Rethink Immigration?" NATIONAL REVIEW, June 22, 1992, p. 30. As it happens, the U.S. contains one particular group that is clearly vulnerable to competition from immigration: blacks. This question has attracted attention for years. Immigration from Europe after the Civil War is sometimes said to have fatally retarded the economic integration of the freed slaves. Conversely, no less an authority than Simon Kuznets felt that the Great Immigration Lull after the 1920s enabled Southern blacks to begin their historic migration to the cities and the economic opportunities of the North.

177.   Vernon M. Briggs. IMMIGRATION POLICY AND THE AMERICAN LABOR FORCE, Baltimore: Johns Hopkins Press, 1984, p. 160. Black workers, of course, are not concentrated in the same labor markets as are Chicanos or Mexican illegal immigrants, but in a number of specific labor markets (e.g., Los Angeles, Chicago, San Antonio, Miami, and Houston) they do compete. Likewise, it is increasingly the case that black workers in urban labor markets in the eastern and north central states are feeling the adverse effects of job competition from illegal immigrants from nations other than Mexico.

178.   Vernon M. Briggs. IMMIGRATION POLICY AND THE AMERICAN LABOR FORCE, Baltimore: Johns Hopkins Press, 1984, p. 248. Unfortunately, however, the anticipated aggregate decline in the size of the youth cohort between 1980 and 1995 masks a serious compositional shift that is taking place within this cohort. Namely, the aggregate decline in the youth cohort reflects a sharp decline in the expected number of white youths. Because the birth rates of blacks and Hispanics did not begin to decline until much later than the rate for whites, and the rate of this decline during the 1960s and 1970s was much slower than that of whites, the number of black and Hispanic youths will continue to increase throughout the 1980s and into the early 1990s. Thus, youth unemployment—which has been a serious national problem since the mid-1960s—will continue to be a serious issue throughout the 1980s for minority youths even though the size of the youth cohort itself will decline sharply. Moreover, given the fact that minorities and immigrants tend to concentrate in the same geo-

graphic—mostly urban—areas, it is likely that many minority youths will have to compete with illegal immigrants and some portion of the growing population of refugees and asylees for entry-level jobs.

179.   Vernon M. Briggs. IMMIGRATION POLICY AND THE AMERICAN LABOR FORCE, Baltimore: Johns Hopkins Press, 1984, p. 255. As for the illegal immigrants who are entering from Mexico and the Caribbean Basin, it appears that they are crowding into the occupations that have shown the greatest decline in employment in recent years. To the extent that this is true, they are in direct competition with poorly skilled citizen workers who are struggling to find work in these same occupations. There is little or no evidence to suggest that illegal immigrants are seeking employment in the expanding occupations of the economy.

180.   Vernon M. Briggs. IMMIGRATION POLICY AND THE AMERICAN LABOR FORCE, Baltimore: Johns Hopkins Press, 1984, pp. 163-164. Another point that must be addressed is the fact that when a shift in the supply of labor takes place, simultaneous wage effects occur. These wage effects are typically overlooked by those who simplistically support only the employment argument—that illegal immigrants for the most part fill jobs that citizens will not take. The presence of a significant number of illegal immigrants in selected labor markets reduces the absolute wage rates below what the market would otherwise have set. It also opens up relative wage gaps between occupations and industries, depending on the degree of participation by illegal immigrants. It is in this context—the artificial suppression of wages due to the presence of illegal immigrants—that the argument that citizen workers are unavailable needs to be reappraised. The argument is, after all, a self-fulfilling prophecy. It is based on induced economic influences rather than the dubious sociological contention that U.S. workers will not do certain types of work. In a normal labor market—one in which an additional, shadow labor force of illegal immigrants is not operative—the supply of labor is generally ample when employers pay competitive wages. Indeed, in a survey taken in San Diego, employers admitted that they could afford to pay the competitive wages needed to attract citizen workers (and could stay in business after doing so), but they indicated that they preferred not to because they could hire illegal immigrants at lower wages. As the authors of the survey concluded, "There is a definite strategy for pulling-in illegal labor from across the border …this strategy is an excellent way to avoid more expensive American labor." Consequently, a significant displacement of workers does occur as a result of the wage effect. [ellipses in original]

181.   Vernon M. Briggs. IMMIGRATION POLICY AND THE AMERICAN LABOR FORCE, Baltimore: Johns Hopkins Press, 1984, p. 163. It is also important to realize that Piore and the other social scientists who have adopted his assertions of a minimal worker displacement effect in the secondary labor market do not provide any direct evidence to support their hypothesis. In fact, it would be very difficult to name a specific occupation in the U.S. economy in which the vast preponderance of workers are *not* citizen workers. Indeed, Undersecretary of Labor Malcolm Lovell, testifying in support of immigration reform, has stated that "in 1981, close to 30 percent of all workers employed in this country, some 29 million people, were holding down the same kind of low-skilled industrial, service, and farm jobs in which illegals typically find employment." Moreover, according to Lovell, "the available data also does not support the claim that Americans will not take low wage jobs. In 1981, an estimated 10.5 million were employed in jobs at or below the minimum wage and 10 million more were earning within about 35 cents of that level." Hence it seems absurd to contend that illegal immigrants do work that citizens will not do when in fact millions of citizen workers are employed in these occupations. Lovell has also pointed out that the unemployment rates for the segments of the labor force that compete most directly with illegal immigrants are consistently higher than the national average—a fact which challenges the notion that citizen workers are not available for secondary-labor-market jobs.

182.   Michael LeMay. FROM OPEN DOOR TO DUTCH DOOR, New York: Praeger Press, 1987, pp. 135-136. Economist Walter Fogel counters, however, that the current flows of undocumented aliens exacerbates the job and income problems of blacks, Hispanics, and other secondary-market workers by reducing the number of jobs available to them, depressing wages for those jobs they do hold, and generally undercutting working conditions as well (*The Unavoidable Issue*: 88). The Rand Study also concludes that the changing job market and projected increases in immigration forecast trouble for many poorly educated Latinos before the turn of the century. They anticipate 3 million new jobs in California by 1995, for example, over half of which will be in white-collar and skilled, high-tech service jobs. Such jobs require skills beyond either immigrants or first-generation native born. Unskilled jobs are expected to grow at a rate far slower than the increase in the Mexican-American population which is expected to triple by the year 2000.

183.   Vernon M. Briggs. IMMIGRATION POLICY AND THE AMERICAN LABOR FORCE, Baltimore: Johns Hopkins Press, 1984, p. 251. Moreover, the effects of automation and computerization, as

well as the prospects for the rapid introduction of robots (at least in manufacturing), imply that future increases in output in the goods-producing sector will likely be accomplished with far fewer labor inputs. Consequently, the growing U.S. labor force has increasingly had to turn to the service industries to find employment. As of 1980, over two-thirds of the nation's nonagricultural labor force was employed in the service sector. Generally speaking, in the past the goods-producing industries provided a disproportionate demand for the nation's unskilled and semiskilled workers while the service sector tended to provide a relatively greater demand for the more skilled and educated workers.

184.   Vernon M. Briggs. IMMIGRATION POLICY
        AND THE AMERICAN LABOR FORCE,
Baltimore: Johns Hopkins Press, 1984, p. 248. Given the limited number of quality jobs that exist at any given time, it is already likely that many job-seekers will not be able to secure the types of jobs they want, and for those who do, it is unlikely that they will advance as rapidly as they hope to or as others have done in the past. Some work-seekers will be bumped downward into jobs for which they are overqualified. Others may be pushed out of the ranks of the employed and into active competition with the poorly qualified and with the least experienced job-seekers for any type of job that might become available. Accordingly, it is unlikely that there will be any shortage of workers for unskilled and semiskilled jobs in the foreseeable future.

185.   Vernon M. Briggs. IMMIGRATION POLICY
        AND THE AMERICAN LABOR FORCE,
Baltimore: Johns Hopkins Press, 1984, p. 250. The use of illegal immigration as a means to supply unskilled workers to the U.S. labor force is totally unjustifiable. When there are no real labor shortages, the illegal immigrants harm the employment and income opportunities of citizen workers; if real shortages exist, the correct course would be to enlarge the flow of legal immigrants and refugees who are unskilled and poorly educated. The labor force of the world is crammed with unskilled workers and refugees who, experience shows, would be more than willing to emigrate to the United States if given the opportunity to fill such a vacuum.

186.   Vernon M. Briggs. IMMIGRATION POLICY
        AND THE AMERICAN LABOR FORCE,
Baltimore: Johns Hopkins Press, 1984, p. 249. Because the size of the nation's youth cohort is expected to decline during the 1980s and because the aspirations of many female and minority workers are rising to ever-higher levels, some analysts have forecast that the nation will soon face a shortage of unskilled and low-wage workers. In many ways it would be a blessing if such a shortage did occur, for it is hard to imaging an

easier economic problem to solve. Given the rapidly declining quality of public education in the United States, however, it is more likely to be the case that many of the nation's youths (especially those in central cities and in rural areas) will be poorly prepared for the jobs that will become available in our increasingly technologically oriented society in the 1980s and 1990s. In 1983 the National Commission on Excellence in Education warned that the decline in the quality of education and training has been so rapid and so pervasive that the long-term welfare of the nation is "in peril." Consequently, when one views the data in that report which show the magnitude of the dropout and pushout problem, as well as the low achievement scores of the graduates of many of the nation's schools, it is hard to imagine that there will ever be a shortage of new job-seekers at the lower end of the skill ladder.

187.   Vernon M. Briggs. IMMIGRATION POLICY
        AND THE AMERICAN LABOR FORCE,
Baltimore: Johns Hopkins Press, 1984, pp. 164-165. In the United States a substantial number of citizen workers face employment and earnings disadvantages. According to one comprehensive study, this number was 40 percent of the people who participated in the labor force in 1980. Not all of these people, of course, compete with illegal immigrants for jobs. It is only in the areas where illegal immigrants are concentrated— and thus essentially only in the secondary labor markets of selected localities (as mentioned earlier, the areas that also receive the largest number of *legal* immigrants) that citizen workers must compete directly. But Los Angeles, San Francisco, Houston, New York City, Chicago, and San Antonio, to name a few of these areas of concentration, are among the largest and most influential labor markets in the United States. Hence, the number of citizen workers who are adversely affected by the presence of illegal immigrants is believed to be substantial.

One of the major ways to increase the number of job opportunities for low-income citizen workers and the rewards that come with earned income, and thus to enhance labor force participation by potential workers in these highly competitive labor markets, is to reduce the uncontrolled inflow of illegal aliens into the existing low-wage sector of the economy. Many of the jobs held by low-wage workers are essential to the operation of our economy. Farmworkers, dishwashers, laborers, garbage collectors, building cleaners, restaurant employees, gardeners, maintenance workers, to name a few occupations, perform useful and often indispensable work. Most of these tasks are not going to go away even if wages do increase. The tragedy is that the remuneration these workers receive is often so poor, and one reason they are underpaid is that an abnormally large pool of would-be workers is available. It is not ordained that workers who do useful things must be

paid poorly. In the normal operation of the labor market, wages increase in response to the demand for essential services. This does not happen, however, when the supply of such workers is excessive. If illegal aliens were flooding the legal, medical, educational, and business executive labor markets of this country, the problem would receive immediate national attention and would be solved. Because it is the nation's blue-collar, agricultural, and service workers who bear most of the burden of the competition with illegal immigrants, however, the issue remains largely unaddressed. Granted, illegal immigrants are not the only cause of unemployment and persistent low-income patterns among certain subgroups of the American labor force, but they certainly are a factor. Any serious full employment strategy for the United States in the 1980s, therefore, will have to include measures to curtail illegal immigration.

188.   Vernon M. Briggs. IMMIGRATION POLICY
        AND THE AMERICAN LABOR FORCE,
Baltimore: Johns Hopkins Press, 1984, p. 164. As for the question, which citizen workers compete more directly with illegal immigrants, all studies and reports unanimously answer, the young and the less skilled (i.e., young people in general, women, and minorities). According to the theory of welfare economics, the government could compensate persons who are hurt by a particular policy (i.e., the toleration of illegal immigrants in the labor market) by taxing those who stand to benefit from it (i.e., those who could buy items or services for less or could hire workers at lower wages), and society as a whole would not suffer. *Only when these transfer payments are actually made,* however—and no policy proposal to this effect has been even remotely suggested—will we have a chance to test this benign hypothesis.

189.   Klaus Fuchs. "Agenda for Tomorrow."
        ANNALS OF THE AMERICAN
ACADEMY OF POLITICAL SCIENCE, November 1993, p. 170. Unskilled and poorly educated illegal aliens unquestionably compete with some unskilled and poorly educated Americans, who are disproportionately black and Latino. But the restrictionists of the 1990s, often relying on the work of economist George Borjas, also assert that an increasing proportion of lawfully admitted immigrants are relatively unskilled and less educated than they used to be.

190.   Alan C. Miller. "Data Sheds Heat, Little
        Light, on Immigration Debate." LOS
ANGELES TIMES, November 21, 1993, p. 1. But these are not boom years. Many academics, most prominently UC San Diego economist George Borjas, say recent immigrants on the whole are less educated

and have fewer skills than native-born Americans and rely more on public services than their predecessors.

A recent census report found that 1 out of every 4 foreign-born adults had less than a ninth-grade education, compared with less than 1 of every 10 native-born. At the same time, the percentage of foreign-born residents with college degrees matched the percentage of native-born, and more foreign-born than native-born Americans had graduate degrees.

191.   "Can We Afford So Many Unskilled Immi-
        grants?" THE NEW YORK TIMES, January
26, 1994, p. A20. This is not surprising. Data from the 1990 Census show that the poverty rate of post-1970 immigrants is 42 percent higher than that of the native born. An immigrant's probability of receiving public assistance, adjusted by the amount of assistance received, is 44 percent greater than that of the native born. High welfare usage, combined with low earnings (meaning low taxes), means that immigrants must run a public-service deficit that is financed by the native born with low welfare and higher earnings (meaning higher taxes).

192.   Peter Brimelow. "Time to Rethink Immigra-
        tion?" NATIONAL REVIEW, June 22, 1992,
p. 30. Just as conservatives tend to think immigration is a natural phenomenon, they also assume vaguely that it must have been ratified by some free-market process. But immigration to the U.S. is not determined by econom-ics: it is determined—or at least profoundly distorted—by public policy. Inevitably, there are mismatches between skills supplied and skills demanded. Which helps explain why—as Borjas demonstrated in Friends or Strangers—welfare participation and poverty rates are sharply higher among the post 1965 immigrants, with some groups, such as Dominicans and other Hispanics, approaching the levels of American-born blacks.

193.   Peter Brimelow. "Time to Rethink Immigra-
        tion?" NATIONAL REVIEW, June 22, 1992,
p. 30. As a result, the post-1965 immigration is not only much bigger than expected: it is also less skilled. And it is becoming even less so—one economist, Professor George J. Borjas, himself a Cuban immigrant, has gone so far as to say, in his 1990 Friends or Strangers: The Impact of Immigrants on the U.S. Economy, that "the skill level of successive immigrant waves admitted to the U.S. has declined precipitously in the past two or three decades." For example, in 1986 less than 4 per cent of the over 600,000 legal immigrants were admitted on the basis of skills.

194.   "New Report Finds Immigration-Generated
        Population Growth." PR NEWSWIRE, Octo-
ber 19, 1992. Among the book's highlights is the find-

ing that the detrimental effects of U.S. population growth are greater than generally believed, largely because of "coastal cramming." Nearly half of the population is crowded onto just 10 percent of the land mass along the coasts. These coastal areas, which are the most ecologically fragile regions of the country and heavily dependent on important resources, are the destination of some three-quarters of the 15 million new immigrants who will enter the United States during the 1990s. (This figure does not include children born after immigrants settle in this country.) "Population growth is choking the very ecosystems that support our existence on this continent. It's like putting a cardiac patient on a high cholesterol diet," said Stein.

195.   Paul Glastris. "Immigration Crackdown." US NEWS & WORLD REPORT, June 21, 1993, p. 34. Another factor driving the debate is growing concern over the costs immigrants impose on government. In the 1980s, policy makers were impressed with studies which showed that immigrants contributed far more federal tax dollars then they consumed in government services. But those studies never fully accounted for the burden on state and local governments. The county of Los Angeles recently produced an influential report showing that immigrants cost the county $800 million annually. Such balance-sheet analyses don't take into account things like higher commercial real-estate taxes paid by immigrant entrepreneurs. But even critics concede that the basic point behind the L.A. report is true: Immigrant use of public services does impose a cost—and many cities are now preparing bills for Uncle Sam.

196.   Donald L. Huddle. "Letter to the Editor." THE NEW YORK TIMES, January 26, 1994, p. A23. "The Unfair Immigration Burden" (editorial Jan. 11) makes clear that New York and only a handful of other states bear an unfair and heavy burden for immigration policies written and regulated in Washington.

Based on five public hearings I conducted in New York City as chairman of the State Senate Committee on Cities last September and October, the costs paid by the state and localities in excess of Federal reimbursement and in lieu of Federal assistance for services to refugees, asylum seekers and other legal immigrants, as well as undocumented aliens, may be greater than ever imagined.

197.   Vernon M. Briggs. IMMIGRATION POLICY AND THE AMERICAN LABOR FORCE, Baltimore: Johns Hopkins Press, 1984, pp. 255-256. As noted in the earlier chapters of this volume, the available research on the settlement patterns of immigrants indicates a strong tendency toward clustering. Legal immigrants and refugees have tended to settle in

the central city labor markets of half a dozen states, and illegal immigrants have shown a pronounced tendency to reside and seek work in these same localities. From the standpoint of the immigrants, this clustering has facilitated their assimilation to the American way of life and the nation's economy. The particular communities that receive immigrants, however, are called upon to provide jobs, housing, and related community services. As indicated earlier, the urban labor markets of California, Texas, and Florida have since the 1960s been the primary destinations not only of immigrants but also of record numbers of citizen migrants. At the other extreme, some of the urban labor markets of New York, Illinois, and New Jersey have been the destinations of many immigrants during periods when the employment opportunities and population of these metropolitan areas have been in a state of secular decline. In both instances immigration has complicated rather than eased the labor market adjustment process. With little or no federal assistance, these few states and localities bear the burdens imposed by the mindlessness of federal immigration policy.

198.   Meredith Burke. "Rising Tide of Immigration Threatens to Sink Everyone." SACRAMENTO BEE, January 7, 1993, p. B9. Ignoring immigration's localized effects is another favorite copout. Immigration and Naturalization Service figures indicate quite clearly which cities and states will be called upon to provide housing, jobs, health care and bilingual education to any specific group admitted. More than 40 percent of Haitians admitted will go to New York state, nearly all to New York City; another third will head to Florida. Nearly 60 percent of Iranians and more than 60 percent of Salvadorans will end up in California.

199.   "National Population Organization Comes to California Speaking Out on the Costs of Immi-gration." PR NEWSWIRE, April 14, 1994. The problem is unsustainable population growth and immigration into California. According to a recent study by Dr. Donald L. Huddle of Rice University, in 1992, immigration cost California taxpayers $18 billion, after subtracting the taxes paid by immigrants. Over the next ten years, unless immigration law and enforcement policies are changed, immigration will cost California taxpayers an average of $45 billion a year!

200.   Leonel Sanchez. "State Immigrants Cost $18.2 Billion in Taxes Last Year, Study Says." SAN DIEGO UNION-TRIBUNE, November 5, 1993, p. A27. Adding fuel to the red-hot immigration debate, a study released yesterday said California's foreign-born population last year cost state taxpayers $18.2 billion in public services and displaced nearly a million U.S.-born workers.

The study warned that the annual cost will soar to $26.5 billion over the next 10 years unless lawmakers stem the flow of legal and illegal immigration.

201.	Robert Bach. "Recrafting the Common Good." ANNALS OF THE AMERICAN ACADEMY OF POLITICAL SCIENCE, November 1993, p. 161. This continuous fluctuation within the labor market leads simultaneously to two apparently contradictory conclusions. As various studies have shown, the net result of immigration in a dynamic economy is virtually zero. But the gross movements of workers within the labor market, with some established workers losing jobs while others gain, have the consequence of creating abundant experiences and accurate accounts of job displacement due to immigration. Communities do not live in the aggregate, nor do people perceive net or balanced outcomes. The continual neglect of the large gains and losses in the labor market leads to an excessively benign account of the impact of economic restructuring on workers in general and, in some cases, of immigration on established residents.

202.	Richard Simon. "1992 Cost of Immigrants $18 Billion, Report Says." LOS ANGELES TIMES, November 5, 1993, p. A3. One point on which Huddle found agreement with most other studies is that the federal government receives most of the taxes paid by immigrants, even though local government and the state provide the bulk of services, such as education and health care.

203.	Donald L. Huddle. "Letter to the Editor." THE NEW YORK TIMES, January 26, 1994, p. A23. More than 20 percent of all immigrants in the United States reside in New York State. That share should rise. Nearly 100,000 immigrants, including 45,000 who are undocumented, come to this state annually. While meeting the needs of legal immigrants is difficult because of meager Federal support, providing services for an illegal alien population estimated at 490,000, for whom the Federal Government provides virtually no reimbursement, is Herculean.

204.	Vernon M. Briggs. IMMIGRATION POLICY AND THE AMERICAN LABOR FORCE, Baltimore: Johns Hopkins Press, 1984, p. 181. In 1982 the National Association of Counties (NACO) stated that its support for amnesty as described in the Simpson-Mazzoli bill was contingent upon two conditions: "that strong enforcement measures, including employer sanctions, be implemented to control future illegal immigration; and that the federal government reimburse state and local governments for additional costs resulting from a legalization program." NACO estimated that the total cost of government cash and medical assistance to the illegal immigrants who would

be granted amnesty under the Simpson-Mazzoli bill (i.e., using January 1, 1980, as an eligibility cutoff date) would be $1.1 billion. It also estimated that over half of this sum—$546.8 million—would be paid by state and local governments. Given the geographical concentration of illegal immigrants, it is likely that this financial burden would be carried by only a few states and local governments. For them, of course, the burden—if it materialized—could be substantial. Local costs could be higher than those estimated by NACO, however, for not only do some states and localities have many more illegal immigrants than others but some have more liberal coverage provisions and more types of social programs than others. In California, for instance, it has been estimated that an am-nesty program would cost the state $1.3 billion. In New York City no specific dollar cost has been computed, but officials believe that the city's total welfare budget could increase by "5 to 10 percent" and that "with legalization, New York City can expect a significant rise in utiliza-tion of municipal hospitals and out-patient clinics, which are 100 percent city-funded, as well as a substan-tial increase in the state and local shares of total Medic-aid, public assistance, and social service expenditures."

205.	Peter Brimelow. "Time to Rethink Immigration?" NATIONAL REVIEW, June 22, 1992, p. 30. Borjas, moreover, was perturbed by the tendency of low-skilled recent immigrants, not necessarily to displace American blacks, but to join them in swelling the ranks of the underclass: "Few issues facing the U.S. are as important, and as difficult to resolve, as the persistent problem of poverty in our midst... The empirical evidence presented here suggests that immigration is exacerbating this problem." [ellipses in original]

206.	"Letters to the Editor." COMMENTARY, August 1993, p. 2. This assumes, of course, that the "family values" of Mexican immigrants really are stronger than those of white Americans. Mr. Fukuyama's own date, however, demonstrate that native-born white Americans have much stronger families than Latin American immigrants in general, and Mexican immigrants in particular. According to Mr. Fukuyama, "Mexican-origin Latinos," with an out-of-wedlock birth rate of 28.9 percent, are *more than twice as likely* as allegedly decadent white Americans to have illegitimate children (the white rate is 13.9 percent). What is more, he concedes that almost twice as many Hispanic families (24.4 percent) as white families (13.5 percent) are headed by a single female parent. Such white families are manifestly much stronger than Hispanic families, Mr. Fukuyama's strained attempt to indict suburban whites by associating their divorce and illegitimacy rates with those of inner-city blacks—

"what has happened among blacks is only an extreme extension of a process that has been proceeding apace among whites as well"—is utterly unconvincing.

207.   "Letters to the Editor." COMMENTARY,
        August 1993, p. 2. Hispanic immigrants,
even in the second and third generation, are significantly more likely than white Americans (and East Asian immigrants) to drop out of school, go on welfare, and end
up in jail, notwithstanding their (exaggerated) greater "family values" and the (equally exaggerated) moral rot "right in the heart of American's well-established white, Anglo-Saxon community." For the nativist caricature of third-world immigrants, Mr. Fukuyama substitutes an equally inaccurate and insulting caricature of native-born white Americans sunk in decadence and indolence. Mr. Fukuyama worries that "the immigrants will be corrupted by" white American habits. Since those habits include far higher rates of school completion and dramatically lower rates of illegitimacy, female-headed families, welfare dependence, and criminality, I for one hope that the immigrants are indeed "corrupted," and soon.

208.   Frank Trejo. "Debate Rates over Economic
        Benefits of Immigrants; Studies Conflict over
Taxes Paid." THE DALLAS MORNING NEWS: NEXUS, January 3, 1994, p. 8A. Last fall investigators for a U.S. Senate subcommittee reported that illegal immigrants are the fastest-growing segment of the federal prison population, currently accounting for 25 percent of inmates.

209.   H.L. Hazelbaker. "How to Repel Immigrants'
        Threat." NEW YORK TIMES, August 30,
1992, Sect 13LI, p. 17. The dangers posed by growing communities of illegal immigrants was graphically exposed by the fact that one-third of the rioters in South-Central Los Angeles were illegal aliens, and the Washington heights riots were orchestrated by drug gangs manned primarily by illegal aliens. The argument that these people are needed is contradicted by good evidence that over the last 20 years immigrants, especially from Latin America, extract more wealth in social services than they create in labor. With unemployment as high as it is among blacks, college and high-school students, it is doubtful that these people are as necessary as some businesspeople content—though no doubt they may be cheaper.

210.   Gene McNary. OPERATIONS OF THE
        BORDER PATROL, Hrg of the Committee
on the judiciary, House of Representatives. August 5, 1992, p. 70. Drug interdiction remains a highly volatile and potentially violent activity along the border. Since 1986, the number of Border Patrol drug

seizures has more than tripled. The value of drugs seized this fiscal year through June is over $1.2 *billion*, twice the value of that seized during the same nine month period just one year ago.

211.   Klaus Fuchs. "Agenda for Tomorrow."
        ANNALS OF THE AMERICAN
ACADEMY OF POLITICAL SCIENCE, November 1993, p. 170. But the restrictionists are obviously correct in asserting that immigration, legal and illegal, at high levels generates tension in the major cities in which immigrants settle. An article by Jack Miles entitled "Blacks v. Browns" in the October 1992 issue of the *Atlantic Monthly*, widely distributed by FAIR and the Center for Immigration Studies, pointed out that more than half of those arrested in the wake of the Los Angeles riots were Latinos and that 40 percent of them already had criminal records. Miles presented a litany of harsh facts concerning the struggle over power and services that have comparable examples in other cities. Black social service workers were let go to make room for bilingual speakers. A janitorial service in downtown Los Angeles has been taken over by nonunionized immigrants, who replaced unionized black workers.

212.   John Dillin. "Panel Studies Impact of New
        Immigrants on US Jobs, Wages." THE
CHRISTIAN SCIENCE MONITOR, May 6, 1993, p. 1. One reason: less-skilled Americans faced more competition from immigrants. Some experts especially worry about the effects of immigration on the nation's cities. They wonder about the impact of pouring large numbers of low-skilled immigrants into cities already facing high unemployment, crime, and poverty.

George High, executive director of the Center for Immigration Studies, warns that "competition between unskilled workers in our cities has contributed to social and racial tensions, especially between immigrants and American minorities.

North agrees. He says competition from immigrants is "extremely hard on the resident working poor."

213.   Charley Reese. "We Should Stop All Immi-
        gration Now." THE ORLANDO SENTINEL,
July 11, 1993, p. G2. Total immigration for 1981 to 1990 was 9.87 million—1.07 million more than a decade of 1901 to 1910. But in that early decade, we had a small population and lots of opportunities. Today, we are 250 million people with shrinking opportunities; deficit-ridden, debt-laden state and national treasuries; chronic unemployment; bulging prisons; a stressed environment; and an infrastructure in need of repairs.

The Center for Immigration Studies says that in 1990 the level of immigration was the equivalent of adding the population of Miami-Hialeah to the United

States. What do you think is going to happen if we keep adding one major metropolitan areas per year, year after year, when there is not now one city in America that doesn't have unemployment, high welfare costs, and a shaky government budget?

Conflict, that's what's going to happen. I once told a friend of mine that his brand of liberalism—the standard, open-your-borders, open-your-purse variety—depended entirely on prosperity. When people have enough for themselves and their families, they don't mind sharing. But when their families start to suffer, competition takes on a hard edge.

214.   Vernon M. Briggs. IMMIGRATION POLICY AND THE AMERICAN LABOR FORCE, Baltimore: Johns Hopkins Press, 1984, p. 249. The societal tension associated with the competition for access to jobs and for advancement in jobs during the 1980-1995 interval will be exacerbated by the need to enlarge the share of jobs, and improve the types of jobs, held by racial and ethnic minorities and by women. Because the civil rights movement and the feminist movement have increasingly turned their attention to economic goals, the labor market has naturally emerged as the primary arena in which to accomplish their objectives. As matters now stand, the BLS projects that the black labor force will grow at twice the annual rate of the white labor force from 1980 to 1995 (2.5 percent versus 1.2 percent per year respectively). The BLS has not issued a long-term projection for Hispanics as a separate group (traditionally they are included in data on whites). But given the fact that fertility rates for Hispanics are much higher than those for blacks, and that a disproportionate number of Hispanics are immigrating to the United States relative to blacks, it is certain that the growth rates for the Hispanic labor force in the next fifteen years will exceed those for blacks. As for women, they are expected to account for over two-thirds of the growth in the labor force during the same period. In 1975, women constituted 40 percent of the labor force, but it is estimated that by 1985 this figure will rise to 45 percent and by 1995, to 47 percent.

215.   Charley Reese. "We Should Stop All Immigration Now." THE ORLANDO SENTINEL, July 11, 1993, p. G2. Congress ought to pass emergency legislation imposing a five-year moratorium on all immigration—legal or otherwise—into the United States. The moratorium should include repeal of asylum laws for political refugees.

Otherwise, that suicide formula of increasing unemployment, immigration and bankrupt governments will collapse the social safety net and produce a poisonous explosion of violence and rancor.

216.   Ruth Conniff. "The War on Aliens." THE PROGRESSIVE, October, 1993, p. 22. "The melting pot is melting down," says Robert Goldsborough, founder and president of the far-right Americans for Immigration Control in Virginia. "The ethnic strife is tearing the country apart. Now you have Asian and Hispanic gangs in Long Beach, California, doing drive-bys and killing each other... You've got Chinese heroin and cocaine gangs being operated by a major drug lord out of Red China. This is destroying the social fabric of America. It's causing ethnic warfare."

217.   Robert Bach. "Recrafting the Common Good." ANNALS OF THE AMERICAN ACADEMY OF POLITICAL SCIENCE, November 1993, p. 161. Much less dramatic social tensions than the all-too-familiar hate crimes and abuses that plague contemporary U.S. life can also lead to conflict. Today's demography creates a social context for misinterpretation of even the most routine interpersonal tensions by turning clashes between individuals into intergroup conflict. The greater the mix of groups, the more likely it is that normal tensions and conflicts will express, by numerical chance, intergroup antagonisms. The rise in conflict between different minority groups, for instance, may result as much from the increase in the number of opportunities to have these encounters as from a significant increase in motivations to harm each other. Under the new demographic diversity, the same number of interpersonal incidents as before can produce a greater number of incidents between different groups.

218.   Nathan Glazer. IMMIGRATION AND U.S. FOREIGN POLICY, San Francisco: Westview Press, 1990, p. 24. The United States has been spared up to now the most extreme consequences of immigration on foreign policy, consequences a good number of countries in the developing world have had to deal with. In some cases, a delicate ethnic balance has been threatened by immigration. This is what has been happening in Assam, as Bengalis move in, often over the international frontier with Bangladesh, with results leading to massacre and a situation of near open rebellion and threatened civil war. In the Punjab, an opposite situation exists, in which Sikh extremists are trying to drive Hindus from the state through terrorism to ensure Sikh dominance. In Lebanon, a delicate balance between various Muslim and Christian groups was upset by the mass entry of Palestinian refugees, which was undoubtedly one factor in the complicated skein of events that has resulted in endless and bloody civil war. The oil-rich Gulf countries have feared the impact of immigrants from other Arab countries—one reason they have preferred workers from Pakistan and India and Korea who cannot participate in local politics. So immigration, which may be seen as only a

means of dealing with labor shortages or fulfilling humanitarian responsibilities, may under certain circumstances threaten the balance of internal politics, and even threaten the subversion of the state.

219.   "Letters to the Editor." COMMENTARY,
          August 1993, p. 2. Unless these facts are
grasped, the extraordinary nature of the current U.S. immigration situation cannot be understood. For, although Mr. Fukuyama does not acknowledge it, the current influx is unique in that it consists overwhelmingly of visible minorities. And, because of those low native-born fertility rates, this is shifting the ethnic balance quickly—from nearly 90-percent white in 1960 to less than 75-percent white in 1990. Plausible scenarios suggest that whites will verge on a minority within the lifetime of children now born. There is no precedent for a country undergoing such a rapid and radical transformation of its ethnic character in the entire history of the world.

220.   Linda Chavez. "Demystifying Multi-
          culturalism." NATIONAL REVIEW, February 21, 1994, p. 26. Multiculturalism is on the advance, everywhere from President Clinton's Cabinet to corporate boardrooms to public-school classrooms. If you believe the multiculturalists' propaganda, whites are on the verge of becoming a minority in the United States. The multiculturalists predict that this demographic shift will fundamentally change American culture—indeed destroy the very idea that America *has* a single unified culture.

221.   H.L. Hazelbaker. "How to Repel Immigrants'
          Threat." NEW YORK TIMES, August 30,
1992, sect 13LI, p. 17. The generally supportive and approving tones describing the local front in the third-world invasion of the United States ("Hispanic Influx Being Felt on East End," July 12) is reprehensible. With the left-wing political culture doing everything it can to discourage assimilation, promote bilingualism and cheapen the value of American citizenship, no one on Long Island or in the nation can afford to be apathetic, let alone passively supportive, of the breakdown of national sovereignty which characterizes United States immigration policy.

In an age of increasing technological sophistication, the United States can not afford to continually accept massive immigration by slash-and-burn third-world peasants. The overload of non-Western immigrants threatens the cultural and political traditions which created this republic and made it the envy of the world.

222.   Linda Chavez. "Demystifying Multi-
          culturalism." NATIONAL REVIEW, February 21, 1994, p. 26. Indeed, multiculturalists hope to ride the immigrant wave to greater power and influence.

They have certainly done so in education. Some 2.3 million children who cannot speak English well now attend public school, an increase of 1 million in the last seven years. Multicultural advocates cite the presence of such children to demand bilingual education and other multicultural services. The Los Angeles Unified School District alone currently offers instruction in Spanish, Armenian, Korean, Cantonese, Tagalog, Russian, and Japanese. Federal and state governments now spend literally billions of dollars on these programs.

223.   Paul Glastris. "Immigration Crackdown." US
          NEWS & WORLD REPORT, June 21, 1993,
p. 34. Beyond the immediate dollars-and-cents concerns of Americans lies another apprehension: that more immigrants will somehow abet the balkanization of the culture. Recent protests by Hispanic students in California universities, demanding the creation of Chicano-studies departments, only fuel the fears of those concerned about immigration.

224.   Joseph Raz. "Multiculturalism: a Liberal
          Perspective." DISSENT, Winter 1994, p. 67.
Only through being socialized in a culture can one tap the options that give life a meaning. By and large, one's cultural membership determines the horizon of one's opportunities, of what one may become, or (if one is older) what one might have been. Little surprise that it is in the interest of every person to be fully integrated in a cultural group. Equally plain is the importance to its members of the prosperity, cultural and material, of that group. Its prosperity contributes to the richness and variety of the opportunities they have access to. This is the first of three ways in which membership in a cultural group affects one's prospects in life.

The second is the fact that a common culture facilitates social relations and is a condition of rich and comprehensive personal relationships. One particular relationship is especially sensitive to this point. Erotic attraction, economic, or certain raw emotional needs can often help overcome even the greatest cultural gaps. But in one's relations with one's children and with one's parents a common culture is an essential condition for the tight bonding we expect and desire. A policy that forcibly detaches children from the culture of their parents not only undermines the stability of society by undermining people's ability to sustain long-term intimate relations, it also threatens one of the deepest desires of most parents, the desire to understand their children, share their world, and to remain close to them.

Finally, being a member of a prosperous cultural community affects individual well-being because, for most people, membership is a major determinant of their sense of who they are; it contributes to what we

369

have come to call their sense of identity. This is not really surprising given that one's culture sets the horizon of one's opportunities. I am what I am, but equally I am what I can become or could have been.

225.   Nathan Glazer. "The Closing Door: is Restrictionism Unthinkable?" THE NEW REPUBLIC, 12/27/93, p. 15. One other element should be mentioned as making up part of the immigration restriction move-ment. One finds in it children of immigrants, and immi-grants themselves, who admire the ability of America to assimilate immigrants and their children, but who fear that the assimilatory powers of America have weakened, because of the legal support to bilingualism in education and voting, because of the power of multicultural trends in education. It is easy to accuse such people of wanting to pull up the drawbridge after they have gained entry. They would answer that they fear the United States is no longer capable of assimilating those now coming as it assimilated them.

226.   Peter Brimelow. "Time to Rethink Immigration?" NATIONAL REVIEW, June 22, 1992, p. 30. Let's be clear about this: The American experience with immigration has been a triumphant success. It has so far transcended anything seen in Europe as to make the application of European lessons an exercise to be performed with care.

But in the late twentieth century, the economic and political culture of the U.S. has changed significantly—from classical liberalism to an interventionist welfare statism. In the previous two hundred years of U.S. history, a number of tried-and-true, but undeniably tough, techniques of assimilation had been perfected. Today, they have been substantially abandoned. Earlier waves of immigrants were basically free to succeed or fail. And many failed: as much as a third of the 1880-to-1920 immigrants returned to their native lands. But with the current wave, public policy interposes itself, with the usual debatable results.

227.   Peter Brimelow. "Time to Rethink Immigration?" NATIONAL REVIEW, June 22, 1992, p. 30. But no natural process is at work. The current wave of immigration, and America's shifting ethnic balance, is simply the result of public policy. A change in public policy opened the Third World floodgates after 1965. A further change in public policy could shut them. Public policy could even restore the status quo ante 1965, which would slowly shift the ethnic balance back.

228.   "Perspective on Immigration." LOS ANGE LES TIMES, April 13, 1994, p. B7. I am a first-generation immigrant. I also have 10 years' experience as an immigration paralegal. I recently joined the staff of Population-Environment Balance out

of a recognition that the United States must encourage a replacement-level fertility rate of 2.1 or lower, concurrently adopt a replacement-level immigration policy of 200,000 people a year and enforce our immigration laws. These measures are necessary to protect the quality of life of Americans of all racial backgrounds.

229.   Ira Mehlman. "The Issue is Immigration; Increasing Opposition to Current US Immigration Policy that Does Not Control Numbers of Immigrants Entering the US." NATIONAL REVIEW, November 29, 1993, p. 26. This misses the simple fact that, unlike the editorial board of the Wall Street Journal, most Americans don't measure the quality of their lives solely by the size of the GNP. Turning what remains of the nation's redwood forests into expensive lawn furniture might be good for the economy. Eliminating environmental protections might maximize profits. The American people would favor neither solely in the name of boosting the GNP.

230.   Wayne Cornelius. "America's New Immigration Law." CENTER FOR US-MEXICAN STUDIES, UNIVERSITY OF CALIFORNIA AT SAN DIEGO, Monograph Series 11, 1983, pp. 58-59. Now, in 1981, the United States finds itself in the ambiguous position of espousing respect for the law as a cornerstone of society, while refusing to make the enforcement of its immigration laws a priority. Until a more meaningful commitment to enforcement is made, illegal migration will continue to undermine the most valued ideals of this nation—the integrity of the law and the fundamental dignity of the individual. It is this undermining of national values that poses the greatest threat to U.S. society, not the displacement of U.S. workers or use of social services by undocumented workers. Jobs taken by undocumented workers sometimes do result in the displacement of American workers, and the presence of these aliens in the work force does have a depressing effect on U.S. labor standards and wages in some locales and some sections of the economy. While these conclusions of the Staff are disputed—at least as to emphasis—by some researchers, no one denies that national ideals are being compromised.

231.   Wayne Cornelius. "America's New Immigration Law." CENTER FOR US-MEXICAN STUDIES, UNIVERSITY OF CALIFORNIA AT SAN DIEGO, Monograph Series 11, 1983, p. 59. Following the Select Commission report, the normative terms used to describe the phenomenon began to enjoy increasing popularity. Several political actors in highly visible forums have recently characterized the problem as one of reasserting national sovereignty. Others have merely cast the problem in terms of reasserting control

over the formulation and execution of immigration policy. Many persons within and outside the federal government perceive that "solving" the problem of undocumented migration has become a test of national will in an age when such will has diminished on many fronts.

232.   Vlae Kershner. "Calculating the Cost of Immigration." THE SAN FRANCISCO CHRONICLE, June 23, 1993, p. A1. That process takes time. While it is commonly believed in this country that the children of immigrants enjoy economic opportunities no different from other natives', University of California at San Diego immigration scholar George Borjas says his recent research indicates that it now takes four generations for immigrants' wages to fully catch up—which means that it could be late in the 21st century before the great-grandchildren of today's immigrants attain average wage levels.

233.   Harold Gilliam. "Bursting at the Seams." SAN FRANCISCO CHRONICLE, February 21, 1993, p. 7. But those benefits will continue with the ethnic and cultural diversity that exists now. Immigrants now in this country have a strong stake in minimizing further immigration, which increases job competition in a shaky economy. A recent Latino National Political Survey poll found that 79 percent of Mexican-born U.S. residents believe there are too many immigrants crossing the borders, and a Wall Street Journal-NBC poll found that 71 percent of the general public feel the same way.

234.   Leonel Sanchez. "State Immigrants Cost $18.2 Billion in Taxes Last Year, Study Says." SAN DIEGO UNION-TRIBUNE, November 5, 1993, p. A27. The Urban Institute concluded earlier this year that a Los Angeles study, which reported that spending on immigrants exceeds revenues from them, was groundless because U.S. citizens, too, generally cost the government more than they contribute.

235.   Larry Rohter. "Debate Rages over Influx of Immigrants." THE DALLAS MORNING NEWS, September 26, 1993, p. 4. Nor does it appear that immigrants make use of services like welfare or unemployment benefits with significantly greater frequency than natives.

"The reason is that these people for the most part are migrating for labor, and when the jobs are not forth-coming, there is a strong tendency for return migration," said Douglas Massey, a University of Chicago sociologist who studies immigration from Mexico, the country that supplies the largest number of new arrivals.

236.   "Letters to the Editor." THE WASHINGTON TIMES, November 13, 1993, p. D2. Studies showing high immigrant labor force participation rates and that immigrants contribute more to public coffers than they take from them support the council's conclusions. Professor Julian Simon of the University of Maryland notes that when the sum of tax contributions to city, state, and federal governments is allowed for, a number of studies show that illegal immigrants pay five to 10 times as much in taxes as they cost in public services they use.

237.   Sidney Weintraub. THE ILLEGAL ALIEN FROM MEXICO, Austin: University of Texas Press, 1980, pp. 24-25. With regard to the direct burden on our social services, this is one of the few areas where the evidence is clear; most illegal workers have taxes deducted from their earnings (in the San Diego study, the interviews indicated that illegals contributed 17 percent of their wages to taxes) while their demands on social services (police costs, hospitals, food stamps, welfare, burial services, education in the public schools) are not great. The San Diego study is a significant one since, as the report notes, "San Diego is the most impacted area in the world by the flow of illegal aliens." San Diego accounts for 43 percent of all border apprehensions of illegal immigrants and 25 percent of apprehensions throughout the nation. The Villalpando study concluded that the cost to provide social services for illegals was $2 million a year, whereas tax contributions amounted to almost $49 million. The exact percentages are less significant than the orders of magnitude.

The Villalpando evidence is supported by the North and Houston inquiry. Based on their interviews with apprehended illegals, 77 percent had social security taxes withheld, 73 percent Federal income taxes, 44 percent hospitalization, and 31 percent even filed income tax returns. This is contrasted with 27 percent using hospitals, 4 percent who collected one or more weeks of unemployment insurance, 4 percent who had children in U.S. schools, 1 percent who secured food stamps, and less than 1 percent who received welfare payments. The requests of school authorities in south Texas for aid for their "impacted" districts suggest that the educational impact may be underestimated in some areas. Again, the exact percentages are less significant (since there would seem to be a natural tendency for the illegals to overstate their payments and understate their use of public serv-ices) than the orders of magnitude. The proposed am-nesty provision would make those affected eligible for such services and would eliminate the reluctance to exercise their rights.

238.   Sidney Weintraub. THE ILLEGAL ALIEN FROM MEXICO, Austin: University of Texas Press, 1980, pp. 25-26. These findings are con-

sistent with the Marshall "work scared and hard" aphorism; one would expect illegal immigrants to be compliant and not demanding. Persons who wish to restrict the inflow of illegals have argued that while the direct costs of social services to illegals may not be high in comparison to what they contribute, there may be nonmeasurable indirect costs. If illegal immigrants displace national labor and the latter must resort to welfare, food stamps, and unemployment insurance, isn't this a cost of the entry of illegals (U.S. Department of Justice, 1976)? This is hypothesis, not fact. One might equally logically argue that if illegals are not displacing national workers, and are contributing more financially than they are receiving in social services, then the illegals are in part financing the costs of the social services for unemployed or underemployed national workers.

239.   Ruth Conniff. "The War on Aliens." THE
        PROGRESSIVE, October, 1993, p. 22. Similarly, costs in social services are disproportionately incurred in communities where there are large numbers of immigrants. But the net economic effect of all immigration—both legal and illegal—is to add wealth to the country, according to the Labor Department study. The solution, Papadimitriou and others argue, is not to clamp down on immigration, but rather for the Federal Government to redistribute the wealth in taxes and income from immigrant labor, and compensate localities that pay the costs.

240.   Donald L. Huddle. "Letter to the Editor." THE
        NEW YORK TIMES, January 26, 1994,
p. A23. Congress must recognize its obligation to New York and other states with significant immigration populations by providing Federal funds commensurate with costs for bilingual instruction and other criminal justice, social service and health programs. Federal authorities must also seriously explore pre-screening aliens traveling to the United States without documentation.

241.   John Judis. "Why Your Wages Keep Falling."
        THE NEW REPUBLIC, February 14, 1994,
p. 26. Under relentless attack from business and facing a hostile administration in Washington, unions lost ground, declining from 31 percent of the nonagricultural work force in 1970 to 26 percent in 1979 to 13 percent today. The effect of this on wages can be calculated by multiplying the loss in the wage premium by the number of workers who might otherwise have been represented by unions. On this basis, Lawrence Mishel and Jared Bernstein of the Economic Policy Institute , the authors of *The State of Working America*, estimate that the collapse of unionism cost blue-collar workers 3.6 percent in real wages from 1978 to 1988.

At a deeper level, business' successful offensive against unions changed the wage structure of the American economy. Instead of unionized workers setting the pace in wages, they became a lagging indicator of the real state of the wage economy. The first tier began to shrink and collapse into the second tier. Workers in the heavily unionized steel industry, for example, saw their wages fall from $20.37 per hour in 1981 to $17.91 per hour in 1987 to $16.87 per hour in 1992 (all these figures are in 1992 dollars). Workers in the second tier began to see their wages driven down to the level of non-unionized laborers and service workers. The wages of partially unionized meat-packing workers went from $13.98 per hour in 1981 to $10.39 per hour in 1987 to $9.15 per hour in 1992. Meanwhile, workers in the third tier, deprived of even the modest protections of the minimum wage, found themselves edging toward subsistence levels. Workers in restaurants and bars— one of the fastest-growing groups in the 1980s—saw their wages fall from $6.14 per hour in 1981 to $5.46 per hour in 1987 to $5.29 per hour in 1992.

242.   John Judis. "Why Your Wages Keep Falling."
        THE NEW REPUBLIC, February 14, 1994,
p. 26. There are plenty of causes: government policies, new technologies and automation, more women in the work force. But the most important, and often overlooked one, is the change that occurred in the rela-tionship between business and labor after the loss of American industrial supremacy. The unfashionable truth is that the decline of American wages has been largely a result of the decline of American labor unions.

243.   Michael LeMay. FROM OPEN DOOR TO
        DUTCH DOOR, New York: Praeger Press,
1987, p. 135. Nor is it so clear that illegals "drive down" wages. In those industries where alien workers are most heavily concentrated wages may already be about as high as they can realistically go. Some economists, like John Kenneth Galbraith and Marvin Smith, argue that such jobs are being filled at what is an "economical wage"—that is, a wage low enough to allow the employer to make a profit. When an employer is faced with the loss of cheap labor, there are other options besides raising wages to be considered: replacing workers with machines, moving the operation overseas, or simply going out of business. When the Bracero Program ended in California, only the lettuce and citrus growers raised their wages in an attempt to attract domestic workers. The tomato growers began using mechanical harvesters, the asparagus growers moved to Mexico, and marginal growers in all crops simply closed down and sold their farms (Crewdson: 266-267).

244.   Larry Rohter. "Debate Rages over Influx of
        Immigrants." THE DALLAS MORNING

NEWS, September 26, 1993, p. 4. During the 1980s, average wages for native-born workers hit a plateau, and those of recently arrived immigrants declined slightly. When David Card, an economist at Princeton University, examined the impact of the arrival of 125,000 Cubans in the 1980 Mariel boatlift, which increased Miami's labor force by 7 percent in an overnight expansion rarely seen in recent American history, he found that "the Mariel influx appears to have had virtually no effect on the wages or unemployment rates of less-skilled workers," whether white or black.

245.   John Judis. "Why Your Wages Keep Falling."
        THE NEW REPUBLIC, February 14, 1994,
p. 29. The solution favored by many labor leaders and liberal Democrats is to restore the pre-1973 status quo. They want to raise the minimum wage (which Clinton has postponed asking Congress to do), reform labor laws, restrict the immigration of unskilled workers and remove incentives for firms to have foreign countries do their manufacturing. While these measures address the causes of wage decline much more directly than do the economists' or Clinton's proposals, they slight the genuine dilemma that American businesses face. If wages were to increase at the rate that they did from 1948 to 1973, many American firms quickly would suffer the fate of Frigidaire or Philco. The world economy is simply a different and less friendly place than it once was.

246.   Michael LeMay. FROM OPEN DOOR TO
        DUTCH DOOR, New York: Praeger Press,
1987, p. 135. Those sweeps, as well as similar studies, have shown that illegal alien workers concentrate in several industries: the garment industry, electronic companies, domestic labor, construction, and agriculture. The Rand Study cited above found Mexican immigrants in California with the following percentages in occupation: 28 percent operatives, 16 percent personal service, 15 percent farm work, 15 percent white collar work, 14 percent skilled labor, and 12 percent general laborers. In terms of industry, 38 percent were in manufacturing, 16 percent were in agriculture, 12 percent in personal service and restaurants, 12 percent in other service jobs, 11 percent in wholesale and retail sales, 5 percent in construction, and 6 percent in "others" (McCarthy and Valdez: 1986).

247.   "At America's Door." THE ECONOMIST,
        July 24, 1993. Immigrants may take some jobs that would otherwise be done by citizens, especially poor blacks; but the evidence is unconvincing. In farm-work, their numbers may sometimes keep wages down; but illegal immigrants also start up businesses, consume goods and services, and create opportunities for others to work. Few of them, even in California, go on the welfare registers for fear of detection. All pay

sales taxes; many go on to pay income tax. The help they get from the government comes mostly in the form of free education for their children, an expense which should eventually earn money for America.

248.   Michael LeMay. FROM OPEN DOOR TO
        DUTCH DOOR, New York: Praeger Press,
1987, pp. 134-135. "Project Jobs," a week-long operation of sweeping raids by the INS, instigated considerable criticism about the use of "gestapo-like" actions, and the arrest of "aliens who turned out to be legal residents" (among them a twelve-year old boy who was a U.S. citizen). Although the INS hailed "Project Jobs" a success, the evidence seemed to be to the contrary. Only a few highly paid illegals were found—an occasional railroad or construction workers earning $9 or $10 per hour. The average salary of the 5,440 employed aliens arrested during the sweep barely reached $190 per week, or less than $10,000 per year—below the poverty level for an average urban family. Of 356 alien workers arrested in New York, three-fourths of whom were not Mexican immigrants, the average weekly income was $174. The Bureau of Labor Statistics stated at the time that it took $251 a week to provide the most basic requirements for a family of four in New York City that year. In Chicago, the average income of all those arrested in the sweep was less than half the city's average hourly wage in manufacturing. The majority of all those arrested throughout the nation during Project Jobs was less than the minimum wage of $3.35 an hour. Most were working in essentially menial jobs (Crewdson: 243).

And few jobs opened by the raids were filled by U.S. citizens thereafter. The Texas Employment Commission found only 42 unemployed citizens who wanted to apply for the 1,105 jobs in that state opened up by the raids, and only 3 of the jobs were actually filled, largely because the wages being offered for the jobs were frequently $1 or $1.50 per hour less than what the INS claimed the arrested aliens were being paid. A similar pattern emerged at a fish-cleaning plant in northern California. The Midwest Steel Company, which lost 114 workers to the INS, was only able to hire 25 replacements. Another steel mill hired 92 workers to replace ones lost to the INS raids and 68 of those quit the first week (Crewdson: 244-45).

249.   Sidney Weintraub. THE ILLEGAL ALIEN
        FROM MEXICO, Austin: University of
Texas Press, 1980, pp. 27-28. According to each of the three major study samples already cited (North and Houstoun, 1976; Villalpando et al., 1977; and Cornelius, 1976), a majority of Mexican illegals worked in agriculture or other occupations requiring minimum skills at the time of apprehension. It would appear that except for California and first employment on entering the United States, the proportion of illegals working in

agriculture is declining. The argument inherent in the view of "leave well enough alone" regarding Mexican illegal immigrants is that they are filling jobs needed in modern societies which nationals do not want. As a woman ranchowner from south Texas contended in what is almost caricature: it is impossible to get anyone but illegals to clean the stables. Or, and this is a variant of this argument, many of the jobs are on the farms and the major unemployment problem in the United States is in the cities, among the youth and minorities. Or, and this is another argument, the "reservation price" of national workers, that price at which it would pay them to give up welfare, is higher than what the occupations into which the Mexicans go can legitimately demand (Reubens, 1978) without the jobs going out of existence or being replaced by labor-saving machinery, as has happened already in much of the country.

250.   Vernon M. Briggs. IMMIGRATION POLICY AND THE AMERICAN LABOR FORCE, Baltimore: Johns Hopkins Press, 1984, p. 162. Most illegal immigrant workers are employed in the secondary labor market of the U.S. economy. It seems that as industrial societies develop, the structure of their labor markets changes. Coexistent with these nations' high-paying, stable, and rewarding jobs are jobs that lack all these features, and comparatively speaking the latter are far less attractive to would-be workers. The quandary for the industrialized nations, therefore, is how to fill the jobs that seem undesirable but that are nonetheless essential to the operation of their economies.

Michael Piore has argued that, in the past, industrialized societies looked toward the margins of the labor force to find workers to fill these jobs, and there they found youths, housewives, and farm-workers as well as the minority groups that for years were denied access to better jobs. Given the developments of the 1970s and early 1980s, however, some of these traditional sources can no longer be depended upon. Many youths, for example, have proven to be undependable because they do not act like permanent workers. Frequently they are "target earners," workers whose income is used to buy a particular object (a car or a stereo) or serves as pocket money, but rarely is needed for room and board (which is often provided by parents). With the rise of the feminist movement and the trend toward smaller families, housewives are increasingly inclined toward career development rather than toward marginal work attachments. Likewise, the dramatic decline in agricultural employment due to extensive mechanization means that there are fewer farmers who can be attracted to work second or off-season jobs in the nonagricultural sector. Finally, of course, the progression of the civil rights movement since the 1960s has been increasingly in the direction of improv-

ing the preparation of minority workers for better jobs and opening up access to a wider range of jobs. It is alleged, therefore, that the above members of the labor force are no longer available or are unwilling to work in the secondary labor market.

251.   Milton Morris. IMMIGRATION—THE BELEAGUERED BUREAUCRACY, Washington, D.C.: The Brookings Institute, 1985, pp. 45-46. A subject of increasing concern to the public and to policymakers at every level of government is coping with the cost of providing immigrants with the basic social services—education, health care, and welfare benefits. One indication of this concern is the steps being taken in an increasing number of localities to monitor these costs and to explore the extent of local governments' responsibilities for providing these services. Another is the several bills introduced in Congress in recent years calling for the federal government to assume responsibility for medical and education costs imposed by immigrants and restricting access by immigrants to various cash assistance programs. In addition, there have been repeated calls for better screening of immigrants to ensure that they do not become public charges and to enforce provisions for the expulsion of legal immigrants who do become public charges within five years of entry.

252.   Larry Rohter. "Debate Rages over Influx of Immigrants." THE DALLAS MORNING NEWS, September 26, 1993, p. 4. Yet data from the 1990 census indicate that while the education gap between native-born workers and immigrants may have widened, newly arrived immigrants are on the average more educated today than at any time in the past.

"There is absolutely no evidence that the quality of immigrants, which is really just a measure of education, has declined," said Marta Tienda, a sociologist and demographer at the University of Chicago.

253.   Jerome Weeks. THE DALLAS MORNING NEWS, March 18, 1994, p. B8. And doggedness, as it turns out, is good for the American economy. when presented with notions about lazy immigrants who burden the welfare system ad steal jobs from Americans, economist Julian Simons has countered that America's most recent arrivals put more into the public coffers than they take out. Like turn-of-the-century Irish and Eastern European immigrants, they start up new companies and stores. They're generally young and industrious with strong family connections.

254.   "Letters to the Editor." COMMENTARY, August 1993, p. 2. It is probably appropriate to compare present-day Mexican immigrants to the several million southern Italians of peasant background who flooded into the United States in the late-19th and

early-20th centuries. This wave of Italian immigrants came with less than ideal cultural baggage: many did in fact suffer from what Edward Banfield (as cited by Mr. Lind) called an "amoral familism" that retarded mobility and educational achievement. Italians, like Mexicans today, had higher rates of truancy, crime, and educational failure than other immigrant groups; they had a knack for organized crime; and their integration into American society was much slower and more painful than for German or Jewish immigrants. Many, moreover, planned not to become U.S. citizens but to return to Italy. And yet today Italian-Americans rank higher than "native" Anglo-Saxons in terms of per-capita income and other measures of socioeconomic success.

255.   Francis Fukuyama. "Immigrants and Family
        Values." COMMENTARY, May 1993, p. 26.
Such facts are highly visible and contribute to the impression among white Americans that Latinos as a whole have joined inner-city blacks to form one vast, threatening underclass. But there are very significant differences among Latino groups. Latinos of Cuban and Mexican origin, for example, who together constitute 65 percent of the Hispanic community, have a 50-percent lower rate of female-headed households than do Puerto Ricans—18.9 and 19.6 percent versus 38.9 percent. While the rate of Puerto Rican out-of-wedlock births approaches that of blacks (53.0 vs. 63.1 percent of live births), the rates for Cuban and Mexican-origin Latinos are much lower, 16.1 and 28.9 percent, respectively, though they are still above the white rate of 13.9 percent.

256.   Francis Fukuyama. "Immigrants and Family
        Values." COMMENTARY, May 1993, p. 26.
Those who fear third-world immigration as a threat to Anglo-American cultural values do not seem to have noticed what the real sources of cultural breakdown have been. To some extent, they can be traced to broad socioeconomic factors over which none of us has control: the fluid, socially disruptive nature of capitalism; technological change; economic pressures of the contemporary workplace and urban life; and so on. But the ideological assault on traditional family values—the sexual revolution; feminism and the delegitimization of the male-dominated household; the celebration of alternative life-styles; attempts ruthlessly to secularize all aspects of American public life; the acceptance of no-fault divorce and the consequent rise of single-parent households—was not the creation of recently-arrived Chicano agricultural workers or Haitian boat people, much less of Chinese or Korean immigrants. They originated right in the heart of America's well-established white, Anglo-Saxon community. The "Hollywood elite" that created the now celebrated Murphy Brown, much like the establishment "media elite" that Republicans enjoy

attacking, does not represent either the values or the interests of most recent third-world immigrants.

In short, though the old, traditional culture continues to exist in the United States, it is over-laid today with an elite culture that espouses very different values. The real danger is not that these elites will become corrupted by the habits and practices of third-world immigrants, but rather that the immigrants will become corrupted by them. And that is in fact what tends to happen.

257.   Linda Chavez. "Demystifying Multi-
        culturalism." NATIONAL REVIEW,
February 21, 1994, p. 26. The impetus for multiculturalism is not coming from immigrants, but from their more affluent and assimilated native-born counterparts. The proponents are most often the elite—the best educated and most successful members of their respective racial and ethnic groups. College campuses, where the most radical displays of multiculturalism take place, are fertile recruiting grounds. Last May, for example, a group of Mexican-American students at UCLA, frustrated that the university would not elevate the school's 23-year-old Chicano-studies program to full department status, stormed the faculty center, breaking windows and furniture and causing half a million dollars in damage. The same month, a group of Asian-American students at UC Irvine went on a hunger strike to pressure administrators into hiring more professors of Asian-American studies. These were not immigrants, or even, by and large, disadvantaged students, but middle-class beneficiaries of their parents' or grandparents' successful assimilation to the American mainstream.

258.   Linda Chavez. "Demystifying Multi-
        culturalism." NATIONAL REVIEW,
February 21, 1994, p. 26. In fact, white males will still constitute about 45 per cent—a plurality—of the workforce in the year 2000. The proportion of white men in the workforce is declining—but primarily because the proportion of white women is growing. They will make up 39 per cent of the workforce within ten years, according to government projections, up from 36 per cent in 1980, Together, white men and women will account for 84 per cent of all workers by 2000—hardly a minority share.

259.   Linda Chavez. "Demystifying Multi-
        culturalism." NATIONAL REVIEW,
February 21, 1994, p. 26. The urge to assimilate has traditionally been overpowering in the United States, especially among the children of immigrants. Only groups that maintain strict rules against intermarriage with persons outside the group, such as Orthodox Jews and the Amish, have ever succeeded in preserving distinct, full-blown cultures within American society.

(It is interesting to note that religion seems to be a more effective deterrent to full assimilation than the secular elements of culture, including language.) Although many Americans worry that Hispanic immigrants, for example, are not learning English and will therefore fail to assimilate into the American mainstream, little evidence supports the case. By the third generation in the United States, a majority of Hispanics, like other ethnic groups, speak only English and are closer to other Americans on most measures of social and economic status than they are to Hispanic immigrants. On one of the most rigorous gauges of assimilation—intermarriage—Hispanics rank high. About one-third of young third-generation Hispanics marry non-Hispanic whites, a pattern similar to that of young Asians. Even for blacks, exogamy rates, which have been quite low historically, are going up; about 3 per cent of blacks now marry outside their group.

260.   Linda Chavez. "Demystifying Multi-
         culturalism." NATIONAL REVIEW, Febru-
ary 21, 1994, p. 26. Nevertheless, multiculturalists insist on treating race and ethnicity as if they were synonymous with culture. They presume that skin color and national origin, which are immutable traits, determine values, mores, language, and other cultural attributes, which, of course, are learned. In the multiculturalists' world view, African-Americans, Puerto Ricans, or Chinese-Americans living in New York City have more in common with persons of their ancestral group living in Lagos or San Juan or Hong Kong than they do with other New Yorkers who are white.

261.   Klaus Fuchs. "Agenda for Tomorrow."
         ANNALS OF THE AMERICAN
ACADEMY OF POLITICAL SCIENCE, November 1993, p. 170. There is considerable evidence to support the conclusion that recent immigrants, and especially their children, are adapting to the American civic culture. President Clinton surely is right in asserting that Los Angeles is not Bosnia. But civic unity and ethnic peace cannot be taken for granted, and he and his administration should begin a careful analysis of which immigration and ethnic policies contribute to civic unity and which do not.

262.   Francis Fukuyama. "Immigrants and Family
         Values." COMMENTARY, May 1993, p. 26.
But it would also seem a priori likely that third-world immigrants should have stronger family values than white, middle-class, suburban Americans, while their work ethic and willingness to defer to traditional sources of authority should be greater as well. Few of the factors that have led to family breakdown in the American middle class over the past couple of

generations—rapidly changing economic conditions, with their attendant social disruptions; the rise of feminism and the refusal of women to play traditional social roles; or the legitimization of alternative life-styles and consequent proliferation of rights and entitlements on a retail level—apply in third-world situations. Immigrants coming from traditional developing societies are likely to be poorer, less educated, and in possession of fewer skills than those from Europe, but they are also likely to have stronger family structures and moral inhibitions. Moreover, de-spite the greater ease of moving to America today than in the last century, immigrants are likely to be a self-selecting group with a much greater than average degree of energy, ambition, toughness, and adaptability.

These intuitions are largely borne out by the available empirical data, particularly if one disaggregates the different parts of the immigrant community.

263.   Roger Hernandez. "Ending Immigration Could
         Destroy American Culture." THE PHOENIX
GAZETTE, August 14, 1993, p. A8. That is going too far. But the contradictory figures should give reasonable people pause in their calls to seal the borders to all comers. An immigration moratorium based on faulty economic data would be a historical tragedy for a nation whose identity is inextricably linked with immigrants. Ending immigration, not immigrants themselves, may turn out to be what destroys American culture.

264.   Myron Weiner. IMMIGRATION AND U.S.
         FOREIGN POLICY, San Francisco:
Westview Press, 1990, p. 193. With the exception of the Indochinese, most Asians did not flee their country. They came primarily because of the superior opportunities for education and employment or to join family members. Asian Americans, to a greater extent than many Europeans who fled intolerable political, social, and economic conditions in the nineteenth and the first half of the twentieth centuries, remain attached to their cultural heritage, which has served them well in the United States. The Asian concern for family loyalty, the importance placed on education, and the emphasis on hard work and discipline have enabled Asian Americans to compete effectively. Most Asian Americans do not reject their past and are keen on transmitting their values to their children.

265.   Barry Chiswick. ILLEGAL ALIENS,
         Kalamazoo: Upjohn Institute for Employment
Research, 1988, p. 4. Research on the labor market ac-tivities of illegal aliens has been hampered by the virtual absence of systematic and reliable data. This is not surprising—illegal aliens have an incentive to avoid revealing their status to an interviewer or in a

questionnaire. As a result, anthropological or ethnographic approaches have sometimes been used by investigators. This type of research is subject to many pitfalls, including the problems inherent in small samples, selective respondents, and respondents reporting what they think the investigator wishes to hear. Others have relied on censored or preselected samples of illegal aliens, such as those who return to their home villages (Cornelius, 1976, and Diez-Canedo, 1980), have applied for social welfare benefits (Van Arsdol *et al.*, 1978), or have been apprehended (North and Houstoun, 1976). Yet with few exceptions, even these techniques have not generated adequate data for labor market analysis.

266.   Leonel Sanchez. "State Immigrants Cost $18.2 Billion in Taxes Last Year, Study Says." SAN DIEGO UNION-TRIBUNE, November 5, 1993, p. A27. Rebecca Clark, a demographer at the Urban Institute, said that estimating the economic cost and benefit of all immigrants is difficult because the necessary numbers are unavailable and leave too much room for assumption.

267.   Michael LeMay. FROM OPEN DOOR TO DUTCH DOOR, New York: Praeger Press, 1987, p. 134. Some of the confusion in this assessment is the result of using different methodologies and economic assumptions in the various analytical studies. The picture that emerges from actual jobs uncovered by INS sweeps substantiates that the impact is at the lower level of jobs and probably is concentrated in largely "undesirable" jobs. Such sweeps are, however, no doubt skewed samples of the total job displacement picture.

268.   Michael LeMay. FROM OPEN DOOR TO DUTCH DOOR, New York: Praeger Press, 1987, p. 134. Studies of the net impact of immigration on government finance are both sketchy and contradictory. A 1980 study by the Urban Institute found that California spent an average $3,254 on each Mexican immigrant household, both legal and illegal, in Los Angeles, and received only $1,515 in tax revenues in return. But a 1982-1983 study by Weintraub indicated that Texas receives about three times as much revenue from illegal aliens as it spends on them. The Rand study found that fewer than 5 percent of California's Mexican immigrants were receiving any form of public assistance in 1980. This compares to an all adult statewide figure of 12 percent. Mexican immigrants' contribution to public revenues exceeds the cost of their service usage, with the sole exception of education. The study concluded that they contributed less than the $2,900 it costs per year to educate a public school student largely because of their low income levels and the relative youth of the immigrants and their children.

269.   Sidney Weintraub. THE ILLEGAL ALIEN FROM MEXICO, Austin: University of Texas Press, 1980, p. 26. Without trying to resolve these debating points, the crux of the argument comes back to the impact of illegal immigrants on the labor market. We think it is fair to state, on the basis of the evidence available, that one can take either view (that illegals seriously adversely affect nonskilled national workers, or that the illegals mostly take jobs nationals will not take), and support the view by partial statistics. The empirical evidence, we believe, is inadequate. Following are some additional arguments relevant to this theme.

270.   Larry Rohter. "Debate Rages over Influx of Immigrants." THE DALLAS MORNING NEWS, September 26, 1993, p. 4. Once again, immigration's critics are saying that the newcomers are a burden, not a boon, over-using public services for which they do not pay taxes.

But the evidence put forth to support these assertions is questionable at best.

Unlike the first decades of the 1900s, when the nation went through a similar influx and debate about immigration, there is now a significant body of research tracking immigrants from the moment they arrive.

Most academic and government studies conclude that the presence of immigrants has some overall benefit; few say they harm the economy.

271.   Alan C. Miller. "Data Sheds Heat, Little Light, on Immigration Debate." LOS ANGELES TIMES, November 21, 1993, p. 1. Anti-immigrant sentiment in California, which is rising in tandem with the state's unemployment rate, is fed by any evidence the newcomers are taking slices out of the living standards of U.S.-born residents. But the evidence on this score, as on virtually all aspects of immigration, is at best ambiguous.

272.   Ruth Conniff. "The War on Aliens." THE PROGRESSIVE, October, 1993, p. 22. Papadimitriou authored a recent Labor Department report on the economic impacts of immigration. "The assumptions about illegal immigration are extraordinary," he says of FAIR's claims. "The analysis is geared toward making a political statement. The real experts in the field make much more guarded and nuanced statements than FAIR."

273.   Ruth Conniff. "The War on Aliens." THE PROGRESSIVE, October, 1993, p. 22. The

economic statistics cited by FAIR, and by almost every other anti-immigration group, come from a study by Dr. Donald Huddle, an economist at Rice University. Huddle's figures, which show that immigrants cost the United States $54 billion a year in social services, have been widely cited in the news as facts.

274.   Alan C. Miller. "Data Sheds Heat, Little Light, on Immigration Debate." LOS ANGELES TIMES, November 21, 1993, p. 1. The most sweeping study was Huddle's, which was released this summer. He looked at the cost to government programs of 19.3 million immigrants—legal and illegal—who arrived in the United States since 1970. He relied heavily on extrapolations from the Los Angeles County study as well as on census figures, academic research and his own controversial surveys of job displacement by immigrants.

275.   Ruth Conniff. "The War on Aliens." THE PROGRESSIVE, October, 1993, p. 22. "We've been trying to get the full report that Don Huddle did, but all we get is a kind of press kit from a group called the Carrying Capacity Network," says Dimitri Papadimitriou, a senior associate at the Carnegie Endowment for International Peace. "I cannot evaluate the figures until I see the full report."

276.   Alan C. Miller. "Data Sheds Heat, Little Light, on Immigration Debate." LOS ANGELES TIMES, November 21, 1993, p. 1. Some longtime immigration specialists dismiss Huddle's work as being anti-immigrant and outside the academic mainstream. They contend that his methodology and assumptions were skewed to drive up cost figures and hold down revenue data.

Jeffrey S. Passel, an immigration specialist with the Urban Institute, said Huddle understated tax revenues paid by immigrants by at least $50 billion—more than enough to offset his total deficit. "You end up with a plus rather than a minus," Passel said.

Passel also said Huddle omitted some tax payments—such as Social Security, unemployment insurance, and state and federal gasoline taxes—and underestimated others by understating incomes and miscalculating tax rates.

277.   Richard Simon. "1992 Cost of Immigrants $18 Billion, Report Says." LOS ANGELES TIMES, November 5, 1993, p. A3. Huddle's earlier studies on immigration also have drawn fire from immigration experts.

Angelo Ancheta, director of the Coalition for Humane Immigrant Rights of Los Angeles, said: "If you're simply looking at government outlays versus tax revenues, that's not a complete picture." He said

studies should include the contributions that immigrants make as consumers, for example.

Huddle acknowledged Thursday that this new report does not include any estimate of Social Security taxes paid by illegal immigrants. Some economists argue that many illegal immigrants have Social Security as well as federal and state income taxes withheld from their pay. Since these workers often do not file tax returns, many do not receive the refunds that legal residents would be entitled to.

278.   Alan C. Miller. "Data Sheds Heat, Little Light, on Immigration Debate." LOS ANGELES TIMES, November 21, 1993, p. 1. More disputed is Huddle's estimate that 25% of immigrants in low-skilled jobs displaced native-born American workers, thus driving up public assistance costs for the native-born by $11.9 billion. Passel and others dispute the 25% figure because Huddle overlooked the jobs and economic growth that immigrants generate by spending money and starting businesses.

279.   "Immigrants Called Drain on Services." HOUSTON CHRONICLE, November 5, 1993, p. 20. The findings issued Thursday by economist Donald L. Huddle of Rice University were challenged by immigrant rights activists.

"Every other report shows that immigrants give much more than they take," said California Assemblyman Richard Polanco, chairman of the Legislature's Latino Caucus.

The report was commissioned by a group that brings together a new coalition seeking to restrict immigration: environmentalists and population control advocates.

280.   "Immigrants Called Drain on Services." HOUSTON CHRONICLE, November 5,1993, p. 20. The findings, however, run counter to the conclusions of other studies—from RAND, the Urban Institute, and others—that immigrants generally do not compete with native-born workers for jobs and are only slightly more likely to receive public assistance than non-immigrants. Other studies also have concluded that illegal immigrants take jobs Americans will not perform, and they create other jobs by spending money in this country.

Polanco said that Huddle underestimated the taxes paid by immigrants.

281.   Roger Hernandez. "Ending Immigration Could Destroy American Culture." THE PHOENIX GAZETTE, August 14, 1993, p. A8. Then there is Huddle's study, funded by a New York-based group that calls itself the Carrying Capacity Network, a population control group, hung up on the notion that we are running out of everything. Again, it is no

surprise that their report found immigrants will make everything run out even faster.

Other studies offer conclusions 180 degrees from what Wilson and Huddle say. Julian Simon, an economist at the University of Maryland, insists that actually the average immigrant family pays $2,500 more in taxes than it takes in from government services. Writing in *The Wall Street Journal*, he said Huddle never took into account business generated by the economic activity of immigrants.

Business Week, too, took the side of immigrants, saying in an editorial, "Immigrants pay an estimated $90 billion in taxes, compared to the $5 billion in welfare they receive.

282.   Vlae Kershner. "Calculating the Cost of Immigration." THE SAN FRANCISCO CHRONICLE, June 23, 1993, p. A1. Two studies are generally cited to show the negative impact of immigrants on the California state government and local jurisdictions, although the accuracy of one of them is a matter of some dispute.

The first, by Los Angeles County, indicated that in 1991-92, the net cost of providing services to recent legal immigrants, amnesty aliens, undocumented immi-grants and citizen children of undocumented immigrants was $807 million more than the county received from them in tax revenue. In addition, immigrant children cost the country's school districts $1.84 billion—23 percent of their entire budget.

The second, commissioned by the state auditor general from a San Diego research firm, estimated that illegal immigrants in San Diego County cost state and local governments $145 million more than the immigrants contribute in taxes.

Extrapolating the results statewide, the authors concluded that undocumented immigrants cost the state and local governments $3 billion. That figure became something of a magic number after the report was released in August and is frequently quoted by those who want immigration restricted.

The study, however, has been attacked as methodologically unsound. Because it is illegal to ask about the immigration status of schoolchildren, principals were asked to estimate the number of undocumented immi-grants in their school based on how many students were enrolled in its Limited English Proficiency program. Enrollment in this program, however, has no known relationship to documentation status, according to Adele de la Torre, a professor in Chicano and Latino studies at California State University, Long Beach.

283.   Alan C. Miller. "Data Sheds Heat, Little Light, on Immigration Debate." LOS ANGELES TIMES, November 21, 1993, p. 1. Two more controversial studies were performed by Richard

A. Parker and Louis M. Rea of San Diego State on the net costs of providing services to undocumented immigrants in San Diego County.

In their initial August, 1992, study, Parker and Rea found that 200,000 illegal immigrants in San Diego County accounted for net state and local costs of $146 million annually. Assuming that the county was home to 5% of California's illegal residents and that other counties accrued similar costs and revenues, the authors pegged the statewide costs of illegal residents at $3 billion.

This was one of the figures Gallegly cited in August, well after the authors' methodology and conclusions had sparked considerable criticism.

In their second study, Parker and Rea concluded that the cost was $244 million in San Diego County and $5 billion statewide.

Many have challenged the number of illegal residents cited by the study. Other projections put the San Diego County total at 100,000 to 150,000.

And Parker's cost and revenue estimates have been challenged by various academicians. Parker's sample of illegal immigrants was particularly controversial: residents of migrant camps in his first study, augmented in his second by those found at such places as medical clinics, social service agencies, soup kitchens, detention facilities and street corners. Hans Johnson, a demographer at the California Research Bureau, said the survey would tend to find the unemployed and lower-paid immigrants. "But if you're working 60 hours a week and you make $10 an hour and you don't frequent any of the places where this survey was conducted, then you're not going to be picked up," he said.

284.   Alan C. Miller. "Data Sheds Heat, Little Light, on Immigration Debate." LOS ANGELES TIMES, November 21, 1993, p. 1. Although this study has drawn less fire than most others, it too has provoked some criticism. An analysis by the Urban Institute, a Washington think tank, found the cost estimates generally too high and the revenue estimates too low, largely because the study underestimated the immigrants' incomes.

Manuel Moreno-Evans, director of the Los Angeles County study, said most of the Urban Institute's findings generally supported the study or cited limitations that the authors had acknowledged.

"We did not include some very significant revenues that should have been included," Moreno-Evans said. "The major reason is that there hasn't really been an agreement on how to apportion them."

285.   Frank Trejo. "Debate Rates over Economic Benefits of Immigrants; Studies Conflict over Taxes Paid." THE DALLAS MORNING NEWS: NEXUS, January 3, 1994, p. 8A. Mr. Simon estimates that the typical immigrant family annually

pays more than $2,000 in taxes above what it uses in public services.

He criticized a Los Angeles County report that said immigrants contributed $139 million in 1992, while costing $947 million in services.

He said that study failed to adequately take into account the federal income taxes paid by immigrants. And Mr. Simon noted that another study by researchers for the Urban Institute found a much different result.

That study found that the deficits attributed to immigrants were exaggerated in the Los Angeles County study, and that long term, immigrants make substantial contributions to their communities.

286.   "Can We Afford So Many Unskilled Immigrants?" THE NEW YORK TIMES, January 26, 1994, p. A20. Anthony Lewis claims in "The Politics of Nativism" (column, Jan. 14) that Julian Simon showed in The Wall Street Journal last year that immigrants do not take the jobs of the native born and that the average immigrant family pays $2,500 more in taxes annually than it receives in public services.

Professor Simon and Mr. Lewis are clearly wrong on both accounts. George Borjas, a national researcher, wrote in the National Review for Dec. 13, 1993, that Mr. Simon's calculation was quite wrong. Mr. Simon has both immigrants and natives running a surplus. Since welfare programs are supposed to redistribute income from some groups to others, both cannot be running a surplus.

287.   "Can We Afford So Many Unskilled Immigrants?" THE NEW YORK TIMES, January 26, 1994, p. A20. Professor Simon's long-held belief that immigrants do not displace Americans in the labor market has been repudiated by a number of careful studies in recent years. A consensus is developing (Huddle, Altonji and Card, Walker, Ellis and Barf) that for each six to seven immigrants, one unskilled or blue-collar job is lost to Americans. As Richard Bean of the University of Texas recently showed, slow growth areas are particularly prone to labor displacement. As in California during the 1990's, many native born, according to Randy Filer in a National Bureau of Economic Research study, end up fleeing the region to avoid job losses and falling wage levels.

288.   Tom Bethell. "Immigration Si; Welfare, No." THE AMERICAN SPECTATOR, November 1993, p. 18. Supporters of immigration have long claimed that immigrants contribute more in taxes than they take in government services, and a leading exponent of this view has been Prof. Julian Simon of the University of Maryland. I have no doubt that he was right in the past—he may still be today. My concern is that his figures may now be out of date. He rebuts recent claims that immigrants take more than they give—a Los Angeles County study, another by Rice University professor emeritus Donald Huddle—with "Census Bureau data for 1970s earnings." Changes in the law since then have no doubt altered the structure of incentives, however. As Congressman Dana Rohrabacher of California put it, since the Immigration Reform and Control Act of 1986 "we have made it more risky for an illegal to apply for a regular job than to apply for government assistance."

289.   Peter Brimelow. "Time to Rethink Immigration?" NATIONAL REVIEW, June 22, 1992, p. 30. Borjas's findings, although well understood among specialists, will be surprising to many conservatives. They contrast sharply with some of Julian Simon's more familiar conclusions. The basic reason: Simon's data were old, reflecting earlier, more traditional immigrant groups—another danger in this rapidly changing area.

290.   Larry Rohter. "Debate Rages over Influx of Immigrants." THE DALLAS MORNING NEWS, September 26, 1993, p. 4. But the Federation for American Immigration Reform, citing other scholars, says that such conclusions are based on outdated assumptions. George J. Borjas, author of *Friends or Strangers: The Impact of Immigrants on the U.S. Economy* and an economics professor at the University of California at San Diego, says the new wave of immigrants is not as skilled as its predecessors.

As a result, he concludes, the newcomers are more likely to become a burden on the state than those who came before.

291.   Peter Brimelow. "Time to Rethink Immigration?" NATIONAL REVIEW, June 22, 1992, p. 30. Another important Simon qualification, unnoticed by his acolytes, is his concept of "negative human-capital externalities." Most recent immigrants have lower skill levels than natives, he notes. If enough of them were to arrive, they could overwhelm and render less effective the higher skills of the natives. "In other words, if there is a huge flood of immigrants from Backwardia to Richonia, Richonia will become economically similar to Backwardia, with loss to Richonians and little gain to immigrants from Backwardia... So even if some immigrants are beneficial, a very large number coming from poorer countries... may have the opposite effect."

This is a crucial theoretical concession. Coupled with the fact that the numbers and type of potential immigrants are unknown, it is the reason Simon quietly declines to follow the logic of his other arguments and endorse completely open borders (as, for

example, the *Wall Street Journal* editorial page has done). [ellipses in original]

292.   "Mass Immigration and the National Interest." SOUTHERN ECONOMIC JOURNAL, October 1993, p. 513. On this and some other points the reader might well look at Julian Simon's The Economic Consequences of Immigration I1 or the recent Urban Institute study, Immigrant Categories and the U.S. Job Market: Do They Make a Difference?, I2 to get alternative views. Briggs is too quick in dismissing the studies of others who find only minor adverse domestic labor markets effects as a result of the "fourth wave" of current mass immigration or who find immigration to be beneficial. Examples include his treatment in chapter 2 of Simon's work and his dismissal in chapter 7 of studies by the Rand Corporation and an earlier study by the Urban Institute.

293.   Alan C. Miller. "Data Sheds Heat, Little Light, on Immigration Debate." LOS ANGELES TIMES, November 21, 1993, p. 1. Huddle, in interviews, supported his findings as being valid and generally accurate. He said he did not consider Social Security taxes paid by immigrants because he did not include benefits collected by immigrants either.

Other taxes were excluded, Huddle said, because the amounts were small or no data was available or they were not in the Los Angeles County study. And he said any corporate tax benefits would have been outweighed by lower wages caused by immigrants, which are not included.

Huddle acknowledged some shortcomings in revenue estimates. But he insisted that the total was only $3 billion—which was more than offset by updated higher figures for benefits received by immigrants.

294.   Leonel Sanchez. "State Immigrants Cost $18.2 Billion in Taxes Last Year, Study Says." SAN DIEGO UNION-TRIBUNE, November 5, 1993, p A27. Huddle's national study was criticized by other researchers and immigrant-rights advocates as exaggerated.

Huddle said he used information from reliable sources, such as the U.S. Census Bureau and municipal governments. He used the same sources for the study he unveiled yesterday in Los Angeles that focused solely on California.

295.   Donald Huddle. "Debate Must Begin with True View of the Costs." HOUSTON CHRONICLE, 8/29/93, p. 1. It is important to realize that almost three-quarters of the above costs are incurred by legal immigrants as opposed to illegal aliens. Therefore, Gov. Wilson was wrong when he singled out illegal immigrants. In fact, newly arriving legal immigrants not only outnumber illegal

immigrants three to one, they also have higher per capita public assistance costs than do illegals—$2,940 vs. $2,103 yearly.

296.   Vernon M. Briggs. IMMIGRATION POLICY AND THE AMERICAN LABOR FORCE, Baltimore: Johns Hopkins Press, 1984, p. 260. It is also vital that the full cost of financing the adjustment of refugees to American economic life be borne by the federal government. Policies that are implemented in the name of the national interest should not impose economic hardship on any specific community or region of the nation or on any particular segment of the labor force.

297.   Frank Trejo. "Rethinking Immigration." DALLAS MORNING NEWS, January 2, 1994, p. 1A. "Immigration policy decisions are made in an isolated federal level. The problem is that the federal government does not take into consideration the local effects of those policies," Mr. Stein said, citing the 1982 Supreme Court decision that mandated public education for all children, regardless of immigration status.

Mr. Stein said the grass-roots sentiment has developed because people feel powerless, because they cannot go to their local officials to complain.

298.   Dan Stein. OPERATIONS OF THE BORDER PATROL, Hrg of the Committee on the Judiciary, House of Representatives, August 5 1992, p. 237. Use of welfare and entitlements by illegal aliens has grown in recent years. As it grows it becomes an encouragement to illegal immigration. Under current law an alien can illegally cross the border, give birth to a child in a public hospital, and acquire a variety of rights through the child, who is regarded as a U.S. citizen. Legislation is essential to clarify that U.S. citizenship is limited to the children of legal residents and to require benefit dispensing agencies to obtain information on immigration status from their clientele and share it with the INS. Not only are the benefits a causal factor in illegal immigration, they are causing a devastating impact on the taxpayers of many states and communities.

299.   Ruth Conniff. "The War on Aliens." THE PROGRESSIVE, October, 1993, p. 22. Goldfarb believes that efforts to crack down on illegal immigrants by cutting off social services will only make matters worse in California, creating an impoverished, outlaw underclass. "People need to understand the phenom-enon of global migration," she says. "Immigrants come here because of conditions in their home countries, for reasons having to do with politics, economics, and war ... No one really believes

that if we take away all their rights and services, that will change immigration." [ellipses in original]

300. Wayne Cornelius. AMERICA'S NEW IMMI-GRATION LAW, Center For US-Mexican Studies, University of California at San Diego, Monograph Series 11, 1983. The consequences of an excessive labor supply can also be understood in narrower economic terms. To be rendered productive, labor must be combined with other factors of production, the supply of which is relatively limited. The availability of some labor above and beyond the ongoing number of jobs produces downward pressure on wages and is likely to stimulate further capital investment; beyond a certain point, however, capital becomes very scarce and hence much more costly; wages reach some minimal floor; and demand for additional output peters out. Should the labor supply continue to increase beyond this point, the social costs of income transfers to the excess will mount. Borne of necessity by the productive sector (capital and employed workers), they will rise steeply on a per-capita basis. This situation is most obvious in a welfare state in which the entire population is entitled to such transfers, paid for out of taxes. But even if the excess labor is denied such benefits—as in the case of unemployed guest workers in many European countries and illegal aliens everywhere—income transfers of some sort will occur if numbers are very large.

301. Paul Glastris. "Immigration Crackdown." US NEWS & WORLD REPORT, June 21, 1993, p. 34. How this issue will be settled is unclear. During his trip to the city last month, Clinton promised Los Angeles officials relief, and liberals like Senate immigration subcommittee chief Edward Kennedy support more generous reimbursements. On the other hand, some conservatives, such as Simi Valley Republican Rep. Elton Gallegly, want a constitutional amendment to deny citizenship to children of illegal immigrants. That would make them ineligible for schooling and nonemergency health care and, Gallegly contends, would reduce the incentive for illegals to cross the border.

302. "Letters to the Editor." THE WASHINGTON TIMES, November 13, 1993, p. D2. Mr. Adelman suggests that his proposed restrictions on illegal immigrants, including reducing eligibility for government services and denying citizenship to their children born in the United States, would deter them from coming to this country. However, lack of employment opportunities in countries such as Mexico and relatively high wages and the availability of jobs in the United States, not government services, account for most immigration. As the U.S. Council of Economic Advisors concluded in 1986, "On the whole,

international migrants appear to pay their own way from a public finance standpoint. Most come to the United States to work, and government benefits do not appear to be a major attraction."

303. J. Michael Cavosie. "Defending the Golden Door: The Persistence of Ad Hoc and Ideological Decision Making in U.S. Refugee Law." INDIANA LAW JOURNAL, Vol. 67: 1992, p. 435. The philosophic underpinning of the Refugee Act of 1980—that all refugees should be treated equally—is ill-served by these recent laws. An egalitarian refugee policy need not, however, be a chimerical pursuit. The following two recommendations should suffice to bring United States policy at least somewhat closer to this goal.

304. Joan A. Pisarchik. "A Rawlsian Analysis of the Immigration Act of 1990." GEORGE-TOWN IMMIGRATION LAW JOURNAL, Vol. 6: 1993, pp. 740-741. At first glance, the lottery system appears to be a less discriminatory and less arbitrary way to determine who will be admitted to the country, compared to past policies, which focused closely on individual and group criteria. Upon closer inspection, however, the lottery is analogous in outcome to past laws although it uses a different process to achieve the result. Instead of specifically excluding certain groups, group identity is specified for those who are desired for admission. The wording of the statute is irrelevant because the result, admission of those deemed acceptable, is the same in both cases.

The 1990 Act and the lottery provision can be analyzed in the same ways in which the earlier acts have been analyzed, as a continuance of classical immigration law and restrictive nationalism. Under this analysis, the 1990 Act first will be looked at in terms of the four factors which are dominant in policy formation: economics, racial moods, nationalism, and foreign policy. Second, as a fifth category, the lottery and the tension between the lottery and the moral and ethical concerns about human migration will be explored. This focuses on the tension between public policy and liberal principles, due to the lottery's emphasis on group identity over that of the individual. Finally, the lottery will be analyzed in Rawlsian terms, using his three principles, with greater emphasis on the difference principle.

305. Joan A. Pisarchik. "A Rawlsian Analysis of the Immigration Act of 1990." GEORGETOWN IMMIGRATION LAW JOURNAL, Vol. 6: 1993, p. 742. The stringent requirements which must be met show that the lottery lacks the randomness that is usually associated with lotteries because the pool has been artificially limited, notably and expressly excluding Mexicans. The exclusion of great numbers of Mexicans, due both the numerical

limits and skill or educational requirements, means that there are proportionally more visas for persons wishing to immigrate from other areas. In addition, Europeans are likely to be better educated than many groups of potential immigrants and more likely to be already employed when they arrive in the United States. This means that those chosen through the lottery will reflect the bias in favor of educated European persons. Instead of desiring a variety of people, the lottery works to maintain uniformity of immigrants, albeit through a disguised process. The criteria and numbers of immigrants allowed per region ensure that the new immigrants will be a fairly homogeneous group resembling their predecessors.

306.   Joan A. Pisarchik. "A Rawlsian Analysis of the Immigration Act of 1990."
GEORGETOWN IMMIGRATION LAW JOURNAL, Vol. 6: 1993, p. 721. As a matter of both international and domestic law, a sovereign has the right to exclude immigrants from its territory. The procedures for exclusion vary from explicit requirements needed for admission, to delineating specific characteristics which, if possessed, will lead to automatic exclusion. In 1990, the United States employed a lottery system to award a portion of its visas. While this policy appears facially neutral, it is merely another procedure by which potential immigrants are excluded. The lottery is not open to all who seek admission. Instead, carefully tailored and highly specific statutory provisions detail those who are eligible to participate.

307.   Joan A. Pisarchik. "A Rawlsian Analysis of the Immigration Act of 1990."
GEORGETOWN IMMIGRATION LAW JOURNAL, Vol. 6: 1993, pp. 742-743. The McCarran-Walter Act prohibited the use of race as an absolute bar to immigration, but the 1990 Act seems to reflect racial considerations and tensions in border states and large cities, arising form the influx of legal and illegal immigrants from Central and South America. Moreover, the 1990 Act ignores population growth and widespread poverty in Central America, and especially in Mexico. This has been accomplished by narrowly tailoring regional definitions and groupings in the 1990 Act and then allowing the Attorney General to establish numerical limits. The non-lottery provisions of the 1990 Act provide for six regions and define them as: (1) Africa; (2) Asia; (3) Europe; (4) North America (other than Mexico); (5) Oceania; and (6) South America, Mexico, Central America, and the Caribbean. The exclusion of Mexico from the North American region and inclusion with Central and South America is highly suspect. Presumably, the preponderance of North American immigration to the United States would be from Mexico. The effect of grouping Mexico with Central and South America is to reduce

proportionately the number of Mexicans who will be able to enter the United States legally. The 1990 Act appears to have grouped the most desperate countries into the same region, thereby severely limiting immigration from them while granting more spaces to areas which are less likely to have as many people desiring to come to the U.S., such as Canada, Europe, and Oceania.

308.   Joan A. Pisarchik. "A Rawlsian Analysis of the Immigration Act of 1990."
GEORGETOWN IMMIGRATION LAW JOURNAL, Vol. 6: 1993, pp. 741-742. The 1990 Act highlights the right of the sovereign to exclude immigrants for any reason. This is the hallmark of classical immigration policy. Economics appear to be the primary motivation behind many of the provisions, especially the lottery, followed by concerns about race and nationalism. Foreign policy considerations appear insignificant, but there is little doubt that the Supreme Court would exercise deference to the legislature if any cases arise under the 1990 Act. Plenary power would seem to remain intact.

Persons wishing to immigrate under any part of the 1990 Act must meet educational requirements, possess skill and experience in some field, or have family members in the United States. Additionally, lottery applicants must have secured employment in the United States prior to admission. This excludes many people from the poorest nations who are unable to meet the requirements and are unlikely to become eligible at any time if they are forced to remain in their native countries. The reality of these requirements is that the immigrants who are eligible for admission will disproportionately reflect the total immigrant population. Only the most qualified persons, according to Western standards, will be admitted, perpetuating the notion of who is desirable and worthy of admission to the United States.

309.   Joan A. Pisarchik. "A Rawlsian Analysis of the Immigration Act of 1990."
GEORGETOWN IMMIGRATION LAW JOURNAL, Vol. 6: 1993, pp. 728-729. If immigration policies were made from behind the veil of ignorance, presumably free migration would be the rule. Those determining policy would be aware of the unequal distribution of resources, but would not know how they would be affected by it. Therefore, they would choose open immigration because they themselves might be the ones wishing to utilize it in the future.

310.   Joan A. Pisarchik. "A Rawlsian Analysis of the Immigration Act of 1990." GEORGE-TOWN IMMIGRATION LAW JOURNAL, Vol. 6: 1993, pp. 729-730. Rawls did not apply his theories

to the global scheme, however, they have been adapted for use in analyzing immigration and global migration. Under the veil of ignorance, no one knows to which society she belongs. However, one would be aware of the unequal distribution of resources and unequal levels of development. Therefore, it is plausible that one would seek a more advantaged society than the one in which she is currently residing. Rawls, *supra* note 55, at 377-82 (applying the theory of justice to nations). *See also* Whelan, *supra note* 42, at 7.

311.   Vernon M. Briggs. IMMIGRATION POLICY
         AND THE AMERICAN LABOR FORCE,
Baltimore: Johns Hopkins Press, 1984, p. 225. Teitelbaum also reverses the equity issue by pointing out that it is law-abiding persons who are actually hurt by the prevailing practices. He argues that "support for such an absolutist position implies an elemental unfairness—the full panoply of legal rights are to be granted to persons who violate the law, but similar rights of appeal are not given to others who respect the law and apply for legal entry but have not yet entered the country."

312.   Vernon M. Briggs. IMMIGRATION POLICY
         AND THE AMERICAN LABOR FORCE,
Baltimore: Johns Hopkins Press, 1984, p. 224. Surely illegal immigrants are entitled to all basic human rights, e.g., the right to humane treatment while in custody, the right of *habeas corpus*, and so no. Yet, realistically, if every technical aspect of due process, including the right of appeal right up to the Supreme Court is to be guaranteed persons walking across an open border or landing in a small boat on an unpatrolled beach, enforceable immigration laws cannot exist in a practical sense.

313.   Sandra Postel. "Carrying Capacity: The
         Earth's Bottom Line." CHALLENGE, March
1994, p. 4. As a result of our population size, consumption patterns, and technology choices, we have surpassed the planet's carrying capacity. This is plainly evident by the extent to which we are damaging and depleting natural capital. The earth's environmental assets are now insufficient to sustain both our present patterns of economic activity and the life-support systems we depend on. If currents trends in resource use continue, and if world population grows as projected, by 2020 per capita availability of rangeland will drop by 22 percent and the fish catch by 10 percent. Together, these provide much of the worlds' animal protein. The per capita area of irrigated land, which now yields about one-third of the global food harvest, will drop by 12 percent. And cropland area and forestland per person will shrink by 21 and 30 percent, respectively.

314.   Charley Reese. " Do Something About
         America's Worst Problems—Stop Immigra-

tion," THE ORLANDO SENTINEL, September 9, 1993, p. A12. Bear in mind that population must always be measured relative to the carrying capacity of the area occupied by the population. Too many people is the point beyond which the area occupied can no longer sustain life.

In the past, surplus population just migrated to a new area. We are descendants of such a migration. What destroyed the world of the Native Americans was not soldiers or congressional policies or treaties not kept—it was uncontrolled immigration. All the bad things that happened to the Native American happened because of population increase from immigration.

And now, it's our turn.

315.   Sandra Postel. "Carrying Capacity: The
         Earth's Bottom Line." CHALLENGE, March
1994, p. 4. It may be the ultimate irony that, in our efforts to make the earth yield more for ourselves, we are diminishing its ability to sustain life of all kinds—humans included. Signs of environmental constraints are now pervasive. Cropland is scarcely expanding any more, and a good portion of existing agricultural land is losing fertility. Grasslands have been overgrazed and fisheries overharvested, limiting the amount of additional food from these sources. Water bodies have suffered extensive depletion and pollution, severely restricting future food production and urban expansion. And natural forests—which help stabilize the climate, moderate water supplies, and harbor a majority of the planet's terrestrial biodiversity—continue to recede.

316.   "Perspective on Immigration." LOS AN
         GELES TIMES, April 13, 1994, p. B7.
Immigration contributes nearly 50% of U.S. population growth, considering immigrants' higher-than-average fertility rates. Every year, about 1 million immigrants enter the United States legally, while an estimated 300,000 arrive and stay illegally. The projected cost of providing universal health care to all existing Americans and legal immigrants is already alarming. Who will finance the cost of future legal immigrants and their U.S.-born children?

317.   "New Report Finds Immigration-Generated
         Population Growth." PR NEWSWIRE, Octo-
ber 19, 1992. The 64-page report titled, "Crowding Out the Future: World Population Growth, U.S. Immigration, and Pressures on Natural Resources," reveals that U.S. population growth has more than offset any environmental and conservation gains achieved in the past 20 years. The report finds that immigration will be the leading source of population growth during the 1990s.

318.   Peter Brimelow. "Time to Rethink
         Immigration?" NATIONAL REVIEW, June
22, 1992, p. 30. American liberalism has survived the loss of its traditional issue, economic management, by improvising new ones. And environmentalism is one of the most important, both because it particularly appeals to the vocal upper middle class and because it appears to necessitate an interventionist government. Yet

the single biggest problem for the environment is the fact that the U.S. population, quite unusually in the developed world, is still growing quickly. Immigration is currently an unusually large factor in U.S. population increase.

319.　Charley Reese. " Do Something About America's Worst Problems—Stop Immigration." THE ORLANDO SENTINEL, September 9, 1993, p. A12. Since we live in the United States, our first step in controlling population growth should be to stop immigration, which is the main source of U.S. population increase.

320.　Henry Ervin. "Illegal Immigration: A Heavy Burden." SAN DIEGO UNION-TRIBUNE, August 29, 1993, p. G3. Authentic immigration reform proposals with teeth in them will almost certainly draw intense fire. Proponents have been accused of racism, elitism, xenophobia or at least a chilly lack of compassion for the less fortunate. Yet through inaction or apathy we do neither our homeland's environment nor our planetary biosphere (including its human members) a favor.

In doing so, we retard the impetus behind population and economic reforms in other nations while seriously reducing the present and future basis for taking care of those who live here now, as well as their native-born descendants. Large number of immigrants, many impoverished, now enter an America ill-equipped to house or employ them adequately. They all too often become an exploited, permanent underclass.

321.　"Anti-immigration Sentiments Rising." BOSTON GLOBE, August 4, 1993, p. 4. "The prospect of easy immigration in the US…helps maintain and indeed even increases fertility rates abroad, which is exactly what we don't want to do," says David Durham, founder of Carrying Capacity Network, a research group focusing on domestic population. "We're not doing the sending countries any good by encouraging them not to look at their carrying capacity." [ellipses in original]

322.　Paul Rauber. "Cribonometry; Overpopulation and the Environment." SIERRA, p. 36. Population stability is not achieved until there is a balance of births and deaths, immigration and emigration. The 1990 Immigration Act, instead of applying the brakes as expected, actually increased immigration, which now accounts for between 30 and 50 percent of the nation's population growth (depending upon one's guess at the level of illegal entry, and on whether the immigrants' subsequent offspring are included in the total). Immigrants also have statistically higher fertility rates, partly because they tend to delay childbirth until arriving in their new home.

323.　Harold Gilliam. "Bursting At The Seams." SAN FRANCISCO CHRONICLE, February 21, 1993, p. 7. Half of the state's population increase comes from net births (the excess of births over deaths). But most of the births that increase the population are attributable to immigration.

Among non-immigrant Californians, the average birthrate in the past decade has been near the replacement level—two children per couple. Immigrants tend to have much larger families, running in some groups close to double that number.

324.　Meredith Burke. "Rising Tide of Immigration Threatens to Sink Everyone." SACRAMENTO BEE, January 7, 1993, p. B9. As illegal (and legal) immigration soared and fertility rates were pulled up by births to immigrant women (over a quarter of all births in California), the Census Bureau kept projecting that our population would peak in the year 2038, then slowly decline. Little wonder that politicians discounted the warnings of population activists of increasing political, economic and environmental stress due to immigration, the major source of U.S. population growth since 1970.

325.　Vernon M. Briggs. IMMIGRATION POLICY AND THE AMERICAN LABOR FORCE, 1984, p. 2. The 1980 census confirmed the reemergence of immigration as a critical national development. It revealed that since 1970, "the number of foreign born Americans has increased sharply after declining [each decade] since 1920" and noted that "one of every 10 people reported speaking a language other than English at home." Commenting on the emerging trend, the demographer Leon Bouvier observed in 1981: "Immigration now appears to be almost as important as fertility insofar as U.S. population growth is concerned."

326.　Hedy Weiss. "U.S. Must Help Stabilize The World's Population." CHICAGO SUN-TIMES, December 10, 1992, p. 45. The effects of such an explosion are mind-boggling. We are living in a finite space that is already plagued by problems of overpopulation and all its longterm fallout, including environmental havoc and war. Think what an increase of more than 100 million people in this country will mean in terms of such basics as housing, energy, transportation, health services, education, jobs and the environment. Consider how it will affect the sheer quality of life. And ponder how the ethnic and racial tensions that plague us now will play out when, as the census report indicates, the percentage of blacks, Hispanics and Asians increases significantly in relation to whites.

327.　Richard Mulcahy. "Feeding an Extra Billion." THE IRISH TIMES, August 3, 1992, p. 8. Whatever chance we have of reversing adverse ecological changes now, we have little hope of doing so with the world population increasing by one million every four days. Apart from the intolerable strain of such a large world population on the limited resources of the Earth, the consequences of overcrowding, unemployment, famine and destitution must lead to horrendous refugee problems and to civil strife and political insta-

bility, with the likelihood of nuclear war as a final act of the holocaust.

328.   Congressman Anthony C. Beilenson
        "Hearing on Population Growth." House Committee on Foreign Affairs, FEDERAL DOCUMENT CLEARING HOUSE CONGRESSIONAL TESTIMONY, September 22, 1993. The impact of overpopulation, combined with unsustainable patterns of consumption, is evident in mounting signs of stress on the world's environment. Under conditions of rapid population growth, renewable resources are being used faster than they can be replaced. Food production, for example lagged behind population growth in 69 out of 102 developing countries for which data are available for the period 1978 to 1989. The burgeoning of the world's population is having an enormous deleterious effect in such other environmental areas as tropical deforestation, erosion of arable land and watersheds, extinction of plant and animal species, and pollution of air, water and land.

329.   Henry Ervin. "Illegal Immigration: A Heavy
        Burden." SAN DIEGO UNION-TRIBUNE, August 29, 1993, p. G3. In late 1991 the United Nations released its first major report on overpopulation and its link to the disastrous deterioration of our global environment. This report laid out the solid scientific evidence connecting human population and consumption patterns with the ongoing environmental problems which make up our daily news.

330.   Sandra Postel. "Carrying Capacity: The
        Earth's Bottom Line." CHALLENGE, March 1994, p. 7. Moreover, a portion of any cropland gains that do occur will be offset by losses. As economies of developing countries diversify and as cities expand to accommodate population growth and migration, land is rapidly being lost to industrial development, housing, road construction, and the like. Canadian geographer Vaclav Smil estimates, for instance, that between 1957 and 1990, China's arable land diminished by at least 35 million hectares—an area equal to all the cropland in France, Germany, Denmark, and the Netherlands combined. At China's 1990 average grain yield and consumption levels, that amount of cropland could have supported some 450 million people, about 40 percent of its population.

331.   "Headline: New Study Prompts
        Environmental Group to Call for Immigration Moratorium." PR NEWSWIRE, June 3, 1993. Current levels of immigration into the United States are the highest they have been in decades, and those numbers continue to rise. Balance says to accommodate increased growth from immigration and natural increase we pave over more than a million acres of farmland annually, we are drawing down our aquifers at 25 percent faster than replacement, and we are losing topsoil 18 times faster than it is being created.

332.   Harold Gilliam. "Bursting At The Seams."
        SAN FRANCISCO CHRONICLE, February 21, 1993, p. 7. Another declining resource is topsoil. Already the exploding population has taken over hundreds of thousands of food-growing acres as cities cover the countryside. A few decades ago Los Angeles County was the top agricultural county in the United States; the sprawling city has long since preempted the available topsoil. Where once there were miles of orange groves beneath snowy mountains, there are now miles of besmogged suburbs, and the mountains are seldom visible.

Central Valley cities are Los Angelizing. From Bakersfield to Fresno to Sacramento and beyond, countless acres of priceless topsoil have been urbanized and removed from food production by the booming population.

333.   Carrie Teegardin. "Census Bureau Paints
        America's Future." THE ATLANTA JOURNAL AND CONSTITUTION, December 4, 1992, p. A1. Population growth in the United States is, in some ways, more troublesome than population growth in the rest of the world, because each American consumes so much more than people in other countries.

334.   Lincoln Chen. "Living Within Limits."
        ISSUES IN SCIENCE AND TECHNOLOGY, December 22, 1993, p. 88. In arguing that poor countries' rapid population growth is pillaging the global commons, Hardin fails to acknowledge the role played by the wealthy countries, whose more slowly growing populations consumer an ever-rising share of the world's resources and emit far higher amounts of pollution.

335.   Henry Ervin. "Illegal immigration: A Heavy
        Burden." SAN DIEGO UNION-TRIBUNE. August 29, 1993, p. G3. Although we in the United States make up less than 5 percent of the world human family, we consume nearly 30 percent of world resources. That rate of consumption more than compensates for our lesser density and lower population growth rate compared to much of the developing world. We have no reason, therefore, to be smug about our role.

336.   "Headline: New Study Prompts Environmental Group to Call for Immigration Moratorium." PR NEWSWIRE, June 3, 1993. "Everyone in the country feels the effects of overpopulation," said Nowak. "Each additional person means more garbage, more air pollution, ore congestion and more urban sprawl while we have less wilderness, less clean water, less open space and an overall declining quality of life."

337.   Lincoln Chen. "Living Within Limits."
        ISSUES IN SCIENCE AND TECHNOLOGY, December 22, 1993, p. 88. Why does Hardin emphasize population, rather than affluence or technology, as the predominant force acting upon our environment? Like a modern-day Malthus, Hardin is basi-

cally a behavioral pessimist. The human appetite for consumption, he argues, is essentially limitless. Our innate and relentless aspiration for material progress inevitably places demands on the physical resource base that cannot be met by changing patterns of consumption or technology, but only by limiting the number of people. To Hardin, it is obvious that the "per capita share of environmental riches must decrease as population numbers increase."

338.   Michael Teitelbaum. "The Population Threat." FOREIGN AFFAIRS, Winter 1993. pp. 65-66. Population growth rates are by no means the only demographic facts of foreign policy significance; at least four others deserve attention. First, populations with high fertility have a powerful and long-lived momentum for continued growth. Even if current high fertility levels declined overnight to the low levels prevailing in industrialized countries, such populations would continue to grow for another half century and would increase by 50 to 100 percent.

This momentum is a consequence of a second strategically significant characteristic of high fertility populations: a high percentage of children. Often nearly half the population consists of children, as compared to about one-fifth in low fertility settings.

Third, most high fertility societies have been experiencing exceptionally rapid urban growth rates, with large cities growing twice as fast as national populations and often doubling in size within only a decade. Mexico City, for example, is now the world's largest urban area, having increased 11-fold in 50 years: from about 1.6 million in 1940, to 5.2 million in 1960, to at least 18 million at present.

339.   Paul Rauber. "Cribonometry; overpopulation and the environment." SIERRA, p. 36. But the onset of the "Baby Boomlet" in the late 1980s popped those comfortable assumptions. Women who did not have children in their 20s turned out not to have forsworn parenthood, but only to have postponed it until their 30s or 40s. By last year the fertility rate had climbed back to 2.1, the highest in the industrialized world. Even at replacement level, the huge number of women of childbearing age—higher now than ever before—provides a "population momentum" that will not subside for at least 40 years.

340.   Lincoln Chen. "Living Within Limits." ISSUES IN SCIENCE AND TECHNOLOGY, December 22, 1993, p. 88. Even if it were desirable and doable, there is no evidence whatsoever that restricting immigration into the United States would have any effect on population growth in other countries. For one thing, immigration into the United States seems to be coming from countries that either have nearly attained replacement fertility levels (such as China) or have greatly reduced their population growth (such as Mexico and the Caribbean countries). More important, Hardin assumes the existence of a feedback loop between immigration and population growth that simply does not exist. There is no reason to believe

that developing countries would solve their population problems because outward migration is curbed.

341.   Henry Ervin. "Illegal Immigration: A Heavy Burden." SAN DIEGO UNION-TRIBUNE, August 29, 1993, p. G3. Yet legal immigration policy is only part of a much larger picture. In order to stabilize and eventually reduce total U.S. populations, we will need to take additional measures to curb illegal entry, offer substantially more family planning resources to developing nations (reducing pressure on our borders) and adopt our own comprehensive domestic blueprint for rapid stabilization.

342.   Michael D'Antonio. "Apocalypse Soon." LOS ANGELES TIMES MAGAZINE, August 29, 1993, p. 18. If the alarm sounded by Kendall, Hardin and others sounds familiar, it is because we have heard this siren before. But as the critics like to point out, 25 years have passed since Stanford ecologist Paul R. Ehrlich published "The Population Bomb," and it has yet to go off. Nearly 20 years have gone by since Donella H. Meadows, Dennis L. Meadows, Jorgen Randers and William W. Behrens III, in "The Limits to Growth," predicted that we would run out of oil in 1992. And it has been almost 200 years since Thomas Robert Malthus, the grandfather of the population prophets, predicted that humanity's number would outstrip the food supply, leading to worldwide starvation.

As far as University of Maryland economist Julian L. Simon is concerned, we should all be more than a little skeptical about the current crop of doomsayers. According to Simon, Henry Kendall is no more correct than Chicken Little. "The problem is that he is probably a total amateur with respect to the fields he's talking about," says Simon. "I wouldn't expect a physicist to know about these issues, but people from the hard sciences often can't seem to resist thinking they are experts in everything."

343.   Michael D'Antonio. "Apocalypse Soon." LOS ANGELES TIMES MAGAZINE, August 29, 1993, p. 18. Although his message may seem extreme, Kendall is not an isolated Cassandra. In the past year, thousands of elite scientists have joined what amounts to an international campaign to convince us that a global disaster is impending. Similar warnings were raised in the 1960s, '70s, and '80s, and the apocalypse never came.

344.   Michael D'Antonio. "Apocalypse Soon." LOS ANGELES TIMES MAGAZINE, August 29, 1993, p. 18. Economist Simon is similarly optimistic about the world's ability to supply a growing population with life-sustaining resources. He points out that many basic goods and services—copper, electricity, even petroleum—are less expensive and more readily available today than they were in the distant past. This is largely because of improvements in the way we find, extract, substitute for and use the Earth's wealth. Simon cites an example of this process

involving West Texas oil. In the 19th Century, some farmers were annoyed by the goo that lay so close to the surface that crops could not be grown. When it was discovered that the petroleum could be refined for high-quality fuel, landowners were able to convert a pesky problem to cash. Technological advance had made some of them rich.

345.   Marguerite Holloway. "Population Pressure." SCIENTIFIC AMERICAN, September 1992, p. 32. Although the growth rate has actually declined from about 2.0 to 1.7 percent during the past 25 years, some 97 million people will be added annually in this decade. Depending on rates of growth, current projections put global population anticipated to take place in the developing world, where 32 percent of the population is younger than 15 years—that is, just coming into childbearing years.

346.   Peter Brimelow. "Time to Rethink Immigration?" NATIONAL REVIEW, June 22, 1992, p. 30. Like the impact of immigration on native workers, the relationship between population and pollution is subtler than it looks. A primitive band of slash-and-burn agriculturists can cause more devastation than a much larger community of modern ex-urbanites with sealed sewage systems and manicured horse farms.

347.   Nathan Glazer. IMMIGRATION AND U.S. FOREIGN POLICY, San Francisco: Westview Press, 1990, p. 15. But increasingly other countries are beginning to respond to the fact that what we do on immigration affects them. Surprising as this may appear to Congress, indignant as this may make them, it is worth exploring how an area of policymaking that has been determined in the past almost entirely by domestic considerations will increasingly have to take into account considerations of foreign policy and the impact of immigration policy on our international relations. (Since it was formulated in 1953, refugee policy, in contrast to immigration policy, has been deeply affected by foreign policy concerns.)

348.   Robert Tucker. IMMIGRATION AND U.S. FOREIGN POLICY, San Francisco: Westview Press, 1990, p. 2. The view that the ethnic composition of the nation is the critical determinant in the shaping of its foreign policy was given recent expression by Nathan Glazer and Daniel P. Moynihan, who declared: "Without too much exaggeration it could be stated that the immigration process is the single most important determinant of American foreign policy. This process regulates the ethnic composition of the American electorate. Foreign policy responds to that ethnic composition. It responds to other things as well, but probably *first of all* to the primal factor of ethnicity."

349.   Nathan Glazer. IMMIGRATION AND U.S. FOREIGN POLICY, San Francisco: Westview Press, 1990, p. 19. These ethnic influences on

foreign policy have, if anything, grown, as ethnic groups are less and less inhibited by fears of disloyalty and charges of "hyphenated Americanism" from engaging in open lobbying and pressures to advance the claims of homelands or countries (such as Israel) that have become symbolic homelands. Senator Mathias might well have had in mind the involvement of his own Greek community in exerting pressure on American policy toward Greece and Turkey.

The rapid creation in the past twenty years of large new ethnic groups as a consequence of our 1965 immigration act has increased the number of ethnic players in American foreign policy. For thirty-five years, the United States could lean toward Pakistan and against India without worrying about domestic pressures— there were no Pakistanis or Indians to pressure their Congressmen. That situation has changed. A half million Asian Indians are now on the scene in the United States, their numbers growing through immigration and natural increase at a rate of more than 20,000 a year. Their leaders will undoubtedly be heard from as we debate additional military aid to Pakistan; in fifteen years, they may be as influential in shaping American policy on issues affecting the military balance between India and Pakistan as a million Greeks have been in the policy debates affecting the military balance between Greece and Turkey.

350.   Robert Tucker. IMMIGRATION AND U.S. FOREIGN POLICY, San Francisco: Westview Press, 1990, p. 8. Nor was it only the immigration of generations past that influenced U.S. postwar policy. The immigration of the 1930s and 1940s did so as well and, though difficult to measure, to a remarkable degree. This influence was due to the refugees who came to this country from Europe before, during, and immediately following the war. The measures, mostly of an ad hoc character, taken in order to deal with the growing number of refugees were the most significant part of immigration policy generally during this period, because the other aspects of immigration policy changed very little. And although the number of refugees admitted during this period was quite modest when judged by the number of immigrants—refugees included—admitted today, their impact on many aspects of U.S. life was enormous. This is generally recognized. What is perhaps less well appreciated is that this influence extended to foreign policy. Postwar thought on foreign policy was in substantial part shaped by the writings of European academics and intellectuals who had fled Europe. In general, this group argued for a much larger role for the United States in the postwar world. That larger role began with, and centered around, Europe.

351.   Nathan Glazer. IMMIGRATION AND U.S. FOREIGN POLICY, San Francisco: Westview Press, 1990, p. 21. While hardly any American, Congressman or otherwise, took note of this perturbation, in Japan the banning of Japanese immigration had an enormous impact. Not many of the Japanese elite were concerned over emigration for themselves—they

did not emigrate—nor were they concerned over the limitation of the economic prospects of poor farmers who were the chief source of emigrants; but they were outraged at the slight to Japanese honor. This crude act of racism mightily strengthened the nationalist xenophobes of Japan and weakened the nascent parliamentary and liberal regime. It was no unimportant factor in the tangled course of developments that led to war in the Pacific.

352. Robert Tucker. IMMIGRATION AND U.S. FOREIGN POLICY, San Francisco: Westview Press, 1990. pp. 2-3. A very different view is expressed by Manfred Jonas in this volume. In his examination of interwar isolationism, Jonas argues that although most historians and political scientists have generally assumed that a significant relationship exists between immigration and foreign policy, the consequences of immigration for foreign policy are difficult to document, and that the record of the interwar period "strongly suggests that the effect of immigration on policy can easily be exaggerated, and that its thrust, in any event, is both more sporadic and more complex than is often assumed."

353. Robert Tucker. IMMIGRATION AND U.S. FOREIGN POLICY, San Francisco: Westview Press, 1990, p. 11. If this projection of the immigration picture for the next two or three decades proves to be reasonably accurate, the impact of a changing ethnic composition on foreign policy will be less significant than the interwar experience appears to have been. This will be the case if only because the proportionate size of the new ethnic and racial groups cannot, with one possible exception, compare with the size of the ethnic groups that affected foreign policy in the interwar period. The Mexican immigrants apart, there is no other immigrant group that forms a cohesive entity and that is likely to be anywhere near the size, proportionately, of the ethnic groups that affected foreign policy in the interwar years. In this respect, it seems quite misleading to speculate about the impact of Hispanic or Asian immigration, assuming thereby that Hispanics or Asians, as such, may be expected to act as cohesive groups. In fact, the reasonable expectation must instead be that they will not do so any more than the Europeans acted as a group. Just as divisions arose among European ethnic groups that reflected the divisions among their respective countries of origin, so also may we expect divisions to arise, whatever their precise character, among Hispanic or Asian immigrant groups. Thus, even if the overall Hispanic and Asian immigration were greater than it is (or promises to become), its potential long-term effects on foreign policy are often markedly exaggerated by the assumption that these groups may act cohesively because they have common interests.

354. Nathan Glazer. IMMIGRATION AND U.S. FOREIGN POLICY, San Francisco: Westview Press, 1990, p. 25. This may seem highly unlikely. The assimilatory power of American society has

been enormous. The fact that the Germans are the largest immigrant ethnic component of the American population, next to the English, Welsh, and Scots, has had hardly any effect on American foreign relations. It did not prevent us from entering into two wars against Germany; if there has been an underground influence of greater sympathy with Germany in American foreign relations as a result of this large component of the American population, it has not been obvious.

355. Robert Tucker. IMMIGRATION AND U.S. FOREIGN POLICY, San Francisco: Westview Press, 1990, p. 10. It is, of course, possible that the above projection will turn out to have been quite misleading and that the numbers of Hispanics (and Asians) will be substantially larger than this projection. Still, barring developments that cannot be foreseen at this time, this seems unlikely. It may well be the case that external pressures to admit still greater numbers of immigrants, above all from the countries of the Caribbean basin, will increase. But it is equally likely that internal pressures to resist admitting even greater numbers will also increase. A standoff of sorts and the maintenance of something close to the status quo therefore seems the most plausible outcome.

356. Peter Hakim. "NAFTA...and After." CURRENT HISTORY, March 1994, p. 1. The converse, however, is not true. Approval does not by any means assure a smooth relationship with either Mexico or Latin America as a whole. Relations with Mexico, particularly, may become more acrimonious as NAFTA is implemented. The contentious issues raised in the debates in the United States over labor protection, environmental cleanup, illegal immigration, and electoral fraud will not go away.

To the contrary, NAFTA has sharply increased the visibility and salience of these and other issues in both the United States and Mexico. Advocacy groups from both sides of the border have become intensely engaged and are working together more closely than ever before. Greater United States involvement in Mexican political affairs seems inevitable. Most of the pressure for change will be directed toward Mexico and much of it will come from groups in the United States, governmental and nongovernmental. This asymmetry will itself be a potential source of conflict.

With presidential elections in Mexico scheduled for August, United States—Mexican relations may come under special strain this year. The central issues will be whether the Mexican government allows for reasonably free and fair elections, and what Washington decides to do to encourage clean elections and how it responds to anything less.

357. Peter Hakim. "NAFTA...and After." CURRENT HISTORY, March 1994, p. 1. So far the Clinton administration has conveyed an ambiguous message. On a trip to Mexico City in December, Vice President Al Gore spoke a great deal about democracy—as much or more than any previous United States leader visiting the country had ever done—but at

the same time he made no specific reference to Mexican elections or Mexican democracy. Although the opposition remains skeptical, the early statements of the official candidate of the ruling Revolutionary Institutional party (PRI), Luis Donaldo Colosio, suggest the electoral playing field may be kept more level than in the past—perhaps because Colosio appears such a sure bet to win and because of the international spotlight that NAFTA has focused on Mexico. The effects of that spotlight were evident in the Mexican government's cautious, even conciliatory approach in dealing with the New Year's Day guerrilla uprising in Chiapas state. It is still too early to assess the longer-term significance of that event, but it has shaken Mexican politics and may well create an even more open atmosphere in the conduct of the country's presidential elections.

358.   Milton Morris. IMMIGRATION—THE
        BELEAGUERED BUREAUCRACY, Washington, D.C: The Brookings Institute, 1985, p. 33. Mexico has emphasized the binational character of the issue and the need for agreement between the two countries on policies that will stem the massive flow of Mexicans crossing the southern border illegally but will not deny Mexicans legal employment in this country. Specifically, Mexico insists that U.S. immigration policy should recognize and respond to the complex economic problems that push Mexicans into this country. Although Mexican authorities have not intervened directly in the deliberations on immigration policy in Congress, the knowledge that Mexico is apprehensive about any significant curtailment of access by its nationals to this country has been a major deterrent to strong legislative or administrative action to curb illegal immigration. Moreover, the issue has been discussed at virtually every meeting of the presidents of the two countries since 1972.

359.   Sidney Weintraub. THE ILLEGAL ALIEN
        FROM MEXICO, Austin: University of Texas Press, 1980, p. 56. However, the current system does benefit many Mexicans and many more Americans than are hurt by it; and it should not be abandoned by the sort of cold-turkey attempt to cut off demand for migrants (by punishing employers) or supply (by reinforcing the border patrol) that was contemplated in the administration's proposal. Cooperative relations with Mexico require that its safety valve not be closed abruptly, but that time for adjustment be given.

360.   Nathan Glazer. IMMIGRATION AND U.S.
        FOREIGN POLICY, San Francisco: Westview Press, 1990, p. 17. Congress did not take much account of these concerns. One suspects the State Department took them more seriously, and we know that at one point in the checkered history of Simpson-Mazzoli, U.S. ambassador to Mexico John Gavin warned of its possible impact on Mexican-American relations. Congress is far more susceptible to domestic pressures, and, after all, what we do about our immigration policy might be thought to be no one's concern but our own. but is it only our concern, and will it continue to be

seen as such by the countries—and there are now many–which provide a flow of legal and illegal immigration to the United States that is of some consequence to *their* internal equilibrium?

361.   Sidney Weintraub. THE ILLEGAL ALIEN
        FROM MEXICO, Austin: University of Texas Press, 1980, p. 34. A unilateral closing of the border by the United States obviously would have repercussions on political relations with Mexico, and Mexico could face a difficult internal problem if its emigration safety valve were closed (Bustamante, 1978a).

362.   Peter Hakim. "NAFTA...and After."
        CURRENT HISTORY, March 1994, p. 1. For the past several years, while NAFTA was being negotiated, debated, and ratified, the United States had good reason to defer the development of a broader policy approach toward Latin America. As long as policy remained undefined toward Mexico, the Latin American country of overwhelmingly greatest importance to the United States, it was hard to develop an approach to the rest of the region. Now that NAFTA has been approved, and has entered into force, the challenge for the Clinton administration is to decide what kind of relationship it wants with Latin American and the Caribbean and how much it is prepared to invest in trying to build it.

363.   Abraham Lowenthal. "Healing the
        Hemisphere." THE RECORDER, April 9, 1993, p. 8. If Latin America's advances of the past five years can be fortified and if cooperative inter-American programs can be built, the United States stands to gain expanded exports and other economic opportunities, some alleviation of immigration pressures, improved international cooperation to resolve key problems, and a better prospect for the success of core U.S. values. Latin America's potential for partnerships with the United States is greater than ever.

364.   Peter Hakim. "NAFTA...and After."
        CURRENT HISTORY, March 1994, p. 1. With new presidents scheduled to take office this year in most Latin American countries—including Brazil, Mexico, Colombia, Venezuela, Chile, and four of five Central American nations—important transformations could surely take place in the region. Yet it is hard to recall a time when the United States has had a more favorable opportunity to shape, with its own policy choices, the future of hemispheric relations. The United States clearly has differences and disagreements over many issues with many Latin American governments, but has no serious clashes or impending confrontations with any of them.

365.   Peter Hakim. "NAFTA...and After."
        CURRENT HISTORY, March 1994, p. 1. Despite these acknowledged advantages, the Clinton administration did not engage in much hemispheric community-building in 1993. Indeed, aside from responding to crises or near-crises in Haiti, Guatemala, and a few other countries, the administration down-

411

played Latin America. By and large, senior policymakers stayed away from the region, and rarely mentioned it in their speeches. The most creative regional program, the Enterprise for the Americas Initiative, which had been initiated by the Bush administration, was deemphasized.

The Clinton administration's approach to Latin America mirrored its more general difficulty in defining and organizing its foreign policy agenda. The president did not travel to the region, but neither did he visit Europe. Latin American policy, moreover, was hostage to NAFTA. Until NAFTA's fate was settled, nothing much could be done to devise a longer-term strategy toward Latin America and the Caribbean.

366.   Peter Hakim. "NAFTA...and After."
        CURRENT HISTORY, March 1994, p. 1.
During the six months it took to negotiate the side pacts, the opposition was able to mobilize an impressive public campaign against the accord. Critics managed to set the terms of the debate, and for most of the year administration advocates found themselves on the defensive. It required an extraordinary eleventh-hour lobbying effort with the intense involvement of both the president and vice president to get a favorable vote on NAFTA in the House of Representatives. But by exercising visible leadership on the issue and achieving a strong come-from-behind victory, Clinton succeeded in erasing any doubts about his own commitment to the agreement. His administration's stock rose considerably in Latin America.

367.   Robert Tucker. IMMIGRATION AND U.S.
        FOREIGN POLICY, San Francisco: Westview Press, 1990, p. 10. The question raised at the outset may be repeated: What will be the long-term effects of the second great immigration on U.S. foreign policy? The answer will depend in the first instance on the magnitude of change in ethnic composition that has already occurred and that may be expected in the years to come. In 1987, the Census Bureau reported the U.S. racial and ethnic composition as follows: white non-Hispanic, 77.6 percent; black, 12.1 percent; Hispanic, 7.9 percent; Asian and other, 2.4 percent. At the same time, the bureau projected the following composition for 2020: white non-Hispanic, 69.5 percent; black, 14.3 percent; Hispanic, 11.1 percent; Asian and other, 5.0 percent. The projection for 2020 assumes the persistence of the present annual rate of immigration (both legal and illegal), roughly the same proportions by regions, and fertility rates of resident and immigrant populations that converge at the present low level (1.9) of the resident population. It is on the basis of these assumptions, then that the proportion of the Hispanic and Asian population will increase from approximately 10 to 11 percent today to an estimated 16 percent in 2020.

368.   Robert Tucker. IMMIGRATION AND U.S.
        FOREIGN POLICY, San Francisco: Westview Press, 1990, p. 12-13. These considerations point to the prospect that the prevailing immigration will

contribute to a more active foreign policy in Latin America and Asia. A changing ethnic composition is occurring today in circumstances that are very different from the circumstances that marked the first great immigration. The first was attended by a foreign policy of isolation, which was in part a response to the circumstance of this earlier migration of European peoples. The second is attended by an activist and interventionist foreign policy, which was well formed before the recent immigration began. And whereas the status of immigrants once discouraged efforts by ethnic groups to influence foreign policy, today the constraints formerly imposed on the "hyphenates" have virtually disappeared. That change has paralleled the change in the status of ethnicity itself from being something to overcome as quickly as possible to something that enjoys a growing measure of toleration and that is, in time, even a cause for celebration.

An interventionist foreign policy and the growth of ethnic groups at home that are no longer bound by many of the constraints of the past need not prove compatible. In certain circumstances, they might even conflict. In the given circumstances, however, it is more likely they will cooperate and serve to reinforce each other. A pre-existing disposition of administrations not only to pursue the cause of human rights but, increasingly, to make human rights almost the centerpiece of policy is likely to be given added momentum by ethnic groups that, on the whole, can be expected to champion the same cause in their respective countries of origin. The intensity with which they may do so will, of course, depend on the circumstances marking their migration to this country, as well as the nature of the relationship between the United States and their home country. Even so, the general expectation must be that they will have an interest in the human rights situation in their home country and that this interest will, on balance, reinforce what has become a basic interest and goal of U.S. foreign policy.

Thus, the broad effect for foreign policy of the second immigration is likely to be the opposite of that of the first, at least when judged in terms of substantive policy. When judged in other terms, however, the two immigrations appear similar in their effects, because in both it is the prevailing foreign policy that is given (or is likely to be given) support.

369.   Robert Tucker. IMMIGRATION AND U.S.
        FOREIGN POLICY, San Francisco: Westview Press, 1990, p. 1. The changed composition of the present immigration must be added to these considerations. Historically, Europe was the source of nearly all immigrants admitted to the United States. Until World War I, it provided almost 9 out of every 10 of the nation's immigrants, with Latin America and Asia seldom contributing more than 8 percent. Today, these proportions are almost exactly reversed, with Europe providing roughly 10 percent of immigrants and Asia and Latin America making up almost 85 percent of the total. And it is unlikely that these proportions will change markedly in the foreseeable future. Although it is expected that the rapid rise in Asian immigration rel-

ative to Latin American immigration will decline, the predominance of Latin America and Asia as the principal sources of future immigrants is expected to persist.

370. Robert Bach. IMMIGRATION AND U.S. FOREIGN POLICY, San Francisco: Westview Press, 1990. p 123. A first step toward answering these questions involves recognizing that, whatever the impact of regional migration on the United States, its effect on the sending country is far greater. Consider, for instance, the numerical impact on the sending country. In 1980, the *total foreign-born population* in the United States amounted to only 6.2 percent of the U.S. population. A similar or even larger share of any one sending country's population, however, has migrated to the United States. Furthermore, the sources of immigration to the United States are distributed among many countries, but for most sending countries, the United States is the sole destination. As a result, fluctuations in U.S. immigration policies may appear—inside the United States—as minor regulatory adjustments; to sending countries the impact of such fluctuations may be substantial. Recent passage of the Simpson-Rodino Immigration Reform and Control Act of 1986, for example, is perceived in Latin America and the Caribbean as a unilateral imposition on their relations with the United States. This is particularly true in Mexico, where U.S. immigration reform has long been a major issue of bilateral concern.

371. Peter Hakim. "NAFTA...and After." CURRENT HISTORY, March 1994, p. 1. Most Latin American governments want the United States to take more initiative in inter-American affairs. and since NAFTA was approved, administration officials are acting like they want to assume greater leadership, as signaled by the vice president's call for a regional summit, repeated statements about forging additional free trade pacts, and frequent reiteration of the idea of hemispheric community. The administration must choose whether to proceed cautiously—on a bilateral, case-by-case basis—or to move more boldly and imaginatively toward a genuinely multilateral, "community-building" approach.

372. Abraham Lowenthal. "Healing the Hemisphere." THE RECORDER, April 9, 1993, p. 8. The American public will not support closer economic ties with Mexico or the rest of Latin America if the United States fails to confront its accumulated domestic agenda. A key question in the 1990s, in effect, is whether the United States itself is ready for inter-American partnership.

373. Abraham Lowenthal. "Healing the Hemisphere." THE RECORDER, April 9, 1993, p. 8. The chances for positive U.S. policies to reinforce Latin American progress and thereby advance U.S. aims depend, however, on revitalizing U.S. economy. The United States cannot successfully implement NAFTA or help build a wider hemispheric economic community if it does not at the same time rejuvenate

its decaying infrastructure, upgrade its technology, enhance the skills of its work force, retrain displaced workers, and assist uncompetitive industries and their communities to adjust to change.

374. Sergio Diaz-Briquets and Sidney Weintraub. MIGRATION IMPACTS OF TRADE AND FOREIGN INVESTMENT: MEXICO AND CARIBBEAN BASIN COUNTRIES. Series on Development and International Migration in Mexico, Central America, and the Caribbean Basin, Vol. 3: 1991, p. xiii. The conclusion that it requires continued economic growth to have a meaningful influence on curtailing emigration has as its corollary that the "cooperative" U.S. policy contained in the Commission's mandate must also be sustained. Although development is essentially an internal responsibility, and Mexico and other countries in the region are taking many needed steps to restructure their economies, the external environment plays a decisive role.

375. Abraham Lowenthal. "Healing the Hemisphere." THE RECORDER, April 9, 1993, p. 8. A third significance of Latin America today is as a prime arena—together with the former Soviet Union and the countries of eastern and central Europe—for the core U.S. values of democrative governance and free market economics. As both democracy and capitalism are severely challenged in the former communist countries, the worldwide appeal and credibility of these ideas may depend importantly on whether our nearest neighbors can make them work.

376. Abraham Lowenthal. "Healing the Hemisphere." THE RECORDER, April 9, 1993, p. 8. Latin America's first significance for the United States is economic. As Latin American countries emerge from recession, the region has once again become the fastest growing market for U.S. exports, as it was in the 1970s. Latin America bought more than $65 billion of U.S. exports in 1992, more than Japan or Germany, and the rate of increase in U.S. exports to Latin America for the last two years has been three times as great as that for all other regions.

Latin America's importance as an export market is all the greater at a time when U.S. dependence on trade has increased and regaining export competitiveness for U.S. firms are also expanding, as prospects for recovery and enlarged markets make Latin America attractive and as investors realize that the region's combination of resources, infrastructure, an educated work force and long experience with market economies make it a better bet than the former communist countries. Latin America also remains the source of nearly 30 percent of U.S. petroleum imports, and several U.S. money center banks still make a significant share of their income in the region.

377. Abraham Lowenthal. "Healing the Hemisphere." THE RECORDER, April 9, 1993, p. 8. Latin America's second importance is its effect on major problems facing American society. The

most dramatic example is narcotics. Latin American countries supply almost all the cocaine, most of the marijuana and an increasing share of the heroin that enters the United States. Although the drug curse can ultimately be reduced only by cutting domestic demand, an effective anti-narcotics campaign will also require enduring cooperation from the Latin American nations where narcotics are cultivated, processed and trafficked. As the site of some of the world's largest rain forests and as leading destroyers of them during the last few years, Latin American countries are also central actors on environmental issues and crucial test cases of the prospects for sustainable development policies.

378.   Robert Bach. IMMIGRATION AND U.S.
         FOREIGN POLICY, San Francisco: West-
view Press, 1990. p 138. In the Haitian and Cuban situations, in addition to the problem of regulation, there was also a strong desire to prevent entire groups from coming to the United States. In the Mariel case, this concern was heightened by the alleged criminal backgrounds of many of those placed on the boats. In the Haitian situation, the problem was to find a foreign policy position that would permit the new arrivals to be treated as refugees without contradicting the vigorous human rights position of the Carter administration.

379.   Stephen Handelman. "Tight Immigration
         Hurts Global Stability." TORONTO STAR,
January 24, 1993, p. F3. But the new, narrow approach to immigration has sharply changed the global landscape.
     If it has not eased the economic pressure on industrialized economies, it has nevertheless increased political tensions. Those refugees whose departure might once have helped relieve the pressure-cooker atmosphere in their home countries now contribute to the tensions which create civil wars and upheavals.

380.   Ranee K. L. Panjabi "The Global Refugee
         Crisis: A Search for Solutions." CALIFOR-
NIA WESTERN INTERNATIONAL LAW JOUR-
NAL, Vol. 21, no. 2: 1990-1991, p. 247. Those of us who enjoy the comforts of secure homes, safe countries and economic well-being have to resolve the problem of the homeless lest it engulf our own lifestyle. It is not solely a matter of charitable humanitarian concern. It is a question of self-interest and self-preservation. It would be a tragic mistake for us to assume that this is really not our problem. Throwing aid money at the crisis will certainly not decrease its intensity, however much it may satisfy our own consciences. Serious international efforts have to be made to create a secure, financially stable life for the millions of frightened, deprived men, women and children in Third World nations. Without this coordinated, dedicated effort on a global scale, the democratic way of life so prized in North America and Western Europe, and the relative economic comfort of a considerable proportion of the population, will have little chance of survival.

381.   Klaus Fuchs. "Agenda for Tomorrow."
         ANNALS OF THE AMERICAN
ACADEMY OF POLITICAL SCIENCE, November 1993, p. 170. Restrictionists also argue that the number of refugees admitted should be sharply reduced from its recent current annual average of around 120,000. FAIR makes the case that current refugee policy is driven to a large extent by domestic politics and foreign policy a conclusion with which few would disagree. FAIR also points out that it is much less expensive for the United States to help support refugees in the other countries than it is to admit them. Perhaps that obligation to take large numbers from the former Soviet Union and Southeast Asia will lessen in the 1990s; they accounted for more than half of those adjusting their status in 1991. But in a world where the United States is attempting to encourage other countries to accept the oppressed victims of ethnic and tribal strife, it is not in a position to make substantial cuts in refugee admissions. Mounting pressures on Europeans to admit refugees from Bosnia-Herzogovina, Azerbaijan, Georgia, Iraq, Iran, and other killing fields will keep the pressure on the United States to accept its fair share. In a world of tremendous uncertainty and resurgent violent nationalisms, it is highly unlikely that the United States will reduce refugee admissions below the 50,000 normal annual flow contemplated by the Refugee Act of 1980. In the meantime, recent refugee admissions dictate that for the next six or seven years, the number of those already in the United States who adjust their status to that of immigrant will average at least 100,000.

382.   Susan George. THE DEBT BOOMERANG:
         HOW THIRD WORLD DEBT HARMS US
ALL, 1992, p. ii. Clearly, the economic policies imposed on debtors by the major multilateral agencies—policies packaged under the general heading of "structural adjustment"—have cured nothing at all. They have, rather, caused untold human suffering and widespread environmental destruction while simultaneously emptying debtor countries of their resources; rendering them each year less able to service their debts, let alone invest in economic and human recovery. The World Bank and the IMF structural adjusters have now had a generous period to impose their plans and cannot complain that their measures have not been given enough time to work. Had these public debt-management officials been corporate executives, with so little to show for themselves, their shareholders would have doubtless sacked them long ago for incompetence. Had they been politicians, they would have been trounced at election time and sent back to where they came from.

383.   Susan George. THE DEBT BOOMERANG:
         HOW THIRD WORLD DEBT HARMS US
ALL, 1992, p. iv. So long as the policies of the rich North represent a mixture of crude carrot-and-stick manœuvres, coupled with basic contempt for the South, its problems and its peoples, we can expect more lethal North-South tensions, more powerful

boomerangs hurtling back at us, a further forced retreat of the rich countries into Fortress America and Fortress Europe. Or we can decide that it is time—high time—we began to live together on this improbable planet as *homo sapiens* a good deal more *sapiens*.

384.   Susan George. THE DEBT BOOMERANG:
         HOW THIRD WORLD DEBT HARMS US
ALL, 1992, p. 28. If we hope to stop the flight of the environmental boomerang, profound change in present debt management policy is the necessary-although not sufficient—condition. We believe debt relief should be combined with measures preventing a return to the same destructive policies that set the infernal machine going in the first place. The most urgent task is to break with the terrible logic of the twentieth-century 'development' model—energy- and resource-intensive, as exploitative of people as it is of their environment.

385.   Susan George. THE DEBT BOOMERANG:
         HOW THIRD WORLD DEBT HARMS US
ALL, 1992, p. 3. Export orientation encourages not only industrial-scale agriculture but also the granting of huge timber and mining concessions, geared to short-term profit with not thought for conserving natural resources. Such concentration of wealth and advantage in few hands leads directly to disregard for the environment, as it leads to poverty and marginalization for the majority. And poverty, too, poses a grave threat to ecological balance. In country after country undergoing structural adjustment, poor people have become poorer still. The survival strategies they are forced to adopt place further pressures on the severely limited, fragile resource bases left at their disposal.

386.   Sergio Diaz-Briquets and Sidney Weintraub.
         MIGRATION IMPACTS OF TRADE AND
FOREIGN INVESTMENT: MEXICO AND
CARIBBEAN BASIN COUNTRIES. Series on
Development and International Migration in Mexico,
Central America, and the Caribbean Basin, Vol. 3:
1991, p. x. There thus remains only one feasible
option—short of leaving bad enough alone and letting
those who wish to come do so—and that is to foster
the economic development of those countries that send
the bulk of undocumented migrants to the United
States. If punishment is not the solution, then perhaps
development is.

387.   Reginald T. Appleyard. INTERNATIONAL
         MIGRATION: CHALLENGE FOR THE
NINETIES, 1991, p. 32. While development would, in
many respects, be a self-serving option for the North,
it is the only viable approach to resolving the North-
South dilemma, including those inequalities that are
legacies of past policies. Raising immigration barriers
alone is no durable solution for, in the absence of a de-
velopmental strategy, income differentials would continue to widen and emigration pressures increase.
Without carefully-planned development, there will almost certainly be a deterioration in the physical environments of many developing countries. The human

environment in many countries of the South is already unsustainable. Rural poverty in Africa and Asia has doubled since 1950. Together with population pressures, it often forces people to cultivate even more marginal lands which further erodes thin soil and depletes shallow water resources. Nearly one billion people already live on drylands being affected by increasing desertification. Lack of water has forced people to move; according to Sadik an estimated 1.7 billion people, spread among 80 countries, are already suffering water shortages. Contrariwise, over-abundance of water, often caused by deforestation of upland watersheds, can and has caused severe floods in lowland regions/countries such as Bangladesh.

388.   Reginald T. Appleyard. INTERNATIONAL
         MIGRATION: CHALLENGE FOR THE
NINETIES, 1991, p. 77. In the absence of appropriate global economic policies which address the enormous income gap between North and South, problems that are symptomatic of the dilemma are unlikely to be resolved. The number of asylum seekers and illegal migrants will therefore almost certainly increase. The propensity for receiving-governments to look for solutions through tighter border controls or through deportation if applications have been rejected, is understandable. But the asylum-seeker/illegal issue will only be resolved by tackling the situations that largely caused it to occur. Widgren has called for new policies to address the current influx of asylum seekers in OECD European countries and has warned that, in their absence, the number could well exceed the number of regular migrants within a few years. Time is running out, he wrote, and solutions are urgently needed to avoid breakdown of the whole institution of asylum. Tighter border controls or annual quotas are directed towards stabilising and controlling the recent rapid increase in numbers; they are not directed towards long-term solutions. Asylum seekers have exploited loopholes in the formal immigration regulations because those regulations prevented their entry.

389.   Reginald T. Appleyard. INTERNATIONAL
         MIGRATION: CHALLENGE FOR THE
NINETIES, 1991, p. 78. In citing Africa as a major problem area, Papademetriou argued that it will be only in policies that address the less-developed societies populations' need for survival, as well as aspirations for economic mobility, that progress towards the long-term control of unauthorised migration can be made. And Tapinos put the issue well when he observed that the impact of international co-operation as an alternative to emigration, at least has the merit of highlighting the fact that the problem of migration is *secondary* to that of development. Development, he claimed, is the only path possible in the longer term.

390.   Reginald T. Appleyard. INTERNATIONAL
         MIGRATION: CHALLENGE FOR THE
NINETIES, 1991, p. 82. Maintaining the *status quo* is the best way to invite the next wave of international migration into the OECD countries which, in turn,

would further stimulate extreme political reactions. What is needed is an *active* policy with respect to international migration and not just a passive *ad hoc* reaction to events as they materialise. A comprehensive development strategy in which international migration is assigned a specific role, represents the most promising direction.

391.   Reginald T. Appleyard. INTERNATIONAL MIGRATION: CHALLENGE FOR THE NINETIES, 1991, p. 77. The Swedish Study Group is one of the few to have carefully studied and then proposed viable long-term solutions to the asylum seeker/illegal and refugee problems. Calling for a holistic approach to the North-South dilemma, the Group proposed that government foreign policy should be *co-ordinated* to encompass development co-operation, refugee and immigration policies. New mechanisms and new solutions to migratory pressures from the Third World countries should be directed towards facilitating the economic and social development of those countries. Indeed, migratory movements could well be stimulated by development programmes without forcing migrants into the "asylum fold."

392.   Nancy Roman. "Policy on Haiti Latest Chapter in Immigration Debate." THE WASHINGTON TIMES, January 17, 1993, p. A6. Mexico would have to expand its job base by an estimated 10 percent annually to keep up with its burgeoning population. The North American Free Trade Agreement, which facilitates the flow of labor across borders, is expected to send millions of Mexicans to the United States.

393.   Sergio Diaz-Briquets and Sidney Weintraub. MIGRATION IMPACTS OF TRADE AND FOREIGN INVESTMENT: MEXICO AND CARIBBEAN BASIN COUNTRIES. Series on Development and International Migration in Mexico, Central America, and the Caribbean Basin, Vol. 3: 1991, p. xiii. The importance of sustaining economic growth over some unquantifiable time period must be emphasized. What we found in study after study was that a short-term increase in income, over one or two years, leads to increased emigration. We came across no study that contradicted this finding. The reason, presumably, is that a modest increase in income makes it possible for people to afford the trip. If, as in the Mexican case, income per person increases by, say, 3 percent after inflation, this adds only $57 to the annual income of the average Mexican. Even this overstates the case; the "average" Mexican, some 50 percent of the population, earns much less than $1,000 a year. An increase in income of $57 or less is not enough to deter the economic incentive to emigrate. But adding 3 percent a year, compounded over 10 or 20 years, might make a difference.

394.   Milton Morris. IMMIGRATION—THE BELEAGUERED BUREAUCRACY, Washington, D.C.: The Brookings Institute, 1985, p. 69.

Mexico is a prime example of a country in which rapid population growth alongside limited economic opportunities has created intense migration pressures. Mexico's annual average growth rate was 0.9 percent between 1910 and 1940, but it shot up to 2.7 percent during 1941-50 and reached an alarming 3.4 percent in 1970; at that rate the country's population would have doubled in about twenty-one years. In 1972 the Mexican government abandoned its pronatalist policies and launched a major family planning effort that yielded impressive results by the end of the 1970s. Although the average for the decade was still up around 3.3 percent, by 1979 the growth rate reportedly had fallen to 2.7 percent.

395.   Milton Morris. IMMIGRATION—THE BELEAGUERED BUREAUCRACY, Washington, D.C: The Brookings Institute, 1985, p. 65. The relationship between economic development and migration is not entirely clear. However, a substantial body of research has suggested that rapid economic development is highly disruptive and forces people to abandon traditional values and life-styles for new ones, replacing much of the labor-intensive modes of production with capital-intensive production and thereby displacing many workers. Accordingly, those who are able to find employment will have increased earnings and thus will be able to afford to emigrate. Economic development also brings with it improved communications, transportation facilities, rapid population growth, rapid urbanization, and heightened public aspirations.

396.   Cesar Conda. "A Flood of Immigration Would Be Cut Sharply by Freer Flow of Trade." SAN DIEGO UNION-TRIBUNE, September 19, 1993, p. G5. These critics couldn't be more wrong; NAFTA is, in fact, a long-term remedy to the problem of illegal Mexican immigration into the United States.

People leave Mexico for one simple reason: Lack of opportunity. The dual forces of "supply-push"—low wages and scarcity of jobs in Mexico—and "demand-pull," relatively higher wages and the abundance of low-skilled, entry-level jobs in the United States—have propelled millions of Mexicans north of the border. The only way to diminish these migratory pressures is to promote economic growth, new and better jobs, and rising wages rates in Mexico. NAFTA would accomplish each of these goals by stimulating a Mexican trade and investment boom. Consider these estimates by the Washington-based Institute for International Economics:

• Economic growth rates in Mexico under the free trade pact could reach as high as 6 percent a year over the next decade.

• This economic expansion will produce an estimated 600,000 new jobs in Mexico over the next ten years, adding 2 percent to total Mexican employment. Mexican wages could rise as much as 16 percent over the next several years.

397.   Cesar Conda. "A Flood of Immigration Would
        Be Cut Sharply by Freer Flow of Trade."
SAN DIEGO UNION-TRIBUNE, September 19, 1993,
p. G5. Indeed, historical evidence suggests a significant
inverse relationship between the rate of economic
growth in Mexico and migratory pressures as measured
by the number of apprehensions at the U.S.-Mexico
border.

Between 1978 and 1981, annual real growth in Mexico averaged a healthy 8.8 percent and, as a result, border apprehensions dropped from a high of 1 million in
1979 to about 840,000 in 1980-81. During 1982-83,
the world-wide recession and commodity price deflation
led to a collapse of the Mexican economy, sending border apprehensions back up to 1.2 million in 1983.
While the Mexican economy recovered somewhat in
1984, it nosedived again in 1986 and apprehensions
soared to a record 1.7 million that year.

The message is clear: A stronger Mexican economy
encourages Mexicans to stay at home. And, as the bi-
partisan Immigration Reform Commission created by
Congress in 1990 concluded, "expanded trade between
the sending countries and the U.S. is the single most
important long-run remedy to the problem."

398.   Vernon M. Briggs. IMMIGRATION POLICY
        AND THE AMERICAN LABOR FORCE,
Baltimore: Johns Hopkins Press, 1984, p. 177. The
United States should carefully reassess its trade and tariff policies that pertain to Mexico and the entire
Caribbean Basin. Efforts to lower the restrictive trade
barriers that presently apply to agricultural and manufacturing imports from these countries are essential.
Such actions would enhance the opportunities for the
export industries of these nations to expand and would
reduce some to the pressures that presently lead to illegal immigration. They would also serve to acknowledge the fact that Mexico in particular, and many other
nations of this region in general, are already major im-
porters of U.S.-made goods.

399.   Sergio Diaz-Briquets and Sidney Weintraub.
        MIGRATION IMPACTS OF TRADE AND
FOREIGN INVESTMENT: MEXICO AND
CARIBBEAN BASIN COUNTRIES, Series on Development and International Migration in Mexico, Central
America, and the Caribbean Basin, Vol. 3: 1991,
p. xii. The saving grace is that incomes do not have to
be identical to act as a deterrent to clandestine
migration. There is a natural desire of most persons to
remain at home, which can be reinforced if economic
hope is offered to would-be migrants and their children.
We suspect, based on the research contained in the
series, that absolute income differentials may matter
less in the migrate-stay calculus than the direction of
economic hope (that is, whether economic conditions
at home are improving or deteriorating). We are not
referring here to improved economic conditions for one
year or two, but sustained over a decade or two.

400.   Cesar Conda. "A Flood of Immigration Would
        Be Cut Sharply by Freer Flow of Trade."

SAN DIEGO UNION-TRIBUNE, September 19, 1993,
p. G5. The critics argue, however, that Mexicans will
continue to seek jobs in the United States because it
will take years, perhaps decades, for NAFTA to close the
current gap in wage rates between the two nations. But,
as the experience of free trade in Europe demonstrates,
wage rates in an immigrant-sending country must simply rise in relation to, and not necessarily equalize
with, that of the immigrant-recipient country in order
to convince people to stay home.

401.   Cesar Conda. "A Flood of Immigration Would
        Be Cut Sharply by Freer Flow of Trade."
SAN DIEGO UNION-TRIBUNE, September 19, 1993,
p. G5. In the short-term, however, NAFTA is likely to
have what international trade economists refer to as the
"J-Curve effect" on Mexico-to-U.S. migration, initially
increasing and subsequently decreasing it. Opening certain import-sensitive Mexican agricultural markets to
U.S. growers would displace thousands of rural Mexican workers, many of whom would migrate to the
United States for jobs. However, a study done for the
World Bank by Levy and Van Winbergen predicts a net
labor release of only 145,000 rural workers out of a total rural work force of 6 million because NAFTA phases
in the tariff reductions for Mexican corn and beans over
15 years. And as the market-oriented reforms of President Carlos Salinas de Gortari take hold and the economy moves into higher gear under NAFTA, these displaced workers would soon be reemployed in new, productive, private sector jobs in Mexico.

402.   Richard Rothstein. "Immigration Dilemmas."
        DISSENT, Fall 1993, p. 457. Today, the ra-
tio of U.S. to Mexican wages is about seven to one,
and the ratio of living standards (measured purchasing
power) is about three to one. As this gap narrows, economic growth and development in Mexico will initially stimulate *increased* emigration to the United
States.

403.   Jorge Castenada. "Can NAFTA Change
        Mexico?" FOREIGN AFFAIRS, Spring
1993, p. 74. While it was hoped that NAFTA would address many of these problems, it has not defused the
end-of-term crisis that Mexico's succession process has
traditionally generated. Granted, the government's expectations, however inaccurate or overblown, touched a
receptive chord among large sectors of the population.
Polls repeatedly indicate strong support for NAFTA, as
well as unfounded reasons for it: a recent survey found
that 45.8 percent of those interviewed believed NAFTA
would make it easier for Mexicans to get jobs in the
United States. Similarly, it has created illusions in the
United States that it would help stem Mexican immigration. Most immigration scholars in both countries
expect NAFTA and the economic policies it will encourage in Mexico to stimulate migratory flows in the
short run, as displaced peasants and laid-off employees
take advantage of large wage differentials and head
north.

404. Jorge Castenada. "Can NAFTA Change Mexico?" FOREIGN AFFAIRS, Spring 1993, p. 66. Overlooked, however, has been the fact that NAFTA itself entails great risks. No country has ever attempted to develop an export manufacturing base by opening its borders so quickly and indiscriminately to more efficient and lower-cost producers. No nation today, not even in the United States, has so willingly sacrificed an industrial policy or an equivalent form of managed trade. By unilaterally renouncing these advantages, Mexico will lose far more jobs in the next few years than it will create. Old industries and agricultural producers will die, be swallowed up or join with foreign ventures, long before the new jobs arrive.

405. Susan George. THE DEBT BOOMERANG: HOW THIRD WORLD DEBT HARMS US ALL, 1992, p. 31. Equally urgent is the task of addressing the US administration's obsession with "free trade," whether for the Western hemisphere through various regional agreements, or for the globe through GATT (General Agreement on Tariffs and Trade). In part, these negotiations are intended to sidetrack debt reduction proposals. They offer indebted country governments the carrot of increased investment and access to Northern markets in exchange for continued docility in playing the debt repayment game. "Free trade" sounds, perhaps, fair and democratic but will inevitably place further strains on the environment and on working people everywhere. All countries must compete to offer the most attractive, least regulated conditions to transnational corporations. "Free trade" is an invitation to multiply *maquiladoras*, based on lowest common denominators.

406. Richard Rothstein. "Immigration Dilemmas." DISSENT, Fall 1993, p. 461. One important reform would be a Mexican development program that goes beyond free trade. If we truly want less Mexican immigration, persuading the Mexican government to slow its agricultural liberalization would be one approach. Failing that, we could underwrite a targeted industrial policy in Mexico, which, in violation of free trade rules, would subsidize the development of small industries in rural areas where peasants are being displaced. Funds spent in this way might be more effective than hiring more border patrol agents.

407. Jorge Castenada. "Can NAFTA Change Mexico?" FOREIGN AFFAIRS, Spring 1993, p. 68. Any Mexican government's performance, as well as the virtues of a new relationship with the United States, must be measured against this background. Under certain conditions, NAFTA provides an opportunity to build a more prosperous, democratic and equitable nation. But NAFTA alone will not modernize Mexico. In the short term especially, the accord as it stands may only exacerbate the country's already stark disparities and dislocations. Rather than speeding and facilitating Mexico's long-awaited and much-hoped-for democratic transition, the near-term effect may be to

slow the momentum for political reform. This must not happen.

408. Jorge Castenada. "Can NAFTA Change Mexico?" FOREIGN AFFAIRS, Spring 1993, p. 71. Much of the problem has been Mexico's inability to hurdle an apparently immovable obstacle to its economic growth: the need for substantial foreign capital injections. Since 1972 Mexico has been unable to overcome this external constraint on growth, except during the ephemeral convergence of exceptional circumstances—high oil prices, cheap and abundant lending, wholesale privatization or high yields in the stock market. The costs of attracting foreign capital—higher interest rates and reduced domestic spending—have become a severe burden and have engendered boom-bust cycles in the economy. Either the economy does not grow or, if it does, immense current account deficits spring up, requiring equivalent magnitudes of capital to finance them. The outcome of each cycle has been a currency devaluation, like those in 1976, 1982, and 1987, or an economic downturn with equally devastating consequences.

409. Jorge Castenada. "Can NAFTA Change Mexico?" FOREIGN AFFAIRS, Spring 1993, p. 75. NAFTA either ignores these problems or leaves their solution to the market. The trade pact presupposes that the amount of money needed to bring together economies and societies as distinct as Mexico, the United States and Canada is not overwhelming and that market forces alone will provide it. In fact the United States will have to retrain tens of thousands of workers and cushion the shock to innumerable communities and factories. Canada is already losing jobs and markets, while Mexico confronts its balance-of-payments difficulties. The three countries will also have to tackle environmental problems and infrastructure deficiencies, along the border and inside Mexico, together with major regional disruptions and a costly process of harmonization.

410. Castenada, Jorge. "Can NAFTA Change Mexico?" *Foreign Affairs,* Spring 1993, p. 73. Many in the United States nonetheless believe that economic integration and NAFTA have moved jobs on a "fast track" to a modernizing Mexico. In fact, the country's disparities are deepening. Ever more dispossessed accompany the growing number of Mexican "yuppies." The loud "sucking noise" of American jobs going south that U.S. presidential candidate Ross Perot ominously announced last fall is, from the Mexican side of the border, singularly difficult to hear.

411. Robert Bach. IMMIGRATION AND U.S. FOREIGN POLICY, San Francisco: Westview Press, 1990, p. 140. The current U.S. position on Central America is to keep displaced persons in the region because of their importance to the future stabilization of the economy and potential usefulness in overthrowing the Sandinista regime. Whereas the early exile campaign against the Castro regime had to be

mounted primarily from Miami, U.S. strategy in Central America is clearly to base operations against the Sandinista regime within the region. As a result, the migration component of U.S. policy toward Central America is dependent upon whether the consolidation of the Sandinista regime leads to a Cuban-like, large-scale outflow or an accommodation occurs that allows those who would normally flee socialist regimes to remain in the country. Similarly, the question in El Salvador is whether and to what extent stabilization of the government can be achieved with reforms that provide opportunities for economic progress within the country. According to some preliminary estimates, however, Central American migration to the United States has already become so important economically, especially as a result of the magnitude of U.S. dollar remittances, that it would be difficult to return the several hundred thousand Central American refugees to their home countries.

412.   Robert Bach. IMMIGRATION AND U.S.
        FOREIGN POLICY, San Francisco: Westview Press, 1990, p.137. Cheap commodities and debt servicing are only two of the most obvious dimensions of regional integration. Migration has been and continues to be another. The current contribution of migration to the region is twofold. To the sending countries, the value of migration is monetary. Increasingly, remittances from migrants working in the United States amount to sending countries' first or second source of foreign exchange earnings. The monetary value of migration has led to explicit promotions of pro-migration policies. The World Bank, for example, concluded in 1984 that

> emigration by the unskilled generally leads to no loss in production, and if there is a scarcity premium on savings and foreign exchange (generated from remittances), then the net benefits from emigration are likely to be large. In fact, it may even be beneficial for countries to facilitate emigration by providing information to potential emigrants and organizing recruitment on an official basis.

413.   Sidney Weintraub. THE ILLEGAL ALIEN
        FROM MEXICO, Austin: University of Texas Press, 1980, pp. 28-29. We can summarize this option. The benefits of doing nothing are that the current system does provide needed labor, frequently below or at the minimum wage, for those who are most unskilled. This rewards them (since they are receiving more than they would at home) and U.S. society as a whole. It affords Mexico a safety valve for economic and political discontent by exporting part of its labor problem and enables Mexico to acquire a substantial number of dollars through remittances.

414.   Sherwood Ross. "Experts Applaud
        Contributions of Illegal Alien Workers." THE REUTER BUSINESS REPORT, March 23, 1993. If the underground system were legalized—along the

lines, say, of the German guest worker plan—skilled Mexican craftsmen would be lured to the United States and would try to settle here permanently, bringing their families.

Instead, Likens says, unskilled workers are attracted to U.S. jobs and sent much of what they earn home to Mexico, energizing that country's economy.

415.   Sherwood Ross. "Experts Applaud
        Contributions of Illegal Alien Workers." THE REUTER BUSINESS REPORT, March 23, 1993. "I don't know how you would ever know if they're being paid the minimum wage," Likens says. "But whatever they're getting paid is more than they earned in Mexico, and they're sending back an enormous amount of money. It's one of Mexico's leading sources of foreign exchange."

416.   Michael D'Antonio. "Apocalypse Soon." *Los Angeles Times Magazine,* August 29, 1993, p. 18. Strict border controls limiting crossings from Mexico would disrupt the economy and political structure of that country, she says. "Given the population growth in Mexico and the economy, they cannot sustain the number of wage earners that will come of age in the near future."

417.   Vernon M. Briggs. IMMIGRATION POLICY
        AND THE AMERICAN LABOR FORCE, Baltimore: Johns Hopkins Press, 1984, p. 11. Conversely, John Kenneth Galbraith, who has long been one of the most outspoken critics of the free-market school, has taken a completely polar stand on the issue of immigration. In 1979 he wrote: "Migration…is the oldest action against poverty. It selects those who most want help. It is good for the country to which they go; it helps break the equilibrium of poverty in the country from which they come. What is the perversity in the human soul that causes people to resist so obvious a good?" Galbraith does not contend that immigration is a panacea for mass poverty or for the extensive variations in standard of living that separate the advanced and less economically developed nations of the world. But he does argue that it should be considered a vital factor in any global strategy to reduce extreme income inequality in the world. [ellipses in original]

418.   Abraham Lowenthal. "Healing the
        Hemisphere." THE RECORDER, April 9, 1993, p.8. The United States will have a better chance of success in solving some of its domestic problems— and especially of creating jobs and managing the rate and impact of immigration—if Latin America becomes more prosperous and inter-American cooperation works. "Intermestic" issues—involving both domestic and international aspects and actors—will be important for the United States in the 1990s. Domestic and foreign policy approaches must be pursued in tandem, not as alternatives.

419.   Cesar Conda. "A Flood of Immigration Would
        Be Cut Sharply by Freer Flow of Trade."

SAN DIEGO UNION-TRIBUNE, September 19, 1993, p. G5. In the final analysis if NAFTA is killed in the Congress, the so-called immigration problem would likely become a national crisis. A weakened Mexican economy could send several million immigrants across the border, double or triple the current rate. Billions of investment dollars would flee from Mexico as investors sought higher rates of return in other countries with growing economies and stable, democratic governments.

420.   Robert Bach. IMMIGRATION AND U.S.
        FOREIGN POLICY. San Francisco: West-
view Press, 1990, p. 134. The consequences of this model of development—trading capital for migration—created a second source of difficulties, which led to a new set of policy interests. Overpopulation was no longer perceived as the major impediment to economic development in Puerto Rico or elsewhere in the region because the economies were growing. Rather, new problems had arisen as the industrialization strategy deployed in Puerto Rico, Mexico, Jamaica, and the Dominican Republic drew vast numbers of people from the countryside without generating sufficient employment in the manufacturing sectors of the urban economy. Industrialization strategies such as those adopted in Puerto Rico and Mexico actually led to a relative decline in available employment.

421.   Robert Bach. IMMIGRATION AND U.S.
        FOREIGN POLICY, San Francisco: West-
view Press, 1990, pp. 133-134. Following World War II, the value of migration was defined within policy models as an explicit source of relief from overpopulation. The best example—and actually the leading policy framework—was the economic development plan adopted for Puerto Rico, "Operation Bootstrap." Policy analysts, supported by Puerto Rican political leaders, embraced the idea that the immigration of excess population from the island to the mainland would alleviate joblessness and poverty caused by overpopulation. Over the next several decades, hundreds of thousands of Puerto Ricans moved to the mainland, forming in the Northeast low-wage, working-class communities significantly different from those established in the 1910s and 1920s. In return, Puerto Rico opened itself to capital investment from the U.S. mainland and, as a result, the island's economy grew at a much higher rate.

422.   "National Population Organization Comes to
        California Speaking Out on the Costs of Im-
migration." PR NEWSWIRE, April 14, 1994. The Immigration Stabilization Act, introduced by Senator Harry Reid (D-NV), if passed, would help solve many of California's problems. "With one stroke of his pen, President Clinton could reduce legal immigration into California by 70%," said Mark W. Nowak, BALANCE's Executive Director. "Accompanied by proven policies to eliminate illegal immigration, this Act alone could ultimately save Californians more than $265 billion over the next decade."

423.   "Headline: New Study Prompts
        Environmental Group to Call for Immigration
Moratorium." PR NEWSWIRE, June 3, 1993. Responding to a study released today by Professor Don L. Huddle of Rice University that estimates immigration into the United States costs more than $40 billion annually, Population-Environment Balance (BALANCE) has called for a temporary, two-year moratorium on immigration so that the United States may evaluate the environmental and economic impact of our current immigration laws.

424.   "Perspective on Immigration," LOS
        ANGELES TIMES, April 13, 1994, p. B7.
Sen. Alan Simpson (R-Wyo.) has introduced a bill to reduce the legal immigration ceiling to a base figure of 500,000 a year—a commendable action, but the ceiling should be much lower. Given our finite fiscal and natural resources, we must aim for an all-inclusive ceiling—legal immigration, amnesty, refugees, etc.—of 200,000 a year.

425.   "Headline: New Study Prompts Environ-
        mental Group to Call for Immigration
Moratorium." PR NEWSWIRE, June 3, 1993. The balance-sponsored moratorium would put a hold on legal immigration for two years, making exceptions for a limited number of non-citizen spouses and minor unmarried children of U.S. citizens who have applied to become citizens prior to May 1, 1992, and a limited number of individually screened refugees and asylees who provide convincing evidence they have a "well-founded fear of persecution."

The all-inclusive limit for both of these categories together would be 100,000 for each of the two years of the moratorium.

426.   Vernon M. Briggs. IMMIGRATION POLICY
        AND THE AMERICAN LABOR FORCE,
Baltimore: Johns Hopkins Press, 1984, pp. 162-163. According to Piore, therefore, it is fruitless to try to restrict illegal immigration so long as the secondary labor market exists. Other scholars have echoed this belief and some have drawn the similar conclusions that illegal immigrants take only the jobs that citizens shun and thus cause a minimum of worker displacement. Consequently, if the United States really wants to reduce the flow of illegal immigrants, Piore argues, it will have to eliminate the labor demand that presently exists in the secondary labor market. He suggests that this could be accomplished by raising the federal minimum wage substantially, by improving the enforcement of job protection laws, and by encouraging through legislation the unionization of many low-wage industries. He is not optimistic, however, that the nation's policymakers will take any of these steps. Thus he believes that as long as it is useful to employers, illegal immigration will continue.

427.   Vlae Kershner. "Calculating the Cost of
        Immigration." THE SAN FRANCISCO
CHRONICLE, June 23, 1993, p. A1. Defenders of

immigration agree there is a problem, but they say the solution is to enforce the labor laws.

"Employers hire undocumented workers because they are easily exploitable," said Valerie Small-Navarro, testifying at an Assembly hearing for the Mexican American Legal Defense and Educational Fund. "If employers were compelled to pay all workers a minimum wage that supports a family above poverty level, overtime, all state and federal taxes due, and provide a safe and healthy work place, the state would eliminate the employers' incentive to hire exploitable unauthorized workers.

428.   Richard Rothstein. "Immigration Dilemmas." DISSENT, Fall 1993, p. 462. Higher labor standards in immigrant industries where native workers don't choose to work would also ameliorate political conflict over the unavoidable presence of undocumented workers. A national health insurance plan, for example, that covered all workers whether here legally or not, would relieve the burden of taxpayers to provide for immigrant health in public emergency rooms and hospitals. Minimum-wage enforcement in immigrant industries, along with a more hospitable climate for union organizing, would put more money into immigrant neighborhoods and increase their tax contributions to the broader community, while reducing immigrant use of welfare, food stamp, and similar benefits.

And also, of course, we could stop eating broccoli.

429.   Wayne Cornelius. AMERICA'S NEW IMMIGRATION LAW, Center for U.S.-Mexican Studies, University of California at San Diego, Monograph Series 11, 1983, p.149. Legalization of their status in the U.S. (under a plan which will minimize the procedural difficulties raised by Thomas Heller and Robert Olson), more vigorous enforcement of minimum wage and fair labor standards laws, and noninterference by immigration authorities in efforts to unionize undocumented workers would all serve to increase the bargaining power of foreign workers in the U.S. labor market. We might thus reduce the immigrants' vulnerability to exploitation as well as their tendency to depress wages and working conditions for some U.S. citizens employed in the same firms. This approach may not affect the level of immigration, but it would substantially reduce the adverse effects of the immigrants' presence in our labor markets.

430.   "House Eases Immigration For Foreign Nurses." CONGRESSIONAL QUARTERLY, October 21, 1989, p. 2808. Jack Brooks, D-Texas, chairman of the Judiciary Committee, said that nurses from some countries currently must wait seven to 14 years to be admitted as immigrants. But they may not stay in the United States for more than five years under their temporary work visas, and many could face deportation at the end of this year unless Congress acts. Nurses from the Philippines have been especially hard-hit by the backlog problem.

431.   "Foreign Nurses Gain Immigration Break." CONGRESSIONAL QUARTERLY, October 7, 1989, p. 2650. Currently, foreign nurses in the special-entry program may remain in this country for five years, with the possibility of a one-year extension. Immigration Subcommittee Chairman Bruce A. Morrison, D-Conn., said, "There is no need or desire to send these individuals. back"

He noted that HR 3259 is largely aimed at nurses from the Philippines, who, without congressional action, face long waiting lists for immigrant slots and likely would be forced to return home.

432.   Arthur Helton. IMMIGRATION AND NATURALIZATION SERVICE MANAGEMENT ISSUES, Hrg of the Committee on the Judiciary, House of Representatives, April 24, 1991, p. 164. Precisely at a time when non-citizenship is soaring in our nation, the INS is complicating the naturalization process by charging excessive fees to U.S. citizenship applicants. Today an immigrant is asked to pay naturalization fees *320%* higher than just 16 months ago. The total charges associated with filling the necessary U.S. citizenship forms have risen from $50 to $160. since December, 1989.

433.   Harry Pachon. IMMIGRATION REFORM, Hrg of the Committee on the Judiciary, Senate, March 3, 1989, p. 129. U.S. citizenship is the often overlooked obstacle to social, economic and political advancement of law abiding, taxpaying permanent residents. Today, one-third of adult Hispanics cannot vote, serve on grand juries or participate fully in the society the live in only because they are not U.S. citizens. While some permanent residents may opt to retain their current nationality, many more are interested in becoming U.S. citizens. Naturalization should be accessible for all people, and today's legislation takes steps to make that a reality for many more people.

434.   Harry Pachon. IMMIGRATION REFORM, Hrg of the Committee on the Judiciary, Senate, March 3, 1989, pp. 126-127. NALEO strongly supports the uniform three-year waiting period for naturalization contained in S. 448. Adjusting the waiting period would serve both the nation and the applicant in several ways.

First, it would help permanent residents move more quickly to U.S. citizenship, which would relieve any pressure on the already stifled second preference category. Since much of today's discussion is revolving around the backlogged preference system, particularly the second preference S. 448's measure would help to abate a potentially disastrous situation—a likely 20 year backlog on second preference for Mexico. With the likely onslaught of nearly 3 million permanent residents from the legalization program, with more than 70 percent being of Mexican origin, allowing them and other permanent residents to apply for U.S. citizenship after three years would permit the reunification of families.

435.   Vernon M. Briggs. IMMIGRATION POLICY
        AND THE AMERICAN LABOR FORCE,
Baltimore: Johns Hopkins Press, 1984, p.178. Certainly no one can argue against the need for more effective enforcement of prevailing labor standards for all workers—citizens or not. But this, it seems, is a weak reed upon which to place the weight of an attack on illegal immigration. To begin with, it is doubtful that most illegal immigrants are legally exploited in the workplace. Some are, but so are some citizens. Greater enforcement efforts might lead to less abuse of the nation's labor laws, but it is doubtful that they would stop the employment of illegal immigrants. After all, these laws are intended to assure that minimum labor standards prevail; that is all that can be enforced. North and Houstoun, for instance, found that 76 percent of the illegal immigrants in their study were paid the minimum wage or more. Most of those who did not receive an equivalent wage were employed in agriculture, which at that time was not covered by minimum-wage legislation. Not surprisingly, North and Houstoun also found that Mexican illegal immigrants are more likely than non-Mexicans to be paid at a rate below the minimum wage. Moreover, while it is true that some labor standard enforcement activities are initiated by government agencies, most of the violations that are reported stem from employee complaints. This the way it has always been and probably always will be. Nevertheless, illegal immigrants are less likely to know how to make such complaints, and even if they do know, they are—given their precarious status in the country—quite unlikely to file complaints.

436.   Vernon M. Briggs. IMMIGRATION POLICY
        AND THE AMERICAN LABOR FORCE,
Baltimore: Johns Hopkins Press, 1984, p. 161. Some illegal immigrant workers are no doubt sought out primarily because they can be exploited. This, however, appears to be the exception rather than the rule. North and Houstoun, for instance, found that 76 percent of the respondents in their study had earned the federal minimum wage or better in the job they held at the time of their apprehension. Even this percentage seems quite low, but it reflects the fact that a disproportionate number of these immigrants were last employed in agriculture. The UCLA study of urban illegal immigrants did not include wage data. It did, however, compute "income" data, which show that on the average its respondents earned about $1,000 a year more than the North-Houstoun interviewees.

437.   Vernon M. Briggs. IMMIGRATION POLICY
        AND THE AMERICAN LABOR FORCE,
Baltimore: Johns Hopkins Press, 1984, p. 178. Although the available data show that the overwhelming majority of illegal immigrants are not legally "exploited" (i.e., they are not paid less than the federal minimum wage and do not work under conditions that are inferior to those that citizen workers encounter), some are. Hence, all the various studies and legislative proposals that have addressed the problem of illegal

immigration have included homilies about the need to enforce existing fair labor standards. Presumably, if these laws were adequately enforced, the need to hire illegal immigrants would recede and illegal immigrants would stop coming.

438.   "Mass Immigration and the National Interest."
        SOUTHERN ECONOMIC JOURNAL, October 1993, p. 513. The argument that runs through this study, that American immigration policy is ad hoc, at best rushing to catch up with external forces, is amply illustrated. The importance given to family reunification is unsurprisingly identified as one of the two great weaknesses of American immigration law. The response to refugee and illegal migration, in recent years to validate illegal settlement with ex post amnesties, is the other. Briggs argues that as a result of these policies the number of immigrants has exceeded any reasonable upper limit, and that the human capital of the immigrants is unsuited for an economy that demands ever higher levels of skill.

439.   "Mass Immigration and the National Interest."
        SOUTHERN ECONOMIC JOURNAL, October 1993, p. 513. Briggs's thesis is that U.S. immigration policy has been driven by short-sighted and ill-conceived political compromise, and that this policy has stimulated a massive inflow of those persons most detrimental to the American labor market, in general, and to the labor market fortunes of native-born minorities, in particular. Briggs introduces this theme on page one, where he defines "mass immigration" as an inflow whose chief characteristic is its quantitative size. He sharpens this definition, however, asserting, "...implicit in the usage of "mass immigration" is disregard for the human capital characteristics of those who enter—especially in relation to the prevailing economic trends and social stresses at work within our nation." [ellipses in original]

440.   Vernon M. Briggs. IMMIGRATION POLICY
        AND THE AMERICAN LABOR FORCE,
Baltimore: Johns Hopkins Press, 1984, p. 244. In contrast to the policies of other immigrant-receiving nations, U.S. immigration policy makes no allowance for cyclical swings in the nation's employment levels. The number of legal immigrants admitted to the United States is fixed; no consideration is given to whether U.S. unemployment levels are high or low, declining or rising. Instead of providing for an administrative agency that would adjust the annual ceiling to meet short-term employment fluctuations, Congress mandated a figure that is reviewed only every couple of decades. Obviously this process makes no allowance for the need to increase the supply of labor during periods of labor shortage and to decrease the supply during periods of labor surplus. With immigration in all its forms accounting in recent years for an influx of over one million persons a year, it can hardly be said that these annual infusions into the U.S. labor force and population are insignificant. Moreover, because these immigrants are concentrated in selected states and urban

labor markets, they undoubtedly give rise to employment and wage conditions that would not prevail in their absence.

441. Vernon M. Briggs. IMMIGRATION POLICY AND THE AMERICAN LABOR FORCE, Baltimore: Johns Hopkins Press, 1984, p. 244. No geographic restrictions are placed upon legal immigrants whereby their admission would be conditional upon their willingness to settle in local labor markets where there are shortages of workers with similar occupational backgrounds or away from areas where there are surpluses. Consequently, immigrants tend to cluster in relatively few cities in relatively few states. Their contribution to these labor markets is therefore purely accidental and may even be detrimental. It can no way be argued that U.S. immigration policy is designed to meet the skill and educational requirements of the local labor markets where legal immigrants tend to reside and seek employment. In sharp contrast to the policies of the few other industrialized nations that admit sizable numbers of immigrants, the U.S. immigration system functions largely without regard for these considerations. During earlier eras, when most of the jobs that needed to be filled were unskilled in nature, there was no need to be particularly concerned about the labor market adjustment of immigrants. As will be shown, however, such a random process is not justified in an era when the number of unskilled jobs is declining (and unskilled workers are in surplus) and the number of skilled jobs is increasing (and skilled workers are in short supply).

442. Wayne Cornelius. AMERICA'S NEW IMMIGRATION LAW, Center for U.S.-Mexican Studies, University of California at San Diego, Monograph Series 11, 1983, p. 74. Our immigration laws have not simply been fitted to short-term, cyclical labor needs, as is often argued. Rather, our immigration history suggests that U.S. immigration laws can be seen as attempts to resolve a variety of dilemmas deriving from contradictions in the political economy—dilemmas such as the conflicting interests of capital and labor, uneven economic development, and a number of more narrowly defined political contradictions. The outcome is a series of policies which are frequently inconsistent and which are at best only momentarily adequate.

443. Frank Kittredge. IMMIGRATION REFORM, Hrg of the Committee on the Judiciary, Senate, March 3, 1989, p. 467. Yet, our present legal immigration laws and policy, rooted in legislation enacted in 1952, have failed to keep up with these evolving needs. As a result, U.S. based employers that need the skills of international personnel confront a variety of disconcerting obstacles in a process characterized by inflexibility, delay, and an absence of predictability. For example, if a visa petition had been filed in the 3rd preference last May, there was a 5 month backlog in this category. Given normal progress, it could have been predicted that this employee would transfer by

year's end. As of today, this petition still is not current, and the company that needed this employee is still waiting. It is now estimated that this employee won't be able to enter the U.S. until the fall of 1989, if all goes well. This handicaps the U.S. firm that needs this professional's services and gives an advantage to the competition.

444. Leonel Sanchez. "State Immigrants Cost $18.2 Billion in Taxes Last Year, Study Says." SAN DIEGO UNION-TRIBUNE, November 5, 1993, p. A27. The study suggested that the United States accept only skilled and professional immigrants and crack down on illegal immigration.

"The highly skilled immigrants are more than paying their way," said the study's author, Donald Huddle, an economics professor at Rice University in Houston. "It's really a question of having a (large) low-skilled population.

445. Vernon M. Briggs. IMMIGRATION POLICY AND THE AMERICAN LABOR FORCE, Baltimore: Johns Hopkins Press, 1984, p. 258. In the 1970s and early 1980s, however, all forms of immigration had increased dramatically, and the 1980 census reported a notable increase in the foreign-born population of the nation. Moreover, the census showed that the composition of the total immigrant population had changed substantially since 1970 in terms of the skills, education, and experiential backgrounds that immigrants were bringing to U.S. labor markets. The magnitude and character of the immigration that has occurred since the 1960s has introduced so many new challenges that it has essentially overwhelmed the nation's extant immigration laws and related administrative procedures. In the absence of any serious effort to forge an immigration policy based on labor market considerations, immigration policy continues to function as a "wild card" among the nation's key labor market policies. Unlike all other categories of economic policy (e.g., fiscal policies, monetary policies, employment and training policies, education policies, and antidiscrimination policies), where attempts are made by policymakers to orchestrate the diverse policy elements into a harmony of action to accomplish particular objectives, immigration policy has been allowed to meander aimlessly.

The United States could probably continue to exempt immigration policy from accountability for its direct efforts on the nation's economic welfare if were not for the major structural changes and external competitive forces that have caused such upheaval in the traditional employment patterns of the nation in recent years. These changes, however, clearly indicate that the nation can no longer afford a policy of inaction.

446. Klaus Fuchs. "Agenda for Tomorrow." ANNALS OF THE AMERICAN ACADEMY OF POLITICAL SCIENCE, November 1993, p. 170. Assuming that Borjas's methodology is sound and his conclusions persuasive, one could still argue against numerical restriction but call for the

United States to choose immigrants based on educational and skill criteria instead of family relationships. The question as to whether lawfully admitted immigrants serve mainly as substitutes for American workers and depress wages and standards for American workers or as complements who help to stimulate an economy through their own skills, hard work, savings, and investment is one that will be examined closely by the Commission on Immigration Reform, created by the 1990 Immigration Act to evaluate its effects.

447.   James Flanihan. "Blaming Immigrants Won't Solve Economic Woes." LOS ANGELES TIMES, August 15, 1993, p. D1. One way to gain border control and economic benefit would be to set up a system of flexible legal immigration that could bring people in when needed for a variety of jobs. Immigration experts say this might be along the lines of the bracero program that brought agricultural laborers from Mexico from wartime 1942 to 1964. The bracero program had faults and was criticized as a cheap-labor scheme, but a new system would have the advantages of being legal and less exploitative.

448.   Vernon M. Briggs. IMMIGRATION POLICY AND THE AMERICAN LABOR FORCE, Baltimore: Johns Hopkins Press, 1984, p. 177. As discussed in Chapter 3, the Simpson-Mazzoli bill sought to exempt Mexico and Canada from the ceiling that in 1976 had been placed on the number of legal immigrants that could be admitted from any one nation each year. The bill proposed maintaining the 20,000-visa ceiling for all other nations, but increasing the limit for Mexico and Canada to 40,000. The Senate bill also outlined a reciprocity agreement whereby Mexico and Canada would be allowed to use each other's unused visas. Since Canada has not in recent years used all 20,000 of its visas, Mexico would stand to gain a significant number of additional visas as a result of this agreement. The increase in available visas would then be used to reduce the massive backlog of Mexican visa requests that currently exists and, it is believed, would help reduce some of the pressures that lead Mexicans to immigrate illegally or that force them to remain illegal if they have already immigrated while waiting for their visa requests to be acted upon. The House version of the bill deleted the reciprocity feature.

This change would help reduce the number of illegal immigrants in the U.S. labor market. In the present author's opinion it was a mistake in 1976 to put legal immigration from Mexico on the same footing as that from other nations. As equitable as it might have seemed at the time, the provision ignored the reality of immigration pressures in Mexico.

449.   Vernon M. Briggs. IMMIGRATION POLICY AND THE AMERICAN LABOR FORCE, Baltimore: Johns Hopkins Press, 1984, p. 249. Thus it is clear that in the last two decades of the twentieth century the labor force of the United States will be confronted with immense internal pressures to change its racial and gender patterns of employment. The effort to

bring about these changes will be hampered if the nation's immigration policy continues to ignore the labor market consequences of its implementation.

450.   Vernon M. Briggs. IMMIGRATION POLICY AND THE AMERICAN LABOR FORCE, Baltimore: Johns Hopkins Press, 1984, p. 250. In addition to the dramatic changes that have taken place in the demographics of the labor supply of the United States since the 1960s, even more consequential long-term changes have been occurring in the demand for labor. The American economy is in the midst of a radical transformation in the types and locations of jobs that are available, and as a result the nation's employment patterns are rapidly changing. Because employment is one of the principal reasons immigrants come to the United States, it is important that the supply of labor provided by immigration be responsive to these emerging trends. If it is not responsive, immigration could retard the formidable adjustment process that confronts the citizen labor force, a process that already involves secular shifts in job opportunities and persistently high unemployment rates.

451.   Sean Minihane. IMMIGRATION REFORM, Hrg of the Committee on the Judiciary, Senate, March 3, 1989, p.134. We believe that a points system is a fair way of selecting independent immigrants and that it is in the national interest. Canada and Australia are already benefiting from the use of a points system: like America, both of these democratic countries share our tradition of receiving immigrants. Further, a points system is inherently flexible and may easily be adjusted to meet the country's labor requirements.

452.   Vernon M. Briggs. IMMIGRATION POLICY AND THE AMERICAN LABOR FORCE, Baltimore: Johns Hopkins Press, 1984, p. 260. The preceding suggestions are predicated on the assumption that a full-scale effort will be mounted to end the flow of illegal immigrants into the United States. If the nation's immigration policies, the entire reform process will be easily circumvented. The various reforms should address both the "push" and the "pull" factors that contribute to illegal immigration. They should include deterrent as well as prevention measures. Enforcement of whatever measures are ultimately adopted should be given high priority in terms of providing the funds and manpower required to fulfill these duties.

453.   Vernon M. Briggs. IMMIGRATION POLICY AND THE AMERICAN LABOR FORCE, Baltimore: Johns Hopkins Press, 1984, p. 260. In sum, U.S. immigration policy needs to be synchronized with all other policies that are designed to accomplish full employment, strengthen the domestic economy, and enhance the development of the nation's human resources. A liberal and nondiscriminatory policy should continue to be a hallmark of American society, but that policy must truly contribute to—not contravene—the nation's domestic economy interests.

454. Sidney Weintraub. THE ILLEGAL ALIEN FROM MEXICO, Austin: University of Texas Press, 1980, p. 53. Where does this ordering of priorities lead us? Because of the contribution the illegals make to the United States economy, our major recommendation is precisely the reverse of the president's. We believe that a significant labor program should be instituted under which visas for temporary work, say, for no more than six to eight months a year, would be given to hundreds of thousands of Mexicans. How many hundreds of thousands can be determined after surveying the United States as to the demand, both in industry and agriculture. There could be agreement at the outset that the number to be admitted would progressively decline over a definite timetable (although we might regret this if projections of shortages in the United States supply of workers in the secondary labor market materialized).

455. Vernon M. Briggs. IMMIGRATION POLICY AND THE AMERICAN LABOR FORCE, Baltimore: Johns Hopkins Press, 1984, p. 243. Immigrants are not ornaments in our society. They are human beings who, regardless of what motivated them to leave their homelands, need to find a means of support in this country. If the current influx of immigrants were of minor proportions, as was the case in the 1930s and 1940s; if the rate of growth of the U.S. labor force were slow; if occupational employment patters were stable; and if the composition of the available labor supply were inconsequential to contemporary economic and social expectations, reconciliation of the nation's immigration policies with its broader economic policies would not be necessary. As will be shown, however, such a reconciliation is long overdue. Labor force parameters have changed significantly in the past twenty years, and it is time to place immigrants within the broader matrix of factors that influence the economic welfare of the nation. Immigration policy is too important to be scrutinized only in terms of its political acceptability. It needs to be held accountable for its economic impacts as well.

456. Vernon M. Briggs. IMMIGRATION POLICY AND THE AMERICAN LABOR FORCE, Baltimore: Johns Hopkins Press, 1984, p. 243. In this concluding chapter, therefore, we will address the reality that the public policymakers of the nation have as yet refused to face—the fact that mass immigration has economic as well as political implications. It is essential that U.S. immigration policy be reconciled with contemporary labor market requirements. To maintain the status quo is to invite an inevitable negative reaction to all forms of immigration. The nation's policymakers cannot continue to treat immigration as a political abstraction that functions in a vacuum devoid of economic implications. On the contrary, immigration is a change-creating process. It is affected by prevailing labor force trends, but it is also capable of influencing the future course of those trends.

457. Vernon M. Briggs. IMMIGRATION POLICY AND THE AMERICAN LABOR FORCE, Baltimore: Johns Hopkins Press, 1984, p. 94. The major reason that the administration of U.S. immigration policy differs so much from that of Australia and Canada is that the duties assigned to respective agencies are so different. In the latter two nations, immigration officers interview prospective immigrants and assess their desirability in largely qualitative terms. These standards vary depending on the state of the receiving country's economy. In 1982, for instance, Canada announced that because it had an unemployment rate of over 12 percent, for the fiscal year 1983 it would sharply reduce the number of immigrants admitted on the basis of their labor market skills (a category called "selected workers") from a target range of 20,000-25,000 to a range of 8,000-10,000. (In fact, the number actually admitted in this category in fiscal 1983 was less than 7,000). Those workers who were admitted in this category were restricted to occupations in which a labor shortage had developed.

458. Vernon M. Briggs. IMMIGRATION POLICY AND THE AMERICAN LABOR FORCE, Baltimore: Johns Hopkins Press, 1984, p. 93. Of the few industrial nations that are admitting legal immigrants on a regular basis, Australia and Canada are most similar to the United States in their settlement histories and institutional structures. As a result, they are usually cited as the two nations whose immigration policies would most likely provide useful lessons for the United States. Yet both of these countries have developed immigration policies that are entirely different from U.S. immigration policy in terms of priorities and operational procedures.

459. Vernon M. Briggs. IMMIGRATION POLICY AND THE AMERICAN LABOR FORCE, Baltimore: Johns Hopkins Press, 1984, p. 250. If by chance the miracle of economic miracles does occur and the United States achieves full employment, and if under these special circumstances labor shortages in certain unskilled occupations do occur, there is a preferable alternative to illegal immigration as a means of filling these needs. That is, of course, to use the front door to the nation's labor force and simply increase legal immigration under the occupational admission categories of the existing immigration statutes. At present, only highly skilled and educated immigrants are admitted under these provisions in response to perceived labor market shortages, but there is no reason why the legal immigration system and the refugee admissions program could not be adapted to meet real shortages of unskilled workers as well.

460. Robert Manley Parker. IMPLEMENTATION OF THE IMMIGRATION ACT OF 1990, Hrg of the Committee on the Judiciary, House of Representatives, May 15, 1991, p. 43. The Immigration Act of 1990 is a significant departure from the law as it has existed since 1906. Title IV of the Act transfers

naturalization authority from the courts to the Attorney General. This is of major concern to the judiciary. Dating from the early years of this century and the initial passage of legislation governing the naturalization of new citizens, the judiciary has played a major role in the naturalization process. The granting of citizenship is one of the most solemn and auspicious events over which a judge presides and the judiciary takes great pride in its role in administering the oath of allegiance to new citizens.

461.   Robert Manley Parker. IMPLEMENTATION
        OF THE IMMIGRATION ACT OF 1990,
Hrg of the Committee on the Judiciary, House of Representatives, May 15, 1991, pp. 44-45. The 1990 legislation fundamentally changes the process by which a new citizen applies for and is bestowed United States citizenship. The federal courts have played an integral role in the naturalization process. The naturalization ceremony, the awarding of certificates of naturalization, and the opportunity for judicial review of denials of eligibility for naturalization all are important aspects of this process that will be irrevocably altered by the 1990 Act. These changes become effective on October 1, 1991. I therefore wish to take this opportunity to address some of the concerns raised by my colleagues in response to the legislative amendments. I am confident that this Subcommittee will consider my remarks carefully, in light of the imminent implementation of the Act.

462.   Robert Manley Parker. IMPLEMENTATION
        OF THE IMMIGRATION ACT OF 1990,
Hrg of the Committee on the Judiciary, House of Representatives, May 15, 1991, pp. 43-44. The 1990 legislation was enacted to streamline the naturalization process by reducing duplicative paperwork and overlapping administrative responsibilities borne both by the federal courts and the Immigration and Naturalization Service. The judiciary does not oppose these efforts, but rather, applauds the accomplishments of the legislature in streamlining the procedure for naturalization. The judiciary, however, has serious concerns with that portion of the Act which potentially would remove the courts from the administration of the oath-taking ceremony. The Act provides that applicants for naturalization can choose to have any United States district court, the Attorney General, or any state court meeting certain requirements administer the oath of allegiance.

463.   Robert Manley Parker. IMPLEMENTATION
        OF THE IMMIGRATION ACT OF 1990,
Hrg of the Committee on the Judiciary, House of Representatives, May 15, 1991, p. 65. I am here to answer any questions and to add for your record some personal viewpoints of a judge from a large district. For your information, my family came from China as immigrants. My father came here in the 1920's. My mother came here in 1940. And one of the greatest pleasures that was had within my family was the fact that my father was naturalized in 1951 before the Federal court where I now sit.

And English is my second language, Chinese being first. I have been very close to my community and with many other immigrant communities, and I know the pulse of the community to the extent that I have traveled abroad a lot and I find that there is a great degree of reverence for the court systems in other countries. It is no less here, I hope. But certainly there is a great degree of reverence for the courts, and to the immigrants, to be naturalized before a court, before a judge, is quite a meaningful thing.

That has transposed itself to my new position of being a judge in a district court where I now have that opportunity to perform naturalization ceremonies, and I find that the dignity and the solemnity of the process through the courts is as I have felt it all along.

I am from a large district. Monday, Tuesday, and Wednesday this week we have our regular naturalization ceremonies. I would be there 2 hours from now to be performing another one. We have two sessions per day all 3 days. Each session has 3,500 people. On Monday, I did perform both ceremonies on Monday and there are 3,500 people in each of these naturalization ceremonies, one in the morning and one in the afternoon.

464.   Robert Manley Parker. IMPLEMENTATION
        OF THE IMMIGRATION ACT OF 1990,
Hrg of the Committee on the Judiciary, House of Representatives, May 15, 1991, p. 46. We believe that the demeanor and presence of a judicial figure lends an aura of solemnity to the oath-taking occasion. Experience teaches that new citizens appreciate the seriousness of the occasion and we should do our utmost to enhance the feelings of pride and dignity upon administration of the oath. The renunciation of allegiance to one sovereign nation and the declaration of allegiance to another is perhaps one of the most important decisions that any human being can be called upon to make. The courts have a tradition enduring almost a century of conducting the administration of the oath of allegiance and that tradition should be allowed to continue. Recent enactments will open the doors of our nation even wider to new citizens, and it is reasonable to anticipate that even greater numbers of applicants will pass through the naturalization process. The availability of an alternative ceremony, to be conducted by the INS, will accommodate that increase in numbers, but it should not supplant the judicial ceremony.

465.   Robert Manley Parker. IMPLEMENTATION
        OF THE IMMIGRATION ACT OF 1990,
Hrg of the Committee on the Judiciary, House of Representatives, May 15, 1991, p. 44. The oath-taking ceremony traditionally has be imbued with a special significance directly attributable to the participation of a judicial officer. Our judges are proud of the special role they play in administering the oath of allegiance to new citizens, and as a body, we do oppose that aspect of the new law which would largely remove the courts from the oath-taking ceremonies. Judge Lew and I are here today to discuss with you the importance of the court's role in administering the oath of allegiance and to advocate preserving the role of the judiciary in the

oath-taking ceremony to the fullest extent practicable, while achieving the goal of the new law of conducting the ceremony in a timely fashion.

466. Robert Manley Parker. IMPLEMENTATION OF THE IMMIGRATION ACT OF 1990, Hrg of the Committee on the Judiciary, House of Representatives, May 15, 1991, pp. 66-67. Well, when you speak to a new group of immigrants, now new citizens, you wonder whether or not they really had a full appreciation of the question or the poll I gave. The second question was: How many of you would like to see the process remain the same, where you will be sworn in in a court or before a Federal judge? Instantaneously, almost everybody's hand went up. And before long, they started waving the flag.

I think that was a pretty clear statement that my position is well stated to this committee.

467. Robert Manley Parker. IMPLEMENTATION OF THE IMMIGRATION ACT OF 1990, Hrg of the Committee on the Judiciary, House of Representatives, May 15, 1991, p. 57. Mr. Chairman, I appreciate this opportunity to appear before the Subcommittee, and I thank you for your attention. As stated, Title IV of the Immigration Act of 1990 will have significant impact on the federal judiciary. We ask this Committee to amend the Act to allow the courts to continue their active role in the naturalization process. Our proposed amendment, which provides for a 45 day period win which the federal courts have exclusive jurisdiction to administer the oath of allegiance, would achieve this result, while at the same time, accomplishing the objective of efficient and timely granting of citizenship in a dignified manner befitting the occasion.

468. Robert Manley Parker. IMPLEMENTATION OF THE IMMIGRATION ACT OF 1990, Hrg of the Committee on the Judiciary, House of Representatives, May 15, 1991, p. 49. We believe that the proposed amendment is a fair compromise, providing the courts the opportunity to conduct the ceremony and the new citizen the opportunity to be naturalized in a timely and dignified fashion.

469. Robert Manley Parker. IMPLEMENTATION OF THE IMMIGRATION ACT OF 1990, Hrg of the Committee on the Judiciary, House of Representatives, May 15, 1991, p.48. One strength of the amendments as proposed is the flexibility it provides. If a particular court is unable to schedule ceremonies within the 45-day period, due to an overcrowded docket, or exceptional circumstances, or if the court chooses to defer to INS for administration of the oath, then the court can waive jurisdiction and the applicant seeking a ceremony in a shorter time frame can participate in an administrative ceremony. Thus, the court can eliminate any potential delays for the applicant by providing a readily available alternative forum for the ceremony.

470. Robert Manley Parker. IMPLEMENTATION OF THE IMMIGRATION ACT OF 1990, Hrg of the Committee on the Judiciary, House of Representatives, May 15, 1991, p.45. I wish to emphasize that we do not oppose the concept of an administrative oath-taking ceremony, *per se*, but rather, we advocate that the first option available to a new citizen should be a judicial oath-taking ceremony, and that an administrative ceremony be the alternative. The Judicial Conference recommendation was not adopted by Congress, and I am here to renew our proposal and to urge the Subcommittee to reconsider this language.

471. Robert Manley Parker. IMPLEMENTATION OF THE IMMIGRATION ACT OF 1990, Hrg of the Committee on the Judiciary, House of Representatives, May 15, 1991, p. 45. The Judicial Conference, at its March 1990 meeting, adopted a resolution which addressed its concerns regarding the naturalization language which eventually became law. That Judicial Conference proposal provides for a 45-day period, commencing after an applicant is declared by INS to be eligible for naturalization, in which the judiciary would have exclusive authority to administer the oath of allegiance. The amendments not only would ensure the expeditious granting of citizenship, but also would ensure the federal courts have the opportunity to conduct the ceremony with the solemnity it deserves. The Judicial Conference proposal is attached as Appendix A.

472. Robert Manley Parker. IMPLEMENTATION OF THE IMMIGRATION ACT OF 1990, Hrg of the Committee on the Judiciary, House of Representatives, May 15, 1991, p. 69. Judge Parker: But that playing field is not level at that point. And I say again, the 45-day limitation placed upon the courts will really address 90 percent of the time problem.

473. Robert Manley Parker. IMPLEMENTATION OF THE IMMIGRATION ACT OF 1990, Hrg of the Committee on the Judiciary, House of Representatives, May 15, 1991, p. 66. I can say that in a large district such as ours the judges enjoy doing it. We have a dislike for losing the ability to do it. We have no backlog in our large district. And whether the ceremony is for 3,500 people that we do regularly or whether it be one or two persons that we do more often than the large ceremonies, we do it all the time at the beck and call of the Immigration and Naturalization Service.

474. Robert Manley Parker. IMPLEMENTATION OF THE IMMIGRATION ACT OF 1990, Hrg of the Committee on the Judiciary, House of Representatives, May 15, 1991, p. 67. I would never like to cast a poor light on Immigration and Naturalization Service. I spoke primarily of the court. If it is the concern of everybody that the court does not have the time to perform the naturalization ceremonies, I would say that there is no backlog in our central district and many of the other large districts with regard to work. It does-

n't take that much time to perform the ceremony, and I think that judges are willing and able to perform it. Whether or not there is a delay, and I saw some of the background information that was provided Congress, I would say many of the districts do have a problem. And I think it is cured, in those smaller districts that have a court problem in managing their time to do their work, with the waiver that we have proposed in the amendment.

475.   Robert Manley Parker. IMPLEMENTATION
          OF THE IMMIGRATION ACT OF 1990,
Hrg of the Committee on the Judiciary, House of Representatives, May 15, 1991, pp. 46-47. The legislative history of the 1990 Act reveals that the revision of the naturalization process is based, in part, upon a premise that the federal judiciary does not accept. One rationale for the shift of the authority to naturalize from the judicial to the executive branch was the argument that the courts, overburdened by crowded dockets, were unable to accommodate the naturalization of new citizens in a timely manner. The Senate Report [accompanying S.358] indicates that the rationale behind the change in naturalization procedures is that certain courts have acute backlogs in conducting swearing-in ceremonies. By shifting responsibilities from the courts to the INS, Congress expected to shorten the waiting period for new citizens, relieve the courts of the naturalization burden, and realize savings of up to $2 million annually because duplicative administrative work performed by the courts would be eliminated.

The drafters looked at the delays attendant to the entire naturalization process and concluded that the delays in the judicial process bore primary responsibility. In fact, it is INS delays in processing certificates of eligibility which often have led some courts to cancel or delay ceremonies. The shift to allowing INS to conduct ceremonies would not, in itself, alleviate the delays for applicants in those areas of the country now experiencing delays. The Judicial Conference would prefer to see this Subcommittee grant the courts an opportunity to demonstrate the judiciary's capability to perform oath-taking ceremonies within a brief statutory time frame. In any district where the workload is too great, the Judicial Conference proposal would all the court to waive its jurisdiction, thus permitting the applicant to proceed directly to the administrative naturalization.

476.   Robert Manley Parker. IMPLEMENTATION
          OF THE IMMIGRATION ACT OF 1990,
Hrg of the Committee on the Judiciary, House of Representatives, May 15, 1991, pp. 49-50. The 1990 Act requires under Section 339 (a) (1) that the clerk of court "issue to each person to whom such an oath is administered a document evidencing that such an oath was administered." We view this provision as creating unnecessarily duplicative paperwork. Such a document will serve no useful function and can only lead to problems regarding its origin and validity. There is no need for the clerk to produce this type of document *if* the new citizen will receive a certificate of naturalization at the ceremony, *as is the present practice.* Our proposed

amendment would require INS to provide the certificate to the courts at the time INS transmits the notice of the applicant's eligibility to take the oath.

477.   Robert Manley Parker. IMPLEMENTATION
          OF THE IMMIGRATION ACT OF 1990,
Hrg of the Committee on the Judiciary, House of Representatives, May 15, 1991, pp. 57-58. We also ask the Committee to favorably consider our request to require the INS to provide naturalization certificates to the courts at the time the INS certifies an applicant as eligible for citizenship. This would eliminate that language in the Act requiring the clerk of court to provide a separate document evidencing the administration of the oath. We believe this would eliminate duplicative paperwork and an unnecessary administrative burden for the courts.

478.   Robert Manley Parker. IMPLEMENTATION
          OF THE IMMIGRATION ACT OF 1990,
Hrg of the Committee on the Judiciary, House of Representatives, May 15, 1991, p. 55. Another significant departure from the existing law is that the 1990 Act requires the district court to conduct a *de novo* review of a denial of an application for naturalization. The new law provides that "a person whose application for naturalization under this title is denied, after a hearing before an immigration officer...may seek judicial review of such denial before the United States District Court for the district in which such person resides....*Such review shall be* de novo, *and the court shall make its own findings of fact and conclusions of law and shall, at the request of the petitioner, conduct a hearing* de novo *on the application.*" (emphasis added). *See* 8 U.S.C. §1421; §310 (c) of the Act. The introduction of *de novo* review is of serious concern. If the intent is to improve the scrutiny that INSS gives applications, it would be more appropriate to reform INS procedures than to refer the applications for *de novo* review by the courts. By requiring courts to conduct *de novo* review, the Act could contribute significantly to increased delays in determining eligibility for naturalization. Moreover, there is not statute of limitations for the filing of a civil action in federal court, and this is an additional problem that will contribute to the workload of an already overburdened federal court system. [ellipses in original]

479.   Robert Manley Parker. IMPLEMENTATION
          OF THE IMMIGRATION ACT OF 1990,
Hrg of the Committee on the Judiciary, House of Representatives, May 15, 1991, p. 56. The fact that the judicial review will not be based upon an administrative record, but rather, will be a *de novo* review, is a significant departure from typical procedures governing review of administrative determinations. Although the Judicial Conference has not yet taken a formal position on this issue, I would ask the Subcommittee to consider amending the 1990 Act to allow the administrative record to be the basis for judicial review of denials of applications for naturalization. This proposal is consistent with the goal of reducing the workload of the

courts and is consistent with the practice under the Administrative Procedures Act, 5 U.S.C. §§701-706. If the courts cannot rely on the administrative record, the immense workload will be extremely burdensome and will not constitute an efficient utilization of already scarce judicial resources.

480.   Robert Manley Parker. IMPLEMENTATION OF THE IMMIGRATION ACT OF 1990, Hrg of the Committee on the Judiciary, House of Representatives, May 15, 1991, pp. 53-54. One likely result of the new Act will be a marked increase in the number of appeals filed in the federal courts, seeking review of INS denials of eligibility for naturalization. Another significant departure from the existing law is the imposition of a time limitation on the decision-making of the immigration officer. Under §336 (b) of the Act (8 U.S.C. §1447), the reviewing officer must issue a final determination within 120 days of the dates of an examination. Failure to comply with this requirement will enable an applicant to apply to the United States district court for a hearing on the matter.

This is a new level of judicial review created by the 1990 Act, and it contrasts with existing procedures, under which one seeking naturalization must exhaust all administrative remedies prior to seeking any judicial remedy. Previously there were not time deadlines imposed on the agency within which a decision must be issued. With the introduction of a statutory deadline, delays under the new Act will actually cause an increase in appeals field in federal court, which appears to be contrary to what sponsors of the 1990 Act envisioned.

481.   Robert Manley Parker. IMPLEMENTATION OF THE IMMIGRATION ACT OF 1990, Hrg of the Committee on the Judiciary, House of Representatives, May 15, 1991, p. 63. The bill as set up; now provides for de novo review on appeal. Now the estimates that I have received from the Administrative Office is that, if we only have 10 percent of those appeals, then we will have 2,000 de novo hearings that will be necessary. This places more demands on INS. they will have to have somebody present at these hearings. Last year, the whole system had 327 appeals. We conduct de novo hearings, and assuming the level of increase goes up because of the 120-day requirement, we could be looking at 2,000 to 3,000 appeals.

482.   Robert Manley Parker. IMPLEMENTATION OF THE IMMIGRATION ACT OF 1990, Hrg of the Committee on the Judiciary, House of Representatives, May 15, 1991, p. 68. But assuming that could be overcome, do you think that choice still isn't maybe the way to go? Judge Parker.

Judge Parker: Mr. Chairman, you have obviously asked the toughest question of all: What is wrong with giving people a choice? That is the first question I asked when this came to my attention. The answer I have to that is these people are really not prepared to make that choice when they are called upon to make it. The people they are dealing with will determine the answer to that question. They have not seen a court cere-

mony. They don't know what is going to be provided for them. They have no way to evaluate at that point the significance that is going to make to them and to their family in looking back on it when he is talking to his grand kids. They are ill-prepared to do that.

483.   Robert Manley Parker. IMPLEMENTATION OF THE IMMIGRATION ACT OF 1990, Hrg of the Committee on the Judiciary, House of Representatives, May 15, 1991, p. 69. Judge Lew: Obviously, I favor giving anybody choices. One of the freedoms that we have is the freedom of choice. But when you talk about the occasion that they are there in court, or before the ceremony, you are talking about the oath. And I will remind you the oath spells out so much. We will speak to the freedoms that they will receive. We will speak of all the benefits they will receive. But the thrust that the court should give them, or the solemnity of the occasion should give them is the thrust of the responsibility they now bear as a citizen. I think the solemnity of the occasion demands that we heighten that fact: The responsibility as a new citizen of this country.

484.   Robert Manley Parker. IMPLEMENTATION OF THE IMMIGRATION ACT OF 1990, Hrg of the Committee on the Judiciary, House of Representatives, May 15, 1991, p. 49. The argument has been offered that judges could still participate in oath-taking ceremonies by traveling to the site of the INS ceremony and participating in that forum. This is not a realistic alternative. In these times of great concern for the demands on the judiciary, judicial resources, and case management, it is counterproductive to set forth a scheme wherein the only means of judicial participation requires the judge to travel to the site of administrative oath-taking ceremonies.

485.   Robert Manley Parker. IMPLEMENTATION OF THE IMMIGRATION ACT OF 1990, Hrg of the Committee on the Judiciary, House of Representatives, May 15, 1991, p. 68. There were people who might have urged us to just simply avoid the court entirely, just make this thing an administrative process. We get our driver's license from an administrative process. We register to vote in an administrative setting. Although the right to vote is a quite remarkable thing, we don't have to go to a court to get that. We just go down to some office in the corner of a courthouse and we register to vote.

486.   Robert Manley Parker. IMPLEMENTATION OF THE IMMIGRATION ACT OF 1990, Hrg of the Committee on the Judiciary, House of Representatives, May 15, 1991, p. 67. I guess, Judge Lew, to answer your question about the solemnity of the occasion and the seriousness of purpose, because this question of administrative naturalization has been with us for, really, several Congresses. Back when Mr. Rodino was with us here, as a matter of fact. And I think that the whole idea was not to reduce that, not to neglect the courts, not to do anything to reduce the im-

portance of that moment, that remarkable moment when they become American citizens. But it was to assist those very people by having a procedure that would be quicker and would yield for them what they are really looking for in the last analysis, a chance to vote, a chance to borrow money, a chance to buy a business, a chance to do the things that only citizens can do.

487.   Robert Manley Parker. IMPLEMENTATION OF THE IMMIGRATION ACT OF 1990, Hrg of the Committee on the Judiciary, House of Representatives, May 15, 1991, p. 68. So the long and short of it was we didn't want to go that route. We didn't want to ignore the courts, for those people who want to have those trappings of the moment. But we didn't want also to ignore the fact there were some people for whom that was important but not as important as just getting the thing done and getting it over with and "Let me move my new life along."

We give them a choice of going the court route, and if it takes 1 week or 2 weeks or 2 months or 20 months, that is their choice. That is what they want. But if they want to have an administrative process, which might offer a little quicker help provided that this committee or somebody decides that when you do it you get your certificate—you ought not to get a document, it seems to me. I mean, how that crept into the law I am not sure. It just seems like wherever you are you ought to get the paper that counts and not have to go back for seconds.

488.   Barry Chiswick. ILLEGAL ALIENS, Kalamazoo: Upjohn Institute for Employment Research, 1988, pp. 3-4. Rather than laying to rest the illegal alien issue, the 1986 Act is a public acknowledgment that past policies failed. There is considerable skepticism that the new policies will succeed. Amnesty, intended to wipe the slate clean, may encourage additional illegal migration in the expectation of fraudulently qualifying for amnesty under the current act, and in the expectation that there will be future amnesties. Employer sanctions may have little if any effectiveness because of the difficulty of enforcement, particularly in the face of the nation's abhorrence of a national identity card system. Skeptics suggest that the promised resources for the enforcement of employer sanctions and for INS border and interior enforcement activities are not likely to be forthcoming. Since the political process failed to provide INS with adequate resources in the past, there is no reason to believe meaningful enforcement resources will be provided in the future.

489.   Tom Morgenthau. "America: Still a Melting Pot?" NEWSWEEK, August 9, 1993, p.16. Bill Clinton's goal, like that of most defenders of continued large-scale immigration, is to drive home the distinction between legal immigration (good) and illegal immigration (very, very bad). Illegal immigration is undeniably out of control. Congress tried to stop it in 1986 with a law called IRCA, the Immigration Reform and Control Act, which was based on a two-

pronged strategy. IRCA offered amnesty and eventual citizenship to an estimated 3.7 million illegal aliens and, at the same time, aimed at shutting down the U.S. job market by making it illegal for employers to hire undocumented aliens. The act has failed. Despite the amnesty, the estimated number of illegals has once again risen to between 2 million and 4 million people. "For the first two years there was a significant drop...because folks thought there was a real law here," says Lawrence H. Fuchs, acting chair of the U.S. Commission on Immigrant Reform. "But the word got out" that IRCA had no teeth, Fuchs says, and the influx resumed. Fuchs concedes that as many as 500,000 illegals now enter this country each year, though he admits it is impossible to know for sure. [ellipses in original]

490.   Donald Huddle. "Debate must begin with true view of the costs." HOUSTON CHRONICLE, August 29, 1993, p. 1. Despite promises to control illegal immigration under the Immigration Reform and Control Act of 1986 by employer sanctions which would fine employers hiring illegal immigrants without proper identification and bring more Border Patrolmen and internal enforcement, our duly elected politicians have cynically failed to provide the resources to do the job. Nor, as required under IRCA, has a secure identifier been developed for employment use despite the widespread use of fraudulent documents by 4 million illegal aliens working in the United States. The Border Patrol is still 2,000 agents below the level authorized by Congress in 1986 and budget restrictions have cut Immigration and Naturalization Service internal investigations of employers hiring illegal aliens to the core. Over 250,000 asylees are released without work permits while they await hearings which could take decades to hear. Fewer than one-third bother showing up for hearings. Most are believed to be economic, not true asylum refugees.

491.   Frank D. Bean. OPENING AND CLOSING THE DOORS, RAND Corporation Press, 1989, p. 53. In addition, a recent study by the GAO (1988d) concluded that "under IRCA, too many documents can be used for employment eligibility purposes to realistically expect employers to control unauthorized employment." It also concluded that the documents used for the Social Security number application and those used for employment authorization are vulnerable to fraud. To date, education of employers on document review and acceptance has been minimal, and the GAO questions the feasibility of educating employers on the large number of acceptable documents. GAO, therefore, recommends reducing the number of documents that can be used for employment authorization and making the Social Security card (after improving its issuance process) the only authorizing document.

492.   Vernon M. Briggs. IMMIGRATION POLICY AND THE AMERICAN LABOR FORCE, Baltimore: Johns Hopkins Press, 1984, p. 184. In all

these countries, therefore, there were fewer applicants for amnesty than had been anticipated. The precise reasons for this are of course unknown. Admittedly, it is very difficult to inform some illegal immigrants of these opportunities. It is also likely that many illegal immigrants are both fearful and distrustful of such offers. Given the experiences of these other nations, it is likely that a sizable number of illegal immigrants in the United States who are eligible for amnesty would not apply for it.

493.   Vernon M. Briggs. IMMIGRATION POLICY
         AND THE AMERICAN LABOR FORCE,
Baltimore: Johns Hopkins Press, 1984, pp. 181-182. Ironically, however, in January 1984 the cost of an amnesty program was cited by David Stockman, the nation's federal budget director, as a reason not to enact the entire bill. This announcement, which came a little over a month after Speaker of the House Thomas P. O'Neill had reversed his opposition to the bill and had promised to allow the House to vote on it, revived the fears that O'Neill had initially expressed—namely, that President Reagan would veto the bill if it was passed. Stockman estimated that the cost of the Senate-passed and House versions of the Simpson-Mazzoli bill would be $10.1 billion and $13.3 billion, respectively, over the period 1984-1989. these costs would accrue primarily as a result of the fact that in time many of the legalized aliens would become eligible for the nation's various social programs. Stockman warned that "both bills create a large new entitlement group of legalized aliens contrary to Administration efforts to control entitlement spending."

494.   Vernon M. Briggs. IMMIGRATION POLICY
         AND THE AMERICAN LABOR FORCE,
Baltimore: Johns Hopkins Press, 1984, p. 184. The serious conceptual flaw in the idea of granting amnesty, however, is the inability to prevent the expectation that once it is given, it will be offered again in the future. The Netherlands has reported that the subject of additional amnesty offers has become a difficult political issue. So far it has refrained from making any new proposals, as have the other nations that provided a one-time amnesty. Admittedly, however, it is a troublesome political concern to refrain from granting it again.

495.   Vernon M. Briggs. IMMIGRATION POLICY
         AND THE AMERICAN LABOR FORCE,
Baltimore: Johns Hopkins Press, 1984, p. 184. Many would, however, and since the main objective of such programs is to reduce the size of the illegal immigrant population of a nation, amnesty could play an important role in the accomplishment of that goal in the United States.

496.   Vernon M. Briggs. IMMIGRATION POLICY
         AND THE AMERICAN LABOR FORCE,
Baltimore: Johns Hopkins Press, 1984, p. 181. In response to these concerns, proponents of an amnesty program have argued that such cost estimates may be

too high. Theoretically, illegal aliens would not be eligible to adjust their status if there was any likelihood of their becoming public charges (in which case they would belong to an excludable class). Also, as Senator Allan Simpson has argued, "These people are not refugees; these people came to the United States for one reason: to work." Hence, Simpson believes, as long as illegal immigrants seek and find work, concerns about the cost of a dependent population will prove to be unfounded.

497.   Vernon M. Briggs. IMMIGRATION POLICY
         AND THE AMERICAN LABOR FORCE,
Baltimore: Johns Hopkins Press, 1984, p. 170. Any strategy to combat illegal immigration must address the need to curtail the demand for illegal immigrant workers. Thus, repeal of the "Texas proviso" and the adoption of a law to make the employment of illegal immigrants an illegal act have served as the natural starting points of all reform movements. An employer sanctions law would set the moral tone. It would define precisely who is in compliance with the laws of the land and who is not. Presently, all employers who hire illegal immigrants are fully within their rights when they do so. An employer sanctions law would clearly indicate that illegal immigrants are not wanted as workers in the United States.

498.   Vernon M. Briggs. IMMIGRATION POLICY
         AND THE AMERICAN LABOR FORCE,
Baltimore: Johns Hopkins Press, 1984, p. 170. Still, the possibility of prosecution would exist. Moreover, there would be some voluntary compliance, and at least the moral weight of the law would be against the employment of illegal aliens. As meaningless as this ban might prove to be, no other reforms will make sense until such a law is on the books.

499.   Keith Crane et al. THE EFFECT OF
         EMPLOYER SANCTIONS ON THE FLOW
OF UNDOCUMENTED IMMIGRANTS TO THE UNITED STATES, Santa Monica: RAND Corporation, April 1990, pp. ix-x. Some indicators continued to show a deterrent effect. The COLEF data indicate a continued decline in the number of people attempting to cross at Canyon Zapata. The number of applicants for asylum exploded to 60,736 from 26, 107 in FY 1987, and 4 of 16 countries registered an increase in the trend for the number of people on the immigration wait list. In addition, in the two-year span after the passage of IRCA, we found that 8 out of 16 countries showed an increase in the trend in the immigrant visa wait list; 5 out of 16, a decline in the trend for the number of business and tourist visas issued.

500.   Wayne Cornelius. AMERICA'S NEW
         IMMIGRATION LAW, Center for U.S.-Mexican Studies, University of California at San Diego, Monograph Series 11, 1983, p. 80. Employer sanctions in the United States will probably not be effective as a deterrent to the employer and hence will not reduce undocumented migration. But this is not to

say that they will have no impact. Any approach which is addressed at the kind of worker employed shifts the onus onto the workers themselves. The federal employer sanctions law will not likely reduce the number of undocumented workers, but it will cause the double "criminalization" of undocumented workers. To obtain a job under the new law, the immigrant will not only have to cross the border without papers but also have to present the employers with bogus documents. As a result, these undocumented workers will be even more vulnerable, even more susceptible to implicit or explicit blackmail by their employers. Furthermore, it is predictable that many undocumented workers, and in some cases the documented, will literally have to pay the price for the legislation. In the initial stages, lay-offs, wage reductions, and up-front payments at the time of employment will be the price that unknown numbers of workers will pay for the "risk" their employers assume in hiring them.

501. Klaus Fuchs. "Agenda for Tomorrow." ANNALS OF THE AMERICAN ACADEMY OF POLITICAL SCIENCE, November 1993, p. 177. Success in substantially reducing illegal migration in the 1990s depends in large part on the willingness of Congress to adopt a secure, reliable system of identifying employees eligible to work. Although the present system is not effective and probably has created some discrimination against foreign-sounding and -looking citizens, the argument remains fierce as to whether a new and secure system to verify job applicants as authorized to work can be phased in and made effective enough to cut back substantially on the migration of illegal aliens, particularly as an unknown and perhaps large proportion of them work in an ethnic cash economy where they may not be asked for identification. A staff report from the Select Commission argued in the affirmative, as did a 1993 report from the Commission on Agricultural Workers, and many experts at hearings and consultations throughout the last decade have as well.

502. Vernon M. Briggs. IMMIGRATION POLICY AND THE AMERICAN LABOR FORCE, Baltimore: Johns Hopkins Press, 1984, p. 173. Other types of worker identification exist, but the point that needs to be made here is that a new identification system must be included in any employer sanctions program if that program is to have a chance to succeed. Yet the members of the Select Commission on Immigration and Refugee Policy—who overwhelmingly endorsed an employer sanctions law—voted only 8 to 7 (one member absent) in favor of coupling the proposed sanctions measure with some form of secure employee identification system. Moreover, this meager majority "was unable to reach a consensus as to the specific type of identification that should be required for verification." Of the ideas that were considered, a counterfeit-proof social security card received the strongest support.

503. Vernon M. Briggs. IMMIGRATION POLICY AND THE AMERICAN LABOR FORCE, Baltimore: Johns Hopkins Press, 1984, p. 172. One suggestion is that a new form of social security card be issued. Since January 1, 1973, citizenship or resident-alien status has been a requirement for eligibility to receive a social security card. The existing card can easily be counterfeited, however. Thus, any new card would have to be unalterable. Special codes have already been developed by cryptographers and computer experts, and it should be easy to use these to verify the citizenship status of any would-be employee. The coded card could be designed like the one that has been issued to resident aliens by the Immigration and Naturalization Service since 1977 (i.e., the ADIT—or Alien Documentation, Identification, and Telecommunications system—card), which includes a photograph, signature, fingerprint, and several rows of coded numbers.

504. Vernon M. Briggs. IMMIGRATION POLICY AND THE AMERICAN LABOR FORCE, Baltimore: Johns Hopkins Press, 1984, pp. 172-173. A social security card—or more specifically a social security number—is already required of virtually everyone as a condition of employment in the private sector. The same is true for most public employees. Thus, the argument against requiring citizens to have identification numbers has already been settled. Like it or not, the social security number has become a national identifier. It serves as a student's ID number on many campuses; it is an individual's driver's license number in eight states; most private health insurance companies use it as a policy number; the Internal Revenue Service uses it to identify taxpayers; and it is the serial number assigned to all persons in the military. The point is that it is absurd to worry about whether something will happen if it has already happened. The only questions that remain are, should social security cards be made noncounterfeitable and should checks be made of these cards to ensure that those who are using them to seek employment are legally entitled to have them.

505. Vernon M. Briggs. IMMIGRATION POLICY AND THE AMERICAN LABOR FORCE, Baltimore: Johns Hopkins Press, 1984, p. 173. David North and Marion Houstoun have studied the identification issue as it relates to the problem of illegal immigration and have recommended a work permit system similar to that used in many other industrialized nations. In another study, however, North developed a unique way to create an identification system that would not require citizenship decisions to be made by employers. Essentially the system would involve the establishment of a nationwide data base. Workers entering the labor force or changing jobs would be required to obtain a work authorization number that would be kept on file at a federal data bank. The number would be issued only after an individual offered some proof that he or she was a citizen or a resident alien. To verify the citizenship eligibility of the newly hired person, employers would only have to call a toll-free data bank number. In return they would receive a transaction

number from the data bank that would indicate their compliance with the employer sanctions provision. The advantage of this system would be that it would not involve any type of card and would not require employers to make a judgment about the eligibility of a job applicant. A would-be worker would have to apply for a work permit at the nearest office of the public employment service. Several types of historical data could be used by the applicant to prove his or her eligibility (e.g., proof of payment of income taxes for a number of past years; proof of payment of social security taxes for a set number of past years; proof of service in the military, government employment, or naturalized citizenship status). An applicant would have to provide at least two types of proof. Only information provided by the applicant would be kept on file. A check of the information provided could be made by comparing it to data already on file in various government data banks. If the computers confirmed the individual's legal presence in the nation, a work permit would be issued.

506.   Wayne Cornelius. AMERICA'S NEW IMMIGRATION LAW, Center for U.S.-Mexican Studies, University of California at San Diego, Monograph Series 11, 1983, p. 124. But as firmly as some Latinos believe that argument, there is no definitive proof that the bill would result in discrimination as a side-effect. None of the studies of employer sanctions laws in other countries and in eleven states of this country have noted any discriminatory side-effects. (Much to the chagrin of advocates of employer sanctions, those studies also found that such laws had little effect in discouraging the employment of illegal immigrants—but that is another issue.)

507.   Austin T. Fragomen, Jr. "Immigration Policy." IN DEFENSE OF THE ALIEN, Vol. 15: 1993, p. 105. Lack of national documentation also increase the incidence of discrimination. I would suggest that policy went astray at that point in the legislative process where the concerns of the civil libertarians rendered the conventional wisdom of the necessity of secure documents untenable.

Moreover, verification as a primary defense against employment of undocumented aliens assumes all employment is in compliance with the law generally. Of course, this is not the case. The "cash" economy is rampant and thrives on the undocumented.

508.   Vernon M. Briggs. IMMIGRATION POLICY AND THE AMERICAN LABOR FORCE, Baltimore: Johns Hopkins Press, 1984, p. 172. Obviously, in order for an employer sanctions law to be enacted it will be necessary to specify exactly what an employer must do to be in compliance. A mere query will not suffice. Because fraudulent documents are readily available both inside and outside the country, traditional forms of identification (i.e., birth certificates, social security cards, drivers' licenses, etc.) are absolutely insufficient. In the absence of some sort of universal identification system, a strong employer sanc-

tions law could lead employers to act in a discriminatory manner toward citizens from the same ethnic groups that comprise the majority of the nation's illegal immigrant population.

509.   Paul Glastris. "Immigration Crackdown." U.S. NEWS AND WORLD REPORT, June 21, 1993, p. 34. Consequently, momentum is building on Capitol Hill to beef up the Border Patrol and improve sanctions against employers who hire undocumented workers, a system almost everyone admits doesn't work. One idea: tamper-proof worker ID cards. Civil liberties groups have successfully opposed this idea on privacy grounds. But Hillary Rodham Clinton's health care task force is considering a national health insurance card that could pave the way.

510.   Vernon M. Briggs. IMMIGRATION POLICY AND THE AMERICAN LABOR FORCE, Baltimore: Johns Hopkins Press, 1984, p. 182. In response to this rapid growth of the illegal immigrant population, the major countries of Western Europe have initiated a series of immigration reforms. Most countries of continental Europe have long relied on the use of work permits. Moreover, Europeans are accustomed to the requirement that they carry identification cards at all times, and they expect to be asked to identify themselves to authorities both on and off the job. Hence, the identification issue has not been a point of contention in Europe. The need for workers to establish their eligibility to work was met in these countries many decades ago.

511.   Vernon M. Briggs. IMMIGRATION POLICY AND THE AMERICAN LABOR FORCE, Baltimore: Johns Hopkins Press, 1984, pp. 174-175, Responding to this and a similar concern expressed by others, the Reverend Theodore Hesburgh, who had served as chairman of the Select Commission on Immigration and Refugee Policy and was also a former chairman of the U.S. Civil Rights Commission, dismissed these fears, however. In 1982 he wrote:

Identification systems to be used upon application for a job and for work purposes are no different from other forms of identification required by our society today and readily accepted by millions of Americans: credit cards which must be checked by merchants; identification cards other than driver's licenses used for cashing checks; social security numbers to open bank accounts, register for school or obtain employment.

...Raising the specter of "Big Brotherism," calling a worker identification system totalitarian or labelling it "the computer taboo" does not further the debate on U.S. immigration policy; it only poisons it. [ellipses in original]

512.   Keith Crane et al. THE EFFECT OF EMPLOYER SANCTIONS ON THE FLOW OF UNDOCUMENTED IMMIGRANTS TO THE UNITED STATES, Santa Monica: RAND Corpora-

tion, April 1990, p. x. For those who expected employer sanctions to halt the flow of undocumented immigrants into the United States in the short run, the evidence clearly shows that such sanctions have not yet been successful. Despite the rhetoric surrounding the passage of IRCA, however, lawmakers appear to have had more modest goals. Yet if the intent was to generate a "large" decline in the flow, employer sanctions have not achieved this goal to date. Congress may wish to *weigh* the cost of continuing employer sanctions against their current level of effectiveness or to *consider increasing the level of enforcement.*

513. Keith Crane et al. THE EFFECT OF EMPLOYER SANCTIONS ON THE FLOW OF UNDOCUMENTED IMMIGRANTS TO THE UNITED STATES, Santa Monica: RAND Corporation, April 1990, p. 68. Based on the wage change results, we find some evidence that the supply of car washers declined in cities with more undocumented immigrants after the imposition of employer sanctions in June 1988. However, in this occupation tips can contribute a sizable amount to total income. Moreover, the results on the change in wage variances do not support this result. We found no evidence of a decline in the supply of labor for dishwashers. We think the data collected on dishwasher wages are more indicative. Food service, in general, is a much more important source of employment than car washes. Furthermore, the wage data for this occupation were more indicative of actual earnings and therefore better reflect the wage necessary to obtain entry-level workers. In short, this analysis does not support the hypothesis that a decline has occurred in the supply of undocumented workers because of employer sanctions.

514. Wayne Cornelius. AMERICA'S NEW IMMIGRATION LAW, Center for U.S.-Mexican Studies, University of California at San Diego, Monograph Series 11, 1983, p. 144. Senator Alan Simpson, the principal author of the employer sanctions legislation pending in Congress, requested the original GAO report on this subject but has not requested any updated information. His staff believes that it is "too soon to tell" about the possible consequences of the recent changes in laws and enforcement strategies in the countries previously studied by the GAO. They note that authorities in Hong Kong reportedly told Attorney General William French Smith that their new identification system designed to prevent illegal immigrants from obtaining employment was "working well." Yet no independent source has confirmed that Hong Kong's worker-identification system has solved its illegal alien "problem" which has been less than monumental in the recent past (an estimated 5,500 illegal aliens were in Hong Kong in 1982). In fact, there is still not a single documented case of successfully using employer sanctions laws to reduce the population of illegal immigrants *anywhere in the world.*

515. Wayne Cornelius. AMERICA'S NEW IMMIGRATION LAW, Center for U.S.-Mex-

ican Studies, University of California at San Diego, Monograph Series 11, 1983, pp. 142-143. Virtually all members of Congress, as well as editorial writers and columnists, have chosen to ignore the fact, pointed out by Kitty Calavita and Carl Schwarz, that this approach to immigration control has already been tried in a dozen U.S. jurisdictions since 1971 and in at least 20 other countries around the world. The results have been practically identical in each case: employer penalties have not reduced the hiring of illegal immigrants and often have created additional problems. The eleven states in this country that have adopted this type of legislation include California and most of the other states that have large concentrations of undocumented immigrants. As Schwarz has reminded us, not a single person has ever been convicted under California's employer sanctions law since its passage in 1971, and nationwide, state-level employer sanctions laws have resulted in only five convictions: one in Kansas, where a convicted employer got a $250 fine; two in Virginia, where the convicted employers received fines of $80 and $44, plus a 30-day suspended jail sentence; and two in Montana against the same corporation, which decided not to contest the $3,200 fine because the legal expenses of an appeal would have exceeded the amount of the penalty.

516. Wayne Cornelius. AMERICA'S NEW IMMIGRATION LAW, Center for U.S.-Mexican Studies, University of California at San Diego, Monograph Series 11, 1983, p. 147. In light of all this evidence, the confidence that most members of Congress and media commentators still place in the employer sanctions concept is noting less than astonishing. Their faith represents a classic example of the "don't let the facts get in the way" approach to public policymaking. The authors of the pending legislation, Senator Simpson and Congressman Mazzoli, have at least practiced the virtue of candor. They have described their bill as a "leap into the dark" but stand by the proposal because, they allege, previous employer sanctions laws have failed to reduce the hiring of illegal immigrants due to a lack of proper enforcement. They argue that with enough money, personnel, and a strong will to enforce, employer penalties can be an effective means of immigration control. Unfortunately, there is still not a shred of evidence to support this claim.

517. Wayne Cornelius. AMERICA'S NEW IMMIGRATION LAW, Center for U.S.-Mexican Studies, University of California at San Diego, Monograph Series 11, 1983, p. 145. Essentially the same picture emerges from all of the other countries studied by the GAO. Employers have devised an endless variety of schemes—and Barbara Strickland's essay includes some examples of them—to evade legal responsibility under employer sanctions laws; and judges are reluctant to impose more than token penalties on these "white-collar criminals," who are usually respected small businessmen in their communities. The few unlucky employers who have been caught and con-

victed have successfully appealed their cases, securing much reduced fines or avoiding penalties altogether. Thus, police and prosecutors are understandably unenthusiastic about investing much time and effort in taking such cases to court.

518.   Vernon M. Briggs. IMMIGRATION POLICY AND THE AMERICAN LABOR FORCE, Baltimore: Johns Hopkins Press, 1984, p. 170. It is debatable, of course, how effective such a law would be. Most proposals state that an employer would be guilty of violating the law only if he or she "knowingly" hired an illegal immigrant. Proving that such "knowledge" was operative is extremely difficult, however. Moreover, it is doubtful that many district attorneys would press for enforcement or that many juries would convict an employer for the offense of providing jobs to anyone. With court dockets already backlogged with serious criminal cases, it is hard to imagine that many employers would ever be brought to trial.

519.   Wayne Cornelius. AMERICA'S NEW IMMIGRATION LAW, Center for U.S.-Mexican Studies, University of California at San Diego, Monograph Series 11, 1983, pp. 144-145. None of the recent changes in laws and enforcement strategies mentioned in the GAO report and trumpeted by defenders of Simpson-Mazzoli can be expected to have a dramatic impact on the situations depicted in that report. If a $20,000 maximum fine failed to deter West German employers from hiring Turkish "illegals," why should a $40,000 fine be more effective? As the GAO reported, German employers "generally appeal administrative fines that the consider too great. Such appeals have generally met with success, as judges have not considered the hiring of illegal aliens a serious violation. Because judges have been lenient,...employers accept the fines as a business cost." [ellipses in original]

520.   Wayne Cornelius. AMERICA'S NEW IMMIGRATION LAW, Center for U.S.-Mexican Studies, University of California at San Diego, Monograph Series 11, 1983, p. 143. Similarly, the major General Accounting Office report cited by several of the contributors to this volume concluded that in all of the 20 countries surveyed by the GAO, "laws penalizing employers of illegal aliens were not an effective deterrent to...illegal employment.... Employers either were able to evade responsibility for illegal employment or, once apprehended, were penalized too little to deter such acts." Clearly, judges do not consider the employment of undocumented workers a serious crime, and they are reluctant to impose penalties. And the more severe the penalty, the less likely it is to be applied, especially criminal fines and jail sentences. [ellipses in original]

521.   Wayne Cornelius. AMERICA'S NEW IMMIGRATION LAW, Center for U.S.-Mexican Studies, University of California at San Diego, Monograph Series 11, 1983, p. 145. But if civil fines are not an effective deterrent, what about criminal penalties? In Germany, for example, employers can be tried as criminals and imprisoned for up to three years for employing illegal immigrants under deplorable working conditions. But when queried by the GAO's investigators, German officials did not know of any employer who had even been imprisoned as a result of such a violation. "Legal proceedings against employers are few because employers and illegal employees cooperate and refuse to testify against one another," the GAO reported. In Canada, court backlogs and excessive costs involved in keeping the illegal immigrant (the prime witness) in Canada for the employer's trial have caused officials to forego prosecuting many employers. In the first nine months of 1981, only 27 employers were prosecuted under Canada's employer sanctions law. Will judges in the United States be any less reluctant to jail employers convicted of hiring unauthorized immigrants? The more severe the penalty, the less likely that judges will apply it in such cases.

522.   Wayne Cornelius. AMERICA'S NEW IMMIGRATION LAW, Center for U.S.-Mexican Studies, University of California at San Diego, Monograph Series 11, 1983, pp. 146-147. Despite what some employers may tell their illegal-immigrant employees, the employer's actual risk of detection and prosecution under the Simpson-Mazzoli Bill will be quite small. When President Jimmy Carter's Attorney General, Griffin Bell, was asked how the Justice Department expected to enforce the Carter administration's proposed employer sanctions law, he replied: "We are traveling on the assumption the Americans are law-abiding people...Once they realize it is now the law that you should not employ an undocumented alien, they will follow the law." The Reagan administration and most of Congress now ask us to make a similar leap of faith. But in all probability, voluntary compliance will not be widespread enough to produce any noticeable reduction in the hiring of undocumented immigrants. [ellipses in original]

523.   Wayne Cornelius. AMERICA'S NEW IMMIGRATION LAW, Center for U.S.-Mexican Studies, University of California at San Diego, Monograph Series 11, 1983, pp. 145-146. Defenders of the Simpson-Mazzoli Bill argue that authorities can maximize the law's effectiveness by encouraging voluntary compliance, which they can allegedly bring about by targeting enforcement efforts on firms know to be "major employers" of illegal aliens. But recent data from several studies of Mexican "illegals" show that the vast majority of them work in small businesses with fewer than 50 employees. Another enforcement strategy under discussion would emphasize highly publicized test cases of prosecution in large cities. However, anti-immigrant hysteria among the general public would probably have to be considerably more intense than at present to guarantee a high level of public tolerance for such "show trials."

524. Barry Chiswick. ILLEGAL ALIENS, Kalamazoo: Upjohn Institute for Employment Research, 1988, p. 145. The 1986 Act introduces "employer sanctions," that is, penalties against employers who knowingly hire illegal aliens. The analysis suggest, however, that at most establishments in 1984 the person in charge of hiring believed that this was already the law of the land. There was little difference in response between the employers identified by an apprehended illegal alien and those randomly selected from directories. This means that the "announcement effect" of the new legislation for deterring the hiring of illegal aliens is likely to be minimal. For the legislation not have a significant impact, substantial resources may have to be devoted to enforcement, and meaningful penalties will have to be imposed. Considering the minimal level of enforcement resources appropriated in the past for immigration control, particularly enforcement away from the border, one may be justifiable skeptical abut future appropriations.

525. Wayne Cornelius. AMERICA'S NEW IMMIGRATION LAW, Center for U.S.-Mexican Studies, University of California at San Diego, Monograph Series 11, 1983, p. 111. Several factors will contribute to a tendency for employer sanctions to increase discrimination against ethnic Americans. First, since the necessity of selective enforcement and a shortage of resources will force the INS to concentrate its enforcement efforts, an employer who hires large number of ethnic workers will run a much greater risk of undergoing investigation. Since such investigations will cost the employers time and money, many of them may attempt to avoid even the possibility of an investigation by reducing the number of ethnic workers that they employ. Since employers are seldom in a position to evaluate the authenticity of documents presented by an employee, many will presume ethnic workers to be illegal and therefore to represent a risk. After the passage of California's employer sanctions law, for example, employers laid off large numbers of Hispanic workers.

526. Wayne Cornelius. AMERICA'S NEW IMMIGRATION LAW, Center for U.S.-Mexican Studies, University of California at San Diego, Monograph Series 11, 1983, p. 111. Employer sanctions will also contribute to discrimination against ethnic Americans by creating a climate of hostility against certain ethnic groups, especially Latinos and Asians. Since INS enforcement priorities overwhelmingly emphasize the Latino and Asian immigrant, they have already created, to a certain extent, the perception that most members of these ethnic groups are "illegal." One sees this hostility demonstrated when people worry about a Hispanic "Quebec" in the United Sates. The perception that the Latino immigrant is somehow linguistically and culturally unassimilable has already gained wide acceptance, despite studies which show that almost no third-generation Hispanics still use Spanish as their dominant language. By singling out Latinos and Asians as potential problems , in the workplace,

employer sanctions will in practice increase popular hostility towards all members of these groups.

527. Joan Biskupt. "Immigration Overhaul Cleared After Last-Minute Flap." CONGRESSIONAL QUARTERLY, November 3, 1990, p. 3753. The license proposal stemmed from a desire to slow the flood of illegal aliens into the country and to give employers, who face penalties for hiring undocumented workers, an easier way to verify that an applicant is here legally. The General Accounting Office reported last spring that employer sanctions are causing widespread bias against foreign-looking workers. *(GAO report, Weekly Report, p. 1005)*

528. Cecelia Munoz. IMMIGRATION AND NATURALIZATION SERVICE MANAGEMENT ISSUES, Hrg of the Committee on the Judiciary, House of Representatives, April 24, 1991, pp. 103-104. Employer sanctions enforcement also suffers from inconsistency and a lack of prioritization. Because the INS has emphasized penalizing employers who fail to fulfill the paperwork requirements of employer sanctions or who have actually hired undocumented workers, rather than educating employers about the anti-discrimination provisions of the law, employers are much more afraid of violating the legal restrictions on hiring than they are of being penalized for discriminating against authorized workers and citizens.

The GAO report, an other studies performed by a wide range of organizations, have shown the human costs of this discrimination—hundreds of thousands of Hispanics have been denied employment opportunities to which they are entitled. Hispanics are one of the fastest growing minorities in the country, and one of the poorest. It is therefore imperative that the INS emphasize the discrimination provisions of IRCA as heavily as the paperwork and hiring requirements. Unfortunately, the agency seems to be moving away from such an approach rather than toward it. The central office recently issued a memorandum to its field operations which, among other things, eliminated the requirement that enforcement personnel make an educational visit to an employer before a fine is imposed.

529. "Letters to the Editor," COMMENTARY, August 1993, p. 2. In my view, employer sanctions are ineffective and unsound. They have given rise to a booming trade in phony documentation. They force employers to play a law-enforcement role, which businesses are ill-equipped to do. Moreover, the evidence shows that these sanctions lead to hiring discrimination against Americans with Asian or Hispanic backgrounds by employers trying to avoid the risk of lawsuit or liability.

530. Wayne Cornelius. AMERICA'S NEW IMMIGRATION LAW, Center for U.S.-Mexican Studies, University of California at San Diego, Monograph Series 11, 1983, p. 146. The Simpson-Mazzoli Bill will exacerbate this problem by giving employers a motive to compensate for a perceived risk

of being fined under an employer sanctions law. As Kitty Calavita's research has revealed, such laws cause deterioration in wages and working conditions for the undocumented and increase the worker's fear of arrest and deportation. Like workplace raids conducted by the Immigration and Naturalization Service, employer sanctions legislation does not reduce the employment of undocumented workers. Such actions only drive the hiring underground. They intensify the immigrants' fear and increase the employer's power to manipulate this fear through threats to call immigration authorities when workers complain about wages or working conditions.

531.   Wayne Cornelius. AMERICA'S NEW
          IMMIGRATION LAW, Center for U.S.-Mexican Studies, University of California at San Diego, Monograph Series 11, 1983, p. 27. As production and service activities are driven underground, the situation of immigrants and domestic minorities working alongside them is likely to deteriorate. Work settings will become more clandestine, and at least part of the increased cost of doing business under the new conditions will be passed on in the form of lower wages. Production can be subcontracted down to illegal sweatshops or to those employing so few workers that they are exempt from the new penalties. Piece-rate homework will become still more common. Violations of fair labor standards laws will become even more difficult to detect.

532.   Barry Chiswick. ILLEGAL ALIENS,
          Kalamazoo: Upjohn Institute for Employment Research, 1988, p. 146. Future flows of illegal aliens will also find their job mobility reduced. As a result of reducing the most effective instrument against employer exploitation, job mobility, it should be expected that the incidence of employer exploitation, in the form of wages below the legal minimum level and undesirable working conditions, will increase in the future.

533.   Barry Chiswick. ILLEGAL ALIENS,
          Kalamazoo: Upjohn Institute for Employment Research, 1988, p. 147. If the deterrent affect of employer sanctions on new illegal migration is not sufficiently strong, wage opportunities in the low-skilled labor market may decrease. This may arise for several reasons. First, the legalized aliens are now likely to have a greater attachment not the U.S. labor market, reducing both season and permanent return migration. This implifies a greater supply of labor to the low-skilled labor market. Second, some, and perhaps many, of the dependent family members whose immigration is sponsored by the now-legalized aliens will enter the labor force. If these are predominantly low-skilled workers, perhaps disproportionately female, the supply of low-skilled workers will expand even further. Third, to the extent that employer sanctions are enforced, employers will have to verify the legal status of each worker hired. The verification process is not without cost. In effect, employer sanctions are the equivalent of a "hiring tax." Relative to wage rates, the "hiring tax"

is more burdensome for low-wage workers in part-time, high turnover, or seasonal jobs. This will reduce the demand for workers in low-wage, low-skilled labor market.

While the intended direct effect of employer sanctions is to raise wages in the low-skilled labor market for workers with legal rights to work in this country, the indirect effects have the opposite impact.

534.   Klaus Fuchs. "Agenda for Tomorrow."
          ANNALS OF THE AMERICAN ACADEMY OF POLITICAL SCIENCE, November 1993, p. 177. The major problem is essentially political and not technical. Despite pubic opinion polls that have consistently shown a large majority of Americans—including Hispanics—supportive of efforts to curtail the flow of unauthorized workers into the United States, a combination of Mexican American advocacy group leaders in coalition with the Black Congressional caucus, civil liberties advocates, and lobbyists for agricultural and other employers have been able to frustrate any attempt to make the system more effective.

535.   Wayne Cornelius. AMERICA'S NEW
          IMMIGRATION LAW, Center for U.S.-Mexican Studies, University of California at San Diego, Monograph Series 11, 1983, pp. 111-112. Finally, employer sanctions and the provision for a national employment identification system create a tremendous potential for the abuse of civil liberties. The existence of such a system will create the temptation to use the identification document for purposes other than determining eligibility for employment, a tendency already manifest in the amendment permitting local police to inquire into immigration status. In recent years, the FBI, IRS, and CIA have abused their powers, and we have no assurance that government agencies will not similarly abuse the employment eligibility card, which would make available an incredible amount of information on any given individual. This response to a perceived problem itself implies much greater risks than does the "problem" which it purports to solve.

536.   Vernon M. Briggs. IMMIGRATION POLICY
          AND THE AMERICAN LABOR FORCE, Baltimore: Johns Hopkins Press, 1984, p. 174. In the congressional debates over the Simpson-Mazzoli bill—especially those in the House of Representatives—this issue proved to be especially worrisome. Many congressmen noted that the U.S. Civil Rights Commission had specifically rejected the idea of establishing any type of national identification system. It had contended that "such a national identity card would provide a tool that could be used to violate the right to privacy of the individual."

537.   Gene McNary. OPERATIONS OF THE
          BORDER PATROL, Hrg of the Committee on the Judiciary, House of Representatives, August 5, 1992, p. 76. To further combat the violence that is imposed upon Border Patrol agents, the Border Patrol is exploring alternative methods currently available to as-

sist in reducing border violence and enhancing the safety of our agents. The Border Patrol is in the process of implementing the use of the expandable side-handle baton. This is designed to offer protection to the officer while allowing a violent or uncooperative offender to be taken into custody without the use of deadly force. The baton training program requires agents to attend and complete 16 hours of basic training to be certified to carry the baton. Agents must also be recertified yearly to retain authorization to carry the baton.

538.   Gene McNary. OPERATIONS OF THE BORDER PATROL, Hrg of the Committee on the Judiciary, House of Representatives, August 5, 1992, pp. 42-43. I pause here to stress that structural changes alone, as reflected by an organization chart, do not guarantee improved performance—only people will. Indeed, as I noted earlier in my statement, our greatest resource is our workforce of talented, dedicated and hard-working employees. In recognition of our need for additional personnel resources, the Department requested, and the U.S. Office of Personnel Management provided, an additional allocation of senior executive service positions.

539.   Gene McNary. OPERATIONS OF THE BORDER PATROL, Hrg of the Committee on the Judiciary, House of Representatives, August 5, 1992, p. 42. Improved coordination at the national level will improve the balance between service and enforcement that is an essential element of our law. Let me stress here that the apparent dichotomy between service and enforcement drawn in the GAO report is a less than precise description of the challenge that the INS faces. When any applicant presents a petition for some benefit under the immigration laws—ranging from a simple request for admission at a port of entry to full naturalization as a citizen—the INS must first establish the validity of that claim under the law. We must ensure that those applying are qualified for the benefit which they seek. An important part of any inspector's or adjudicator's responsibilities is to detect and deny unjustified claims, and to report any evidence of fraud. That decision is the critical link that prevents any clear truncation between services and enforcement of the immigration laws. To that end, I have centralized control of the INS Service Centers. This will provide greater uniformity in adjudicating petitions and applications.

540.   William Gadsby. IMMIGRATION AND NATURALIZATION SERVICE MANAGE-MENT ISSUES, Hrg of the Committee on the Judiciary, House of Representatives, April 24, 1991, p. 6. The area requiring the most immediate attention is the critical need for financial and budgeting reforms. We reported that because of poor financial information, INS could not determine how much it had spent. Without control of spending, INS frequently adjusts the budgets, thereby constraining managers' ability to carry out their programs because they do not have good information on resource availability and priorities. We

recommended that the Attorney General, together with OMB, establish a group of top experts from Federal agencies and from the private sector to work with the Commission to design and implement an effective financial management system by the end of this fiscal year.

541.   David Masci. "Groups Line Up on Both Sides Of Border Fee Proposal," CONGRESSIONAL QUARTERLY, December 1, 1990, p. 4003. "The INS traditionally gets stiffed at budget time," Ray said, "and a $2 crossing fee could raise up to $600 million annually." That would increase by two-thirds the fiscal 1991 INS budget of $900 million.

542.   Tom Bethell. "Immigration, Si; Welfare, No." AMERICAN SPECTATOR, November 1993, p. 18. Crossing the border into the U.S. you go through a turnstile, and an INS official gives you a practiced glance. I showed a driver's license but was told you don't even have to do that. They have a "profile" of likely illegals and do little more than occasional spot checks. So many people are coming across that a huge increase in the bureaucracy would be needed to permit a more thorough inspection. It's the same with cars heading north on the interstate. Sometimes they are stopped and searched, but when that happens the highway instantly becomes a parking lot, and the Mexicans coming across for day-labor and housework in San Diego are three hours late on the job. Then there are complaints to the local politicians.

So, as far as I could see, there really isn't much of a border at all. It's an obstacle that most of the time is "flattened by market forces—the heavy volume of passengers who are crossing at every minute. The potential exists to turn it into a substantial barrier, but the cost of doing so is presumably reckoned to be higher than the benefits. I think I like it that way. If immigration is such a big problem, why does one not hear more complaints about it in San Diego?

543.   Wayne Cornelius. AMERICA'S NEW IMMIGRATION LAW, Center for U.S.-Mexican Studies, University of California at San Diego, Monograph Series 11, 1983, p. 141. The hard reality is that neither the U.S. nor the governments of the main source countries now have the capacity to shut off or sharply reduce the flow simply by policy decision or legislative fiat. The United States cannot build a wall around its economy, hoping to cut off new entries of foreign workers, so that it can concentrate on legalizing those who are already here as permanent settlers. Short of a full-scale militarization of the border, no policy will prevent a continued influx into this country of Mexican migrants who cannot meet the stringent criteria for admission as permanent legal residents, usually because they lack immediate relatives who are U.S. citizens. These people will come legally if they have a legal-entry option, illegally if they do not. So the issue of reducing the size of the illegal component in this flow remains. Attaining that objective is extremely difficult at a time when the U.S. is mired in an economic

depression and when two out of three Americans, according to a 180 Gallup poll, believe that the U.S. should halt *all* immigration until the unemployment rate falls below five percent—which many economists doubt will happen again in this century.

544. "At America's Door." THE ECONOMIST, July 24, 1993, pp. 11-12. Even if it had, it could not do so. Such a huge country, endowed with space, freedom and relative prosperity, has always been a magnet to the world. It still is. It remains, too, the only first-world country that shares a 2,000-mile border with the third world. The pressures of this connection—dirt roads up against bright lights—will always be intense. They can be relieved,, in the long term, only by free-trade agreements such as NAFTA, which will help to increase prosperity and rationalise jobs on either side of the border. A richer region to the south is the best palliative for fears of immigration.

545. Richard Rothstein. "Immigration Dilemmas." DISSENT, Fall 1993, p. 461. Total border control is an unrealizable dream; it is impossible to calculate immigration flows to match domestic employment needs; and a variety of uncontrollable and unpredictable economic, political, and social developments in sending countries will, in any event, have a lot to do with the actual level of immigration. As candidate Clinton realized, we can't hope to design a coherent immigration policy. But there are piecemeal policies we can implement that address some of the problems, at least around the edges.

546. Michael Lemay. FROM OPEN DOOR TO DUTCH DOOR, New York: Praeger Press, 1987, p. 126. The recent wave of immigration and the sizable illegal flow have demonstrated with sharp clarity one aspect of current immigration policy: the U.S. is no longer able to control its borders. Depiction of the border as a "tortilla curtain" or a "revolving door" illustrate a degree of frustration about our lack of ability to keep out those who wish to enter illegally, keep close count and track of those allowed in legally but temporarily to ensure that they leave when their visas expire, and keep up with the tide of illegals who daily pour in and out of the country.

The INS lacks sufficient border guards and equipment to stop the influx of illegals entering at an estimated rate of four per minute. There are fewer border patrol officers on duty along the 2,000 miles of Mexican-U.S. border than there are policemen on the day shift in Philadelphia. The agency's enforcement budget for 1985 comes to only $366 million for a staff of 7,599—less than a third the number of officers in New York City's police force (*Time*, July 8, 1985). Its ponderous and archaic operations result in foreigners who wish to enter legally having to wait years for approval. This state of affairs induces attempts at illegal entry. Members of Congress have characterized the INS as the "worst agency in government" (*The Wall Street Journal*, May 9, 1985: 1-2).

The INS has been treated with worse than benign neglect. Its agents have been left without enough gasoline to carry out routine patrols. Its record-keeping remains so outdated and outmoded as to be literally useless. What other agency of government would be allowed to drift along for two and one-half years without a permanent director?

547. Milton Morris. IMMIGRATION—THE BELEAGUERED BUREAUCRACY, Washington, D.C: The Brookings Institute, 1985, pp. 107-108. The Border Patrol—the unit within the INS that is responsible for preventing unauthorized entries and for apprehending those who enter the United States illegally in the border region—has never had the means to carry out this task effectively. Although the Border Patrol has apprehended over a million illegal entrants a year in at least three of the years since 1977, another million or more probably succeed in entering illegally each year. Part of the problem is that the Border Patrol is small and has limited resources at its disposal to cope with the border management task. In fiscal year 1981 the daily on-duty force averaged about 2,690 officers on the immediate border, or a maximum of roughly 900 persons per shift (not allowing for leaves, illnesses, and the like) to patrol almost 2,000 miles of Mexican-U.S. border. And in spite of the growing concern about illegal border crossings, the number of Border Patrol positions authorized for 1983 was only thirty-four more than the number for 1980.

548. T. J. Bonner. OPERATIONS OF THE BORDER PATROL, Hrg of the Committee on the Judiciary, House of Representatives, August 5, 1992, p. 144. Considering the current and predictable resources of the border Patrol, control of illegal immigration at the border is virtually impossible. Transferring agents from traffic checkpoints and other inland areas to the border would do nothing to change this situation. In fact, even a shoulder-to-shoulder army of Border Patrol agents lined along the perimeter of our nation would be unable to control illegal immigration at the border, as smugglers would easily be able to breach that defense by directing large masses of undocumented migrants toward a single location. Traffic checkpoints situated at strategic areas where main smuggling routes converge, and inland stations located at other critical areas, are an efficient utilization of limited resources, and are vital to the accomplishment of the Border Patrol's mission.

549. Michael Lemay. FROM OPEN DOOR TO DUTCH DOOR, New York: Praeger Press, 1987, p.128. The Iranian student debacle and the Haitian and Cuban boat people flooding ashore demonstrated the inability of the U.S. to control its borders. And the thousands who do enter legally daily leave behind a paper trail of about 50 million files with which the INS is simply incapable of coping. It has no idea of who comes, leaves or overstays. Its disastrous record-keeping results from use of 19th century tools and approaches to the data handling and processing as-

pects of the agency's tasks. It is, indeed, remarkable and ironic that an immensely rich and technologically advanced nation like the United States is no longer able to keep out those from other countries who wish to come here. Anyone with the desire to cross and the physical stamina to do so is apparently able to do so with impunity.

550.	Milton Morris. IMMIGRATION—THE BELEAGUERED BUREAUCRACY, Washington, D.C: The Brookings Institute, 1985, pp. 120-121. Confronted with court decisions outlawing or restricting some of this basic investigative procedures, the INS often has attempted to conform by discontinuing the offending practices. More significantly, these legal developments, as well as the high cost and labor-intensive nature of the investigative activities in the interior of the country, have prompted the INS to reduce its emphasis on apprehending and expelling deportable aliens already in the country and to stress instead increased efforts to prevent illegal entries. They have also prompted INS officials to try to focus more on combating organized illegal schemes like smuggling, sham marriages, and the production of fraudulent documents than on apprehending individual deportable aliens within the country.

These are rational decisions, given the demands on the INS and the resources at its disposal, but they signify a partial abandonment of a vital part of the enforcement responsibility. Moreover, the diminishing effectiveness of the internal control efforts of the INS—especially the declining likelihood that a deportable alien in the country will be apprehended and expelled—makes the immigrant flow more difficult to manage because illegal residence comes to be perceived as almost risk free and therefore a good investment by those abroad who seek employment here.

551.	David Masci. "Groups Line Up on Both Sides Of Border Fee Proposal," CONGRESSIONAL QUARTERLY, December 1, 1990, p. 4003. The INS has yet to announce any plans. But Hispanic Americans have voiced concerns that the fees would unfairly hit poor Mexicans and other Latin Americans whose lifestyles and livelihoods straddle the border.

"The people who live near the border are going to bear the brunt of these fees," said Cecilia Muñoz, a policy analyst for the National Council of La Raza, a Hispanic-American immigration-rights group. While agreeing that more inspectors are needed at the border, she said that people who work, shop and visit relatives in the United States have "ties that we should be encouraging, not discouraging by charging an entry fee."

552.	Cecelia Munoz. IMMIGRATION AND NATURALIZATION SERVICE MANAGEMENT ISSUES, Hrg of the Committee on the Judiciary, House of Representatives, April 24, 1991, p. 104. *Border Violence*—Due to understaffing and a lack of training, violence instigated by INS Border Patrol officers is increasing. Last year, for example, an unarmed 15-year-old boy was shot and killed by Border Patrol agents. Harassment of anyone who fits the stereotype of an Hispanic is common. This harassment can involve being stopped and questioned or being detained. Hispanic citizens have been forced across the border into Mexico by enforcement officials who are not satisfied with their proof of identity.

553.	Roberto Martinez. BORDER VIOLENCE, Hrg of the Committee on the Judiciary, House of Representatives, September 29, 1993, p. 265. Over the last ten years human and civil rights violations have run the gamut of abuses imaginable. From shootings that have left dozens of men and boys dead and injured, to sexual and physical abuse, including several rapes by US Border Patrol agents. The most common abuse we document is physical abuse. Although shootings are less frequent now, victims of physical abuse are found to be suffering more severe injuries than ever before.

At the present time, besides severe physical abuse cases, we are also experiencing an increase in arrests and abuses against US citizens by both US Border Patrol and US Customs. Both US citizens and legal residents are often either excluded from entering the United Sates at the ports of entry or when stopped by Border Patrol are not given the benefit of the doubt as to their citizenship. They are often accused of falsifying their documents or accused of buying them illegally. Even original birth certificates and green cards are confiscated as fraudulent documents leaving the victim with the financial burden of having to go through a lengthy process of applying for a new document.

554.	Aryeh Neier. OPERATIONS OF THE BORDER PATROL, Hrg of the Committee on the Judiciary, House of Representatives, August 5, 1992, p. 203. Undocumented migrants who enter or are living in the United States may be deportable or excludable, but their immigration status does not lessen their entitlement to respect for their basic human rights. As an institution, the INS needs to redirect its mission to emphasize the promotion and protection of human rights in the fulfillment of its responsibility to enforce U.S. immigration laws. This policy must be conveyed, through example and training, to all INS personnel. The INS must make clear to its personnel that failure to respect the legally protected human rights of any person will be punished.

555.	Cecelia Munoz. IMMIGRATION AND NATURALIZATION SERVICE MANAGEMENT ISSUES, Hrg of the Committee on the Judiciary, House of Representatives, April 24, 1991, pp. 104-105. Enforcement officials receive little training in the civil and human rights standards to which they should adhere. In addition, they often suffer from a sense of siege because they are so outnumbered by the flow of the undocumented across the southern border. Despite this understaffing at the border, the GAO has noted that Border Patrol agents are becoming increasingly involved in nonborder control activities which should be covered by the Investigations Division. The

nonborder activities in which the Border Patrol is engaged include investigating drug smuggling organizations, enforcing employer sanctions, and identifying and taking into custody criminal aliens. Border Patrol units were found 300 miles north of the border." Commissioner McNary recently testified before the House Appropriations Subcommittee on Commerce, Justice, State and Judiciary that he has ordered Border Patrol activities to be limited to a 50-mile distance to alleviate this stretching of resources.

Border violence may soon be exacerbated, however, by certain provisions of ImmAct '90. The Act expands the arrest authority of the INS and expressly authorizes the use of firearms by enforcement officials.

556. Michael Lemay. FROM OPEN DOOR TO DUTCH DOOR, New York: Praeger Press, 1987, p. 131. The underfunding of the INS compels it to engage in various secondary enforcement activities to locate illegal entrants: stopping traffic at checkpoints, watching air, bus and rail terminals, inspecting farms, ranches and areas of employment, and following up on specific leads. Such activities, however, pose more problems regarding the civil rights of individuals and numerous instances occur where such rights are likely to be abused. Enforcement begins to take on a perverse quality—we tend to apprehend and return those aliens who are truthful; the ones who avoid apprehension and remain among us are the ones most likely to be those who can successfully dissemble (Bennet, D., 1985: 8). The 1986 law does increase funding and staffing for the Border Patrol but probably still insufficiently so to substantially reduce this aspect of the problem.

557. Peter Visclosky. IMPLEMENTATION OF THE IMMIGRATION ACT OF 1990, Hrg of the Committee on the Judiciary, House of Representatives, May 15, 1991, p. 17. Earlier this year, with the Subcommittee's assistance, I secured a General Accounting Office study to determine the percentage of Indiana INS applicants who reside in Northwest Indiana. Unfortunately, I was informed by the GAO that the study could not be performed because INS's record-keeping is inadequate. As you can imagine, I found this very disturbing. The lack of records calls into question whether INS is adequately meeting its legal mandate to serve the public and whether government funds are being spent with necessary care.

Mr. Chairman, the problems with inadequate INS service in Northwest Indiana are only indicative of the problems that other communities across the nation are experiencing. According to a January, 1991 GAO report on INS management, the average processing time nationwide for various applications continues to exceeded INS' own 4-month requirement, and lengthy processing delays of cases continue to occur at several district offices. As a nation of immigrants, the United States cannot allow the delays, poor recordkeeping, ad other mismanagement problems to continue.

558. Aryeh Neier. OPERATIONS OF THE BORDER PATROL, Hrg of the Committee on the Judiciary, House of Representatives, August 5, 1992, pp. 218-219. One way it does so is by maintaining an unresponsive complaint process. The INS boasts, as noted above, that it receives only one complaint of abuse for every 17,000 arrests. That figure misleads the public into thinking that there is a meaningful and well-publicized means for filing complaints. In fact, the complaint system now in place is a well-kept secret that most victims of Border Patrol abuse never learn about and those who do often fear to use. Among the persistent problems with the complaint procedures are the lack of a complaint form; the lack of a comprehensive and systematic procedure for informing the public of its right to complain; inadequate staffing in comparison to the number of INS employees; employment of investigators who have past ties to the INS or a bias in favor of the agency; the failure to notify complainants of the status and disposition of their complaints; the lack of an adequate appeals process; and the lack of meaningful guarantees to ensure that reprisals are not taken against those who file complaints. Again, this last is especially important. It allows us to see the small number of complaints in a different light: that is, it is more a consequence of an effective means of intimidation than a tribute to lack of abuse.

559. Aryeh Neier. OPERATIONS OF THE BORDER PATROL, Hrg of the Committee on the Judiciary, House of Representatives, August 5, 1992, p. 219. The INS covers up for agent misconduct by filing intimidating criminal misdemeanor or felony charges against victims of abuse. While most undocumented migrants who are arrested by the Border Patrol are given "voluntary departure," and bussed to the border, the Border Patrol has the power to put undocumented migrants into deportation proceedings, or to charge them criminally with illegal entry or another federal crime. This power has been abused and serves to deter victims of abuse from pursuing complaints.

560. Aryeh Neier. OPERATIONS OF THE BORDER PATROL, Hrg of the Committee on the Judiciary, House of Representatives, August 5, 1992, p. 218. The most outrageous explanation for Border Patrol misconduct is the agency's willingness to cover for almost any form of egregious abuse by its agents. The agency seems far more interested in protecting the reputation of its agents than in protecting the human rights of the million or more people with whom it comes into contact each year.

561. Aryeh Neier. OPERATIONS OF THE BORDER PATROL, Hrg of the Committee on the Judiciary, House of Representatives, August 5, 1992, p. 221. The attitude that is reflected in such efforts to dismiss criticism does not encourage us to believe that the INS is capable of reforming itself. External pressure from the Congress; and structural change, as in the establishment of the independent Board of Re-

view that we have proposed, are required. It shames this nation of immigrants when we deal abusively with strangers at our borders seeking entry either because they are fleeing persecution or because they are seeking economic advancement and a better life. Again, we are not urging changes in our laws dealing with immigrants. We are urging that the law should be enforced in a manner that is becoming to a lawful society.

562.   T. J. Bonner. OPERATIONS OF THE BORDER PATROL, Hrg of the Committee on the Judiciary, House of Representatives, August 5, 1992, pp. 159-160. Despite these allegations and documented cases over the years, very few institutional changes have been implemented to prevent and/or respond to abusive and illegal behavior. It appears that the U.S. Border Patrol and the Immigration and Naturalization Service (INS) are so overwhelmed by the pressures of having to enforce immigration laws in the U.S. that they have ignored violations of law by some agents of the Border Patrol or failed to enact policies and procedures to prevent such behavior.

563.   Arnold Torres. OPERATIONS OF THE BORDER PATROL, Hrg of the Committee on the Judiciary, House of Representatives, August 5, 1992, p. 19. And just let me draw your attention to another management problem that has implications for border violence. GAO reports that the INS lacks access to essential data, and that information management is a systemwide problem for this agency. The information management system at the INS is missing essential data which hampers its ability to perform many core functions, such as the control and management of financial resources.

A key to addressing the problem or border violence is accountability through accurate and efficient management of complaint information. The quality of the internal complaint process has important implications for the agency's ability to identify and correct violence problems.

564.   Aryeh Neier. OPERATIONS OF THE BORDER PATROL, Hrg of the Committee on the Judiciary, House of Representatives, August 5, 1992, p. 706. An independent Board of Review, with an independent staff to receive and investigate complaints would be sensitive to this question and could devise procedures to allow complainants to file their complaints in a manner that would minimize the risk of reprisals. There is no way to determine how many complaints would emerge, or their seriousness, unless such procedures are adopted. Also, there is no way to assure complainants that they would not face reprisals without the creation of an Independent Board of Review. Such a Board would establish methods of disseminating information about the filing of complaints and ways to persuade potential complainants that complaints may be made safely. If such a Board had the power to compel the production of evidence, it could assure complainants that a good faith effort would be made to investigate the merits of their complaints.

565.   Aryeh Neier. OPERATIONS OF THE BORDER PATROL, Hrg of the Committee on the Judiciary, House of Representatives, August 5, 1992, pp. 208-209. Part of the reason that the issue has not aroused greater concern is that most victims of Border Patrol abuse either have no opportunity to or are afraid to report the abuses they suffered. The majority are undocumented migrants who, following arrest by the Border Patrol, sign voluntary departure agreements and are quickly repatriated. Neither the right to file a complaint nor instructions on how to do so are routinely communicated to persons in INS custody. Moreover, many fear that if they report Border Patrol abuses they will face reprisals such as being criminally charged with illegal entry or another crime, or being placed in deportation proceedings instead of being offered voluntary departure. Under those circumstances they risk detention as well as restrictions on their ability to enter lawfully or live in the United States in the future.

566.   Cecelia Munoz. IMMIGRATION AND NATURALIZATION SERVICE MANAGEMENT ISSUES, Hrg of the Committee on the Judiciary, House of Representatives, April 24, 1991, pp. 105-106. *Detention Practices*—The GAO concluded that serious problems exist at several INS detention facilities because of inadequate levels of staff and security. NCLR has been involved with a working group with the INS focusing on one of the more alarming INS detention practices, the detention of children and youth. The focus of the working group has been to provide alternatives to the detention of minors. For any period in which a minor is detained, however, conditions should meet recognized child welfare standards. Currently, many children and youth are detained in large facilities grossly inadequate to meet their needs. In some cases, children are detained on a long-term basis in juvenile halls designed for the incarceration of juvenile delinquents. In other cases, they are housed in unlicensed shelter facilities. The staffing, education, meals, and recreation provided to these minors are often minimal. In addition, many of these minors have fled their homelands in very traumatic circumstances and require mental health care that the INS is unable to provide. NCLR applauds Commissioner McNary's personal commitment to resolving these problems through the working group, but is concerned that funding limitations may impede the speedy resolution of these issues.

567.   Arthur Helton. IMMIGRATION AND NATURALIZATION SERVICE MANAGEMENT ISSUES, Hrg of the Committee on the Judiciary, House of Representatives, April 24, 1991, p. 158. On the issue of detention, we estimate that currently about 50,000 aliens are detained each year in INS facilities across the country. While some are criminal offenders awaiting deportation, we estimate that about 10,000 are persons seeking political asylum in the United States because of fear of persecution in their home countries. These groups are sometimes confined

together due to lack of available space. According to the January, 1991 GAO report, the INS has failed to meet the increased need for additional detention facilities.

568. Vernon M. Briggs. IMMIGRATION POLICY AND THE AMERICAN LABOR FORCE, Baltimore: Johns Hopkins Press, 1984, pp. 175-176. Unfortunately, in neither the work of the Select Commission on Immigration and Refugee Policy nor the debates on the Simpson-Mazzoli bill was any attention given to the voluntary departure system as a factor that contributes to illegal immigration. It is doubtful, however, that any policy to stop illegal immigration will ever be taken seriously so long as there is virtually no chance that a penalty will be imposed on offenders. Until all illegal immigrants are identified, records are kept, and repeat offenders are subjected to formal deportation hearings (which would permanently preclude them from legal immigrant status), aliens will have no reason even to ponder the risks of immigrating illegally.

569. H. L. Hazelbaker. "How to Repel Immigrants' Threat." NEW YORK TIMES, August 30, 1992, sect 13LI, p. 17. The failure of the Suffolk County government to take steps to aid in repelling this invasion of our nation is more than disconcerting. It is despicable. For a Town Councilman to state that "we have no choice but to welcome them" is an admission of governmental and moral bankruptcy. You don't welcome people who have violated our law and threaten our national cohesion and institutions. The correct response for governmental leaders, and indeed all citizens, is to inform the I.N.S. whenever these people are identified, so they may receive the only benefit they have any claim to—a fast return trip to their country of origin.

570. Vernon M. Briggs. IMMIGRATION POLICY AND THE AMERICAN LABOR FORCE, Baltimore: Johns Hopkins Press, 1984, p. 176. Relying more heavily on legal procedures, however, will be costly and time-consuming and will necessitate an increase in the INS budget. Nevertheless, these costs, as well as the expense of acquiring more detection hardware, must be weighed against the costs of allowing the growth of the nation's illegal immigrant population to continue unabated. It is the present author's view that it would be far less costly to assume a strong posture of prevention than to respond to the social costs of illegal immigration after they accumulate.

571. Vernon M. Briggs. IMMIGRATION POLICY AND THE AMERICAN LABOR FORCE, Baltimore: Johns Hopkins Press, 1984, p. 12. Of course, numerous other theories of immigration from various social science disciplines are far more elaborate in their designs and assumptions. Many of these theories, however, contradict each other. Some stress the economic motivations of the individuals involved, but most introduce other sociopolitical factors as well. Some stress institutional practices by businesses and

governments that focus on demand for labor objectives; others focus upon supply factors that propel people to leave their homelands; and obviously some emphasize both "push" and "pull" processes. Some are explicitly Marxist in their belief that capitalist economic development triggers emigration motivations within the "have not" nations of the world. Thus, the debate among academicians in search of an explanation for the causes of immigration is endless. Rather than devote attention to a fruitless review of the various theories and their respective deficiencies, or attempt to adopt any particular theoretical approach, this study will focus on immigration policy—not immigration theory—and on the evolution of its influences upon the labor force of the United States. This approach accepts the wisdom of John Dunlop, who has poignantly observed: "Theories are intellectually exciting and challenging but their relevance and application to policy making is scarcely within the reach of most researchers." In fact, Dunlop asserts, the tools of analysis used by researchers and those used by policymakers are frequently separated by "millions of light years."

572. Vernon M. Briggs. IMMIGRATION POLICY AND THE AMERICAN LABOR FORCE, Baltimore: Johns Hopkins Press, 1984, pp. 11-12. Frankly stated, there is pitifully little in the economic literature that can serve as a theoretical basis for explaining the causes of immigration. The standard approach to this question among economists rests upon the neoclassical assumption that the operation of supply-and-demand forces will lead to tendencies that seek an equilibrium position. Immigration from nations with a slow rate of growth and surplus labor into nations with higher growth rates and labor shortages is viewed as a self-adjusting process in which spatial differences between the demand for and supply of labor are automatically reconciled. The efforts of a nation like the United States to protect its labor force from the adverse effects (i.e., competitive forces that depress wages and reduce living standards) of unlimited immigration are viewed as self-defeating, for in the absence of market forces to reduce wages and lower work standards, business will invest in capital-intensive rather than labor-intensive forms of technology. The resulting unemployment is attributed to the strength and selfishness of existing trade unions or the prevalence of government-imposed protective legislation that inhibits the equilibrium adjustment process. In other words, reliance upon much of this theoretical construct is tantamount to acceptance of the necessity of keeping labor costs cheap and living standards low for most workers. Small wonder, therefore, that even the "Chicago school of economics" is reluctant to embrace unlimited immigration as a desirable course for public policymakers to pursue.

573. Frank D. Bean. OPENING AND CLOSING THE DOORS, RAND Corporation Press, 1989, p. 73. There are at least two reasons to expect that many (possibly most) ineligible workers will remain here. First, the growing disparities in job oppor-

tunities and wages between the United States and the various countries of origin, as well as political and social unrest in some of these countries make undocumented immigrants unlikely to leave voluntarily, even if their job opportunities or wages fall here. A second reason is the family ties that some remaining undocumented individuals have with legal or IRCA—legalized immigrants.

574.   Wayne Cornelius. AMERICA'S NEW IMMIGRATION LAW, Center for U.S.-Mexican Studies, University of California at San Diego, Monograph Series 11, 1983, pp. 10-11. It would appear, at first sight, difficult for an economic theory predicated on a tendency toward market equilibrium to account for such a process: the migratory flow should grind to a halt when demand for labor in the receiving country bottoms out. However, a continued flow of immigrants in a period of rising domestic unemployment is regulated by the market mechanism operating in its most rational form. Leaving aside the temporary excess that may occur as the result of information lag, of conjunctional downturn, or of the intrusion of non-economic factors—as when migrant workers succeed in gaining the right to stay in the receiving country when not needed or to bring in dependents—two processes come into play. First, the extreme wage differential between the two countries, in combination with the fact that the workers initially think of themselves as migrants rather than settlers, insures that workers from the periphery, who intend to maintain their original low standard of living and to transfer their savings to the country of origin, expect that they will be able to sell their labor at such a low price that they will always find a buyer, even in a period of high native unemployment. And, in fact, their calculations are quite correct. As the flow continues, displacement occurs; the excess thus formed consists not of immigrants but of natives. The replacement of the latter by the former is rational from the point of view of the receiving economy as a whole, since the displaced native is commonly entitled to income transfers. Secondly, the wide gap in the income of individual workers living in countries at very different levels of development stems not only from wage differentials, but also from substantial differences in income from collective goods provided by the respective countries. Notwithstanding their many discomforts and problems, advanced industrial societies with liberal regimes provide their residents with many more universally prized valuables such as disease-free environments, freedom from arbitrary exactions, or sheer entertainment and variety of life, than do less-developed countries. In some sense, the lower the wage income of the immigrant worker in the receiving country, the more prominently access to collective goods not available at home figures in that person's total income As indicated earlier, the preservation of such collective goods is one of the factors which determines the necessity of restriction; but access to them cannot be easily denied to anyone physically present in the society. Overall, the pressure for entry can be thought of as permanent, and some will always squeeze through.

575.   Vernon M. Briggs. IMMIGRATION POLICY AND THE AMERICAN LABOR FORCE, Baltimore: Johns Hopkins Press, 1984, p. 158. The primary reason for illegal immigrants to come to the United States is to search for jobs, and studies show that by and large they are successful. Other motivations, such as criminal activity or income maintenance support from available income transfer programs, appear to be relatively inconsequential. thus, the impact of illegal immigrants on the U.S. labor market has repeatedly surfaced as one of the most critical and controversial issues surrounding the whole subject.

576.   Vernon M. Briggs. IMMIGRATION POLICY AND THE AMERICAN LABOR FORCE, Baltimore: Johns Hopkins Press, 1984, p. 185. Since the time of the Pilgrim Fathers, some immigration to the United States has been motivated by reasons other than the desire for economic improvement. Among the immigrants admitted to the United States there have often been individuals and groups who were seeking to escape persecution in their homelands. Thus the subject of refugee accommodation is not a new one for the nation. Having paid homage to tradition, however, it is necessary to indicate that the issue of accepting refugees at a time when the nation's immigration policy was essentially to open its doors to virtually all who sought entry is entirely different from the issue of refugee accommodation today, for now there is a complex regulatory system in place to determine eligibility for admission within the scope of an overall annual admissions ceiling as well as individual country ceilings. In terms of U.S. history, then, refugee policy was of no real consequence in the policy formulation process prior to the 1920s, but since the mid-1930s it has become one of the most perplexing issues ever to confront policymakers.

577.   Vernon M. Briggs. IMMIGRATION POLICY AND THE AMERICAN LABOR FORCE, Baltimore: Johns Hopkins Press, 1984, pp. 151-152. The main force behind Mexican Immigration—especially the illegal inflows—has always been the lure of the United States as "a promised land." Acting as a network of information, "word of mouth" accounts of better job opportunities, high wages, and improved living conditions circulate from returnees and from letters that often contain remittances (which in the aggregate total in the tens of millions of dollars each year) to family members who remain behind. These tales are often exaggerated or at least tend to minimize negative aspects of the experience. The verbal and written accounts, the reality of the remittances, and the immigrants' visits home add to the desires of others to emigrate. It does not take much information for many Mexicans in the northern and central sections of the country to realize that in purely economic terms life in the United States is likely to offer far more options than the arduous and stifling life of perpetual poverty that faces most who choose to remain in Mexico.

578. Vernon M. Briggs. IMMIGRATION POLICY AND THE AMERICAN LABOR FORCE, Baltimore: Johns Hopkins Press, 1984, pp. 156-157. In fact, some scholars have examined this issue and are convinced that the lack of credible deterrence is no accident. They argue that the United states actually wants to have illegal immigrants on hand to keep the labor market for unskilled workers in constant surplus. In 1982, while the Simpson-Mazzoli bill was pending before Congress, for instance, on observer reported that many Mexicans "commonly assume that the U.S. economy's demand for foreign labor is ineradicable, even in a recession; and many maintain a Marxist world-view leading them to believe business interests dominate Congress and, thus, would never allow Congress to pass or to enforce stiff employer sanctions."

579. Michael Lemay. FROM OPEN DOOR TO DUTCH DOOR, New York: Praeger Press, 1987, p. 126. Milton Morris, the director of research for the Joint Center for Political Studies in Washington, D.C., recently pointed out the anomaly implicit in our national attitude towards immigration policy: "We are opposed to illegal immigration in principle, but we really object to the idea of the INS arresting some hardworking guy and taking away his chance to make a living" (The Wall Street Journal, May 9, 1985: 1). the war against illegal immigration often makes the INS an unpopular agents in a nation that proudly sees itself as a melting pot. By keeping the INS weak we are simultaneously able to pursue two contradictory immigration policies: a stated policy of selective immigration, and an actual one of quite liberal immigration. as we shall see more fully below, the very vagueness of some of the language contained in the newly enacted Immigration Reform and Control Act of 1986, which seems to have been essential for its successful passage, retains the status of ambiguity in immigration policy.

580. Wayne Cornelius. AMERICA'S NEW IMMIGRATION LAW, Center for U.S.-Mexican Studies, University of California at San Diego, Monograph Series 11, 1983, p. 148. Nothing that the U.S. government has done in the last 100 years has appreciably reduced the demand for Mexican and other foreign labor in our economy. Given this track record, this country may today be facing the alternatives of immigration regulated by market forces or militarization of the border, coupled with the kinds of internal controls on population movement that some European countries have but that most Americans would find intolerable. This type of governmental "cure" seems, on the basis of existing evidence, worse than the perceived "illness."

581. Lincoln Chen. "Living Within Limits." ISSUES IN SCIENCE AND TECHNOLOGY, December 22, 1993. p. 88. Hardin does not answer the question of how rich countries will prevent immigrants from slipping across the border. So far, efforts to stem the flow of traffic-whether in drugs or people—from South to North America have been notoriously ineffective. It remains unclear whether immigration can be restricted without resorting to draconian methods and without the cooperation of sending or transit countries.

582. Vernon M. Briggs. IMMIGRATION POLICY AND THE AMERICAN LABOR FORCE, Baltimore: Johns Hopkins Press, 1984, p. 4. Despite the fact that the immigration policies of most nations have sought to restrict the inflow of persons, these attempts have often failed. Illegal immigration has become a common phenomenon on virtually every continent. Sometimes, during periods of labor shortages, governments decide to supplement their domestic labor forces temporarily with nonimmigrant foreign workers. It is estimated that in 1980 some 20 million persons lived and worked in countries of which the were not citizens, nor did they intend, or would they usually be allowed, to become citizens.

583. Vernon M. Briggs. IMMIGRATION POLICY AND THE AMERICAN LABOR FORCE, Baltimore: Johns Hopkins Press, 1984, p. 128. In many ways illegal immigration is a dilemma that is inherent in a free society. It is unlikely that the United Sates will ever be able to stop completely the flow of persons who enter the country illegally. Yet the problem is not one that can be ignored simply because of the difficulties that may be encountered in designing appropriate policy responses. The policy objective, therefore, is not to stop illegal immigration but rather to bring the flow under control by significantly reducing both its scale and its adverse effects. Laws against speeding on the nation's highways have not stopped all speeders, but they have probably reduced the incidence of speeding from what it would be in their absence. Moreover, laws against speeding have enabled law enforcement officials to focus attention upon the most serious offenders. The same expectations can be expressed in policy measures aimed at controlling illegal immigration. The fact that there are presently no meaningful deterrents to illegal immigration at least implicitly signals to people of other countries that the United States is not really committed to enforcing its immigration statutes. Until this incongruity is rectified, it will be impossible to say that the nation has a coherent immigration policy.

584. William Gadsby. IMMIGRATION AND NATURALIZATION SERVICE MANAGEMENT ISSUES, Hrg of the Committee on the Judiciary, House of Representatives, April 24, 1991, p. 8. GAO found that over the past decade weak management systems and inconsistent leadership have allowed serious problems to go unresolved. Without coherent overall direction and basic management reforms, the organization has been unable to effectively address certain enforcement responsibilities and longstanding service delivery problems.

585. Harry Pachon. IMMIGRATION REFORM, Hrg of the Committee on the Judiciary, Senate, March 3, 1989, pp. 177-178. The major problem underlying the management difficulties plaguing the INS is the lack of a clearly stated, cohesive immigration policy. That is, we have no overall concept of what we hope to achieve as a nation through immigration. And, in the absence of a clear congressional mandate, the courts have taken up the policy-making role. Increasingly, America's important immigration policies are being made by judges rather than by the elected representatives of the people.

586. Cecelia Munoz. IMMIGRATION AND NATURALIZATION SERVICE MANAGEMENT ISSUES, Hrg of the Committee on the Judiciary, House of Representatives, April 24, 1991, p. 98. We concur with these findings. The Hispanic community has firsthand experience with the human impact of the INS' infrastructural problems. The reports generally divide these effects into two categories—**service delivery problems** and **enforcement problems**. In terms of service delivery, despite the fact that expenditures for adjudications have nearly doubled since 1986, lengthy backlogs exist in many INS districts for the adjudication of naturalization, asylum, and adjustment of status petitions. In addition, many potential applicants are confused or misinformed about these programs due to a lack of INS outreach. On the enforcement side, officials have been increasingly overburdened as they have been charged with the responsibility of controlling illegal immigration, enforcing employer sanctions, deporting criminal aliens, and interdicting international drug traffickers. In addition, the two INS divisions enforcing these policies, the Border Patrol and the Investigations Division, have overlapping duties that are not clearly prioritized or managed by the central office. As a result, programs have been implemented inefficiently and inconsistently.

587. Milton Morris. IMMIGRATION—THE BELEAGUERED BUREAUCRACY, Washington, D.C: The Brookings Institute, 1985, p. 114. Experiences like these illustrate the inadequacy of the most basic element in the administration of immigration policy—the INS data-gathering system. Undoubtedly the INS problem is partly a result of the rapidly rising number of aliens entering the country, but it also reflects the long-standing inattention to these needs by both the executive branch and Congress. Other units within the government that must maintain current information on large numbers of individuals, such as the Social Security Administration and the Federal Bureau of Investigation, have been able to maintain reasonably effective and reliable data systems.

588. Warren Leiden. IMMIGRATION AND NATURALIZATION SERVICE MANAGEMENT ISSUES, Hrg of the Committee on the Judiciary, House of Representatives, April 24, 1991, p. 81. Lack of case tracking and frequency of file loss compound inefficiency and delay. INS is in desperate need of a file tracking system. While INS has made efforts to upgrade its information technology, the current system is grossly inadequate and inefficient. Perhaps the most persistent problem is that there is no mechanism for documenting receipt of applications at the district office level or for tracking those applications when they are remoted elsewhere for adjudication.

589. Michael Lemay. FROM OPEN DOOR TO DUTCH DOOR, New York: Praeger Press, 1987, pp. 129-130. Problems of corruption flow naturally from the tremendous pressures for immigration coupled with the restrictions of legal immigration and the inefficiency of the INS. Nor is the problem limited to the INS. The State Department and immigration lawyers share in the extensive nature of corruption associated with the whole immigration process. Immigrants seeking the legal right to live here are often desperate to do so. Compliance with the legal process involved often necessitates using an immigration lawyer—a legal specialty currently booming. High demand for entry has led to practices that are openly fraudulent or questionably legal, and a situation wherein the field of immigration law has a tarnished reputation. INS officials estimate that about 30 percent of all permanent-resident petitions are fraudulent, with corrupt or incompetent lawyers often to blame. To legally gain a green card, an immigrant must be qualified to fill a job for which there is a shortage of U.S. workers, to be a refugee facing persecution at home, or be related to a U.S. citizen or permanent resident. Each category breeds its own schemes or scams. Among the easiest and most popular is the phony marriage. In one year, of 111,653 who applied for resident status through marriage, 30 percent were found to be fraudulent. One district director estimates that half such marriages would turn out to be phony if investigators had enough time to check them all thoroughly ("Quiz Traps Fraudulent Immigrants," *The Cumberland Sunday Times,* November 3, 1985: A3).

590. Michael Lemay. FROM OPEN DOOR TO DUTCH DOOR, New York: Praeger Press, 1987, pp. 130-131. The State Department's visa issuing procedures have also contributed to the problem and have involved allegations of widespread corruption. In 1980, temporary visas were issued to 12 million persons. INS records substantiate only 10 million left. Visa overstayers are an undoubtedly increasing problem largely beyond the resources of the INS to control. In part, this is due to the fact that the State Department is granting such temporary visas to more "bad risk" applicants. This practice contributes to the low morale of the INS. It is also costly. David North, a noted immigration researcher, noted that for the foreign service officer to check whether or not to issue or deny a visa costs the government an average of $3.37. The cost of the INS to inspect arriving passengers was only 42 cents. But for the border patrol to catch a visa overstayer once in the country, North estimated that it cost $43.38—if indeed it ever did catch them. Some State

Department officials estimate that between 20,000 and 50, 000 visas are sold annually (Crewdson: 136-37).

Similar problems of extensive corruption plague the INS. A notorious case in 1971 established that an INS inspector took bribes to let undocumented aliens in. In four years time, the government's attorneys concluded, he had supplement his annual salary of $24,000 with more than $250,000 in bribes and proceeds from selling visitor's visas, green cards, border crossing cards, and the like. In the early 1970s an in-house investigation called "Operation Clean Sweep" opened criminal cases on 217 past and present INS officers, involving the taking of bribes, violations of civil rights, fraud against the government, with devastating evidence of alien and narcotics smuggling, perjury, rape, robbery, extortion of money and sex, influence peddling, and the misappropriation of government funds and property (Crewdson: 150-71).

591. Michael Lemay. FROM OPEN DOOR TO DUTCH DOOR, New York: Praeger Press, 1987, p. 128. Another problem is the ease with which INS documents can be counterfeited. Undocumented aliens exploit the confusion of INS green cards by counterfeiting them. California's "Silicon Valley" is awash in such cards, which sell openly on the streets for $50 to $100 and have been used as far north as Milwaukee, Wisconsin where officials have seen dozens of such fake green cards used by illegal workers.

592. Michael Lemay. FROM OPEN DOOR TO DUTCH DOOR, New York: Praeger Press, 1987, p. 128. Nor do all such undocumented aliens need fake green cards to get across. Many use perfectly legal "crossing cards." Mexicans who wish to remain in the U.S. for up to seventy-two hours to shop or visit a friend must have a border-crossing card. Needless to say, the demand for them is high, and those seeking them often begin lining up outside the INS offices at the border the day before they make their application.

593. Cecelia Munoz. IMMIGRATION AND NATURALIZATION SERVICE MANAGE-MENT ISSUES, Hrg of the Committee on the Judiciary, House of Representatives, April 24, 1991, p. 97. **A decentralized management structure that lacks lines of accountability**—Despite Commissioner McNary's efforts, the INS remains a fragmented agency that hands over too much authority to its regional and district offices. This decentralization results in policy making at the regional and district levels that often contradicts instructions from the central office, and leads to inconsistencies in service delivery and enforcement.

594. Michael Lemay. FROM OPEN DOOR TO DUTCH DOOR, New York: Praeger Press, 1987, p. 128. Associated with the INS's inability to control our borders are the problems of the agency's low level of morale and high degree of corruption.

The agency suffers from a severe reputation problem. It is often perceived as more of an enemy

than the illegal aliens it attempts to arrest and send back. Its officers are sometimes made to feel like social outcasts. This understandably depresses morale. And when agents catch the same persons over and over again, it makes the job frustrating and seemingly meaningless. Agents complain of feeling like "we're just truant officers going after people playing hooky from Mexico," others "like the Dutch boy with his thumb in the dike." (*The Wall Street Journal,* May 9, 1985: 6-7).

595. Michael Lemay. FROM OPEN DOOR TO DUTCH DOOR, New York: Praeger Press, 1987, p. 128. The morale problem is exacerbated by the ease with which illegal aliens can be smuggled in and obtain counterfeit documents. Smuggling in aliens is a big business along the Mexican border—rivaling in size and profitability even drug smuggling. Alien smuggling arrests in recent years have tripled.

596. Aryeh Neier. OPERATIONS OF THE BORDER PATROL, Hrg of the Committee on the Judiciary, House of Representatives, August 5, 1992, p. 218. Low morale also results from the perceived futility of enforcing U.S. immigration laws. The agents know that most of the undocumented whom they arrest will be sent back to Mexico without charge or punishment and that man will soon attempt to reenter the United States without authorization. Agent frustration may explain some incidents of abuse for which no other discernible motive is obvious. It may also explain agents' zeal for narcotics interdiction. The administration routinely asserts that fighting "the war on drugs" is one of our highest national priorities. Border Patrol agents are rewarded for their anti-narcotics efforts with high powered weapons and technology to which they would not otherwise have access. Also, because of the harsh penalties associated with narcotics arrests, agents do not have the same feelings of frustration and futility they have when they arrest undocumented migrants.

597. Frank Morris. "Re: Legal Immigration Reform." THE SOCIAL CONTRACT, Summer 1991, pp. 131-132. These differing view about the reasons for the poor performance of the INS, along with the lack of public support for increased funding of administrative activities, help to explain why there have been only modest increases in the INS budget for most of the past decade, even though its problems are widely acknowledged. The growth of the budget, from $87.3 million in 1969 to $501.3 million in 1984 (see table 4-2), is due in large part to inflation and the overall increase in government spending during this period. The real budget increases have been modest increments that have allowed the INS to improve only slightly the routine conduct of enforcement responsibilities.

598. Cecelia Munoz. IMMIGRATION AND NATURALIZATION SERVICE MANAGE-MENT ISSUES, Hrg of the Committee on the Judi-

ciary, House of Representatives, April 24, 1991, p. 97. **Deplorable Financial Management**—Lack of fiscal accountability and control hampers the ability of INS management to address program weaknesses. Program resources are not targeted to program needs. In addition, the GAO has estimated that millions of dollars in revenue could be lost due to inaccurate and unreliable financial recordkeeping.

599.   Dan Stein. IMMIGRATION AND NATURALIZATION SERVICE MANAGEMENT ISSUES, Hrg of the Committee on the Judiciary, House of Representatives, April 24, 1991, pp. 180-181. Money alone is not enough. As I mentioned earlier, a commitment to a clearly stated immigration policy which reflects the national interest is required. To meet this goal, new laws and congressional initiatives will be necessary. For example, Congress must revise current legal immigration law regarding the number of immigrants the U.S. should accept, and the basis on which they should be selected. Although the 1990 immigration act purported to accomplish such a task, all it succeeded in doing was to increase dramatically the overall numbers of immigrants. A comprehensive legal immigration policy should be based on the following sound principles:
• Equal opportunity—The adoption of a policy that selects people on the basis of objective individual merit, not family connections, is in keeping with the best traditions of an egalitarian society.
• National interest—While immigration, a voluntary act, is almost always in the best interests of the person immigrating, the adoption of an objective point system (awarding points for skills and merit) would ensure that immigration also serves the interests of society.
• Nuclear family—Traditionally, the most important social institution in the U.S. has been the nuclear family. Although extended family connections are important in our society, immigration law cannot offer assurances to those who voluntarily migrate to this county that entire extended families can be reconstituted here.

600.   Amnesty International. REASONABLE FEAR: HUMAN RIGHTS AND UNITED STATES REFUGEE POLICY, Amnesty International USA: New York, March 1990, p. 16. The cases of asylum seekers presented in this report indicate bias in Immigration and Naturalization Service decisions to grant or deny asylum. United States Government immigration statistics support charges of bias. The Bureau of Human Rights and Humanitarian Affairs, in particular, appears to be biased against refugees and asylum seekers of certain nationalities. This bureau has an option to evaluate every asylum application in terms of current conditions in the applicant's country. People fleeing from one of several countries with severe or widespread human rights abuses during recent years have had little chance to obtain asylum in the

United States. The most compelling evidence of bias compiled by Amnesty International, U.S.A. appears in cases of Salvadoran, Guatemalan, and Haitian asylum seekers.

601.   Lawyers Committee for Human Rights. HUMAN RIGHTS AND U.S. FOREIGN POLICY: REPORT AND RECOMMENDATIONS, Lawyers Committee for Human Rights: New York, 1992, p. 7. Following the adoption of Section 582, the State Department reported that no countries receiving U.S. security assistance were consistent violators of internationally recognized human rights. The State Department's report provided only cursory information on how the assistance was being used to improve the human rights performance of recipient governments. The failure of Section 582 to generate a more meaningful examination of the human rights records in recipient countries demonstrates the continued reluctance of the executive branch to treat these legislative requirements seriously. The circumvention of these statutory requirements indicates the need for a reexamination of the entire process.

602.   Amnesty International. REASONABLE FEAR: HUMAN RIGHTS AND UNITED STATES REFUGEE POLICY, Amnesty International USA: New York, March 1990, p. 4. Government bias against asylum seekers from particular countries appears to be a worldwide pattern. Different governments may reflect biases against nationals from different countries. Amnesty International USA's investigation of individual asylum cases in this country reveals a bias, also strongly indicated by the United States Government's own statistics, against asylum seekers coming to the United States in large numbers from countries with persistent, widespread human rights abuses: Guatemala, Haiti and El Salvador. The following report, which does not present comprehensive data on asylum seekers in the United States focuses on Guatemalans, Haitians, and Salvadorans whose cases have come to Amnesty International's attention.

603.   Amnesty International. REASONABLE FEAR: HUMAN RIGHTS AND UNITED STATES REFUGEE POLICY, Amnesty International USA: New York, March 1990, p. 4. Today, 10 years after enactment of the United States Refugee Act, an overwhelming body of evidence has emerged to show a continuing pattern of bias in this country's asylum policy. Amnesty International USA has communicated its concerns for many hears to officials of the State Department and to Immigration and Naturalization Service authorities and other officials of the Justice Department. No substantive response has been received to date, and people with reasonable fears for their lives continue to be denied protection.

ABERNETHY, VIRGINIA D.
PhD, Anthropology and Economics. Associate Professor of Psychiatry, School of Medicine, Vanderbilt University

ANDERSON, ANNELISE.
Senior Research Fellow at the Hoover Institution

ANTONOVICH, MICHAEL D.
Board of Supervisors, County of Los Angeles

APPLEYARD, REGINALD T.
Director, Centre for Migration and Development Studies, University of Western Australia

ARBOLEDA, EDUARDO.
Deputy Representative, UNHCR Branch Office, Mexico City, Mexico

BACH, ROBERT L.
Associate Professor of Sociology and the Director of the Institute for Research on Multiculturalism and International Labor at the State University of New York, Binghampton

BARNES, FRED.
Staff writer, *New York Times*

BARTLEY, ROBERT L.
Editor of the *Wall Street Journal*

BEAN, FRANK D.
Professor of Sociology, University of Texas at Austin. Director of Research on Immigration Policy at the Urban Institute

BENOIT, JEAN-PIERRE.
Department of Economics and School of Law, New York University

BERMAN, JASON
President, Recording Industry Association of America

BETHELL, TOM.
Visiting fellow, Hoover Institution

BEYLER, GREGG A.
Director of Asylum, Asylum Division, Immigration and Naturalization Service

BHAGWATI, JAGDISH.
Professor of Economics and Political Science, Columbia University

BIRNBAUM, JEFFREY H.
Staff writer, *Wall Street Journal*

BOCK, ALAN W.
Senior Columnist for *The Orange County Register*, a Daily Newspaper Published in Southern California

BONNER, T. J.
National President, National Border Patrol Council, AFGE, AFL-CIO

BORJAS, GEORGE J.
Professor of Economics, University of California; author of *Friends or Strangers: The Impact of Immigrants on the U.S. Economy*

BOUVIER, LEON F.
Adjunct Professor of Demography at Tulane School of Public Health; Former Consultant to the U.S. House of Representatives Select Committee on Population and the Select Committee on Immigration and Refugee Policy

BOWER, KAREN.
Law student, Georgetown University Law Center

BRADLEY, BILL.
Democratic U.S. Senator, New Jersey

BRIGGS, VERNON M.
Professor of Human Resource Economics at the New York State School of Labor and Industrial Relations at Cornell University; Labor Economist in the New York State School of Industrial and Labor Relations at Cornell University

BRIMELOW, PETER.
Senior Editor at *Forbes*

BROWN, WAYNE.
Executive Director, Louisville Orchestra

BUNTING, GLENN F.
Staff Writer, *Los Angeles Times*

BUSTAMANTE, JORGE A.
President of El Colegio de la Frontera Norte in Tijuana

CALAVITA, KITTY.
Sociologist of Law at Middlebury College, Vermont

CASTEL, JACQUELINE R.
Member of University of Toronto Faculty of Law

CAVOSIE, J. MICHAEL.
Law Student, University of Indiana School of Law at Bloomington

CHAPMAN, STEPHEN.
Columnist, *Chicago Tribune*

CHISWICK, BARRY R.
Chair, Economics Department, University of Illinois at Chicago; Research Professor in the Department of Economics and the Survey Research Laboratory at the University of Illinois at Chicago

CIPRIANI, LINDA.
Instructor of International Law, South Central Institute of Politics and Law, Wuhan, China

CLAPP, PRISCILLA.
United States Department of State

CLARK, REBECCA L.
  Demographer at the Urban Institute

CLARK, TOM.
  Coordinator, InterChurch Committee for Refugees,
  Toronto, Canada

CLINTON, BILL.
  United States President

COOK, JAMES.
  Economics Writer, *Forbes* Magazine

COOPER, MARY H.
  Policy researcher

CORDTZ, DAN.
  Staff Writer, *Financial World*

CORNELIUS, WAYNE A.
  Professor of Political Science and Director of the
  Center for U.S.-Mexican Studies at the University
  of California, San Diego

CRANE, KEITH.
  The Rand Corporation

CUOMO, MARIO
  Governor, New York

CUTLER, BLAYNE
  Staff writer, *American Demographics*

DEFFENBAUGH, REV. RALSTON H., JR.
  Executive Director, Lutheran Immigration and
  Refuge Service

DE FREITAS, GREGORY.
  Professor of Economics, Hofstra University

DELAHANTY, REV. PATRICK.
  Migration and Refugee Service, Catholic Chari-
  ties, Archdiocese of Louisville

DELBRUCK, JOST.
  Professor of German Constitutional Law, International Law, and European Community Law,
  Christian-Albrechts-Universität, Kiel, Germany;
  Visiting Professor of International Law and European Community Law, Indiana University School
  of Law at Bloomington

DEL OLMO, FRANK.
  Editorial Writer for the *Los Angeles Times*

DIAZ-BRIQUETS, SERGIO.
  Research Director of the United States Commis-
  sion for the Study of International Migration and
  Cooperative Economic Development; also with
  the Consulting Firm of Casals and Associates in
  Washington, D.C.

DOMINQUEZ, JORGE I.
  Professor of Government and a Member of the Ex-
  ecutive Committee of the Center for International
  Affairs at Harvard University

EDMONSTON, BARRY.
  Senior Research Associate in the Population Studies Center of The Urban Institute

FALLOWS, JAMES.
  Washington editor of *The Atlantic Monthly*

FEINSTEIN, DIANNE.
  Democratic Senator, California

FELD, KENNETH.
  President and CEO, Ringling Bros-Barnum and
  Bailey Circus

FIERMAN, JACLYN.
  Economics Writer

FLANIGAN, JAMES.
  Staff Writer, *Los Angeles Times*

FLEMING, THOMAS.
  Editor of *Chronicles*, a Magazine on American
  Culture Published by the Rockford Institute in
  Rockford, Illinois.

FOSSEDAL, GREGORY A.
  Media Fellow at the Hoover Institution and chairman of the Alexis de Tocqueville Institution

FRAGOMEN, AUSTIN T., JR.
  Staff Member of Fragomen Del Rey and Bernsen,
  P.C.

FRENZEN, NEILS W.
  Chairperson of the Board of the Coalition for Humane Immigrant Rights

FREY, BARBARA.
  Executive Director of the Minnesota Lawyers International Human Rights Committee

FRIEDMAN, THOMAS L.
  Staff Writer, *New York Times*

FUCHS, LAWRENCE H.
  Meyer and Walter Jaffe Professor of American Civ-
  ilization and Politics and Chairman of American
  Studies at Brandeis University

FULLERTON, MARYELLEN.
  Professor of Law, Brooklyn Law School

GADSBY, J. WILLIAM.
  Director, Federal Management Issues, General
  Government Division, General Accounting Office

GALLEGLY, ELTON.
  U.S. Representative (R-California)

GARCIA Y GRIEGO, MANUEL.
  Demographer and Historian Who Directs the Pro-
  gram on U.S.-Mexican Relations at the Centro de
  Estudios Internacionales of El Colegio de Mexico,
  Mexico City

GEORGE, SUSAN.
  Associate Director of The Transnational Institute,
  Amsterdam, the Netherlands

GLAZER, NATHAN.
  Professor of Education and Sociology at Harvard
  University

GLUCK, SUZANNE.
  Law Student

GOLDBERG, PAMELA.
Full-time Adjunct Professor of Law, City University of New York Law School at Queens College

GOLDBERG, SUZANNE B.
Staff Attorney, Lambda Legal Defense and Education Fund, New York, New York

GOMEZ, ARTURO SANTAMARIA.
Political Commentator and Professor at the University of Mazatlan, Mexico

GORDAN, ALAN.
Eastern Executive Secretary, Directors Guild of America

GREENWOOD, MICHAEL.
Professor of Economics, University of Colorado at Boulder

GRIFFEN, RODMAN D.
Policy Researcher, *Congressional Researcher*

HAMILL, PETE.
Columnist for *Esquire,* a Monthly Men's Magazine; Author of *Loving Women*

HAMMOND, DONALD.
Senior Vice Chairman, Committee on Migration and Refugee Affairs of Interaction

HARDIN, GARRETT.
Emeritus Professor of Human Ecology, University of California, Santa Barbara

HELTON, ARTHUR C.
Director, Refugee Project, Lawyers Committee for Human Rights, New York, New York

HING, BILL ONG.
Associate Professor of Law, Director of Immigrant Legal Resource Center, Stanford University

HOPKINS, ROBERT N.
Demographer and Contributing Editor to *Conservative Review*, a Journal of Opinion Published by the Council for Social and Economic Studies in Washington, D.C.

HOY, IAN.
Former Legal Intern with UNHCR Branch, Ottawa, Canada

HUDDLE, DONALD L.
Professor Emeritus of Economics at Rice University

IDELSON, HOLLY.
Staff writer, *Congressional Quarterly Weekly Report*

JAMES, DANIEL.
President, Mexico-United States Institute

JASPER, WILLIAM F.
Contributing Editor to *The New American*, a Conservative News and Opinion Magazine

KAURZLARICH, RICK.
Deputy Assistant Secretary, Bureau of European and Canadian Affairs, Department of State

KEELY, CHARLES B.
Social Demographer in the Department of Geography at Colgate University

KELLY, NANCY.
Clinical Instructor in Immigration Law, Harvard Law School; Attorney for the Women Refugees Project of Cambridge and Somerville Legal Services and Harvard Immigration and Refugee Program

KENNEDY, PAUL.
Professor of History, Yale University

KERN, ROSEMARY.
Vice-president, Economics and Social Institute

KHOA, LE XUAN.
President, Indochina Resource Action Center

KIRSCHTEN, DICK.
Staff writer, *National Journal*

KITTREDGE, FRANK.
President, National Foreign Trade Council

KLIEN, DIANNE.
Staff Writer, *Los Angeles Times*

KLIEN, JEFFREY.
Staff Writer, *Mother Jones*

KOH, HAROLD HONGJU.
Gerard C. and Bernice Latrobe Smith Professor of International Law, Yale Law School

KORNHAUSER, LEWIS A.
School of Law, New York University

KRALY, ELLEN PERCY.
Social Demographer in the Department of Geography at Colgate University

LAWSON, EUGENE.
Deputy Undersecretary, Bureau of International Labor Affairs, U.S. Department of Labor

LEE, BENNETT J.
Law Student, Georgetown University Law Center

LEIDEN, WARREN R.
Executive Director, American Immigration Lawyers Association

LEMAY, MICHAEL.
Professor of Political Science at Frostburg State College

LOEB, PENNY.
Staff Writer, *U.S. News and World Report*

LUMBY, CATHERINE.
Staff Writer, *The Sydney Morning Herald*

LUTTON, WAYNE.
Immigration Writer

MCCORMICK, ELIZABETH MARY.
Law Student, Georgetown University Law Center

MCNARY, GENE.
Commissioner, Immigration and Naturalization Service

MANDEL, MICHAEL J.
Associate Economics Editor, *Business Week*

MARTIN, DAVID.
Henry L. and Grace Doherty Professor of Law and F. Palmer Weber Research Professor of Civil Liberties and Human Rights, University of Virginia

MARTIN, JOHN L.
Research Director, Center for Immigration Studies

MARTIN, SUSAN FORBES.
Executive Director of the U.S. Commission on Immigration Reform

MARTINEZ, ROBERTO.
Director, U.S.-Mexico Border Program for the American Friends Service Committee in San Diego

MEHLMAN, IRA.
Director of Media Outreach for the Federation of American Immigration Reform

MEYER, JACK A.
President, New Directions for Policy

MILLER, GREG.
Staff Writer, *Los Angeles Times*

MILLER, MONIQUE.
Executive Director of Carrying Capacity Network, Washington, D.C.

MINIHANE, SEAN.
National Chairman, Irish Immigration Reform Movement

MINTER, SHANNON.
Symposium Editor and Law Student, Cornell Law School

MONTOYA, RICARDO ANZULDUA.
Center for U.S.-Mexican Studies at the University of California, San Diego

MOUSSALLI, MICHEL.
International Protection, United Nations High Commissioner for Refugees

MULLANE, HUGH G.
Law student, Georgetown University Law Center

MUNOZ, CECELIA.
Senior Immigration Policy Analyst, National Council of La Raza

NATIONAL COUNCIL OF LA RAZA.
National Council of La Raza is One of the Largest National Hispanic Organizations. It Provides Policy Analysis, Lobbying, and Public Information Programs on Behalf of Americans of Hispanic Descent

NEAL, DAVID L.
Managing editor, *Columbia Human Rights Law Review,* 1988-89

NEIER, ARYEH.
Executive Director of the Americas Watch

NELSON, ALAN C.
Commissioner of the Immigration and Naturalization Service from 1982 to 1989

NORTH, DAVID.
New TransCentury Foundation

NORTON, RICHARD E.
Director, Facilitation, Air Transport Association of America

PACHON, HARRY.
National Director, National Association of Latino Elected and Appointed Officials; Kenan Professor of Politics, Pitzer College

PACKARD, RON.
Member of the U.S. House of Representatives from California

PADAVAN, FRANK.
State Senator, New York

PANJABI, RANEE K. L.
Associate Professor of History, Memorial University, Canada

PARKER, ROBERT MANLEY.
Chief Judge, U.S. District Court, Eastern District of Texas

PASSEL, JEFFREY S.
Demographer and Senior Research Associate at The Urban Institute

PIORE, MICHAEL J.
Professor of Economics, Massachusetts Institute of Technology

PISARCHIK, JOAN A.
Law Student, Georgetown University Law Center

PLAVIN, DAVID.
Director of Aviation for the Port Authority of New York and New Jersey

POTANCO, RICHARD G.
Assistant Speaker Pro Tem of the California State Assembly

PORTES, ALEJANDRO.
Professor of Sociology at the Johns Hopkins University

RIVERA-BATIZ, FRANCISCO L.
Director of the Institute for Urban and Minority Education and Associate Professor of Economics and Education at Columbia University

RODRIGUEZ, RICHARD.
Writer for Pacific News Service

ROGERS, ROSEMARIE.
Professor, Tufts University

ROHTER, LARRY.
Staff Writer, *New York Times*

ROTHSTEIN, RICHARD.
Policy Analyst

RUMBAUT, RUBEN G.
Professor of Sociology, San Diego State University

RYSCAVAGE, REV. RICHARD, S.J.
Executive Director, Migration and Refugee Service, U.S. Catholic Conference

SAVAGE, DAVID G.
Staff Writer, *Los Angeles Times*

SCHIFTER, RICHARD.
Former U.S. assistant Secretary of State for Human Rights and Humanitarian Affairs. 1985-1992

SCHWARZ, CARL E.
Professor of Political Science and Public Law at Fullerton College, California; Faculty Research Associate of the Center of U.S.-Mexican Studies at the University of California, San Diego

SCORCA, MARC.
Executive Vice President, Opera America

SEIB, GERALD F.
Policy Analyst, *Wall Street Journal*

SHARRY, FRANK.
Executive Director, National Immigration Forum

SCHMIDT, PAUL WICKHAM.
Staff Member of Jones, Day, Reavis and Pogue of Washington, D.C.

SHENFIELD, JAMES.
Director of the Washington Institute for Policy Studies

SILVERSTEIN, KEN.
Staff Writer, *Scholastic Update*

SIMCOX, DAVID E.
Director of the Center for Immigration Studies

SIMON, JULIAN L.
Professor of Business Administration, University of Maryland

SPRAUGE, STEPHAN.
Secretary-Treasurer, American Federation of Musicians

STACY, PALMER.
President, Americans for Immigration Control

STEIN, DANIEL A.
Executive Director of the Federation of American Immigration Reform, Washington, D.C.

STRICKLAND, BARBARA K.
Legal Affairs Consultant Based in Mexico City

SUDO, PHIL.
Staff Writer, *Scholastic Update*

SUHRKE, ASTRI.
Director of Research, Department of Social Science and Development, Michelsen Institute, University of Bergen, Norway

SULLIVAN, TERESA.
University of Texas at Austin

TAMPOSI, ELIZABETH.
Assistant Secretary for Consular Affairs, Department of State

TEFERRA, TSEHAYE.
Director, Ethiopian Community Development Council, Inc.

TORRES, ARNOLD.
Policy Consultant, State of California

TUCKER, ROBERT.
Christian A. Herter Professor of American Foreign Policy and Director of the American Foreign Policy Program at the Johns Hopkins School of Advanced International Studies in Washington, D.C.

UDAGAMA, DEEPIKA.
Legal Fellow with the Minnesota Lawyers International Human Rights Committee

VAGELOS, ELLEN.
Law Student, Fordham University

VINSON, JOHN.
President of the American Immigration Control Foundation

VISCLOSKY, PETER.
Member of the House of Representatives from the State of Indiana

VON STERNBERG, MARK.
Attorney, Catholic Legal Immigration Network, Inc., New York, New York

WARNER, DAVID.
Member of the Editorial Board of the International Journal of Refugee Law

WATTENBERG, BEN J.
Senior Fellow at the American Enterprise Institute

WEINER, MYRON.
Ford International Professor of Political Science in the Department of Political Science, Massachusetts Institute of Technology

WEINTRAUB, SIDNEY.
Dean Rusk Professor and Director of the Program for U.S.-Mexico Policy Studies at the Lyndon B. Johnson School of Public Affairs at the University of Texas at Austin

WEISS, MICHAEL D.
Adjunct Professor of Law at the University of Houston

WEITZHANDLER, ARI.
Law Student, University of Colorado Law School

WILLIAMS, DAVID.
Deputy Assistant Secretary for Employment and Training, Department of Labor

WILKINSON, TRACY.
Staff Writer, *Los Angeles Times*

WYDEN, RON.
Member of the House of Representatives from the
State of Oregon

ZINSMEISTER, KARL.
Scholar at the American Enterprise Institute

ZUCKERMAN, KARL D.
Executive Vice President, Hebrew Immigrant Aid
Society

CHAPTER VI

BIBLIOGRAPHY

BOOKS

Abernethy, Virginia D. *Population Politics.* New York: Plenum Press, 1993.

Anderson, Annelise. "What Should Our Immigration Policy Be?" *The World and I.* January 1994, pp. 363-369.

Appleyard, Reginald T. *International Migration: Challenge for the Nineties.* Geneva, Switzerland: International Organization for Migration, 1991.

Bach, Robert L. "Immigration and U.S. Foreign Policy in Latin America and the Caribbean." Robert W. Tucker et al. "Preface." *Immigration and U.S. Foreign Policy.* Boulder: Westview Press. 1990, pp. 123-149.

Bayo, Francisco R. "Discussion." *Demography and Retirement.* Eds. Anna Rappaport and Sylvester Schieber. Westport, Conn: Praeger, 1993, pp. 49-52.

Bean, Frank D., et al. *Opening and Closing the Doors: Evaluating Immigration Reform and Control.* Washington, D.C.: Rand Corporation and the Urban Institute Press, 1989.

Bock, Alan W. "Illegal Immigration Should Be Legalized." *Immigration OpposingViewpoints.* San Diego: Greenhaven Press, 1990, pp. 176-181.

Bouvier, Leon F. *Peaceful Invasions: Immigration and Changing America,* Lanham, Maryland: University Press of America, 1992.

Briggs, Vernon M. "Political Confrontation with Economic Reality: Mass Immigration in the Postindustrial Age," in *Elephants in the Volkswagen.* Ed. Lindsey Grant. New York: W. H. Freeman and Company, 1992, pp. 72-84.

Briggs, Vernon M. *Immigration Policy and the American Labor Force.* Baltimore: Johns Hopkins Press, 1984.

Calavita, Kitty. "Employer Sanctions Legislation in the United States: Implications for Immigration Policy." *America's New Immigration Law: Origins, Rationales and Potential Consequences.* Ed. by Wayne A. Cornelius and Ricardo Anzaldua Montoya . San Diego: Center for U.S.-Mexican Studies, University of California, 1983, pp. 73-81.

Chiswick Barry R. *Illegal Aliens: Their Employment and Employers.* Upjohn Institute for Employment Research: Kalamazoo, Michigan, 1988.

Chiswick, Barry R. "Illegal Immigration and Immigration Control," in *U.S. Immigration Policy Reform in the 1980s.* Eds. Francisco L. Rivera-

Batiz, Selig L. Sechzer, and Ira N. Gang. New York: Praeger, 1991, pp. 45-64.

Cornelius, Wayne A. "Simpson-Mazzoli vs. the Realities of Mexican Immigration." *America's New Immigration Law: Origins, Rationales and Potential Consequences.* Ed. by Cornelius, Wayne A. and Montoya, Ricardo Anzaldua. San Diego: Center for U.S.-Mexican Studies, University of California, 1983, pp. 139-150.

Crane, Keith, et al. *The Effects of Employer Sanctions on the Flow of Undocumented Immigrants to the United States.* Washington, D.C.: Rand Corporation and the Urban Institute Press, 1990.

DeFreitas, Gregory. "Economic Implications of Immigration Law Reform," in *U.S. Immigration Policy Reform in the 1980s.* Eds. Francisco L. Rivera-Batiz, Selig L. Sechzer, and Ira N. Gang. New York: Praeger, 1991, pp. 117-130.

del Olmo, Frank. "Simpson-Mazzoli: Implications for the Latino Community." *America's New Immigration Law: Origins, RAtionales and Potential Consequences.* Ed. by Wayne A. Cornelius and Ricardo Anzuldua Montoya . San Diego: Center for U.S. Mexican Studies, University of California, 1983, pp. 123-128.

Dominquez, Jorge I. "Immigration as Foreign Policy in U.S.-Latin American Relations." Robert W. Tucker et al. "Preface." *Immigration and U.S. Foreign Policy.* Boulder: Westview Press, 1990, pp. 150-169.

Edmonston, Barry. "Discussion." *Demography and Retirement.* Eds. Anna Rappaport and Sylvester Schieber. Westport, Conn: Praeger, 1993, pp. 57-71.

Fallows, James. "Immigrants Do Not Threaten American Culture." *Immigration: Opposing Viewpoints.* Ed. William Dudley. San Diego: Greenhaven Press, 1990, pp. 74-79.

Fleming, Thomas. "Immigrants Threaten American Culture." *Immigration: Opposing Viewpoints.* San Diego: Greenhaven Press, 1990, pp. 66-73.

Fuchs, Lawrence H. "From Select Commission to Simpson-Mazzoli: The Making of America's New Immigration Law." *America's New Immigration Law: Origins, Rationales and Potential Consequences.* Ed by Wayne A. Cornelius and Ricardo Ansaldua. San Diego: Center for U.S.-Mexican Studies, University of California, 1983, pp. 43-52.

Garcia y Griego, Manuel. "Employer Sanctions: Political Appeal, Administrative Dilemmas." *America's New Immigration Law: Origins, Rationales and Potential Consequences.* Ed. by Wayne A. Cornelius and Ricardo Anzaldua Montoya. San Diego: Center for U.S.-Mexican Studies, University of California, 1983, pp. 53-71.

George, Susan. *The Debt Boomerang: How Third World Debt Harms Us All.* Boulder: Westview Press, 1992.

Glazer, Nathan. "New Rules of the Game." ed. by Robert W. Tucker et al. *Immigration and U.S. Foreign Policy.* Boulder: Westview Press, 1990, pp. 15-25.

Goss, Stephen C. "Discussion." *Demography and Retirement.* Eds. Anna Rappaport and Sylvester Schieber. Westport, Conn: Praeger, 1993, pp. 53-56.

Hamill, Pete. "Illegal Immigration Is Not a Crisis." *Immigration: Opposing Viewpoints.* San Diego: Greenhaven Press, 1990, pp. 165-170.

Hardin, Garrett. *Living Within Limits,* New York: Oxford University Press, 1993.

Hardy, Dorcas R., and C. Colburn Hardy. *Social Insecurity.* New York: Villard Books, 1991.

Hopkins, Robert N. "Third World Immigrants Cannot Adapt to the U.S." *Immigration: Opposing Viewpoints.* San Diego: Greenhaven Press, 1990, pp. 234-241.

James, Daniel. *Illegal Immigration: an Unfolding Crisis.* New York: University Press of America, 1991.

Jasper, William F. "Illegal Immigration Is a Crisis." *Immigration: Opposing Viewpoints.* San Diego: Greenhaven Press, 1990, pp. 157-164.

Kennedy, Paul. *Preparing for the Twenty-First Century.* New York: Random House, 1993.

Kingston, Eric R., and Edward D. Berkowitz. *Social Security and Medicare.* Westport, Conn: Auburn House, 1993.

Kraly, Ellen Percy. "U.S. Refugee Policies and Refugee Migration Since World War II." Robert W. Tucker et al. "Preface." *Immigration and U.S. Foreign Policy.* Boulder: Westview Press, 1990, pp. 73-98.

LeMay, Michael. *From Open Door to Dutch Door.* New York: Praeger, 1987.

Martinez, Roberto. "Illegal Immigrants Are Victims of Crime." *Immigration: Opposing Viewpoints.* Ed. William Dudley. San Diego: Greenhaven Press, 1990, pp. 96-99.

Meyer, Jack A., and Rosemary Kern. "Economic and Social Implications of Demographic Change," in *Demographic Change and the American Future.* Eds. R. Scott Fosler, William Alonso, Jack A.

Meyer, and Rosemary Kern. Pittsburgh: University of Pittsburgh Press, 1990. pp. 79-132.

Morris, Milton. *Immigration: The Beleaguered Bureaucracy.* Washington, D.C.: The Brookings Institution, 1985.

National Council of La Raza. "Third World Immigrants Are Adapting to the U.S." *Immigration: Opposing Viewpoints.* San Diego: Greenhaven Press, 1990, pp. 226-233.

Portes, Alejandro. "Of Borders and States: A Skeptical Note on the Legislative Control of Immigration." *America's New Immigration Law: Origins, Rationales and Potential Consequences.* Ed. by Wayne A. Cornelius and Ricardo Anzaldua Montoya. San Diego: Center for U.S.-Mexican Studies, University of California, 1983, pp. 17-32.

Preston, Samuel H. "Demographic Change in the United States, 1970-2050." *Demography and Retirement.* Eds. Anna Rappaport and Sylvester Schieber. Westport, Conn: Praeger, 1993, pp. 19-48.

Rappaport, Anna M., and Sylvester J. Schieber. "Overview." *Demography and Retirement.* Eds. Anna Rappaport and Sylvester Schieber. Westport, Conn: Praeger, 1993, pp. 1-18.

Rivera-Batiz, Francisco L. "Introduction," in *U.S. Immigration Policy Reform in the 1980s.* Eds. Francisco L. Rivera-Batiz, Selig L. Sechzer, and Ira N. Gang. New York: Praeger, 1991, pp. 1-16.

Rumbaut, Ruben G. "Passages to America." *America at Century's End.* Ed. Alan Wolfe. Berkeley: University of California Press, 1991, pp. 208-244.

Schieber, Sylvester J. "Can Our Social Insurance Systems Survive the Demographic Shifts of the Twenty-First Century?" *Demography and Retirement.* Eds. Anna Rappaport and Sylvester Schieber. Westport, Conn: Praeger, 1993, pp. 111-150.

Schulz, James H. *The Economics of Aging.* Fifth Ed. New York: Auburn House, 1992.

Schwarz, Carl E. "Employer Sanctions Laws: The State Experience as Compared with Federal Proposals." *America's New Immigration Law: Origins, Rationales and Potential Consequences.* Ed. by Wayne A. Cornelius and Ricardo Anzaldua Montoya. San Diego: Center for U.S.-Mexican Studies, University of California, 1983, pp. 83-102.

Simcox, David E. "Sustainable Immigration: Learning to Say No," in *Elephants in the Volkswagen.* Ed. Lindsey Grant. New York: W. H. Freeman and Company, 1992, pp. 166-177.

Simon, Julian L. *The Economic Consequences of Immigration.* Cambridge, Mass: Basil Blackwell with the Cato Institute, 1989.

Simon, Julian L. "Immigrants Help the U.S. Economy." *Immigration: Opposing Viewpoints.* Ed. William Dudley. San Diego: Greenhaven Press, 1990, pp. 80-84.

Simon, Julian L. *Population Matters: People, Resources, Environment, and Immigration.* New Brunswick: Transaction Publishers, 1990.

Stacy, Palmer, and Wayne Lutton. "Illegal Immigrants Cause Crime." *Immigration: Opposing Viewpoints.* Ed. William Dudley. San Diego: Greenhaven Press, 1990, pp. 90-95.

Statement of the International Alliance of Theatrical Stage Employees. *Admission of O and P Non-Immigrants.* Hearing before the Subcommittee on International Law, Immigration, and Refugees of the Committee on the Judiciary. House of Representatives. October 9, 1991, pp. 82-89.

Stewart, David W. *Immigration and Education.* New York: Lexington Books, 1993.

Strickland, Barbara K. "Immigration Reform and Legal Rights: A Critical Analysis of the Simpson-Mazzoli Bill." *America's New Immigration Law: Origins, Rationales and Potential Consequences.* Ed. by Wayne A. Cornelius and Ricardo Anzaldua Montoya. San Diego: Center for U.S.-Mexican Studies, University of California, 1983, pp. 103-114.

Sutcliffe, Bob. "Immigration and the World Economy." *Creating a New World Economy.* Ed. Gerald Epstein, et al. Philadelphia: Temple University Press, 1993, pp. 84-107.

Torres-Gil, Fernando. "Separating Myth from Reality." *The California-Mexico Connection.* Ed. Abraham F. Lowenthal and Katrina Burgess. Stanford: Stanford University Press, 1993, pp. 164-175.

Tucker, Robert W., Charles B. Keely, and Linda Wrigley. Eds. *Immigration and U.S. Foreign Policy.* Boulder: Westview Press, 1990.

Tucker, Robert W., et al. "Preface." *Immigration and U.S. Foreign Policy.* Boulder: Westview Press, 1990.

Vinson, John. *Immigration Out of Control: The Interests Against America.* Monterey, Virginia: American Immigration Control Foundation, 1992.

Wattenberg, Ben J., and Karl Zinsmeister, "The U.S. Should Encourage Immigration." *Immigration: Opposing Viewpoints.* Ed. William Dudley. San Diego: Greenhaven Press, 1990. 113-120.

Weintraub, Sidney, and Stanley R. Ross. *The Illegal Alien from Mexico: Policy Choices for an Intractable Issue.* Austin, Texas: Mexico-United States Border Research Program, The University of Texas, 1980.

PERIODICALS

"Headline: New Study Prompts Environmental Group to Call for Immigration Moratorium." *PR Newswire.* June 3, 1993.

"Immigration Costs California $18.2 Billion in 1992." *PR Newswire.* November 4, 1993.

"National Population Organization Comes to California Speaking out on the Costs of Immigration." *PR Newswire.* April 14, 1994.

"Population Growth." *BNA International Environment Daily.* June 8, 1993.

"Why Our Borders Are Out of Control." *Newsweek,* August 9, 1993, p. 25.

Arboleda, Eduardo, and Ian Hoy. "The Convention Refugee Definition in the West: Disharmony of Interpretation and Application." *International Journal of Refugee Law.* Vol. 15: 1993, pp. 66-90.

Barnes, Fred. "No Entry." new republic. November 8, 1993. pp. 10-14.

Bartley, Robert L. Reply to an Article by Peter Brimelow. *National Review.* February 1, 1993. pp. 32-33.

Benoit, Jean-Pierre and Lewis A. Kornhauser. "Unsafe Havens." *The University of Chicago Law Review.* Vol. 59, no. 4: Fall 1993, pp. 1421-1464.

Bethell, Tom. "Immigration Si; Welfare, No." *American Spectator.* November 1993, pp. 18-19.

Beyer, Gregg A. "Establishing the United States Asylum Officer Corps: A First Report." *International Journal of Refugee Law.* Vol. 4, no. 4: 1992, pp. 454-485.

Bhagwati, Jagdis. "Behind the Green Card." (Review of *The Economic Consequences of Immigration* by Julian L. Simon) *The New Republic.* May 14, 1990, pp. 31-39.

Borjas, George J. Reply to an Article by Peter Brimelow. *National Review.* February 1, 1993, pp. 29-30.

Bouvier, Leon F., and John L. Martin. "Four Hundred Million Americans!" *The Social Contract.* Spring 1993, pp. 183-191.

Bower, Karen. "Recognizing Violence Against Women as Persecution on the Basis of Membership in a Particular Social Group." *Georgetown Immigration Law Journal.* Vol. 7: 1993, pp. 173-206.

Brimelow, Peter. "Does the Nation-State Exist?" *The Social Contract.* Summer 1993, pp. 299-34.

495

Brimelow, Peter. Response to Simon, Borjas, Wattenberg, Stein, and Bartley. *National Review.* February 1, 1993, pp. 33-34.

Castel, Jacqueline R. "Rape, Sexual Assault and the Meaning of Persecution." *International Journal of Refugee Law.* Vol. 4, no. 2: 1992, pp. 39-56.

Cavosie, J. Michael. "Defending the Golden Door: The Persistence of Ad Hoc and Ideological Decision Making in the U.S. Refugee Law." *Indiana Law Journal.* Vol. 67: 1992, pp. 411-439.

Chen, Lincoln. "Living within limits." *Issues in Science and Technology.* December 22, 1993, p. 88.

Cipriani, Linda. "Gender and Persecution: Protecting Women Under International Refugee Law." *Georgetown Immigration Law Journal.* Vol. 7: 1993, pp. 511-548.

Clapp, Priscilla. "The Future of Refugee Policy." *In Defense of the Alien.* Vol. 15: 1993, pp. 106-111.

Clark, Tom. "Human Rights and Expulsion: Giving Content to the Concept of Asylum." *International Journal of Refugee Law.* Vol. 4, no. 2: 1992, pp. 188-203.

Conniff, Ruth. "The War on Aliens." *The Progressive.* October, 1993, p. 22.

Cook, James. "The More the Merrier." *Forbes.* April 2, 1990, pp. 77-81.

Cordtz, Dan. "The Fraying Welcome Mat." *Financial World.* November 9, 1993, pp. 58-65.

Cutler, Blayne. "Wanted: More Irving Berlins." (Review of *The Economic Consequences of Immigration* by Julian L. Simon) *American Demographics.* June 1990, p. 12.

D'Antonio, Michael. "Apocalypse Soon." *Los Angeles Times Magazine.* August 29, 1993, pp. 19-20+.

Delbruck, Jost. "A Fresh Look at Humanitarian Intervention under the Authority of the United Nations." *Indiana Law Journal.* Vol. 67: 1992. pp. 887-901.

Diaz-Briquets, Sergio, and Sidney Weintraub. "Migration Impacts of Trade and Foreign Investment: Mexico and Caribbean Basin Countries." *Series on Development and International Migration in Mexico, Central America, and the Caribbean Basin.* Boulder: Westview Press. Vol. 3: 1991.

Ellul, Jacques. "No Limits to Population Growth?" *The Social Contract.* Spring 1993, pp. 180-182.

Fierman, Jaclyn. "Is Immigration Hurting the U.S.? *Fortune.* August 9, 1993, pp. 76-79.

Fossedal, Gregory A. Review of *The Economic Consequences of Immigration* by Julian L. Simon.

The American Spectator. February 1990, pp. 45-46.

Fragomen, Austin T., Jr. "Immigration Policy." *In Defense of the Alien.* Vol 15: 1993, pp. 101-105.

Frey, Barbara, and Deepika Udagama. "Assisting Indigent Political Asylum Seekers in the United States: A Model for Volunteer Legal Assistance." *Hamline Law Review.* Vol. 13: 1990, pp. 661-672.

Fullerton, Maryellen. "A Comparative Look at Refugee Status Based on Persecution Due to Membership in a Particular Social Group. *Cornell International Law Journal.* Vol. 26: 1993, pp. 505-563.

Gilliam, Harold. "Bursting At The Seams." *The Social Contract.* Summer 1993, pp. 263-265.

Glastris, Paul. "Immigration Crackdown." *U.S. News and World Report.* June 21, 1993, p. 34.

Gluck, Suzanne. "Intercepting Refugees at Sea: An Analysis of the United States' Legal and Moral Obligations." *Fordham Law Review.* Vol. 16: 1993, pp. 865-893.

Goldberg, Pamela. "Anyplace but Home: Asylum in the United States for Women Fleeing Intimate Violence." *Cornell International Law Journal.* Vol. 26: 1993, pp. 565-604.

Goldberg, Suzanne B. "Give Me Liberty or Give Me Death: Political Asylum and the Global Persecution of Lesbians and Gay Men." *Cornell International Law Journal.* Vol. 26: 1993, pp. 604-623.

Gomez, Arturo Santamaria. "The Porous U.S.-Mexico Border." *The Nation.* October 25, 1993, pp. 458-462.

Graham, Otis L., and Roy Beck. "Immigration's Impact On Inner City Blacks." *The Social Contract.* Summer 1992, pp. 215-216.

Gurr, Ted Robert. "Drowning In A Crime Wave." *The Social Contract.* Spring 1993, pp. 157-158.

Harrison, Lawrence. "Those Huddled Unskilled Masses." *he Social Contract.* Summer 1992, pp. 222-224.

Helton, Arthur C. "America Must Offer Oppressed a Haven." *The National Law Journal.* May 10, 1993, p. 30.

Helton, Arthur C. "Courts Have an Obligation to Protect the Rights of Aliens and Refugees." *The National Law Journal.* September 14, 1992, pp. 19-21.

Helton, Arthur C. "The Mandate of U.S. Courts to Protect Aliens and Refugees Under International Human Rights Law." *The Yale Law Journal.* Vol. 100: 1991, pp. 2335-2346.

Helton, Arthur C. "Refugees and Human Rights." *In Defense of the Alien.* Vol 15: 1993, pp. 143-148.

Helton, Arthur C. "Toward Harmonized Asylum Procedures in North America: The Proposed United States-Canada Memorandum of Understanding for Cooperation in the Examination of Refugee Status Claims from Nationals of Third Countries." *Cornell International Law Journal.* Vol 26: 1993, pp. 737-747.

Helton, Arthur C. "Uncontrolled Right of Entry Poses a Threat." *The National Law Journal.* May 3, 1993, pp. 15-16.

Hing, Bill Ong. "The Tempest-Tossed: New Groups of Refugees and Asylum-seekers Test Our Historic Generosity of Spirit." *Stanford Lawyer.* Fall 1993, pp. 18-19+.

Huddle, Donald, and David Simcox. "Red Ink from Abroad." *The World and I.* January 1994, pp. 381-393.

Kelly, Nancy. "Gender-Related Persecution: Assessing the Asylum Claims of Women." *Cornell International Law Journal.* Vol. 26: 1993, pp. 625-674.

Kennan, George F. "U.S. Overpopulation Deprives The Planet of A Helpful Civilization." *The Social Contract.* Spring 1993. 192-194.

Kirschten, Dick. "Catch-Up Ball." *National Journal.* August 7, 1993, pp. 1976-1979.

Klien, Jeffrey. "Nativist Son." *Mother Jones.* November/December 1993, p. 3.

Koh, Harold Hongju. "The Human Face of the Haitian Interdiction Program." *Virginia Journal of International Law.* Vol. 33: 1993, pp. 483-490.

Lee, Bennett J. "The Immigration ad Naturalization Service: In Search of the Necessary Efficiency." *Georgetown Immigration Law Journal.* Vol. 6: 1992, pp. 519-543.

Loeb, Penny, et al. "To Make a Nation." *U.S. News and World Report.* 4 Oct 1993, pp. 47-54.

Lumby, Catherine. "A Poor Record on Human Rights." *The Sydney Morning Herald* included in *World Press Review.* April 1992, p. 35.

Mandel, Michael J. "Does America Need More 'Huddled Masses'? Yes." (Review of *The Economic Consequences of Immigration* by Julian L. Simon) *Business Week.* March 12, 1990, p. 20.

Martin, David A. "Asylum Case Law: How the New Regulations Can Help." *In Defense of the Alien.* Vol. 14: 1992, pp. 132-141.

Martin, David A. "Strategies for a Resistant World: Human Rights Initiatives and the Need for Alternatives to Refugee Interdiction." *Cornell International Law Journal.* Vol. 26: 1993, pp. 753-770.

Martin, David. "Interdiction, Intervention, and the New Frontiers of Refugee Law and Policy." *Virginia Journal of International Law.* Vol. 33: 1993, pp. 473-481.

Martin, Susan Forbes. "U.S. Immigration Policy: Challenges for the 1990s." *National Strategy Reporter.* Fall 1993, pp. 1-5.

McCarthy, Barbara. "Memo From The San Diego Border." *The Social Contract.* Spring 1993, pp. 174-176.

McCormick, Elizabeth Mary. "HIV-Infected Haitian Refugees: An Argument Against Expulsion." *Georgetown Immigration Law Journal.* Vol. 7: 1993, pp. 149-171.

McNary, Gene. "INS Response to Immigration Reform." *In Defense of the Alien.* Vol. 14: 1992, pp. 3-13.

Mehlman, Ira. "Avoiding The Obvious." *The Social Contract.* Summer 1992, pp. 228-231.

Mehlman, Ira. "The Issue Is Immigration." *National Review.* November 29, 1993, pp. 26-28.

Minter, Shannon. "Sodomy and Public Morality Offenses under U.S. Immigration Law: Penalizing Lesbian and Gay Identity." *Cornell International Law Journal.* Vol. 26: 1993, pp. 771-818.

Morganthau, Tom. "America: Still a Melting Pot?" *Newsweek.* August 9, 1993, pp. 16-23.

Morris, Frank. "Re: Legal Immigration Reform." *The Social Contract.* Summer 1991, pp. 188-190.

Moussali, Michel. "Prospects for Refugee Protection in the 1990s." *In Defense of the Alien.* Vol. 15: 1993, pp. 127-132.

Mullane, Hugh G. "Political Asylum: Determining Standards of Review." *Georgetown Immigration Law Journal.* Vol. 6: 1993, pp. 87-106.

Neal, David L. "Women as a Social Group: Recognizing Sex-Based Persecution as Grounds for Asylum." *Immigration and Nationality Law Review.* 1990. 217-271. (As reprinted from *Columbia Human Rights Law Review.* 20:203. {1988}).

Packard, Ron. "Congressman Speaks On Illegal Immigration." *Border Watch.* December 1993, p. 6.

Panjabi, Ranee K. L. "The Global Refugee Crisis: A Search for Solutions." *California Western International Law Journal.* Vol. 21, no. 2: 1990-1991, pp. 247-263.

Piore, Michael J. "Give Me Your Skilled." (Review of *The Economic Consequences of Immigration* by Julian L. Simon) *New Leader.* May 14, 1990, pp. 26-27.

Pisarchik, Joan A. "A Rawlsian Analysis of the Immigration Act of 1990." *Georgetown Immigration Law Journal.* Vol. 6: 1993, pp. 721-744.

Reese, Charley. "Immigration Hurts Us All." *The Social Contract*. Spring 1992, p. 181.

Rodriguez, Richard. "In California, Hysteria Hides Immigration Truth." *National Catholic Reporter*. 10 Sep 1993, p. 12.

Rogers, Rosemarie. "The Future of Refugee Flows and Policies." *International Migration Review*. Vol. 26, no. 4: Winter 1992, pp. 1112-1143.

Rothstein, Richard. "Immigration Dilemmas." *Dissent*. Fall 1993, pp. 455-462.

Scheuer, James. "A Disappointing Outcome." *The Social Contract*. Summer 1992, pp. 203-206.

Schifter, Richard. "Enhancing Our Human Rights Effort." *International Law and Politics*. Vol. 24: 1992, pp. 1287-1296.

Schmidt, Paul Wickham. "Business-related Provisions of the Immigration Act of 1990." *In Defense of the Alien*. Vol. 15: 1993, pp. 7-30.

Shenfield, James. "New Blood." (Review of *The Economic Consequences of Immigration* by Julian L. Simon) *National Review*. September 3, 1990, pp. 42-43.

Silverstein, Ken. "The Labor Debate." *Scholastic Update*. November 19, 1993, pp. 16-17.

Simon, Julian L. "The Case for Greatly Increased Immigration." *Public Interest*. Winter 1991, pp. 89-103.

Simon, Julian L. "Immigrants and Alien Workers." *Journal of Labor Research*. Winter 1992, pp. 73-78.

Simon, Julian L. Reply to an Article by Peter Brimelow. *National Review*. February 1, 1993, pp. 27-29.

Simon, Julian L., Stephen Moore, and Richard Sullivan. "The Effect of Immigration on Aggregate Native Unemployment: An Across-City Estimation." *Journal of Labor Research*. Summer 1993, pp. 299-316.

Stein, Daniel A. "Immigration Dilemma: Humanity vs. Terrorism: America Must Remain a Haven." *The National Law Journal*. May 3, 1993, pp. 15-16.

Stein, Dan. Reply to an Article by Peter Brimelow. *National Review*. February 1, 1993. p. 32.

Stein, Dan. "States, Counties Foot Bill for Unchecked Immigration." *The Social Contract*. Summer 1991, pp. 199-200.

Sudo, Phil. "The Golden Door." *Scholastic Update*. November 19, 1993, pp. 2-5.

Suhrke, Astri. "A Crisis Diminished: Refugees in the Developing World." *International Journal: Canadian Institute of International Affairs*. Spring 1993, pp. 215-239.

Tanton, John, and Wayne Lutton. "Immigration and Crime." The Social Contract. Spring 1993, pp. 159-167.

Tanton, John, and Wayne Lutton. "Welfare Costs For Immigrants." *The Social Contract*. Fall 1992, pp. 6-15.

Teitelbaum, Michael S. "New Polemics On Immigration." *The Social Contract*. Spring 1992, pp. 182-183.

Thomas, Rich, and Andrew Murr. "The Economic Cost of Immigration." *Newsweek*. August 9, 1993, pp. 18-19.

Vagelos, Ellen. "The Social Group That Dare Not Speak Its Name: Should Homosexuals Constitute a Particular Social Group for Purposes of Obtaining Refugee Status? Comment on *Re: Insudi*. *Fordham International Law Journal*. Vol. 17: 1993, pp. 229-276.

Von Sternberg, Mark R. "Political Asylum and the Law of Internal Armed Conflict: Refugee Status, Human Rights and Humanitarian Law Concerns." *International Journal of Refugee Law*. Vol. 5, no. 2: 1993, pp. 153-182.

Warner, Daniel. "We Are All Refugees." *International Journal of Refugee Law*. Vol. 4, no. 3: 1992, pp. 365-372.

Wattenberg, Ben J. Reply to an Article by Peter Brimelow. *National Review*. February 1, 1993, pp. 30-32.

Weiner, Myron. "Introduction: Security, Stability and International Migration." *International Migration and Security*. Boulder: Westview Press. 1993. (As originally published in *International Security*. Vol. 17, no. 3: Winter 1992/93.)

Weiss, Michael D. "Sisyphean Policy: Borders and Bureaucracies." *The World and I*. January 1994, pp. 317-379.

Weitzhandler, Ari. "Temporary Protected Status: The Congressional Response to the Plight of Salvadoran Aliens." *University of Colorado Law Review*. Vol. 64: 1993, pp. 249-275.

NEWSPAPERS

"Immigration's Impact On Nation's Resources." *New York Times*. October 15, 1993, p. A34.

"Perspective on Immigration." *Los Angeles Times*. April 13, 1994, p. B7.

"The 'I-Word' Creates Tense Environment at Sierra Club." *San Francisco Chronicle*. March 30, 1994, p. A10.

Abcarian, Robin. "Immigration Talk Borders on Environmental Dramatics." *Los Angeles Times*. November 10, 1993, pp. E1, 3.

Antonovich, Michael D. Letter. *Wall Street Journal.* September 10, 1993, p. A19.

Birnbaum, Jeffrey H. "Clinton Administration Gearing Up for Effort to Strengthen Barriers to Illegal Immigration." *Wall Street Journal.* June 29, 1993, p. A20.

Bradley, Bill. "NAFTA Opens More Than a Trade Door." *Wall Street Journal.* September 16, 1993, p. A20.

Brimelow, Peter. "Time To Rethink Immigration?" *National Review.* June 22, 1992, pp. 30-46.

Bunting, Glenn F. "Plan for National Guard at Border Gains Support." *Los Angeles Times.* October 19, 1993, pp. A3, 24.

Bustamente, Jorge A. "Mexico-Bashing: A Case Where Words Can Hurt." *Los Angeles Times.* August 13, 1993, p. B7.

Chapman, Stephen. "Immigrant Myths and the Recurrent Urge to Exclude." *Chicago Tribune.* July 25, 1993, Sec. 4, p. 3.

Clark, Rebecca L., and Jeffrey S. Passell. "Studies Are Deceptive." *New York Times.* September 3, 1993, p. A23.

Conda, Cesar. "A Flood of Immigration Would Be Cut Sharply by Freer Flow of Trade." *San Diego Union-Tribune.* September 19, 1993, p. G5.

D'Antonio, Michael. "Apocalypse Soon." *Los Angeles Times.* August 29, 1993, p. 18.

Dowling, Katherine. "Social Security: A Widening Gap." *Atlanta Constitution.* January 25, 1994, p. A11.

Ervin, Henry. "Illegal Immigration: a Heavy Burden." *San Diego Union-Tribune.* August 29, 1993, p. G3.

Feinstein, Dianne. "We Can Get a Grip on Our Borders." *Los Angeles Times.* June 15, 1993, p. A11.

Flanigan, James. "Blaming Immigrants Won't Solve Economic Woes." *Los Angeles Times.* August 15, 1993, pp. D1, 4.

Frenzen, Neils W. "Do We Want to Be Like Kuwait?" *Los Angeles Times.* August 12, 1993, p. B7.

Friedman, Thomas L. "Clinton Seeks More Powers To Stem Illegal Immigration." *New York Times.* July 28, 1993, p. A13.

Gallegly, Elton. Letter. *Wall Street Journal.* December 6, 1993, p. A15.

Glazer, Nathan. "Keep the Borders Open." (Review of *The Economic Consequences of Immigration* by Julian L. Simon) *New York Times Book Review.* January 14, 1990, Sec. 7, p. 28.

Huddle, Donald. "Debate Must Begin with True View of the Costs." *Houston Chronicle.* August 29, 1993, p. 1.

Huddle, Donald L. "A Growing Burden." *New York Times.* September 3, 1993, p. A23.

Huddle, Donald L. Letter. *New York Times.* January 26, 1994, p. A14.

James, Daniel. "Bar the Door." *New York Times.* July 25, 1992, p. 21.

Kershner, Vlae. "A Hot Issue for the '90s—California Leads in Immigration–and Backlash." *The San Francisco Chronicle.* June 21, 1993, p. A1.

Klien, Dianne. "Majority in State Are Fed Up With Illegal Immigration." *Los Angeles Times.* September 19, 1993, pp. A1, 30.

Klien, Dianne. "State Puts New Edge on Immigration Debate." *Los Angeles Times.* September 6, 1993, pp. A1, 29.

Kotkin, Joel. "Is Fascism Back in Fashion?" *Washington Post.* January 2, 1994, p. C4.

Lewis, Anthony. "The Politics of Nativism." *New York Times.* January 14, 1994, p. A29.

Martin, John L. Letter. *Wall Street Journal.* September 10, 1993, p. A19.

Miller, Greg. "Immigrant Costs Overstated, Study Finds." *Los Angeles Times.* September 3, 1993, pp. B1, 4.

Miller, Monique. Letter. *Washington Post.* January 13, 1994, p. A26.

Nelson, Alan C. "A Governor's Brave Stand On Illegal Aliens." *New York Times.* August 23, 1993, p. A15.

Padavan, Frank. Letter. *New York Times.* January 26, 1994, p. A14.

Polanco, Richard G. "Cut the Rhetoric and Work on Solutions." *Los Angeles Times.* August 13, 1993, p. B7.

Reese, Charley. "Do Something About America's Worst Problems—Stop Immigration." *The Orlando Sentinel.* September 9, 1993, p. A12.

Richman, Sheldon. "Population Means Progress, Not Poverty." *Washington Post.* September 1, 1993, p. A23.

Rohter, Larry. "Revisiting Immigration and the Open-Door Policy." *New York Times.* September 19, 1993, Sec. 4, p. 4.

Rowen, Hobart. "Overpopulation Remains World's Defining Crisis." *Washington Post.* April 4, 1993, pp. H1, 5.

Sanchez, Leonel. "State Immigrants Cost $18.2 Billion in Taxes Last Year, Study Says." *San Diego Union-Tribune.* November 5, 1993, p. A27.

Savage, David G. "Temporary Visas Used to Stay in U.S. Indefinitely." *Los Angeles Times.* March 8, 1993, pp. A1, 5.

Seib, Gerald F. "In Tense Times, It's Easy to Hit At Immigrants." *Wall Street Journal.* October 27, 1993, p. A18.

Sharry, Frank. Letter. *Washington Post.* January 27, 1994, p. A26.

Shepard, Scott. "As Boomers Get Older, Nation Faces Hard Choice." *Atlanta Constitution.* March 31, 1993, p. E6.

Silk, Leonard. "Head Off a Trade War." *New York Times.* February 4, 1993, p. A23.

Simon, Julian L. "The Nativists Are Wrong." *Wall Street Journal.* August 4, 1993, p. A8.

Simon, Richard. "1992 Cost of Immigrants $18 Billion, Report Says." *Los Angeles Times.* November 5, 1993, p. A3.

Stein, Dan. Letter. *New York Times.* January 26, 1993, p. A14.

Stein, Dan. Letter. *Wall Street Journal.* September 10, 1993, p. A19.

Wilkinson, Tracy. "Will Democracy's Growth Stanch Migrant Flow, Even Prompt a Return?" *Los Angeles Times.* October 18, 1993, p. A11.

GOVERNMENT DOCUMENTS

"Clinton Announces Policy On Illegal Immigration." *Congressional Quarterly Weekly Report.* July 31, 1993, pp. 2082-2083.

Americas Watch. *Border Violence.* Hearing before the Subcommittee on International Law, Immigration, and Refugees of the Committee on the Judiciary. House of Representatives. (Y4.J 89/1: 103/14) September 29, 1993, pp. 120-165.

Beilenson, Congressman Anthony C. "House Committee on Foreign Affairs, Hearing on Population Growth." *Federal Document Clearing House Congressional Testimony.* September 22, 1993.

Berman, Jason. *Admission of O and P Non-Immigrants.* Hearing before the Subcommittee on International Law, Immigration, and Refugees of the Committee on the Judiciary. House of Representatives. October 9, 1991, pp. 145-156.

Bonner, T. J. *Border Violence.* Hearing before the Subcommittee on International Law, Immigration, and Refugees of the Committee on the Judiciary. House of Representatives. (Y4.J 89/1: 103/114) September 29, 1993, pp. 68-71.

Bonner, T. J. *Operations of the Border Patrol.* Hearing before the Subcommittee on International Law, Immigration, and Refugees of the Committee on the Judiciary. House of Representatives. (Y4.J 89/1: 102/66) August 5, 1992, pp. 143-153.

Brown, Wayne. *Admission of O and P Non-Immigrants.* Hearing before the Subcommittee on International Law, Immigration, and Refugees of the Committee on the Judiciary. House of Representatives. October 9, 1991, pp. 41-42.

Church World Service, Immigration and Refugee Program. *Reauthorization of Appropriations FOR the Refugee Act of 1980.* Hearing before the Subcommittee on International Law, Immigration, and Refugees of the Committee on the Judiciary. House of Representatives. (Y4.J 89/1: 102/21) July 25, 1991, pp. 181-201.

Clinton, Bill. "Protecting U.S. Borders Against Illegal Immigration." *U.S. Department of State Dispatch.* August 9, 1993, pp. 561-565.

Cooper, Mary H. "Immigration Reform." *Congressional Quarterly Researcher.* September 24, 1993, pp. 842-863.

Deffenbaugh, Rev. Ralston H., Jr. *Reauthorization of Appropriations for the Refugee Act of 1980.* Hearing before the Subcommittee on International Law, Immigration, and Refugees of the Committee on the Judiciary. House of Representatives. (Y4.J 89/1: 102/21) July 25, 1991, pp. 109-129.

Delahanty, Rev. Patrick. *Reauthorization of Appropriations for the Refugee Act of 1980.* Hearing before the Subcommittee on International Law, Immigration, and Refugees of the Committee on the Judiciary. House of Representatives. (Y4.J 89/1: 102/21) July 25, 1991, pp. 143-163.

Feld, Kenneth. *Admission of O and P Non-Immigrants.* Hearing before the Subcommittee on International Law, Immigration, and Refugees of the Committee on the Judiciary. House of Representatives. October 9, 1991, pp. 135-145.

Gadsby, J. William. *Immigration and Naturalization Service Management Issues.* Hearing before the Subcommittee on International Law, Immigration, and Refugees of the Committee on the Judiciary. House of Representatives. (Y4.J 89/1: 102/8) April 24 and May 1, 1991, pp. 5-7.

Golodner, Jack. *Admission of O and P Non-Immigrants.* Hearing before the Subcommittee on International Law, Immigration, and Refugees of the Committee on the Judiciary. House of Representatives. October 9, 1991, pp. 109-132.

Gordan, Allen. *Admission of O and P Non-Immigrants.* Hearing before the Subcommittee on International Law, Immigration, and Refugees of the Committee on the Judiciary. House of Representatives. October 9, 1991, pp. 78-79.

Griffen, Rodman D. "Illegal Immigration." *Congressional Quarterly Researcher.* April 24, 1992, pp. 362-383.

Hammond, Donald. *Reauthorization of Appropriations for the Refugee Act of 1980.* Hearing before the Subcommittee on International Law, Immigration, and Refugees of the Committee on the Judiciary. House of Representatives. (Y4.J 89/1: 102/21) July 25, 1991, pp. 85-92.

Helton, Arthur C. *Immigration and Naturalization Service Management Issues.* Hearing before the Subcommittee on International Law, Immigration, and Refugees of the Committee on the Judiciary. House of Representatives. (Y4.J 89/1: 102/8) April 24 and May 1, 1991, pp. 152-160.

Idelson, Holly. "Clinton's Immigration Changes Aim to Stop Abuses." *Congressional Quarterly Weekly Report.* July 31, 1993, p. 2061.

Jiminez, Maria. *Border Violence.* Hearing before the Subcommittee on International Law, Immigration, and Refugees of the Committee on the Judiciary. House of Representatives. (Y4.J 89/1: 103/14) September 29, 1993, pp. 239-242.

Kaurzlarich, Rick. *Admission of O and P Non-Immigrants.* Hearing before the Subcommittee on International Law, Immigration, and Refugees of the Committee on the Judiciary. House of Representatives. October 9, 1991, pp. 22-33.

Khoa, Le Xuan. *Reauthorization of Appropriations for the Refugee Act of 1980.* Hearing before the Subcommittee on International Law, Immigration, and Refugees of the Committee on the Judiciary. House of Representatives. July 25, 1991, pp. 132-138.

Kittredge, Frank. *Immigration Reform.* Hearing before the Subcommittee on Immigration and Refugee Affairs of the Committee on the Judiciary. United States Senate. (Y4.J 89/2: S. Hrg. 101-607) March 3, 1989, pp. 467-480.

Lawson, Eugene. *Immigration Reform.* Hearing before the Subcommittee on Immigration and Refugee Affairs of the Committee on the Judiciary. United States Senate. (Y4.J 89/2: S. Hrg. 101-607) March 3, 1989, pp. 281-297.

Leiden, Warren R. *Immigration and Naturalization Service Management Issues.* Hearing before the Subcommittee on International Law, Immigration, and Refugees of the Committee on the Judiciary. House of Representatives. (Y4.J 89/1: 102/8) April 24 and May 1, 1991, pp. 69-91.

Martinez, Roberto. *Border Violence.* Hearing before the Subcommittee on International Law, Immigration, and Refugees of the Committee

on the Judiciary. House of Representatives. (Y4.J 89/1: 103/14) September 29, 1993, pp. 265-268.

McNary, Gene. *Admission of O and P Non-Immigrants.* Hearing before the Subcommittee on International Law, Immigration, and Refugees of the Committee on the Judiciary. House of Representatives. October 9, 1991, pp. 10-22.

McNary, Gene. *Immigration and Naturalization Service Management Issues.* Hearing before the Subcommittee on International Law, Immigration, and Refugees of the Committee on the Judiciary. House of Representatives. (Y4.J 89/1: 102/8) April 24 and May 1, 1991, pp. 35-46.

McNary, Gene. *Implementation of Immigration Act of 1990.* Hearing before the Subcommittee on International Law, Immigration, and Refugees of the Committee on the Judiciary. House of Representatives. May 15, 1991, pp. 72-80.

McNary, Gene. *Operations of the Border Patrol.* Hearing before the Subcommittee on International Law, Immigration, and Refugees of the Committee on the Judiciary. House of Representatives. (Y4.J 89/1: 102/66) August 5, 1992, pp. 68-96.

Minihane, Sean. *Immigration Reform.* Hearing before the Subcommittee on Immigration and Refugee Affairs of the Committee on the Judiciary. United States Senate. (Y4.J 89/2: S. Hrg. 101-607) March 3, 1989, pp. 131-137.

Munoz, Cecilia. *Immigration and Naturalization Service Management Issues.* Hearing before the Subcommittee on International Law, Immigration, and Refugees of the Committee on the Judiciary. House of Representatives. (Y4.J 89/1: 102/8) April 24 and May 1, 1991, pp. 92-110.

Neier, Aryeh. *Operations of the Border Patrol.* Hearing before the Subcommittee on International Law, Immigration, and Refugees of the Committee on the Judiciary. House of Representatives. (Y4.J 89/1: 102/66) August 5, 1992, pp. 203-221.

Norton, Richard E. *Immigration and Naturalization Service Management Issues.* Hearing before the Subcommittee on International Law, Immigration, and Refugees of the Committee on the Judiciary. House of Representatives. (Y4.J 89/1: 102/8) April 24 and May 1, 1994, pp. 113-120.

Pachon, Harry. *Immigration and Naturalization Service Management Issues.* Hearing before the Subcommittee on International Law, Immigration, and Refugees of the Committee on the Judiciary. House of Representatives. (Y4.J 89/1: 102/8) April 24 and May 1, 1991, pp. 163-171.

Pachon, Harry. IMMIGRATION REFORM. Hearing before the Subcommittee on Immigration and Refugee Affairs of the Committee on the Judiciary. United States Senate. (Y4.J 89/2: S. Hrg. 101-607) March 3, 1989, pp. 125-129.

Packard, Rep. Ron. OPERATIONS OF THE BORDER PATROL. Hearing before the Subcommittee on International Law, Immigration, and Refugees of the Committee on the Judiciary. House of Representatives. (Y4.J 89/1: 102/66) August 5, 1992, pp. 10-12.

Parker, Robert Manley. IMPLEMENTATION OF IMMIGRATION ACT OF 1990. Hearing before the Subcommittee on International Law, Immigration, and Refugees of the Committee on the Judiciary. House of Representatives. May 15, 1991, pp. 42-72.

Plavin, David. *Immigration and Naturalization Service Management Issues.* Hearing before the Subcommittee on International Law, Immigration, and Refugees of the Committee on the Judiciary. House of Representatives. (Y4.J 89/1: 102/8) April 24 and May 1, 1991, pp. 124-135.

Reid, Senator Harry. "The Math on Immigration, US Jobs." *Roll Call.* February 7, 1994.

Ryscavage, Rev. Richard, S.J. *Reauthorization of Appropriations for the Refugee Act of 1980.* Hearing before the Subcommittee on International Law, Immigration, and Refugees of the Committee on the Judiciary. House of Representatives. (Y4.J 89/1: 102/21) July 25, 1991, pp. 39-63.

Scorca, Marc. *Admission of O and P Non-Immigrants.* Hearing before the Subcommittee on International Law, Immigration, and Refugees of the Committee on the Judiciary. House of Representatives. October 9, 1991, pp. 42-50.

Sprauge, Stephan. *Admission of O and P Non-Immigrants.* Hearing before the Subcommittee on International Law, Immigration, and Refugees of the Committee on the Judiciary. House of Representatives. October 9, 1991, pp. 104-108.

Stein, Dan. *Operations of the Border Patrol.* Hearing before the Subcommittee on International Law, Immigration, and Refugees of the Committee on the Judiciary. House of Representatives. (Y4.J 89/1: 102/66) August 5, 1992, pp. 225-235.

Stein, Dan. *Reauthorization of Appropriations for the Refugee Act of 1980.* Hearing before the Subcommittee on International Law, Immigration, and Refugees of the Committee on the Judiciary. House of Representatives. (Y4.J 89/1: 102/21) July 25, 1991, pp. 222-230.

Tamposi, Elizabeth. *Implementation of Immigration Act of 1990.* Hearing before the Subcommittee on International Law, Immigration, and Refugees of the Committee on the Judiciary. House of Representatives. May 15, 1991, pp. 80-95.

Teferra, Tsehaye. *Reauthorization of Appropriations for the Refugee Act of 1980.* Hearing before the Subcommittee on International Law, Immigration, and Refugees of the Committee on the Judiciary. House of Representatives. (Y4.J 89/1: 102/21) July 25, 1991, pp. 85-92.

Tobias, Robert. *Border Violence.* Hearing before the Subcommittee on International Law, Immigration, and Refugees of the Committee on the Judiciary. House of Representatives. (Y4.J 89/1: 103/14) September 29, 1993, pp. 64-66.

Torres, Arnold. *Operations of the Border Patrol.* Hearing before the Subcommittee on International Law, Immigration, and Refugees of the Committee on the Judiciary. House of Representatives. (Y4.J 89/1: 102/66) August 5, 1992, pp. 13-14.

Visclosky, Peter. *Implementation of Immigration Act of 1990.* Hearing before the Subcommittee on International Law, Immigration, and Refugees of the Committee on the Judiciary. House of Representatives. May 15, 1991, pp. 15-18.

Wheeler, Bruce. *Border Violence.* Hearing before the Subcommittee on International Law, Immigration, and Refugees of the Committee on the Judiciary. House of Representatives. (Y4.J 89/1: 103/14) September 29, 1993, pp. 93-95.

Williams, David. *Implementation of Immigration Act of 1990.* Hearing before the Subcommittee on International Law, Immigration, and Refugees of the Committee on the Judiciary. House of Representatives. May 15, 1991, pp. 96-109.

Wyden, Ron, and Kenneth Feld. *Admission of O and P Non-Immigrants.* Hearing before the Subcommittee on International Law, Immigration, and Refugees of the Committee on the Judiciary. House of Representatives. October 9, 1991, pp. 135-145.

Wyden, Ron. *Implementation of Immigration Act of 1990.* Hearing before the Subcommittee on International Law, Immigration, and Refugees of the Committee on the Judiciary. House of Representatives. May 15, 1991, pp. 18-38.

Zuckerman, Karl D. *Reauthorization of Appropriations for the Refugee Act of 1980.* Hearing before the Subcommittee on International Law, Immigration, and Refugees of the Committee on the Judiciary. House of Representatives. (Y4.J 89/1: 102/21) July 25, 1991, pp. 67-80.